A CHRONOLOGY OF THE LIFE OF SIR ARTHUR CONAN DOYLE

MAY 22nd to JULY 7th 1930

2018 Revised and Expanded Edition

A Detailed Account Of The Life And Times Of The Creator Of Sherlock Holmes

By

Brian W Pugh

First edition published in 2009
© 2009
Brian W. Pugh

Second edition published in 2012
© 2012
Brian W. Pugh

Third edition published 2014
© 2014
Brian W. Pugh

Fourth edition published 2018
© 2018
Brian W. Pugh

The right of Brian W Pugh to be identified as the author of this work has been asserted by him in accordance with the Copyright, Designs and Patents Act 1998. All rights reserved. No reproduction, copy or transmission of this publication may be made without written permission. No paragraph of this publication may be reproduced, copied or transmitted save with the written permission or in accordance with the provisions of the Copyright Act 1956 (as amended). Any person who does any unauthorised act in relation to this publication may be liable to criminal prosecution and civil claims for damage.

Paperback ISBN - 978-1-78705-346-5
ePub ISBN – 978-1-78705-347-2
PDF ISBN - 978-1-78705-348-9

MX Publishing Ltd., 335 Princess Park Manor, Royal Drive,
London, N11 3GX
www.mxpublishing.co.uk

Cover design by Brian Belanger

Cover photograph courtesy of The Arthur Conan Doyle Collection, Toronto Public Library.

Title page: pastel portrait by Carole A Skinner of Lewes, Sussex.

This book is dedicated to my partner Christine
for her continued support and encouragement

FOREWORD

A chronology is not a biography, but it can play an essential role in researching and understanding someone's life. At its best a chronology strips away speculation and equivocation, focusing on specific facts, dates, and events. It fills in the details that get overlooked in broader biographical works. These details can provide vital links in a chain of discovery about a person.

Sir Arthur Conan Doyle was notoriously careless with dates and numbers. Most of his correspondence is undated, and a majority of his biographies lack specific source citations. This makes it dangerous to rely on any single book, or even several books, about his life. Yet constantly searching through the numerous Conan Doyle biographies is tedious work.

Fortunately this *Chronology of the Life of Sir Arthur Conan Doyle* cites the sources for each listed event. It becomes a sort of master index to Conan Doyle biographical material. For example, the *Chronology* identifies seven sources that discuss the wounding of Sir Arthur's son during World War I. Four biographers state that he was wounded on 1 July 1916 and sent back to England. Two others mention the incident without giving a specific date. A final source notes that Conan Doyle received a telegram on 7 July with news of the wounding.

By themselves the *Chronology* entries provide a valuable summary of biographical reporting. When used as an index to their corresponding sources, they offer a timesaving cross-reference to scholars searching for more information. As such this *Chronology* could be described as the ultimate Conan Doyle reference work. It is an indispensable resource for anyone doing serious research.

Randall Stock
Editor, *The Best of Sherlock Holmes* (www.bestofsherlock.com)

Note from the author: - Randall is probably best known for his website, and for his checklists of Conan Doyle manuscripts and other rarities. He has presented papers about Conan Doyle at Harvard and at the University of Minnesota, written a number of articles for the BSJ, and contributed chapters to the BSI Manuscript Facsimile series for So *Painful a Scandal* (2009)), *Bohemian Souls* (2011), *The Wrong Passage* (2012), *Irregular Stain* (2013), Out *of The Abyss* (2014), *Dancing To Death* (2016) and *Trenches* (2017).

A CHRONOLOGY OF THE LIFE OF SIR ARTHUR CONAN DOYLE

The Chronology does not pretend to be complete and is, of course, a progressive work. Additional dates will be added as identified, with addenda supplements being issued at intervals, as required. The object of this publication is to collect in chronological order the events of the life of Sir Arthur Conan Doyle. This not only lists the dates applicable to Sir Arthur, but also to his family. No doubt some scholars will dispute some of the dates stated and I have accordingly listed at the end of this book the works that have been consulted for the sources.

All dates that appear in each of the sources quoted, have, I hope, been included. Biographical sources differ over the dates of many of the events of ACD's life. Where such disagreements occur all of the alternative dates have been given in their appropriate chronological location, together with an indication in square brackets as to which source(s) support each dating. Where alternative dates exist, an asterisk (*) included after the source bracket as follows:

Asterisk Information: Entries with (*2) indicates that this is one of two entries for that event, derived from alternative or conflicting information or facts. (*3) indicates three entries, and so on. Where sources do not date certain events, these appear at the beginning of each year and indicated n.d.; other events that have no dates are inserted in the relevant part of the year and again indicated n.d.

Since the private publication of *A Chronology of the Life of Sir Arthur Conan Doyle* first appeared in 2000, numerous new sources were consulted, the original text and index were greatly revised, expanded and corrected, and it was then published in 2009, in the 2012 edition was completely revised, corrections were made and a further sources were consulted. The 2014 edition was again completely revised; further corrections were made, with new sources added, this was followed in 2016 by the *Addenda and Corrigenda*, the 2009, 2012, 2014 editions and the *Addenda and Corrigenda* were all published by MX Publishing Ltd. This new 2018 edition is a completely revised text and includes all of the revisions and corrections that were made previously plus the information and maps included in the *Addenda and Corrigenda*. Also included is the information and sources located during research from 2016. New photographs have been added to those already published and *The Times* is now listed in the sources with the date of publication.

There are a great number of entries stating ACD was at Southsea, ACD at Undershaw, ACD at Windlesham etc. The dates for these entries are taken from letters by ACD and are dated, so it can only be assumed that he was at the address given.

Abbreviations Used: Arthur Conan Doyle is as ACD. PLSS = The Portsmouth Literary and Scientific Society. UNLSS = The Upper Norwood Literary and Scientific Society.

The index covers the Chronology pages 1 – 205 & 209 – 225 only. Any Sherlock Holmes title which contains the words *The Adventure of* as in *The Adventure of the Blue Carbuncle* will be found within the index as *Blue Carbuncle, The*.

For full details of the works cited within the chronology and the bibliography section, I would suggest that *A Bibliography of A. Conan Doyle* by Richard Lancelyn Green and John Michael Gibson, 1983 or 2000, *A Bibliographic Listing of Stories, Poems, and Other Writings of A. Conan Doyle* by Phillip G. Bergem, 2007 and *A Doylean and Sherlockian Checklist of The Strand Magazine* compiled by Phillip G. Bergem, 2007, are consulted.

I would be very grateful for any further dates and information that could be included in any future reprints of this chronology. I will continue to collect further information and issue an Addenda and Corrigenda as and when required, contact me at Brian W. Pugh, 20, Clare Road, Lewes. Sussex. BN7 1PN England or by email: brianpugh140@btinternet.com

ACKNOWLEDGEMENTS

I am indebted to Sir Arthur Conan Doyle's autobiography, all the authors of the biographies and other sources used, and of course without *A Bibliography of A. Conan Doyle* by Richard Lancelyn Green and John Michael Gibson this chronology would never have been attempted. Not forgetting *A Bibliographic Listing of Stories, Poems, and Other Writings of A. Conan Doyle* by Philip G Bergem, a real gem of a publication.

I would also like to thank Philip & Jane Weller, Mrs. G. Doyle and my partner Christine for their support and encouragement in what started out as only a few page summary, to what you are now reading. I would like to thank Paul Spiring, for his research for our 2008 publication; *On The Trail of Arthur Conan Doyle: An Illustrated Devon Tour*, the research results are included in the Chronology. To Horace Coates and Roger Johnson for their advice and guidance on the presentation of the original version of the Chronology. To Marcus Geisser for putting me in touch with Vincent Delay, who in turn obtained permission from Bibliothèque cantonale et universitaire to use the photographs as listed. I would also like to thank Mark Doyle, Alistair Duncan and Derek Barnard for supplying corrections to the first edition, and Christopher Roden for his assistance in compiling the 2012 edition. Thanks also for their contributions to the 2014 edition go to Doug Wrigglesworth, Ken Cooper and Bill Barnes. I would like to acknowledge Phil Bergem, Oscar Ross, Mattias Boström, Michael Morton, Mark Alberstat, Roger Straughan, Leonie Paterson (Royal Botanic Garden Edinburgh Archives), The Arthur Conan Doyle Collection at Toronto Public Library, and Alexis Barquin at The Arthur Conan Doyle Encyclopedia: https://arthur-conan-doyle.com and to Randall Stock for the Foreword and his suggestions for improvement on the text.

Thanks also go to Geraldine Beare for compiling the index.

Photographs in this publication are from the following.

The Arthur Conan Doyle Collection at Toronto Public Library – front cover, 208 mourners at funeral, 227 ACD & family at Nielsen Park, Sydney, Australia; 228 6th Royal Sussex Volunteer Regiment, 229 at the Blue Mountains

Courtesy of Bibliothèque cantonale et universitaire – Fonds manuscripts – Fond A. Conan Doyle. Lausanne, 239 Jean Conan Doyle, Mary Doyle & family photograph, 240 ACD in fancy dress, in uniform & with Kingsley, 241 all, 242 all, 243 all, 244 Adrian Denis, Major Wood & Jean, 260 Undershaw under construction.

Courtesy of Hull City Council, ©2012 Hull Maritime Museum: Hull Museums, page 238 top photo.

arthur-conan-doyle.com – 226 Dame Jean, ACD graduating, 227 ACD leaving St. Giles, ACD with top hat and cane, 228 Prince Henry Tour, 229 Jasper Park, 230 both photos, 231 both photos, 290 both photos.

The remaining photographs are from the collection of the author: title page, foreword page, 206, 207, 208 two grave markers, 226 service of thanks giving and certificate of graduation, 239 Louise Conan Doyle, 240 ACD & Jean at Apiary, 244 Windlesham & Racing medal, 245 all, 259, 260 Undershaw, 261 all, 289 both photos, 295, 321, 323, 324 both photos, 366.

On Line Sources for Newspapers

The Times:	http://infotrac.galegroup.com library membership number required
British:	www.britishnewspaperarchives.co.uk subscription required
New Zealand:	www.paperspast.natlib.gov.nz free access
Australia:	http://trove.nla.gov.au/newspaper free access
Cricket:	http://cricketarchive.com subscription required

Contents

	The Family Tree	Page 57	1894
Page 1	1755 – 1809	Page 58	1894
Page 2	1818 – 1829	Page 59	1894
Page 3	1830 – 1844	Page 60	1894
Page 4	1844 – 1855	Page 61	1894
Page 5	1855 – 1860	Page 62	1894 – 1895
Page 6	1861 – 1866	Page 63	1895
Page 7	1866 – 1869	Page 64	1895
Page 8	1869 – 1873	Page 65	1895
Page 9	1873 – 1875	Page 66	1895 – 1896
Page 10	1875 – 1876	Page 67	1896
Page 11	1876 – 1877	Page 68	1896
Page 12	1877 – 1878	Page 69	1896 – 1897
Page 13	1878 – 1879	Page 70	1897
Page 14	1879 – 1880	Page 71	1897
Page 15	1880	Page 72	1897
Page 16	1880	Page 73	1897
Page 17	1880	Page 74	1897 – 1898
Page 18	1880 – 1881	Page 75	1898
Page 19	1881	Page 76	1898
Page 20	1881 – 1882	Page 77	1898 – 1899
Page 21	1882 – 1883	Page 78	1899
Page 22	1883	Page 79	1889
Page 23	1883 – 1884	Page 80	1889
Page 24	1884	Page 81	1889 – 1900
Page 25	1884 – 1885	Page 82	1900
Page 26	1885	Page 83	1900
Page 27	1885	Page 84	1900
Page 28	1885 – 1886	Page 85	1900
Page 29	1886	Page 86	1900
Page 30	1886	Page 87	1900 – 1901
Page 31	1886 – 1887	Page 88	1901
Page 32	1887 – 1888	Page 89	1901
Page 33	1888	Page 90	1901
Page 34	1888	Page 91	1901
Page 35	1888 – 1889	Page 92	1901
Page 36	1889	Page 93	1901 – 1902
Page 37	1889	Page 94	1902
Page 38	1889	Page 95	1902
Page 39	1889 – 1890	Page 96	1902
Page 40	1890	Page 97	1902 – 1903
Page 41	1890	Page 98	1903
Page 42	1890 – 1891	Page 99	1903
Page 43	1891	Page 100	1903
Page 44	1891	Page 101	1903
Page 45	1891	Page 102	1903 – 1904
Page 46	1891 – 1892	Page 103	1904
Page 47	1892	Page 104	1904
Page 48	1892	Page 105	1904
Page 49	1892	Page 106	1904 – 1905
Page 50	1892	Page 107	1905
Page 51	1893	Page 108	1905
Page 52	1893	Page 109	1905
Page 53	1893	Page 110	1905 – 1906
Page 54	1893	Page 111	1906
Page 55	1893	Page 112	1906
Page 56	1893 – 1894	Page 113	1906 – 1907

Page 114	1907	Page 171	1921
Page 115	1907	Page 172	1921
Page 116	1907	Page 173	1921 – 1922
Page 117	1907	Page 174	1922
Page 118	1907 – 1908	Page 175	1922
Page 119	1908	Page 176	1922
Page 120	1908	Page 177	1922
Page 121	1908 – 1909	Page 178	1922 – 1923
Page 122	1909	Page 179	1923
Page 123	1909	Page 180	1923
Page 124	1909	Page 181	1923
Page 125	1909	Page 182	1923
Page 126	1910	Page 183	1923 – 1924
Page 127	1910	Page 184	1924
Page 128	1910	Page 185	1924
Page 129	1910	Page 186	1924 – 1925
Page 130	1910 – 1911	Page 187	1925
Page 131	1911	Page 188	1925
Page 132	1911	Page 189	1925
Page 133	1911	Page 190	1925 – 1926
Page 134	1911	Page 191	1926
Page 135	1912	Page 192	1926
Page 136	1912	Page 193	1926 – 1927
Page 137	1912 – 1913	Page 194	1927
Page 138	1913	Page 195	1927 – 1928
Page 139	1913	Page 196	1928
Page 140	1913	Page 197	1928
Page 141	1913 – 1914	Page 198	1928 – 1929
Page 142	1914	Page 199	1929
Page 143	1914	Page 200	1929
Page 144	1914	Page 201	1929
Page 145	1914	Page 202	1929
Page 146	1914	Page 203	1929
Page 147	1914 – 1915	Page 204	1930
Page 148	1915	Page 205	1930
Page 149	1915	Page 206	Photographs
Page 150	1915 – 1916	Page 209	Other dates of interest
Page 151	1916	Page 226	Photographs
Page 152	1916	Page 232	An Arctic Voyage in 1880
Page 153	1916 – 1917	Page 239	Photographs
Page 154	1917	Page 246	Maps
Page 155	1917	Page 259	Residences of ACD
Page 156	1917 – 1918	Page 260	Photographs
Page 157	1918	Page 262	Where Are They Buried?
Page 158	1918	Page 264	Statues and Plaques
Page 159	1918 – 1919	Page 271	ACD & Cricket
Page 160	1919	Page 289	Cricket Photographs
Page 161	1919	Page 291	ACD & Football
Page 162	1919 – 1920	Page 294	Innes Doyle & Cricket
Page 163	1920	Page 296	Biographies etc.
Page 164	1920	Page 300	Facsimile Manuscripts
Page 165	1920	Page 301	Bibliography
Page 166	1920	Page 322	Minor Contributions
Page 167	1920	Page 324	Photographs
Page 168	1920	Page 325	Works Consulted
Page 169	1920 – 1921	Page 366	About The Chronologist
Page 170	1921	Page 367	Index

Doyle Family Tree

James Doyle married Catherine Tynan
b. c.1755
d. c.1845

Children

Catherine
b. c.1794
d. 3 May 1827

James
b. Aug. 1795
d. 21 Nov 1824

John (HB)
b. April 1797
d. 2 Jan 1868
m. Marianne Conan
m. 13 Feb 1820
b. c.1795
d. 11 Dec 1839

William
b. 1799

Anna Maria
b. 6 August 1801
d. 11 Sept 1866

Michael
b. 1803
Baptised 4 Jan 1804

Richard (Dicky)
b. Sept 1824
d. 11 Dec 1883

Children of John (HB) and Marianne Conan

James Edmund William
b. 22 Oct 1822
d. 3 Dec 1892
m. Jane Hawkins
b. c.1835
d. 27 May 1925

Henry Edward
b. c.1827
d. 17 Feb 1892
m. Jane Ball
b. c.1818
d. 10 April 1905

Francis (Frank)
b. c.1829
d. c.1843

Adelaide
b. c.1831
d. 2 April 1844

Charles Altamont
b. 25 March 1832
d. 10 Oct 1893
m. Mary Foley
b. 8 July 1837
d. 30 Dec 1920

Children of James Edmund William and Jane Hawkins

Ann Martha (Annette)
b. 24 Jan 1821
d. 17 Oct 1899

Children of Charles Altamont and Mary Foley

Ann Mary Frances (Annette) Conan
b. 22 July 1856
d. 13 Jan 1890

Catherine Amelia Angela
b. 22 April 1858
d. 20 Oct 1858

Arthur Ignatius Conan
b. 22 May 1859
d. 7 July 1930
m. (1) Louise Hawkins
b. 10 April 1857
d. 4 July 1906
m. (2) Jean Leckie
b. 14 March 1874
d. 27 June 1940
[continued on next page]

Mary Helena Monica
b. 4 May 1861
d. 3 June 1863

Caroline Mary Burton (Lottie)
b. 22 Feb 1866
d. 3 May 1941
m. Leslie William Searles Oldham
b. c.1870
d. 28 July 1915
[see next page 1]

Constance Amelia Monica (Connie)
b. 4 March 1868
d. 8 June 1924
m. Ernest William Hornung
b. 7 June 1866
d. 22 March 1921
[see next page 2]

John Francis Innes Hay (Innes)
b. 31 March 1873
d. 19 Feb 1919
m. Clara Schwensen
b. 29 March 1881
d. 3 Nov 1930
[see next page 3]

Jane Adelaide Rose (Ida)
b. 16 March 1875
d. 1 July 1937
m. Nelson Foley
b. 1850
d. 3 Jan 1909
[see next page 4]

Bryan Mary Julia Josephine (Dodo)
b. 2 March 1877
d. 8 Feb 1927
m. Charles Cyril Angell
b. 1873
d. 30 Sept 1937
[see next page 5]

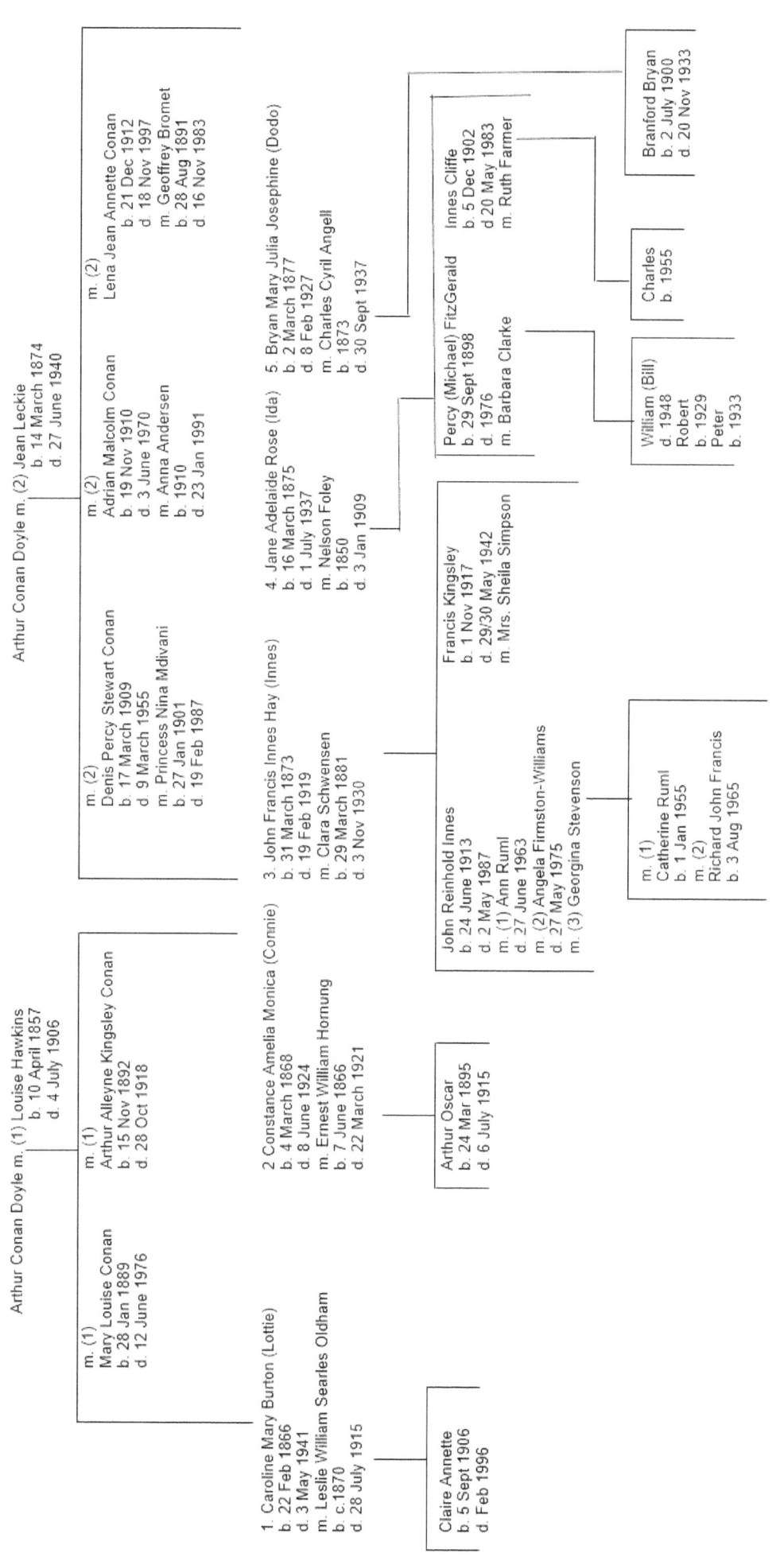

A CHRONOLOGY OF THE LIFE OF SIR ARTHUR CONAN DOYLE
May 22nd 1859 to July 7th 1930

Asterisk Information: Entries with (*2) indicates that this is one of two entries for that event, derived from alternative or conflicting information or facts. (*3) indicates three entries, and so on. Sources that do not date certain events appear at the beginning of each year; events that have no dates are inserted in the relevant part of the year and indicated n.d.

1755
n.d.   Birth of James Doyle (*c*.1755). [124,202] {Note: at some stage James Doyle married Catherine Tynan.}

1794
n.d.   Birth of Catherine Doyle daughter of James and Catherine Doyle (*c*.1794). [124,202]

1794/95
n.d.   Birth of Marianne Conan [68,200,202] (*c*.1795) [124] or Marianna. [202]

1795
n.d.   Birth of James Doyle. [202] (*2)
August   Birth of James Doyle son of James and Catherine Doyle. [124] (*2)

1797
n.d.   Birth of John Doyle (HB). [202] (*2)
April   Birth of John Doyle (HB) son of James and Catherine Doyle. [68,124,200,203] (*2)
April 26   John Doyle (HB) baptised. [124,200]

1799
n.d.   Birth of William Doyle son of James and Catherine Doyle. [124,202]

1801
n.d.   Birth of Anna Doyle. [202] (*2)
August 6   Birth of Anna Maria Doyle daughter of James and Catherine Doyle. [124] (*2)

1803
n.d.   Birth of Michael Doyle son of James and Catherine Doyle (*c*.1803). [124,202]

1804
January 4   Michael Doyle baptised. [124]

1807
n.d.   Birth of William Foley, father of Mary Josephine Foley. [68,203] (*2)

1808
n.d.   Birth of Catherine Pack. [202] (*3)

1808/09
n.d.   Birth of Catherine Pack. [68] (*3)

1809
n.d.   Birth of William Foley. [200] (*2)
n.d.   Birth of Catherine Pack. [200] (*3)

1818/19
n.d.   Birth of Jane Isabella Ball. [68,200,202]

1820
n.d.   John Doyle (HB) married Marianna Conan. [180,202] (*3)
February   John Doyle (HB) married Marianne Conan (*3) at St. Andrew's Church, Dublin. [215] (*2)
February 13   John Doyle (HB) married Marianne (or Mary Ann) Conan (*3) at St. Andrew's Church, Dublin [124] John Doyle (HB) married Marianne Conan. [68,200] (*2)

1821
n.d.   Birth of Ann Martha Doyle (Annette) daughter of John and Marianna Doyle. [202,203] (*2)
January 24   Birth of Ann Martha Doyle (Annette) daughter of John and Marianne Doyle [124] Ann Martha Doyle also known as Annette and Sister Ignatius Aloysius daughter of John and Marianne Doyle. [68,200] (*2)

1822
n.d.   John and Marianne Doyle probably arrived in London and rented a house at 60 Berners Street. [214,215]
n.d.   Birth of James William Edmund Doyle, son of John and Marianne Doyle. [180,202,203,215] (*3)
October   Birth of James Edmund William Doyle, son of John and Marianne Doyle. [124] (*3)
October 22   Birth of James William Edmund Doyle, son of John and Marianne Doyle. [68,200] (*3)
n.d.   Birth of Richard Doyle, son of John and Marianne Doyle. [215] (*3)

1824
n.d.   Birth of Richard Doyle (Dicky). [180,202] (*3)
September   Birth of Richard Doyle (Dick or Dicky), son of John and Marianne Doyle. [68,124,200,203] (*3)
n.d.   Death of James Doyle. [202] (*2)
November 21   Death of James Doyle. [124] (*2)

1825
November 3   Birth of George Turnavine Budd. [151]
December 28   Birth of Emily Butt (later Emily Hawkins). {Date as noted on grave.} (*2)
December 30   Birth of Emily Butt, later married Jeremiah Hawkins, mother and father of Emily (Nem), Louise and John (Jack). [124] (*2)

1827
n.d.   Birth of Henry Edward Doyle, son of John and Marianne Doyle. [68,124,180,200,202,203,215]
n.d.   Death of Catherine Doyle. [202] (*2
May 3   Death of Catherine Doyle. [124] (*2)

1828
n.d.   Birth of Francis (Frank) Doyle (c.1828), son of John and Marianne Doyle. [68,200,202] (*2)

1829
n.d.   Birth of Francis (Frank) Doyle, son of John and Marianne Doyle. [124,180,215] (*2)

1830
n.d.   Birth of Adelaide Doyle (c.1830) daughter of John and Marianne Doyle. [202] (*2)

1831
n.d.   Birth of Adelaide Doyle daughter of John and Marianne Doyle. [68,180,200,124] (*2)

1832
n.d.   Birth of Charles Altamont Doyle. [14,180] (*2)
March 25   Birth of Charles Altamont Doyle [68,124,200,202,203,215] (*2) born in Bayswater, London. [124]

1833
n.d.   John and Marianne Doyle, with their family were living at 17 Cambridge Terrace, London [214,215] or John and Marianna Doyle were living at 17 Cambridge Terrace, London. [180,202]

1835
n.d.   William Foley married Catherine Pack, father and mother of Mary Josephine Elizabeth Foley. [68,202,203] (*2)
April 24   William Foley married Catherine Pack, father and mother of Mary Josephine Elizabeth Foley [200] (*2) at St. Andrews's Church, Dublin. [124]
n.d.   Birth of Jane Henrietta Hawkins. (c.1935) [202] (*2)

1835/36
n.d.   Birth of Jane Henrietta Hawkins. [68,200] (*2)

1837
n.d.   Birth of Mary Foley. [14,16,202] (*3)
June 4   Birth of Mary Josephine Elizabeth Foley. [200] (*3)
July 8   Birth of Mary Josephine Elizabeth Foley. [68,124,200,203] (*3)
December 2   Birth of Joseph Bell at 22 St. Andrew Square, Edinburgh. [2010]

1839
n.d.   Birth of Catherine Foley. [202,203]
n.d.   Elizabeth and Michael Conan, sister and brother of Marianne Conan were also living at 17 Cambridge Terrace, London. [215]
n.d.   Death of Marianna (Conan) Doyle. [202,203] (*3)
April 19   Birth of Catherine (Kate) Agnes Mullin Foley. [200]
December 3   Death of Marianne (Conan) Doyle at 17 Cambridge Terrace, London. [68,200] (*3)
December 11   Death of Marianne (Conan) Doyle [124,215] (*3) aged 44. [215]
December 16   Funeral of Marianne (Conan) Doyle at Norwood Cemetery, Norwood Road, Lambeth, London. [781]

1840
n.d.   Death of William Foley. [68,200,203]

1843
n.d.   Death of Francis (Frank) Doyle. [68,200,202]
June 15   Funeral of Francis (Frank) Doyle at Norwood Cemetery, Norwood Road, Lambeth, London. [781]

1844
n.d.   Death of Adelaide Doyle. [180,202] (*2)

1844
April 2   Death of Adelaide Doyle at 17 Cambridge Terrace, London. [68,124,200] (*2)
April 6   Funeral of Adelaide Doyle at Norwood Cemetery, Norwood Road, Lambeth, London. [781]

1845
n.d.   Death of James Doyle (c.1845). [202]

1846
May 12   Michael Conan married Susan Frances Field at St. Pancras Church, London. [124]

1847
April   Catherine Foley with her daughters, Mary and Catherine moved from Ireland to Edinburgh and found accommodation at 27 Clyde Street. [202]

1849
n.d.   Charles Altamont Doyle was one of the assistants to Robert Matheson, Chief Surveyor for Scotland. [124]
n.d.   Charles Altamont Doyle briefly lodged with Catherine Foley at 27 Clyde Street, Edinburgh. [202] (*2)
n.d.   Charles Altamont Doyle moved to Edinburgh and started work with the Scottish Office of Works; he lodged at Nelson Street [124] with Katherine Foley (née Pack), [180] he became one of the assistants to Robert Matheson, Chief Surveyor for Scotland. [124]
n.d.   Charles Altamont Doyle lodged with Catherine Foley, mother of Mary, at 8 Scotland Street, Edinburgh. [68,200,215]

1850
n.d.   Charles Altamont Doyle lived at Abercromby Place, Edinburgh. [68,200]
n.d.   Birth of Nelson Foley. [202]

1851
March   John Doyle and sons were living at 17 Cambridge Terrace, London. [68,200]
March 13   Birth of George Newnes. [189]
March 30/31   Catherine Foley with her daughters, Mary and Catherine were living at 27 Clyde Street, Edinburgh, and Charles Altamont Doyle was a boarder. [216] (*2)

1852
n.d.   Charles Altamont Doyle lived at 5 Nicholson Street, Edinburgh. [68,200]

1854
August 2   Birth of Emily (Nem) Hawkins, sister of Louise and John (Jack). [124,200]

1855
n.d.   Charles Altamont Doyle married Mary Foley [2,5,15,215] (*4) at St. Mary's Roman Catholic Cathedral, Edinburgh. [215]
n.d.   Charles Altamont Doyle, youngest son of John Doyle (the political cartoonist HB) married Mary Josephine Foley, the daughter of his Irish landlady, Katherine Foley, in Edinburgh. [99] (*4)
July 31   Charles Altamont Doyle youngest son of John Doyle married Mary Josephine Foley his Irish landlady's daughter, the marriage took place at St. Mary's Cathedral, Edinburgh [5,11,14,68,200,203] (*4) at St. Mary's Church, Edinburgh. [202]

1855

July 31	Charles Altamont Doyle married Mary Josephine Foley at Edinburgh's Roman Catholic Cathedral of St. Mary [180] they continued to live at Nelson Street. [124] (*4)

1856

n.d.	Birth of Annette Mary Frances Conan Doyle (Nan), daughter of Charles and Mary Doyle. [14,15,17,20,180] (*4)
July	Birth of Ann Mary Frances Conan (Annette). [215] (*4)
July 22	Birth of Annette Mary Frances Conan Doyle (Nan) [202] at 1 South Nelson Street, Edinburgh. [16,68,200] (*4)
July 22	Birth of Ann Mary Frances (Annette) Conan Doyle [124,203] known as Tottie when young. [203] (*4)

1857

July 23	Ann Mary Frances (Annette) Conan Doyle baptised at St. Mary's Church [202] at St. Mary's Cathedral, Broughton, Edinburgh. [124]
n.d.	Doyle family resided at 1 South Nelson Street, Edinburgh. [68,200]
n.d.	Birth of Louise Hawkins. [202] (*4)
April 6	Birth of Louisa (Louise) Hawkins. [33] (*4)
April 10	Birth of Louise Hawkins (Touie) Rosebrook Cottage, Dixton, Monmouthshire. [68,124,200] (*4)
September 10	Birth of Louise Hawkins (Touie) in Dixton, Monmouthshire. [163] (*4)

1858

n.d.	Doyle family resided at 5 Nelson Street, Edinburgh. [68,200]
n.d.	Birth of Catherine Amelia Angela Doyle, daughter of Charles and Mary Doyle, she died in the same year of hydrocephalus. [180,203] (*3)
April	Birth of Catherine Emelia Angela Doyle. [14,17,202] (*3)
April 22	Birth of Catherine (or Katherine) Amelia Angela Doyle at 5 Nelson Street, Edinburgh. [5,16,68,124,200,215] (*3)
October	Death of Catherine Doyle aged 6 months. [202] (*2)
October 20	Death of Catherine Amelia Angela Doyle at 5 Nelson Street, Edinburgh, [16,68,200] she died of hydrocephalus. [124,215] (*2)

1859

n.d.	Doyle family resided at 11 Picardy Place, Edinburgh. [68,200]
n.d.	Birth of John (Jack) Hawkins. [202] (*2)
April 24	Birth of John (Jack) Hawkins, brother of Emily (Nem) and Louise. [124,200] (*2)
May 22	Birth of Arthur Ignatius Conan Doyle [203] at 11 Picardy Place, Edinburgh [124,202,215,220,2010] at 4:55a.m. [202] he was baptized into the Roman Catholic religion, and given the name Conan to help perpetuate the name of his childless godfather and great-uncle Michael Conan. [3,14,68,100,124,180,200] (*2)
May 22	Birth of Arthur Ignatius Conan Doyle second child of Charles Doyle and Mary (Foley) Doyle. [20,99] (*2)
May 24	ACD baptised Arthur Ignatius Conan Doyle [202,220] at St. Mary's Cathedral, Broughton, Edinburgh, [124,215] baptised a catholic. [99]

1860

October 4	Birth of Sidney Paget. [189]

1861

April 7	Charles Altamont Doyle, his wife Mary, daughter Annette and son ACD, plus Catherine Foley and her daughter Catherine were living at 11 Picardy Place, Edinburgh. [115,202]
April 7	Jeremiah Hawkins and his wife Emily were living with their family, Jeremiah, Mary, John, Louisa and Emily at Leckhampton, Gloucester. [324]
n.d.	Birth of Mary Monica Henrietta Doyle, daughter of Charles and Mary Doyle. [17,180,203] (*5)
May	Birth of Mary Doyle at 11 Picardy Place, Edinburgh. [202] (*5)
May 4	Birth of Mary Monica Henrietta Doyle. [16] (*5)
May 4	Birth of Mary Helena Harriet Doyle at 11 Picardy Place, Edinburgh. [68,200] (*5)
May 4	Birth of Mary Helena Monica Henrietta (Harriet) Doyle. [124] (*5)

1862

n.d.	Doyle family resided at 3 Tower Bank, Portobello, Edinburgh. [5,14,68,200,202]
n.d.	Death of Catherine Foley. [203] (*3)
May	Death of Catherine Foley aged fifty-two at 3 Tower Bank, Portobello, Edinburgh. [202] (*3)
June 3	Death of Mary Monica Henrietta Doyle. [16] (*5)
June 3	Death of Mary Helena Harriet Doyle. [68,200] (*5)
June 7	Death of Katherine (Catherine, Kate) Foley at 3 Tower Bank, Portobello, Edinburgh [68,200] aged fifty-three. [124] (*3)

1863

n.d.	Death of Mary Helena Monica Henrietta Doyle, she died of laryngitis. [180,203,215] (*5)
June	Death of Mary Doyle. [202] (*5)
June 3	Death of Mary Helena Monica (Harriet) Doyle [68,200] she died of laryngitis at Wilson's Park, Portobello, Edinburgh. [124,200] (*5)

1864

n.d.	Early 1864 and not yet five years old, ACD wrote his first story of thirty-six words involving a Bengal tiger. [203] (*2)

1865

n.d.	ACD wrote his first literary creation, the story of a Bengal tiger [202] containing thirty-six words, written at the age of six. [99,215] (*2)

1866

n.d.	ACD lived with Mary Burton at Liberton Bank House, Edinburgh. [5,14,68,200]
February 6	Henry Edward Doyle married Jane Isabella Ball at the Spanish Chapel, Charles Street, Marylebone, London. [68,124,200]
n.d.	Birth of Caroline Mary Burton Doyle (Lottie), daughter of Charles and Mary. [17,180] (*4)
February	Birth of Caroline Mary Burton Doyle (Lottie), daughter of Charles and Mary. [215] (*4)
February 15	Birth of Caroline Mary Burton Doyle (Lottie) at Liberton Bank, Edinburgh. [124] (*4)
February 22	Birth of Caroline Mary Burton Doyle (Lottie) [203] at Liberton Bank, Edinburgh. [16,68,200,202,203] (*4)
March	Caroline Mary Burton Doyle (Lottie) baptised at St. Mary's Cathedral, Broughton, Edinburgh. [124]
April 23	Birth of Alfred Herbert Wood, later to become ACD's secretary. [109,235]
n.d.	Birth of E.W. Hornung. [202] (*2)

1866

June 7	Birth of E.W. Hornung. [68,124,200] (*2)
Summer	ACD and his mother took a holiday in King's County, Ireland; they stayed with some 'well-to-do' relations. [202]
n.d.	ACD with his mother spent a few weeks in Lismore, County Waterford, Ireland. [14]
n.d.	The Doyle family moved to 3 Sciennes Hill Place, Edinburgh. [202]
n.d.	ACD attended Newington Academy, Edinburgh. [5,14,68,200,215] (*2)
Autumn	ACD attended Newington Academy, Salisbury Place, Edinburgh. [202] (*2)
n.d.	Death of Anna Maria Doyle. [202] (*2)
September 11	Death of Anna Maria Doyle. [124] (*2)

1867

Autumn	ACD left Edinburgh for England to start his Jesuit education at Hodder House. [203]
September 15	ACD was enrolled at Hodder House, the preparatory school for Stonyhurst. [215] (*4)
October 13	ACD at Hodder House the preparatory school for Stonyhurst College, earliest letter dated 13 October sent from ACD to his mother. [141,203]

1868

n.d.	Doyle family resided at 3 Sciennes Hill Place, Edinburgh. [11,20,39,68,200]
n.d.	ACD's sister Annette was working as a governess in Portugal. [124]
January	Death of John Doyle (HB) at 54 Clifton Gardens, Maida Vale, London. [202] (*2)
January 2	Death of John Doyle (HB) [215] at 54 Clifton Gardens, London. [68,124,200,203] (*2)
January 8	Funeral of John (HB) Doyle at Norwood Cemetery, Norwood Road, Lambeth, London. [781]
n.d.	Birth of Constance Amelia Monica (Connie) Doyle, daughter of Charles and Mary. [14,17,20,180] (*3)
March	Birth of Constance Amelia Monica (Connie) at Sciennes Hill Place, Edinburgh. [202] (*3)
March 4	Birth of Constance Amelia Monica Doyle (Connie) [16,68,124,200,203,215] at 3 Sciennes Hill Place, Edinburgh. [68,200] (*3)
n.d.	ACD entered and boarded at Hodder Preparatory School, Lancashire, paid for by Mary Doyle [99] (*3) and then onto adjacent Stonyhurst College, Lancashire. [124,180,215]
March 28	ACD at Hodder House. [203]
May	ACD made his first communion at Hodder House. [202,203]
Summer	ACD spent the summer holidays from Hodder House at home in Edinburgh. [203]
n.d.	ACD entered Hodder House. [99] (*3)
September 15	ACD entered Hodder Preparatory School [68,200,202,220,801] (*3) for two years education under the Jesuits, this being the preparatory school for Stonyhurst College, both in the Ribble Valley, Lancashire, it was here that ACD distinguished himself as a storyteller and athlete. [7]
September	ACD began his studies at Stonyhurst College. [203] (*4)
December 13	ACD at Hodder House. [203]
Christmas	ACD spent Christmas at Hodder House. [202,203]

1869

May 30	ACD at Hodder House. [203]
August 1	End of the school year ACD returned home for the holiday period. [203]
September	ACD returned after his annual summer holiday to Stonyhurst College. [203]
September 19	ACD at Stonyhurst College. [203]
November 14	ACD at Stonyhurst College. [203]

1869

November 21	ACD at Stonyhurst College. [203]
Christmas	ACD at Stonyhurst College. [203]

1870

n.d.	Birth of Leslie William Searles Oldham. [68,124,200]
n.d.	ACD entered Stonyhurst College and remained there for five years, a Catholic public school run by Jesuits. [7,99,215] (*4)
January 7	ACD at Stonyhurst College. [203]
January 30	ACD at Stonyhurst College. [203]
March 6	ACD at Stonyhurst College. [203]
March 20	ACD at Stonyhurst College. [203]
July	ACD entered Stonyhurst College and remained there for five years. [5,68,200] (*4)
August 22	Birth of Bertram Fletcher Robinson in Wavertree, Liverpool. [153]
Autumn	ACD entered Stonyhurst College. [202] (*4)
Autumn	ACD at Stonyhurst College. [203]
October	ACD wrote his first recorded poem *The Students Dream*. [202]
October 31	ACD at Stonyhurst College. [203]
November 25	ACD at Stonyhurst College. [203]
November 29	ACD at Stonyhurst College. [203]
December 6	ACD at Stonyhurst College. [203]
Christmas	ACD spent Christmas at Stonyhurst College. [203]

1871

n.d.	Bryan Charles Waller arrived in Edinburgh and studied medicine at Edinburgh University's medical school. [180]
April 2/3	Charles Altamont Doyle, his wife Mary, daughters Caroline and Constance and Kate Foley were living at 3 Sciennes Hill Place, Edinburgh. [116]
April 2/3	ACD at Stonyhurst College. [205,217]
April 2/3	James and Selina Leckie were living at New Kidbrooke, Kent. [217]
April 11	ACD at Stonyhurst College. [203]
May 27	Kate Foley, ACD's maternal aunt sailed from London on board the *Abbey Holme* for Brisbane, Australia. [1014]
August 30	ACD at Sciennes Hill Place, Edinburgh for the college holiday. [203]
Autumn	ACD returned to Stonyhurst College. [203]
September 13	Kate Foley arrived on board the *Abbey Holme* at Brisbane, Australia. [1014]
October 10	ACD at Stonyhurst College. [203]
October 31	ACD at Stonyhurst. [203]

1872

n.d.	Birth of John Francis Innes Hay Doyle, son of Charles and Mary Doyle. [20] (*3)
n.d.	Birth of Richard Barry-Doyle [69] second cousin of ACD. [3]
May	ACD at Stonyhurst College. [203]
July 21	ACD was confirmed by Bishop Richard Roskell of Nottingham at Stonyhurst College. [202]
August	ACD at Stonyhurst College. [203]
Christmas	ACD at Stonyhurst College. [203]

1873

n.d.	Birth of Charles Cyril Angell. [68,200]
March	ACD at Stonyhurst College. [203]
n.d.	Birth of John Francis Innes Hay Doyle. [99,180] (*3)
March 31	Birth of John Francis Innes Hay Doyle [202,203] at 3 Sciennes Hill Place, Edinburgh. [9,14,16,17,68,124,200] (*3)
April	ACD at Stonyhurst College. [203]

1873

June	ACD at Stonyhurst College. [203]
July	ACD at Stonyhurst College. [203]
July	ACD's final term at Stonyhurst College. [202]
July 14	Death of Jeremiah Hawkins, husband of Emily Hawkins. [124]
September	ACD at Stonyhurst College. [203]
October	ACD at Stonyhurst College. [203]
November	ACD and another student at Stonyhurst, Arthur Roskell, launched a journal titled the *Stonyhurst Figaro*. [203,215]
November 14	ACD wrote the poem *The Passage of the Red Sea*. [99,202]

1874

n.d.	Birth of Jane Adelaide Rose Doyle (Ida). [20] (*3)
n.d.	James William Edmund Doyle married Jane Henrietta Hawkins at Our Lady of the Rosary, Marylebone Road, London. [68] (*3)
n.d.	James Doyle married Jane Henrietta Hawkins. [202] (*3)
February 12	James William Edmund Doyle married Jane Henrietta Hawkins [200] (*3) at Our Lady of the Rosary, Marylebone Road, London. [124]
February 16	Shrove Monday ACD played cricket. [203]
n.d.	Birth of Jean Leckie. [202] (*3)
March 14	Birth of Jean Leckie at 3 Kidbrook Terrace, Kidbrook, Kent. [68,200,203] (*3)
May 25	Whit Monday ACD played cricket. [203]
June	ACD at Stonyhurst College. [203]
June 18	ACD probably watched a cricket match at Preston. [203]
Autumn	ACD entered his final year at Stonyhurst. [202,203]
September	ACD at Stonyhurst College. [203]
November	ACD visited and stayed with his Uncle and Aunt, Richard and Annette Doyle at 7 Finborough Road, London. [32] (*4)
November 21	ACD arrived in London at Euston Station and stayed with Aunt Annette and Uncle Richard at 7 Finborough Road, London. [233] (*4)
Christmas	ACD visited London and stayed with his Uncle Richard Doyle the artist and Aunt Annette [5,14,99,180,202] (*4). During his time in London, he saw Henry Irving in *Hamlet* at the Lyceum [99,215] he visited St. Paul's Cathedral, Westminster Abbey, the Tower of London and Madame Tussaud's waxworks in the Baker Street Bazaar. [25,124,215]
December	During the Christmas break in late December 1874 to early January 1895, ACD spent some time with Uncle Richard and Aunt Annette at their home at 7 Finborough Road, London [203,215] (*4) and with Uncle James and Aunt Jane probably at 54 Clifton Gardens, London. [124,141,203]

1875

n.d.	Birth of Jean Leckie. [124] (*3)
n.d.	Bryan Charles Waller was lodging with Charles Doyle and his family at 2 Argyle Park Terrace, Edinburgh. [5,11,20,39,68,11,20,124,180,200,2010]
n.d.	Birth of Jane Adelaide Rose (Ida) Doyle, daughter of Charles and Mary Doyle. [180,203] (*3)
March 16	Birth of Jane Adelaide Rose (Ida) Doyle [215] daughter of Charles and Mary Doyle at 2 Argyle Park Terrace, Edinburgh. [14,16,17,68,124,200,202] (*3)
n.d.	Annette Conan Doyle departed for Portugal to be a governess. [203]
May 14	ACD at Stonyhurst College. [203]
June	At the Matriculation Examination for June, ACD passed with in the honours division. [191,203] he was placed eighty-first. [99] (*4)
June 5	Trial exams at Stonyhurst began. [203]
June	ACD at Stonyhurst College. [203]
June 28	Exams began at Stonyhurst College, these lasted for nearly a fortnight. [203]
July	ACD at Stonyhurst College. [203]

1875

July	ACD passed London Matriculation Examination at Stonyhurst College [14] passed with honours. [203,215] (*4)
July 28	ACD passed London Matriculation Examination at Stonyhurst College. [202] (*4)
n.d.	ACD passes his final exams at Stonyhurst College and is sent on a final year at a Jesuit school at Feldkirch, Austria, he began to question his Catholic faith. [99] (*4)
August 3	ACD left Stonyhurst College. [801]
September	ACD stayed in Liverpool with a family called the Rockcliffes on route to Stella Mautina, Feldkirch, Austria. [202,203]
September	ACD attended Stella Matutina (Stonyhurst branch school) in Feldkirch, Austria, from sometime in September 1875 until 28 June 1876. [141] (*3)
n.d.	ACD attended Stella Matutina (Stonyhurst branch school) Feldkirch, Austria, for one year. [68,200] (*3)
Autumn	ACD attended the Jesuit school at Feldkirch in Austria. [3,7,14] (*3)
October	ACD edited the *Feldkirchian Gazette*. [6,99]
November	ACD edited the *Feldkirchian Gazette*. [6,99]
Winter	ACD began his studies at Edinburgh University. [1] (*6)
Christmas	ACD spent Christmas at Feldkirch. [203]

1876

January	ACD at Feldkirch. [203]
March	ACD at Feldkirch. [203]
March	Birth of George Edalji. [18,189]
April	ACD at Feldkirch. [203]
April	Charles Altamont Doyle left his government job in Edinburgh. [141,202]
May	ACD at Feldkirch. [203]
May 30	ACD at Feldkirch. [203]
June	Charles Altamont Doyle retired from the Scottish Office of Works. [124,180,203]
June 1	ACD at Feldkirch. [203]
n.d.	Charles Altamont Doyle sent to Blairerno, a nursing facility, to receive treatment for alcoholism and suffering from epilepsy. [15,99]
n.d.	Birth of Bryan Mary Julia Josephine Doyle (Dodo). [20] (*5)
June	Mary Doyle (ACD's mother) was living at Masongill, Thornton in Lonsdale, Yorkshire. [202]
June	ACD left Feldkirch. [3,215] (*3)
June 26	ACD travelled from Feldkirch to Lindau. [1819]
June 27	ACD travelled from Lindau to Rorschach and then on to Basel, where he stayed overnight. [1819]
June 28	ACD travelled from Basle to Paris, where he visited he uncle Michael Conan and aunt Susan in Avenue Wagram, he stayed with them for several weeks. [1819]
n.d.	ACD stayed for a while in Paris, France with godparents Michael and Susan Conan at avenue de Wagram. [124] (*5)
June	At the end of June, ACD spent several weeks with Uncle Michael Conan and Aunt Susan at 65 Avenue de Wagram, Paris. [3,4,68,202,203,215] (*5)
July	ACD probably visited his Uncle Michael Conan and Aunt Susan in Paris. [141] (*5)
Summer	ACD left Feldkirch. [2] (*3)
n.d.	ACD left Feldkirch, Austria. [99] (*3)
n.d.	ACD finished his school education. [124]
Summer	ACD on his way back to Edinburgh from Feldkirch visited his godfather and grand-uncle Michael Conan at 65 Avenue de Wagram, Paris. [86] (*5)
August	ACD visited his Godfather and uncle, Michael Conan in Paris. [2] (*5)
n.d.	ACD arrived back in Edinburgh. [124]

1876

Summer	ACD arrived back at 2 Argyle Park Terrace, Edinburgh. [202]
September 9	ACD at 2 Argyle Park Terrace, Edinburgh. [203]
September	ACD was at home at 2 Argyle Park Terrace, Edinburgh cramming for the bursary that he won, but he did not get. [141]
n.d.	ACD entered Edinburgh University's medical school. [180] (*6)
n.d.	ACD enrolled at the University of Edinburgh Medical School. [7,11,15,21,39] (*6)
n.d.	ACD decides to become a doctor and enrols at Edinburgh University (*6) on the advice of Bryan Charles Waller with whom the Doyles are now lodging in Edinburgh. [99]
October 25	ACD commenced his studies in medicine at Edinburgh University. [182] (*6)
October	ACD enrolled at Edinburgh University to study medicine on the advice of Bryan Charles Waller, while at the University he met Dr Joseph Bell, on whom Holmes was largely based and also Professor Rutherford, later a model for Professor Challenger. [2,3,5,7,14,20,68,200,202,203,215] (*6)

1877

n.d.	Bryan Charles Waller inherited Masongill estate in North Yorkshire. [180]
March	After polishing up on his French, German and moral philosophy for a preliminary examination, ACD gained a worthy pass. [202]
n.d.	Birth of Bryan Mary Julia Josephine (Dodo) Doyle, daughter of Charles and Mary Doyle. [180] (*5)
March	Birth of Bryan Mary Doyle (Dodo). [17] (*5)
March 2	Birth of Bryan Mary Julia Josephine Doyle (Dodo) [202,203,215] at 2 Argyle Park Terrace, Edinburgh. [5,14,16,68,124,200] (*5)
April 6	Bryan Mary Julia Josephine (Dodo) Doyle baptised at St. Mary's Cathedral, Broughton, Edinburgh [124] St. Mary's Church. [202]
May 18	ACD attended the Botanical class at the Royal Botanic Garden Edinburgh {RBGE} in order to graduate in medicine at the University of Edinburgh. [1131]
May 21	ACD attended the Vegetable Histology & Practical Botany class at the Royal Botanic Garden Edinburgh {RBGE} in order to graduate in medicine at the University of Edinburgh. [1131]
May 23	ACD attended the Vegetable Histology & Practical Botany class at the RBGE. [1131]
May 28	ACD attended the Vegetable Histology & Practical Botany class at the RBGE. [1131]
May 29	ACD attended the Botanical class at the RBGE. [1131]
May 30	ACD attended the Botanical class at the RBGE. [1131]
May 30	ACD attended the Vegetable Histology & Practical Botany class at the RBGE. [1131]
June 4	ACD attended the Vegetable Histology & Practical Botany class at the RBGE. [1131]
June 5	ACD attended the Botanical class at the RBGE. [1131]
June 6	ACD attended the Vegetable Histology & Practical Botany class at the RBGE. [1131]
June 8	ACD attended the Botanical class at the RBGE. [1131]
June 11	ACD attended the Vegetable Histology & Practical Botany class at the RBGE. [1131]
June 12	ACD attended the Botanical class at the RBGE. [1131]
June 13	ACD attended the Vegetable Histology & Practical Botany class at the RBGE. [1131]
June 15	Owing to illness ACD did not attend the Botanical class at the RBGE. [1131]
June 18	ACD attended the Vegetable Histology & Practical Botany class at the RBGE. [1131]
June 19	Owing to illness ACD did not attend the Botanical class at the RBGE. [1131]

1877

June 20	ACD attended the Vegetable Histology & Practical Botany class at the RBGE. [1131]
June 22	ACD attended the Botanical class at the RBGE. [1131]
June 25	Owing to illness ACD did not attend the Vegetable Histology & Practical Botany class at the RBGE. [1131]
June 26	ACD attended the Botanical class at the RBGE. [1131]
June 27	ACD attended the Vegetable Histology & Practical Botany class at the RBGE [1131]
June 29	ACD attended the Botanical class at the RBGE. [1131]
July 2	ACD attended the Vegetable Histology & Practical Botany class at the RBGE. [1131]
July 3	ACD attended the Botanical class at the RBGE. [1131]
July 4	ACD attended the Vegetable Histology & Practical Botany class at the RBGE. [1131]
July 6	ACD attended the Botanical class at the RBGE. [1131]
n.d.	Bryan Charles Waller leased 23 George Square, Edinburgh, as a consulting pathologist with all the Doyles as residents. [5,7,11,20,39,68,124,200] (*2)
August	In August or early September, the Doyle family probably moved to 23 George Square, Edinburgh. [202] (*2)
n.d.	ACD spent a holiday in the Isle of Arran. [3,14,21] (*2)
August 29	ACD arrived at East Knowe, Brodick, Arran, Scotland [203] he stayed at the home of Miss Fullerton in East Knowe in the hills above Brodick, Arran. [141]
August	ACD spent a holiday on the Isle of Arran [202] (*2). His sister Lottie and his Stonyhurst friend Jimmy Ryan originally accompanied him. Ryan did not stay as long as the others, and was replaced in the lodgings by ACD's sister Connie and his father for a short time. [202]
September 6	ACD on the Isle of Arran. [203]
September 17	ACD met Dr Joseph Bell on the Isle of Arran. [203]
September 18	ACD at the Isle of Arran. [203]
November 1	ACD commenced studying at the University of Edinburgh. [128] (*6)
n.d.	ACD became surgeon's clerk to Joseph Bell at Edinburgh University. [99,180] (*3)

1878

n.d.	ACD began to read widely in spiritualism. [99]
March 2	Birth of Bryan Mary Julia Josephine Doyle (Dodo). (*5) [Date taken from grave headstone]
April	ACD became a doctor's assistant to Dr Charles Richardson in Sheffield; this lasted for three weeks. [202] (*5)
n.d.	While still a student ACD took a job, as doctor's assistant with Dr Richardson in Sheffield lasting 3 weeks. [215] (*5)
Spring	While still a student ACD took a part time job lasting 3 weeks assisting Dr Richardson at Sheffield, [68] Dr Charles Sidney Richardson, Nelson Terrace, 80 Spital Hill, Sheffield. [192,200,203] (*5)
May 18	ACD arrived in London. [203]
May 19	ACD dined with Uncle James and Aunt Jane at Clifton Gardens, London. [203] (*2)
n.d.	ACD spent a few weeks with Aunt Jane Doyle, Uncle Henry Doyle and Uncle James Doyle at their home at 54 Clifton Gardens, Maida Vale, London. [2,3,14,39,68,124,200] (*2)
May 22	ACD saw Henry Irving in *Louis XI*. [203,215]
May 25	ACD saw the guards parade. [203]
n.d.	ACD visited his Uncle Dick in Finborough Road, Chelsea. [215] (*2)
May 26	ACD at Finborough Road, London with Uncle Richard Doyle and Aunt Annette Doyle. [203] (*2)

1878

May 27	ACD attended a cricket match at Lord's where the Australians defeated England. [203]
May 28	ACD spent the day at Westminster Aquarium. [203]
May 28	ACD dined at 54 Clifton Gardens, London. [203]
May 29	ACD visited the Royal Academy. [203]
June 11	ACD in London. [203]
June 18	ACD in London. [203]
July	ACD working as an assistant to Dr Henry Francis Elliot of Cliffe House, Ruyton-XI-Towns, Shropshire [203] Dr Elliott. [215] (*3)
n.d.	During July or August, ACD played cricket for Ruyton and took 7 wickets for 11 runs. [203]
August 23	ACD at Ruyton-XI-Towns. [203]
Summer	ACD student assistant for four months with Dr Henry Francis Elliott or Elliot in the village of Ruyton-XI-Towns, Shropshire. [2,7,14,20,39,68,200,202] (*3)
n.d.	While still a student ACD took a part-time job, lasting 3 weeks, as student assistant to Dr Richardson at Sheffield (*5) and then became surgeon's clerk to Joseph Bell. [7,10,14,20,202] (*3)
n.d.	ACD became clerk to Dr Joseph Bell at Edinburgh University. [7,14] (*3)
n.d.	ACD became an outpatient clerk for Dr Bell at the Royal Infirmary. [202]
n.d.	ACD was temporary medical assistantship with Dr Richardson at Sheffield (*5) and Dr Hoare at Birmingham. [99]
October	ACD returned to Edinburgh University. [14]
October 10	ACD with Dr Elliott at Ruyton-XI-Towns, Shropshire. [203] (*3)
October 19	ACD's final letter sent to his mother from Ruyton-XI-Towns. [203]

1879

n.d.	Charles Doyle entered an institution Fordoun House, near Fordoun north of Montrose, Scotland. He was a manic-depressive, alcoholic and epileptic. [14]
n.d.	Charles Doyle entered an institution near Fordoun north of Montrose, Scotland. [16]
n.d.	Charles Altamont Doyle admitted to Blairerno House, Drumlithie (New Mill), Kincardineshire a home for intemperates. [124,180]
May	ACD finished his second year of clinical study. [202]
June 2	ACD arrived in Birmingham. [203]
June 3	ACD in Birmingham. [203]
n.d.	ACD became an assistant to Dr Reginald Ratcliff Hoare at his surgery, Clifton House, Aston Road, Birmingham [202,215] in June. [203] (*3)
Summer	In the summer or possibly spring, ACD was a student assistant to Dr Reginald Ratcliff Hoare at 63 Aston Road North, Aston, Birmingham. [2,68,200] (*3)
Summer	ACD student assistant to Dr Reginald Ratcliff Hoare at Clifton House, Aston Road, Birmingham, from the middle of March until February 1880. [3,5,7,39] (*3)
n.d.	ACD experimented on himself with gelseminum, or yellow jasmine, the results of which were published in the *British Medical Journal*. [202] (*3)
n.d.	ACD was experimenting on himself with gelseminum. [215] (*3)
June	ACD was experimenting on himself with gelseminum. [203] (*3)
September	ACD at Clifton House, Aston Road, Birmingham as assistant to Dr Reginald Hoare. [18]
n.d.	*The Mystery of Sasassa Valley* published in *Chambers's Journal*. [99] (*2)
September 6	*The Mystery of Sasassa Valley* published in *Chambers's Journal*. [6,31,180,196,198,202,215] (*2)
n.d.	*Gelseminium as Prism* published in the *British Medical Journal*. [99] (*3)
n.d.	*Gelseminum as a Poison* published in the *British Medical Journal*. [215] (*3)
September 20	*Gelseminum as a Poison* published in the *British Medical Journal*. [6,18,180,196,202] (*3)
December	Death of Michael Conan in Paris, great-uncle of ACD. [202] (2*)

1879

December 3	Death of Michael Conan at his home, 65 avenue de Wagram, Paris, he was buried in the Paris cemetery of Saint Ouen. [124] (2*)

1880

January	ACD attended a lecture in Birmingham "Does Death End All?" [4,203] His first spiritualist lecture [100] probably given by a local spiritualist group. [20]
January	ACD showed his first interest in spiritualism and the paranormal. [14]
January 30	ACD in Birmingham. [203]
February 6	ACD attended a ball. [203]
February	ACD in Lerwick, Scotland. [203]
n.d.	ACD served in the capacity of surgeon for seven months on board the whaling ship *Hope* of Peterhead. [99,180] (*4)
February 27	ACD signed on as ship's surgeon on the Greenland whaler *Hope*. [144,202] (*4)
February 28	ACD set sail from Peterhead on board the Greenland whaler *Hope*. [99,144,202,215]
February 28	ACD served as ship's surgeon on the Greenland whaler *Hope* of Peterhead for seven months [2,7,10,14,15] (*4) February to September. [11,68,200]
February 28	ACD sailed at 2 o'clock on board the *Hope* for Shetland. [336]
February 29	*Hope* arrived in Lerwick at 7:30p.m. [336] {Note: this entry in the Log is dated Sunday March 1, an error by ACD as 1880 was a leap year, so he arrived on Sunday 29 February.}
March	ACD served as ship's surgeon on the Greenland whaler *Hope* of Peterhead for six months. [5] (*4)
March 1	*Hope* in Lerwick harbour. [336]
March 2	*Hope* in Lerwick harbour. [336]
March 3	ACD and Captain Gray went ashore at Lerwick and enlisted the Shetland hands at George Reid Tait's, the draper, clothier and shipping agent. [336]
March 4	ACD went ashore at Lerwick went to the Queen's Hotel and the Commercial Hotel. [336]
March 5	ACD and Captain Gray went ashore for dinner with George Tait after playing billiards at the Queen's Hotel. [336]
March 6	ACD did nothing all day as it was raining and blowing hard. [336]
March 7	The engineer of the *Windward* had crushed his two forefingers yesterday, and ACD dressed them before breakfast. [336]
March 8	ACD went ashore with Captain Gray and watched a football match between Orkney and Shetland. They met the Captains of *Jan Mayen*, *Nova Zembla* and *Erik*; they all went to the Queen's Hotel after the match. [336]
March 8	ACD wrote a letter to his mother thanking her for her letters, parcels and updating her on his news. [336]
March 9	ACD went ashore with Captain Gray. [336]
March 9	ACD arrived at Lerwick on board the *Hope* in the Shetland Islands. [202] (*2)
March 10	A north wind prevented the *Hope* sailing, went ashore in the evening and played billiards. [336]
March 10	ACD left Lerwick on the Shetland Islands. [202,203] (*2)
March 11	*Hope* left Lerwick about 1 o'clock and came to anchorage about seven in a little inlet. [336] (*2)
March 12	*Hope* was still anchored owing to a high gale. [336]
March 13	*Hope* left its anchorage and set sail in high winds and heavy rain. [336]
March 14	*Hope* all day under steam and sail. [336]
March 15	*Hope* first under steam and sail, and then under sail alone. [336]
March 15	ACD sighted the first seal. [99] (*2)
March 16	*Hope* still under sail. [336]
March 16	ACD reached the ice. [203] (*2)
March 17	*Hope* under steam and first encountered ice (*2), ACD spent the morning up the crow's nest. [336]

1880

March 18	*Hope* north of Jan Mayen, ACD and crew saw their first seal, a bladdernose. [336] (*2)
March 19	*Hope* travelling through thick haze and drizzle. [336]
March 20	About a couple of hundred seals visible from the crow's nest. [336] (*2)
March 20	ACD saw his first real pack of seals. [203] (*2)
March 21	*Hope* had to lay to all day owing to thick haze. [336]
March 22	The fog lasted all day so the *Hope* had to lay to. [336]
March 23	*Hope* under steam, blowing a gale all day. [336]
March 24	The crew of the *Hope* sighted an enormous pack of seals. [336]
March 25	*Hope* took up her position, mounting boats and cleaning guns. [336]
March 26	ACD saw the young seals suckling, hurt his hand boxing with Stewart, stuffed old Keith's tooth and cured young Keith's collywobbles. [336]
March 27	*Hope* was steaming a little, rifles were issued, Haggie Milne health improving. [336]
March 28	Haggie Milne taken ill again, ACD had dinner on board the *Eclipse*. [336]
March 29	Thick day with a driving snow. [336]
March 30	Nothing much doing, the *Windward* came alongside the *Hope* and Captain Murray came aboard, ACD sparred with Colin and Stewart. [336]
March 31	Very little doing all day, a heavy swell had set in. [336]
n.d.	Bryan Charles Waller and the Doyles were living at 15 Lonsdale Terrace, Edinburgh. [7,39] (*2)
April	Mary Doyle and family were living at 15 Lonsdale Terrace, Edinburgh. [68,200] (*2)
April	Charles Altamont Doyle was a boarder at Blairerno, Glenbervie, Kincardine, Scotland. [68,200]
April 1	The swell continued and the *Hope* steamed for a while. [336]
April 2	The swell was still on. [336]
April 3	ACD took part in the first seal hunt. [99,202,203,215] (*2)
April 3	Hunting started on 3 April [202] (*2), during the hunting season ACD fell into the water and was then nicknamed 'the great northern diver' by Captain John Gray of the *Hope*, the total catch by the *Hope* was 2 Greenland whales and 3,614 seals, ACD own 'gamebag' was 55 seals. [99,202]
April 3	The swell was still on, while getting over the ships side ACD, fell in the sea, he succeeded in killing a couple seals, and the crew took 760 seals. [336]
April 4	ACD was working on the pack ice all day and fell into the sea three times, the crew took about 460 seals. [366]
April 5	ACD nearly lost his life when he fell from a large piece of ice. [203,215]
April 5	ACD working again, he fell into the sea yet again, after he had killed a seal, the crew took about 400 seals. [336] {Note: this entry is dated Monday 6 April in the Log, but the 5 April was a Monday.}
April 6	ACD shot an eleven-foot long sea elephant. [203]
April 6	ACD working on the pack ice, although he did not fall into the sea, the Captain called him "the Great Northern Diver." ACD shot two large bladdernoses, also called Sea Elephants. The crew took 270 young and 58 old seals. [336]
April 7	ACD off Jan Mayen's Island in the Arctic Circle. [203,215]
April 7	A poor day, very few seals about, only 133 taken. Crew member Andrew Haggie Milne seriously ill. [336]
April 8	The *Active* collected letters from the *Hope*, only about 30 seals taken, gale in the evening. [336]
April 9	The gale continued with a heavy swell, ACD did nothing but sleep and write up his log. [336]
April 10	Andrew Milne almost beyond help, gale and heavy swell continued. [336]
April 11	Andrew Milne died, about 60 seals were taken. [336]
April 12	Andrew Milne buried at sea, about 60 seals were taken. [336]
April 13	*Hope* had to lay to all day owing to the continuing gale, ACD did some fine boxing, no seals taken. [336]

1880

April 14	About 80 seals taken, making the total to about 2450, ACD stood at the forecastle all day reporting progress. [336]
April 15	Beautiful fine day only about 46 seals taken, ACD assisted in shooting 2 bladdernoses. [336]
April 16	*Hope* was steaming northwest to locate seals, only took half a dozen. [336]
April 17	*Hope* was steaming south, only took half a dozen seals. [336]
April 18	A snowy drizzly day, ACD shot a seal in the morning, in the evening he attended a Methodist meeting. [336]
April 19	*Hope* was steaming north, the crew got a few bladdernoses. [336]
April 20	*Hope* was steaming northeast. [336]
April 21	Heavy cross sea and swell, nothing to do. [336]
April 22	Heavy swell still on, took 13 seals of which ACD shot 2, he claims to have shot about 15 in all. [336]
April 23	A total of 36 seals were taken, of which ACD took 11, making 26 in all. [336]
April 24	*Hope* was steaming northwest, picked up 17 young seals, no shooting today, ACD sparred in the morning. [336]
April 25	22 young seals taken, ACD shot 7 young seals, total taken by the crew so far 2502, boxed with Stewart in the evening. [336]
April 26	*Hope* was sailing north and northwest all day looking for old seals; ACD did some boxing in the evening. [336]
April 27	*Hope* was steaming north and northwest all day. [336]
April 28	*Hope* came across heavy ice. [336]
April 29	*Hope* steaming north all day. [336]
April 30	*Hope* steaming northeast. [336]
May 1	*Hope* crew took 69 seals. [336]
May 2	*Hope* steaming north in showers, heavy ice, snow and wind. [336]
May 3	The hunting boats were lowered at about 6a.m., ACD's boat took 27 seals, at 2p.m. dinner was taken and then the boats were lowered again, this time ACD's boat took 28 or so seals, total for the ship taken during the day was 540 old seals. [336]
May 4	Again the boats were lowered at 6a.m., ACD took 7 seals, total for the day was 275 old seals. [336]
May 5	*Hope* steaming northeast, the crew took 71 seals. [336]
May 6	*Hope* steaming southwest, heavy swell and no sign of seals. [336]
May 7	*Hope* sailing northeast, no sign of seals. [336]
May 8	*Hope* steaming northwest, no sign of seals. [336]
May 9	*Hope* steaming northwest, no sign of seals. [336]
May 10	*Hope* steaming north, thick rain and wind, no sign of seals. [336]
May 11	*Hope* steaming north, heavy gale, no sign of seals. [336]
May 12	A beautiful day with blue sky, no sign of seals. [336]
May 13	Seals sighted but no hunting. [336]
May 14	Boats were lowered at 9a.m.; ACD's boat took 5 seals, 119 seals taken by the crew. [336]
May 15	32 seals taken by the crew, *Hope* steaming and sailing north. [336]
May 16	*Hope* steaming north, no seals found. [336]
May 17	*Hope* steaming about 100 miles west of Spitzbergen, 6 seals taken. [336]
May 18-20	From 18 to 20 heavy gale blowing. [336]
May 21	No seals sighted. [336]
May 22	Birthday of ACD, he became of age. [336]
May 23	*Hope* sailing west. [336]
May 24	Strong winds, no seals sighted. [336]
May 25	Stronger winds, no seals sighted. [336]
May 26	Fine day but no seals sighted. [336]
May 27	No seals sighted. [336]
May 28	*Hope* steaming north and northeast, no seals sighted. [336]
May 29	No seals sighted. [336]

1880

May 30	2 ground seals taken. [336]
May 31	No seals sighted. [336]
June 1	One bladdernose taken. [336]
June 2	*Hope* sailing west and south, no seals sighted. [336]
June 3	No seals sighted. [336]
June 4	No seals sighted. [336]
June 5	One sea elephant shot. [336] {Note: this entry is dated Saturday June 6, whereas it should be Saturday June 5.}
June 6	One narwhal taken, 2 rare ducks were shot by the captain. [336]
June 7	ACD went aboard the *Eclipse*. [336]
June 8	No seals sighted, ACD went bird shooting, he shot a roach and loon. [336]
June 9	No seals sighted, ACD went bird shooting, he took a roach and 6 snowbirds. [336]
June 10	No seals sighted, ACD shot a kittiwake, a maulie and 3 loons. [336]
June 11	Jack Williamson, crew member, suffered a terrible blow to his head, ACD stitched the wound. [336]
June 12	Crew shot a bear; ACD went aboard the *Eclipse* for dinner. [336]
June 13	*Hope* sailing west and south west. [336]
June 14	Jack Williamson doing very well. [336]
June 15	Thick fog, no seals sighted. [336]
June 16	Many narwhals seen during the evening. [336]
June 17	No seals sighted, ACD and Mathieson hunted a bear, ACD wounded the bear but it ran off. [336]
June 18	Buchan, crew member shot a bear and two cubs, no seals sighted. [336]
June 19	Many narwhals seen, but no seals. [336]
June 20	*Hope* anchored up. [336]
June 21	*Hope* anchored up. [336]
June 22	*Hope* anchored up. [336]
June 23	*Hope* steaming south and east. [336]
June 24	Hard gale blowing. [336]
June 25	Strong wind blowing, *Hope* steaming north. [336]
June 26	One Greenland whale taken. [336]
June 27	No seals sighted. [336]
June 28	No seals sighted. [336]
June 29	ACD shot a burgy, a snowbird and 5 loons, *Hope* laying to. [336]
June 30	No seals sighted, *Hope* laying to, ACD went aboard the *Eclipse*. [336]
July 1	*Hope* laying to in a thick fog, one large Narwhal taken by Colin McLean the first mate. [336]
July 2	*Hope* still laying to in a thick fog. [336]
July 3	Fog had cleared and the *Hope* was heading north and northwest. [336]
July 4	*Hope* sailing north and then south. [336]
July 5	No seals sighted. [336]
July 6	ACD went aboard the *Eclipse*, then went shooting and shot 7 loons, a roach, a kittiwake, a snowbird and a flaw rat, saw 2 Sea Swallows. [336]
July 7	*Hope* steaming south. [336]
July 8	Crew took a whale. [336]
July 9	No seals sighted. [336]
July 10	*Hope* heading north, no seals sighted. [336]
July 11	No seals sighted. [336]
July 12	ACD went aboard the *Eclipse* for dinner and then aboard the *Eira* where ACD was photographed among a distinguished group on the quarterdeck. [336]
July 13	*Hope* steaming south. [336]
July 14	*Hope* steamed and sailed south and south west, foggy all day. [336]
July 15	Thick fog all day. [336]
July 16	Still foggy, ACD went aboard the *Eclipse*. [336]
July 17	Thick fog, *Hope* steaming south and east. [336]

1880

July 18	Heavy wind blowing. [336]
July 19	Blowing a gale all day. [336]
July 20	*Hope* steaming south and west. [336]
July 21	Thick fog again, anchored up, ACD and the captain went aboard the *Eclipse* in the evening. [336]
July 22	*Hope* still anchored owing to thick fog. [336]
July 23	*Hope* steaming south and south west, under sail at night. [336]
July 24	*Hope* steaming south west. [336]
July 25	A very clear day, *Hope* steaming west, under sail at night. [336]
July 26	*Hope* sailing west and south west. [336]
July 27	*Hope* sailing south, south west. [336]
July 28	Heavy wind, thick fog and ice everywhere. [336]
July 29	*Hope* anchored up waiting for better weather, *Hope* steamed south east later in the day when the weather cleared, but fog grew thicker, *Hope* anchored up again. [336]
July 30	*Hope* steaming south, south east, 2 bladdernose seals shot, 1 by ACD. [336]
July 31	*Hope* steaming west, south west. [336]
August 1	No entry in diary. [336]
August 2	Hunted 4 bottlenose whales, but they got away. [336]
August 3	*Hope* sailing west. [336]
August 4	No seals sighted. [336]
August 5	*Hope* sailing southwest. [336]
August 6	*Hope* steaming east, southeast for Shetland. [336]
August 7	*Hope* under steam in thick fog. [336]
August 8	Sighted land at about 8p.m. that proved to be the north end of Faeroe Island. [336]
August 9	Clear day with blue sky and bright sun, all hands on the lookout for land. [336]
August 10	Land sighted, *Hope* under steam, passed Lerwick heading for Peterhead. [336]
August 10	The *Hope* returned to Scotland. [203]
August 11	Saw Rattray Head, *Hope* less than 10 miles from Peterhead. [336]
August 12	The *Hope* arrived back in Peterhead. [144] (*2)
August	Mid-August ACD arrived back in Peterhead on board the *Hope*. [202] (*2)
n.d.	ACD became an agnostic. [14]
n.d.	ACD stayed a few weeks in Edinburgh. [202]
September	ACD arrived back in Edinburgh. [14]
October	ACD arrived back in Edinburgh. [5]
n.d.	ACD was student medical assistant to Dr Hoare in Birmingham. [7,20,68,200] (*3)
October	In October or early November ACD returned to work with Dr Hoare in Aston, Birmingham. [202] (*3)
November 16	ACD was working with Dr Hoare in Aston, Birmingham. [203] (*3)
Autumn	ACD returned to his studies in Edinburgh. [15]
December	*The American's Tale* published in the Christmas issue of *London Society*. [6,99,196,198,202]
December	ACD working in Birmingham. [203]
Christmas	ACD spent Christmas in Aston, Birmingham. [203]

1881

n.d.	ACD attended a lecture in Birmingham titled "Does Death End All?" [15,29,180,202]
January	ACD working in Aston, Birmingham. [203]
February 27	ACD working in Birmingham. [203]
March 29	Birth of Clara Schwensen, (the future wife of Innes Doyle). [68,124,200]
April	*A Night among the Nihilists* published in *London Society*. [6,196,198]
April	Jean E. Leckie was living with her family at The Avenue, Eltham, Kent. [68,200] (*2)

1881

April 3/4	James Leckie his wife Selina with their family Jean, Malcolm, Patrick and Sara were living at The Avenue, Eltham, Kent. [219] (*2)
April	James E. Doyle and his wife Jane were living at 54 Clifton Gardens, London. [68, 200] (*2)
April 3/4	James E. Doyle and his wife Jane were living at 54 Clifton Gardens, London. [219] (*2)
April	Annette Doyle and her brother Henry E. Doyle were living at 7 Finborough Road, London. [68,200] (*2)
April 3/4	Annette Doyle and her brother Henry E. Doyle were living at 7 Finborough Road, London. [219] (*2)
April	Mary Doyle, ACD, Innes, Jane and Bryan were living at 23 George Square, Edinburgh. [215]
n.d.	Bryan Charles Waller and the Doyle family were living at 15 Lonsdale Terrace, Edinburgh. [5,11,14,20,68,200,2010] (*3)
April	Mary Doyle, Dodo, Connie, Innes, Ida and ACD were living at 15 Lonsdale Terrace, Edinburgh, leased by Dr Waller (*3) Charles was at Blairerno, Annette was in Portugal and Lottie was in Les Andelys, France. [202]
April 3/4	Mary J.E, Doyle, ACD, Constance, Innes, Jane and Bryan Mary were living at 15 Lonsdale Terrace, Edinburgh. [206] (*3)
April	Charles Altamont Doyle was institutionalised at Blairerno House, Drumlithie, Aberdeenshire. [203,215] (*3)
April	Charles Altamont Doyle was a boarder at Blairerno, Glenbervie, Kincardine, near Fordoun, Scotland. [58] (*3)
April 3/4	Charles Altamont Doyle was a boarder at Blairerno, Glenbervie, Kincardineshire. [207,215] (*3)
Spring	ACD visited Dr Budd in Bristol, Budd was in financial difficulties and had hoped ACD could help him out. [2,3]
June	ACD was living at 15 Lonsdale Terrace, Edinburgh. [203]
June	ACD took his Bachelor of Medicine (MB) and Master of Surgery (CM) exams. [203]
June	ACD on holiday with friends in Lismore, Co. Waterford, Ireland. [202]
June	ACD probably attended a fancy fair and rose show at Ballyin Gardens, Lismore, Miss Elmore Weldon also attended. [202]
July	ACD visited Ballygally, Lismore, Co. Waterford, Ireland. [203]
July	ACD on holiday with friends and visited relations in Lismore, Co. Waterford, Ireland. [14,21,51]
July 1	ACD played cricket for Lismore against the 25th Regiment. [202]
July	ACD played cricket for Lismore against Cahir. [202]
July	ACD sent off *The Gully of Bluemansdyke* to an editor. [203]
July/August	In July or August, ACD and friends visited the Isle of May. [21,202]
n.d.	ACD received his MD in biology. [99]
August	ACD graduated from Edinburgh University as Bachelor of Medicine (MB) and Master of Surgery (CM). [2,14,15,20,99,180,215] (*4)
August 1	ACD graduated as Bachelor of Medicine (MB) and Master of Surgery (CM). [7,68,128,200,202] (*4)
August 1	ACD gained a MB, CM with First Class Honours at Edinburgh University. [182] (*4)
August	ACD graduated with an MB from the University of Edinburgh. [128] (*4)
September	ACD was a medical assistant to Dr Hoare in Birmingham. [7,68,200]
September	ACD's sister Caroline (Lottie) was working as a governess in Portugal. [124]
September	ACD visited George Budd in Bristol. [203]
October	ACD in Liverpool. [203]
October	ACD served as surgeon on board the steamer *Mayumba* to West Africa. [180] (*3)
October 14	*After Cormorants with a Camera* published in the *British Journal of Photography* on 14 & 21 October. [6,21,196,198,202]

1881

October 22	From 22 October 1881 – January 1882, to ACD served as ship's doctor on board the SS *Mayumba* leaving Liverpool to Madeira – Teneriffe – Canary – Sierra Leone – Monrovia Cape Palmas (Liberia) Elmira. Cape Coast Castle, Accra, Addah, Quittah – Little Popo. Whydah (Dahomey), Lagos, Bonny, Fernando Po. Victoria and Old Calabar. During this voyage ACD suffered severe fever. [99] (*3)
October 22	ACD made second voyage as ships doctor this time on a cargo steamer the SS *Mayumba* heading for West Africa [2,7,14,21,31,202,215] end of October [15] October to January. [11,68,68,99,200,203] (*3)
October 29	The SS *Mayumba* reached Madeira, and then called at Tenerife [21,92] Grand Canary and Old Calabar. [21]
November 9	The SS *Mayumba* arrived in Freetown, Sierra Leone. [2024]
November 18	ACD almost died of fever while on board the SS *Mayumba*. [10,14] Mid-November. [15]
November 18	The SS *Mayumba* arrived in Lagos, Nigeria where he was seriously ill with a fever, probably malaria. [2024]
November 22	ACD on board SS *Mayumba* at Bonny River, Nigeria. [203]
November 27	The SS *Mayumba* reached the end of the Africa trip at Fernando Po. [92,144,202]
Christmas	*The Gully of Bluemansdyke* published in the Christmas issue of *London Society*. [6,196,198]
Christmas	*That Little Square Box* published in the Christmas issue of *London Society*. [6,196,198]

1882

n.d.	ACD renounced the Catholic faith. [99]
n.d.	Charles Altamont Doyle confined at Fordoun House because of his alcoholism and epilepsy. [15]
January	Middle of January ACD arrived back in Liverpool. [15,203] (*3)
January 12	ACD on board the SS *Mayumba* arrived back in Liverpool. [99] (*3)
January 14	ACD arrived back in the Port of Liverpool. [2,7,10,14,21,31,202,215] (*3)
February	February-March ACD was living in Birmingham. [232] (*4)
February	From February to April ACD was a medical assistant to Dr Hoare in Birmingham [7,14,68] probably the branch practice at The Elms, Gravelly Hill, Birmingham. [200,202,203] (*4)
n.d.	ACD visited his aunt and uncles in London to discuss his future. [3,7,15,215]
March	ACD at The Elms, Gravelly Hill, Birmingham. [203] (*4)
March	ACD at Aston, Birmingham. [18,215,884] (*4)
March	ACD sent off the 46 page manuscript of *Bones, The April Fool of Harvey's Sluice* to James Hogg editor of *London Society*. [203]
March 25	*Notes on a Case of Leucoythaemia* published in *Lancet*. [6,196]
March	ACD completed writing *Our Derby Sweepstake*. [203]
March 31	*On the Slave Coast with a Camera* published in the *British Journal of Photography* on 31 March & 7 April. [6,21,196,198]
April	*Bones, The April Fool of Harvey's Sluice* published in *London Society*. [6,99,196,198]
May	*Our Derby Sweepstake* published in *London Society*. [6,196,198]
n.d.	ACD went into medical practice with Dr George Budd in Plymouth. [99] (*5)
May	May-June ACD was living in Plymouth. [232] (*5)
Spring	ACD joined the medical practice of Dr Budd in Plymouth. [2,14,215] (*5)
May	ACD joined the medical practice of former fellow student Dr George Turnavine Budd at 1 Durnford Street, Stonehouse, Plymouth. ACD lived with Budd and his wife at 6 Elliot Terrace, The Hoe, Plymouth. [7,15,39,68,200,202] (*5)
June	ACD was working with Dr Budd in Plymouth. [203] (*5)
June	ACD visited Tavistock and Dartmoor. [21] (*2)
June	ACD left Plymouth on board an Irish steamer for Portsmouth. [215]

1882

June	At the end of June ACD left Plymouth to set up own practice [15] late June. [202]
June	At the end of June ACD arrived in Southsea. [15] (*5)
June	ACD worked as a general practitioner in Southsea, Portsmouth, Hampshire, at 1 Bush Vilas, Elm Grove. [124,180,203]
n.d.	ACD moved to Southsea and set up his own practice, his brother Innes joined him and helped out in the practice. [99] (*5)
June 24	ACD arrived in Southsea. [7,8,202] (*5)
June 24	ACD had lodgings in Southsea, Hampshire for one week. [68,200,202]
July	ACD arrived in Portsmouth (Southsea). [2] (*5)
July	ACD arrived at Portsmouth to set up his own practice at Bush Villa, Southsea. [99] (*5)
July	From July 1882 until December 1890 ACD was living in Southsea, Portsmouth. [232]
July 1	ACD opened his practice at 1 Bush Villas, Elm Grove, Southsea [7,8,20,68,200,202,215] (*2) Innes Doyle was resident with ACD as schoolboy and surgery page, [8,14,15,20,203,215] (*3) Innes was educated at Hope House, Green Road. [215] (*2)
n.d.	Innes Doyle was living with ACD at Bush Villas (*3) and was educated at Hope House Day School, Green Road, Southsea. [124] (*2)
July 2	ACD at 1 Bush Villas, Elm Grove, Southsea. [1125]
July 10	Innes Doyle was living with ACD at 1 Bush Villas, Elm Grove, Southsea. [202]
July 17	Innes Doyle arrived at 1 Bush Villas, Elm Grove, Southsea. [203]
July 28	*Up an African River with the Camera* published in the *British Journal of Photography.* [6,21,196,198]
August	ACD visited Tavistock and Dartmoor. [21] (*2)
September	ACD set up his practice in Southsea. [4] (*2)
September	Innes Doyle resident with ACD as schoolboy and surgery page. [11] (*3)
n.d.	Bryan Charles Waller retired to Masongill, North Yorkshire. [180]
n.d.	ACD's mother Mary, with his brother and sisters move to a cottage on Dr Bryan Charles Waller's Masongill estate in Yorkshire. [99] (*3)
n.d.	Mary Doyle resident at Masongill Cottage on the Waller estate at Masongill, Yorkshire. [5,14,15]
September 2	*That Veteran* published in *All the Year Round.* [6,196,198,202]
September 20	ACD at 1 Bush Villas, Elm Grove, Southsea. [1125]
October	ACD at Southsea. [203]
October 11	ACD at 1 Bush Villas, Elm Grove, Southsea. [1125]
November 2	ACD treated Mr Robinson who was thrown from his horse outside the Bush Hotel, Southsea. [339]
November 3	*Dry Plates on a Wet Moor* published in the *British Journal of Photography.* [6,21,196,198]
November 13	ACD at 1 Bush Villa, Elm Grove, Southsea. [1125]
December	*A Few Technical Hints* published in the *British Journal of Photography Almanac for 1883.* [6,21] (*2)
December	ACD at Southsea. [203]
December 5	ACD attended Portsmouth Literary and Scientific Society (PLSS) meeting. [6]
Christmas	ACD's mother stayed at 1 Bush Villas, Elm Grove, Southsea. [202,203]
Christmas	*My Friend the Murderer* published in the Christmas issue of *London Society.* [6,196,198]

1883

n.d.	Charles Altamont Doyle institutionalised. [5,17]
n.d.	*A Few Technical Hints* published in the *British Journal of Photography Almanac.* [198] (*2)
n.d.	ACD taken on as medical examiner for the Gresham Life Assurance Society. [202,203]

1883

n.d.	*J. Habakuk Jephson's Statement* published. [180] (*2)
n.d.	*The Captain of the Pole-star* published in *Temple Bar*. [99] (*2)
January	*The Captain of the Pole-star* published in *Temple Bar*. [6,196,198] (*2)
January 12	*Trial of Burton's Emulsion Process* published in the *British Journal of Photography*. [6,21,196,198]
February	ACD at Southsea. [203]
February	ACD's sisters, Annette and Lottie were in Portugal working as governesses. [203]
February 9	ACD was called in after the death of Mrs Cantello at 99 Grosvenor Street, ACD pronounced life to be extinct. [340]
n.d.	ACD spent two days in London buying furniture. [203]
March	*Life and Death in the Blood* published in *Good Words*, original title *The Fishes of the Blood*. [6,198,202,203]
March 12	ACD treated Mr Warburton and Mr Peel who were thrown from their carriage at the corner of Elm Grove and Grove Road. [341]
March 13	ACD attended PLSS meeting. [6]
March	Willie Burton and a friend called Davies visited ACD over Easter, they went on a local photography expedition, [202] {Note: the outcome of this was *Where to Go with the Camera. Southsea: Three Days in Search of Effects*.}
March 31	ACD at Southsea. [203]
March 31	*Gentlemanly Joe* published in *All The Year Round*. [6,196,198]
June	ACD sent the manuscript of *Statement of J. Habakuk Jephson M.D.* to *Cornhill Magazine*. [203]
June	ACD at Southsea. [18]
n.d.	Mary Doyle resident in Masongill Cottage on the Waller estate at Masongill, Yorkshire. [16,68,200,215]
Summer	ACD's mother moved from Edinburgh to Masongill Cottage. [202] (*3)
Summer	ACD joined the local Southsea Bowling Club. [202,215]
June 15	ACD at Southsea. [203]
n.d.	ACD attended Smith, Elder & Co's full dress dinner at The Ship, Greenwich, London. [203]
June 16	*The Week. Topics of the Day* published in *The Medical Times*. [6]
June 22	*Where to Go with the Camera. Southsea: Three Days in Search of Effects* published in the *British Journal of Photography*. [6,21,196,198]
July 11	*The Winning Shot* published in *Bow Bells*. [6,196,198]
July 20	*The "New" Scientific Subject* published in the *British Journal of Photography*. [6,21,196,198]
July 22	Death of Susan Conan at her home at 65 avenue de Wagram, Paris. [124]
August 17	*Where to Go with the Camera. To the Waterford Coast and Along It* published in the *British Journal of Photography* on 17 & 24 August. [6,21,196,198]
October 19	ACD at 1 Bush Villas, Elm Grove, Southsea. [1125]
October 27	ACD set the broken leg of John Malone. [342]
November 2	Frederick Purchase, Arthur George Rowe and Thomas Chiverton appeared at Portsmouth Police Court charged with assaulting John Malone, they were remanded on bail. [1102]
November 6	ACD attended PLSS meeting and was nominated for membership. [6,8,20]
November	ACD became a member of the PLSS. It was at this time that ACD met General Alfred Drayson. [15,180,202] (*2)
November 20	ACD joined and attended a meeting of the PLSS [6,14,8,20] (*2), at Penny Street Lecture Hall, Portsmouth. [343]
November	ACD at Southsea. [203]
November 29	It was announced in The Evening News (Portsmouth) that 'at the next meeting of the Portsmouth Literary and Scientific Society, which will be held at the Penny Street Lecture Hall, Portsmouth, on Tuesday evening, the 4th December, Dr Conan Doyle will read an interesting paper, titled "The Arctic Seas."' [982]
n.d.	*Selecting a Ghost* published. [180] (*2)

1883

December	*Selecting a Ghost. The Ghosts of Goresthorpe Grange* published in *London Society*. [6,196,198] (*2)
December	ACD at Southsea. [203]
December 3	ACD attended and spoke at PLSS meeting, the talk was titled "The Arctic Seas". [7] (*2)
December 4	ACD attended and spoke at PLSS meeting, the talk was titled "The Arctic Seas", [6,8,14,99,202,203,215] (*2) held at Penny Street Lecture Hall, Portsmouth, Hampshire [8,99,215] held at the Sailor Boy's Room at the Soldiers' [982]
December 7	ACD attended the trial of Frederick Purchase and Arthur Rowe who were charged with having committed a violent assault on John Malone, ACD attended as a witness. [344]
December 7	Frederick Purchase and Arthur George Rowe were found guilty of assaulting John Malone and were sentenced to two months imprisonment, Thomas Chiverton was fined. [1103]
December 10	Richard (Dicky) Doyle had a fit and fell down at the Athenaeum Club, London. [124]
n.d.	Death of Richard Doyle. [203] (*2)
December 11	Death of Richard Doyle (Dick, Dickie or Dicky) at 7 Finborough Road, London [8,68,124,200] (*2) at the Athenaeum Club. [202]
December 17	Richard (Dicky) Doyle was buried at St. Mary's Roman Catholic Cemetery, Kensal Green, London [124], at Kensal Green Cemetery [345] ACD attended the funeral. [345a]
Late 1883	Mary Doyle (ACD's mother) together with Connie, Ida and Dodo moved to Masongill, North Yorkshire, (*3) Innes joined them during his school holidays. [124,180,203]
Christmas	*An Exciting Christmas Eve; or My Lecture on Dynamite* published in the Christmas issue of *Boy's Own Paper*. [6,196,198]
Christmas	*The Silver Hatchet* published in the Christmas issue of *London Society*. [6,196,198]
December	ACD arrived in Birmingham to visit Dr Hoare. [203] {Note: there is some confusion here with ACD's letters, see source 203 page 215.}
December 31	ACD travelled to Birmingham to ring in the New Year with Dr Hoare and his family, he was joined there with fifteen year-old Connie Doyle. [203]

1884

n.d.	ACD began his first novel *The Firm of Girdlestone*. [6,99,202]
January	ACD still in Birmingham. [203]
January	ACD at Southsea with his sister Constance (Connie). [203]
January	*J. Habakuk Jephson's Statement* published in *The Cornhill Magazine*. [6,196,198,202,203] (*2)
January	*The Heiress of Glenmahowley* published in *Temple Bar*. [6,196,198]
January 5	ACD at 1 Bush Villas, Elm Grove, Southsea. [1125]
January 5	ACD attended and spoke at PLSS meeting [6] Connie also attended. [203]
January 6	ACD and Connie attended a dance given by a Mr Reynolds. [203]
January 15	ACD attended PLSS meeting [21] at Penny Street Lecture Hall. [346]
February	ACD at Southsea. [203]
n.d.	ACD sent off the manuscript of *The Blood-Stone Tragedy* to *Cassell's*. [203]
February	ACD confined to bed at Bush Villas with a bladder infection. [202,203]
February 12	ACD attended and spoke at PLSS meeting [6,8] at Penny Street Lecture Hall. [347]
February	*The Blood-Stone Tragedy* published in *Cassell's Saturday Journal*. [203] (*2)
February 16	*The Blood-Stone Tragedy* published in *Cassell's Saturday Journal*. [6,197,198] (*2)
February 26	ACD attended and spoke at PLSS meeting [6] at Penny Street Lecture Hall. [348]

1884

February 27	ACD at 1 Bush Villas, Elm Grove, Southsea. [1125]
March 2	At Southsea ACD had completed and sent off to publishers *The Blood-Stone Tragedy* and *Barrington Cowles* (*Cassell's Saturday Journal*), *Our Midnight Visitor* (*Temple Bar*), *A Day on the Island* (*Photographic Journal*) and *The Man with the Mattock* [re-titled later as *A Pastoral Horror*] (*Cornhill*). [203]
March 11	ACD at 1 Bush Villas, Elm Grove, Southsea. [1125]
Early spring	ACD visited the Isle of Wight with his sisters Annette, Caroline and their friend Jessie Drummond. [8,21]
April	ACD at Southsea. [203]
April 12	*John Barrington Cowles* published in *Cassell's Saturday Journal* on 12 & 19 April. [6,196,198,202] (*2)
April	*John Barrington Cowles* published in *Cassell's Saturday Journal*. [20,203] (*2)
April 14	ACD watched the Volunteer Review at Portsmouth [8,21] with Innes they walked four miles to see a review of sixteen thousand volunteer soldiers on Portsdown Hill. [203]
April	ACD played cricket for Portsmouth XI against Royal Engineers; he scored 27. [203]
April	ACD played cricket for Portsmouth XI against United Service; he scored 11. [203] (*2)
April 19	ACD played cricket for Portsmouth XI against United Services at United Services Recreation Ground, Portsmouth; he scored 11, match drawn. [235] (*2)
April 25	*A Day on "The Island"* published in the *British Journal of Photography*. [6,8,21,196,198]
April 29	ACD attended the AGM of the PLSS at the Soldiers' Institute, Penny Street, Portsmouth [349] and was voted on to the Council of the PLSS. [8]
May 10	ACD played cricket for Portsmouth Borough against Southsea Rivals at North End, Portsmouth. [8]
May 15	ACD played cricket for Portsmouth Borough against Ordnance Survey at County Ground, Southampton; he scored 15, match drawn. [235]
May 17	*The Cabman's Story. The Mysteries of a London "Growler"* published in *Cassell's Saturday Journal*. [6,196,198]
May 21	ACD played cricket for Portsmouth Borough against the Royal Artillery [8], at United Services Recreation Ground, Portsmouth; he scored 27 and 2, match drawn. [235]
May 23	*Easter Monday with the Camera* published in the *British Journal of Photography*. [6,8,21,196,198]
May 28	ACD's sisters Lottie and Annette arrived in Liverpool and visited ACD at Southsea; they all spent some time on the Isle of Wight. [202]
June 10	ACD played cricket for Portsmouth Borough against the Hampshire Regiment [8] at United Services Recreation Ground, Portsmouth; he scored 44 and took 1 wicket, match drawn. [235]
June 24	ACD at 1 Bush Villas, Elm Grove, Southsea. [1125]
July 28	ACD played cricket for Portsmouth Borough against Royal Artillery at St. George's, Portsmouth; he scored 12 and took 1 catch, Portsmouth Borough won. [235]
August 20	ACD played cricket for South Hampshire against United Services Portsmouth at Hilsea, Portsmouth; he scored 22 and 11, match drawn. [235]
August 20	*The Tragedians* published in *Bow Bells*. [6,196,198]
September	ACD visited Arran. [21] (*2)
Autumn	ACD visited Arran. [21] (*2)
September 22	ACD dressed the wound of an employee of Mr Burton of St. Pauls Square, he was accidently stabbed by one of his companions. [350]
October	Emily Hawkins with her daughter and son, Louise and John (Jack) were lodging at 2 Queens Gate, Osborne Road, Southsea. [8]

1884

October 14	At a meeting at the Blue Anchor, Kingston Cross, Portsmouth, ACD became a founding member and player of Portsmouth Football Club (PAFC) [202] he often played in goal and also used the name "A.C. Smith" when playing as a fullback. [8,14,107,202]
November 11	ACD attended PLSS meeting [6,31] at Penny Street Lecture Hall. [351]
November 15	ACD played in goal for PAFC against Hayling Island at North End, PAFC won 5-1. [107]
November 24	ACD at Southsea. [18]
November 25	ACD attended PLSS meeting [6]
November 29	*The Remote Effects of Gout* published in *Lancet*. [6,196,198]
December 9	ACD attended PLSS meeting. [6]
December 13	ACD played in goal for PAFC away against Havant, PAFC won 2-0. [107]
December 27	ACD played in goal for PAFC against Cowes at North End, drew 2-2. [107]
n.d.	ACD attended the Cornhill's end of year dinner at the Ship Tavern, Greenwich. [202] (*2)
n.d.	ACD attended a fish dinner at the Ship Hotel, Greenwich with James Payn and George Du Maurier. [14] (*2)
Christmas	*Crabbe's Practice* published in the Christmas issue of *Boy's Own Paper*. [6,99,196,198,202,215]

1885

n.d.	ACD became interested in spiritualism with General Drayson. [7] (*2)
n.d	The idea for *Micah Clarke* was conceived. [6,99]
January	*The Man from Archangel* published in *London Society*. [6,196,198,203]
January	ACD at Southsea. [203]
January 17	ACD played in goal for PAFC against Mr Pares's Team, Sunflowers at East Hants Ground, PAFC lost 2-0. [107]
January 24	ACD played in goal for PAFC against Havant at North End, PAFC won 7-2. [107]
January 31	ACD played in goal for PAFC away against Chichester, PAFC lost 4-2. [107]
February	ACD was working on his MD thesis. [203]
February	ACD at 1 Bush Villas, Elm Grove, Southsea. [1125]
February 2	ACD presided at a committee meeting of Portsmouth Cricket Club held at the Blue Anchor, Kingston Cross, Portsmouth. [1164]
February 7	ACD played in goal for PAFC away against Hayling Island, PAFC won 3-0. [107]
February 11	The Portsmouth Cricket Club held their annual general meeting at the Albany Hotel, Commercial Road, Portsmouth, and a resolution was passed to make the Blue Anchor Hotel, Kingston Cross, Portsmouth its headquarters in future, also during the same meeting ACD was elected Captain for the coming season. [8]
February 14	ACD played in goal for PAFC at North End against Southsea, PAFC won 1–0. [107]
March	Emily Hawkins, her daughter Louise and son John (Jack) were lodging at 2 Queens Gate, Osborne Road, Southsea. [8,124,163]
March	ACD took John (Jack) Hawkins as a resident patient [15,20,202] ACD subsequently developed a friendship with Louise, sister of John. [180]
March 3	ACD attended PLSS meeting. [6]
March 7	ACD played in goal for PAFC at North End against Fareham, drew 2-2. [107]
March 23	ACD played for PAFC (position unknown) away against Cowes, PAFC won 3-1. [107]
March 25	ACD attended the annual dinner of the Portsmouth Waltonian Angling Society held at the Golden Fleece, Commercial Road, Portsmouth. [1165]
March 25	John (Jack) Hawkins, briefly a resident patient with ACD, died of cerebral meningitis. [8,99,124,200,202,215]
March 27	Funeral of John (Jack) Hawkins at Highland Road Cemetery, Southsea, Hampshire. [8,163]

1885

March 27	During the evening ACD was interviewed by the police regarding the death of John (Jack) Hawkins. [163]
March 31	ACD attended a meeting of the PLSS. [8]
April	ACD submitted his MD thesis *An Essay Upon the Vasomotor Changes of Tabes Dorsalis*. [183]
April	ACD became engaged to Louise Hawkins. [215]
April 2	ACD attended PLSS meeting. [6,31]
April 3	ACD attended a smoking concert held by Portsmouth Cricket Club at the Blue Anchor Hotel, Kingston Cross, Portsmouth. [1166]
April 3	*Strange Tale of the Sea* published in *The Boston Herald*. [198]
April 29	ACD attended the first annual general meeting of Portsmouth Football Club held at the Blue Anchor Hotel, Kingston Cross, Portsmouth. [1167]
May	ACD was in Eastbourne, Sussex. [202]
n.d.	Charles Altamont Doyle committed to Sunnyside at the Montrose Royal Lunatic Asylum. [15,16,20,203] (*7)
May	Charles Altamont Doyle committed to Montrose Royal Lunatic Asylum. [5,215,2010] (*7)
May	Charles Altamont Doyle was committed to Montrose Royal Lunatic Asylum (Sunnyside), Kincardineshire (now Angus), Scotland until January 1892. [68,200] (*7)
May	Charles Altamont Doyle entered Montrose Royal Mental Hospital (Sunnyside). [124] (*7)
May 2	*The Lonely Hampshire Cottage* published in *Cassell's Saturday Journal*. [6,196,198]
May	Charles Altamont Doyle obtained some alcohol and became violent; he was then committed to the Royal Lunatic Asylum, Montrose and was a resident of Sunnyside House. [215] (*7)
May 9	ACD played cricket for Portsmouth Borough against Southsea Rivals at North End Cricket Ground, Portsmouth, he scored 1 and 2, match drawn. [235]
May 20	ACD attended the AGM of the PLSS at Portsmouth Lecture Hall. [352]
May 26	Charles Altamont Doyle acquired some liquor, became violent and attempted to leave Blairerno House; he was transferred to the Montrose Royal Asylum (Sunnyside). [124,180,202] (*7)
May 26	Charles Altamont Doyle admitted as a private patient to Montrose Asylum. [152] (*7)
June	ACD and Emily Hawkins, mother of Louise, travelled to Monmouth to draw up a marriage settlement with the Hawkins family solicitor, [202] settlement date 25 July 1885. [33]
July	ACD awarded MD degree from the University of Edinburgh. [5,7,15,68,200,215] (*5)
July	*The Great Keinplatz Experiment* published in *Belgravia Magazine*. [6,198]
July 15	ACD was with the Southsea Bowling Club that played against Newport Bowling Club at Newport, it is unclear if he played but Southsea Bowling Club lost. [1168]
July 17	*Where to Go with the Camera: Arran in Autumn* published in the *British Journal of Photography*. [6,21,196,198]
July 18	ACD played cricket for Theatre Royal against Fun of the Bristol at Governor's Green, Portsmouth, he scored 65 and took 1 wicket, Theatre Royal won. [235]
July 29	ACD played bowls for Southsea Bowling Club against Newport. [8,202]
August	ACD half way through writing *The Firm of Girdlestone*. [6]
n.d.	ACD obtained his doctorate from Edinburgh University. [180] (*5)
August 1	ACD awarded MD degree from the University of Edinburgh. [47,202] (*5)
August 1	ACD received his MD, the title of his thesis, *On Vasomotor Influences in Tabes Dorsalis*. [182] (*5)
August 1	At the Summer Sessions of Edinburgh University at the U.P. Synod Hall, Castle Terrace, Edinburgh, ACD received his M.B. and C.M. [353] (*5)

1885

August 3	ACD played cricket for Stonyhurst Wanderers against Stonyhurst College at Stonyhurst College Ground, Clitheroe, he scored 8 not out, Stonyhurst Wanderers won [235] for Old Stonyhurst (Wanderers) against Stonyhurst College. [66,202]
n.d.	ACD married Louise (Touie) Hawkins. [203] (*4)
August 5	ACD married Louise (Touie) Hawkins at Masongill; they travelled to Dublin for honeymoon [7,15] (*4), he also played cricket with an Old Stonyhurst team. [5,15]
August 6	ACD married Louise (Touie) Hawkins [99,180] at the Parish Church of Thornton-in-Lonsdale, near Masongill, Yorkshire by the Revd. S.R. Stable, there were several witnesses: Bryan Waller, Emily Hawkins, Julia Waller, J.F. Innes H. Doyle, Mary J. Doyle and Constance A.M. Doyle. [124,215] (*4) Soon after their honeymoon Innes left Bush Villas to go to Richmond School, Richmond, Yorkshire, [14,202] (*2) it is interesting to note that Bryan Waller had also been a pupil at this school. [124,202]
August 6	ACD married Louise (Touie) Hawkins at Thornton-in-Lonsdale Parish Church, Yorkshire [6,7,8,14,20,68,163,1194] (*4), St. Oswald's Church, Thornton-in-Lonsdale, West Yorkshire [200,202,2010] they travelled in Ireland for honeymoon. [14,124,215]
n.d.	Innes Doyle left Southsea to attend a public school in Yorkshire. [2,10,31] (*2)
n.d.	ACD joined the Stonyhurst Wanderers cricket team for a short tour of Ireland. [202]
August 10	From August 10 to 15, ACD accompanied the Stonyhurst Wanderers cricket team on their third tour, visiting Ireland as part of his honeymoon. [6]
August 10	ACD played cricket on 10 & 11 for Stonyhurst Wanderers against Phoenix at Phoenix Cricket Club Ground, Phoenix Park, Dublin, he scored 15, Stonyhurst Wanderers won. [235]
August 12	ACD played cricket on 12 & 13 for Stonyhurst Wanderers against Dublin University at College Park, Dublin, he scored 24 and took 1 catch, Stonyhurst Wanderers won [235] for Old Stonyhurst (Wanderers) against Dublin University. [66,220]
August 14	ACD played cricket on 14 & 15 for Stonyhurst Wanderers against Leinster at Observatory Lane, Rathmines, Dublin, he scored zero and 10 and took 1 catch, Stonyhurst Wanderers won [235] for Old Stonyhurst (Wanderers) against Leinster Club at Rathmines, Dublin. [66,220]
August 24	ACD and Louise left Kingston (near Dublin), Ireland on board a Royal Mail steamer to return to England. [1141]
September	In the first week of September ACD played cricket for Portsmouth Cricket Club against Sarisbury. [8]
September 15	At the Bush Hotel, Southsea a presentation of a handsome dinner service was made to ACD by Southsea Bowling Club. [354] (*2)
September 17	Southsea Bowling Club presented ACD with a dinner service as a slight token of the esteem in which Conan Doyle was held by the members. [8] (*2)
October 3	ACD played in goal for PAFC away against Havant, won 3-0. [107]
October 15	As a guest ACD attended the dinner of Crystal Palace Bowling Club at the Crystal Palace Tavern. [1169]
October 17	ACD played as a back for PAFC at North End against Hilsea Artillery Ramblers, PAFC won 2-0. [107]
October 17	ACD attended the Crystal Palace Bowling Club dinner in Fratton. [8]
October 24	ACD played as a back for PAFC away against the Argyll & Sutherland Highlanders, PAFC lost 8-0. [107]
October 29	ACD as Vice-Chairman attended the annual closing dinner of Southsea Bowling Club at the Bush Hotel. [355]
October 30	*With a Camera on an African River* published in the *British Journal of Photography*. [6,21,196,198]
November	*The Wanderers' Irish Tour* (poem) published in *Stonyhurst Magazine*. [6,198]

1885

November	ACD completed writing *The Firm of Girdlestone*. [6]
November 4	ACD at 1 Bush Villas, Elm Grove, Southsea. [1125]
November 7	ACD played as a full back for PAFC away against Chichester, won 4-1. [107]
November 10	ACD attended PLSS meeting [6,8] ACD attended the inaugural meeting of the 1885-86 session of the PLSS at the Penny Street Lecture Hall, Portsmouth. [1142]
November 14	ACD played in goal for PAFC at North End against Stubbington House, PAFC won 3-0. [107]
November 16	Charles Altamont Doyle had the first of his epileptic seizures. [124]
November 22	ACD played as a back for PAFC away against Midhurst, PAFC won 3–2. [107]
December 1	ACD's sister Constance (Connie) was working as a governess in Portugal. [124]
December 5	ACD played as a full back for PAFC at Garrison Barracks Ground against Wimborne, PAFC lost 2-1. [107]
December 8	ACD attended and spoke at PLSS meeting [6,8], at the Penny Street Lecture Hall, Portsmouth. [1143]
December 9	ACD played as a back for PAFC at North End against Horndean, PAFC won 4–1. [107]
December	*The Fate of the Evangeline* published in Christmas issue of *Boy's Own Paper*. [6,196,198]
Christmas	*The Parson of Jackman's Gulch* published in the Christmas issue of *London Society* as *Elias B. Hopkins. The Parson of Jackman's Gulch*. [6,196,198]
December 26	ACD played in goal for PAFC away against Fareham, PAFC won 2–0; this was a morning kick off. [107]
December 26	ACD played as a back for PAFC at Garrison Recreation Ground against the Worcestershire Regiment, PAFC won 3-0; this was an afternoon kick off. [107]
December 28	ACD played as a full back for PAFC at North End against Havant, PAFC won 6–4. [107]
December 30	ACD played for PAFC (position unknown) at Forton against the Royal Marines Light Infantry, PAFC won 10–0. [107]

1886

n.d.	ACD became interested in spiritualism with General Drayson and Mr Ball [3,10,20] (*2) and began attending psychic meetings in Southsea. [99]
n.d.	ACD's mother paid a lengthy visit to Southsea. [202]
January 2	ACD played as a full back for PAFC at North End against Sunflowers, PAFC won 2–0. [107]
January 9	ACD played as a full back for PAFC at North End against Cowes, drew 2–2. [107]
January 9	ACD attended to the injuries incurred by Mr Charles Smithers when he fell through an open cellar door. [356]
n.d.	ACD gave a lecture on Thomas Carlyle at the PLSS. [202] (*2)
January 19	ACD attended PLSS meeting and spoke on Thomas Carlyle and his Works [6,7,8,47] (*2) at the Small Hall of the Soldiers' Institute. [357]
January 24	ACD held a spiritualist sitting with Mr Ball. [3]
January 25	ACD played as a full back for PAFC at Garrison Recreation Ground against the 93rd Regiment, PAFC lost 4–2. [107]
January 26	ACD at Southsea. [18]
January (end)	ACD played as a full back for PAFC at North End against Hilsea Artillery Ramblers, PAFC won 6–0. [107]
January 30	ACD played as a full back for PAFC away against Horndean, PAFC won 4–0, ACD scored 1 goal. [107]
February 13	ACD played in goal for PAFC at Garrison Recreation Ground against Stubbington Lodge School, PAFC won 3–1. [107]
February 20	ACD played as a full back for PAFC at Forton against RMLI, PAFC won 6–0. [107]

1886

February 27	ACD played as a full back for PAFC at North End against Hayling Island, PAFC won 7–1. [107]
March 2	ACD attended and spoke at PLSS meeting [6] at the Penny Street Lecture Hall. [358]
March 6	ACD played for PAFC (position unknown) at North End against Petersfield, PAFC won 13–1. [107]
March	ACD spent six weeks of March and April writing *A Tangled Skein* (*A Study in Scarlet*). [203,215] (*4)
March	During March and April *A Study in Scarlet* was written. [6] (*4)
n.d.	ACD began writing *A Study in Scarlet*. [99] (*4)
March 8	ACD started writing *A Study in Scarlet*. [202] (*4)
March 13	ACD played in goal for PAFC away against Portsmouth Grammar School, drew 1–1. [107]
March 16	ACD attended and spoke at PLSS meeting [6,31] at the Lecture Hall, Penny Street. [359]
March 20	ACD played in goal for PAFC at Officers' Recreation Ground against HMS *Marlborough*, PAFC lost 1–0. [107]
March 27	ACD played as a full back for PAFC away against Petersfield, drew 1–1. [107]
April	*Touch and Go: A Midshipman's Story* published in *Cassell's Family Magazine*. [6,198]
April 1	ACD was voted to the chair at a meeting of over twenty athletic clubs to discuss their requirements of the proposed recreation ground at North End, Portsmouth. [360]
April 11	ACD probably dispatched *A Study in Scarlet* to the *Cornhill Magazine* but it was rejected. [202]
April 15	ACD spoke at a meeting in Southsea in support of kindness to animals, he spoke in favour of vivisection [6,7] at St. Simon's School Room, Clarendon Road, Southsea. [361]
May	ACD at Bush Villa, Southsea. [18]
May	From mid-May ACD played cricket regularly for Portsmouth Cricket Club, scoring 22, 41, 42 and 25 in successive games. [8]
May 3	ACD attended a meeting of the PLSS at St. Vincent Lodge, Kent Road, Southsea. [362]
May 17	ACD played cricket for Portsmouth Borough against United Services Portsmouth at United Services Ground Portsmouth, he scored 8, took 1 wicket and 1 catch, United Services Portsmouth won. [235]
May 26	ACD played cricket for Majilton Gay City Company against United Services Portsmouth at United Services Ground, Portsmouth, he scored 8, match drawn. [235]
June 23	ACD played cricket for Portsmouth Cricket Club against Fareham at Fareham, he scored zero in both innings. [8]
June	ACD spoke in support of Sir William Crossman, Liberal candidate for Portsmouth. [6,14,21,202]
June 25	ACD attended a Liberal Unionist meeting at the Amphitheatre, Gunwharf Road, Portsmouth. [363]
July 2	ACD attended a meeting held by the Unionists at the Beneficial Society's Hall, Portsea. [364]
July 26	ACD played bowls for Southsea Bowling Club against Newport Bowling Club at The Ground attached to the Bush Hotel; the match was won by Southsea. [365]
July 29	ACD played cricket for Portsmouth Borough against Royal Artillery Northern Division at United Services Recreation Ground, Portsmouth, he scored 3 and took 2 wickets, Portsmouth Borough won. [235]
August 4	ACD played cricket for South Hampshire Rovers against Brixton Wanderers at Hilsea, Portsmouth, he scored 6, match drawn. [235]

1886

August 25	ACD played cricket for Portsmouth against the Royal Sussex Regiment at the United Service Cricket Ground, Portsmouth, he scored 31 and took 5 wickets, Portsmouth won. [2085]
August 26	ACD played cricket for Portsmouth Borough against Fareham at Catisfield, Fareham, he scored 12 and took 5 wickets, Portsmouth Borough won. [235]
August 28	ACD played cricket for Portsmouth Borough against United Services Portsmouth at United Services Recreation Ground, Portsmouth, he scored zero and took 1 wicket, match drawn, A.H. Wood played for Portsmouth Borough, he scored 22. [235]
September	Ward, Lock & Company bought the copyright of *A Study in Scarlet* for £25. [202] (*3)
September 8	ACD played cricket for Portsmouth Borough against Sarisbury at Hilsea, Portsmouth, he scored 47, match drawn, A.H. Wood played for Portsmouth Borough, he scored 115, took 3 wickets and 1 catch. [235]
October	ACD elected as joint Secretary of the PLSS. [8,202]
October 2	ACD played in goal for PAFC at Portsmouth against Woolston Works, result unknown. [107]
October 9	ACD played as a back for PAFC at Garrison Recreation Ground against the 2nd Worcestershire, PAFC lost 3–1. [107]
October 16	ACD played in goal for PAFC at Garrison Recreation Ground against Fareham, PAFC won 5–0. [107]
October 30	ACD played in goal for PAFC away against Petersfield, Portsmouth Senior Cup round one, PAFC won 6-1. [107]
October	Ward Lock & Company bought the copyright of *A Study in Scarlet* for £25 [8] end of October. [203] (*3)
October 30	Ward, Lock & Co. bought the copyright of *A Study in Scarlet* for £25. [215] (*3)
November 3	ACD played as a full back for PAFC at Garrison Recreation Ground against United Services Men's Garrison, PAFC lost 3–2. [107]
November 6	ACD played as a full back for PAFC at Garrison Recreation Ground against the Worcestershire Regiment, PAFC lost 1–0. [107]
November 8	ACD attended the first meeting of the Portsmouth House of Commons Debating Society at the Lower Hall of the Protestant Buildings. [366]
November 13	ACD played as a back for PAFC away against Portsmouth Grammar School, PAFC won 5–2, ACD scored an own goal. [107]
November 17	ACD played as a back for PAFC at Garrison Recreation Ground against the Royal Irish Rifles, drew 1–1. [107]
November 19	*Testing Gas Pipes for Leakage* published in *Gas and Water Review*. [6,198,202]
November 23	ACD attended PLSS meeting [6] at the Penny Street Lecture Hall. [367]
November 24	ACD was called to 31 Green Road, Southsea to attend to five year old Lizzie Slatterie, but death took place before he arrived. [368]
November 27	ACD played in goal for PAFC at Hilsea against 2/1 Welsh Division RA, PAFC won 3–0. [107]
December 6	ACD attended the Portsmouth House of Commons Debating Society at the Portsmouth Institute, Portsmouth. [369]
December 7	ACD attended and spoke at PLSS meeting [6] at the Sailor Boys' Room, Soldiers Institute. [370]
December 15	ACD played as a full back for PAFC at Garrison Recreation Ground against Blandford, PAFC won 3–2, Hampshire Senior Cup round one. [107]
December 18	ACD played as a back for PAFC at Garrison Recreation Ground against Portsmouth Grammar School, PAFC won 3–0, Portsmouth Senior Cup round two. [107]
December 21	ACD attended PLSS meeting [6] as Joint Secretary at the Penny Street Lecture Hall, Portsmouth. [371]
December	ACD was attending General Harward during his illness. [372]

1886

Christmas — *Cyprian Overbeck Wells. A Literary Mosaic* published in the Christmas issue of *Boy's Own Paper*. [6,196,198]

1887

n.d.	Ann (Annette), ACD's sister, went to Brazil. [124]
n.d.	ACD began the novel *Micah Clarke*. [203]
January	ACD and his friend Henry Ball started to experiment in telepathy. [14,20,180]
January 8	ACD attended and spoke at PLSS meeting. [6]
January 8	*Uncle Jeremy's Household* published in *Boy's Own Paper* from 8 January to 19 February. [6,196,198]
January 15	ACD played as a back for PAFC at Garrison Recreation Ground against the Royal Irish Rifles, PAFC won 1–0 [107]
January 18	ACD attended a meeting of the PLSS at the Penny Street Lecture Hall, Portsmouth. [373]
January 18	Mrs Conan Doyle with other ladies attended the children at a free meal for 150 girls at St. Paul's, Southsea. [374]
January 24	ACD held his own psychic sitting. [20]
January 24	ACD, Henry Ball, General Harward, his daughter Annie and Louise Conan Doyle attended a psychic sitting at Kingston Lodge, Portsmouth [202] ACD was invited by Lieutenant-General Thomas Harward to attend a séance at Kingston Lodge, Portsmouth, the group comprised of ACD, his wife Louise, Henry Ball, Thomas Harward and his 22 year old daughter Nancy. [1135]
January 26	ACD initiated as a Freemason of the Phoenix Lodge No 257, Southsea, Portsmouth [7,8,14,97,202] 110 High Street. [8,68,200]
February 1	ACD attended PLSS meeting. [6]
February 2	ACD, Henry Ball, General Harward, his daughter Annie and Louise Conan Doyle attended a second psychic sitting at Kingston Lodge, Portsmouth. [202]
February 5	ACD played as a back for PAFC at United Services Officers' Ground against Freemantle, PAFC won 2–0. [107]
February 12	ACD played as a back for PAFC at United Men's Ground against the Royal Irish Rifles, PAFC won 4–2. [107]
February 15	ACD attended PLSS meeting. [6]
February 23	ACD passed into the Phoenix Lodge 257, Southsea, Hampshire. [97]
March	ACD at Bush Villa, Southsea, Hampshire. [18]
March 1	ACD attended and spoke at PLSS meeting. [6]
March 5	ACD played as a back for PAFC away against Portsmouth Grammar School, PAFC won 5–1. [107]
March 15	ACD attended PLSS meeting [6] at the Penny Street Hall, Portsmouth. [375]
March 19	ACD played in goal for PAFC away against Petersfield, drew 1–1. [107]
March 23	ACD played in goal for PAFC at United Services Men's Ground against Mr Richard's Garrison Team, PAFC won 2–0. [107]
March 23	ACD raised in to the Phoenix Lodge 257, Southsea, Hampshire. [97]
March 26	ACD played in goal for PAFC at United Services Recreation Ground against Woolston Works, PAFC won 1–0, Portsmouth & District Challenge Cup. [107]
April 8	ACD played in goal for PAFC at United Services Recreation Ground against HMS Marlborough, PAFC won 2-0. [107]
April 18	ACD took part in the ceremonies of the day at the Freemason's Hall, Landport, Portsmouth. [376]
April 26	ACD attended and spoke at PLSS meeting [6] at the Penny Street Lecture Hall. [377]
May 25	ACD played cricket for Portsmouth Borough against Fareham at Catisfield, Fareham, he scored 2 and zero, and took 2 wickets and 1 catch, match drawn. [235]
June 16	ACD held a sitting at Bush Villa with Henry Ball and Percy Boulnois. [202]
Summer	ACD played regularly for Portsmouth Cricket Club. [8]
July	ACD at Bush Villa, Southsea, Hampshire. [18]

1887

n.d.	ACD began writing *Micah Clarke*. [6,99] (*2)
July	ACD started writing *Micah Clarke*. [202] (*2)
July 2	ACD declared his conviction in believing in spiritualism in a letter in *Light*. [14,203]
July 2	*A Test Message* published in *Light*. [6,18,196,1135]
July 13	ACD played cricket for Fareham against Ockley at Catisfield, Fareham, he scored 2 and 2 and took 1 wicket, match drawn. [235]
July 14	ACD at Bush Villa, Southsea, Hampshire. [18]
August 5	ACD's last recorded séance. [202]
August 20	ACD at Southsea. [1135]
October	*Dreamland and Ghostland* published in three volumes by George Redway. [6,196]
October 21	ACD held a meeting of the PLSS at Bush Villas. [8]
October 29	ACD played as a full back for PAFC at Men's Recreation Ground against Hilsea Ramblers, PAFC lost 3–1. [107]
n.d.	*A Study in Scarlet* published in *Beeton's Christmas Annual*. [99] (*2)
November	*A Study in Scarlet* published in *Beeton's Christmas Annual*. [6,124,180,196,198,202,215,1195] (*2)
November 2	ACD played as a full back for PAFC at Recreation Ground, Portsmouth against Chichester G & AC, PAFC lost 3–0. [107]
November 12	ACD played in goal for PAFC at Recreation Ground, Portsmouth against the Royal Scots Greys, PAFC won 3–0. [107]
November 22	ACD attended PLSS meeting, ACD related several humorous anecdotes regarding The Old Portsmouth Theatre. [6]
November 25	ACD attended a meeting at the residence of the Mayor (Mr Albert Addison) to make preliminary arrangements for a town banquet to Mr Walter Besant, to be held on 19 January 1888. [378]
December 2	ACD attended a General Committee Meeting at the Guildhall, Portsmouth with the Mayor (Mr Albert Addison) to make arrangements for the proposed town banquet to Mr Walter Besant. [379]
December 6	ACD attended PLSS meeting and spoke about "Three years residence in the Congo" [6] at the Sailor Boys' Room, Soldiers' Institute. [380]
December 8	ACD represented the Liberal-Unionists at Westminster Town Hall, London [8] ACD represented the Liberal Unionist of Portsmouth at the conference of Liberal Unionists at Westminster Town Hall; he then subsequently attended a banquet at St. Stephen's Hall. [381]
December 20	ACD attended and spoke at PLSS meeting, "Our Knowledge of the Brain". [6,8] (*2)
December 21	ACD attended and spoke at PLSS meeting, "Our Knowledge of the Brain" by Dr C.C. Claremont. [7] (*2)
Christmas	*Corporal Dick's Promotion (An Epic of the Egyptian Campaign)* (poem) published in *Boy's Own Paper*. [6,196,198]
Christmas	ACD had completed writing *Micah Clarke*. [202]
December	*The Stone of Boxman's Drift* published in the Christmas issue *Boy's Own Paper*. [6,196,198]
December 24	ACD played in goal for PAFC at United Service Men's Ground against Sunflowers, PAFC won 2–0. [107]

1888

n.d.	Annette Mary Frances Conan Doyle died. [7] (*4)
January 7	ACD played in goal for PAFC at Officers' Recreation Ground against Hilsea Ramblers, PAFC lost 1–0 in the Portsmouth Senior Cup Semi-Final. [107]
January 19	ACD and Louise attended a civic banquet for Walter Besant at the Victoria Hall [8] at the Victoria Hall, Commercial Road. [382]
January 23	ACD attended the AGM of the Portsmouth Cricket Club at the Albany Hotel where he was elected as captain. [383] (*2)

1888

January 25	At the annual general meeting of the Portsmouth Cricket Club held at the Albany Hotel, ACD was re-elected Captain. [8] (*2)
January 25	ACD played as a full back for PAFC at Officers' Recreation Ground against Hilsea Ramblers, PAFC lost 4–0 in the Portsmouth Senior Cup Semi-Final. [107]
January 31	ACD attended PLSS meeting and spoke on the reporting style of Howells and James in America [6] ACD attended a lecture given by Mr A.W. Jerrard, headmaster of Portsmouth Grammar School at the Guildhall before members of the PLSS. [384]
February 4	ACD played in goal for PAFC at Bar End Cricket Ground against Woolston Works, PAFC lost 1–0 in the Hampshire Senior Cup. [107]
February 14	ACD attended PLSS meeting and spoke [6,21] at the Guildhall, High Street, Portsmouth. [385]
February 20	ACD attended PLSS meeting and a talk, the talk was 'Travels in Bolivia'. [6] (*2)
February 28	ACD attended PLSS meeting and a talk 'Travels in Bolivia' at the Guildhall, High Street, Portsmouth. [386] (*2)
February 29	ACD sent *Micah Clarke* to his publishers. [203]
March 1	ACD at Southsea. [203]
n.d.	ACD invited his father Charles to provide six pen and ink drawings for the Ward Lock & Co. book edition of *A Study in Scarlet*. [180,202,203]
March 13	ACD attended PLSS meeting [6] at the Guildhall, High Street, Portsmouth. [387]
March 17	ACD played in goal for PAFC at Hilsea Recreation Ground against Portsmouth Grammar School, drew 0–0 in the Portsmouth Senior Cup Final First Round. [107]
March 27	ACD attended PLSS meeting and spoke about the English language. [6]
April	Between April and July ACD had written *The Mystery of Cloomber*. [202]
April 12	ACD at Southsea. [203]
April 14	ACD attended PLSS meeting held at Bush Villas. [8]
April 17	ACD attended a grand combined Conservative and Liberal-Unionist demonstration at the Amphitheatre in Gunwharf Road, Portsmouth. [8,215]
April 21	ACD at Bush Villa, Elm Grove, Southsea, Hampshire. [18]
April 24	As Assistant Honorary Secretary ACD read the PLSS Nineteenth Annual Report; a resolution to admit ladies was carried [6,8] at the AGM at the Guildhall, High Street, Portsmouth. [388]
April 27	ACD was called upon in his professional capacity to give evidence at a Coroner's inquest held in the Barley Mow public house, Castle Road, Southsea. [8]
May 24	ACD played cricket for Portsmouth Borough against Royal Artillery Hilsea at United Services Recreation Ground, Portsmouth, he scored 21, took 1 wicket and 1 catch, Portsmouth Borough won. [235]
May 27	ACD played cricket for Portsmouth Borough against Royal Artillery Gosport at United Services Recreation Ground, Portsmouth, he scored 5, Royal Artillery won. [235]
June	*John Huxford's Hiatus* published in *The Cornhill Magazine*. [6,196,198]
June 6	ACD played cricket for Portsmouth Borough against United Services Portsmouth at United Services Recreation Ground, Portsmouth, he scored 3 and took 2 catches, United Services Portsmouth won. [235]
June 16	ACD played cricket for Portsmouth Borough against Royal Engineers at United Services Recreation Ground, Portsmouth, he scored 49 not out and took 2 wickets, Portsmouth Borough won. [235]
June 26	ACD played cricket for Portsmouth Borough against Fareham at Hilsea, Fareham, he did not bat, Portsmouth Borough won, A.H. Wood played for Portsmouth Borough, he did not bat but took 5 wickets and 1 catch. [235]

1888

June 28	ACD played cricket for Portsmouth Borough against Ryde at Quarr Hill, Ryde, he scored 37, Ryde won. [235]
July	*A Study in Scarlet* book edition published by Ward, Lock & Co., London, this included six pen and ink drawings by Charles Doyle. [215] (*2)
July 2	*A Study in Scarlet* book edition published Ward, Lock & Co., London. [6] (*2)
July 6	ACD played cricket for Portsmouth Borough against Southsea Rovers at Hilsea, Portsmouth, he scored 49, Portsmouth Borough won. [235]
July 14	ACD played cricket for Portsmouth Borough against South Lancashire Regiment at United Services Recreation Ground, Portsmouth, he scored 19. Portsmouth Borough won. [235]
July 19	ACD played cricket for Portsmouth Borough against Fareham at Catisfield, Fareham, he scored 7 and zero, match drawn. [235]
July 24	ACD played cricket for Portsmouth Borough against Ordnance Survey at County Ground, Southampton, he scored 5 and 36, match drawn. [235]
August	*On the Geographical Distribution of British Intellect* published in *The Nineteenth Century*. [198]
August 4	ACD played cricket for Portsmouth Borough against Royal Engineers at United Services Recreation Ground, Portsmouth, he scored 29 and took 7 wickets, Royal Engineers won. [235]
August 9	ACD played cricket for South Hampshire Rovers against Ye Olde Carawan at Adhurst St. Mary, he scored zero, match drawn, A.H. Wood played for South Hampshire Rovers, he scored 35 and took 4 wickets and 1 catch. [235]
August 25	ACD played cricket for Portsmouth Borough against South Lancashire Regiment at United Services Recreation Ground, Portsmouth, he scored 17 and took 8 wickets, match drawn. [235]
August 30	ACD played cricket for Portsmouth Borough against Southampton at United Services Recreation Ground, Portsmouth, he scored 4 and did not bat in second innings, match drawn, A.H. Wood played for Portsmouth Borough, he scored 7 in the first innings and did not bat in the second innings, he took 2 wickets. [235]
August 30	*The Mystery of Cloomber* published in *The Pall Mall Budget* 30 August–8 November. [6,198]
September 1	ACD played cricket for Portsmouth Borough against Dorset Regiment at United Services Recreation Ground, Portsmouth, he scored 20 and did not bat in second innings, match drawn. [235]
September 13	ACD played cricket for In the Ranks Dramatic Company against Border Regiment at United Services Recreation Ground, Portsmouth, he scored 82 not out and took 1 wicket, In the Ranks Dramatic Company won. [235]
September 14	ACD played cricket on 14 & 15 for Portsmouth Borough against Winchester at County Ground, Southampton, he scored 13 and 32 and took 2 wickets and 1 catch, Winchester won, A.H. Wood played for Portsmouth Borough, he scored 12 and 4 and took 1 wicket. [235]
September 17	Caroline (Lottie), ACD's sister visited Southsea before travelling onto Paris in November with ACD and Emily, Louise's elder sister. [124]
September 24	Formation of the Hampshire Psychical Society, ACD was joint vice-president, [6,8] this took place at a special meeting of members held at Holy Trinity Schoolrooms, Northam Road, Southampton, ACD was elected a Vice-President. [982,1170]
September 29	A report was published in the *Hampshire Telegraph* on the formation of the Hampshire Psychical Society that was held on 24 September. [6,8,982]
October 13	ACD played as a full back for PAFC at United Services Men's Ground against the Royal Engineers (Chatham), PAFC lost 6–0. [107]
October 27	ACD played as a full back for PAFC at United Services Men's Ground against the United Services, drew 1–1. [107]

1888

October 29	ACD attended a meeting of the Portsmouth Jewish Literary and Debating Society at the Synagogue, Queen Street, Portsea, where he read a paper titled "Thomas Carlyle". [389]
October 31	ACD attended a presentation to the Mayor of Portsmouth (A. Addison Esq.) at the Guildhall, Portsmouth. [390]
November 1	ACD played as a full back for PAFC at United Services Men's Ground against the South Yorkshire Regiment, PAFC won 2–0. [107]
November 1	ACD among many others attended a presentation to the Mayor of Portsmouth (A. Addison) and Mrs Addison at the Guildhall, Portsmouth. [1171]
November 3	ACD played as a full back for PAFC at Men's Recreation Ground against United Services Men's Team, PAFC lost 3–0, Portsmouth Senior Cup first round. [107]
November	ACD visited Versailles, Le petit Trianon, Louvre, Pantheon, Luxembourg, Tour D'Eiffel, Musée de Clunny, Invalides, Musée Grévin, Le Cirque Nouvelle, the Huguenots at the Grand Opera, Panorame de Bastille and Panorame de Gravelotte. [203]
November 14	ACD returned home from Paris. [203]
November 20	ACD at Southsea. [203]
November 20	ACD attended PLSS meeting and lectured on "The Genius of George Meredith" [6,7,8,48,99,202,203], held at the Portsmouth Guildhall. [982]
November 21	ACD travelled to London to discuss cuts to *Micah Clarke* with his publisher [202] lunched with Andrew Lang at the Savile Club. [203]
December 4	ACD attended PLSS meeting with Mrs and Miss Doyle. [6,8]
December 13	ACD played as a full back for PAFC at United Services Men's Ground against Winchester, PAFC won 2–0. [107]
n.d.	*The Mystery of Cloomber* published. [99] (*3
December	*The Mystery of Cloomber* published. [203] (*3)
December 17	*The Mystery of Cloomber* published by Ward and Downey, London. [6,180] (*3)
December 18	ACD attended PLSS meeting and spoke on the Eiffel Tower as a gigantic act of vandalism. [6,8] (*2)
December 18	ACD spoke at some length on the Eiffel Tower [203] (*2) Louise also attended the meeting at the Guildhall, High Street, Portsmouth. [391]
December 19	ACD sent another instalment of *Micah Clarke* to his publisher. [203]
December 19	ACD at Southsea. [203]
December 19	ACD played as a full back for PAFC at United Services Men's Ground against Fareham, PAFC won 6–0. [107]
December 22	ACD played as a full back for PAFC at United Services Men's Ground against United Services Men's Team, drew 0–0. [107]
n.d.	*The Bravoes of Market-Drayton* accepted by Chambers. [203]
End of year	At the end of 1888 ACD was working on *Angels of Darkness*, a drama in three acts, based on the second part of *A Study in Scarlet*, this was never completed. [6]

1889

n.d.	Annette Mary Frances Conan Doyle died of influenza. [5,20] (*4)
n.d.	ACD resigned from the Freemason Phoenix Lodge No 257, Portsmouth. [8,14,68,200]
n.d.	ACD demitted from the Phoenix Lodge 257, Southsea, Hampshire. [97]
January	ACD at Southsea. [203]
January 8	ACD played as a full back for PAFC at Aldershot against the King's Royal Rifles, PAFC won 4–0 in the Hampshire Senior Cup second round. [107]
January 15	ACD attended and spoke at PLSS meeting [6] at the Guildhall. [392]
January 16	ACD at Bush Villas, Southsea. [884]
January 19	ACD played as a full back for PAFC away against Fareham, PAFC won 3–1. [107]

1889

n.d.	Birth of Mary Louise Conan Doyle. [99] (*4)
January	Birth of Mary Louise Conan Doyle daughter of ACD and Louise. [180] (*4)
January 23	Birth of Mary Louise Conan Doyle daughter of ACD and Louise. [33] (*4)
January 24	ACD examined James Godding who had been injured while demolishing the walls of the building of Manufactures Alliance at the junction of Commercial Road and Edinburgh Road, Landport. [393]
January 26	ACD played as a full back for PAFC at Men's Recreation Ground against the Yorkshire Regiment, PAFC lost 1–0. [107]
January 28	Birth of Mary Louise Conan Doyle [7,8,14,15,16,47,68,124,200,202,203,215] (*4) at 1 Bush Villas, Southsea, Hampshire [124,215] delivered by ACD [202,215] delivered by ACD at 6:15a.m. [203]
January 28	ACD completing the final revision of *Micah Clarke*. [202]
February	ACD at Southsea. [203]
February 2	ACD played as a full back for PAFC at North End against the YMCA, PAFC won 3–1. [107]
February 8	ACD attended an exhibition of "mesmeric force" in Southsea, given by Professor Milo de Meyer [6,7,15,20,180,] at the Portland Hall, [202] ACD attended a séance given by Professor Milo de Meyer at the small hall of the Portland Hall, Southsea. [980,982]
February 14	ACD at Southsea. [203]
February 23	ACD played as a full back for PAFC at Men's Recreation Ground against Portsmouth Grammar School, PAFC won 2–0 in the Hampshire Senior Cup semi-final. [107]
February 25	*Micah Clarke* published by Longmans, Green, and Co., London. [6,99,202] (*3)
n.d.	*Micah Clarke* published. [7,124,180,215] (*3)
February 26	*Micah Clark* published. [203] (*3)
February 26	ACD at Southsea. [203]
February 26	ACD attended PLSS meeting and lecture. [8,202]
February 28	George Turnavine Budd died in Plymouth. [151]
February 29	ACD attended and spoke at PLSS meeting. [6]
March	ACD at Southsea. [203]
March 2	ACD played as a full back for PAFC at County Ground, Southampton against the Royal Engineers (Aldershot), PAFC lost 5–1 in the Hampshire Senior Cup Final [107] played at Southampton. [8]
March 26	ACD attended PLSS meeting and spoke on the carved images of Easter Island. [6,394]
March 26	ACD attended a meeting of the subscribers to The Portsmouth and South Hants Eye and Ear Infirmary at the Guildhall. [395]
n.d.	ACD was writing *The White Company*. [7] (*3)
Easter	ACD took a brief holiday at a house on Emery Down in the New Forest, Hampshire; his companions were General Drayson, Mr Henry Percy Boulnois and Dr Vernon Ford [3,6,9] Drayson, Stratton Boulnois and Dr Vernon Ford [203] towards the end of April [8,202] at the end of April [124] and started writing *The White Company*, [6,99] (*3)
April	ACD played cricket for Portsmouth Cricket Club during April and May. [8]
April 27	ACD played cricket for Portsmouth Borough against South Lancashire Regiment at United Services Recreation Ground, Portsmouth, he scored 6 and took 1 catch, South Lancashire Regiment won. [235]
May 3	ACD played cricket on 3 & 4 for Southsea Rovers against United Services Portsmouth at United Services Recreation Ground, Portsmouth; he scored 6 and took 3 wickets, match drawn. [235]
n.d.	ACD played cricket for Portsmouth against the Royal Artillery scoring 111 not out. [202] (*2)

1889

May 11	ACD played cricket for Portsmouth Borough against Royal Artillery Southern Division at United Services Recreation Ground, Portsmouth, he scored 111 not out and did bat in second innings, Portsmouth Borough won. [235] (*2)
May 14	ACD read the Twentieth Annual Report and balance sheet at PLSS meeting [6] at the Guildhall. [396]
May 15	ACD played cricket for Portsmouth Borough against United Services Portsmouth at United Services Recreation Ground, Portsmouth, he scored 3 and took 2 wickets, United Services Portsmouth won. [235]
n.d.	Louise, with baby Mary, joined her mother Emily Hawkins for a holiday on the Isle of Wight. [202]
May 24	ACD played cricket on 24 & 25 for South Hampshire Rovers against United Services Portsmouth at United Services Recreation Ground, Portsmouth; he scored 29 and 24 and took 3 catches, match drawn. [235]
May 29	ACD played cricket for Portsmouth Borough against Fareham at Catisfield, Fareham, he scored 20 not out and 25, taking 2 wickets and 1 catch, match drawn. [235]
June 1	ACD played cricket for South Hampshire Rovers against Royal Navy at United Services Recreation Ground, Portsmouth, he scored 61 and took 3 wickets, South Hampshire Rovers won, A.H. Wood played for South Hampshire Rovers, he scored 4 and took 1 wicket. [235]
June 3	ACD played cricket on 3 & 4 for Corinthians against United Services Portsmouth at United Services Recreation Ground, Portsmouth, he scored 16 and did not bat in second innings and took 7 wickets and 1 catch, Corinthians won. [235]
June 5	ACD attended an address by Mr A.J. Balfour, M.P. at the Workingmen's Conservative Club, Arundel Street, Landport. In the evening at Barrard's Amphitheatre, Gunwharf Road, ACD attended a second address by Balfour. [397] (*2)
June 5	A.J. Balfour, a future Prime Minister, visited Portsmouth, lunch was taken at the George Hotel, followed by a visit to the Conservative Club, in the evening at the Amphitheatre; ACD seconded the resolution of thanks. [6,8,21,202,203] (*2)
June 8	*Micah Clarke* published in the *Manchester Weekly Times Supplement,* 8 June–28 September. [198]
June 14	ACD played cricket for Portsmouth Cricket Club against Southampton Cricket Club in the Hants County Cricket Challenge Cup at Hilsea. [398]
June 18	ACD played cricket for South Hampshire Rovers against Hampshire Hogs at County Ground, Southampton, he scored 5 and took 2 wickets, match drawn. [235]
June 19	ACD played cricket for Portsmouth Borough against Havant at Havant Park, Havant, he scored zero and took 1 wicket, Havant won. [235]
June 22	ACD played cricket for Portsmouth Borough against Royal Artillery Southern Division at United Services Recreation Ground, Portsmouth, he scored 14, took 3 wickets and 1 catch, match drawn. [235]
June 27	ACD played cricket for Southsea Rovers against Royal Marine Artillery at United Services Recreation Ground, Portsmouth, he scored 26 and took 1 catch, match drawn. [235]
June 29	ACD played cricket for Portsmouth Borough against Dorset Regiment at United Services Recreation Ground, Portsmouth, he scored 4 and took 6 wickets, match drawn. [235]
July 4	ACD played cricket for Portsmouth Borough against Southampton at Hilsea, Portsmouth, he scored zero and did not bat in second innings and took 6 wickets, Southampton won, A.H. Wood played for Portsmouth Borough, he scored 1 and took 1 wicket. [235]

1889

July 9	ACD played cricket on 9 & 10 for Corinthians against United Services Portsmouth at United Services Recreation Ground, Portsmouth, he scored 4 and 30, he took 1 wicket and 1 catch, match drawn. [235]
July 13	ACD played cricket for South Hampshire Rovers against United Services Portsmouth at United Services Recreation Ground, Portsmouth, he scored 1 and 4, match drawn. [235]
July 24	ACD played cricket for Portsmouth Borough against Havant at Hilsea, Portsmouth, he scored 20 and took 1 catch, Portsmouth Borough won. [235]
July 27	ACD played cricket for South Hampshire Rovers against Portsmouth Grammar School at Hilsea, Portsmouth, he scored 10 and took 1 wicket, match drawn, A.H. Wood played for Portsmouth Grammar School, he scored 44 and 19 and took 2 catches. [235]
August 3	The *Pall Mall Gazette* announced that ACD and a few gentlemen were about to establish and embark in a periodical. [399]
August 6	ACD played cricket for Portsmouth Borough against Ryde at Quarr Hill, Ryde, he scored 10, and took 1 wicket and 1 catch, match drawn. [235]
n.d.	ACD spent some time in the New Forest to continue work on his historical novel. [202] (*2)
Summer	ACD spent several weeks in the New Forest researching for his next book. [15] (*2)
August 19	ACD started writing *The White Company*. [202] (*3)
August 24	*The Bravoes of Market Drayton* published in *Chambers's Journal*. [6,196,198,202]
August 30	ACD attended a dinner and meeting with Joseph Marshall Stoddart, editor of *Lippincott's Monthly Magazine,* Oscar Wilde and an Irish MP, Thomas Patrick Gill at the Langham Hotel, Portland Place, London, the outcome of his meeting resulted in ACD writing *The Sign of the Four* and Oscar Wilde writing *The Picture of Dorian Gray*. [6,14,15,31,47,99,202,203,215]
September	ACD started writing *The Sign of the Six* or *The Problem of the Sholtos* [202] {Note: later to become *The Sign of the Four*.}
September	The Hampshire Psychical Society formed with ACD and Professor William Barrett as Vice-Presidents. [163]
September 30	ACD completed writing *The Sign of the Four*. [202] (*2)
September	During September and October *The Sign of Four* was written. [6,99]
October	By early October ACD had finished *The Sign of the Four*. [203] (*2)
n.d.	*The Sign of Four* published. [180] (*4)
October 12	ACD purchased 50 ordinary shares and one Founders share, total cost £225, in the Portsmouth and South Hampshire Electricity Supply Company. [8]
October 12	ACD was a member of the Portsmouth and South Hants Electrical Supply Company. [400]
October 15	ACD was listed as a founder member of the House-to-House Electric Light Company Ltd., investing £250. [401]
October 27	*The Firm of Girdlestone. A Romance for the Unromantic* published in *The People*, October 27 1889 until 13 April 1890. [6,198]
October 30	ACD at 1 Bush Villas, Elm Grove, Southsea. [1125]
November 2	ACD played as a full back for PAFC away against Petersfield, PAFC won 3–0. [107]
November 7	ACD at 1 Bush Villas, Elm Grove, Southsea. [1125]
November 11	ACD at 1 Bush Villas, Elm Grove, Southsea. [1125]
November 13	ACD was one of the umpires at a football match between Albion Athletic and Post Office (Portsmouth) in the Minor Cup Second Round played at the Governor's Green, Portsmouth. [1037]
November 20	ACD played as a full back for PAFC at United Services Men's Ground against Stubbington House School, PAFC won 1–0. [107]
November 23	ACD played as a full back for PAFC away against Fareham, PAFC won 5–0. [107]

1889

November 30	ACD played as a full back for PAFC at Hilsea against Portsmouth Grammar School, PAFC won 6–0. [107]
December 3	ACD attended a meeting of the PLSS at the Guildhall, where Major-General Drayson spoke about "The Art of Killing". [402] ACD and his wife attended PLSS meeting with General Drayson who lectured on "The Art of Killing". [8]
December 28	ACD played as a full back for PAFC away against the Royal Engineers (Aldershot), PAFC lost 3–2 in the Hampshire Senior Cup second round. This was ACD's last appearance for Portsmouth Association Football Club. [107]

1890

n.d.	*The Strand Magazine* established. [99] (*2)
n.d.	*The White Company* published. [180] (*2)
January	ACD's sister Annette seriously ill in Lisbon. [202]
January	*The Ring of Thoth* published in *The Cornhill Magazine*. [6,196,198]
January	*Mr. Stevenson's Methods in Fiction* published in *The National Review*. [6,198]
January 10	Mary Doyle, ACD's mother arrived in Lisbon to visit Annette. [202,203]
January 11	ACD at 1 Bush Villas, Elm Grove, Southsea. [1125]
January	Innes Doyle succeeded in his preliminary examination to enter the Royal Military Academy at Woolwich. [202,203]
n.d.	Death in Portugal of ACD's sister Ann (Annette). [99,180] (*4)
January 13	Death of ACD's sister Annette Mary Frances Conan Doyle [124,202,203,215] (*4) aged 33 [124] she died of influenza [124,215] she died of influenza aggravated by pneumonia at 24 Rua de Sacramento à Lapa, Lisbon. [23,68,200,203] at 24 Rua do Sacramento do Lapa. [124]
January 22	ACD attended the Portsmouth Cricket Club AGM at the Albany Hotel. [403] (*2)
January 29	ACD attended the Portsmouth Cricket Club's annual general meeting at the Albany Hotel. [8] (*2)
January 29	It was reported that ACD was secretary of a committee to set up a testimonial for Mr H. Percy Boulnois for his forthcoming departure. [404]
January 30	ACD at 1 Bush Villas, Elm Grove, Southsea. [1125]
n.d.	*The Sign of Four* Published. [99] (*4)
February	*The Sign of the Four* published in *Lippincott's Monthly Magazine*. [6,31,198,202,215] (*4)
February	*The Sign of Four* published. [202] (*4)
February	ACD at Southsea. [203]
February 4	ACD attended PLSS meeting. [6]
February 7	Mary Louise Conan Doyle, daughter of ACD and Louise, baptised at the Church of St. James, Milton, Portsmouth. [124] (*2)
February 7	ACD subscribed £1:1s to the Boulnois presentation fund. [405]
February 20	ACD was required to attend an inquest in Portsmouth. [8]
March 1	ACD attended a presentation to Mr H.P. Boulnois at the Grosvenor Hotel, Southsea. [406]
March 1	*Mysteries and Adventures* published by Walter Scott, London. [6]
n.d.	*The Captain of the Pole-star* published. [20,99,180] (*3)
March 6	*The Captain of the Polestar and Other Stories* published by Longmans, Green, and Company. [202] (*3)
March 6	*The Captain of the Polestar and Other Tales* published by Longmans, Green, and Company, London. [6] (*3)
March 13	ACD at Southsea [203] at 1 Bush Villas, Elm Grove, Southsea. [1125]
March 14	ACD at Bush Villa, Southsea. [884]
March 15	ACD presented the Portsmouth Association Challenge Cup to the winners of the final Freemantle who beat Geneva Cross one nil. [407]
April 1	ACD attended PLSS meeting and spoke on mesmerism and hypnotism. [6,215]
n.d.	*The Firm of Girdlestone* published. [99,180,202] (*2)
April 15	*The Firm of Girdlestone* published by Chatto & Windus, London. [6] (*2)

1890

April 25	ACD played cricket on 25 & 26 for United Services at Portsmouth against MCC; he scored 20 and took 1 catch. [31]
April 29	ACD attended a political speech and seconding of the resolution to adopt the Hon. Evelyn Ashley as Liberal Unionist candidate at the Esplanade Hotel, Southsea [6] ACD attended a large gathering of members of the Portsmouth Liberal Unionist Committee and their Conservative allies at the Esplanade Hotel, Southsea. [408]
April	At the end of April took a holiday with General Drayson, Dr Vernon Ford and Mr Boulnois at Emery Down near Lyndhurst, Hampshire. [124]
May 13	ACD attended the AGM of the PLSS at the Guildhall. [409]
May 21	ACD played cricket for Hampshire Rovers against Fareham at Hilsea, Portsmouth, he scored 8 and then 11 not out, he took 7 wickets, match drawn. [235]
May 30	ACD played cricket on 30 and 31 for Hampshire Rovers against United Services Portsmouth at United Services Recreation Ground, Portsmouth; he scored 22 and took 6 wickets, match drawn. [235]
June 4	ACD at 1 Bush Villas, Elm Grove, Southsea. [1125]
June 16	ACD played cricket on 16 & 17 for Hampshire Rovers against South Lancashire Regiment in Jersey, he scored 22 and 26, and took 5 wickets, Hampshire Rovers won. [235]
June 18	ACD played cricket for Hampshire Rovers against Victoria College, Jersey at the Victoria College Ground, St. Helier, Jersey, he scored 28 and took 4 wickets, match drawn. [235]
June 19	ACD played cricket for Hampshire Rovers against Jersey in Jersey, he scored 6, match drawn. [235]
July 2	ACD played cricket on 2 and 3 for Portsmouth against United Services at United Service Recreation Ground, he scored 40 and 2 and took 4 wickets in the first innings and 6 wickets in the second innings, Portsmouth won. [410]
July	ACD completed writing *The White Company*. [6,8,99,202] (*2)
July 5	ACD at Southsea and he completed writing *The White Company*. [203] (*2)
July 7	Mary Louise Conan Doyle, daughter of ACD and Louise, baptised. [8] (*2)
July 11	ACD played cricket on 11 & 12 for Hampshire Rovers against United Services Portsmouth at United Services Recreation Ground, Portsmouth; he scored zero and 14 and took 4 wickets, United Services Portsmouth won. [235]
July 16	ACD played cricket on 16 & 17 for United Services Portsmouth against Incogniti at the United Services Cricket Club, he took 1 wicket but did not bat, match drawn. [411]
August	ACD visited Berlin to investigate claim by German physician Robert Koch, that he had found a cure for tuberculosis [15,180] (*6) ACD correctly rejected the claim. [15] (*2)
August 18	ACD played cricket for Hampshire Rovers against Green Jackets at St. Cross, he scored 3, match drawn. [1969] {Note: St. Cross ground at Winchester.}
August 20	ACD played cricket on 20 & 21 for United Services Portsmouth against Free Foresters at United Services Recreation Ground, Portsmouth; he scored 4 and 1, and took 4 wickets and 1 catch, Free Foresters won. [235,412]
August 22	ACD played cricket on 22 & 23 for United Services Portsmouth against Crystal Palace at United Services Ground, Portsmouth, he scored 7 and 18 and took 2 wickets, match drawn. [235]
August	ACD played cricket for the United Services against MCC [6] (*2)
August 25	ACD played cricket on 25 & 26 for United Services Portsmouth against MCC at United Services Recreation Ground, Portsmouth, he scored 20 and took 1 catch, match drawn, A.H. Wood played for United Services Portsmouth, he scored 16 and took 5 wickets. [235] (*2)

1890

August 28	ACD played cricket on 28 & 29 for Hampshire XI against Hampshire Colts at Winchester College Ground, he scored 6 and 4, and took 2 catches, Hampshire XI won, A.H. Wood played for Hampshire XI, he scored 2 and then 7 not out and took 4 wickets. [235]
September	*A Physiologist's Wife* published in *Blackwood's Edinburgh Magazine.* [6,198]
September 9	ACD played cricket for United Services Portsmouth against South Hampshire, he scored 3 and 15, and took 1 wicket, match drawn [235] South Hampshire won. [413]
September 15	ACD played cricket for Portsmouth Borough against Winchester at County Ground, Southampton, he scored 5 and 2, and he took 4 wickets, Winchester won, A.H. Wood played for Portsmouth Borough, he scored zero and 13 and took 1 wicket and 2 catches. [235]
September 23	ACD attended the AGM of subscribers to the Eye and Ear Infirmary at the Grand Jury Room, New Town Hall, Portsmouth. [414]
September 24	ACD presided over the AGM [8] of the Portsmouth Association Football Club at the Albany Hotel, Landport, Mr A.H. Wood was elected as captain. [415]
October	ACD visited Berlin to investigate claim by bacteriologist Robert Koch to have found a cure for tuberculosis. [3,4,6,] (*6)
October	Innes was living at Bush Villas after failing the final stage of his exams; he then attended Portsmouth Grammar School. [202]
October 1	*The Sign of Four* published by Spencer Blackett, London [6] in October. [203]
October 13	ACD finished writing the play *Angels of Darkness*. [202]
October 25	The PLSS committee held their pre-season meeting at Bush Villas. [8]
November	ACD visited Berlin to investigate Koch's tuberculin cure. [7,48,215] (*6)
November 8	ACD was an umpire in the Association Junior Cup Final (Hants) between Portsmouth and Geneva Cross from Netley Hospital at the Hilsea ground. [416]
November 15	ACD left England for Berlin. [796]
November 16	ACD visited Berlin to investigate claim by bacteriologist Robert Koch to have found a cure for tuberculosis [7,8,202] (*6). On arrival ACD visited the British embassy to see if he could obtain a ticket for the Koch demonstration, but they could not help. ACD then visited Koch's home to see if could obtain a ticket but was told that he was unavailable. ACD unsuccessfully attempted to attend the lecture by Robert Koch in Berlin but could not obtain a ticket, so he mingled with the crowd to attempt to gain entry but was unsuccessful. He met with Dr Henry Hartz, an American doctor from Detroit, who offered to share his notes of the lecture with ACD. In the afternoon after the lecture ACD met Dr Henry Hartz and read his notes closely, making his own copy. [796]
n.d.	ACD visited Berlin to investigate claim by Robert Koch about his cure for tuberculosis. [99] (*6)
November	ACD visited Berlin to investigate claim by bacteriologist Robert Koch to have found a cure for tuberculosis (*6) but ACD correctly rejected the claim. [14] (*2)
November 17	ACD at the Central Hotel, Berlin. [18]
November 17	ACD visited Dr von Bergmann's clinic with Dr Hartz. [796]
November 19	ACD returned to London from Berlin. [48]
November 22	ACD returned to Southsea. [7,14,15,48]
November 22	ACD arrived back in Southsea from Berlin. [796]
November 24	In a local newspaper ACD announced that he would be leaving for the continent. [7,15]
November 26	ACD at Bush Villa, Southsea. [1834]
November 28	It was announced that ACD would be leaving Southsea next month for Vienna and then settle down in London, he had recently visited Berlin. [417]
November 30	Caroline Mary Burton Doyle (Lottie) heard of ACD's determination to leave Southsea, Lottie was in Lisbon at the time. [124,203]
December	*The Duello in France* published *The Cornhill Magazine.* [6,196,198]
December	*Dr. Koch and his Cure* published in *The Review of Reviews.* [6,198]

1890

December 6	*The Surgeon of Gaster Fell* published in *Chambers's Journal* on December 6, 13, 20 & 27. [6,196,198] (*2)
n.d.	*The Surgeon of Gaster Fell* published in *Chambers's Journal*. [180] (*2)
December 12	ACD attended a farewell dinner on his behalf at the Grosvenor Hotel, Southsea prior to leaving Southsea. [2,7,20,31,36,48,202,215,418] (*3)
December 12	The Portsmouth Literary and Scientific Society of Portsmouth marked their appreciation of the value of ACD's position as a townsman and their regret at his forthcoming departure entertained him to dinner at the Grosvenor Hotel, Southsea. [982] (*3)
December 13	Farewell dinner to ACD at the Grosvenor Hotel, Southsea. [8,14] (*3)
December	ACD left general practice in Southsea. [7] (*4)
December 15	ACD left his Southsea practice. [68] (*4)
December 18	ACD left his practice in Southsea, Hampshire. [7,48,124,203] (*4)
December	ACD and Louise spent a couple of nights in a lodging house in Southsea. [202]
December	ACD and Louise spent some time with the Hoares in Birmingham. [202]
December	*A Pastoral Horror* published in *The People*. [203] (*2)
December 21	*A Pastoral Horror* published in *The People*. [6,198] (*2)
Christmas	The first issue of *The Strand Magazine* published. [215] (*2)
Christmas	ACD and Louise spent Christmas at Masongill [215] after visiting Dr and Mrs Hoare in Birmingham. [5,7,8,14,15,48,202]
December 31	ACD and Louise left England for Vienna. [48] (*4)
n.d.	At the end of 1890 ACD and Louise left for Vienna. [12] (*4)
n.d.	ACD spent some time in Vienna studying ophthalmology. [99]

1891

n.d.	ACD played cricket for the Allahakbarries against Shere. [1146]
n.d.	ACD began his long association with the firm of A.P. Watt, literary agents. [99]
n.d.	George Newnes founded *The Strand Magazine*. [203] (*2)
January	George Newnes launched the first issue of *The Strand Magazine*. [215] (*2)
January	*The White Company* published in *The Cornhill Magazine* from January to December. [6,196,198]
January 3	ACD and Louise left England for Vienna. [7] (*4)
January 4	ACD and Louise left Victoria Station for their journey to Vienna. [202] (*4)
January 5	ACD and Louise arrived in Vienna to study eye medicine but his plans fell through [2,4,6,7,12,15,20,48,68,200,215] and stayed at the Hotel Kummer. [203] (*2)
January 6	ACD and Louise arrived in Vienna and stayed at the Hotel Kummer. [202] (*2)
n.d.	After a short stay at the Hotel Kummer ACD and Louise moved to a cheaper pension run by Madame Bonfort at Universitat Strasse 6. [202] (*2)
January 6	ACD and Louise moved to a cheaper pension run by a Madame Bomfort, Pension Bomfort, Universität Strasse 6, Vienna [203] Universitaet Strasse 6, Vienna. [215] (*2)
January 6	ACD started writing *The Doings of Raffles Haw*. [6,202,215] (*2)
n.d.	ACD started writing *The Doings of Raffle Haw*. [203] (*2)
January 12	Nem Hawkins (Emily, sister of Louise) started out for Algiers. [203]
January 13	ACD in Vienna. [203]
January 23	ACD completed writing *The Doings of Raffles Haw*. [6,202,215]
January	Charles Altamont Doyle was moved to the Royal Edinburgh Asylum [203] (*2) or Edinburgh Royal Asylum. [2010]
January 23	Charles Altamont Doyle was moved to the Royal Edinburgh Asylum. [152] (*2)
January 29	ACD and Louise attended an Anglo American Ball in Vienna. [203]
January 30	ACD in Vienna. [203]
February	ACD in Vienna. [203]
February	*The Song of the Bow* (poem) published in *The Cornhill Magazine*. [6,198]
February	*Our Midnight Visitor* published in *Temple Bar*. [6,196,198]

1891

March	*The Voice of Science* published in the third issue of *The Strand Magazine*. [6,99,194,195,196,198,202]
March 9	ACD left Vienna [7,68] and travelled to Paris via Venice and Milan. [202,215]
March 9	ACD travelled to Semmering. [2,12,14,48]
March 10	ACD travelled to Venice. [2,12]
March 16	ACD travelled to Milan. [2,12]
March 19	ACD arrived in Paris. [2,7,12,86]
n.d.	*A Straggler of '15* published. [180,203] (*2)
March 21	*A Straggler of '15* published in *Black and White*. [6,196,198] (*2)
March 24	ACD arrived in London. [2,86,202,215]
n.d.	ACD left his Southsea practice (*4) and moved to London and opened an eye practice at 2 Upper Wimpole Street, few clients visited and he decided to give medicine. [99]
March	ACD and his family moved to London, he rented rooms at 23 Montague Place, Bloomsbury [124,180] with consulting rooms at 2 Upper Wimpole Street. [124]
March 24	On or about 24 March ACD and Louise moved into a rented flat at 23 Montague Place, Bloomsbury, London, at the same time ACD took a front room with part use of a waiting room at 2 Devonshire Place, near Harley Street for his practice. [233]
March 24	ACD was residing at 23 Montague Place, Russell Square, London. [7,12,14,20,39,48,68,200,202]
March	By the end of March ACD was living at Montague Place, London and was attempting to establish himself as an eye specialist at 2 Upper Wimpole Street, London. [320]
March	At the end of March ACD took a large flat at 23 Montague Place, London. [15]
March	At the end of March ACD rented a consulting room at 2 Devonshire Place, London. [8]
March/April	ACD at 2 Upper Wimpole Street, London and lodging at 23 Montague Place, Russell Square, London. [203]
April	April-June ACD was living at 23 Montague Place, London. [232]
April 1	ACD opened practice as an eye specialist at 2 Upper Wimpole Street, London. [48]
April 1	ACD applied for admission to the Reading Room of the British Museum, Great Russell Street, London. He gave his address as 23, Montague Place and his profession/occupation as physician. [789]
April	ACD sent *A Scandal in Bohemia* to his agent A.P. Watt. [202] (*2)
April 3	ACD sent *A Scandal in Bohemia* to his agent A.P. Watt. [2,6,163] (*2)
April	A.P. Watt sent the manuscript of *A Scandal in Bohemia* to the editor of *The Strand Magazine*. [99,202]
April 5	Mary J.E. Doyle and Bryan Mary (Dodo), mother and sister of ACD, were living at Masongill Cottage, Masongill, Thornton-in-Lonsdale, Yorkshire, Bryan Charles Waller was living at Masongill House. [117,124]
n.d.	Caroline (Lottie) and Constance (Connie) were governess's in Portugal. [124]
April 5	ACD and Louise were living 23 Montague Place, Bloomsbury, London. [118]
April 5	ACD's daughter Mary was living with Emily Hawkins (mother of Louise), Louisa Butt, Jeremiah and Emily Hawkins (son and daughter) of Emily at Emanuel Road, Southsea, Hampshire. [119]
April 5	Charles Altamont Doyle was a patient at Sunnyside, Hillside, Montrose Royal Lunatic Asylum. [120]
April 5	John Francis Innes Hay Doyle at the Royal Military Academy, Woolwich. [204]
April 5	James Leckie with his wife Selina and their family, Jean, Malcolm, Patrick and Sarah, were living at Glebe House, The Glebe, Lee. [119]
April 5	ACD opened practice as an eye specialist at 2 Devonshire Place, London. [8,10]
April 6	ACD opened practice as an eye specialist at 2 Upper Wimpole Street, London. [7,14,68,200,202]

1891

April 6	ACD opened practice as an eye specialist at 2 Devonshire Place, London. [2,7,20] {Note: in 1994 this was found to actually be 2 Upper Wimpole Street, off Harley Street, London.} [12]
April 10	ACD completed writing *A Case of Identity*. [6,20]
April 11	*A Case of Identity* sent to A.P. Watt. [202]
April 20	ACD completed writing *The Red-Headed League*. [6]
April 20	*The Red-Headed League* reached A.P. Watt. [20,202]
April 27	ACD completed writing *The Boscombe Valley Mystery*. [6]
April 27	*The Boscombe Valley Mystery* sent to A.P. Watt. [20]
May 4	ACD seriously ill with a severe bout of influenza [2,6,12,14,15,48,124,215] (*3) for three weeks. [202]
May 10	*The Song of the Bow* (poem) published in *The Sun*. [198]
May 14	ACD was seriously ill with a severe bout of influenza. [20] (*3)
May 18	*The Five Orange Pips* dispatched to A.P. Watt. [202]
May	ACD gave up medicine to write full time. [2,48,215] (*4)
June	ACD gave up medicine to write full time [7,20,215] (*4) and moved to 12 Tennison Road, South Norwood. [33,124,180,215] (*4)
June 1	ACD signed a contract with *Good Words* to write a story for the special Christmas edition, this was *Beyond the City*. [2,6]
June 25	ACD left 23 Montague Place and moved to 12 Tennison Road, South Norwood [7,12,14,20,39,68,200,202] at the end of June. [48] (*4)
June 25	Sherlock Holmes made his debut in *The Strand Magazine*. [1972]
June 25	ACD moved into 12 Tennison Road, South Norwood. [2,320] (*4)
June 28	*The Franklin's Maid* (poem) published in *The Sun*. [198]
June 30	ACD played cricket for Norwood Club away at Addiscombe, he scored 22 [320] for Norwood Club against Addiscombe at Norwood Green, he scored 21, match drawn. [235]
n.d.	From July 1891 until 1896 ACD was living at 12 Tennison Road, South Norwood, London. [232] (*4)
July	The Sherlock Holmes short stories began to appear in *The Strand Magazine*. [180]
n.d.	The first six of *The Adventures of Sherlock Holmes* published in *The Strand Magazine*. [99]
July	*A Scandal in Bohemia* published in *The Strand Magazine*. [6,31,99,194,195,196,198,202,203,215]
July 1	ACD played cricket for Norwood Club at home to the Surrey Club and Ground, he scored zero [320] at Norwood Green, he scored zero, Surrey Club and Ground won. [235]
July 3	ACD played cricket for Norwood Club against Willesden at Norwood Green, he scored zero, Norwood Club won. [235]
July 4	ACD played cricket for Norwood Club against Oakleigh Wanderers at Norwood, he scored 15 and took 1 wicket, Norwood Club won. [235]
July 7	ACD bought 250 shares in Newnes Ltd. [2]
July 8	The manuscript of *Beyond the City* delivered to ACD's agent. [6,202]
July 12	*The Doings of Raffle Haw* published in the *Pittsburgh Commercial Gazette,* 12 July – 23 August. [198]
n.d.	ACD played cricket for Norwood Club against Norbury Park, he scored 32 and took 5 wickets. [320]
July 15	ACD played cricket for Norwood Club against The Erratics at Norwood Green, he scored 27 and took 2 wickets and 1 catch, Norwood Club won. [235]
July 16	The Society of Authors celebrated the adoption of the American Copyright Act with a dinner at the Hotel Metropole, London, among those attending were ACD, Brete Harte, Thomas Hardy, Walter Besant, Rider Haggard and Oscar Wilde. [982,1972]
July 18	ACD played cricket for Norwood Club against Hornsey at Norwood Green, he scored 2, match drawn. [235]

1891

July 22	ACD played cricket for Norwood Club against Northbrook at Norwood Green, he scored 2, match drawn. [235]
July 26	*The Colonel's Choice* published in *Lloyd's Weekly Newspaper*. [6,198]
August	ACD had been seriously ill with a severe bout of influenza (*3) and decided to give up medicine and write full time. [10] (*4)
August	ACD gave up medicine to write full time. [10,53,203,215] (*4)
August	ACD and family lived at 12 Tennison Road, South Norwood. [15,203]
August	*The Red-Headed League* published in *The Strand Magazine*. [6,194,195,196,198,215]
August	ACD assisted Miss Joan Paynter a nurse from Torquay to locate her fiancé. [99]
August 1	ACD played cricket for Norwood Club against Granville (Lee) at The Cedars, Lee, he scored 2, Granville (Lee) won. [235]
August 3	ACD played cricket for Norwood Club against Willesden at Toleys Cricket Ground, Willesden, he scored 6 and took 3 wickets, match drawn. [235]
August 8	ACD played cricket for Norwood Club against Addiscombe at Sandilands, Croydon, he scored zero, match drawn. [235]
August 8	*Woman's Wit* published in the *Baltimore Weekly Sun*. [198]
August 10	ACD sent *The Adventure of the Man with the Twisted Lip* to his literary agent. [202]
August 12	ACD played cricket for Norwood Club against Windsor Home Park at Windsor Park, Windsor, he scored 18 and took 1 catch, Norwood Club won. [235]
August 15	ACD left England with Norwood Club for a short cricket tour of Holland. [2,202,320]
August	ACD toured Holland with the British cricket team. [63] (*3)
Summer	ACD toured Holland playing cricket and football for the local South Norwood teams. [14] (*3)
August 18	*The White Company* published in America by John W. Lovell Company. [6,99]
August 26	ACD arrived back in England after the cricket tour. [2] (*2)
August 26	ACD returned to England after the cricket tour of Holland. [320] (*2)
August 28	Birth of Geoffrey Rhodes Bromet. [68,200]
September	*A Case of Identity* published in *The Strand Magazine*. [6,194,195,196,198]
September 2	ACD played cricket for Norwood Club against East Dulwich at Norwood Green, he scored 33 and took 1 wicket, match drawn. [235]
September 21	ACD at 12 Tennison Road, South Norwood. [884]
September 28	ACD and family, including his sister Connie, were living at Tennison Road, South Norwood. [203]
October	ACD applied to join the Reform Club; he was proposed by James Payn and seconded by the surgeon Malcolm Morris. [202]
October	*The Boscombe Valley Mystery* published in *The Strand Magazine*. [6,194,195,196,198]
October 5	ACD signed the contract with Cassell & Company which gave them the English and Colonial book rights for *The Doings of Raffles Haw*. [982]
n.d.	ACD saw Zola's *Thérèse Raquin* at the Royalty Theatre, London. [202]
October 14	ACD saw Zola's 'Therése Raquin' in London. [203]
October 14	ACD at South Norwood. [203]
October 26	*The White Company* published by Smith, Elder, & Co., London [6,99,202] in three volumes. [203]
October 28	ACD and Louise were invited to a dinner by James Payn, also present was Baron von Tauchnitz [202] also Baroness Tauchnitz and George Buckle. [203]
October 29	ACD at South Norwood. [203]
October	During October and November ACD was writing *The Blue Carbuncle, The Speckled Band, The Noble Bachelor, The Engineer's Thumb* and *The Beryl Coronet*. [20,202,203]
November	ACD at South Norwood. [203]
November	*The Five Orange Pips* published in *The Strand Magazine*. [6,194,195,196,198] (*2)

1891

n.d.	*The Five Orange Pips* published. [180] (*2)
November 11	ACD at South Norwood. [203]
November 14	ACD and Connie visited Innes at Woolwich. [203]
November 16	ACD bought 200 shares in *Tit Bits*. [2]
November 18	ACD photographed at work in his South Norwood home by David Thomson. [203]
November 29	*A Sordid Affair* published in *The People*. [6,198]
December	*The Man with the Twisted Lip* published in *The Strand Magazine*. [6,194,195,196,198]
December	ACD featured in *Portraits of Celebrities at different times of their Lives* in *The Strand Magazine*. [6,195,198]
December	Between December 1891 and February 1892, ACD was writing *The Refugees*. [6,99,203,215]
December 3	ACD bought 15 shares in *Tit Bits*. [2]
December 7	ACD at South Norwood. [203]
December 8	ACD at 12 Tennison Road, South Norwood. [884]
December 12	*The Doings of Raffles Haw* published in *Answers*, 12 December 1891–27 February 1892. [6,196,198]
December 15	*Between Two Fires* published in *Gentlewoman*. [202] (*2)
December 19	*Between Two Fires* published in *The Gentlewoman*. [6,196,198] (*2)
December 22	ACD at South Norwood. [203]
Christmas	Over Christmas ACD completed writing *The Copper Beeches*. [202]
Christmas	*Beyond the City. The Idyll of a Suburb* published in *Good Cheer* (*Good Words*), the special Christmas edition of *Good Words*. [6,198,202]
Christmas	*A False Start* published in the Christmas issue of *The Gentlewoman*. [6,198]
December 27	ACD dined at the Langham Hotel with the Bouluois family. [203]

1892

n.d.	Constance (Connie) returned to England. [124]
n.d.	ACD played cricket at The Hague, Holland. [10] (*3) [Note: this was probably the cricket tour in 1891.}
January	ACD was at work on *The Refugees*. [99]
January	*The Adventure of the Blue Carbuncle* published in *The Strand Magazine*. [6,194,195,196,198]
January	Charles Altamont Doyle transferred to The Edinburgh Royal Infirmary for three months, then on to The Crighton Royal Institution. [14,20] (*4)
January	Charles Altamont Doyle committed to Royal Edinburgh Asylum (Morningside) until May 1892. [68,200,202] (*4)
January 2	*Out of the Running* published in *Black and White*. [6,196,198]
January	ACD attended his first Idler's soirée [202] where he met J.M. Barrie, Jerome K. Jerome, Barry Pain, Zangwill, Robert Barr and Robertson. [203] (*2)
January 4	A dinner was held to celebrate the birth of *The Idler* at Pagani's, Great Portland Street, London, among those that attended the dinner were; ACD, J.M. Barrie, I. Zangwill, Jerome K. Jerome, F.W. Robinson, Eden Phillpots and George Hutchinson. [982] (*2)
January 6	ACD at South Norwood. [203]
January 8	Dined again with some of those he met at an earlier Idler's dinner. [203]
January 20	Charles Altamont Doyle was transferred from Montrose to Morningside Asylum. [124] (*4)
January 23	Charles Altamont Doyle was transferred from the Montrose Royal Asylum to the Royal Edinburgh Asylum. [180] (*4)
January 30	*The Gamut of Humour* published in *The Speaker*. [6,198]
January	J.M. Barrie stayed with ACD at Tennison Road for a weekend at the end of January. [202,203]
February	A shortened version of *Micah Clarke* was published in *Longman's School Magazine*, February–December. [6]

1892

February	*The Adventure of the Speckled Band* published in *The Strand Magazine*. [6,194,195,196,198]
February 1	ACD at South Norwood. [203]
February 4	ACD at South Norwood [203], at 12 Tennison Road, South Norwood. [1125]
February 6	*The Storming Party* (poem) published in *The Speaker*. [6,198]
n.d.	Death of Henry Doyle. [202,203] (*2)
February 17	Death of Henry Edward Doyle, he was buried at St. Mary's Roman Catholic Cemetery, Kensal Green, London. [68,124,200] (*2)
February 18	*De Profundis* published in *The Independent*. [198]
February 22	ACD attended the funeral of Henry Doyle at St. Mary's Cemetery, Kensal Green, London. [419]
February 26	ACD at South Norwood. [203]
February 27	ACD visited George Meredith at his Box Hill home near Dorking in Surrey with J.M. Barrie and Arthur Quiller-Couch ("Q"). [9,202]
March	*De Profundis* published in *The Idler Magazine*. [6,196,198,202]
March	*The Adventure of the Engineer's Thumb* published in *The Strand Magazine*. [6,194,195,196,198]
March 2	ACD sent the script of *A Straggler of '15* to Henry Irving. [202]
March 5	Henry Irving accepted the script of *A Straggler of '15*, and soon paid ACD £100 for exclusive rights. [202]
March 5	*The Doings of Raffles Haw* published by Cassell & Company, London. [6]
March 5	*The Great Brown-Pericord Motor* published in the *Ludgate Weekly Magazine*. [6,198]
n.d.	ACD, J.M. Barrie and Arthur Quiller-Couch visited George Meredith at Boxhill, Surrey. [202] (*2)
March 6	ACD, J.M. Barrie and Arthur Quiller-Couch visited George Meredith at Boxhill, Surrey. [203] (*2)
March 7	ACD at South Norwood. [203]
March 12	*The Frontier Line* (poem) published in *The Speaker*. [6,198]
March 12	*The Adventure of the Noble Bachelor* published in *The Courier-Journal* (Louisville). [198]
March 13	ACD completed writing *The Refugees*. [202]
March	ACD took a brief holiday in Scotland, staying in Edinburgh; he visited J.M. Barrie at Kirriemuir and spent one week fishing at Alford in Aberdeenshire. [4,7,14] (*4)
n.d.	ACD visited Edinburgh and then on to The Forbes Arms, Alford, Aberdeenshire where he visited J.M. Barrie at Kirriemuir. [203] (*4)
April	Between April and June ACD was writing *The Great Shadow*. [6,99]
April	*The Adventures of the Noble Bachelor* published in *The Strand Magazine*. [6,194,195,196,198]
Easter	ACD travelled to Scotland for a spot of fishing with J.M. Barrie at Kirriemuir, he stayed from 16 to 19 April. [202] (*4)
April 16	ACD arrived at Kirriemuir, Scotland and stayed with J.M. Barrie at his residence Strathview. [982] (*4)
April 16	*The Adventure of the Beryl Coronet* published in *The Indianapolis News*, on 16 & 23. [198]
April 30	*The Engineer's Thumb* published as *Strange Adventure* in the *Baltimore Weekly Sun*. [198]
May	ACD was the President of the PLSS. [322]
May	*A Talk with Dr. Conan Doyle* published in *The Bookman* (London). [198]
May	*The Adventure of the Beryl Coronet* published in *The Strand Magazine*. [6,194,195,196,198]
May 4	ACD at 12 Tennison Road, South Norwood. [1834]
May 7	ACD at 12 Tennison Road, South Norwood. [884]
May 14	ACD played cricket for Norwood Club against Croydon at Norwood Green, he scored zero and took 5 wickets, Norwood Club won. [235]

1892

May 14	*A Regimental Scandal* published in *The Courier-Journal*. [6,198]
May	ACD was elected the president of the UNLSS at the AGM. [320]
May 20	ACD played cricket on 20 & 21 for Hampshire Rovers against United Services Portsmouth at United Services Recreation Ground, Portsmouth, he scored zero and 1, and took 2 wickets, Hampshire Rovers won, A.H. Wood played for Hampshire Rovers, he scored 31 and 28, he took 3 wickets and 1 catch. [235]
May	Charles Altamont Doyle transferred to the Crichton Royal Asylum, Dumfries [203,215] (*5) or Crichton Royal Institution. [2010]
May 23	Charles Altamont Doyle transferred to the Crichton Royal Asylum, Dumfries. [152] (*5)
May 26	Charles Altamont Doyle transferred to the Crichton Royal Asylum, Dumfries. [124] (*5)
May 28	ACD played cricket for Norwood Club against Dulwich at Norwood Green, he scored 14 and took 1 wicket, match drawn. [235]
May 31	Charles Altamont Doyle committed to The Crichton Royal Institution, Dumfries, Dumfriesshire [68,200,202] (*5), was transferred from the Royal Edinburgh Asylum to the Crichton Royal (mental) Hospital, Dumfries. [180] (*5)
May 31	ACD attended the Incorporated Society of Authors at the Holborn Restaurant, London. [1196]
June	It was announced that ACD was a committee member of the Lowell Memorial. [1197]
June	*The Adventure of the Copper Beeches* published in *The Strand Magazine*. [6,194,195,196,198]
June	ACD was writing *Silver Blaze, The Cardboard Box* and *The Yellow Face*. [202]
June 6	ACD played cricket for Norwood Club against Forest Hill at Norwood Green, he scored 48 and took 3 wickets, Norwood Club won. [235]
June 11	ACD played cricket for Norwood Club against Plaistow at Norwood Green, he scored 11, match drawn. [235]
June 16	ACD's membership to the Reform Club was confirmed. [202] (*2)
n.d.	ACD joined the Reform Club, 104 Pall Mall, London. [181] (*2)
June 18	ACD played cricket for Norwood Club against Norbury Park at J.W. Hobbs Ground, Norbury, he scored 3 and took 3 wickets, Norwood Club won. [235]
June	ACD took a holiday in Norway with his sister Connie, sister-in-law Nem, Josephine Hoare (daughter of Dr Hoare) and Jerome K. Jerome. [202] (*3)
June 21	ACD played cricket for Emeriti against Beaumont College at Beaumont College Ground, Old Windsor, he scored 3 and took 4 wickets and took 1 catch, Emeriti won. [235]
June 22	ACD played cricket for Norwood Club against Croydon at Fairfield Ground, Croydon, he scored 16, took 1 wicket and 1 catch, Norwood Club won. [235]
June 25	ACD played cricket for Norwood Club against The Grecians at Norwood Green, he scored 79, Norwood Club won. [235]
June 27	ACD played cricket for Emeriti against Hampstead at Lymington Road, Hampstead, he scored 15, match drawn. [235]
June 29	ACD played cricket for Norwood Club against Addiscombe at Sandilands, Croydon, he scored 18 and took 1 catch, Norwood Club won. [235]
July	*The Glamour of the Arctic* published in *The Idler Magazine*. [6,196,198]
July 4	ACD played cricket for Norwood Club against The Erratics at Norwood Green, he scored 25 and 19 and took 1 wicket and 1 catch, match drawn. [235]
July 6	ACD played cricket for Norwood Club against Willesden at Norwood Green, he scored 19 and took 4 wickets and 1 catch, Norwood Club won. [235]
July 7	ACD played cricket for Norwood Club against MCC at Merchant Taylors' Ground, Northwood, he scored 4 and then 1 not out, match drawn. [235] (*2)
July	ACD played cricket for the Norwood Club against MCC. [63] (*2)
July 8	ACD played cricket for Norwood Club against S. Ellis' XI at Norwood Green, he scored zero and took 2 wickets and 1 catch, match drawn. [235]

1892

July 20	ACD played cricket for Norwood Club against Sutton at Cheam Road, Sutton, he scored 4 and took 5 wickets, Norwood Club won. [235]
July 30	ACD played cricket for Norwood Club against Norbury Park at Norwood Green, he scored 9, Norwood Club won. [235]
Summer	*A Question of Diplomacy* published in *The Illustrated London News*, Summer & Jubilee Number. [6,99,196,198]
Summer	ACD with his sister Constance (Connie), his sister-in-law Nem and Josephine (Joey) Hoare, daughter of Dr Hoare, visited Norway with Jerome K. Jerome. [15,124,180,215] (*3)
August	ACD with family visited Norway with Jerome K. Jerome where he skied for the first time, ACD later he introduced cross-country skiing in Switzerland. [3,4,14] (*3)
August	*A Day with Dr. Conan Doyle*, an interview with ACD by Harry How published in *The Strand Magazine*. [6,195,198,215]
August 1	ACD played cricket for Norwood Club against South Croydon at Norwood Green, he scored zero and took 7 wickets and 2 catches, Norwood Club won. [235]
August 5	*Out of the Running* published in *Bow Bells*. [198]
August 6	ACD played cricket for Norwood Club against Dulwich College at Turney Road, Dulwich, he scored 104 not out, Norwood Club won [235] against Dulwich. [320]
August 10	ACD played cricket for Norwood Club against Roving Friars at Norwood Green, he scored 26 and took 2 wickets and 1 catch, Norwood Club won. [235]
August 13	ACD played cricket for Norwood Club against Epsom [320] at Epsom Down, Epsom, he scored 40, match drawn. [235]
August 17	ACD played cricket for Norwood Club against Addiscombe at Norwood Green, he scored 29 and took 5 wickets, match drawn. [235]
September 1	ACD played cricket for The Idlers against Norwood Club, the Idlers team also included Robert Barr, E.W. Hornung, Alfred Wood and Innes Doyle. [63] (*4)
September 3	ACD played cricket for Norwood Club against Granville (Lee) at Norwood Green, he scored 10, match drawn. [235]
n.d.	ACD captained The Idlers cricket team that included Jerome K. Jerome, Robert Barr, E.W. Hornung, Innes Doyle and Alfred Wood playing against his local Norwood club. [202] (*4)
September 6	ACD played cricket for The Idlers against Norwood Club at Norwood Green, he scored 17 and took 3 wickets, match drawn. Also in the Idlers team were A.H. Wood who scored 8 and took 1 catch, Innes Doyle scored 25 and E.W. Hornung who scored 10. Jerome K. Jerome was officiating as scorer and did not play, [235] ACD was the captain of The Idler team. [124] (*4)
September 7	ACD played cricket for The Idlers against Norwood Club at Norwood, he scored 17 and took 4 wickets; also in the Idlers team were Alfred Wood who scored 8 and took 1 catch, Innes Doyle scored 25 and E.W. Hornung who scored 10, Jerome K. Jerome was officiating as scorer and did not play. [320] (*4)
September	*Lot No. 249* published in *Harper's Monthly*. [6,198]
September	ACD at 12 Tennison Road, South Norwood. [18]
September 12	H.M.S. "*Foudroyant*" (poem) published in the *Daily Chronicle* as "*For Nelson's Sake*" H.M.S. *Foudroyant*. [6,198] (*2)
September	H.M.S. "*Foudroyant*" published the *Daily Chronicle*. [203] (*2)
October 1	*The Great Shadow* published in *The Saturday Globe,* 1 October–5 November. [198]
October 12	ACD attended the funeral of Alfred Tennyson at Westminster Abbey, as did among others including, Mr Irving, Miss Ellen Terry, Mr Henry James, Mr Thomas Hardy, Revd. S. Baring-Gould and Mr J.M. Barrie. [1198]
October 14	*The Adventures of Sherlock Holmes* published by George Newnes, Ltd., London. [6] (*2)

1892

n.d.	*The Adventures of Sherlock Holmes* published. [180,202,215] (*2)
October 19	ACD attended and spoke at meeting of the UNLSS. [6] (*2)
October 19	ACD attended a lecture delivered at the Royal Normal College for the Blind before the UNLSS by Dr Benham of Oxford. [420] (*2)
October 21	Caroline (Lottie) returned to England [3,124] she arrived at Shadwell Basin and took up residence with her brother ACD, at 12 Tennison Road, South Norwood. [188]
n.d.	*The Great Shadow* published. [180,203] (*2)
October 31	*The Great Shadow* published in *Arrowsmith's Christmas Annual*. [198] (*2)
November	*Jelland's Voyage* published in *Phil May's Illustrated Winter Annual*. [6,196,198]
November	ACD at South Norwood. [203]
November 2	ACD lectured on "The Genius and Writings of George Meredith" at a meeting of UNLSS. [2,6]
November 10	ACD attended the Authors' Club dinner at St. James's Place. [1972]
n.d.	Birth of Arthur Alleyne Kingsley Conan Doyle, son of ACD and Louise. [99] (*4)
November	Birth of Arthur Alleyne Kingsley Conan Doyle (known as Kingsley), son of ACD and Louise. [180] (*4)
November 15	Birth of Arthur Alleyne Kingsley Conan Doyle, son of ACD and Louise, [14,16,17,68,124,200,202,203,215,236] (*4) at 12 Tennison Road, South Norwood. [68,124,200]
November 16	Birth of son Arthur Alleyne Kingsley Conan Doyle. [33] (*4)
November 16	ACD attended and spoke at meeting of UNLSS. [6]
n.d.	Mary Doyle, mother of ACD, was living at Masongill Cottage, Masongill, Yorkshire. [180]
December	*The Los Amigos Fiasco* published in *The Idler Magazine*. [6,196,198]
December	ACD gave lectures in Scotland and visited J.M. Barrie at Kirriemuir. [15]
December	ACD was probably writing *The Musgrave Ritual*. [202]
December	*The Adventure of Silver Blaze* published in *The Strand Magazine*. [6,194,195,196,198,202]
December	ACD, Jerome K. Jerome and E.W. Hornung visited the Black Museum at New Scotland Yard. [15] (*3)
December 2	ACD, Jerome K. Jerome and E.W. Hornung were given a tour of the basement room at Scotland Yard by Dr Gilbert, the Medical Officer of Newgate and Holloway prisons. [67,163,208] (*3)
n.d.	Death of James Doyle. [202,203] (*2)
December 3	Death of James William Edmund Doyle. [68,124,200] (*2)
December 8	ACD attended a special gathering at the Authors' Club where between fifty and sixty authors and their friends dined together under the presidency of Mr Oswald Crawfurd held at Whitehall Court, London. [982]
December 8	ACD read *The Curse of Eve* at a meeting of the Authors' Club [1974] (*2)
December 10	ACD was invited by Dr Philip Gilbert, physician of Newgate and Holloway prisons, to visit Scotland Yard's crime museum, ACD took Jerome K. Jerome and Willie Hornung with him. [202] (*3)
December 12	*Critics and Criticism. Two Types of Reviews* published in the *Morning Leader*. [198]
December 14	ACD attended and spoke at meeting of UNLSS. [6]
December 16	ACD attended a dinner at the Reform Club. [132]
December 22	ACD at the Reform Club, Pall Mall, S.W., London. [18]
December 22	Arthur Alleyne Kingsley Conan Doyle baptised at St. Mark's Church, South Norwood. [236,320]
December 23	Mary J.E. Doyle was at Masongill Cottage, Yorkshire. [203]
n.d.	ACD in collaboration with J.M. Barrie was working on the comic operetta, *Jane Annie; or, The Good-Conduct Prize*. [203]
December 29	ACD at 12 Tennison Road, South Norwood. [884]

1893

Early 1893	ACD and Louise took a holiday in Switzerland and visited the Reichenbach Falls, [3,4,20,180], ACD visited Davos. [99]
n.d.	ACD joined the Beckenham Golf Club. [1134]
n.d.	Connie Doyle met E.W. Hornung. [203]
n.d.	Caroline, ACD's sister, returned home to South Norwood from Portugal. [99]
n.d.	ACD played cricket for the Allahakbarries against Shere. [1146]
n.d.	*The Refugees* published. [180] (*2)
January	*The Refugees. A Tale of Two Continents* published in *Harper's New Monthly Magazine* from January to June. [6,198] (*2)
January	*My First Book VI. – Juvenilia* published in *The Idler Magazine*. [6,99,196,198]
January	*The Adventure of the Cardboard Box* published in *The Strand Magazine*. [6,194,195,196,198]
January	ACD at South Norwood. [203]
January 4	ACD attended meeting of UNLSS [3,6] ACD chaired the meeting where William Fletcher Barrett gave a lecture titled "The Psychical Research Society". [320]
January 4	ACD at the Reform Club. [1834]
January 10	ACD attended a meeting of the Authors' Club. [1134]
January 13	ACD attended the Vagabonds' Club monthly dinner at the Holborn Restaurant, London. [421]
January 25	ACD attended meeting of UNLSS and spoke on the next war [6] chaired the meeting where a Russian exile, Mr Felix Volkhovski, gave a lecture, ACD also spoke at this meeting and voiced he opinion on the next war. [320]
n.d.	ACD became member of the Society of Psychical Research [202] from 1893 until 1930. [133] (*4)
n.d.	During January or very early February ACD joined the Society for Psychical Research. [320] (*4)
n.d.	*The Adventure of the Yellow Face* published. [180] (*2)
February	*The Adventure of the Yellow Face* published in *The Strand Magazine*. [6,194,194,196,198] (*2)
February	ACD was listed as a new member of the Society for Psychical Research. [1135]
February 8	ACD attended meeting of UNLSS and spoke of Ibsen and Tolstoi. [6]
February 12	ACD attended the ninth annual dinner of the Playgoers Club at the Criterion Restaurant, Piccadilly, London, Mr H. Irving was the principle guest. [1134]
February 15	*A Chat with Dr. Conan Doyle* published in *Cassell's Saturday Journal*. [6,196]
February 25	*An Arizona Tragedy* (*The American's Tale*) published in *The Minneapolis Journal*. [198]
March	*The Adventure of the Stockbroker's Clerk* published in *The Strand Magazine*. [6,194,195,196,198]
March 8	ACD attended and spoke at meeting of UNLSS. [6]
March 9	It was reported in *The Royal Cornwall Gazette* that 'Sherlock Holmes, otherwise Dr Conan Doyle, the famous novelist, accompanied by his friend the "doctor" was present in Cornwall, and on Thursday {2 March} joined in a game of golf on the links at Lelant.' [1134]
n.d.	During March/April ACD commenced work on *The Final Problem*. [203,320]
April	*The Adventure of the "Gloria Scott"* published in *The Strand Magazine*. [6,194,195,196,198]
n.d.	Innes obtained his commission with the Royal Field Artillery. [200]
April 4	It was announced that John Francis Innes Hay Doyle had been promoted from the Gentleman Cadets to Second Lieutenant. [1199,1762]
April 6	ACD at South Norwood. [203]
April 7	It was announced in *The Morning Post* (London) that the Booksellers' Trade dinner would be held on 15 April, ACD was among others that intended to attend. [422,1134]

1893

April 8	It was announced in *The Glasgow Herald* that ACD had promised to deliver a lecture on "George Meredith," and possibly to read a second paper on "Some Young Writers," at the great summer gathering of young people which is to be held in Lucerne from 5 to 19 August (1893). [1134]
April 15	ACD attended the Booksellers' Trade Dinner at the Holborn Restaurant. [203,1200]
April 17	ACD was at the Reform Club, London. [1134]
April 19	ACD attended the premier of *A Woman of No Importance*, at play by Oscar Wilde, at the Haymarket, London. [1134]
May	*Jane Annie or, The Good Conduct Prize* was premiered at the Savoy Theatre, London. [202] (*3)
May 13	From 13 May–1 July the comic opera *Jane Annie: or, The Conduct Prize* by J.M. Barrie and ACD was performed at the Savoy Theatre, London. [6,215] (*3)
May 13	ACD and J.M. Barrie attended the opening night of *Jane Annie* at the Savoy Theatre, London. [320]
May 13	*Jane Annie: or, The Good Conduct Prize* played for the first time at the Savoy Theatre, London. [423] (*3)
May 13	It was announced that Mr E.W. Hornung would be marrying the sister of Dr Conan Doyle. [424]
May	*The Adventure of the Musgrave Ritual* published in *The Strand Magazine*. [6,194,195,196,198]
n.d.	*The Refugees* published. [99] (*2)
May 17	*The Refugees* published by Longmans, Green, and Co., London. [6,196] (*2)
May 22	ACD played cricket for Norwood Club against Chislehurst at Norwood Pavilion Ground, he scored 10 [320] Norwood Club won [221], at Norwood Green, he scored 10 and took 1 catch, match drawn. [235]
May 25	ACD was re-elected to serve a second term as president of the UNLSS. [320]
June	*The Green Flag* published in *The Pall Mall Magazine*. [6,198]
June	*The Adventure of the Reigate Squire* published in *The Strand Magazine*. [6,99,194,195,196,198]
June	*Jane Annie, The Good Conduct Prize* performed at the Savoy Theatre, London. [99]
June 3	ACD's play *Foreign Policy* based on his story *A Question of Diplomacy*, was performed at Terry's Theatre, London. [6,99,202,1134]
June 3	ACD played cricket for Norwood Club 1st team against Dulwich 1st team at Norwood Pavilion Ground, Norwood Club won [222], at Norwood Green, he scored zero. [235]
June 6-9	ACD's play *Foreign Policy* performed at Terry's Theatre, London on 6-9 June. [6,99]
June 17	ACD played cricket for Norwood Club 1st team against Forest Hill 1st team at Norwood Pavilion Ground, Norwood Club won [223] at Norwood Green, he scored 8 and took 1 catch. [235]
June 21	It was reported in *The Birmingham Daily Post* that M. Jules Claretie, the manager of the Théâtre Français, has been elected an honorary member of the Reform Club. He was proposed by Mr Livesey, and supported by Sir John Robinson and Dr Conan Doyle. [1134]
June 24	ACD at South Norwood. [203]
June 24	ACD played cricket for Norwood Club against London & Westminster Bank at Norwood Pavilion Ground, Norwood Club won [224] at Norwood Green, he scored 3, match drawn. [235]
June 28	ACD played cricket for Norwood Club against Epsom probably at Norwood Pavilion Ground, Epsom won, ACD scored 38. [225]
June 30	ACD attended the annual meeting of the International Arbitration and Peace Association at Westminster Palace Hotel, London. [1838]

1893

July	*The Adventure of the Crooked Man* published in *The Strand Magazine*. [6,194,195,196,198]
July 1	The last two performances this season of *Jane Annie, The Good Conduct Prize* at the Savoy Theatre, London. [1201]
July 1	It was announced that *Janie Annie or, The Good Conduct Prize* would be withdrawn on 2 July at the Savoy Theatre, London. [425]
July 1	ACD attended a dinner at the Egyptian Hall, The Mansion House, London [1202] held by the Lord Mayor. [1838]
July 3	ACD played cricket for Norwood Club against Croydon during Norwood Cricket Week, implying that the game was played at Norwood Pavilion Ground, match drawn [226] at Norwood Green, he scored zero. [235]
July 4	ACD played cricket for Norwood Club against Brixton Wanderers during Norwood Cricket Week, implying the game was played at Norwood Pavilion Ground, Norwood Club won [227] at Norwood Green, he scored 16 and took 1 catch. [235]
July 8	ACD played cricket for Norwood Club against Forest Hill at Norwood Green, he scored 37, Norwood Club won. [235]
July 15	ACD played cricket for Norwood Club 2nd team against Addiscombe 2nd team at Addiscombe Ground, Norwood Club won. [228]
July 22	ACD played cricket for Norwood 2nd team against Grecians 2nd team at Norwood Pavilion Ground, Norwood Club won. [229]
July 24	From 24–29 July the comic opera *Jane Annie: or, The Good Conduct Prize* by J.M. Barrie and ACD was performed at the Theatre Royal, Newcastle-upon-Tyne. [6]
July 27	ACD played cricket for Dr Thomson's XI against Dr Law's XI the Thorpe Asylum Ground, St. Andrew's, Norfolk, he took 8 wickets for 9 runs and scored 12, Dr Thomson's XI won. [2022]
August	At the beginning of August ACD and his wife were staying at the Hotel de l'Europe in Lucerne, Switzerland. [145]
August	Early August ACD and Louise travelled to Lucerne to join Dr Henry Lunn's inter-religious conference in the church of Lucerne. [1819]
n.d.	ACD started writing *The Stark Munro Letters* while he was in Switzerland. [6]
Summer	ACD and Louise on tour in Switzerland [4,124,215], ACD lectured in Lucerne in August, staying at the Hotel de l'Europe and then the Riffel Alp Hotel, Zermatt, it was during this trip that ACD and Louise visited the Reichenbach Falls near Meiringen [124,215] while their parents were in Switzerland, Mary and Kingsley stayed with Granny Hawkins, Nem and Jeremiah Hawkins in the Reigate area. [124]
Summer	While in Switzerland ACD visited the Findelen Glacier with Silas Hocking. [6]
n.d.	ACD visited Meiringen and the Reichenbach Falls. [15]
August	*The Great Shadow* and *Beyond the City* published by J.W. Arrowsmith, London. [6]
August	*Pennarby Mine* (poem) published in *The Pall Mall Magazine*. [6,196,198]
August	*The "Slapping Sal"* published in *Vagabond's Annual (Arrowsmith's Summer Annual)*. [6,196,198]
August	*The Adventure of the Resident Patient* published in *The Strand Magazine*. [6,194,195,196,198]
August	ACD and Louise travel to Switzerland [14] they stayed at the Hôtel de l'Europe in Lucerne. [31]
August 7-12	ACD and Louise stayed at the Hôtel de l'Europe, Lucerne. [1819]
August 9	ACD gave a lecture on George Meredith at the Old Catholic Church, Lucerne, Switzerland [31,145] or at the Hôtel de l'Europe [202] gave a lecture on "Fiction as Part of Literature. [1819] (*2)
August 10	ACD lectured in Lucerne "Fiction as a part of Literature", at the Old Catholic Church [3,6,15,20,1838] (*2) ACD and Louise then moved on and stayed at the Rifel Alp Hotel, Zermatt. [15]

1893

August 12	ACD crossed the Gemmi Pass towards Zermatt. [1819]
August	ACD and Louise stayed at the Berghotel Schwarenberg. [1819]
August 18	In Visp ACD met the tour party from Lucerne, Hocking, Dawson, Howatt et al. [1819]
August	ACD and the tour party arrived at the Riffelalp Hotel, Zermatt. [1819]
August	ACD joined Hocking and Dawson for an excursion to find the Findel Glacier. [1818]
August 28	ACD and Louise returned to England. [1819]
August 28	ACD back in England. [145]
n.d.	Louise Conan Doyle diagnosed as suffering from tuberculosis. [99,180] (*7)
n.d.	A few weeks after returning to England from Switzerland, Louise became ill and was diagnosed with what was called then galloping consumption, this was confirmed by Sir Douglas Powell. [124] (*7)
n.d.	On their return to England from Switzerland, Louise was diagnosed as suffering from tuberculosis and not expected to live longer than a few months. [15,33] (*7)
September	*The Adventure of the Greek Interpreter* published in *The Strand Magazine*. [6,194,195,196,198]
September 9	ACD played cricket for Norwood Club against Kenley at Norwood Green, he scored zero, match drawn. [235]
n.d.	Constance (Connie) Doyle married E.W. Hornung. [99,203] (*3)
September 27	ACD's sister Constance (Connie) Doyle married E.W. (Willie) Hornung [23,68,124,200] at the Roman Catholic Church of St. Edward's, Place Street, London [124,202], the service was performed by Revd. Father Butler [1838], at St. Peter's and St. Edward's Church, Westminster, London, ACD gave away the bride; Mr Gilbert Parker was best man. The bridesmaids were her sisters, Miss Doyle, Miss Ida Doyle and Miss Hornung, sister of the groom. The reception was held at Whitehall Rooms, Hotel Metropole after which they left for their honeymoon in Paris and Normandy. [426] (*3)
Summer	Constance (Connie) Doyle married E.W. Hornung. [14] (*3)
October	*The Adventure of the Naval Treaty* published in *The Strand Magazine* in October and November. [6,194,195,196,198]
October	ACD and Louise stayed at the Curhaus Hotel, The Grand Hôtel and Pension Belvedere in Davos, Switzerland. [68]
October 4	ACD attended meeting of UNLSS. Read a paper "Some facts about fiction". [6]
October 5	ACD delivered speech on his medical career at the dinner of the Edinburgh University Club of Manchester [6] he was the guest of the Manchester Edinburgh University Club at their annual dinner at the Queen's Hotel, Manchester. [427,1838]
October 6	ACD lectured on "Facts About Fiction" at the Sale Public Hall [428] Sale Public Hall, Manchester. [1838]
n.d.	Death of Charles Altamont Doyle. [99] (*2)
October 10	Death of Charles Altamont Doyle at The Crighton Royal Institution, Dumfries, Scotland [14,15,20,68,124,200,202,203] at the Crichton Royal (mental) Hospital, Dumfries, Scotland, he died aged sixty-one during an epileptic seizure. [180,215] (*2)
October	ACD at the Reform Club, Pall Mall, London. [203]
October	Louise diagnosed as suffering from consumption confirmed by Douglas Powell. [203] (*7)
October 11	ACD attended meeting of UNLSS [6] Frederic Myers gave a talk "Recent Evidences as to Man's Survival of Death." [6,202]
October 17	ACD lectured "Facts From Fiction" for the Kingston Literary Society at St. James's Hall, Kingston. [2019]
October 24	It was advertised that ACD would lecture at the Rotunda Lecture Hall on 29 October. [429] {Note: no report of this lecture located.}

1893

October 28	It was advertised that ACD would lecture on "Facts About Fiction" at the Storey Institute Lecture Society, Lancaster on 2 November. [430] {Note: no report of this lecture located.}
October 29	ACD gave a talk "Facts About Fiction" at the Picton Lecture Hall, Liverpool. [92]
October 29	*The Case of Lady Sannox* published in *The Courier-Journal*. [6,198]
November	*The Case of Lady Sannox* published in *The Idler Magazine*. [198]
November	ACD joined the British Society for Psychical Research. [14,20,203] (*4)
November	ACD applied to join the Society for Psychical Research. [15] (*4)
November	From November 1893 to summer 1894, ACD and Louise spent their time in Davos, Switzerland, staying at the Curhaus Hotel, Grand Hôtel and Pension Belvedere. [200] (*2)
November	Louise Conan Doyle was diagnosed as suffering from tuberculosis. [8,215] (*7)
November 1	Louise and her sister Emily left for Davos, [202,215] they spent the winter of 1893-94 in the Alps at Davos Platz, Switzerland, ACD and Lottie joined them later. [124]
November 1	It was advertised that ACD would lecture on "Facts About Fiction" at Caledonia Road Church, Glasgow on 23 November. [431] {Note: no report of this lecture located.}
November 2	Louise and her sister Emily were staying at the Kurhaus Hotel, Davos. [202,1819]
November 5	ACD at 12 Tennison Road. [1834]
November 7	ACD lectured on "Facts About Fiction" at Harborne and Edgbaston Institute at Harborne, Birmingham. [432]
November 11	*A Lay of the Links* (poem) published in *Today*. [6,196,198]
November 12	ACD at 12 Tennison Road. [1834]
November 13	ACD at the Reform Club, London. [18]
November 14	ACD lectured on "Facts About Fiction" at Bradford Mechanics' Institute, Bradford. [433] (*2)
November 15	ACD gave a talk in Bradford. [203] (*2)
November 15	ACD lectured on "Facts About Fiction" for Leeds Mechanics' Institute at the Albert Hall, Leeds. [434] (*2)
November 16	ACD gave a talk in Leeds. [203] (*2)
November 16	ACD lectured on "Facts About Fiction" at Cleveland Literary and Philosophical Society [435] in Corporation Road, Middlesbrough. [1838] (*2)
November 17	ACD gave a talk in Middlesbrough. [203] (*2)
November 17	ACD lectured on "Facts About Fiction" at the Music Hall, Surrey Street, Sheffield [436] lectured to the Literary and Philosophical Society at the Music Hall, Surrey Street, Sheffield. [1838] (*2)
November 18	ACD gave a talk in Sheffield. [203] (*2)
November 19	ACD in Liverpool. [203]
November 19	ACD gave a talk in Liverpool. [92,203]
November 20	ACD in Liverpool. [203]
November 20	ACD lectured on "George Meredith, Novelist and Poet" at the New Windsor Chapel, Salford, Manchester. [437]
November 21	ACD gave a talk in Edinburgh [203] on "George Meredith, Novelist and Poet" held at the Edinburgh Philosophical Institute, Edinburgh [1172] in Queen Street Hall, Edinburgh. [1838]
November	ACD gave a lecture in Glasgow. [203] {Note: this was probably on 23 November that was advertised on November 1, no report of this lecture located.}
November 24	ACD lectured on "Facts About Fiction" at the Kinnaird Hall, Dundee [438,1838] after the lecture Lord Provost Low (Sir James Low) entertained ACD and friends at Mount Rosa, 45 Seafield Road, Broughty Ferry, Dundee. [1838]
November 26	*The Final Problem* published in *The Courier-Journal*. [198]

1893

November	ACD was staying in Newcastle-on-Tyne. [203]
November 26	ACD lectured on "Facts About Fiction" for the Tyneside Sunday Lecture Society at the Tyne Theatre, Newcastle. [439]
November 27	It was advertised that ACD would lecture on "Facts About Fiction" for the Queen's Park Lecture Association at Queen's Park U.P. Church, Glasgow on 28 November. [440] {Note: no report of this lecture located.}
November 29	ACD gave a lecture, "Facts About Fiction", at the Inverness Music Hall, Inverness. [2106]
December	ACD among others subscribed to the James Russell Powell Fund, Powell was the American poet, critic and diplomat. [1838]
December 1	ACD lectured on "Facts About Fiction" at Watt Museum Hall, Greenock, Scotland [441] under the auspices of Greenock Philosophical Society. [1838]
December 3	ACD lectured on "Facts About Fiction" before the Leeds Sunday Society in Leeds [1173] at the Coliseum Theatre, Cookridge Street, Leeds. [1838]
December 4	ACD lectured on "Facts About Fiction" at the Mechanics' Hall, Nottingham. [442]
December 6	ACD lectured on "Facts About Fiction" for the Literary and Philosophic Club at the Victoria Rooms, Bristol. [443]
December 8	ACD completed his lecture tour and was in London. [444]
December	Louise Conan Doyle was diagnosed as suffering from tuberculosis and was given only a few months to live; ACD took her to Davos, Switzerland. [4] (*7)
Late 1893	Louise Conan Doyle was diagnosed by Dr Dalton as suffering from tuberculosis and was given only a few months to live, [14,20] (*7) ACD took her to Davos, Switzerland, where the climate offered some hope of a cure. [8,14] Louise and the two children lived at the Kurhaus Hotel, Davos [3,20,203] or the Curhaus Davos Hotel. [15]
December 9	ACD left London for Davos. [445]
December 10	ACD arrived at the Kurhaus Hotel, Davos Platz [202] arrived at the Curhaus Hotel, the list of arrivals at the hotel included Dr and Mrs Conan Doyle, London and Miss Doyle, London. [1819]
December	*The Adventure of the Final Problem* published in *The Strand Magazine*. [6,180,194,195,196,198,203,215] (*2)
December	*The Final Problem* was possibly published on 12 or 13 December. [320] (*2)
December 13	*The Memoirs of Sherlock Holmes* published by George Newnes Ltd., London. [6] (*2)
n.d.	ACD gave a reading of *The Curse of Eve* at the Authors' Club. [15,203,320] (*2)
December 14	*Alpine Walk* published in *The Independent*. [6,196,198]

1894

Early 1894	Arrived in America for visits to the major cities Chicago, Indianapolis, Cincinnati, Toledo, Detroit and Milwaukee. [110]
n.d.	*The Memoirs of Sherlock Holmes* (twelve stories) published. [99,180] (*2)
January 7	ACD at Davos Platz, Switzerland. [18]
January 13	ACD at Davos. [884]
January 23	ACD at the Kurhaus Hotel, Davos, Switzerland, he had been suffering from a kind of influenza quinsy for nearly a week. [202, 203]
n.d.	ACD visited the Swiss Alps, skiing at Davos, mountain air beneficial to Louise. [99]
January	ACD started writing *The Stark Munro Letters* during his stay in Switzerland. [99]
January	ACD completed writing *The Stark Munro Letters*. [6]
January 23	ACD nearing the end of writing *The Stark Munro Letters*. [215]
February	Mid February ACD moved to the Grand Hotel and Pension Belvedere. [202]
February 15	ACD, Louise and Emily moved to the Grandhotel und Pension Belvédère, Davos. [1819]

1894

n.d.	ACD and the Branger brothers skied from Davos and Arosa. [2,99] (*5)
March	ACD made the crossing from Davos to Arosa. [124] (*5)
Late March	ACD with the Branger brothers on skis, crossed from Davos to Arosa. [3] (*5)
March 20	ACD became the first Englishman to cross the 2,440m Maienfelder Furka Pass above Davos, Switzerland and ski down the other side. [224] (*5)
March 22	ACD at the Belvedere Hotel, Davos, Switzerland. [203]
March 23	ACD with the Branger brothers on skis crossed the Furka Pass to Arosa. [14,15,202,203,215] (*5)
March 23	ACD with Tobias and Johannes Branger set out from Davos-Platz to Frauenfeld in order to climb to the Maienfelder Furgga, they stayed the night in Arosa. [1819]
March 24	ACD and the Branger brothers returned to Davos. [1819]
March 24	ACD at the Belvedere Hotel, Davos, Switzerland. [203]
March 24	*The Ballad of the "Eurydice."* (*The Home-Coming of the Eurydice*) (poem) published in *The Speaker*. [6,198,202]
April	ACD and Louise returned to England [124] in the third week of April ACD, Louise and Emily returned to England [1819] travelling from Switzerland via Paris [86] staying at the Hotel Byron, Paris. [202]
April	*The Doctors of Hoyland* published in *The Idler Magazine*. [6,196,198]
April 21	*Paris in 1894: A Superficial Impression* published in *The Speaker*. [6,198]
April 30	ACD at the Reform Club, London. [18]
May 2	ACD at 12 Tennison Road, South Norwood. [18]
May 2	ACD visited the Reform Club, London. [203]
May 3	ACD dined with the *Pall Mall Magazine* staff, Willie Hornung also attended [203] at the Grand Hotel, London to celebrate the first birthday of the *Pall Mall Magazine*. [2012]
May 4	ACD visited The Royal Academy of Arts and the Independent Theatre. [203]
May 5	ACD attended The Royal Academy of Arts dinner [203] at Burlington House, London [1203] attended the Annual Dinner of the Royal Academy at the Academy. [446]
May 5	*Before My Bookcase* published 5 May to 20 June in *Great Thoughts*. [198]
May 11	ACD attended the annual general meeting of UNLSS held at the Welcome Lecture Hall, Westow Street, Upper Norwood; it was at this meeting that ACD resigned as chairman. [320]
May 14	ACD played cricket for Norwood Club at home against the London and Westminster Bank, ACD scored zero. [320]
n.d.	ACD played cricket for Norwood second eleven against the Spencer team. [320]
Summer	ACD and Louise were living at 12 Tennison Road, South Norwood. [124]
Summer	ACD and family spent the summer at Maloja. [2,68,200]
Summer	Late Summer ACD returned to London. [68,200]
Summer	ACD attended a banquet for the American naval historian Captain Alfred Mahan. [202] (*3)
May 24	ACD attended a banquet at St. James's Hall, London for Rear-Admiral Erben, Captain Mahan and officers of the United States Navy ship *Chicago*. [1204] (*3)
May 24	ACD attended a complimentary banquet given to Rear-Admiral H. Erben at St. James's Restaurant. [447] (*3)
May 31	ACD, who was accompanied by Miss Doyle, attended and spoke at a dinner of the Society of Authors held at the Venetian Room, Holborn Restaurant, London, [9,202,1205] {Note: Miss Doyle was probably Ida Doyle.} [124]
June	*Sweethearts* published *The Idler Magazine*. [6,196,198]
June	*A Sordid Affair* published in *Illustrated Home Guest*. [198]
June	ACD accompanied Frank Podmore and Dr Sydney Scott from the Society for Psychical Research on a field trip to Dorset [20] they stayed at the Coach and Horses Hotel, Charmouth. [202]

1894

June	*An Alpine Pass On "Ski"* published in *The Strand Magazine*. [194] (*3)
June 3	ACD at 12 Tennison Road, South Norwood. [884]
June 4	ACD at 12 Tennison Road, South Norwood. [99]
June 16	ACD played cricket for Norwood Club against Caterham at Norwood Green, he did not bat, Norwood Club won. [235]
June 26	ACD at 12 Tennison Road, South Norwood. [884]
June	ACD subscribed to the Westport Catastrophe with a £2:2s donation. [1206]
n.d.	*The Lord of Chateau Noir* published. [180] (*2)
July	*The Lord of Chateau Noir* published in *The Strand Magazine*. [6,194,195,196,198] (*2)
July	Early July ACD played cricket for Norwood Club against Croydon during the Norwood Cricket Club week, he scored 40, Norwood Club won. [1940]
July 3	ACD played cricket for Norwood Club against Crystal Palace at Norwood in the second match of the cricket week, he scored zero and took 5 wickets, Crystal Palace won. [1941] (*3)
n.d.	ACD played cricket for Norwood Club against Crystal Palace and took 5 wickets. [320] (*3)
July 4	ACD played cricket for Norwood Club against "the well known Crystal Palace Eleven", he took 5 wickets. [448] (*3)
July 4	ACD played cricket for Norwood Club against Mitcham at Norwood, he scored 5 and took 2 wickets, Mitcham won. [1941]
July	ACD played cricket for the Norwood Club against MCC. [63] (*3)
July 5	ACD played cricket for Norwood Club against MCC at Merchant Taylors' Ground, Northwood, he scored 4 and zero, and took 1 wicket and 1 catch, MCC won. [235] (*3)
July 7	*An Actor's Duel* and *The Winning Shot* published by John Dicks, London. [6]
July 11	ACD at 12 Tennison Road, South Norwood. [884]
July 12	ACD played cricket for Norwood Club against MCC, he scored 4, MCC won. [237] (*3)
n.d.	*My First Book* published by J.B. Lippincott. [9] (*2)
August	*My First Book* published in *McClure's Magazine*. [198,203] (*2)
August 2	ACD played cricket for Norwood Club against Croydon, he scored 45, due to heavy rain the play was abandoned leaving the match as a draw. [1942]
August 6	The Gentlemen of Holland cricket team began a short English tour with a match against Norwood Club at Norwood. Norwood Club won, ACD scored 64 for Norwood [1207] (*2)
August 6	ACD played cricket for Norwood Club against Gentlemen of Netherlands at Merchant Taylors' School Ground, Northwood, he scored 64 and took 2 catches, match drawn. [235] (*2)
n.d.	ACD played cricket for Norwood Club against Burlington Wanderers, he scored 100. [320]
August 18	ACD played cricket for Norwood Club against Northbrook at Norwood Green, he scored 35 and took 6 wickets, Norwood Club won [235]
August 25	ACD played cricket for Thorpe Asylum against Lowestoft Visitors at Thorpe Asylum, he scored 65, the Asylum won. [2013,2022]
August 30	ACD played cricket for Norfolk County Asylum against 1st King Dragoon Guards at Thorpe Asylum, he scored 1 in the first innings and 30 in the second innings and he took all 10 wickets for 15 runs, the Asylum won. ACD was on visit to Dr Thomson of the asylum. [2014]
September 1	ACD played cricket for Norwood against Granville at Norwood, he scored 20 and took 1 wicket, Granville won. [2018]
September 8	ACD played his last game of cricket for Norwood Club against F. Loud's XI at Norwood, ACD scored 5, Norwood Club won. [320]
September	Louise Conan Doyle returned to Davos, Switzerland [203] ACD joined her for Christmas. [180]
September	*Juvenilia* published in *My First Book* by Chatto & Windus, London. [6,196]

1894

September 21	First performance of *Waterloo*, a play by ACD based on *A Straggler of '15* performed at Prince's Theatre, Bristol starring H.B. Irving as Corporal Brewster. [6,99,202,203,215,1208]
September	ACD embarked on a tour of the United States [180,203] end of September [110] (*3)
September 23	ACD and Innes left Southampton on the steamship *Elbe* for lecture tour of America. [9,15,73,202,242,320] (*3)
n.d.	The first Brigadier Gerard story written, *How the Brigadier Came to the Castle of Gloom*, ACD read it during his lecture tour of America. [6]
October	ACD and Innes embarked for New York. [2,4] (*3)
October	*A Chat with Conan Doyle* published in *The Idler Magazine*. [198]
October	*The Stark Munro Letters* published in *The Idler Magazine* from October 1894 to November 1895. [6,99,196,198]
October 2	ACD and Innes arrived in New York for an American tour [9,15,73,111,124,202,203,215] on board the *Elbe*. [96,215]
n.d.	ACD and Innes made a successful tour of America. [99]
October 2	ACD and Innes toured the Northeast United States from October 2 to December 8. [68,73,200]
October 2	ACD attended the play *Shenandoah* performed at the Academy of Music, New York. [9]
October 4	*The Favourite Quotation* published in *New Age*. [198]
October 4	ACD attended an informal luncheon at the Lotos Club, New York. [9]
October 6	ACD explored the Parkman Land (The Adirondack region), he stayed at Bungalow Bay, Saranac Lake. [9]
October 7	Death of Oliver Wendell Holmes in Boston. [110,203]
n.d.	ACD spent a day hunting in the Adirondacks. [202] (*2)
October 8	ACD takes part in a hunting trip in the Adirondacks. [9] (*2)
October 9	ACD and Innes back in New York after a exploring the Parkman Land, they stayed at the Aldine Club. [9]
October 10	ACD lectured at the Calvary Baptist Church, Calvary [9] the 1,506-seat auditorium of the Calvary Baptist Church on West 57th Street, New York. [110,202] (*2)
October 11	ACD lectured at the 1,500-seat Calvary Baptist Church, New York. [215] (*2)
October 11	ACD left New York for Chicago [9,202] and stayed at the Grand Pacific Hotel, Chicago. [202]
October 12	ACD and Innes arrived in Chicago and stayed at the Grand Pacific Hotel. [9]
October 12	ACD lectured at the Twentieth Century Club, Michigan Avenue, Chicago. [9,73,202]
October 13	ACD attended a literary luncheon at the Union League Club, Chicago. [9]
October 14	ACD watched the play "Aladdin Jr." at the Opera House, Chicago. [9]
n.d.	ACD left Chicago for further talks in Indianapolis, Cincinnati, Toledo, Detroit and Milwaukee. [202]
October 15	ACD and Innes arrived at 5:30p.m. at Union Station, Indianapolis [73] and stayed at the Denison Hotel, Indianapolis. [73,150]
October 15	ACD lectured at the opening of the Monterfiore Lecture course at Plymouth Congregational Church, Indianapolis. [9,73]
October 16	ACD and Innes visited the Indiana State Soldiers and Sailors Monument on the Circle, Indianapolis. [73]
October 16	ACD left Indianapolis for Cincinnati. [9]
October 16	ACD and Innes arrived in Cincinnati at 6p.m. after leaving Indianapolis at 3p.m.; they stayed at Burnet House at the corner of Third and Vine Streets. [9]
October 17	ACD lectured at the Odd Fellows Hall, Cincinnati. [9]
October 17	ACD and Innes spent the day sight-seeing in Cincinnati. [9]
n.d.	ACD attended and spoke at the farmers' Fellowship Club, Chicago. [202] (*2)
October 18	ACD made a speech at the Fellowship Club, Chicago. [9,203] (*2)
October 19	ACD lectured at the National Union League, Toledo. [9]

1894

October 20	ACD left Toledo for Detroit. [9]
October 20	ACD and Innes arrived in Detroit at 2:10p.m. and stayed at the Russell House Hotel. [9]
October 21	On 21 and 22 October ACD and Innes sightseeing in Detroit. [9]
October 22	ACD at the Russell House, Detroit, Michigan. [2053]
October 22	ACD lectured at the Detroit Church of Our Father, Detroit. [9]
October 23	ACD left Detroit for Chicago. [9]
n.d.	*Round the Red Lamp* published. [180] (*2)
October 23	*Round the Red Lamp* published by Methuen & Co., London. [6,9,99] (*2)
October 25	ACD lectured at the Plymouth Congregational Church, Milwaukee. [9,203]
October 26	ACD attended a luncheon at 2 Bank Street, Chicago. [9]
October 26	ACD lectured at the Central Music Hall, Chicago. [9,203]
October 27	ACD left Chicago for Brooklyn. [9]
October 29	ACD attended a dinner in his honour at the Hamilton Club, 146 Remsen Street, Brooklyn. [9]
October 29	ACD lectured at the Academy of Music, Brooklyn. [9]
October 30	ACD lectured at the Northampton City Hall, Northampton, Massachusetts. [9]
October 30	ACD dined at the Greek Revival Mansion, Round Hill, off Elm Street, Northampton, Massachusetts. [9]
October 30	ACD arrived in Boston, USA. [231]
n.d.	ACD placed a wreath at the grave of Oliver Wendell Holmes at the Mount Auburn Cemetery, Cambridge, Massachusetts. [202] (*3)
October 31	ACD placed a wreath at the grave of Oliver Wendell Holmes at the Mount Auburn Cemetery, Cambridge, Boston. [9] (*3)
October 31	ACD lectured at the Association Hall, Boston [9] at the auditorium of the Boston YMCA. [231]
n.d.	The *Brigadier Gerard* stories first appeared. [180]
November	*Real Conversation…* published in *McClure's Magazine*. [198]
November	*The Medal of Brigadier Gerard* published in *The Strand Magazine*. [194] (*2)
November 1	ACD visited the grave of Oliver Wendell Holmes. [203] (*3)
November 1	ACD lectured at the Association Hall, Worcester, Massachusetts. [9]
November 1	ACD attended a reception at 1017 Main Street, New Worcester after an earlier lecture. [9]
November 2	ACD at Worcester, Massachusetts. [203]
November 2	ACD arrived in Amherst and stayed at the Amherst House. [9]
November 2	ACD lecture at the College Hall, Amherst. [9,203]
November 3	ACD lectured at the Slater Memorial Hall, Norwich, Connecticut. [9,203]
November 5	ACD arrived in Washington and stayed at The Arlington. [9]
November 5	ACD lectured at the Metzerott Music Hall, Washington. [9,203]
November 6	ACD left Washington for Baltimore and visited the marble monument to Edgar Allan Poe at the corner of Fayette and Greene Streets, West Baltimore. [9]
November 6	ACD returned to Washington and was entertained at the National Capital Press Club, The Loughran Building, E Street. [9]
November 6	ACD lectured at the National Capital Press Club, Washington. [9]
November 8	ACD visited Philadelphia, being entertained by Craige Lippincott at 218, South Nineteenth Street. [9]
November 9	ACD at Newark, New Jersey, stayed with the Lippincotts. [203]
November 9	ACD lectured at the Essex Lyceum, Newark, New Jersey. [9]
November 10	At Trenton ACD watched an American football game at the State Fair Grounds. [9]
November 10	ACD lectured at the Musical Fund Hall, Philadelphia. [9]
November 10	*The Parasite* published in *Harper's Weekly* 10 November–1 December. [6,198]
November 10	ACD has dinner at the Philadelphia home of Dr James William White. [9]
November 10	*A Foreign Office Romance* published in *The Indianapolis News*. [198]
November 11	ACD left Philadelphia for New York. [9]
November 12	ACD lectured at the Daly's Theatre, New York. [9]

1894

November 12	ACD lectured at the home of John Kendrick Bangs at Yonkers. [9]
November 12	ACD spoke at the Yonkers Lawn Tennis Club titled "Readings and Reminiscences". [149]
November 13	ACD played a round of golf with John Kendrick Bangs at the St. Andrew's Club at Yonkers. [9]
November 13	ACD lectured at the Music Hall, Orange. [9]
November 14	ACD lectured at Daly's Theatre, New York. [9]
November 14	ACD lectured at the Lotos Club, New York. [46]
November 15	ACD lectured at the Alexander Hall, Princeton. [9]
November 15	ACD gave lecture at Daly's Theatre, New York. [9]
November 16	ACD lectured at Daly's Theatre, New York. [9]
November 16	ACD lectured at Trinity Place Public School, New Rochelle. [9]
November 17	*Los Amigos Fiasco* published in *The Minneapolis Journal*. [198]
November 17	ACD attended a dinner and made a speech at the Lotos Club, New York. [4,9,110,2053] (*2)
November	ACD bought 1000 shares in McClure's publishing business for £1030. [203]
November 18	ACD attended the Lotos Club dinner. [203] (*2)
November 19	ACD had lunch with S.S. McClure at the Aldine Club, New York. [9]
November 19	ACD lectured at the Association Hall, Boston. [9]
November 20	ACD lectured at the Association Hall, Boston. [9,203]
November 20	ACD left Boston for Rochester. [203]
November 21	ACD arrived in Rochester [203] and stayed at the Powers Hotel at Main and Fitzhugh Streets. [9]
November 21	ACD lectured at the YMCA Music Hall, Rochester. [9,203]
November 22	ACD arrived in Elmira and stayed at the Rathbun House Hotel. [9]
November 22	ACD lectured at the all-female college at Elmira. [9,203]
November 23	ACD lectured at the Glen Falls Opera House, Glen Falls. [9,203]
November 24	ACD lectured at the First Reformed Church, Schenectady. [9,203]
November 25	ACD travelled from Schenectady, New York to Niagara Falls arriving late at night and stayed at the Prospect Hotel. [9]
November 25	ACD visited Niagara Falls. [9,203] (*2)
November 26	ACD visited Niagara Falls and surrounding area, he then travelled to Toronto arriving at about 5:30p.m. [9] (*2)
November 26	ACD and Innes arrived at Toronto and stayed at 281 Sherbourne Street, the residence of Dr Latimer Pickering and his wife. [9]
November 26	ACD lectured at the Massey Music Hall, Toronto. [9,203]
November 26	It was advertised that the first performance in London of *A Story of Waterloo* would take place at the Lyric Theatre on 17 December for the benefit of the Newport Market Refuge. [449] {Note: the venue was changed, see entry for 17 December 1894.}
November 27	ACD lectured at the Woman's Union Hall, Buffalo. [9,203]
n.d.	ACD spent Thanksgiving with Rudyard Kipling at his house called Naulakha, outside Brattleboro, Vermont. [202] (*2)
November 28	ACD spent three days with Rudyard Kipling at Brattleboro, Vermont [9] spent two days. [203] (*2)
n.d.	ACD played golf with Beatty Balestier (Kipling's brother-in-law) against Rudyard Kipling against Innes in Vermont, the game was won by Kipling and Innes. [202] (*2)
November 29	ACD played golf with Rudyard Kipling against Innes and Balestier (Kipling's brother-in-law) in Vermont. [124] (*2)
November 29	In his absence ACD was re-elected to the board of the Davos Literary and Scientific Society. [1819]
November 30	ACD and Innes left Brattleboro on the afternoon train to Morristown, New Jersey. [9]
November 30	ACD gave a lecture at St. Bartholomew's School for boys in Morristown. [9]
n.d.	The first of the many Brigadier Gerard stories were written late 1894. [99]

1894

December	*How the Brigadier Won His Medal* published in *The Strand Magazine* as *The Medal of the Brigadier*. [6,195,196,198,203] (*2)
n.d.	*An Alpine Pass on "Ski"* published. [99] (*3)
December	*An Alpine Pass on "Ski"* published in the *Strand Magazine*. [6,195,196,198] (*3)
December 1	ACD lectured at the Paterson's Association Hall, Paterson, New Jersey. [9]
December 3	ACD lectured at Flushing, Queens County. [9]
December 3	*The Parasite* published by Acme Library, A. Constable & Co., London. [6,198]
December 5	ACD lectured at the Town Hall, Jamaica, Queens County. [9]
December 6	ACD lectured at the First Presbyterian Church in Jersey City. [9]
December 6	In the evening ACD attended a farewell dinner at the Aldine Club, New York. [2,14,31,110,111] (*2)
December 7	ACD had lunch at the Aldine Club, New York with Hamilton W. Mabie. [9]
December 7	In the evening ACD attended a farewell dinner at the Aldine Club, New York [6,9,203,231] (*2) Captain J.F.I.H. Doyle also attended. [1794]
December 8	ACD and Innes on board the Cunard liner *Etruria* left New York at 16.00hrs. [4,14,15,73,96,111,203,215,1795]
December 13	*The Stark Munro Letters* published in *Leslie's Illustrated Weekly News*. [198]
n.d.	Ida engaged to be married to Nelson Foley. [203]
December 14	ACD on board the SS *Etruria*. [203]
December 15	ACD and Innes arrived in Liverpool. [9,15,73,96,203,215]
December 17	The play, *A Story of Waterloo* opened with a charity matinee at the Garrick Theatre, London [6,1209] for the benefit of the Newport Market Refuge and Industrial Schools; ACD witnessed the performance from a private box. [450]
Winter	ACD sent Louise, Kingsley and Mary to Davos. [1819]
Winter	Louise and children, Mary and Kingsley, spent the winter in Davos [124] on route they visited Paris and San Remo (probably Naples); Caroline (Lottie) joined them at Davos. [124]
December	ACD left 12 Tennison Road, South Norwood. [322]
December 17	ACD joined Louise and children who were staying at the Grand Hotel Belvedere, Davos. [202] (*2)
December 19	ACD and his wife left England for Davos [451] for the Grandhotel Belvédère. [1819]
December	ACD and Louise in Davos. [68,200]
Christmas	ACD joined his family in Davos [124] (*2) and stayed at the Grand Hotel Belvedere, Davos [215] (*2) joined Louise, Kingsley, Mary and Lottie. [1819]
Christmas	ACD and Louise stayed at the Grand Hotel, Davos, Switzerland. [14,15]
Christmas	*A Foreign Office Romance* published in "The Young Man" and "The Young Woman". [6,196,198]
December 27	ACD at Davos Platz, Switzerland. [18]
December 29	Lottie as part of the indoor entertainment committee of the Grandhotel Belvédère took part in organising the childrens fancy-dress ball, her own costume was that of a fairy. [1819]
Winter	During the winter of 1894-95 ACD laid out a golf course at Davos. [124,202]

1895

n.d.	ACD and Louise spent most of 1895 in Switzerland and Egypt. [2]
n.d.	Bertram Fletcher Robinson joined the Reform Club 104 Pall Mall, London. [181]
January	*How to Make a Really Happy New Year. Oh! The Happiness of a Smile* published in *Demorest's Family Magazine*. [198]
January	*The Green Flag* published in *McClure's Magazine*. [198]
January	*A Forgotten Tale* (poem) published in *Scribner's Magazine*. [6,198]
January 8	ACD entered a sledge race between the teams of the Grand Hotel Belvédère and the Hotel Buol on the Klosters route (less than two miles) with a time of 7 minutes and 56 seconds, he finished 13th and last place. [1819]

1895

January 8	In the evening ACD took part in a billiards competition at the Belvédère. [1819]
January 12	ACD acted as goalkeeper in a bandy game against St. Moritz. [1819] {Note: bandy is a team winter sport played on ice, a form of hockey.}
January 14	ACD attended a fancy-dress ball at the Hotel Belvédère in his new dress as a Viking, Lottie was dressed as a marguerite. [1819]
January 16	ACD and Lottie attended the Bal Poudré at the Hotel Victoria. [1819]
January 17	ACD gave a reading from his own works at the Grandhotel Belvédère. [1819]
January 19	ACD presented Mrs Katherine Symonds with the "Challenge Cup" for the sledge race at the Hotel Boul. [1819]
January	*The Recollections of Captain Wilkie* published in *Chambers's Journal*. [202] (*2)
January 19	*The Recollections of Captain Wilkie* was published in *Chambers's Journal* on 19 & 26 January. [6,196,198] (*2)
January 19	ACD arrived in Davos. [203]
January 23	ACD gave a little fête at Davos. [203]
January 24	ACD stayed at the Grand Hotel Belvedere, Davos, Switzerland [78,203] completed writing *How the Brigadier held the King* and *How the King held the Brigadier*. [202,203]
January 24	Lottie attended a ball in Davos. [203]
January 25	ACD and Lottie attended the bachelor's ball at the Hotel Belvédère. [1819]
February 2	*The Poor* published in *Great Thoughts*. [198]
February 2	ACD and Miss N. Piers jointly took part in the mixed pairs sledge race, they finished second to last. [1819]
February 7	ACD made a Cavaliere, or Knight, of the Order of the Crown of Italy by King Umberto I of Italy. [78] (*2)
February 8	ACD at the Grand Hotel Belvedere, Davos-Platz. [1834]
February 12	ACD at Davos, Switzerland. [203]
February 13	ACD and Louise invited their friends to a tailing party at Clavadel where they organised a ski race, ACD or Mr Wilson won the men's race, Lottie won the ladies race and finished sixth out of seventeen in the Ladies Handicap race. [1819]
February 13	ACD was staying in Davos, a snowshoe race was held at St. Moritz where the Canadian snowshoe competed against the Norwegian ski, Miss Conan Doyle (Lottie) won the ladies race using the snowshoe. [452]
February 18	ACD at the Grand Hotel Belvedere, Davos [798] or Hotel Belvedere, Davos Platz, Switzerland. [884]
February 19	*Impartial Opinions from England* published in *The New York Times*. [198]
March	*Literary Aspects of America* published in *The Ladies Home Journal*. [198]
March 3	ACD attended the sledger's dinner at the Huguenins. [1819]
March 5	ACD with Tobias and Johannes Branger made an expedition starting from Davos to St. Moritz, they stayed overnight at the Posthotel Löwen, Mühlen. [1819]
March 6	ACD and the Branger brothers left Mühlen for St. Moritz, they stayed at the Kulm Hotel. [1819]
March 22	ACD at Davos, Switzerland. [203]
March 24	Birth of Oscar Hornung, son of Willie and Constance (Connie) Hornung [24,68,124,200,202] Arthur Oscar Hornung. [203]
March 27	ACD at Davos, Switzerland. [203]
March	ACD confined to his room for six days with a sore throat. [203]
n.d.	*The Exploits of Brigadier Gerard* published in *The Strand Magazine*. [99]
April	*How the Brigadier Held the King* published in *The Strand Magazine*. [6,194,195,196,198]
April 27	ACD attended the annual dinner of the London Press Club at the Freemasons' Tavern, Great Queen Street, London. [453]
May	*What are the Benefits of Bicycling?* published in *Demorest's Family Magazine*. [198]

1895

May	*How the King Held the Brigadier* published in *The Strand Magazine*. [6,194,195,196,198]
May	ACD returned to England for a short while. [202,203]
n.d.	Grant Allen recommended Hindhead, Surrey as being beneficial for those suffering from tuberculosis. [322] (*4)
May	ACD met Grant Allen who was living in Hindhead, Surrey and found the air to beneficial, recommended Hindhead for its therapeutic air, which may have helped Louise in her recovery or improve her health. [3,8,124,202,203] (*4)
May 4	ACD attended the Royal Academy banquet at Burlington House, London [1210] given by the Academicians. [202,203]
n.d.	ACD's play *Waterloo* performed starring Henry Irving. [180] (*2)
May 4	*Waterloo* a play by ACD based on *A Straggler of '15* performed at the Lyceum Theatre, London with Henry Irving in the role of Corporal Brewster. [6,99,202,1211] (*2)
May 6	Innes played cricket for Royal Artillery Officers against Sweet Seventeen at Redlands Sports Ground, Weymouth, he scored 2, Sweet Seventeen won. [235]
n.d.	ACD purchased land at Hindhead. [99] (*5)
n.d.	ACD paid a deposit on a plot of land at Hindhead. [202] (*5)
May 25	ACD back in Davos, Switzerland. [203]
n.d.	ACD, Louise and the family stayed at the Hotel Kursaal, Maloja. [202]
June	*How the Brigadier Slew the Brothers of Ajaccio* published in *The Strand Magazine*. [6,194,195,196,198]
June	While in Davos ACD with mountaineers P. and L. Whiteway took over the chairmanship of the sub-committee for the organisation of tableaux vivants (living pictures) during social events. They organised two events, one in July and another one in September. [1819]
June 6	Death of Jeremiah Hawkins, son of Emily Hawkins. [124]
June 23	ACD and Louise in Maloja they stayed at the Hôtel-Kursaal [68,200] or the Engadin Hôtel Kursaal de La Maloja. [1819]
July	*How the Brigadier Came to the Castle of Gloom* published in *The Strand Magazine*. [6,194,195,196,198]
July 2	ACD at Maloja, Switzerland and working on *Rodney Stone*. [203]
July	ACD at the Grand Hotel Belvedere, Davos Platz, Switzerland. [18]
Summer	ACD helped lay out a golf course at Davos. [2]
August	*How the Brigadier Took the Field against the Marshal Millefleurs* published in *The Strand Magazine*. [6,194,195,196,198]
August 5	Innes played cricket for Townley Park against Merton at John Innes Recreation Ground, Merton Park, he scored 8, Merton won. [235]
Summer	ACD and Louise left Davos for Maloja near St. Moritz. [14]
n.d.	Louise had returned to Switzerland, Caroline (Lottie) joined her and they then visited Caux where ACD joined them. [124]
Summer	ACD and Louise spent the summer at Maloja near St. Moritz [15]
Summer	ACD and Louise were at Maloja, Switzerland [124], Caroline (Lottie) returned to England [124], ACD and Louise then travelled to Caux near Lake Geneva, then to Rome and at the end of the year to Egypt. [180]
n.d.	ACD and Louise spent some time in Caux. [2]
n.d.	While at Caux, ACD started writing *Rodney Stone*. [6]
n.d.	ACD purchased land at Hindhead, Surrey to build a new home for Louise [99,203] the Southsea architect and friend of ACD, J.H. Ball, designed and built what would become Undershaw. [8] (*5)
Autumn	On a short visit to England ACD heard from Grant Allen that the air of Hindhead in Surrey had cured him of consumption, and may help Louise, (*4) ACD purchased a piece of land and engaged J.H. Ball as architect and chose a builder. [2] (*5)
Autumn	ACD, Louise and Caroline (Lottie) left Caux and stopped for a few days in Rome before leaving Brindisi by boat for Egypt. [124]

1895

September	*How the Brigadier was Tempted by the Devil* published in *The Strand Magazine*. [6,194,195,196,198]
September	ACD completed writing *Rodney Stone*. [6]
September	ACD and Louise at Caux, Switzerland. [200]
September 2	ACD at Maloja, Switzerland. [18]
September 2	It was reported that J.M. Barrie and his wife were staying at the Engadine, Maloja as guests of ACD and his wife, they left soon after to attend the funeral of Barrie's mother and sister that was held on 6 September. [1158]
September 5	*The Stark Munro Letters* published by Longmans, Green, and Co., London. [6]
September 6	*The Stark Munro Letters* published by D. Appleton and Co. [203]
September 7	ACD at Maloja, Switzerland [203,215] and had completed writing *Rodney Stone*. [203] (*2)
n.d.	ACD had completed writing *Rodney Stone*. [202] (*2)
n.d.	ACD stayed at the Grand Hotel Victoria, Glion, Montreux. [202]
September 14	ACD at Maloja, Switzerland. [203]
September 15	*The Stark Munro Letters* published. [99]
September	In the third week of September the Doyles left Maloja for Caux where they stayed at the Grand Hotel, Caux. [1819]
September 29	ACD at Caux, Switzerland. [203]
September 30	ACD at the Grand Hotel, Caux. [18]
October	ACD and Louise spent the month in Caux. [4,6,14,15,68]
October	Grant Allen recommended Hindhead, Surrey for its therapeutic air, which may have helped Louise recover. [14,15] (*4)
October	ACD purchased land at Hindhead, Surrey to build a house, J.H. Ball the Southsea architect and friend of ACD designed and a Guildford builder built what would become Undershaw. [14,15] (*5)
October	*The Surgeon of Gaster Fell* published in *The People's Home Journal* in October and November. [198]
n.d.	ACD returned briefly to England. [202]
October 1	ACD probably returned briefly to England and reached 23 Oakley Street, Chelsea on 2 October. [203]
October 10	ACD wrote a letter from 23 Oakley Street, Chelsea instructing Mr Harrison, publisher at *The Strand Magazine*, to prepare galley sheets for the first publication of the Brigadier Gerard stories in England, France, Germany and America. [837]
October 16	ACD attended the first night of Arthur Wing Pinero's new comedy, *The Benefit of the Doubt* at the Comedy Theatre, London. [1156]
October 25	ACD back at Caux, Switzerland. [203]
n.d.	ACD left Switzerland for Egypt. [203]
November	*A Night Among the Nihilists* published in *Good Literature*. [198]
November	*Novelists on their Works* published in *The Ludgate*. [198]
n.d.	ACD, Louise and Lottie travelled to Egypt from Lucerne through Milan, Florence, Rome and Naples, where they visited Nelson Foley and on to Brindisi. [202]
n.d.	ACD, Louise and Lottie travelled through Italy, staying for a few days in Rome, before moving on to Brindisi to catch a boat for Cairo where they stayed at the Mena House Hotel. [215]
November	ACD visited Rome whilst travelling from Lucerne through Italy to Brindisi in order to reach Egypt. [78]
November	ACD and Louise took a trip to Egypt. [68,200]
November	ACD arrived at Brindisi and then took a boat to Egypt. [4,14,68]
November	ACD and Louise stayed at the Mena House Hotel, seven miles from Cairo. [2,3,14,15,202]
n.d.	ACD and Lottie climbed the Great Pyramid. [202,215]
November 2	ACD at the Mena House Hotel, Cairo, ACD and Lottie ascended the pyramid. [203]

1895

November 4	ACD at Mena House Hotel, Cairo. [1834]
November 6	The Doyles left Caux for Italy, after a few days in Rome, the family left Brindisi by ship to Egypt to spend the winter in Cairo. [1819]
November 27	ACD in Cairo. [203]
December	*How the Brigadier Played for a Kingdom* published in *The Strand Magazine*. [6,194,195,196,198]
December 10	ACD in Cairo. [203]
n.d.	ACD's sister Jane (Ida) married Nelson Foley. [203] (*3)
December 16	ACD's sister Jane (Ida) married Nelson Foley at Thornton-in-Lonsdale, the witnesses were J.F.I. Hay Doyle (Innes), Bryan Charles Waller, B.M. Doyle (Dodo) and Mary J.E. Doyle. [124] (*3)
December 17	Jane (Ida) Doyle married Nelson Foley [203] at St. Oswald's Church, Thornton-in-Lonsdale, West Riding, Yorkshire. [16,68,200] (*3)
End of 1895	At the end of 1895 ACD, Louise and Caroline (Lottie) reached Egypt and stayed at the Mena House Hotel near the Pyramids. [124]
December 30	ACD in Cairo. [203]
December 30	ACD at the Mena House Hotel, Pyramids, Cairo. [18]
December 31	ACD and Louise travelled up the Nile to Sudan. [3,99,203] (*4)
December 31	ACD and Louise stayed at the Mena Hotel, near the Pyramids, Egypt. [99]

1896

n.d.	*Rodney Stone* published. [99,180] (*2)
January	*Rodney Stone* published in *The Strand Magazine* from January to December. [6,194,195,196,198] (*2)
January	ACD celebrated the New Year with Louise and Lottie in Cairo. [15,6]
n.d.	While in Egypt, ACD started writing *Uncle Bernac*. [6]
n.d.	ACD, Louise and Lottie travelled up the Nile on board the *Nitocris*. [202,215] (*4)
January	ACD took Louise and his sister Caroline (Lottie), on a voyage down the Nile [180] with a visit to Wadi Halfa. [124] (*4)
January 3	ACD and Louise travelled up the Nile to Sudan, [2,4,14,20] on board Thomas Cook's paddle steamer *Nitocris*, [14,15] (*4) during this time a short war broke out between the British and the Dervishes, ACD acted briefly as war correspondent for *The Westminster Gazette*. [1,2,4,15,21,215] (*2)
n.d.	ACD and Colonel Lewis set out on a trip into the desert to see an old Coptic monastery fifty miles from Cairo, they also visited Natron Lake, a salt lake. [124,215]
January 7	ACD and Louise visited the temples of Luxor. [99,215]
January 13	ACD in the area of the Mahdi forces and travelled to Korosko where he inspects the beginnings of a railway [99] stayed at Dendour for the night. [202]
January 14	ACD at Korosko. [202]
January 15	ACD visited a village beyond Korosko. [202]
January 15	ACD and Louise attended a ball in Cairo hosted by Lord and Lady Cromer. [1212]
January 16	ACD arrived at Wadi Halfa. [202]
January 17	ACD at Wady Halfa. [99,203]
January 18	*Cycle Notes: Dr. Conan Doyle on Cycling* published in *Scientific American*. [198]
January 23	ACD on board Cook's Nile Steamboat Services at Assiout. [203]
January 27	ACD probably returned to Cairo. [203]
February 5	ACD in Cairo. [203]
February 8	*On the Egyptian Frontier* published in *The Speaker*. [6,198]
February 15	*Christmas 1895* (poem) published in *Today*. [6,196,198]
n.d.	*Brigadier Gerard* published. [99]
February 15	*The Exploits of Brigadier Gerard* published by George Newnes Ltd., London. [6]

1896

February 19	Mary and Kingsley were staying at Reigate, Surrey. [124]
March 3	ACD in Cairo. [203]
March 19	ACD in Cairo. [203]
April 1	Innes was promoted from Second Lieutenant to Lieutenant. [1763]
April	ACD, Louise and Caroline (Lottie) returned to England. [2,15,20]
April 1	ACD and Louise stayed at the Assouan Hotel, Egypt. [155]
n.d.	ACD acted as briefly as a war correspondent for *The Westminster Gazette*. [99,124] (*2)
April 1	From 1 April until 11 May, ACD worked for *The Westminster Gazette*. [202,203]
April 1	*Before the Campaign. I. A Letter from Cairo* published in *The Westminster Gazette*. [198]
April 2	ACD and five correspondents left Aswan for Korosko. [215]
April 7	*Before the Campaign: II. Can the Fella Fight?* published in *The Westminster Gazette*. [198]
April 9	*From Cairo to Akasheh. Letters from Egypt. – III.* published in *The Westminster Gazette*. [198]
April 10	ACD and Louise stayed in Korosko, Egypt. [6,99,156]
April 13	*The Scene at Assouan. Letters from Egypt – IV.* published in *The Westminster Gazette*. [198]
April 16	ACD left Wady Halfa. [454]
April 17	ACD at Wady Halfa. [203]
April 20	*Correspondents and Camels. Letters from Egypt – V.* published in *The Westminster Gazette*. [198,203]
April 27	*From Assouan to Korosko. Letters from Egypt – VI.* published in *The Westminster Gazette*. [198]
April	ACD left Egypt for England. [203]
Late April	ACD, Louise and Caroline (Lottie) returned to England [180,215], as Undershaw, Hindhead was not completed; ACD and his family rented Grayswood Beeches in nearby Haslemere. [124] (*4)
May	ACD and family resided at Grayswood Beeches, Haslemere as Undershaw was not completed. [14,16,68,200] (*4)
May	ACD returned from Egypt, his new house at Hindhead was still not completed, [8] so he took the furnished house called Greyswood Beeches [215] (*4) where he remained until early 1897 when he moved Moorlands boarding house. [18]
May	ACD and family resided at Greywood Beeches, Haslemere [3] as Undershaw was not completed, or Greyswood Beeches. [39] (*4)
May 1	ACD arrived in London from Egypt. [203]
May 1	ACD a guest at the Royal Academy Banquet at Burlington House, London. [2,10,14]
May 2	For the weeks ending 2, 9, and 16 May, a Mrs and Miss Leckie were staying at the Grosvenor Hotel, Southsea. [8]
n.d.	ACD moved temporarily into rooms at 44 Norfolk Square, off Hyde Park, London. [202] (*2)
May 4	ACD moved into rooms at 44 Norfolk Square, Hyde Park, London. [203] (*2)
May 9	Innes played cricket for Royal Artillery Devonport against Ottery St. Mary at Salston Field, Ottery St. Mary, he scored 7, Ottery St. Mary won. [235]
May 11	*The Outlook from Sarras* published in *The Westminster Gazette*. [203]
n.d.	For six weeks during May and June ACD and Louise stayed at 4 Southsea Terrace, Southsea. [202]
May 14	ACD visited Southsea and played cricket for Hampshire Rovers, he stayed for a few weeks in Southsea. [8,15]
May 14	ACD played cricket for Hampshire Rovers 2nd XI against the Army Service Corps at the Recreation Ground, Portsmouth, he scored 36 and Rovers won. [455]
May 16	ACD visited Southsea and took temporary residence at 4 Southsea Terrace. [8]

1896

n.d.	ACD played cricket for Hampshire Rovers, he scored 84 not out and took 2 wickets. [202] (*2)
May 25	ACD played cricket on 25 & 26 for Hampshire Rovers against United Services Portsmouth at United Services Recreation Ground, Portsmouth; he scored 84 not out and 16 and took 2 wickets, match drawn. [235] (*2)
May 27	Innes played cricket for Royal Artillery Devonport against Devonshire Regiment at Devonport, he scored 3, Devonshire Regiment won. [235]
May 30	Miss Doyle and a Miss Hawkins were occupying separate apartments at 4 Southsea Terrace. [8]
n.d.	At the end of May it was announced that ACD was on a visit to Southsea. [456]
June	From June 1896 until July 1912, ACD owned South View Lodge, 53 Kent Road, Southsea; he never lived there, but leased it out. [68,200] (*3)
June 12	ACD at 4 Southsea Terrace, Southsea. [1834]
June 13	ACD, Miss Doyle and Miss Hawkins were listed as being at 4 Southsea Terrace, Southsea. [457]
June 15	ACD chaired the annual dinner of the New Vagabond Club for distinguished lady writers at the Holborn Restaurant. [1213]
June 27	*A Rover Chanty* (poem) published in *The Speaker*. [6,198]
June	ACD purchased South View Lodge, 50 Kent Road, Portsmouth for £1,800 [202] purchased Southview Lodge, he put down a £500 deposit with a mortgage of £1,300, which he repaid in full by 1901. [215] (*3)
June 28	While in Southsea ACD purchased South View Lodge, 53 Kent Road, Southsea [8,68] there is no evidence that he ever lived there. Dr A.V. Ford rented the property from ACD. [39] (*3)
n.d.	ACD spoke at the Authors' Club. [31,203] (*2)
June 29	ACD made a speech at the Authors' Club. [6,50,202] (*2)
July 1	ACD returned to Hindhead after spending a few weeks in Southsea. [8]
July 4	*The Conan Doyle Banquet at the Author's Club. Dr. Doyle tells of the Story of his Career* published in *Queen*. [6]
n.d.	ACD and the family resided at Grayswood Beeches, Haslemere, Surrey. [202]
July	ACD attended a dinner held by the Authors' Club. [1972]
July 9	ACD and the family resided at Greyswood Beeches, Haslemere, Surrey. [203]
July 20	It was announced that "Dr A. Conan Doyle has removed from Southsea to Grayswood Beeches, Haslemere." [458]
July 24	ACD played cricket on 24 & 25 for Hampshire Rovers against United Services Portsmouth at United Services Recreation Ground, Portsmouth; he scored 44, Hampshire Rovers won. [235]
July 29	ACD at Grayswood Beeches, Haslemere. [459]
Summer	ACD and the family resided at Grayswood Beeches, Haslemere, Surrey. [34]
Summer	ACD completed writing *Uncle Bernac*. [6]
August 10	ACD played cricket on 10 & 11 for Hampshire Rovers against Littlehampton at the Sportsfield, Littlehampton, he scored 17 and 7, Littlehampton won, playing for Hampshire Rovers were A.H. Wood who scored 12 and 20 and took 3 wickets, and Innes Doyle who scored 7 and then 16 not out and took 2 catches. [235]
August 11	Bryan Waller married Ada Roberts. [202]
August 12	While on leave from Topsham near Exeter, Devon, Innes visited ACD at Grayswood Beeches; they played tennis and visited Undershaw. [124]
August 15	ACD played cricket for Haslemere at Lythe Park against East Lyss. [63]
August 17	ACD played cricket on 17 & 18 for Hampshire Rovers against Kensington at Hilsea, Portsmouth, he scored 28 and took 2 wickets, match drawn, in the Rovers team was A.H. Wood who scored 100 and took 1 wicket. [235]
August 18	ACD at Greyswood Beeches, Haslemere, Surrey. [203]
August 22	Innes played cricket for Royal Artillery Devonport against Shobrooke at Shobrooke Park, Shobrooke, he scored 12 and zero and took 2 wickets, Shobrooke won. [235]

1896

August 22	*Dr. Conan Doyle on Cycling* published in *Hub*. [6,198]
August 24	ACD played cricket on 24 & 25 for Hampshire Rovers against Old Malvernians at Hilsea, Portsmouth, he scored 15 and did not bat in second innings, he took 1 wicket and 1 catch, match drawn, in the Rovers team was A.H. Wood who scored 12 and 2 and took 4 wickets. [235]
August 26	ACD played cricket for Haslemere against Godalming. [63]
September 17	ACD played cricket for the Authors against the Press at Lord's, he scored 101 not out and took 2 wickets, match drawn. [235,1214]
October	*The Three Correspondents* published in *The Windsor Magazine*. [6,196,198,202]
October	ACD and the family moved into Undershaw, Hindhead. [4,99] (*7)
October 10	ACD applied to become a member of the London Library, St. James's Square, London, S.W, the subscription was £3. He gave his address as Greyswood Beeches, Haslemere and occupation/position as Letters; he was introduced by Arthur Griffith. [814]
October 25	ACD attended a pre-supper séance. [202]
November 7	ACD at Greyswood Beeches, Haslemere, Surrey. [18]
November 13	*Rodney Stone* published by Smith, Elder & Co., London. [6]
November 20	ACD attended a dinner at Frascati's Restaurant in Oxford Street, London that was held by the Omar Khayyam Club [1822]
November 20	ACD was at the Omar Khayyam Club. [31]
November 20	*The Field Bazaar* published in *The Student* Edinburgh, Volume 11, pp. 35-6 as *The Memoirs of Sherlock Holmes. "The Field Bazaar"*. [6,198]
December 2	ACD attended a dinner given by the Royal Societies' Club at the Royal Academy. [460]
December	The Hindhead and Hankley Common Golf Club was formed. [125,322] (*2)
December 7	The Hindhead and Hankley Common Golf Club was formed. [1174] (*2)
December 9	ACD attended the Christmas dinner of the New Vagabond Club at the King's Hall, Holborn Restaurant. [1215]

1897

n.d.	ACD joined The Hindhead and Hankley Golf Club. [125,322]
January	*Uncle Bernac – A Memory of the Empire* published from January to March in *The Cosmopolitan*. [198]
January	ACD and family moved from South Norwood to temporary accommodation in Surrey. [180]
January	ACD and the family moved into the Moorlands Hotel, Hindhead as Undershaw was still not completed. [3,14,68,200,202,215,322]
January	*Whaling in the Arctic Ocean* published in *The Strand Magazine* as *The Life on a Greenland Whaler*. [6,194,195,196,198]
January	*Tales of the High Seas. No. I. The Governor of St. Kitt's* published in *Pearson's Magazine*. [196]
January	*Captain Sharkey I. How the Governor of St. Kitt's came Home* published in *Pearson's Magazine* as *Tales of the High Seas: No. I – The Governor of St. Kitt's*. [6,198]
January	ACD purchased a Norfolk breed horse named Brigadier. [202,203]
January	ACD at the Reform Club, Pall Mall, S.W. London. [18]
January 4	ACD at Greyswood Beeches, Haslemere, Surrey. [18]
January 8	*Uncle Bernac* published in the *Manchester Weekly Times* from 8 January to 5 March. [6,196,198]
n.d.	ACD donated £4250 over a seventeen month period to *Light* newspaper. [240]
January 22	Innes visited ACD and his family, it was about this time that ACD and his family were living at Grayswood Beeches, Haslemere. [124]
January 24	ACD and Innes walked to Hindhead to see how the new house was progressing. [124]
January 31	ACD and family were living at Moorlands, Hindhead, Surrey. [203]

1897

February 1	ACD visited Innes at Exeter to meet the Hamiltons as Innes had some designs on their daughter Dora. [203] (*2)
February	ACD travelled to Exeter to meet the family of Miss Dora Hamilton, whom Innes wanted to marry. [4] (*2)
February 3	ACD attended a dinner held by the Royal Societies' Club at St. James's Street, London to welcome Dr Nansen. [461]
February 5	ACD attended a reception for the Norwegian explorer of the Arctic, Fridtjof Nansen at the Royal Albert Hall, London. [203]
February 6	*A Ballad of the Ranks* (poem) published in *The Speaker*. [6,198]
February 8	ACD at Moorlands, Hindhead. [884]
February 9	Mary Conan Doyle attended a children's fancy dress ball at the Portsmouth Town Hall, she was dressed as Little Red Riding Hood. [462]
February 10	ACD attended the annual dinner of the Society of Authors at the Holborn Restaurant, London. [1216]
February 13	ACD made a speech at the Irish Literary Society annual dinner at the Café Monico, London. [6,203]
February 19	ACD and family were living at Moorlands, Hindhead, Surrey. [203]
March	ACD attended a dance at Exeter and meet Innes and his girlfriend, Dora Hamilton, and her family. [202]
March	ACD was elected to the Omar Khayyam Club. [463]
March	*Captain Sharkey II. The Dealings of Captain Sharkey with Stephen Craddock* published in *Pearson's Magazine* as *Tales of the High Seas: No. 2 – The Two Barques*. [6,196,198]
March 1	ACD gave a reading from his own works, under the patronage of the Lord Mayor and Lady Mayoress at the Queen's Hall, Langham Place, London in aid of the Mansion House Indian Fund, Sir Walter Besant presided [1217] ACD gave a reading for the Indian Fund. [203]
March 6	It was announced that ACD would attend an entertainment at Grosvenor House, Upper Grosvenor Street, London in aid of funds of the Metropolitan Association for Befriending Young Servants on 25 March [1218] {Note: no report of this lecture located.}
n.d.	ACD met Jean Leckie. [99] (*5)
Spring	ACD met Jean Leckie. [203] (*5)
March	Probably during March, ACD met Jean Leckie. [124] (*5)
March 15	ACD met and fell in love with Jean Leckie, later to become his wife. [3,4,14,15,17,180,202,203,322] (*5)
March 17	ACD gave a lecture on the Irish Brigade. [203]
March 20	*The Blind Archer* (poem) published in *The Speaker*. [6,198]
March 27	ACD lectured on the Irish Brigade before members of the Irish Literary Society at the Society of Arts Rooms, John Street, Adelphi, London. [464]
March 28	ACD lectured on "The Irish Brigade" (The Wild Geese) to the Irish Literary Society, London. [4,6]
March 30	ACD attended a dinner at the Merchant Taylors' Hall, Threadneedle Street, London [465] held by the Needle Makers Company. [1219]
April	*The Output of Authors* published in *Pearson's Magazine*. [198]
May	*Captain Sharkey III. How Copley Banks slew Captain Sharkey* published in *Pearson's Magazine* as *Tales of the High Seas: No. 3 – The Voyage of Copley Banks*. [6,196,198]
May	*The Tragedy of the Korosko* published in *The Strand Magazine* from May to December. [6,194,195,196,198,322]
May	ACD at the Reform Club, London. [203]
May	ACD subscribed to the Robert Louis Stevenson memorial fund. [1220]
May 8	ACD played cricket for Eastbourne against Thirteen Local Clubs he scored 49, Eastbourne won. [466]
May 12	Innes played cricket for Royal Artillery Devonport against Exeter at The County Ground, Exeter, he scored 2 and took 1 catch, Exeter won. [235]

1897

May 14	*Uncle Bernac* published by Smith, Elder, & Co., London. [6] (*2)
n.d.	*Uncle Bernac* published. [99,203] (*2)
May 14	ACD was staying at the Claremont, Grand Parade, Eastbourne. [203]
May 18	ACD gave a reading of his own works at Southsea [203] the Portland Hall, Southsea in aid of the funds of the Portsmouth and South Hants Eye and Ear Infirmary. [467]
May 19	Innes played cricket for Royal Artillery Devonport against Blundell's School at Blundell's School, Tiverton, he scored 11, Blundell's School won. [235]
May 22	ACD visited William Waldorf Astor at Cliveden, Maidenhead, Buckinghamshire for the weekend. [203]
May 26	Innes played cricket for Royal Artillery Devonport against Devonshire Regiment at Topsham Barracks, Exeter, he scored 15 and took 1 catch, he did not bat in the second innings, match drawn. [235]
n.d.	About the middle of the year ACD met Jean Leckie. [4] (*5)
June 1	*Waterloo* starring Henry Irving performed at the Prince of Wales Theatre, London in aid of the Prince of Wales's Jubilee Fund. [468]
June 5	Innes played cricket for Royal Artillery Devonport against Wonford House at Wonford House, Exeter, he scored 25, Royal Artillery Devonport won. [235]
June 9	Innes played cricket for Royal Artillery Devonport against Devonshire Regiment at Topsham Barracks, Exeter, he scored 4 and took 1 catch, Devonshire Regiment won. [235]
June 12	ACD played cricket for Hampshire Rovers against Royal Navy at United Services Recreation Ground, Portsmouth, he scored 19, Royal Navy won. [235]
June 13	ACD took the chair at a dinner of the Irish Literary Society at the Café Monico, Regent Street, London. [202]
June 17	ACD played cricket on 17 & 18 for Hampshire Rovers against Leighton at Leighton, Wiltshire, he scored 42 in the first innings and 9 not out in the second innings, he took 2 wickets and took 2 catches the result was a draw. [2008]
June 19	ACD played cricket for the Allahakbarries against the Artists at Broadway, Worcester. [1146]
June 24	ACD played cricket for Eastbourne against South Lynn at The Saffrons, Eastbourne, he scored 2 and took 2 wickets, South Lynn won. [1943]
June 25	*Waterloo* performed for the Colonial and Indian troops at the Lyceum Theatre. [469]
June 28	ACD among many others attended a reception on the stage at the Lyceum Theatre, London given by Sir Henry Irving. [985]
n.d.	From 1897 until 1907 ACD was living at Undershaw, Hindhead, Surrey. [232]
About June	ACD and the family moved into Undershaw, Hindhead. [2,10,20,39,68,200] (*7)
July 1	Innes played cricket for Royal Artillery Devonport against Honiton at Topsham Barracks, Exeter, he scored 51 not out, match drawn. [235]
July 3	Innes played cricket for Royal Artillery Devonport against 4th Battalion Devonshire Regiment at Topsham Barracks, Exeter, he scored 5, 4th Battalion Devonshire Regiment won. [235]
July 5	ACD at the Claremont, Grand Parade, Eastbourne where Nelson and Ida Foley joined him. [203]
July 6	Nelson and Ida left Eastbourne. [203]
July 10	Innes played cricket for Royal Artillery Devonport against St. Matthew's at Topsham Barracks, Exeter, he scored 2 and took 1 wicket, St. Matthew's won. [235]
July	*The Striped Chest* published in *Pearson's Magazine* as *Tales of the High Seas: No. IV – The Striped Chest*. [6,196,198]
July 19	ACD play cricket on 19 & 20 for Eastbourne against Surrey Club & Ground at The Saffrons, Eastbourne, he scored 4, took 1 wicket and I catch, match drawn. [1944]
July 23	*Waterloo* closed at the Lyceum Theatre. [470]

1897

July	Innes joined ACD, Louise and the Mam at Eastbourne, Sussex, they then travelled to Goodwood Races [215] and then onto Portsmouth for the Albert Yacht Club Jubilee Ball at the Portland Hotel, Jean Leckie was at the party [202,215] but it appears not ACD. [124]
July 30	ACD, Miss Doyle, Dr and Mrs Vernon Ford, Mrs and Miss Leckie were invited to the Royal Albert Yacht Club Ball at the Town Hall, Portsmouth. [2023]
August 2	ACD played cricket on 2 & 3 for Eastbourne against Plaistow at The Saffrons, Eastbourne, he scored 67, took 3 wickets and 1 catch, Eastbourne won. [1945]
August 4	ACD played cricket on 4 & 5 for Eastbourne against Old Yverdonians at The Saffrons, Eastbourne, he scored 6 and took 2 wickets, Eastbourne won. [1946]
August 4	Innes played cricket for 73rd Battery Royal Artillery against 19th Battery Royal Artillery at Topsham Barracks, Exeter, he scored 27 and took 1 catch, 73rd Battery Royal Artillery won. [235]
August 6	ACD played cricket on 6 & 7 for Eastbourne against Uppingham Rovers at The Saffrons, Eastbourne, he scored 12 not out, took 1 and 5 wickets, Eastbourne won. [1947]
August 6	ACD at the Authors' Club. [18]
August 9	ACD played cricket on 9 & 10 for Hampshire Rovers against Littlehampton at the Sportsfield, Littlehampton, he scored 16 and 3, and took 6 wickets, Littlehampton won, A.H. Wood scored 1 for the Rovers and took 7 wickets. [235]
August 11	ACD played cricket on 11 & 12 for Eastbourne against Old Cholmelians at The Saffrons, Eastbourne, he scored 15, Eastbourne won. [1948]
August 16	ACD played cricket on 16 & 17 for Eastbourne against Reigate Priory at The Saffrons, Eastbourne, he scored zero and 48, took 1 wicket, drawn match. [1949]
August 18	ACD played cricket on 18 & 19 for Eastbourne against Incogniti at The Saffrons, Eastbourne, he scored 4 and took 6 wickets, Eastbourne won. [235]
August 20	ACD at Claremont, Eastbourne. [884]
August 23	ACD played cricket on 23 & 24 for MCC against Eastbourne at The Saffrons, Eastbourne, he scored 35 and 27, and took 1 wicket, MCC won. [235] (*3)
August	ACD played cricket for Eastbourne against MCC, MCC won, ACD scored 35 and 27. [203] (*3)
Summer	ACD played cricket for Eastbourne Town CC against MCC. [63] (*3)
Summer	ACD and the family moved into Undershaw, Hindhead. [14] (*7)
August 25	ACD played cricket on 25 & 26 for Eastbourne against Old Malvernians at The Saffrons, Eastbourne, he scored 1 and took 1 wicket, drawn match. [1950]
August 27	ACD at Claremont, Eastbourne. [243] (*2)
August	ACD at the Claremont, Grand Parade, Eastbourne. [203] (*2)
August 30	ACD played cricket on 30 & 31 for Eastbourne against Peripatetics at The Saffrons, Eastbourne, he scored 35 and 1, took 1 wicket, Peripatetics won. [1951]
September	ACD stayed at the Hotel Albermarle, Piccadilly, London. [203]
September 9	ACD played cricket for Norfolk County Asylum against CEYMS (Church of England Young Men's Society) at The Asylum, he scored 44, The Asylum won. [2022]
September	ACD, Louise and son Kingsley took a holiday at the Royal Links Hotel, Cromer, Norfolk. [57] (*2)
September 16	ACD stayed at the Royal Links Hotel, Cromer, Norfolk. [203] (*2)
October	ACD at Morley's Hotel, Trafalgar Square, London, W.C. [18]
October	Innes Doyle (ACD's brother), Emily Hawkins (ACD's mother in law) and Emily Hawkins (sister in law) visited Undershaw. [123]
October	Innes visited ACD at Morley's Hotel, Trafalgar Square, London. [124]
October 1	*The Fiend of the Cooperage* published in the *Manchester Weekly Times*. [6,20,196,198]

1897

October 7	ACD attended a lecture by Mr Frederick G. Jackson at the Royal Societies' Club, St. James's Street, London. [1221]
October 11	ACD visited Undershaw to check on progress. [203]
October 16	Innes, Louise and Emily (Nem) Hawkins shopping in London and then to the theatre in Drury Lane. [124]
Autumn	ACD and the family moved into Undershaw, Hindhead. [16] (*7)
October	ACD and the family moved into Undershaw, Hindhead. [3,33,15,68,200] (*7)
October 17	ACD and the family moved into Undershaw, Hindhead. [202] (*7)
October 19	ACD and family moved into Undershaw. [203,322] (*7)
October 22	ACD at the Reform Club, Pall Mall, S.W., London. [18]
October 22	Innes stayed at Undershaw for the first time. [124,322]
October 23	ACD owned a horse named Brigadier; Innes rode him on this day. [124]
October 24	ACD riding Brigadier and Innes riding a grey rode to Chiddingfold to visit Dr Butler and his wife. [124]
n.d.	Late October Emily Hawkins and her daughter Emily visited Undershaw. [123]
n.d.	ACD founded the Undershaw Football Club. [124]
November 9	Henry Buchanan visited Undershaw. [123,322]
November 17	E.W. Hornung with his wife Constance (Connie) and son Oscar visited Undershaw from the 17 until 22 November. [123,322]
November 18	ACD, Louise, Innes, Connie, Willie and Oscar Hornung, Kingsley and Mary at Undershaw, Hindhead, Surrey. [124]
November 19	Henry Buchanan was a visitor at Undershaw. [322]
November 22	Willie Hornung and his wife Connie sailed to Genoa on board the Norddeutscher Lloyd line's SS *Königin Luise*, the ship visited Genoa and passed Etna arriving in Naples in December. They were met by the Foleys on their steam launch and taken to La Gaiola; they stayed at Villa Foley until January 1898 when they moved to Rome with Ida Foley. [1028]
November 26	Miss Jean Leckie dined at Undershaw. [124,215,322]
December 6	Miss Leckie took tea at Undershaw. [124,322]
December 6	Innes, ACD, Miss Leckie and Miss Halahan walked to Waggoner's Wells near Hindhead. [124,215,322]
December 7	Innes broke his collarbone while hunting near Hindhead. [202]
December 10	ACD gave a reading of his own works at a meeting of the Haslemere Microscope and Natural History Society. [34]
n.d.	Bryan Mary Doyle (Dodo) became engaged to be married to Charles Angell. [203]
December 16	ACD read a paper "The Story of the Irish Brigade" at a meeting of Portsmouth Literary Scientific Society in the Grand Jury Room, Town Hall, Portsmouth. [1038]
December 17	Sidney Paget visited Undershaw from 17 to 23 December. [123,124,203,322]
December 18	ACD and Sidney Paget hunted with Lord Leconsfield. [124]
December 18	ACD spent the morning hunting. [203]
December 18	Archie L. Langman visited Undershaw from 18 to 20 December. [123,124]
December 20	Sidney Paget began painting ACD's portrait. [124,203,322]
December 22	ACD, Sidney Paget, Miss Leckie and Miss Halahan went hunting at Elstead. [124,215]
December 23	Sidney Paget left Undershaw. [124]
December 23	Emily Hawkins and Emily (Nem) Hawkins, Louise's mother and sister visited Undershaw. [124]
December 24	Christmas Eve, children's party at Undershaw. [124]
December 25	Family party at Undershaw, ACD, Louise, Kingsley, Mary Louise, Mary Doyle, Emily (Nem) Hawkins, Caroline (Lottie), Innes and Miss Sladen. [124]
December 26	Innes went for a walk with Lottie, Miss Halahan, Miss and Mr Samson, took tea at Moorlands. [124]
December 26	A.R. Williams (trustee at the time dealing with the Hawkins estate) visited Undershaw from 26 until 30 December. [123,124,322]

1897

December 28	'William, The Engineer' at Undershaw fainted in the Engine House and burnt himself very badly about the right foot. [124,202]

1898

n.d.	*The New Catacomb. (The Burger's Secret)* published in *The Sunlight Year Book*. [6,196,198]
n.d.	Jane (Ida) Doyle became engaged to Nelson Foley. [4,14]
January	ACD at Undershaw. [203]
January	*Cremona. A Ballad of the Irish Brigade (poem)* published in *The Cornhill Magazine*. [6,196,198]
January	*My Favorite Novelist and His Best Book* published in *Munsey's Magazine*. [6,198]
January 1	*With the Chiddingfolds* (poem) published in *The Speaker*. [6,198]
January 17	*The Confession* published in *The Star*. [6,198,202]
January 17	Mr & Mrs J.M. Barrie visited Undershaw. [123]
January 28	ACD presided over a large meeting at the Hindhead Hall to assure the Government of support in the making the forthcoming International Press Conference effective. [1039]
n.d.	*The Tragedy of Korosko* published. [99,180] (*2)
February 1	*The Tragedy of the Korosko/A Desert Drama* published by Smith, Elder, & Co., London. [6,203] (*2)
February 7	Dr & Mrs Vernon Ford and son from Southsea visited Undershaw. [123]
n.d.	ACD travelled to Italy with his brother-in-law E.W. Hornung. [180]
February 14	The play *Waterloo* opened at the Lyceum Theatre, London with Sir Henry Irving in the lead role. [471]
March	ACD visited Italy and was appointed Cavaliere of the Crown of Italy, (an honorary knighthood). [14] (*2)
March 5	*The Old Huntsman* (poem) published in *The Speaker*. [6,198]
March 10	ACD took the chair of the New Vagabond Club at the Holborn Restaurant, Anthony Hope was the guest. [472]
March 13	John Kendrick Bangs visited Undershaw. [123]
March 23	Death of Dr Reginald Ratcliff Hoare in Aston, Birmingham. [326]
March 24	Charles Frohman arrived in England on board the ship *St. Louis*. [322]
March 25	Death of James Payn (editor of *Cornhill Magazine*). [203,322,1222]
n.d.	Death of James Payn late March. [202]
March 26	ACD completed writing *The Man with the Watches*. [322]
March 27	*The Groom's Story* (poem) published in *The Sun*. [198]
March 30	ACD attended the funeral of James Payn [203,1223] at St. Saviour's Church [322] Warrington Crescent, London. Henry James, Henry Rider Haggard, Sir Wemyss Reid and Sir John Robinson also attended. Payn was buried at Paddington Cemetery, Willesden. [322,1223]
March 31	ACD at Undershaw. [203]
n.d.	E.W. Hornung (ACD's brother-in-law) created A.J. Raffles and in 1899 dedicated the first stories to ACD. [11,14]
April	*The Groom's Story* published in *The Cornhill Magazine*. [6,196,198]
April 1	ACD completed writing *The Story of the Sealed Room*. [202,322]
April 2	*The Late Mr. James Payn. A Tribute from Dr. Conan Doyle* published in *The Illustrated London News*. [198,322]
April	ACD, H.G. Wells, E.W. Hornung and George Gissing visited Rome. [78,202]
April 4	ACD left England for Italy where he stayed for time with Willie and Connie Hornung who were based in Rome; he then headed back home via Gaiola, a small island off Naples, and stayed with his brother-in-law Nelson Foley. [322]
April 8	ACD arrived in Rome for a short stay, in the evening he dined with Willie Hornung, George Gissing and H.G. Wells at the Trattoria Colonna. [1028]
April 22	ACD was back in England. [322]

1898

May 4	ACD attended the first performance of the play *Medicine Man* by H.D. Traill and Robert Hichens and starring Henry Irving and Miss Ellen Terry at the Lyceum Theatre, London. [322,2083]
May 11	Mary Josephine Elizabeth Doyle (ACD's mother) visited Undershaw. [123]
May 17	ACD was visited by a deputation from the Portsmouth Conservatives to attempt him to lure him into politics. [322]
May 19	ACD decided against the idea of entering politics. [322]
May 20	Charles Cyril Angell (future husband of Bryan Mary Julia Josephine Doyle, ACD's sister) visited Undershaw. [123]
May 23	Archie Langman visited Undershaw. [123]
May 24	*Waterloo* performed at Her Majesty's Theatre in aid of the Prince of Wales Fund. [473]
May 28	ACD played cricket for Grayshott against Liphook at Grayshott Hall and scored 37. [63]
May	ACD donated £2:2s to the London Fund for the Relief of the Distressed in the West and South West of Ireland. [1830]
May 30	ACD played cricket on 30 & 31 for Hampshire Rovers against United Services Portsmouth at United Services Recreation Ground, Portsmouth; he scored 16 and 11, and took 2 wickets, match drawn. [235]
June	E.W. Hornung dedicated *The Amateur Cracksman* 'To A.C.D., this form of flattery.' [203]
June	*The Beetle Hunter* published in *The Strand Magazine*. [6,194,195,196,198]
June 3	ACD attended the Anglo-American banquet at the Hotel Cecil, London. ACD was a member of the Anglo-American Committee. [322,1224]
June 4	ACD played cricket for Grayshott against Lychmere at Grayshott Hall and scored 43 not out. [63]
June 7	It was announced that ACD was part of the Privy Council of the Anglo-American Committee. [2015]
n.d.	*Songs of Action* published. [124,322] (*2)
June 8	*Songs of Action* published by Smith, Elder, & Co., London. [6] (*2)
June 11	ACD played cricket for the Allahakbarries against the Artists at Broadway, Worcester, he scored 46, the Allahakbarries won. [1146]
June 13	Julia Angel, sister of Charles Cyril Angell visited Undershaw. [123]
June 16	ACD attended the annual dinner of the New Vagabond Club at the King's Hall, Holborn Restaurant. [1225]
June 17	Innes visited ACD, Louise and the Mam at Morley's Hotel, Trafalgar Square, London, watched a cricket match at Lord's, in the evening they were joined by Cyril Angell and his sister, Julia. [124]
June 20	ACD at Undershaw. [2053]
June 21	ACD signed the petition in support of a new opera house in London. [1226]
June 28	Innes played cricket for Royal Artillery Devonport against 4th Battalion Devonshire Regiment at Topsham Barracks, Exeter, he scored 3, match drawn. [235]
July	Willie Hornung and Connie returned to England. [1028]
July	*The Man with the Watches* published in *The Strand Magazine*. [6,194,195,196,198,322]
July	*The King of the Foxes* published in *The Windsor Magazine*. [6,196,198]
July 6	ACD played cricket for Haslemere against Petworth at Lythe Hill Park, he scored 17 and took 3 wickets. [63]
July 20	ACD played cricket for Hindhead School against Churt. [63]
July 22	ACD played cricket on 22 & 23 for Hampshire Rovers against United Services Portsmouth at United Services Recreation Ground, Portsmouth, he scored 28, and there was no play on the final day, match drawn. [235]
July 26	James Ryan and Elizabeth C. Ryan visited Undershaw. [123]
August	ACD spent four days with Major Arthur Griffiths at The Cottage, Telfont Evias, near Salisbury. [203]

1898

August	*The Story of the Lost Special* published in *The Strand Magazine*. [6,194,195,196,198,322]
August 1	ACD played cricket for his own team, "Dr Conan Doyle's XI" against Haslemere [63] for Undershaw (Dr Conan Doyle's Eleven) at Haslemere, he scored 16, Undershaw won. [1952]
August 3	ACD played cricket for Undershaw (Dr Conan Doyle's Eleven) against Mr Turle's Eleven, he scored 5, Undershaw won. [1953]
August 4	ACD played cricket for his own team "Dr Conan Doyle's XI" against Churt [63] for Undershaw (Dr Conan Doyle's Eleven) he scored 12, Undershaw won. [1954]
August 4	Alfred Wood and Philip Trevor visited Undershaw. [123]
August 5	ACD played cricket for Undershaw (Dr Conan Doyle's Eleven) against Captain Clark's Eleven at Beacon Hill, he scored 4, Undershaw won. [1954]
August 15	ACD played cricket for Haslemere against Northchapel. [63]
September	*The Story of the Sealed Room* published in *The Strand Magazine*. [6,194,195,196,198,322]
September	ACD attended a dinner on Salisbury Plain with Commander-in-Chief, Lord Wolseley. [202]
September 17	*An Impression of the Army* published in *The Speaker*. [6,198]
n.d.	Birth of Percy Fitzgerald (Michael) Foley son of Nelson and Jane (Ida) Foley. [202] (*2)
September 29	Birth of Percy Fitzgerald (Michael) Foley son of Nelson and Jane (Ida) Foley. [124] (*2)
October	*The Story of the Black Doctor* published in *The Strand Magazine*. [6,194,195,196,198]
October 6	ACD at Undershaw. [2053]
October 9	Bryan Mary Doyle ACD's sister visited Undershaw, as did Mrs Josephine Ratcliff Hoare and Joey Ratcliff Hoare, wife and daughter of Dr Reginald Ratcliff. [123]
October 28	ACD was approached by the Liberal Unionists who wished him to represent them, but he refused. [322]
November	*The Story of the Club-Footed Grocer* published in *The Strand Magazine*. [6,194,195,196,198]
November 12	Thomas Wemyss Reid visited Undershaw. [123]
November 15	ACD attended and spoke at the national conference of Liberal Unionist in Manchester [2005] at the Free Trade Hall, Manchester. [2016]
November 18	Mr & Mrs Stratten Boulnois visited Undershaw. [123]
November 19	*Master* (poem) published in *The Living Age*. [6,198]
December	*The Retirement of Signor Lambert* published in *Pearson's Magazine*. [6,196,198]
December	*The Story of the Brazilian Cat* published in *The Strand Magazine*. [6,194,195,196,198]
December	*A Shadow Before* published in *The Windsor Magazine*. [6,196,198]
December	ACD was elected to Ireland's National Literary Society. [322]
December 10	ACD chaired a Christmas dinner of the New Vagabond Club at the Great Hall of the Hotel Cecil, London. [322,1227]
December 14	Nelson Foley (ACD's brother in law) visited Undershaw. [123]
December 17	Innes arrived at Undershaw for Christmas. [124]
December 22	Connie arrived at Undershaw. [124]
December 23	ACD and family celebrated moving into Undershaw by holding a fancy-dress ball at the Brecon Hill Hotel, Hindhead [6] or Beacon Hill Hotel, Hindhead [16,322] some of the guests were dressed as characters from his works [6] at a nearby hotel [203] at the Beacon Hotel. [202] (*2)

1898

December 23	ACD held a grand fancy-dress ball was held at the Hindhead Beacon Hotel, the guests included Mr & Mrs Grant Allen (cardinal & Japanese lady), Mrs J. Grant Allen (Japanese), Mr & Mrs Stratten Boulnois (gentleman of Queen Elizabeth's time & poudre Louis XIV), Miss Doyle (Marguerite), Mr Innes Doyle (Sir Gervas Jerome), Mr L Driver (study in scarlet), Miss Driver (Little maid of Arcady), Mr & Mrs Vernon Ford (QC & silver blaze), Miss Leckie (one of the Queens Maries), Mrs E.W. Hornung (Charlotte Corday), Oscar Hornung (Little Boy Blue), Mrs Leuchers (Madame Pompadour), Miss Leuchers (Christmas rose), Archie Langman (Lieutenant, Middlesex Yeomanry), Captain and Mrs Trevor (Conan Doyle & Geisha girl) Mary Doyle (Forget-me-not) and Dr & Mrs Conan Doyle (Viking & poudre). [124] (*2)
December 26	ACD attended the Boxing Day meet with the Chiddingfold Hounds; they assembled at The Royal Huts, Hindhead. [34]
December 28	ACD attended the second annual social tea at the Grayshott Institute on December 28 & 29 and read from his own works. [34]
December	Innes travelled from Haslemere to Masongill by train for the New Year. [124]

1899

n.d.	William Gillette began a thirty-three year stint starring as Sherlock Holmes in a play by Gillette and ACD. [99]
January	ACD at Undershaw. [203]
January	ACD took the chair at a public meeting held at the Congregational Hall, Hindhead where the first thoughts of a Hindhead Golf Club arose. [124]
January	ACD spoke at a woman's meeting in the Hindhead Free Church Hall. [124]
January	Emily Hawkins, mother of Louise, was probably living at The Cottage, Hindhead. [124]
January	*The Story of the Japanned Box* published in *The Strand Magazine*. [6,194,195,196,198]
January 20	ACD at Undershaw. [203]
January 27	ACD elected as a member of the Liberal Union Club, 6 Great George Street, London. [1228]
January 28	ACD presided over a meeting "The Peace Crusade" held at the Hindhead Hall. [1229] (*3)
January 28	Speeches by ACD and Mr Bernard Shaw on "Disarmament and Arbitration", at the Czar's Peace Proposition held at Hindhead [2,6,14,20,203] ACD chaired the meeting at the Congregational Hall, Tower Road, Hindhead. [125] (*3)
January	ACD took the chair in support of W.T. Stead's campaign in favour of the 'Czar's Note on National Disarmament' held at the Hindhead Free Church Hall. [20,124,202] (*3)
January 31	ACD chaired a meeting of the Authors' Club at 3 Whitehall Court. [474]
February	ACD at Undershaw. [203]
n.d.	ACD and Innes had lunch with the Leckies at Blackheath. [203]
February	*The Story of the Jew's Breastplate* published in *The Strand Magazine*. [6,194,195,196,198]
February	A slight accident occurred at the electrical works at Undershaw, the engine room caught fire, but the flames were quickly extinguished, the clothes of the driver, Mr William Simmonds, were slightly burned. [121]
February 11	ACD presented a talk "Reading from my Books" at Toynbee Hall, London. [322,1230]
February 26	Hesketh Prichard and Kate O'Brian Prichard visited Undershaw. [123]
March	ACD attended a meet of the Chiddingfold Hunt. [34]
March	ACD supported the Beacon Hotel, Hindhead in a successful application for a drinks licence. [34]
March 6	ACD spoke at a meeting presided by the Lord Mayor of London held at the Mansion House, London to consider proposals to celebrate the millenary of Alfred the Great. [1231]

1899

March	*The Story of B. 24* published in *The Strand Magazine*. [6,194,195,196,198]
March 19	*A True Story of the Tragedy of Flowery Land* published in *The Courier-Journal*. [6]
n.d.	*A Duet* published. [99] (*3)
March	*A Duet* published by Grant Richards. [202,203] (*3)
March 23	*A Duet with an Occasional Chorus* published by Grant Richards, London. [6] (*3)
April	ACD attended a private dinner for Lord Wolseley and War Office aides. [202]
April	*The Usher of Lea House School* published in *The Strand Magazine* as *The Story of the Latin Tutor*. [6,194,195,196,198]
April	Innes Doyle joined the Royal Horse Artillery [202] and was posted in India. [200]
April 10	From 10 April to 15 April *Halves* a prologue and three acts by ACD, based on the story by James Payn, first performed at His Majesty's Theatre, Aberdeen. [6,99,122] (*2)
April	*Halves* opened in Aberdeen. [203] (*2)
April 10	ACD at Undershaw. [203]
n.d.	ACD's sister Bryan Mary Julia Josephine (Dodo) married the Revd. Charles Angell. [203] (*4)
April 11	Bryan Mary Julia Josephine (Dodo) married Charles Cyril Angell [203] (*4) at St. Oswald's Church, Thornton-in-Lonsdale, West Riding, Yorkshire. [68,200]
April	ACD's sister Bryan Mary (Dodo) married Charles Angell. [202] (*4)
April	ACD's sister Bryan Mary Julia Josephine (Dodo) married Charles Cyril Angell [3,14,16,17] (*4) at the Parish Church of Thornton-in-Lonsdale, witnesses at the marriage were Innes Hay Doyle, Mary Doyle, Willie and Connie Hornung and Julia Angell (Cyril's sister). [124]
April 15	ACD attended the play *Robespierre* starring Henry Irving at the Lyceum Theatre, London. [475]
April 19	Innes arrived in Bombay, India [124] he joined the Royal Horse Artillery in India. [202]
Spring	ACD travelled through Italy with E.W. Hornung and visited H.G. Wells. [15]
May	ACD was elected chairman of the Authors' Club. [1972]
May	ACD at the Reform Club, Pall Mall, S.W., London. [18]
May	ACD at Undershaw. [18,44,203]
May	William Gillette visited ACD at Undershaw, Hindhead, Surrey. [14,15,78,215]
May	*The Story of the Brown Hand* published in *The Strand Magazine*. [6,194,195,196,198]
May 3	Charles Cyril Angell and Bryan Mary Angell visited Undershaw. [123]
May 9	ACD played cricket for Mitcham against Surrey Colts at the Oval, he scored 6, match drawn. [1955]
May 15	ACD played cricket on 15 & 16 for Incogniti against Aldershot Division at Officers Club Services Ground, Aldershot, he scored 17 and took 1 catch, match drawn. [235]
May 16	ACD at Undershaw. [203]
May 18	ACD played cricket on 18 & 19 for Hampshire Rovers against United Services, Portsmouth at United Services Recreation Ground, Portsmouth; he scored 11 and 3, and took 2 wickets, Hampshire Rovers won. [235]
May 19	Innes arrived in Bombay, later in the year he was joined by his sister Caroline (Lottie) at Umballa. [124]
May	ACD was on the committee of the William Black Memorial Fund. [1232]
May 22	ACD played cricket, he scored 53 and took 10 wickets, teams unknown. [203,215]
May 22	ACD at Undershaw. [203]
May 24	ACD played cricket on 24 & 25 for Incogniti against Uppingham at Upper Field, Uppingham School, he scored 6, match drawn. [235]
May 31	Mr & Mrs Charles Cyril Angell visited Undershaw. [123]

1899

June	ACD was elected as a member of the MCC, he was proposed by Mr (later Sir) F.E. Lacey and seconded by Captain E.G. Wynyard. [1124]
June	ACD played cricket for Incogniti on schools tour against Clifton College, Sherborne School, East Gloucester and Cheltenham College. [63]
June 1	ACD played cricket for the Authors against the Artists at Denmark Hill, he scored 5, the Authors won. [235]
June 3	It was announced that the Cheltenham College Cricket team would play Incogniti at the College Ground, Cheltenham on 9 & 10 June. [1116]
June 3	ACD played cricket for Incogniti against Clifton College at Clifton College Close Ground, Clifton, he scored 4 and took 4 wickets, Clifton College won. [235,1148]
June 5	ACD played cricket on 5 & 6 for Incogniti against Sherborne School at Sherborne School, Sherborne, he scored 7 and took 1 catch, match drawn. [235]
June 7	It was advertised that *Halves* would be performed for the first time in London on 10 June at the Garrick Theatre. [1233]
June 8	ACD played cricket for Incogniti against East Gloucester at Charlton Park, Gloucester, he scored 67 and took 3 wickets, Incogniti won [1117], played at East Gloucester Cricket Club Ground, Cheltenham, match drawn. [235]
June 9	ACD played cricket on 9 & 10 for Incogniti against Cheltenham College at the Clifton College Close Ground, Cheltenham, he scored 43 and took 3 wickets, Incogniti won. [235,1118,1148]
June	ACD at Undershaw. [203]
June 10	It was announced that ACD was a visitor at the Queen's Hotel, Cheltenham. [476]
June 10	*Halves* was performed at the Garrick Theatre, London from 10 June-4 August. [6,1234,2053]
June 11	ACD played cricket for Incogniti against Clifton at Clifton, Bristol, he scored 4 and took 4 wickets, Clifton won. [477]
June 12	*Sherlock Holmes*, a drama in four acts, by ACD and William Gillette and starring William Gillette, was performed as a copyright performance at the Duke of York's Theatre, St. Martin's Lane, London. [6,31,99,202,322]
June 12	ACD attended and gave a talk at a dinner of the Anglo-African Writers' Club held at the Grand Hotel, London. [85,322]
June 17	ACD at Undershaw. [203]
June 18	ACD at Undershaw. [203]
June	Mid-June ACD hired his butler Thomas Rodney Cleeve, his wife Elizabeth Cleeve was employed as parlour maid. [322]
June 22	ACD and Louise attended a large garden party at the Authors' Club. [478]
June 23	ACD played cricket for C.M. Tuke's XI against Incogniti at Chiswick Park, Chiswick, he scored 15, Incogniti won. [235]
June 24	ACD played cricket for Incogniti against Blackheath at The Rectory Field, Blackheath, he scored 1 and took 2 wickets, match drawn. [235]
June 28	ACD was a guest at a supper party given by the proprietor of *Punch* at their new offices in Bouverie Street, London. [479]
June 30	ACD played cricket for the Allahakbarries against the Artists at Broadway, Worcestershire. [481]
July	*Sir Nigel's Song* published in the *Souvenir of the Charing Cross Hospital Bazaar* as *A Soldier's Prayer*. [6]
July	ACD at Undershaw. [203]
July 1	*The Arab Steed* (poem) published in the *Daily News Weekly*. [6,196,198]
July 1	ACD played cricket for Grayshott against Farnham. [63]
July 5	ACD played cricket for MCC & Ground against Richmond at Richmond he scored zero and took 1 wicket, MCC won [56], or MCC against Richmond at Old Deer Park, Richmond, match drawn. [235]
July 19	ACD played cricket for MCC against Dorking at Cotmandene, Dorking, he scored 9 and took 3 wickets, match drawn. [235]

1899

July 20	ACD at Undershaw. [203]
July 21	ACD played cricket on 21 & 22 for Hampshire Rovers against United Services, Portsmouth; [203] he scored 55 and took 1 catch, Hampshire Rovers won. [235]
July 24	ACD at Undershaw. [203,322]
July 24	ACD played cricket on 24 & 25 for MCC against Wiltshire at Trowbridge Cricket Club Ground [203]; he missed the first innings but scored 6 in the second innings and took 1 catch, Wiltshire won. [235,322]
July 26	*Halves* reached its 50th performance at the Garrick Theatre, London. [480]
July 28	ACD played cricket for MCC against Oaklands Park at Oaklands Park Cricket Club Ground, Weybridge, he scored 53 and took 2 wickets, MCC won. [235]
July 29	ACD played cricket for Grayshott against Shottermill. [63]
August	ACD held his August cricket week; he staged games against Haslemere, Grayshott and other local clubs. [202,322,1146]
August 3	ACD read his new Brigadier Gerard story at Hindhead. [203] read from an unpublished book at a Bazaar held at the Rectory Gardens, Haslemere. [482]
August 4	*Halves* closed at the Garrick Theatre, London, due to resume in September. [483]
August 4	ACD played cricket for MCC against Surbiton at Surbiton, he scored 1 and took 2 wickets, Surbiton won. [235]
August 21	ACD played cricket for Incogniti against Hampshire Hogs at County Ground, Southampton, he scored 16, match drawn. [235]
August 23	ACD played cricket on 23 & 24 for Incogniti against Hampshire Rovers at Hilsea, Portsmouth, he scored 89 and took 3 wickets, 1 of which was that of A.H. Wood, match drawn, A.H. Wood played for Hampshire Rovers, he scored 8 and took 1 wicket. [235]
August 25	ACD played cricket on 25 & 26 for Incogniti against Bournemouth at Dean Park, Bournemouth, he scored 31 and zero and took 4 wickets in both innings, match drawn. [235]
August 30	ACD played cricket on 30 & 31 for MCC & Ground against Cambridgeshire at Lord's, he took 7 wickets [63,1146] (*2), including a hat trick [56,322,1235]. MCC against Cambridgeshire, he did not bat but took 7 wickets in the first innings and 1 wicket in the second innings, match drawn. [56,235]
September	ACD at Undershaw. [203]
September	Caroline (Lottie) Doyle left England on board the SS *Egypt* to join Innes in India [3,14,202] (*2), it was in India that she met and married Captain Leslie Oldham. [3,14]
September 29	Caroline (Lottie) left England for India to join Innes. [203] (*2)
October	*The Croxley Master* published in *The Strand Magazine*, October–December. [6,194,195,196,198]
October 3	ACD lectured at the Westbourne Park Institute, London [1236] lectured at the Westbourne Chapel. [484]
October 5	ACD lectured at the Cambridge Hall, Southport under the auspices of the local YMCA [485]
October 7	It was announced that ACD would gave a lecture at the Town Hall, Newbury for the Guildhall Club on 13 October. [487]
October 7	It was announced that ACD would give a lecture at the opening meeting of the Literary Society Lectures on "Sidelights on History" at St. James's Hall, Kingston on 10 October. [804]
October 10	ACD lectured for the Kingston Literary Society at St. James's Hall, Kingston on "Sidelights on History." [807]
October 11	The Boer War began. [3,202,215]
October 11	ACD was staying at the Reform Club, London. [202]
October	ACD at Undershaw. [203]
October	Sir Francis and Lady Jeune entertained ACD at their home Arlington Manor, Berkshire. [486]
October 13	ACD gave a reading from his own works at the Town Hall, Newbury. [487a]

1899

n.d.	Death of Ann Martha Doyle. [202] (*2)
October 17	Death of Ann (Annette) Martha Doyle [203] (*2) at the Common House, Church Street, Kensington, London. [68,124,200]
October 18	*Who's That Calling?* (poem) published in the *Daily News*. [6,198]
October 20	It was advertised that ACD would lecture at the Great Hall, Tunbridge Wells on 27 October, reading from his own works, with comments. [811]
October 20	ACD gave a reading "Sidelights of History" at the opening of the Literary and Philosophical Society's Session at the Royal Institution Assembly Rooms, Bath. [488] {Note: this was an afternoon lecture.}
October 20	ACD gave a lecture at the Clifton Subscription Lectures held at the Victoria Rooms, Clifton, Bristol; the lecture was titled "Sidelights of History". [322,489] {Note: this was an evening lecture.}
October 23	*Sherlock Holmes* starring William Gillette opened in Buffalo, New York [203], opened at the Star Theatre, Buffalo, New York [31], and the then did a brief tour in Rochester, Syracuse, Scranton and Wilkes-Barre en route to New York's Garrick Theatre. [322]
n.d.	Death of Mr Grant Allen. [202] (*2)
October 25	Death of Mr Grant Allen. [6] (*2)
October 26	ACD presented the prizes of the Victoria Cricket Association held at the Champion Hotel, Aldersgate Street, London. [490]
October 27	At the Great Hall, Tunbridge Wells ACD gave some readings from his own works and made some comments. [1162]
October 29	ACD at Undershaw. [809]
October	ACD contributed £10:10s to the Transvaal War Fund. [1237]
October 31	It was advertised that ACD would give readings from his own works, with comments, including an extract from an unpublished story, at Hampstead Conservatoire (close to Swiss Cottage Station) tonight, 31 October at 8.30. [2045] {Note: no report of this lecture located.}
November 6	*Sherlock Holmes* a play by ACD and William Gillette and starring William Gillette performed at the Garrick Theatre, New York from 6 November until 16 June 1900. [31,99,184,202,215,322,323]
November 6	ACD took the chair at the Lord Wolseley banquet [202,203] ACD presided at the Authors' Club dinner held at 3 Whitehall Court, London [1238], guest of honour was Lord Wolseley. [322]
November 8	ACD at Undershaw. [203]
November 22	Mary Doyle, mother of ACD, was living at Masongill Cottage. [203]
November 23	ACD attended one of Sir Henry Thompson's octave dinners. [203]
November 24	ACD dined with Nugent Robinson. [203]
November 27	ACD entertained the Bishop of London at the Authors' Club. [203]
November 30	ACD attended the Royal Society Anniversary Meeting at Burlington House and the dinner of the Royal Society at the Metropole. [203,1239]
December	ACD at Undershaw. [18,203]
December	ACD volunteered for service in South Africa, but was rejected. [2,5,7,15]
December	ACD applied to join the army to fight against the Boers but was rejected because of his age. [99,180]
December	*The Crime of the Brigadier* published in *The Cosmopolitan*. [198]
December	*My First Guinea* published in *Pearson's Magazine*. [198]
December 18	ACD attended the New Vagabond Club ladies dinner at the Holborn Restaurant. [491]
December 25	Mary Doyle at Masongill Cottage. [203]
December 26	ACD at Undershaw. [203]

1900

n.d.	ACD gave a presentation speech at Saint Mary's Hospital, London. [113]
January	ACD gave a speech in Edinburgh. [203]
January	ACD made out his Will. [203,322]

1900

January	ACD at Undershaw. [203]
January	*How the Brigadier Slew the Fox* published in *The Strand Magazine* as *The Crime of the Brigadier*. [6,194,195,196,198]
January 3	*The Début of Bimbashi Joyce* published in *Punch*. [6,196,198]
January 6	It was announced that ACD had volunteered his services with the Langman Field Hospital. [492]
January 22	Speech by ACD at the Authors' Club, "Conan Doyle's Views on the War". [6]
n.d.	ACD was invited to become an Honorary Member of the Irvine Burns Club. [1823]
February	*Hilda Wade. XII. The Episode of the Dead Man Who Spoke* published in *The Strand Magazine*. [6,196,198]
February	ACD at 6 Stanhope Terrace, Hyde Park, London. [203]
February 3	In a letter by ACD from Undershaw to the Irvine Burns Club he accepted the invitation to become an Honorary Member of the club. [1823]
February 7	ACD listed in *The Times* as A. Conan Doyle M.D., M.C.H., physician with the Langman Hospital. [1240]
February 18	ACD sailed for South Africa. [5] (*5)
February 19	ACD at the Reform Club, London. [18]
n.d.	ACD accompanied the volunteer-staffed Langman Hospital as an unofficial supervisor to support British forces in the Boer War. [99]
February 21	ACD attended a luncheon given by Mr John Langman in honour of His Royal Highness the Duke of Cambridge at Claridge's Hotel, London. [493]
February 21	The Duke of Cambridge at the headquarters of the St. George's Rifles, Davies Street, London [1241] to inspect the Langman Hospital Company [7] John L. Langman sent a field hospital to South Africa at his own expense, staff included Mr A. Langman (son of John Langman), ACD [1241] and Cleeve, ACD's butler. [202,322]
February 22	ACD listed in *The Times* as being on the committee of the Atlantic Union. [1242]
February 28	SS *Oriental* set sail from London. [494, 495] (*5)
February 28	ACD sailed from Tilbury on the *Oriental* with the Langman Hospital [154,215] ACD sailed from Tilbury on the P&O liner *Oriental* for South Africa. [2,3,4,7,10,14,15] (*5)
February 28	ACD set sail from Tilbury for Cape Town with the Langman Hospital [124,180] (*5) from the Royal Albert Docks [322,1243], soon after Louise went to Naples and probably stayed with Nelson and Ida Foley on Gaiola. [99,124,202]
n.d.	Louise was in Naples. [14]
February	At the end of February ACD sailed on the *Oriental* for South Africa. [6] (*5)
March	*Playing with Fire* published in *The Strand Magazine*. [6,194,195,196,198,202]
March 2	ACD arrived on board the SS *Oriental* in Queenstown, Ireland and took on board the 3rd Battalion Royal Scots (Edinburgh Light Infantry Militia) left at 4p.m. [1243] 3rd Militia Battalion, Royal Scots Fusiliers. [154] (*2)
March 2	SS *Oriental* arrived in Queenstown, Ireland at 6a.m. and left at 3p.m. [494] (*2)
March 9	SS *Oriental* anchored off St. Vincent, part of the Cape Verde group, ACD went ashore at 11 o'clock, in the afternoon ACD played cricket for the ship's eleven against St. Vincent, ACD took 3 wickets, ship's eleven won. [337,494]
March 9	ACD at sea on route for South Africa [203] passed Cape St. Vincent. [154]
March 11	On board the SS *Oriental* ACD gave a lecture on the war. [494]
March 21	ACD arrived at Cape Town, [7,10,14,15,202] (*3) stayed at the Mount Nelson Hotel. [202,322] (*2)
March 21	ACD served with the Langman Hospital in South Africa until 11 July. [68,200]
March 21	SS *Oriental* arrived in Table Bay, Cape Town at 10p.m. [494] (*3)
March 22	ACD arrived at Cape Town, [154,215] (*3) stayed at the Mount Nelson Hotel, [10,154] (*2)
March 26	ACD left Cape Town by ship travelling to East London. [154,215,322] (*3)

1900

March 26	The Langman Field Hospital sailed from Cape Town for East London. [7,10,14] (*3)
March 26	SS *Oriental* left Cape Town for East London at 6:30a.m. [494] (*3)
n.d.	*The Green Flag* published. [180] (*3)
March	*The Green Flag* published by Smith, Elder & Co. [202] (*3)
March 27	*The Green Flag and Other Stories of War and Sport* published by Smith, Elder & Co., London. [6] (*3)
March 28	ACD at sea off East London. [202,203]
March 28	SS *Oriental* arrived at East London at daybreak, ACD and Mr Langman went ashore and stayed at a hotel in East London. [494]
March 28	ACD arrived in East London. [7,10,154]
March 28	The Langman Hospital disembarked at East London. [495]
March 29	The Langman Hospital left East London by special Langman Hospital train at 5:30p.m. [494]
March	ACD and the Langman Hospital travelled on two trains from East London to Bloemfontein. [154]
March 30	The Langman Hospital train stopped for breakfast at Cathcart, left at 10:30a.m. [494]
March 30	The Langman Hospital train arrived at Queenstown at 1p.m. left at 1:30p.m. [494]
March 30	The Langman Hospital train arrived at Sterkstroom at 5:30p.m. [494]
March 31	The Langman Hospital train arrived at Burgersdrop at 6:30a.m. [494]
April	*My Friend the Villain* published in *The Hearthstone*. [198]
April 1	The Langman Hospital train passed through Olive. [494]
April 2	The Langman Hospital train arrived at Bethulie at 2p.m. In the evening ACD, Archie Langman, Robert O'Callaghan (surgeon) and Charles Blasson went walking, ACD shot a dove. [494]
April	ACD was in Bloemfontein. [124]
April 2	ACD was in Bloemfontein at the Langman Hospital. [2,3,4,6,14,15]
April 2	The Langman Hospital train arrived in Bloemfontein [154,202,203,495] (*2) arrived at 5p.m. [7,10,322]
April 3	The Langman Hospital train left Bethulie at midday. [494]
April 3	The Langman Hospital train arrived at Springfontein at 4:30p.m. [494]
April 3	ACD at Bloemfontein. [203]
April 4	The Langman Hospital train arrived in Bloemfontein at 5:30a.m. [494] (*2)
April 5	ACD attended a meeting of an emergency Masonic lodge, Rising Star Lodge No. 1022, English Constitution at Bloemfontein. [202]
April 6	*A First Impression* published in *The Friend*. [198]
April	The Langman Hospital commandeered the premises of The Ramblers Club of Bloemfontein. [202,322]
April 8	The 35 tent Langman Hospital opened at the Ramblers Cricket Club ground. [494,495]
April 8	The Langman Hospital opened in Bloemfontein. [154]
April 10	ACD dined at headquarters. [203]
April 11	Lord Roberts inspected the hospital. [495] (*2)
April 13	Lord Roberts inspected the hospital. [494] (*2)
April 14	ACD took part in some cricket practice in the nets. [494]
April 16	*Conan Doyle in "Luck"* published in the *Daily News*. [6,198]
April 20	ACD at the Langman Field Hospital, South African Field Force. [203,215]
April 22	ACD joined the hospital unit as a doctor at the Langman Hospital, Bloemfontein in South Africa. [3]
April 22	ACD, Archie Langman and Mr Bennett Burleigh of the *Daily Telegraph* left Bloemfontein to see the fighting at Springfield. [494]
April 24	ACD watched Bloemfontein waterworks being recaptured. [202]
May 1	ACD and Archie Langman left Bloemfontein with the troops to see if they see any fighting. [494]

1900

May 1	ACD left Bloemfontein with Lord Roberts for Pretoria. [7]
May 1–7	ACD with the British Army in the field and saw Brandfort captured. [2]
May 2–7	ACD with Archie Langman visited the Front and observed the advance of Lord Roberts. [99]
May 4	Lady Roberts inspected the hospital. [494]
May 7	ACD returned to Bloemfontein. [7]
May 8	ACD and Archie Langman returned from the front. [494]
May 10	Charles Blasson (dresser) started his fortnight's clerking with ACD. [494]
May 16	It was announced that the marriage between Captain Leslie Oldham, Royal Engineers, of Jubbulpore, Central Provinces and Caroline Mary Doyle, sister of Dr Conan Doyle of Hindhead, would take place in the Autumn. [496]
May 19	ACD was captain of a Langman Hospital football team that played against the Imperial Yeomanry Field Hospital at Bloemfontein, South Africa, the result was a 1-1 draw. [494]
May 23	Charles Blasson went for a ride on ACD's Basuto pony. [494]
May 24	ACD attended and read *The Brigadier and The Fox* at a Grand Evening Concert to celebrate the 81st birthday of Queen Victoria, held at the Town Hall, Bloemfontein. [335]
June 4	ACD and others were arrested for shooting at a spring buck; they were released when their names had been taken, ACD played billiards in the evening. [494]
June 5	ACD at the Langman Hospital, South African Field Force, Bloemfontein. [18,884,1244]
June 5	Pretoria, the capital of the Transvaal captured by the British. [180]
June 14	ACD gave Blasson a cheque for £5:5s for doing his work for him. [494]
June 16	*Sherlock Holmes* completed its run of 256 performances at the Garrick Theatre, New York; it was then taken on tour from October 1900 – 30 March 1901. [322,323]
June 22	ACD left by train and visited Pretoria. [7,10,322] (*5)
June 23	ACD left Bloemfontein for Pretoria. [203,215] (*5)
June 23	ACD visited Pretoria. [3] (*5)
June 24	ACD left Bloemfontein for Pretoria. [494] (*5)
June	ACD visited Johannesburg. [7]
June 27	ACD visited Pretoria. [203] (*5)
June 27	ACD was granted an interview by Lord Roberts. [99,215]
June	At the end of June ACD met Lord Roberts in Pretoria. [2,202]
n.d.	Birth of Branford Bryan Angell son of Cyril and Bryan Mary (Dodo) Angell. [202] (*2)
July 2	Birth of Bryan Branford Angell born, only son of Cyril and Bryan Mary (Dodo) Angell. [68,124,200] (*2)
July 3	ACD returned from Pretoria. [494]
July 4	ACD returned to Bloemfontein. [7,10,202,322]
July 5	ACD left Bloemfontein [1246] for Cape Town. [322]
July 6	ACD at the Langman Hospital, South African Field Force. [203]
July 6	ACD left Bloemfontein to return to England. [4,494]
July 6	*Mr. Burdett-Coutts's Charges* published in *The Times*. [198]
July 7	*Mr. Burdett-Coutts's Charges* published in the *British Medical Journal* as *The War in South Africa. The Epidemic of Enteric Fever at Bloemfontein.* [6,196,198]
July 7–10	ACD at the Mount Nelson Hotel, Cape Town where he met Lord Milner. [2]
July	ACD sailed from South Africa on board the SS *Briton* and returned to England. [15,202] (*2)
July 11	ACD sailed from Cape Town, South Africa on the liner the SS *Briton* (*2) during this return trip to England ACD met Bertram Fletcher Robinson. [2,3,6,7,10,14,15,124,202,203,215,322] (*2)
July 27	ACD arrived in Southampton on board the Union Castle Company's steamer *Briton* from Cape Town. [1245] (*2)

1900

July	Late July ACD was back in London. [202]
July 28	ACD and Bertram Fletcher Robinson arrived in Southampton on board the SS *Briton*. [79] (*2)
n.d.	ACD appeared as a witness in front of the independent South African Hospital Commission. [202] (*2)
July 30	ACD was questioned before the South African Hospitals Commission at Burlington Gardens, London. [322,1247] (*2)
August	*An Impression of the Regency* published in *Frank Leslie's Popular Monthly*. [6,99,198]
August	Early August ACD arrived home. [203]
August	ACD rejoined his family at Undershaw. [14,15]
August	ACD back home at Undershaw. [124]
August 8	ACD played cricket on 8 & 9 for MCC against Hertfordshire at Lord's; he scored 1, match drawn. [235]
August 9	ACD was busily engaged in completing his history of the Boer War. [1248]
n.d.	ACD stayed at Morley's Hotel, Cockspur Street, London. [215] {Note: Morley's Hotel was actually located at Trafalgar Square.}
August 13	ACD played cricket on 13 & 14 for MCC against Buckinghamshire at Lord's; he scored 6 and took 3 wickets, MCC won. [235]
August 15	ACD played cricket on 15 & 16 for MCC against Wiltshire at Lord's; he scored 34 and 3, Wiltshire won. [235,497]
August 17	ACD played cricket on 17 & 18 for MCC against Cambridgeshire at Lord's, he scored 33 and 6, he took 1 wicket, match drawn. [235,1249]
August 18	It was announced that ACD would attend the unveiling of the Admiral Blake statue at Bridgewater followed by a dinner at the Town Hall on 4 October. [498] {Note: reports of the unveiling do not include ACD as attending.}
August 21	It was announced that the marriage between Captain Leslie Oldham of the Royal Engineers, Jubbulpore, Central Providences, India and Caroline Mary (Lottie), daughter of the late Charles Altamont Doyle, artist, and sister of Dr A. Conan Doyle will be celebrated on Monday next, 27 August, at Dagshai in the Himalayas. [499]
August 23	ACD played a first class cricket match on 23, 24 & 25 for MCC against London County at Crystal Palace Park, there was no play on the first day; he scored 4 and zero and took the wicket of W G Grace, who had scored 110, this being his only first class wicket, MCC won. In this match ACD made his debut in First-Class Matches and. [56,71,202,235,322]
August 27	ACD at Undershaw. [203]
August	Caroline (Lottie) Doyle, ACD's sister, married Captain Leslie Oldham in India. [202] (*2)
August 27	Caroline (Lottie) Doyle, ACD's sister, married Leslie Searles Oldham. [16,68,200,203] Captain in the Royal Engineers; they married at Nagpur, India, [124] (*2) or at Jubbulpore {now known as Jabalpur}, India. [787]
n.d.	ACD wrote *The Great Boer War*. [99]
August 29	ACD played cricket for Haslemere against Northchapel at Lythe Park and scored 78. [63]
September	*Days with the Army* published in *The Strand Magazine* as *A Glimpse of the Army*. [6,194,195,196,198]
September	ACD at Undershaw. [203]
September	ACD played cricket for Haslemere against Northchapel. [34]
September 1	ACD played cricket for Haslemere against Petersfield at Lythe Park and took 8 wickets. [63]
September	ACD was adopted as the Liberal Unionist candidate for Edinburgh Central. [322]
September 8	It was announced that the Edinburgh Unionists had decided to invite Dr Conan Doyle to contest one of the divisions of the city. [500]

1900

September 15	It was announced that Lieutenant J.F.I. Doyle (Innes) was promoted to the rank of Captain. [501]
September 21	ACD at 27 Rue des Batignolles, Paris. [884]
September 24	ACD at Dunard, Grange Loan, Edinburgh. [18]
September 24	ACD arrived in Edinburgh and was adopted as the Unionist candidate. [502]
September 24	ACD was adopted by the Central Edinburgh Liberal Union Association as their candidate in the contest against Mr G.M. Brown for Edinburgh Central. [202,1250]
September 24	ACD made speech accepting the nomination as Conservative and Liberal Unionist candidate for the Central Division of Edinburgh. [3,6,15]
September	Between 25 September & 24 October the UK General Election took place. [976]
September 26	ACD addressed a meeting at St. Paul's Hall, St. Leonards Street, Edinburgh. [503]
September	ACD spoke at the Operetta House, Edinburgh; he did 14 speeches in 3 days. [215]
September 28	ACD addressed a meeting of bakers at the works of Young Brothers, Pleasance and in the evening addressed a meeting at the Operetta House, Edinburgh as the Unionist candidate. [504]
September	*Some Military Lessons of the War* published in *The Cornhill Magazine*. [202] (*2)
October	ACD at the Old Waverley Hotel, Edinburgh. [18,203]
October	ACD at Undershaw. [18]
October	*Some Military Lessons of the War* published in *The Cornhill Magazine*. [6,196,198] (*2)
October 1	Dr Joseph Bell shared the platform with ACD at the Literary Institute in Edinburgh to lend his support to ACD as prospective Union candidate. [14,31,215] (*2)
n.d.	ACD stood as Liberal Unionist Party parliamentary candidate for Central Edinburgh [180] ACD an unsuccessful Liberal Unionist parliamentary candidate for Edinburgh central. [99]
October 4	ACD stood for Parliament for Central Edinburgh. [200]
October 4	The UK General Elections took place in Edinburgh Central where ACD was an unsuccessful candidate. [977]
n.d.	ACD was an unsuccessful Liberal Unionist parliamentary candidate for Edinburgh Central. [99] (*2)
October	ACD was an unsuccessful Liberal Unionist parliamentary candidate for Central Edinburgh [14] (*2) the count was, G.M. Brown (L) 3,028 and A. Conan Doyle 2,459 [3,6,15,1251] he lost by 569 votes. [180,215]
October 8	It was announced that ACD had left Edinburgh for Manchester. [505]
October 9	ACD at Reform Club, London. [884]
October 13	ACD at the Reform Club, London. [18,202]
October 16	ACD at Undershaw. [203]
October 17	ACD at Undershaw. [18]
October 22	ACD attended a dinner of the Authors' Club; the chair was occupied by Mr Rider Haggard. [506]
n.d.	*The Great Boer War* published. [180,202] (*2)
October 23	*The Great Boer War* published by Smith, Elder, & Co., London. [6] (*2)
October 25	ACD made a speech "Mr Winston Churchill and Dr Conan Doyle on the War" at the annual dinner of the Pall Mall Club, St. James [3,6,15,79,202,203] at St. James's Square. [322]
November	ACD at the Reform Club, Pall Mall, London. [18]
November	ACD at Undershaw. [18]
November 5	ACD chaired a meeting for Winston Churchill at the Pall Club, St. James's Hall, London. [202] (*2)

1900

November 5	ACD attended a lecture by Winston Churchill titled 'The War As I Saw It' held at St. James's Hall, London. [507] (*2)
November 11	Alfred H. Wood visited Undershaw. [123]
November 12	ACD made a speech on the war as Chairman of the Authors' Club at a dinner [6,322,1972] ACD attended a dinner at the Authors' Club at Whitehall Court, London. [508] (*2)
November 13	ACD made a speech on the war as Chairman of the Authors' Club at a dinner. [7] (*2)
November 15	ACD presided at the opening banquet of the Vagabond Club [1252] ACD attended a dinner at the opening of the New Vagabond Club at the Holborn Restaurant, London. [509]
December	ACD at Undershaw. [18]
December 15	*A Gaudy Death* published in *Tit-Bits*. [198]
December 15	ACD attended the New Vagabond Club Christmas banquet at the Hotel Cecil [1253] ACD attended a dinner of the New Vagabond Club at the Hotel Cecil, London. [510]
December 17	ACD presided at a meeting of the Authors' Club [1254] ACD attended a dinner at the Authors' Club at Whitehall Court, London. [511]
Late 1900	ACD formed the Undershaw Rifle Club. [3,6,14,202,203,215,322] (*2)
Christmas	ACD at Undershaw. [203]
December 29	It was reported that ACD was hard at work starting a shooting club and range near his house at Hindhead, and he had already secured nearly 100 members. [512]

1901

n.d.	ACD formed the Undershaw Rifle Club [7,10] launched the Undershaw Rifle Club. [203] (*2)
n.d.	Dr Joseph Bell shared platform and supported ACD as prospective Union candidate at Edinburgh. [4,10] (*2)
January	ACD spent three days at the Ashdown Forest Hotel, Forest Row, Sussex. [203]
January	ACD at Undershaw. [18,203]
January	*The Military Lessons of the War: A Rejoinder* published in *The Cornhill Magazine*. [6,196,198]
January	Innes posted to Peking. [99]
January	ACD addressed the members of the Whitefriars Club on "The Art of Fiction". [1824]
January 6	Josephine Ratcliff Hoare visited Undershaw. [123]
January 14	Claire Foley, daughter of Nelson and Jane (Ida) visited Undershaw. [123]
n.d.	Birth of Nina Mdivani. [200] (*2)
January 27	Birth of Nina Mdivani future wife of Denis Conan Doyle. [964] (*2)
February	ACD at Undershaw. [203]
February 11	ACD presided at a meeting of the Authors' Club where Mr John Langman was the chief guest. [513]
March	*Strange Studies from Life: I The Holocaust of Manor Place* published in *The Strand Magazine*. [6,194,195,196,198]
March 2	Herbert John Bennett was found guilty and sentenced to death at the Old Bailey for the murder of his wife, the trial commenced on 25 February and at some time ACD did attend the trial. [514]
March 8	It was announced that ACD arrived in Torquay last week. [515] {Note: no further information on this visit located.}
March 8	ACD became a member of the Athenaeum Club, London. [79,202]
March 9	ACD made a speech made at Hindhead Hall on the war [6,1255] he was presented with a silver rose bowl inscribed 'Arthur Conan Doyle, who at a great crisis – in word and in deed – served his country'. [6,79,202,322]
March	ACD took a short holiday with Bertram Fletcher Robinson at the Royal Links Hotel, Cromer, Norfolk. [3,6,14,15,20,21,49,203,215] (*7)

1901

March	ACD wrote to Greenhough Smith at *The Strand*, saying he that he had a 'real creeper' of a story to sell him. [215]
March	ACD gave a dinner at the Athenaeum Club, London; guests included J.M. Barrie, Winston Churchill and Anthony Hope. [3,203]
Mid-March	ACD spent several days with his mother at the Ashdown Forest Hotel, Forest Row, Sussex. [79] (*2)
March 16–17	ACD spent the weekend at the Ashdown Forest Hotel, Forest Row, Sussex [202] (*2) or Ashdown Park Hotel. [322]
March 21	Herbert John Bennett was hanged at Norwich Prison by James Billington assisted by his son Thomas Billington. [169]
March 23	ACD in Edinburgh. [79]
March 23	In the afternoon ACD was admitted as an honorary member of the Lodge of Edinburgh (St. Mary's Chapel) No. 1. [516]
March 23	ACD was the guest of honour at The Edinburgh Burns Club evening dinner at the Balmoral Hotel, Edinburgh; he proposed the main toast, "The Immortal Memory". [4,6,79,99,203,517]
March 24	ACD in Edinburgh. [79]
n.d.	ACD accepted an honorary membership in The Lodge of Edinburgh (Mary's Chapel) No. 1 (96 George Street) Edinburgh. [68] (*3)
March 24	ACD made a speech "Dr Conan Doyle and the Freemasons" on being received as an honorary member of St. Mary's Chapel, No 1, Edinburgh, The Grand Lodge of Scotland. [6,8,14] (*3)
March 25	ACD accepted an honorary membership in The Lodge of Edinburgh (Mary's Chapel) No. 1 (96 George Street, Edinburgh. [200] (*3)
March 25	*The Edinburgh Burns Club Dinner. Address by Dr. Conan Doyle* published in *The Scotsman*. [198]
March 31	Bryan Charles Waller and his wife Ada were at Masongill House, Thornton in Lonsdale, Yorkshire. [218]
March 31	ACD, Jean Leckie and Mary J. Doyle (ACD's mother) stayed at the Ashdown Forest Hotel, Forest Row, Sussex [68,83,200,218] or the Ashdown Park Hotel. [322]
March 31	Louise Conan Doyle and her mother Emily Hawkins stayed at The Boltons Boarding House, Torquay. [68,83,200,218,322]
March 31	Mary Conan Doyle and Kingsley Conan Doyle (daughter and son of ACD) at Undershaw, Hindhead, Surrey being taken care of by Louise's sister Emily Hawkins. [68,83,200,218,322]
March 31	Bryan (Dodo) Mary Angell (ACD's sister) stayed at Whitesmith Buildings, Hawksdale near Carlisle with her 8 month old son and sister in law Julia Angell [68,200]
March 31	Charles Cyril Angell (husband of Bryan Mary) was a boarder at Hindhead School, Churt, Surrey. [68,83,200]
March 31	Willie and Constance (Connie) Hornung with their son Arthur Oscar were at 9 Pitt Street, Kensington, London. [218]
March 31	James Leckie with his wife Selina and sons Malcolm and Patrick were living at Glebe House, The Glebe, Lee. [218]
March	At the end of the month, ACD was staying at Rowe's Duchy Hotel, Princetown, Dartmoor with Fletcher Robinson researching for *The Hound of the Baskervilles*. [6] (*6)
April	*Strange Studies from Life: II The Love Affair of George Vincent Parker* published in *The Strand Magazine*. [6,194,195,196,198]
April	ACD at Undershaw. [18]
April	*The Immortal Memory* printed by R. Mitchell and Sons, Edinburgh for private circulation. [6]
April	ACD and Bertram Fletcher Robinson stayed at Rowe's Duchy Hotel, Princetown, Dartmoor, Devon. [203] (*6)

1901

April 2	ACD stayed at Rowe's Duchy Hotel, Princetown, Devon, writing *The Hound of the Baskervilles* with the assistance of Bertram Fletcher Robinson. [3,21,31,49,215] (*6)
April 8	It was announced that ACD was a financial donor to The Society of Authors Pension Fund. [518]
April 18	It was announced in *The Times* that ACD was part of the organising committee for a dinner given to Sir John Tenniel to be held on 12 June. [1256]
April 23	It was reported that ACD had accepted the post of one of the stewards at the Dinner of the Society of Authors to be held on 1 May at the King's Hall of the Holborn Restaurant. [1257]
April	At the end of April, ACD and Bertram Fletcher Robinson stayed in Cromer. [46] (*7)
April 26	From April 26 to 30, ACD and Bertram Fletcher Robinson stayed at the Royal Links Hotel, Cromer, Norfolk [57] (*7), they booked out on Tuesday 30 April [16], ACD then made his way to London. [185]
April 26–29	ACD stayed for four days at Cromer, Norfolk with Bertram Fletcher Robinson. [99] (*7)
April 27	It was announced that ACD would accompany a party of American and Colonial visitors, members of the Atlantic Union, who will be shown round The Temple, Portsmouth on 4 May. [519] {Note: no report of this event located.}
April 27	From April 27 to 30, ACD and Bertram Fletcher Robinson stayed at the Royal Links Hotel, Cromer, Norfolk [57] April 27-28. [202] (*7)
April 28	ACD and Bertram Fletcher Robinson stayed at the Royal Links Hotel, Cromer, Norfolk [61] (*7) on a golfing holiday. [322]
April 28	ACD and Bertram Fletcher Robinson stayed at the Royal Links Hotel, Cromer, Norfolk [79,62]. (*7) On Sunday the breeze was blowing too strongly to play golf [61], this could have been when they started to discuss *The Hound of the Baskervilles*, from the hotel, ACD wrote to his mother 'Fletcher Robinson came here with me and we are going to do a small book together The Hound of the Baskervilles---a real creeper.' [79]
April 28	From the Royal Links Hotel he wrote to Greenhough Smith, the editor of *The Strand Magazine*, with the stipulation that my friend Fletcher Robinson's name must appear with mine. ACD requested £50 per thousand words. [79]
April 30	ACD gave a dinner at the Athenaeum Club, London; one of the guests was Winston Churchill. [61,322]
May	*The Great Boer War* published in *The Wide World Magazine* from May 1901 to June 1902. [6,198,322]
May	*Strange Studies from Life: III The Debatable Case of Mrs. Emsley* published in *The Strand Magazine*. [6,194,195,196,198]
May	ACD wrote to Greenhough Smith asking for £100 per thousand words if Sherlock Holmes was the principle character in *The Hound of the Baskervilles*. [79]
May	ACD at the Athenaeum, Pall Mall, London, S.W. [18]
May 1	The annual dinner of the Society of Authors was held at the Kings Hall of the Holborn Restaurant, London. [1258] {Note: ACD might have attended, see 18 April, but he is not mentioned in the report of the dinner.}
May 8	ACD attended a dinner at Gray's Inn The Master of the Bench. [1259]
May 16	Mr & Mrs Charles Cyril Angell visited Undershaw, as did Laura Hornung (wife of John Peter [Pitt] Hornung). [123]
May 16	ACD played a first class cricket match on 16, 17 & 18 for MCC against Leicestershire at Lord's [63,1260], he scored 1 and then 32 not out, MCC won. [235]
May 16	ACD had supper with Winston Churchill at the House of Commons, London. [79]
May 20	ACD presided at a Ladies Dinner given by the Authors' Club [84] at the Hotel Cecil. [1261]

1901

May 20	ACD played cricket for the Allahakbarries against the Artists at Kensington Park [63] at St. Quintin's Park, Kensington, he scored 91 and took 8 wickets, the Allahakbarries won. [235]
May 23	ACD played a first class cricket match on 23 & 24 for MCC against Derbyshire at Lord's the match was scheduled for 3 days but was completed in 2 days [63,1262] he scored 28, MCC won. [235]
May 25	*Tit-Bits*, the sister publication to *The Strand Magazine* announced that 'presently [Mr Conan Doyle] will give us an important story to appear in the Strand, in which the great Sherlock Holmes is the principle character'. [61,202]
May 25	ACD arrived at the railway station at Newton Abbot, Devon where he was collected by Henry (Harry) Baskerville and taken to Park Hill House, Ipplepen. [185]
May 26	ACD was staying at Park Hill House Ipplepen, the home of Bertram Fletcher Robinson, ACD probably attended church with Fletcher Robinson and family. [185]
May 27	Probably on 27, 28, 29 and 30 May, ACD and Fletcher Robinson toured Dartmoor gathering information for *The Hound of the Baskervilles*, they were driven by Henry (Harry) Baskerville. [185]
Late May	Nearly half of *The Hound of the Baskervilles* was written – that is approximately 25,000 words. [79]
May 30	ACD was elected as honorary member of The Portsmouth Literary and Scientific Society (PLSS). [520]
May 31	ACD and Fletcher Robinson visited Dartmoor, probably stayed at Rowe's Duchy Hotel, Princetown. [185] (*6)
May	End of May, ACD visited Dartmoor with Bertram Fletcher Robinson. [46]
June	*A British Commando. An Interview with Conan Doyle* by Captain Philip Trevor published in *The Strand Magazine*. [6,194,195,198,203,322]
June	ACD drafted the second half of *The Hound of the Baskervilles*. [80]
June 1	ACD almost halfway through writing *The Hound of the Baskervilles*. [202]
June 1	ACD probably visited the mighty bog on Dartmoor. [61]
June 1	ACD and Bertram Fletcher Robinson were staying at Rowe's Duchy Hotel, Princetown, Dartmoor. [63,80] (*6)
June 1	ACD wrote a letter (postmarked Sunday 2 June) to his mother saying that he owed Fletcher Robinson the idea of the Hound and that they did 14 miles over the Moor. He also states that tomorrow (Sunday) we drive 6 miles to Ipplepen where R's (Fletcher Robinson) parents live. He then goes onto give details of his plans for the next few days. [61]
June 2	ACD and Bertram Fletcher Robinson were staying at Rowe's Duchy Hotel, Princetown, Dartmoor. [61] (*6)
June 2	ACD probably visited Ipplepen home of the parents of Fletcher Robinson, and stayed overnight. [185]
June 2	ACD visited Ipplepen home of the parents of Bertram Fletcher Robinson. [61,80]
June 3	ACD probably left Ipplepen driven by Henry (Harry) Baskerville for Newton Abbot Railway Station and caught a train for Sherborne. [185]
June 3	ACD played cricket on 3 & 4 for Incogniti against Sherborne School [61,63,80,202], at Sherborne School, he scored 11 and took 4 wickets in first innings and 3 in second innings, match drawn, A.H. Wood played for Incogniti, he scored 57 and took 3 wickets. [186,235]
June 5	ACD played cricket on 5 & 6 for Incogniti against Lansdown at Coombe Park, Bath [61,80] or Combe Park [63] or Lansdown Cricket Club Ground, Combe Park, Bath, he scored 5 and took 2 wickets, match drawn, A.H. Wood played for Incogniti, he scored 36 and took 2 wickets. [235]
June 6	There is a payment in ACD's bankbook, to Fletcher Robinson – one of many, varying in amount, over the next three years – of £3. [61]

1901

June 7	ACD played cricket on 7 & 8 for Incogniti against Cheltenham College at the College Ground, Cheltenham [61,63,80] he scored 23 and 13, he took 1 wicket, match drawn [187,235] A.H. Wood played for Incogniti, he scored 38 and 20 and took 5 wickets. [22,36]
June 10	ACD back home at Undershaw, Hindhead, Surrey. [61,63]
June	ACD stayed at Morley's Hotel, Trafalgar Square, London while playing cricket at Lord's [80]
June 13	ACD played cricket on 13 & 14 for MCC against W.G. Grace's team at Lord's [63] against London County. [202,1263] (*2)
June 13	ACD played a first class cricket match on 13 & 14 for MCC against London County at Lord's, the match was scheduled for 3 days but was completed in 2 days, he scored 21 not out and 10, London County won. [235] (*2)
June 15	It was reported that Dr A. Conan Doyle was staying at the Queen's Hotel, Cheltenham. [521] {Note: ACD played cricket at Cheltenham on 7 & 8 June, so the report is most likely referring to that period.}
June 17	The proof of the second instalment of *The Hound of the Baskervilles* returned, 'The Problem/Sir Henry Baskerville' (chapters 3 & 4) ACD informed the editor of *The Strand Magazine* that the third instalment was nearly finished (chapters 5 & 6). [80]
June 17	ACD played cricket on 17 & 18 for MCC against Minor Counties at Lord's [56] he scored 7 and 8 and took 2 wickets, Minor Counties won. [235]
June 21	ACD played cricket for the Authors against the Artists in Esher [63] at New Road, Esher, he scored 2 and took 5 wickets, the Artists won. [235]
June 24	ACD sent the fourth and fifth instalments to of *The Hound of the Baskervilles* ('The Stapletons of Merripit' to 'The Light on the Moor' chapters 7 & 8) to *The Strand Magazine*. [79]
June 24	ACD played cricket on 24 & 25 for MCC against the Grange Club at Lord's, he scored 4 and 1 [63,1264] Gentlemen of MCC against Grange Club, Grange won. [235]
June 26	ACD played cricket for the Gentlemen of Marylebone Cricket Club against the Royal Navy at Lord's; he scored 31, The Gentlemen won. [63,235]
June 29	ACD played cricket for MCC against the Royal Military College at Camberley [63] at Royal Military Academy Ground, Camberley, he scored zero, match drawn. [235]
June	At the end of June the fourth and fifth instalments (chapters 7 to 9) of *The Hound of the Baskervilles* sent to *The Strand Magazine*. [80]
July 4	ACD made a hot air balloon ascent with Percival Spencer on board the *City of York* from Crystal Palace. They reached a height of 6,000 feet and landed 25 miles away outside of Sevenoaks, Kent. [98] The flight took 1 hour 45 minutes and reached a maximum altitude of 6,500 feet the balloon landed at Kemsing near Sevenoaks, Kent. [99,203] (*2)
July	ACD attended a dinner at the Devonshire Club to honour Mr Langman. [1825]
July	Jean Leckie won a bronze medal as a vocalist in the London Academy of Music's public examination, her friend Lily Loder-Symonds was awarded a silver medal for her harp playing. [202]
July 10	ACD attended a dinner given by the Liberal Unionist Association in London [1265] at the Criterion Restaurant, London. [522]
July 12	ACD at Undershaw. [884]
July n.d.	ACD played cricket for Hampshire Rovers against R.M.A. at the Officers' Ground, Portsmouth, he scored 10 and took 4 wickets, R.M.A. won. [523] (*2)
July 17	ACD played cricket for Hampshire Rovers against Royal Marines at Royal Marines Ground, Eastney, Southsea, he scored 10 and took 4 wickets, match drawn. [235] (*2)
July 18	It was reported in *The Times* that The Undershaw Rifle Club (Hindhead, Haslemere) of which ACD was the President and had 186 members and was affiliated to the National Rifle Association. [322,1266]

1901

July 19	On 19 & 20 ACD played cricket for Hampshire Rovers against United Services at United Services Ground, Portsmouth; he scored 24 and 25, match drawn, A.H. Wood played for Hampshire Rovers, he scored 83 and 23 and took 3 catches. [235,524]
n.d.	ACD and Louise spent four days in Southsea. [203]
July 24	ACD attended a dinner at the Hotel Cecil, London. [1267]
August	*The Hound of the Baskervilles* published in *The Strand Magazine* from August 1901 to April 1902. [6,194,195,196,198,322] (*2)
n.d.	*The Hound of the Baskervilles* published in *The Strand Magazine*. [99,180] (*2)
August 5	Alfred H. Wood visited Undershaw. [123]
August 9	ACD played cricket on 9 & 10 for MCC against Norfolk at County Ground, Lakeham [63] he scored 16 and took 4 wickets, the match was drawn [235], Jean Leckie was staying not far away at the Marlborough Hotel in Southwold. [202]
August 13	Ida Foley and her son, Percy, visited Undershaw. [123]
August 14	ACD played cricket on 14 & 15 for MCC against Dorsetshire at Lord's, he scored 4 not out and took 1 wicket, match drawn. [63,235]
August 15	Claire Foley joined her mother and brother at Undershaw. [123]
August 16	ACD played cricket on 16 & 17 for MCC against Wiltshire at Lord's [63,1268] and scored 4 not out and 33, he took 1 wicket, Wiltshire won. [235]
August 22	William Gillette arrived in Liverpool and then travelled to London. [525]
August 23	ACD played cricket on 23 & 24 for MCC against Oxfordshire at Lord's [1269] and scored 31 not out and zero, he took 2 wickets, MCC won. [235]
August 31	ACD played cricket for MCC against London Playing Fields at Lord's, he scored 53, match drawn [63,235,1270]
September	*Boer Critics on 'The Great Boer War'* published in *The Cornhill Magazine*. [6,196,198]
September	ACD at Undershaw. [18]
September	ACD at the Athenaeum, Pall Mall, London, S.W. [18]
September 2	The play *Sherlock Holmes* opened in Liverpool [322] from 2-8 September [323] 2-7 September. [6]
September 9	The play *Sherlock Holmes* starring William Gillette was performed at the Lyceum Theatre, London; Charles Chaplin appeared as the page [31,78,184,202,215,322] from 9 September-11 April 1902. [6]
September 14	ACD was a judge at a competition to find the man with the world's best physique held at the Royal Albert Hall, London [202,1271] the Sandow Competition named after the pioneering bodybuilder Eugen Sandow [322] ACD, Eugen Sandow and Sir Charles Lawes were the judges and the winner was W.L. Murray (Nottingham), second D. Cooper (Warwick) and third A.C. Smith (Middlesex) [1772]
October	*A Hunting Morning* published *Current Literature,* New York. [6,198]
October 26	ACD attended the opening of a drill hall for the 5th West Middlesex R.V. Regiment at Hendon. [1272]
October	ACD was a Director of Raphael Tuck & Sons, Ltd. [202,1272]
n.d.	ACD had taken rooms the Authors' Club at 2 Whitehall Court, London. [203]
n.d.	ACD at 16 Buckingham Street, WC, London. [203]
November	ACD was at the Reform Club, London. [203]
November 4	ACD attended and spoke at a dinner at the Authors' Club, E.W. Hornung also attended. [1273]
November 12	ACD made a speech "Typhoid and the Army" at the Royal United Service Institution. [6,203]
November 28	ACD attended the national Thanksgiving Day dinner with the American Society at the Hotel Cecil, London. [1990]
December	ACD purchased one of few hundred privately printed copies of *The Tale of Peter Rabbit* by Beatrix Potter. [1147]

1901

December 1	ACD attended and delivered an address at the annual sacred service in connection with the Edinburgh, Leith and Granton Lifeboat Fund held at the Edinburgh Palace Theatre. [526]
December 2	ACD attended and proposed the toast of "The Imperial Forces" at a dinner in Edinburgh. [527]
December 6	ACD was in Edinburgh for the annual Walter Scott Club dinner. [322]
December 25	The American Members of the company performing *Sherlock Holmes* at the Lyceum spent Christmas Day at Undershaw. [528]
December 27	ACD at Undershaw. [203]

1902

n.d.	ACD made a speech at a Centenary dinner for Madame Tussaud's. [25]
n.d.	ACD rejoined The Freemason Phoenix Lodge No 257, Portsmouth. [8,68,97,200]
n.d.	ACD made a hot air balloon ascent from Crystal Palace in South London and landed at Sevenoaks in Kent. [4,14,15,215] (*2)
n.d.	ACD's daughter, Mary, was sent to Prior's Field boarding school, Godalming, Surrey. [124,202]
n.d.	ACD invited to dine with Lord Roseberry. [203]
n.d.	ACD invited to dine with Lady Jeune to meet Princess Christian. [203]
January	ACD at Undershaw. [203]
January 7	ACD attended one of Sir Henry Thompson's famous 'octave' dinners in London. [4,10,202]
January 7	*The War in South Africa – Its Cause and Conduct* conceived. [6]
January 9	ACD commenced writing *The War in South Africa – Its Cause and Conduct*. [6]
n.d.	*The War in South Africa: its Cause and Conduct* published. [180]
January 16	*The War in South Africa – Its Cause and Conduct* published by Smith, Elder, & Co., London. [6,202,322]
January 21	ACD attended the AGM of Raphael Tuck & Son at Winchester House, London. [1274]
January 22	ACD attended a dinner with Joseph Chamberlain. [4,203]
January 28	ACD at Undershaw. [2053]
January 30	ACD attended a performance of a play titled *Sherlock Holmes* by William Gillette at the Lyceum Theatre, London, staged for King Edward VII and Queen Alexandra, ACD appeared on the stage with William Gillette after the final act. [78]
January 30	ACD at the Athenaeum Club, London, S.W. [18]
January 31	ACD at Undershaw. [18]
February	ACD at Undershaw. [18,203]
February	Innes with the 79th Battery Harrismith, Orange River Colony. [203]
February 6	ACD at the Athenaeum Club, London. [884] {Note: this letter was dated incorrectly as 16 February by *The Times*.}
February	ACD was awarded life membership to the Nova Scotia Historical Society for his patriotic work for the Empire. [322] (*2)
February 10	ACD at the Athenaeum Club, London. [1275]
February 11	ACD was elected a life member of Nova Scotia Historical Society in recognition of patriotic for the Empire in writing *The War in South Africa: Its Cause and Conduct*. [529] (*2)
February 20	ACD at Undershaw. [18,203]
March	ACD at Undershaw. [18]
March 1	ACD at Undershaw. [203]
March 10	ACD at Undershaw. [884]
March 10	ACD attended a dinner at the Authors' Club. [1991]
March 11	ACD was one of many guests at the opening night of the play *The Princess' Nose* by Henry Arthur Jones at the Duke of York's Theatre, London. [322]

1902

March 14	Jean Leckie's birthday, ACD and Jean spent it together. [203]
March 17	ACD attended and addressed the National Sporting Club anniversary dinner at the National Sporting Club, Covent Garden, London. [2086]
March 25	*The Hound of the Baskervilles* published by George Newnes Ltd., London. [6,322]
March 26	ACD physically and mentally exhausted, his doctor ordered him to rest. [78]
March 26	ACD in a letter, postmarked 26 March, to William Gillette, ACD states that he intends going on a voyage on 11 April. [78]
April	ACD was notified that he would receive a knighthood in the forthcoming Honours List. [4,203]
April 9	ACD at the Athenaeum Club, London. [18]
April	ACD travelled on board the RMS *Austral* from Tilbury for Naples to visit Nelson and Ida Foley on Gaiola [215] (*2), while in Italy ACD began work on the *Brigadier Gerard* stories. [215]
April 10	ACD sailed for Naples, Italy on board RMS *Austral* [3] sailed from Tilbury near London. [78,202] (*2)
April	ACD on board the RMS. *Austral*. [203]
April 11	The play *Sherlock Holmes* completed its run at the Lyceum Theatre, London. [6] (*2)
April 12	The play *Sherlock Holmes* completed its run of 216 performances at the Lyceum Theatre, London. [322,323] (*2)
April 17	ACD on board RMS *Austral*. [2053]
April 20	ACD on the island at Naples. [203]
April	ACD visited Nelson and Jane (Ida) Foley on Gaiola. [124]
April	ACD took a few weeks holiday with Ida and Nelson Foley on their little island of Gaiola in the Gulf of Gaeta [4,14] and afterwards went to Sicily, Venice, the Italian lakes and Switzerland. [4]
April – May	ACD stayed with Nelson and Jane (Ida) Foley on the Island in the Bay of Naples. [3,202]
May 7	ACD probably left Naples travelling to Florence, Milan, Venice, Como, Maloja, St. Moritz, Davos, Zurich, Divonne and Paris to London. [203]
May	ACD returned to England towards the end of May. [3] (*2)
May 26	The play *Sherlock Holmes* was performed in Liverpool between 26 and 31 May. [322,323]
May 28	ACD probably arrived home at Undershaw. [203]
May 31	ACD returned to England. [202] (*2)
June	ACD at Undershaw. [203]
June 1	Lottie Oldham (ACD's sister) visited Undershaw. [123]
n.d.	ACD at Hall Barn, Beaconsfield, Bucks. [203]
June	ACD was offered the position of one of the Deputy Lord Lieutenants of the County of Surrey. [203]
June	ACD played cricket for the Authors against Royal Engineers at Chatham, he took 5 wickets. [202,1146]
June	ACD at the Athenaeum, Pall Mall, London. [18]
June 2	The following announcement appeared in the Classified Adverts in *The Times*: Dr Conan Doyle would be much obliged to any officers or their relatives who would forward him PARTICULARS of ACTIONS in SOUTH AFRICA during the LAST SIX MONTHS. Such documents would be treated as confidential, and returned. Address Undershaw, Hindhead. (This was intended to help ACD in gathering material for the preparation of a further, updated impression of his book: *The Great Boer War* (Smith, Elder & Co.), which had initially been published on 23 October 1900. The 17th impression was published on 11 October 1902). [1276]
June	ACD may have attended the two-day cricket match between England and Australia at Lord's on 12 and 13 June. [203]
June 14	ACD at Undershaw. [203]

1902

n.d.	ACD at the Golden Cross Hotel, Charing Cross, London. [203]
June 16	ACD took the chair at a dinner at the Authors' Club at Whitehall Court, London. [1277]
June 20	ACD received a letter from Lord Salisbury confirming that he would receive a knighthood [4] ACD accepted the knighthood with reluctance. [15]
June 23	ACD played a first class cricket match on 23 & 24 for MCC against Derbyshire at Lord's the match was scheduled for 3 days but was completed in 2 days [1278], he scored zero and did not bat in second innings, MCC won. [235]
June 26	It was announced in *The Times* that ACD would receive a knighthood; he was listed as A. Conan Doyle, Esq., M.D. [1279]
June 30	ACD played cricket for the Authors against the Artists at Esher, Surrey, the Artists won [322] at New Road, Esher, he scored 13 and did not bat in the second innings, and took 3 wickets, match drawn. [235]
July 3	ACD and Louise attended a reception given by Sir Henry Irving on stage at the Lyceum Theatre, London, the guests numbered upwards of 500. [1280]
July 11	ACD and Louise attended a reception to meet the Colonial Premiers at Grafton Galleries, London. [1281]
July 11	ACD was gazetted to be Deputy Lieutenant of the County of Surrey. [530]
July 14	ACD played a first class cricket match on 14, 15 & 16 for MCC against London County at Crystal Palace Park [1282], ACD scored 43 and zero. ACD passed his previous highest First Class score of 32, London County won [235] W.G. Grace played for London County and scored 131. [1282]
July 14	ACD and W.G. Grace witnessed the first lady to navigate an airship, Mrs Stanley Spencer, she successfully navigated the Merlin airship around the polo ground at the Crystal Palace. [1076]
July 17	ACD as a director attended the first annual general meeting of Raphael Tuck & Sons (Ltd.) at Salisbury House, Finsbury Circus. [1283]
July 17	ACD presided at a meeting of the New Vagabond Club at the Criterion Restaurant, London. [1283]
July 25	ACD played cricket on 25 & 26 for the Gentlemen of Marylebone Cricket Club against Royal Engineers at Lord's and scored 1 and took 2 wickets and 1 catch, MCC won. [235,1284]
July 25	The Athenaeum Club entertained at dinner the members of the Order of Merit, ACD attended with among others including Lord Roberts, J.M. Barrie, Sir Henry Irving and Rudyard Kipling. [1132]
July 28	ACD attended a dinner at the Authors' Club, H. Rider Haggard presided and ACD was the chairman of the club. [322,1285]
August	*How the Brigadier Lost His Ear* published in *The Strand Magazine*. [6,194,195,196,198]
August 2	ACD played cricket for the Undershaw team against Eashing at Haslemere, he scored 19 and took 2 wickets, Undershaw won. [2087]
August 6	ACD knighted by King Edward VII. [7] (*4)
August 7	ACD played cricket the Undershaw team against Broadwater at Broadwater, he scored 11 and took 8 wickets, Undershaw won. [2088]
August 8	ACD played cricket for the Undershaw team against Lynchmere at Lynchmere, he scored 61 and 5, he took 5 wickets and 1 catch, Undershaw won. [2089]
August 9	ACD knighted by King Edward VII at Buckingham Palace (*4) he was also appointed a Deputy Lieutenant of Surrey. [3,7,20,233] (*2)
August 10	Alfred H. Wood visited Undershaw. [123]
August 13	ACD played cricket on 13 & 14 for MCC against North Devon at North Devon Club Ground, Sandhills, Instow, he scored 5, took 2 wickets and 1 catch, match drawn. [235]
August 15	ACD played cricket on 15 & 16 for MCC against R.W. Sealy's XI at Golf Links Road, Westward Ho!, he scored 64 and took 3 wickets and 1 catch, MCC won. [235]
August 16	ACD probably at Teignmouth, Devon. [203]

1902

n.d.	Touie and her mother spent some time at the Clytonville Hotel, Margate. [203]
August 18	ACD was due to play cricket for the MCC play Devon at Kelly College Ground, Tavistock, but owing to heavy rain the match appears to have been cancelled. [2090]
August 20	ACD played cricket on 20 & 21 for MCC against Teignbridge at Teignbridge; he scored 1 and 31, MCC won. [235]
August 25	ACD played cricket on 25 & 26 for MCC against Cornwall at Boscawen Park, Truro, Cornwall; he scored 7 and 4, and took 3 catches, MCC won. [235]
August 27	ACD played cricket on 27 & 28 for MCC against Sidmouth at Belmont Grounds, Sidmouth, he scored 7 and 27, he took 1 wicket, Sidmouth won. [235]
August	It was noted in *The Sidmouth Herald* on 30 August that ACD and Miss Conan Doyle were staying at The Royal York Hotel, Sidmouth for 2 weeks. [1149]
n.d.	ACD met Jean Leckie in Exeter where they viewed Innes' old barracks. [202,203]
September	ACD was entertained by Sir George Newnes at his home, Hollerday House, Lynton, Devon, ACD then made the main speech when a life-size marble bust of Sir George Newnes was unveiled at the Town Hall, Lynton, Devon. [210]
September 6	ACD made the main speech when a life-size marble bust of Sir George Newnes was unveiled at the Town Hall, Lynton, Devon. [322,1286]
September 7	ACD at Lynton, Devon. [203]
September 12	ACD donated a cheque for £1000, being the balance of profit from his South Africa pamphlets, to the University of Edinburgh as a bursary in the faculty of medicine only available for students from South Africa. [531]
September	ACD presented a silver statue of a civilian rifleman standing on a pedestal, which he offered for annual competition among the rifle clubs of Surrey, Sussex and Hampshire. The trophy would not be won outright, but ACD would give the members of the winning teams medals. [1287]
October	ACD at Undershaw. [203]
October 16	ACD attended a luncheon presented by the Pilgrims at the Carlton Hotel, London. [532]
n.d.	ACD was knighted for his services to the Crown during the Boer War. [99] (*4)
October 24	ACD knighted by King Edward VII at Buckingham Palace he was knighted mainly for his writing on The Boer War; (*4) he was also appointed a Deputy Lieutenant of Surrey, [68,14,15,78,180,200,202,203,215,322,1288] (*2)
October 25	ACD at Undershaw. [203]
October 25	In the evening ACD attended the coming of age dinner of the London Press Club at the Trocadero Restaurant, London. [1289]
October 27	*A Duet*, a duologue, a comedy in one act based on *A Duet* by ACD performed at the Steinway Hall, London. [6]
November	*How the Brigadier Saved an Army* published in *The Strand Magazine* as *How the Brigadier Saved the Army*. [6,194,195,196,198]
November 6	It was reported that ACD was 'spending a golfing holiday at the Peak resort at present.' [533] {Note: the resort of Buxton.}
November 8	It was reported that 'Sir A. Conan Doyle the popular novelist was staying at Buxton on a short visit for the benefit of his health. He spent a good deal of last week on the golf links and this week is making excursions in the neighbourhood.' [534]
November 14	ACD addressed the Boys' Empire League at Holborn Town Hall, Holborn. [85]
November 19	ACD at Undershaw. [99]
November	Innes returned home from South Africa after more than four years' service abroad, he was met from the boat train at Waterloo by ACD, Louise and Connie. [215] (*2)
November 22	Innes returned to England from South Africa arriving at Southampton, the Mam, ACD and Constance (Connie) met him at Waterloo Station, London, they then returned to Undershaw. [124,202] (*2)

1902

November 24	ACD attended a dinner of the Authors' Club at Whitehall Court, Captain Percy Scott was principal guest, Captain Doyle also attended. [1290]
November 27	ACD attended a dinner held by the New Vagabond Club held at the Trocadero Restaurant, London. [535]
November 28	ACD visited the bazaar of the Queen's Edinburgh Rifle Volunteer Brigade that was held to raise £12,000 to erect a new headquarters in the city. [1291] (*2)
November 28	ACD opened the third day's proceedings of the Queen's Volunteer Brigade bazaar held in the Waverley Market, Edinburgh. [536] (*2)
November 28	ACD attended a dinner held by the Morayshire Club, Edinburgh where he proposed a toast "To the memory of our Scottish soldiers who had not come home." [537]
December	*How the Brigadier Rode to Minsk* published in *The Strand Magazine*. [6,194,195,196,198]
December 2	It was reported that 'Sir Arthur Conan Doyle has accepted the presidency of the Boys' Empire League.' [538]
December 5	Birth of Innes Cliffe Foley. [200] (*2)
December	Birth of Innes Cliffe Foley, Nelson and Jane (Ida) Foley's second son. [124] (*2)
December 15	ACD chaired a dinner of the Authors' Club, Whitehall Court, London. [1292]
December 17	ACD was the President of the Boys Empire League. [1293]
December 25	Innes and Bryan Mary (Dodo), with the children, attended church at Churt. [124]
December 26	Constance (Connie) arrived at Undershaw and Bryan Mary (Dodo) left. [124]

1903

n.d.	ACD's son Kingsley was sent to Sandroyd School, Oxshott Heath, Surrey. [124]
n.d.	*A Duet (A Duologue)* published by Samuel French, London. [6]
n.d.	*Author's Edition* (thirteen volumes) published by D. Appleton (New York) and Smith, Elder and Company (London). [6]
January	*Brigadier Gerard at Waterloo* published in *The Strand Magazine* in January and February. [195,198]
January	*How the Brigadier Bore Himself at Waterloo – I. The Story of the Forest Inn* published in *The Strand Magazine*. [6,194,196]
n.d.	ACD gave a gift of £1,000 to the University of Edinburgh. [202] (*2)
January 4	ACD gave a gift of £1,000 to the University of Edinburgh for the foundation of a prize in the faculty of medicine, to be awarded annually to the most distinguished graduate, MB, Ch.B from South Africa. [1294] (*2)
January 5	ACD gave a silver basket as a wedding present to Mr Brodrick M.P. and Miss Madeleine Cecilia Carlyle Stanley [1295], ACD attended the wedding and reception of Hon. W. St. John Brodrick to Miss Madeleine Cecilia Carlyle Stanley at St. Georges, Hanover Square, London, the reception was held at the home of Sir Francis and Lady Jeune in Harley Street, London. [1077]
January 17	ACD at Undershaw. [884]
January 27	It was announced that Sir A. Conan Doyle as president of the Boys' Empire League had offered a prize of £10 for a patriotic song suitable for boys. [539]
January 31	ACD donated £5: 5s to the Cricketers National War Fund. [1296]
February	*How the Brigadier Bore Himself at Waterloo – II. The Story of the Nine Prussian Horsemen* published in *The Strand Magazine*. [6,194,196,198]
February 12	ACD presided at a meeting of the Executive Committee of the Boys' Empire League held at the Chapter House, St. Paul's Cathedral, London. [540]
February	ACD showed an interest in forming the Union Jack Club. [1297]
n.d.	ACD spoke for the Union Jack Club for soldiers and sailors in London. [203] (*3)
February	ACD attended a gala evening at the Union Jack Club, London. [202] (*3)

1903

February 25	ACD attended a luncheon and meeting at the Mansion House, London in support of the proposed Union Jack Club, he donated £50 to the fund [1298] (*3) or £100. [202]
March	ACD had completed writing the stage version of *Brigadier Gerard*. [202]
March	*How the Brigadier Triumphed in England* published in *The Strand Magazine* as *The Brigadier in England*. [6,194,195,196,198]
March 18	ACD at The Limes, Wallingford, Oxfordshire. [1834] {Note: Reverend Charles Cyril Angell lived at The Limes with his wife Bryan Mary (Dodo) and son Branford Bryan, Charles Angell was the curate of nearby North Stoke with Ipsden and Newnham Murren from 1903 to 1906.}
March 23	ACD called before the Royal Commission on the War in South Africa and gave evidence on the enteric epidemic at Bloemfontein. [113] (*2)
March 24	ACD gave evidence at the Royal Commission on the War in South Africa held at St. Stephen's House, Westminster. [154,1299] (*2)
March 25	ACD at Undershaw. [1834]
March 25	ACD opened a bazaar at the Public Hall, Godalming in aid of the Wesleyan Chapel. [541]
March 25	ACD kicked off a football match between a local Hindhead team and the Portsmouth team (he did not actually play), Portsmouth won 3-0. Afterwards the teams were entertained at the Royal Huts Hotel, Hindhead. [542]
March	By 31 March ACD had written *The Empty House*. [322]
n.d.	ACD visited Birmingham and purchased a 10-horse power Wolseley; he then drove it back to Undershaw. [203] (*3)
n.d.	ACD purchased a ten-horse power Wolseley; he collected the car at Birmingham and drove the 150 miles back to Undershaw. [3,202] (*3)
Spring	ACD purchased a five-seater 10-horsepower, dark blue with red wheels Wolseley car from Wolseley Tool and Motor Car Company in Birmingham, ACD drove the 140 miles from Birmingham back to Hindhead. [215] (*3)
April	ACD at 16 Buckingham Street, London. [203]
April	*Arthur Conan Doyle* (an article/interview) published in *The Bookman*. [198]
April	*How the Brigadier Captured Saragossa* published in *The Strand Magazine* as *How the Brigadier joined the Hussars at Conflans*. [6,194,195,196,198]
April 3	ACD at Undershaw. [2053]
April 11	It was announced that the Revd. Joseph McKim of Swinhope Rectory, Lincolnshire had won the prize for the best song suitable for boys. [543]
April 15	ACD completed writing *The Norwood Builder*. [322]
April 27	ACD completed writing *The Solitary Cyclist*. [322]
April 30	ACD attended the first performance of *Dante* starring Henry Irving at Drury Lane Theatre, London. [2046]
May	*The Last Adventure of the Brigadier* published in *The Strand Magazine* as *How the Brigadier said Goodbye to his Master*. [6,194,195,196,198]
May 2	ACD held a rifle shooting competition at Undershaw [322,1300] invited were rifle clubs from Surrey, Sussex and Hampshire, [254] the challenge trophy, a silver statuette of a typical civilian rifleman, presented by Mr Langman, was won by the London and South-Western Railway Rifle Club with the runners-up being the Undershaw team. [322,1300]
May 8	ACD took Kingsley back to school. [202]
May 9	ACD on holiday at Hill House Hotel, Happisburgh, Norfolk [202] (*2) visited his mother who was staying with Willie and Connie Hornung at East Ruston. [202]
May 9	It was announced that the King had made several appointments to the Hospital of St. John of Jerusalem in England, including that of Sir Arthur Conan Doyle to be a Knight of Grace. [544]
May 14	ACD on holiday at Hill House Hotel, Happisburgh, Norfolk. [31,50,203,1834] (*2)
May 16	ACD was back in London. [202]

1903

May 20	ACD at the Grand Hotel, Trafalgar Square, London. [2027]
May 22	ACD played cricket for the Authors against the Artists at Esher, Surrey [71], at New Road, Esher, he scored 28 and took 1 wicket, the Authors won. [235,1146]
May 23	ACD played cricket for the Authors against Esher at Esher, Surrey [71], he scored 29 and Esher won. [1078,1146]
May 25	ACD presided at the annual ladies dinner of the Authors' Club in the grand hall of the Hotel Cecil, London. [545]
May 28	ACD played a first class cricket match on 28 & 29 for MCC & Ground against Kent at Lord's [1301] the match was scheduled for 3 days but completed in 2 days, ACD scored 3 and then 16 not out, Kent won. [235]
May 28	ACD attended the first annual concert of the Boys' Empire League at St. James's Hall, London. [1301]
June	ACD joined The Royal Automobile Club. [202]
June	*The Leather Funnel* published in *The Strand Magazine*. [6,194,195,196,198]
June 3	ACD completed writing *The Dancing Men*. [322]
June 5	ACD played cricket for the Allahakbarries against Royal Engineers (Chatham) at Chatham, he scored 29 not out and took 5 wickets. [1956]
June 19	ACD attended the first annual dinner of the Pilgrims Society at Prince's Restaurant, Piccadilly, London. [800]
June 26	ACD played cricket on 26 & 27 for MCC against 1st Army Corps at Officers Club Services Ground, Aldershot; he scored 13 and 10, and took 2 catches, 1st Army Corps won. [235]
June 29	ACD chaired the last house dinner of the season of the Authors' Club at Whitehall Court. [1302]
n.d.	*The Episodes of Marge: Memoirs of a Humble Adventuress* by H. Ripley Cromarsh (the pen name of ACD's sister, Bryan Mary Doyle) published. {photocopy in the collection of Brian W. Pugh.} [203] (*2)
July	*The Episodes of Marge: Memoirs of a Humble Adventuress* by H. Ripley Cromarsh (the pen name of ACD's sister, Bryan Mary Doyle) published by Grant Richards. [6] (*2)
July	ACD made a donation of £100 to supply a bedroom named Lady Conan Doyle bedroom at the Union Jack Club. [1303]
July	ACD at Undershaw. [18]
July 1	ACD attended the wedding of Anthony Hope Hawkins to Miss Elizabeth Somerville Sheldon at St. Bride's Church, Fleet Street, London. [1992]
July 4	ACD played a cup cricket match for Grayshott against Blackmoor. [63]
July 6	ACD played cricket for the Authors against the Artists at Frensham Hill, Farnham, he scored 25 and took 3 wickets, the Artists won. [235]
July 8	ACD at the Golden Cross Hotel, London. [1834]
July 8	ACD played cricket for MCC against Bedford Grammar School at Bedford School Ground, he scored zero, match drawn. [235]
July 9	ACD played cricket for MCC against Bedford Modern School at Bedford Modern School Ground, he scored 15 and took 1 wicket, MCC won. [235]
July 10	ACD played cricket for MCC against Bedford County School at Bedford County School Ground, he scored 30, MCC won. [235]
July 11	John and Mary Langman visited Undershaw. [123]
July 14	ACD played cricket for MCC against Oatlands Park at Oatlands Park Cricket Club Ground, Weybridge, he scored 82, match drawn. [235]
July 18	ACD played a cup cricket match for Grayshott against Linchmere and scored 37 [63] l'Anson Cup final at Lynchmere Cricket Ground, he scored 37, took 1 wicket and 1 catch, Grayshott won. [235]
July 19	Josephine Ratcliff Hoare visited Undershaw, as did Alfred H. Wood. [123]
July 20	ACD played cricket on 20 & 21 for MCC against Gentlemen of Warwickshire at Warwick Cricket Club Ground; he scored 11 and 1, match drawn. [235]

1903

July 22	ACD played cricket on 22 & 23 for MCC against Leamington Town at Leamington Cricket Club Ground; he scored 1 and took 1 wicket, match drawn. [235]
July 24	ACD played cricket for MCC against Coventry and North Warwickshire at The Butts Ground, Coventry, he scored 22 not out and did not bat in second innings, he took 1 wicket and 1 catch, match drawn. [235]
July 25	ACD played cricket for MCC against Rugby Town at Rugby Town Club Ground, he scored 65 and took 1 wicket, MCC won. [235]
July 25	The play *Sherlock Holmes* starring Cuyler Hastings as Holmes opened at His Majesty's Theatre, Brisbane. [1013]
July 26	ACD completed writing *Black Peter* and began work on *Charles Augustus Milverton*. [322]
July 28	ACD presided at the annual dinner of the Atlantic Union [1304] at the Hotel Cecil, London. [322]
August	ACD made another donation this time of £50 for a "Lady Conan Doyle Bedroom" to the Union Jack Club. [1305]
August	ACD at Undershaw. [18]
August	ACD with W.G. Jones patented a device called the Sculptograph. [202,322]
August 2	Constance (Connie) and E.W. Hornung visited Undershaw. [123]
August 3	Miss Catherine (Kate) Foley, maternal aunt of ACD and sister of Mary Josephine Foley who married Charles Altamont Doyle, attended the last performance of the play *Sherlock Holmes* as a guest of the management at His Majesty's Theatre, Brisbane. It appears that she was living on Kent Street, near Tenerife Park, Brisbane. [1014]
August 5	George Guggisberg visited Undershaw. [122,322]
August 5	ACD played cricket for the Undershaw team against Grayshott at Grayshott, he scored 23 and took 1 wicket, Undershaw won. [2091]
August 6	ACD played cricket for the Undershaw team against Broadwater at Godalming, he scored 8 and took 3 wickets and 1 catch, Undershaw won. [2091]
August	ACD stayed at The Royal York Hotel, Sidmouth. [1149]
August 14	ACD played cricket on 14 & 15 for MCC against Sidmouth at Belmont Grounds, Sidmouth, he scored zero and 4, match drawn. [235]
August 17	ACD played cricket on 17 & 18 for MCC against United Services at Devonport; he scored 3 and 35, MCC won. [235]
August 19	ACD played cricket on 19 & 20 for MCC against Teignbridge at Teignbridge, he scored zero, match drawn. [235]
August 21	ACD played cricket on 21 & 22 for MCC against Devon at Kelly College Ground, Tavistock, Devon; he scored 8, MCC won. [235]
August 24	ACD played cricket on 24 & 25 for MCC against Instow at North Devon Cricket Club Ground, Sandhills, Instow; he scored 9, MCC won. [235] (*2)
August 24	ACD played cricket on 24 & 25 for MCC against North Devon at Instow. [546] (*2)
August 26	ACD played cricket on 26 & 27 for MCC against R.W. Sealy's XI at Golf Links Road, Westward Ho! he scored 96 not out, match drawn. [235]
September 2	E.W. Hornung and his wife Constance (Connie) visited Undershaw. [123]
September 5	ACD at Undershaw. [18]
September 15	ACD at Undershaw [1027] and completed writing *The Six Napoleons*. [322]
September 22	*The Adventures of Gerard* published by George Newnes Ltd., London [6,202]
September 24	*Author's Edition* (twelve volumes) published by Smith, Elder & Co., London. [6]
n.d.	*The Adventure of the Empty House* published. [180] (*2)
September 26	*The Adventure of the Empty House* published in *Collier's Weekly*. [198] (*2)
September 26	At a meeting held at Grayshott near Hindhead to consider the massacres in Macedonia, ACD proposed a resolution to urge the Government to carry out reforms and maintain order. [1306]
n.d.	*The Return of Sherlock Holmes* published in *The Strand Magazine*. [99,203]

1903

October	*The Adventure of the Empty House* published in *The Strand Magazine*. [6,194,195,196,198,215]
October 6	Sir Henry Irving performed *Waterloo* at the Haymarket Theatre, London. [1307]
October 8	ACD presided over the Executive Committee of the Boys' Empire League at Chapter House, St. Paul's Cathedral, London. [85]
October 15	ACD attended a dinner of the Pilgrims of London at Claridge's Hotel, London. [1308]
October 22	ACD attended a political meeting at the Town Hall, Leamington. [1309]
n.d.	George Edalji sentenced to seven years hard labour for horse and cattle mutilations. [180] (*3)
October 23	George Edalji sentenced to 7 years penal servitude (*3), the sentence carried out at Lewes prison and then Portland prison. [3] (*3)
October 26	ACD presided at a dinner of the Authors' Club. [1770]
October 31	*The Adventure of the Norwood Builder* published in *Collier's Weekly*. [198]
November	George Edalji sentenced to 7 years penal servitude. [4,6] (*3)
n.d.	ACD became interested in the George Edalji case. [99]
November	*The Adventure of the Norwood Builder* published in *The Strand Magazine*. [6,194,195,196,198]
November 4	ACD was a guest at the Royal Musselburgh Golf Club and during the visit he played a couple of rounds on the Links. [547]
November 4	ACD attended a meeting of Lodge Canongate Kilwinning at their chapel in St. John Street, Edinburgh. [548]
November 4	ACD left Edinburgh for London late evening. [549]
November 7	ACD's assent to stand as the Unionist candidate in the Hawick Burghs constituency was formally published at a meeting in Galashiels. [6]
November 9	ACD completed writing *The Three Students*. [322]
November	ACD consented to the Liberal Unionist candidate. [322]
November	ACD donated £1000 to Edinburgh University for the purpose of founding a scholarship for South African students. [322]
November 14	ACD accepted the nomination as Unionist candidate in the Hawick Burghs constituency. [202,1310]
November 18	ACD had lunch in London with S.S. McClure. [50]
November 19	ACD attended a dinner at Grays Inn. [1993]
November 25	ACD at Undershaw. [2026]
November 26	ACD at Undershaw. [2026]
November 27	It was reported that ACD had donated £2:2s and was added to the Melville Testimonial Committee. [2047]
November 30	ACD addressed the Authors' Club [85], he was among those present at a dinner to meet the famous cricketer C.B. Fry; E.W. Hornung was in the chair. [988]
December	*The Adventure of the Dancing Men* published in *The Strand Magazine*. [6,194,195,196,198]
December 5	*The Adventure of the Dancing Men* published in *Collier's Weekly*. [198]
December 7	ACD attended a meeting of the Unionists at the Music Hall, Edinburgh. [550]
December 8	ACD gave a recital of selections from his works held at the Victoria Hall, Selkirk [551], the proceeds from his recital were given to the New Bridge Bazaar fund for the new traffic bridge over the river Ettrick at Selkirk. [990]
December 9	ACD addressed a meeting at Hawick in connection with his adoption as candidate for the Border Burghs in opposition to Mr Thomas Shaw. [203,1311]
December 10	As the prospective Unionist candidate for the Border Burghs, ACD made a speech on Tariff Reform at Galashiels, Scotland. [6]
December 12	ACD met the Selkirk Unionist Party in Selkirk. [989]
December 12	ACD opened the bazaar held at the Victoria Hall, Selkirk [552], he opened the third day of the Selkirk New Bridge bazaar held at the Victoria Hall, Selkirk. [991]
December 13	Amy J. Ratcliff Hoare visited Undershaw. [123]

1903

December 14	ACD at Undershaw. [884]
December 17	ACD attended the centenary of the founding of Madam Tussaud's waxwork museum. [322]
December 21	At the Surrey County Football Association Council meeting it was announced that ACD promised a cup for the newly-instituted Minor Competition. [553]
December 22	ACD in London. [203]
December 25	ACD at Undershaw. [203]
December 26	*The Adventure of the Solitary Cyclist* published in *Collier's Weekly*. [198]
December 28	ACD at Undershaw. [18]

1904

n.d.	ACD played cricket for MCC against Cambridgeshire at Lord's, he took 7 wickets. [10] (*2) {Note: ACD has this wrong in his autobiography, the match actually took place on 30 & 31 August 1899.}
n.d.	ACD and Bertram Fletcher Robinson joined Our Society (The Crimes Club) in London. [77]
n.d.	ACD was made a member of the Crimes Club (Our Society). [99]
January 1	ACD at Undershaw. [203]
January	*The Adventure of the Solitary Cyclist* published in *The Strand Magazine*. [6,194,195,196,198]
January 9	It was announced that ACD and an MCC XI would play cricket in the Scottish Borders at Hawick June 21, Gala 22 June, Selkirk 23 June and South of Scotland on 24 & June. [554]
January	ACD was part of the General Committee for presenting a National Testimonial to Superintendent Melville [1312] the retiring head of Scotland Yard's Special Branch. [202] (*2)
January 18	ACD, the Duke of Westminster and others attended Westminster City Hall and were elected to the committee in charge of a testimonial fund in honour of William Melville. [322] (*2)
January 18	ACD attended a house dinner at the Authors' Club, Whitehall Court. [1313]
January 23	ACD attended a dinner at the Charlton Hotel to celebrate the twentieth anniversary of the establishment of the *Financial News*. [1994]
n.d.	ACD donated £10:10s in aid of the disaster at Bloemfontein. [1995]
January 26	ACD addressed the electors at Galashiels. [1314]
January 27	ACD addressed the electors at Selkirk. [1315]
January 28	Lecture by ACD, "The Life and Times of Gibbon" at Hawick Theatre. [6]
January 30	*The Adventure of the Priory School* published in *Collier's Weekly*. [198]
February	*The Adventure of the Priory School* published in *The Strand Magazine*. [6,194,195,196,198]
February	ACD at the North British Station Hotel, Edinburgh. [18]
February 3	ACD at the Athenaeum Club, London. [18]
February 5	ACD at Undershaw. [18]
February 8	ACD was a Vice-President of the Dickens Fellowship; he attended the birthday anniversary of Charles Dickens held at the Memorial Hall, Farringdon Street, London. [1316]
February 20	It was announced that Mr F. Carruthers Gould had succeeded ACD as President of the Boys' Empire League. [555,1317]
February 27	*The Adventure of Black Peter* published in *Collier's Weekly*. [198]
March	*The Adventure of Black Peter* published in *The Strand Magazine*. [6,194,195,196,198]
March	ACD completed writing *The Missing Three-Quarter*. [322]
March 2	ACD at Sheringham, Norfolk. [884]
March 3	ACD visited Hawick and met with members of the Burgh Ward Committee in the smaller hall of the Exchange Buildings and delivered a short address. [1006]
March 4	ACD addressed the electors at Edinburgh [1318] at the Synod Hall, Edinburgh. [556] (*2)

1904

March 5	ACD was elected as a Hon. Vice-President of the Scottish Border Amateur Athletic Association at the AGM held at Buccleuch Hotel, Hawick. [1007]
March 12	ACD at the Great Northern Victoria Hotel, Bradford, attended a dinner and made a speech for the Bradford Textile Society. [203]
March 15	ACD took Jean out for a car ride for the day. [203,322]
March 16	ACD at the Golden Cross Hotel, London. [203]
March 17	It was announced that ACD had been appointed Hon. Vice-President (among others) of the Border Amateur Athletic Association. [557]
March 19	Innes returned from South Africa, he was met by ACD and Kingsley at Southampton. [202]
March 26	*The Adventure of Charles Augustus Milverton* published in *Collier's Weekly*. [198]
March 27	ACD and Innes played a round of golf at Hankley. [124,202]
March 27	Motoring accident happened at Undershaw involving ACD and Innes. [124,202,322] (*3)
March	ACD and Innes were involved in a motoring accident in Surrey. [6] (*3)
March 28	ACD and Innes spent three days playing golf at Sheringham, Norfolk. [202] (*2)
n.d.	Innes visited Sheringham, Norfolk with ACD, some of the Leckie family joined them. [215] (*2)
March 31	The Leckie's arrived at Undershaw. [202]
April	*The Adventure of Charles Augustus Milverton* published in *The Strand Magazine*. [6,194,195,196,198]
April 8	ACD and J.M. Barrie were Vice-Presidents of The Ravens Dramatic Club, Surrey. [558]
April 9	At the Hindhead Free Church a meeting was held to formally found the new Hindhead Golf Club [322], (date taken from information shown in the club by the author), held in the schoolroom of the Hindhead Free Church [125], later ACD became the first President. [104]
April 14	It was reported that ACD had consented to become one of the Vice-Presidents of the Hawick and Wilton Cricket Club. [559]
April 20	ACD attended the annual dinner of the Incorporated Society of Authors at the Hotel Cecil. [1319]
April 20	It was reported that ACD was a member of the "Ends of the Earth Club", New York. [2006]
April	ACD was part of the committee of the Compatriots' Club. [1320]
April 22	ACD attended a dinner at the Trocadero to welcome MCC's Australian team on their return from Australia. [1321]
April	ACD completed and submitted *The Abbey Grange* to *Collier's Weekly* and *The Strand Magazine*. [322] (*2)
April 26	ACD completed writing *The Adventure of the Abbey Grange*. [2025] (*2)
April 30	*The Adventure of the Six Napoleons* published in *Collier's Weekly*. [198]
May	*The Adventure of the Six Napoleons* published in *The Strand Magazine*. [6,194,195,196,198]
May	ACD attended and was one of the speakers at the seventh annual dinner of the London Border Counties Association held at the Hotel Cecil, London. [1008]
May	ACD donated one guinea to the Surrey (Princess of Wales) Imperial Yeomanry Fund. [2020]
May 2	ACD played a first class cricket match on 2, 3 & 4 for MCC against London County at Lord's [1322]; he scored 10 not out and 31, London County won. [235]
May 10	ACD gave speech at a banquet of The London Scottish Border Counties Association. [6]
May 14	ACD played cricket for Esher against Marlborough Blues at New Road, Esher, he scored 3, match drawn, Innes Doyle also played for Esher and scored 8. [235]

1904

May 16	ACD played a first class cricket match on 16 & 17 for MCC against Kent [1323], at Lord's, the match was scheduled for 3 days but was completed in 2 days, he scored zero and 5 not out, MCC won. [235]
May 20	ACD played cricket for the Authors against the Artists at Esher, Surrey [71] at New Road Esher, he scored 27 and took 5 wickets and 1 catch, the Authors won, also playing for the Authors were Innes Doyle who scored 15 and E.W. Hornung who scored 3. [235]
May 20	It was reported that Lady Conan Doyle and Mrs Thomas Hardy had consented to adjudicate on the new "Tatler" Prize Competition for the photographs of the three most beautiful children in the British Isles. [560]
May 21	ACD played cricket for the Authors against Esher at Esher, he scored 8, Esher won. [2092]
May 23	ACD at Undershaw. [1834]
May 24	Innes took Louise and her sister Emily to His Majesty's Theatre to see *Darling of the Gods* starring Herbert Beerbohm Tree, and then for dinner at the Grand Hotel. [124,215]
May 25	It was reported that ACD broke a finger while playing cricket for the Authors at Esher. [561] {Note: this would have been on May 21 in the match between the Authors and the Artists.}
May 28	Leslie and Caroline (Lottie) Oldham arrived in England from India. [124]
May 30	ACD and E.W. Hornung attended a dinner of the Authors' Club at their clubhouse in Whitehall Court. [1324]
June	*The Adventure of the Three Students* published in *The Strand Magazine*. [6,194,195,196,198]
June 1	Innes took Emily (Nem) Hawkins and Mary Conan Doyle to the Military Tournament. [124]
June 7	Innes was presented to King Edward VII. [124]
June	Early June, Nelson and Jane (Ida) Foley arrived in London from Gaiola. [124]
June	On the weekend of 11/12 June Lord Burnham entertained a house party at Hall Barn near Beaconsfield, Buckinghamshire, among the guests were ACD and Mr H.B. Irving. [1831]
June 16	ACD attended the Cornet's dinner held at the Town Hall, Hawick. [1009]
June 18	ACD attended the second annual banquet of The Pilgrims Club, a group founded in August 1902 to encourage better relationship between Britain and the USA. This banquet took place at the Savoy Hotel, and it honoured Field Marshall Earl Roberts of Kandahar, Pretoria and Waterford, the President of the Club, with Mr Choate, the U.S. Ambassador presiding, also present was Bertram Fletcher Robinson. [322,1325]
June 19	ACD was the guest of Sir Robert Cranston, the Lord Provost of Edinburgh, and tea in the afternoon with the Alake of Abeokuta. [1010]
June 21	ACD played cricket for MCC (Sir A. Conan Doyle's XI) against Hawick at Hawick he scored zero, MCC won [562] at Buccleuch Park, Hawick A.H. Wood played for MCC, he scored 54 and took 1 catch. [235]
June 22	ACD played cricket for MCC (Sir A. Conan Doyle's XI) against Gala at Galashiels, he scored 10, MCC won [563] at Mossilee, Galashiels, A.H. Wood played for MCC, he scored 58 and took 1 catch and stumped 3. [235]
June 23	ACD played cricket for MCC (Sir A. Conan Doyle's XI) against Selkirk at Philiphaugh, Selkirk he scored 35 and zero and took 1 catch, MCC won [235,564] A.H. Wood played for MCC, he scored zero and took 2 catches. [235]
June 24	ACD played cricket on 24 & 25 for MCC (Sir A. Conan Doyle's XI against South of Scotland at Galashiels, he scored 8 and took 3 wickets [565], MCC won, at Mossilee, Galashiels, A.H. Wood played for MCC, he scored 56 and took 1 catch and 1 stump. [235]
June 29	ACD elected as a representative of the Liberal Union Club Council at the special general meeting held at the Hotel Metropole, London. [1326]

1904

July	*The Adventure of the Golden Pince-Nez* published in *The Strand Magazine*. [6,194,195,196,198]
July	The Prince of Wales laid the foundation stone of the Union Jack Club at 91 Waterloo Road, London. [189]
July 7	ACD played cricket for MCC against Haverford College at Lord's; he scored 41 not out, and took 1 catch, Haverford College won. [235]
July 13	ACD played cricket for Lythe Hill against Marlborough Blues at Lynchmere Cricket Ground, Lynchmere, he scored 4 and took 6 wickets, Marlborough Blues won. [235]
July 14	ACD attended a meeting of the Liberal Unionist Council held at the Imperial Theatre, London in the afternoon. [1327]
July 14	ACD attended a public meeting of the Liberal Unionist Council at the Albert Hall, London in the evening. [1327]
July 17	ACD paid his first visit to Our Society (Crimes Club). [31]
July 18	ACD as a director attended the annual general meeting of Raphael Tuck & Sons (Ltd.) at Salisbury House, Finsbury Circus. [1328]
July 19	ACD played cricket for Lythe Hill against Incogniti at Lynchmere Cricket Ground, Lynchmere, he scored 7 and zero and took 2 wickets, match drawn. [235]
July 20	Before opening the Hindhead Bazaar, ACD delivered a speech on religion [6] the Free Church bazaar. [1329]
August 1	Leslie & Lottie Oldham visited Undershaw. [123]
August	*The Adventure of the Missing Three-Quarter* published in *The Strand Magazine*. [6,194,195,196,198]
August 4	Gordon Guggisberg visited Undershaw. [123]
August 12	ACD played cricket on 12 & 13 for MCC against Devon Dumplings at County Cricket Ground, Exeter; he scored zero and 8, MCC won. [235,566]
August 15	ACD played cricket on 15 & 16 for MCC against Exmouth at Exmouth; he scored zero and 32 and took 1 catch [567], at The Maer Ground, Exmouth, MCC won. [235]
August 23	Innes met the Mam at Liverpool Street and took her to stay with Mrs Hoare in Westbourne Terrace. [124]
September	*The Adventure of the Abbey Grange* published in *The Strand Magazine*. [6,194,195,196,198] (*2)
September 9	ACD left King's Cross, London for Edinburgh. [1330]
September 10	ACD attended a Unionist picnic and made an address held at Gala House, Galashiels [568], ACD made a speech at an open air demonstration held by the Galashiels Unionist Association at the Galahouse Grounds. [1331]
September 16	ACD at Undershaw. [884]
September 17	ACD at Grand Hotel, Trafalgar Square, London. [884]
September	Louise Conan Doyle was one of two judges in a competition held by the *Tatler* magazine to find the prettiest child in England. [322]
September 22	ACD was in Southwark Police Court in response to summons issued on behalf of William George Jones, his partner in the Sculptograph, the summons was ultimately withdrawn. [322]
October 1	ACD ordered a new 20-horse-power car from the Dennis Company in Guildford. [202]
October	ACD was the chief guest at the annual dinner of the Norwich Medico-Chirurgical Society. [2007]
October 4	ACD attended the annual dinner of the Norwich Medic-Chirurgical Society at the Maid's Head Hotel, Norwich. [2021]
October 15	ACD made a speech on the common ground of all Christian religions at the stone-laying ceremony at the new Wesleyan Church, Hindhead. [6]
October 17	ACD presided over a meeting at the Town Hall, Galashiels. [569]
October 18	ACD presided over a meeting at the Town Hall, Hawick and spoke on the Tariff Reform. [1011]

1904

October 21	ACD presided over a meeting under the auspices of the Imperial Union at the Town Hall, Galashiels. [570]
October 25	ACD attended a dinner with the Pilgrims at the Savoy Hotel, London. [1332]
November 8	ACD attended the wedding of Miss Phyllis Lindsay Watson and Mr E.D. Holland at St. George's Church, Hanover Square, London. [1012]
November 25	ACD at Undershaw. [18]
November 29	ACD addressed a meeting under the auspices of the Imperial Union at Hawick. [571]
December	Innes took command of number six depot RFA (Royal Field Artillery) at Seaforth near Liverpool. [322]
December 5	ACD presided at a dinner of the Authors' Club, E.W. Hornung also attended. [1333]
December	*The Adventure of the Second Stain* published in *The Strand Magazine*. [6,194,195,196,198,322]
December 16	ACD presided at a lecture at the Caxton Hall for the Compatriots' Club. [1334]
Winter	Motoring accident in Surrey involving ACD and Innes. [3,15] (*3)
Christmas	ACD at Undershaw, also Lottie and her husband Captain Leslie Oldham. [203,215]
December 31	*The Adventure of the Abbey Grange* published in *Colliers Weekly* (USA). [2025]

1905

n.d.	*The Adventure of the Abbey Grange* published. [180] (*2)
n.d.	ACD became the first President of The Hindhead Golf Club, [124,322] from 1905 until 1907. [125,180]
n.d.	ACD presented a gunnery challenge cup to the Royal Navy at Portsmouth, the Channel Fleet Shooting Trophy. [3,10]
January	ACD was part of the committee of the Boz Club. [1335]
January	ACD at Undershaw. [203]
January 16	ACD attended a dinner of the Authors' Club at Whitehall Court, C.B. Fry presided. [1336]
January 17	ACD at Undershaw. [99]
January 25	ACD accepted an honorary membership to The Lodge Canongate Kilwinning (No. 2), Edinburgh. [200]
January 26	ACD attended a Burns celebration at the Constitutional Club. [572]
January	*The Adventure of the Second Stain* published in *Collier's Weekly*. [322]
January 28	*The Adventure of the Second Stain* published in *Collier's The National Weekly*. [198]
January 31	ACD addressed a meeting at the Victoria Hall, Selkirk. [573]
February	Mr A.H. Wood, M.A., formerly a master at Portsmouth Grammar School was appointed private secretary to ACD. [1040]
February 7	ACD was offered Honorary Degree of D.D. by the Senatus Accademicus, Edinburgh. [1337]
February 8	It was announced that Lady Conan Doyle had left London for San Remo. [1996]
February 25	It was reported that ACD had been suffering from overwork, and had been ordered a rest cure for two or three weeks. [1997]
March 7	*The Return of Sherlock Holmes* published by George Newnes Ltd., London. [6]
n.d.	*An Address to The Edinburgh University Tariff Reform League (The Fiscal Question)* published. [99]
March 22	It was reported that ACD had entered his ROC motor cycle for the International Motor Cycle Cup to be held on the Isle of Man, the eliminating trials to take place on 31 May with race being on 18 June. [574]
March 27	ACD at Tower Hotel, Hawick. [884]
March 30	ACD addressed a meeting of electors at the Masonic Hall, Galashiels. [575]
March 31	ACD addressed a meeting of electors at Union Street Hall, Galashiels. [576]

1905

April	*The Fiscal Question (Tariff Reform)* published by W. Henderson, Hawick. [6,198]
April 1	ACD addressed a meeting of electors in Galashiels. [577]
April 3	ACD addressed a meeting of electors at the Town Hall, Hawick. [578]
April	ACD received an honorary doctorate (LL.D.) from Edinburgh University. [215] (*5)
April 7	At the Edinburgh University Graduation Ceremonial, ACD was bestowed the Degree of LL.D. [6,7,200] (*5)
April 7	ACD was awarded his honorary degree LL.D. by Edinburgh University. [182,203,322] (*5)
April 8	ACD at the Balmoral Hotel, Edinburgh. [18]
n.d.	Death of Jane (Ball) Doyle. [202] (*2)
April 10	Death of Jane Isabella (Ball) Doyle at her home 98 Lansdowne Road, London, she was buried in the same grave as Annette at St. Mary's Roman Catholic Cemetery, Kensal Green, London. [68,124,200] (*2)
April 15	ACD driving a 10hp Wolseley car won a road trial at Hindhead [35,202,215] hosted by the West Surrey Automobile Club a hill climbing handicap, the hill was two miles and 1500 yards long with an average gradient of 1 in 20. [2103.
April 15	ACD was the guest of the Lyceum Club. [579]
April 19	ACD visited the Whitechapel area of London with Our Society (Crimes Club). [25,31] (*2)
April 19	ACD, Professor Churton Collins, H.B. Irving, Dr Crosse, S. Ingleby Oddie and three City detectives visited Jack the Ripper murder scenes in the Whitechapel area of London. [67] (*2)
April 29	ACD at Undershaw. [884]
May	Louise and daughter Mary took a trip to Paris. [202]
May	ACD made a loan of £100 to keep The Hindhead Golf Club afloat [125,322] around the same time Alfred H. Wood joined the golf club [322]
May	ACD at the Royal Pier Hotel, Southsea [203] with Louise. [202]
May	ACD entered a 9hp ROC motorcycle at the Isle of Man International Cup race trials [103,202], T. Tessier [102] or Tom Silver [103] were entered as the riders, 18 entries were received, 11 were weighed in, 4 succumbed to either machine failure or rider error in practice. [102] {Note: it appears that the ROC did not take part in the race.}
May 5	ACD attended a farewell dinner at the Mansion House, London in honour of the outgoing U.S. Ambassador to Britain, Joseph Hodges Choate. [322]
May 11	ACD presided at a meeting of the Tariff Reform League at Guildford, Surrey. [580]
May 16	ACD attended the annual dinner of the Society of Authors at the Hotel Cecil. [1338]
May 19	ACD played cricket for the Authors against the Artists at New Road, Esher, he scored 24 and took 5 wickets, the Authors won, A.H. Wood played for the Authors and scored 116 and stumped 2. [235]
May 20	ACD caught speeding in his car at Shalford, Surrey. [130,202,322]
May 22	The Royal Medical and Chirurgical Society of London celebrated its centenary with a dinner at the Hotel Cecil, London, which was attended by the Prince of Wales; ACD is listed among the guests, [202,322,1339] a toast was to 'Literature and Science', ACD replied for Literature. [203]
May 26	ACD played cricket on 26 and 27 for Hampshire Rovers against United Services at the Officers' Recreation Ground, Portsmouth. A.H. Wood was also in the same team, ACD scored 78 and then 35 not out, he took 2 catches, A.H. Wood scored 34, the result was a draw. [1041]
May 31	The ROC entered by ACD for the International Motor Cycle Cup on the Isle of Man did not turn up for the trials. [581]
June	ACD at Undershaw. [18]

1905

June 2	ACD attended a reception at Lansdowne House, London. [582] {Note: he may have attended an address by Mr Belfour at the Albert Hall, London before the reception.}
June 3	ACD fined £5 for speeding at Shalford Court. [130] (*2)
June 3	ACD summoned at Guildford County Session for speeding at a greater speed than 20 mph on the Portsmouth Road, Shalford, he was fined £5. [322,1340] (*2)
June 3	ACD attended a luncheon held by the Unionist Parliamentary candidates at the Hotel Metropole, London. [1340]
June 5	*Waterloo* performed at the Theatre Royal, Drury Lane, London. [6]
June 10	Henry Irving's farewell performance as Corporal Brewster in the play *Waterloo* at the Theatre Royal, Drury Lane, London. [981]
June 15	*Waterloo* performed at His Majesty's Theatre, London [6] this was the last performance in London and in this play by Henry Irving. [981]
June 22	ACD played cricket for Gentlemen of Marylebone Cricket Club against Royal Navy at Lord's, he scored 1 run, and took 1 catch, Gentlemen won. [235]
June 23	ACD played cricket on 23 & 24 for MCC against Wiltshire at Lord's; he scored 24, and took 1 catch, MCC won. [235]
June 23	ACD was a speaker at the Pilgrims Banquet at Claridge's Hotel, London, [1341] to welcome the new U.S Ambassador to Britain, Whitelaw Reid, the guests also included Henry Irving, Rudyard Kipling, H. Rider Haggard and Lord Hallam Tennyson. [322]
June 29	ACD played cricket for the Authors against the Actors at Lord's, he scored 2, the Actors won [71]; he scored 2, match drawn. [235]
June 29	ACD presided at the Authors' Club ladies' dinner at the Hotel Cecil. [1342]
July 7	ACD attended the second annual business meeting of the Tariff Reform League held at Caxton Hall, Westminster, London. [1343]
July 8	ACD and Jean attended the garden party given by the London County Council at the Royal Botanic Gardens, Regents Park, London. [1998]
July 13	ACD played cricket for Hythe Hill against Incogniti at Lynchmere Cricket Ground, Lynchmere, he scored 17 and zero, match drawn, A.H. Wood played for Hythe Hill, he scored 29 and then 34 not out, he took 1 catch [235] or Lythe Hill against Incogniti at Haslemere, won by Incogniti. [1957]
July 15	ACD played cricket for Haslemere against Wilts Regiment at Lythe Hill Park and took 7 wickets. [63]
July 20	ACD as a director attended the annual general meeting of Raphael Tuck & Sons (Ltd.) at Salisbury House, Finsbury Circus. [1344] (*2)
July 21	ACD played cricket for Hampshire Rovers against United Services at the Officers' Recreation Ground, Portsmouth. A.H. Wood was also in the same team, ACD scored zero and A.H. Wood scored 19, but the result is unknown. [1042]
July 28	ACD at Undershaw. [203]
July 28	ACD had lunch with Reg Smith and Admiral Percy Scott in London. [203]
July 28	ACD at Grand Hotel, Trafalgar Square, London. [884]
July 29	ACD chaired for the annual Authors Dinner. [203]
July 31	ACD played cricket for the Undershaw team against Haslemere at Haslemere, he scored 65 and took 1 wicket. [2093]
n.d.	Alfred H Wood was elected to the committee of The Hindhead Golf Club. [125]
Summer	ACD commenced writing another novel, *Sir Nigel*, a prequel to *The White Company*. [99,215]
August	ACD attended the fourth annual general meeting of Raphael Tuck & Sons. [322] (*2)
August 1	ACD played cricket for the Undershaw team against Broadwater at Broadwater, he scored 42, Undershaw won. [2093]
August 2	ACD played cricket on 2 & 3 for the Undershaw team against Frensham Hill at Frensham Hill, he scored 44 not out, Undershaw won. [2093]

1905

August 3	Ida Foley visited Undershaw. [123]
August 4	ACD played cricket on 4 & 5 for the Undershaw team against Lythe Hill at Lythe Hill, he scored zero and 24, Undershaw won. [2093]
August 7	At the dinner of The Chiddingfold Hunt, ACD proposed the toast. [6]
August 11	It was reported that ACD was in Dover, Kent and was staying at the Grand Hotel. [583]
August	At Undershaw, ACD entertained the officers of the French navy. [3,14] (*2)
August 13	ACD entertained representatives from the French navy at Undershaw. [124,202,1345] (*2)
August 15	ACD presented The West Surrey Automobile Club Challenge Cup to E. Williams at a gymkhana held at Prior's Field, Compton, Surrey. [35]
n.d.	ACD was a witness at the wedding of Fredrick Guggisberg and Decima Moore. [202] (*2)
August 16	ACD acted as best man at the wedding of Miss Decima Moore the well-known actress and Major Frederick Gordon Guggisberg of the Royal Engineers. [245,322] (*2)
August 18	ACD played cricket for MCC against Hythe at Hythe, he scored 1, result unknown. [2094]
August 19	Emily Hawkins, ACD's mother in law, visited Undershaw. [123]
August 20	ACD caught speeding in his car at Folkestone, Kent. [131,202]
August 26	ACD played a cup cricket match for Grayshott against Liss. [63]
August 26	ACD fined £10 plus 9 shillings costs at the Folkestone Police Court for speeding in Folkestone, ACD did not attend the court. [124,131,215,322] (*3)
August 26	At the Court in Folkestone, Kent ACD, who was not present, pleaded guilty through his solicitor to driving his car at the speed of 26 miles per hour on the Cheriton Road, he was fined £10 and costs [584], he was fined £10 and 4 shillings costs or a months hard labour. [585] (*3)
August 31	ACD played cricket for Cricket Golfers against Golf Cricketers at Lord's [1346], he scored 11 and 1; he took 4 wickets, match drawn. [235]
September	ACD caught and fined for speeding. [14] (*3)
September 2	ACD at Undershaw. [18]
September 8	ACD attended a meeting of the Tariff Reform at the Exchange Hall, Hawick. [586]
September 9	ACD attended a meeting in the afternoon of the Tariff Reform at the Gala Park, Galashiels and again in the evening at the Town Hall. [587]
September 13	ACD attended the first performance of the play *Clarice* at the Duke of York's Theatre, London staring William Gillette. [1820] {Note: the actual date is taken from the *London Daily News* 13 September 1905.}
October	ACD completed writing *Sir Nigel*. [99,215]
October 10	ACD was possibly in Liverpool. [322]
October 13	Death of Sir Henry Irving in Bradford (borne 6 February 1838). [1347]
October 17	Revival of the play *Sherlock Holmes* starring William Gillette at the Duke of York's Theatre, London. [322,1348]
October	During mid October, the play *Sherlock Holmes* starring William Gillette opened at the Duke of York's Theatre, London for 47 performances. [184]
October 18	ACD attended the annual meeting of the Northern Tariff Reform Federation at Newcastle. [588]
October 18	The body of Sir Henry Irving was cremated at Golders Green Crematorium, Hendon, London. [983]
October 19	Sholto Wood and Amy Ratcliff Hoare visited Undershaw. [123]
October 20	ACD attended the funeral of Sir Henry Irving at Westminster Abbey, London his ashes laid to rest at Poets' Corner, Westminster Abbey, London. [1349]
n.d.	It was reported that ACD had won the monthly medal competition at Hindhead Golf Club. [1999]
October 25	It was announced that ACD was part of the committee of the Olympia Sports Club. [1958]

1905

October 28	ACD at Undershaw. [18]
November 2	ACD at Undershaw. [1350]
November 4	ACD attended the marriage of Miss A. Harvey and Mr Harry Brittain at Brompton Oratory. [589]
November 20	ACD attended a house dinner at the Authors' Club held at 3 Whitehall Court, E. W. Hornung and A. Hope Hopkins attended. [1351]
November 21	ACD attended the Liberal Unionist Council Conference in Bristol. [590]
November 27	ACD at Undershaw, he finished writing *Sir Nigel*. [202,203]
November 28	ACD addressed a meeting of electors at the Victoria Hall, Selkirk. [591]
Late 1905	Malcolm Leckie, brother of Jean Leckie, visited Undershaw. [123] (no date in the guest book).
n.d.	*Sir Nigel* published in *The Strand Magazine*. [99] (*2)
December	*Sir Nigel* published in *The Strand Magazine* from December 1905 to December 1906. [6,194,195,196,198,322] (*2)
December 1	At Haslemere ACD made a speech on Tariff Reform. [6]
December 2	ACD at Undershaw. [18]
December 6	ACD spoke at a meeting as Unionist candidate at Hawick. [1043]
December 8	ACD addressed a meeting of electors at Hawick. [592]
December 10	*Sir Nigel's Song* published in *Associated Sunday Magazines*. [198]
December 25	Death of Emily (Butt) Hawkins, mother of Louise [33,124,202,203] at The Cottage, Hindhead. [593]
December 27	ACD at Undershaw. [18]
December 28	ACD attended the funeral of Emily Hawkins at Reigate Borough Cemetery, Reigate, Surrey. [594]
December 30	ACD was unanimously adopted as Unionist candidate for the Hawick Burghs. [1352]

1906

n.d.	*The Secret of the Moor Cottage* by H. Ripley Cromarsh (the pen name of ACD's sister, Bryan Mary Doyle) published by Small, Maynard & Company. {photocopy in the collection of Brian W. Pugh.} (*2)
n.d.	ACD donated a prize (cup) to be competed for annually at the National Rifle Associations rifle-shooting competition. [14,17]
n.d.	ACD took an involved interest in Divorce Law Reform Movement. [15]
n.d.	Kingsley Conan Doyle at Eton. [124]
n.d.	Alfred H Wood was elected Hon. Treasurer of The Hindhead Golf Club. [125]
January	*Sir Nigel's Song* published in *The Strand Magazine* as *A Soldier's Prayer*. [6,196]
January 4	ACD attended a meeting of electors at the Volunteer Hall, Galashiels. [595]
January 8	ACD addressed the workers at the factory of Messrs William Watson & Sons, Hawick. [596]
January 8	ACD made a speech on "Exposition of Unionist Principles" at Hawick Town Hall. [6]
January 10	ACD addressed the mill workers at Selkirk. [597]
January	Between 12 January & 8 February the UK General Election took place. [978]
January 15	ACD addressed a meeting of electors at the Volunteer Hall, Selkirk. [598]
January 16	ACD addressed a meeting of electors at the Victoria Hall, Selkirk. [599]
January 17	ACD stood again for Parliament as prospective member for the Scottish constituency of the Border Burghs, he was again defeated [99,180,200,202] ACD 2,444 votes, Thomas Shaw 3,133 votes. [215] (*3)
January 17	The UK General Elections took place at Hawick Burghs where ACD was an unsuccessful candidate. [979] (*3)
January 18	ACD was the unsuccessful Unionist candidate in Hawick at the General Election. ACD 2,444 votes, Thomas Shaw 3,133 votes. [3,6,14,125,1353] (*3)
January 18	ACD and Innes at the Tower Hotel, Hawick. [203]
January 19	ACD at the Grand Hotel, Trafalgar Square, London. [322]

1906

January 26	ACD at the Grand Hotel, Trafalgar Square, London. [18,202]
February 14	ACD at Undershaw. [884]
March 1	ACD attended the New Vagabonds Ladysmith Dinner at the Hotel Cecil, London. [1020,1021]
March 3	The romantic comedy in four acts, *Brigadier Gerard* by ACD opened at the Imperial Theatre, London starring Lewis Waller, [6,99,203,322,1354] (*2) it ran for 114 performances [322] from 3 March-12 May. [6]
March 8	*Brigadier Gerard* opened at the Imperial Theatre, London. [202] (*2)
March 10	ACD was probably at 7 Horton Street, Kensington, the home of E.W. Hornung. [884]
March	William Payne who stole photographs belonging to ACD from a Pickfords van was sentenced to three-months hard labour at Worship Street Court. [1079]
April	ACD at Undershaw. [18]
April	ACD gave a gift of £50 to The Hindhead Golf Club and loaned a further £100 without security. [125,322]
April 6	ACD attended a Pilgrims banquet at the Savoy Hotel, London. [1355]
April 19	ACD at the Grand Hotel, Trafalgar Square, London. [203]
April 23	ACD chaired the annual general meeting of the Authors' Club. [1972]
April 23	ACD attended the inaugural meeting of the Central London Branch of the Jewish Territorial Organization at Steinway Hall, Lower Seymour Street, London. [1356]
May	ACD at Undershaw. [203]
May	In the middle of May *Brigadier Gerard* moved to the Lyric Theatre, London. [203]
May 5	ACD attended a banquet at the Grand Hall, Hotel Cecil, London, held by the London Society of East Anglians. [1974]
May 14	*Brigadier Gerard* opened at the Lyric Theatre, London from 14 May-27 June. [6]
May 19	ACD played cricket for the Authors against the Artists at New Road, Esher, he scored 2, the Artists won, also in the Authors team were Innes Doyle who scored 51 and E.W. Hornung who scored 1. [235]
May 24	ACD attended a dinner to Lord Milner at the Hotel Cecil, London. [322,1357]
May 26	ACD played cricket for MCC & Ground against R.M.C. (Sandhurst) at Sandhurst, he scored zero and took 1 catch, MCC & Ground won. [1959]
May 28	Louise accompanied Innes to the Imperial Theatre, London to see *Brigadier Gerard* where they met Lewis Waller. [322] (*3)
May 29	Louise accompanied Innes to the theatre in London. [215] (*3)
May 29	Innes, Louise and Mary went to see ACD's play, *Brigadier Gerard* where they met Lewis Waller. [124,202] (*3)
June	*An Incursion into Diplomacy* published in *The Cornhill Magazine*. [6,99,196,198]
June	ACD at Undershaw. [203]
June 8	ACD at the Grand Hotel, London. [203]
June 8	ACD proposed the Magistrates at the Surrey County Dinner. [203]
June 8	ACD attended a dinner held by the new High Sheriff (Mr R. Collingwood Forster at the Hotel Cecil, London. [600]
June 8	ACD chaired an extraordinary general meeting of the Authors' Club. [1972]
June	ACD attended a ladies night at the Authors' Club. [202] (*2)
June 11	ACD presided at a ladies' dinner at the Authors' Club held at the Criterion. [203,1358] (*2)
June 12	In Gilbert and Sullivan's *A Trial by Jury* the cast included ACD and Anthony Hope as members of the jury, W.S. Gilbert played the part of The Associate. This was performed in the afternoon at Drury Lane Theatre, London as part of the Ellen Terry Jubilee. [1150]
June	ACD unveiled a memorial tablet to Henry Fielding. [202] (*2)

1906

June 15	ACD unveiled a memorial tablet to Henry Fielding at Widcombe Lodge, Bath. [1359] (*2)
June 15	ACD made a speech on the life and work of Henry Fielding at the Guildhall, Bath. [6,203]
June 21	Claire Foley, Nelson Foley's daughter and Jane's (Ida) stepdaughter, married Martin Henze in Naples, Italy. [124]
June	*Brigadier Gerard* closed at the Lyric Theatre, London. [203]
June 30	ACD attended the Hindhead Golf Club Exhibition Match and official opening. [124,125,202]
July	*An Incursion into Diplomacy* published by Smith, Elder & Co., London. [6]
July 3	ACD at Undershaw. [884]
July 4	At 03:00hrs Louise, the first Lady Conan Doyle died aged 49 at Undershaw, Hindhead, Surrey [3,4,6,11,14,15,20,68,78,200,202,203,215,322,1360] she died from the effects of chronic tuberculosis. [124,180]
July 6	The funeral of Louise took place at St. Luke's Church, Grayshott, the service was conducted by the Vicar, the Revd. J.M. Jeakes and the Revd. C.C. Angell (brother-in-law of Louise), chief mourner was ACD, accompanying him were Miss Hawkins (Louise's sister), Captain Innes Doyle, Mr E.W. Hornung and Mr A.W. Wood (ACD's secretary). [124,202,203,322,1361]
July 7	Stratten Boulnois visited ACD at Undershaw to pay his respects. [124]
July 23	ACD as a director attended the fifth annual general meeting of Raphael Tuck & Sons (Ltd.) at Salisbury House, Finsbury Circus. [1362]
Summer	ACD had a miniature railway or monorail running in the grounds of Undershaw. [3,14]
July 31	Kingsley completed his last term at Sandroyd. [124,202]
August 3	ACD at the Ashdown Forest Hotel, Forest Row, Sussex, [18,124,202] Ashdown Park Hotel. [322]
August 10	Innes joined ACD at the Ashdown Forest Hotel; they then dined at the Leckie's home, Monkstown, Crowborough, [124,202,215] Ashdown Park Hotel. [322]
August 18	ACD spent the weekend at Crowborough and played in the competition in connection with the Beacon Golf Club, he returned a score of 86, with a handicap of 1. [601]
September	Kingsley commenced his studies at Eton. [322]
September	Birth of Claire Annette Oldham, daughter of Leslie and Caroline (Lottie) Oldham. [124] (*2)
September 5	Birth of Claire Annette Oldham, daughter of Leslie and Caroline (Lottie) Oldham. [68,200,203] (*2)
September 6	ACD at the Old Waverly Temperance Hotel, Edinburgh. [203]
September	ACD took a short break in Dunbar, Scotland [14]
September 7	ACD at the Roxburgh County Hotel, Dunbar. [203]
September 14	Innes who was in Scotland, was informed that he being posted to the 95th Battery at Aldershot, Hampshire. [124]
September 14	ACD, Innes and Kingsley were at the Roxburghe Hotel, Dunbar, Scotland. [202]
September 15	Innes travelled to Dunbar, Scotland, and met ACD and Kingsley who were staying at the Roxburgh Hotel. [124]
September 16	ACD, Kingsley and Innes took tea with Lewis Waller and others [124] in Edinburgh. [202]
September 17	Kingsley and Innes left Scotland, Innes returning to Liverpool, and Kingsley to Eton. [124,202]
October	ACD at Undershaw. [203]
October	ACD loaned Hindhead Golf Club £100. [125]
October 1	*Sir Nigel* published in America by McClure, Philips & Co. [99]

1906

October 12	ACD was at The Lodge, Crowborough. [1027] {Note: the letter is written on ACD's personal letterhead, Undershaw, Hindhead, Surrey, with the address The Lodge, Crowborough and the date Oct 12/06 in his handwriting and was sent to Kingsley. The letter is bordered in black indicating that he was still in mourning for his wife Louise who died on 4 July 1906.
October	George Edalji released after serving three years of seven-year sentence. [99,180,215] (*4)
October 19	George Edalji was released from prison. [15,31,322] (*4)
October 19	Innes spent the weekend at Undershaw. [322]
October 20	ACD, Innes, Bertram Fletcher Robinson, Alfred Wood and his nephew Sholto Wood played golf at Hindhead. [124,129,202,215,322]
October 21	ACD and Innes drove to Godalming and took Mary out for tea. [124,215]
October 21	Innes returned to Aldershot where he was based. [322]
November 5	*Brigadier Gerard* was performed at Savoy Theatre, New York from 5-17 November. [6]
November 14	ACD attended a dinner held by the Motor Union of Great Britain and Ireland at the Hotel Great Central, Marylebone Road, London. [1363]
n.d.	*Sir Nigel* published. [180] (*2)
November 15	*Sir Nigel* published by Smith, Elder & Co., London. [6,99,322] (*2)
November 19	Innes travelled by train from Woolwich to Haslemere, ACD, Mary Conan Doyle and Miss Julia Pocock at Undershaw. [124]
November 21	Innes joined the Hindhead Golf Club for six months. [124]
November 22	ACD at Undershaw. [18]
November 26	Hindhead Golf Club held an invitation only competition where ACD presented the prizes. [322]
n.d.	George Edalji was released from prison. [202] (*4)
December	*Through the Magic Door* published in *Cassell's Magazine* from December 1906 to November 1907. [6,198,202]
December	ACD took up the cause of George Edalji, unjustly imprisoned in 1903 for cattle maiming. [3,4,6,14,15,31,203,322]
December 2	ACD attended a committee meeting of Hindhead Golf Club. [125]
December 12	ACD, Innes, Bryan Mary (Dodo) Angell and Jean Leckie went to the Scala Theatre, London. [124,322]
December 22	Innes travelled to Undershaw, Mary and Kingsley Conan Doyle at Undershaw. [124]
Christmas	The family spent their last Christmas at Undershaw, guests included Lewis Waller and his brother Victor. [124,202,203,322]
December 26	ACD chaired a special general committee meeting of Hindhead Golf Club. [125]
December 28	Churton Collins of Our Society (Crimes Club) visited ACD at Undershaw. [31,202,322]

1907

n.d.	*The Secret of the Moor Cottage* by H. Ripley Cromarsh (the pen name of ACD's sister, Bryan Mary Doyle) published. [203] (*2)
n.d.	*Waterloo* (or *A Story of Waterloo*), a play based on *A Straggler of '15* by ACD published by Samuel French Ltd., London. [6]
n.d.	George Edalji released from prison. [99] (*4)
January	ACD met George Edalji at the Grand Hotel, Charing Cross, London. [3,14,202]
January	ACD and George Edalji consulted Mr R.D. Yelverton at his chambers at Pump Court, Temple, London. [1364]
January	*The Story of Mr. George Edalji* published. [180]
January 3	ACD travelled to Great Wyrley to interview Revd. Edalji. [215]
January 7	ACD at Monkstown, Crowborough. [18]
January 11	*The Case of Mr. George Edalji* published in *The Daily Telegraph* on 11 and 12 January. [6,99,198,202,215]

1907

January 13	ACD at Undershaw. [18]
January 14	ACD at Undershaw. [18]
January 15	ACD visited the Home Secretary, Herbert Gladstone to discuss the Edalji evidence. [202,322]
January 17	ACD at Undershaw. [99]
January 18	ACD at the Grand Hotel, Trafalgar Square, London. [18]
January 19	*The Case of George Edalji: A Question for Opthalmologists* published in the *British Medical Journal* and *Lancet*. [6,196,198]
January 20	*The Story of Mr. George Edalji* published by T. Harrison Roberts, London. [6,198,322]
January 21	Death of Bertram Fletcher Robinson at 44, Eaton Terrace, London. [153,322,1365]
January 22	ACD a guest at the New York Vagabond Club Christmas dinner at the Hotel Cecil, Strand, London. [85]
January 23	ACD at Monkstown, Crowborough. [884]
January 24	Memorial service in memory of Bertram Fletcher Robinson held at St. Clement Danes, Strand, London. [322,1366]
January 24	Bertram Fletcher Robinson was buried at St. Andrew's Church, Ipplepen, Devon; the coffin was of polished oak and bore the inscription "Bertram Fletcher Robinson, Died 21st January 1907, Aged 37 years." Henry Baskerville was one of the bearers, floral tributes included one from Sir & Lady Conan Doyle. [1769]
January 25	ACD at the Grand Hotel, Trafalgar Square, London. [18]
January 29	ACD at Undershaw. [203]
February 9	ACD had an interview with the Home Secretary regarding the George Edalji case. [602]
February 9	ACD at the Grand Hotel, London. [884]
February 16	P. Stewart Leckie, brother of Jean Leckie, visited Undershaw. [123]
February	*The Tailor of Wallingham* by H. Ripley Cromarsh (the pen name of ACD's sister Bryan Mary Doyle) published in *The All-Story Magazine*, Volume 7 number 2. {photo copy in the collection of Brian W. Pugh.}
n.d.	ACD unwell at Undershaw. [124,322]
February 21	ACD was taken ill at Undershaw. [203]
February 26	Innes visited ACD at Undershaw, still unwell, not very fit. [124]
February 27	ACD better, Ptomaine subsiding. [124,203]
March	ACD announced his forthcoming marriage to Jean Leckie. [124]
March	*The Croxley Master* published by McClure, Philips & Co., New York. [6]
March 3	ACD probably arrived at Monkstown, Crowborough. [203]
March 4	ACD went out for the first time after his illness. [202,322,1367]
March 4	ACD at Monkstown, Crowborough. [18]
March 6	ACD left Hindhead for Crowborough where he stayed for a few days. [202,322,1368]
n.d.	ACD visited Monkstown, Crowborough for a few days. [203]
March 15	ACD at Undershaw. [203]
March	ACD became a Vice-President of the Surrey Liberal Unionists Association. [1369]
April 1	Mr & Mrs (Ida) Nelson Foley visited Undershaw. [123]
April 7	*The Times* announced in the Wills and Bequests that: 'Dame Louisa Doyle, of Undershaw, Hindhead, Surrey, who died on July 3, aged 49, has been granted to Sir Arthur Conan Doyle, her husband. The estate is valued at £454.' [322,1370]
April 7	ACD was received the Honorary Doctor of Laws degree (LL.D). [68] (*5)
April 8	ACD attended the monthly dinner of the Authors' Club at 4 Whitehall Court. [2048]
April 11	Mr & Mrs Charles Cyril Angell and their son Bryan Branford Angell visited Undershaw. [123]

1907

April 13	ACD at the Grand Hotel, London. [203]
April 15	ACD attended the annual general meeting of the Authors' Club. [1972]
April 15	ACD attended a dinner and reception held by Earl and Countess Beauchamp at their residence in Belgrave Square, London. [1371]
April 22	ACD presided at a public dinner held by the Society of Somerset Men at the Café Monica, Piccadilly Circus, London. [322,1372]
April 23	ACD attended the funeral of Viscount Midleton at Peper Harow Church, Godalming, Surrey. [1373]
May	George Edalji pardoned. [3,17,202,215]
May 1	It was announced that ACD had donated 10 shillings to the National Flag and London Schools Fund. [2049]
May 8	ACD attended the annual dinner of the Society of Authors at the Criterion Restaurant, London. [322,1374]
May 12	ACD read a paper "The Edalji Case" at a meeting of Our Society (Crimes Club). [77,202]
May 13	ACD played a first class cricket match on the 13, 14 & 15 for MCC against Derbyshire at Lord's, there was no play on the 14 owing to heavy rain [1375] he scored 19 and then 8 not out and took 1 catch, MCC won. This was to be ACD's last appearance in first-class matches. [235]
May 15	ACD at the Grand Hotel, London. [203]
May 18	George Edalji was exonerated. [202]
May 18	ACD at Undershaw. [884]
May 20	ACD at Undershaw. [884]
May 24	ACD at Undershaw. [884]
May 25	ACD played cricket for Hampshire Rovers against United Services at United Services Ground, Portsmouth, he scored 4 and 8, drawn match. [1960]
May 27	ACD attended the annual meeting of the Children's County Holiday Fund at the Hotel Metropole, London. [1376]
May 28	ACD at the Grand Hotel, Trafalgar Square, London. [18]
May 30	ACD at Undershaw. [18]
May 30	Innes visited ACD at Undershaw, ACD still not very fit. [124]
May 31	ACD played cricket for the Authors against the Artists at Esher, Surrey, he scored 36 and took 4 wickets, the Authors won [603], or for E.W. Hornung's XI against the Artists, he scored 26 took 4 wickets and 1 catch, E.W. Hornung's XI won. Also playing for E.W. Hornungs team were Innes Doyle who scored 1 and took 1 catch and E.W. Hornung scored zero. [235]
June 6	ACD played cricket on 6 & 7 for MCC against Hampstead at Lord's; he scored 35 and took 1 catch, A.H. Wood played for MCC, he scored 14 and took 1 catch, MCC won. [235,1961]
June 10	ACD at Undershaw. [18]
June 19	ACD played cricket for MCC against Egypt and The Sudan at Lord's, he scored 47, match drawn. [235]
June 21	ACD attended a dinner at the Dorchester House, London. [1377]
June 22	Bram Stoker visited Undershaw on 22 and 23 June. [123]
June 24	ACD at Ely-place, Holborn, E.C., London. [18]
June 27	ACD was among thousands of members and friends of the Salvation Army that filled the Albert Hall, London to welcome General Booth on his return from Canada. [1112]
July	King Edward VII officially opened the Union Jack Club, 91 Waterloo Road, London. [189]
July 8	The Mam, ACD, Innes, Mary Conan Doyle, Jean Leckie, Willie and Constance (Connie) Hornung, Cyril and Bryan Mary (Dodo) Angell gathered at Hornton Street, the home of Willie and Constance, for the seventieth birthday of the Mam, after dining at the Gaiety, they all went to see *Mrs. Wiggs of the Cabbage Patch*. [124,202]

1907

July 9	In the *Daily Express* it was announced the engagement of ACD and Jean Leckie and that the marriage was to take place in September. [322]
July 10	The Conan Doyle Cup was won at the Bisley meeting by Mr C.E. Fidgeon. [1378]
July 11	ACD attended the unveiling of a bronze bust of Mr William Ernest Henly in the crypt of St. Paul's Cathedral, London. [1379]
July 12	ACD played cricket on 12 & 13 for MCC & Ground against Leamington at Leamington; he scored 9 and took 3 wickets and 1 catch, MCC won [604] played at Arlington Avenue, Leamington Spa, he did not bat in the second innings. [235]
July	ACD at the Regent Hotel, Royal Leamington Spa. [18]
July 15	ACD at Leamington. [884]
July 15	ACD played cricket for MCC & Ground against Coventry & North Warwickshire at Stoke, he scored 11, MCC won [605] at Bulls Head Ground, Coventry. [235]
July 15	Kingsley, Mary and Nem left Undershaw. [124]
July 17	ACD played cricket on 17 & 18 for MCC & Ground against Warwickshire Gentlemen at Warwick, in the first innings he scored 37 not out and 30 in the second innings, he also took 2 wickets, the result was a draw. [1773]
July 22	ACD as a director attended the sixth annual general meeting of Raphael Tuck & Sons (Ltd.) at Salisbury House, Finsbury Circus. [322,1380]
July 29	ACD played cricket on 29 & 30 for MCC against Royal Navy at Lord's; he scored 36 and 43 and took 1 catch, A.H. Wood played for MCC, he scored 10 and 9 and stumped 4 [235] Royal Navy won. [1962]
August 5	Jean Leckie with her brother Malcolm Leckie and her friend Lily Loder-Symonds visited Undershaw. [123,322]
August 9	ACD played cricket on 9 & 10 for MCC against Wiltshire at Lord's; he scored 27 and 9, Wiltshire won. [235]
August 14	ACD played cricket for MCC against Royal Academy of Arts at Lord's, he scored 56 and took 4 wickets [235] MCC won. [1963]
August 14	ACD at Monkstown. [884]
August 15	ACD played cricket for the Authors against the Actors at Lord's, he scored 4 and took 1 wicket, the Actors won, the Authors team included F.G. Guggisberg who scored 56, A.H. Wood zero, A.A. Milne 5, P.G. Wodehouse 1 and E.W. Hornung 7 not out. [235,1381]
August 21	ACD played cricket for MCC & Ground against London Playing Fields at Lord's, he scored 2 and took 3 wickets, match drawn. [235,1382]
August 26	Innes was at Aldershot and was visited for tea by Mary Conan Doyle, Kingsley Conan Doyle, Mary Storr and Jack, and Norah Alexander; they all watched polo and cricket. [124]
August 28	ACD visited Great Wyrley, Staffordshire to investigate the Edalji case. [1383]
August 30	ACD was at the Grand Hotel, Trafalgar Square, London. [1005]
August 31	ACD was at Undershaw. [1005]
August 31	ACD, Jean Leckie, Mr Leckie, Malcolm Leckie, Mary Conan Doyle and Kingsley Conan Doyle visited Innes at Aldershot for Sports Day. [124]
September	Members of the Authors' Club presented ACD with a silver mounted lemonade jug inscribed 'To Sir Arthur Conan Doyle, Chairman of the Authors' Club from his fellow members.' [1972]
September 2	ACD was at the Grand Hotel, Trafalgar Square, London. [1005]
September 4	ACD was at Undershaw. [1005]
September 5	ACD was at Undershaw. [1005]
September 6	ACD was interviewed by a representative of the *Birmingham Gazette & Express* at Undershaw regarding the Edalji case. [2064]
September 12	ACD attended the play *The Sins of Society* at the Drury Lane Theatre, London, [322]
September 14	ACD was at Undershaw. [1005]

1907

September 17	Innes on Autumn Manoeuvres and then left for ACD's wedding-eve dinner party at The Gaiety Restaurant [124,202,322] the party consisted ACD, Innes, John and Archie Langman, Alfred Wood, Major Guggisberg, Captain Trevor, Cyril Angell, Willie Hornung and A.C.R. Williams. [322]
n.d.	ACD married Jean Leckie. [180] (*2)
September 18	ACD married Jean Leckie (the second Lady Conan Doyle) the wedding was held at 1:45p.m. at St. Margaret's Church, Westminster, Innes Doyle was best man and Cyril Angell married them, only about thirty guests were present [1796], the reception was held at Whitehall Rooms, Hotel Metropole at 2:45p.m., some 250 guests were present, among them Jerome K. Jerome, Bram Stoker, J.M. Barrie, George Newnes, Max Pemberton, Herbert Greenhough Smith and George Edalji. [3,4,6,10,11,14,15,20,68,124,200,202,203,215,322] (*2)
September	ACD and Jean spent September 21 & 22 at the Hotel Regina, Paris as two days of their honeymoon [86] they went on to visit Berlin, Venice, Rome and Constantinople. [215]
September	By the end of September Mary Conan Doyle was in Dresden, Saxony studying music. [124]
October 9	ACD and Jean at the Hotel Royal Danieli, Venice. [203]
October 11	ACD and Jean left Venice for Rome. [203]
October 11	ACD and Jean in Rome. [203]
October 13	ACD in Rome and attended a performance of the play *Sherlock Holmes* at the Manzoni Theatre. [606]
October 14	It was announced that Messrs. Hampton had recently let on lease Undershaw. [1787] {Note: it did not mention who leased the house.}
October 14	ACD left Rome for Naples and arrived on the same day. [606]
October 14	ACD and Jean arrived in Naples and stayed and Parkers Hotel. [203]
October 14-21	ACD stayed in Naples. [606]
October 21	ACD was at the Hotel Du Vesuve, Naples. [1005]
October 21	ACD and Jean left Naples for Constantinople, touching Athens and Smyrna on the way. [203]
October	ACD and Jean spent some time at Smyrna. [203]
October 26	ACD on board the steamer *Paquebot Stambul*. [606]
October 26	ACD and Jean arrived in Constantinople. [203]
October 27	ACD probably disembarked the *Paquebot Stambul* at Constantinople. [606]
n.d.	*Through the Magic Door* published. [180,202]
November	During their honeymoon ACD received The Order of the Second Class of the Medjidieh and his wife received the Order of the Chevekat from Sultan Abdul-Hamid in Constantinople [6,14] (*3) or the Order of the Mejidie and the Shefkat Nisham. [202]
November 1	ACD and Jean visited Constantinople and attended the Selamlik, the Sultan decorated ACD with the second class of the Medjidieh, and his wife the second class of the Nichan-i-Chefakat. [68,1384] (*3)
November 1	ACD received the Order of the Medjidie, second class (also called the Mecidi Nishani) from the Ottoman Grand Sultan Abdul Hammid II; Lady Jean was also awarded the Order of Nichan-I-Chefakat, second class (Shefkat Nishani or the Order of Charity. [200,203] (*3)
November 2	ACD and Jean stayed at the Pera Palace, Constantinople. [202,203]
November 8	It was announced that Windlesham had been connected to the National Telephone Company's Tunbridge Wells exchange during October. [862]
November 10	ACD and Jean stayed at the Hotel Regina, Palace Rivoli, Paris. [203]
November 14	ACD and Jean travelled from Paris to London. [203]
November 15	ACD and Jean stayed at the Hotel Metropole, London. [203]
n.d.	Undershaw was let, ACD and Jean moved to Crowborough, Sussex. [124]
November	Mid-November ACD and Jean returned to Windlesham. [202]
November 16	ACD and Jean at Windlesham. [203]

1907

November 20	*Through the Magic Door* published by Smith, Elder & Co., London. [6]
November 30	Innes Doyle visited Mary Conan Doyle for a few days in Dresden. [124]
n.d.	From 1907 until his death in 1930, ACD was living at Windlesham, Crowborough, Sussex. [232]
Late 1907	ACD and Jean moved into Windlesham, Hurtis Hill, Crowborough. [16,68,200] (*2)
December 4	Death of Robert Leckie, brother of Jean Leckie. [124]
December 6	It was reported that ACD had recently become the Vice-President of the Crowborough Rifle Club. [607]
December 13	ACD addressed the members of the Whitefriars Club at their Christmas dinner at the Tracadero, London. [1826]
December 18	The New Vagabond Club gave a "homecoming" Christmas dinner for ACD and Jean at the Hotel Cecil [1385], due to a bereavement Jean was unable to attend. [975]
December 19	ACD attended the Authors' Club Christmas Dinner. [2050]
December	ACD at Windlesham. [203]
December	Mary Conan Doyle spent Christmas in Dresden. [124,215]
December	Kingsley spent Christmas with Willie and Constance (Connie) Hornung at West Grinstead Park. [124]
December 25	*The Times* announced that Canon Edward Carus Selwyn, D.D., the retiring headmaster of Uppingham School had taken over Undershaw, Hindhead. [322,1386]

1908

n.d.	ACD and Jean moved into Windlesham, Hurtis Hill, Crowborough. [52,99] (*2)
n.d.	ACD honoured at the Encaenia, Oxford. [7]
n.d.	ACD elected as a vice-president of The Beacon Brass Band, Crowborough. [127]
January	Kingsley Conan Doyle spent some time at Windlesham, Crowborough, Sussex. [124]
January	ACD subscribed ten guineas to the Veteran Relief Fund. [1832]
January 25	ACD at Windlesham. [884]
January 27	ACD became a vice-president of the Research Defence Society. [1387]
n.d.	Death of Sidney Paget. [99] (*2)
January 28	Death of Sidney Paget [189] in Margate, Kent after a long illness aged 47. [1388] (*2)
February	ACD resigned as President of Hindhead Golf Club. [1964]
February 21	ACD attended a demonstration by the Congo Reform Association at Queen's Hall. [2000]
February 22	ACD and Jean attended the wedding of Miss Marie Mandina Botha and Mr Robert Crawford Hawkins at the Dutch Church, Austin Friars, London. [2017]
March	*The Strand Magazine* published *A Pot of Caviare*. [6,124,194,195,196,198,202]
March 4	ACD at Windlesham. [203]
April	ACD wrote *The Adventure of Wisteria Lodge*. [6]
April 8	ACD chaired the annual general meeting of the Authors' Club held at Whitehall Court. [1972]
April 10	Jean opened a bazaar at Tunbridge Wells, Kent [203] ACD said a few words before Jean opened the sale in connection with the Gentlewoman's Industrial Guild at the Pump Room, Tunbridge Wells. [863]
April 11	ACD at Windlesham. [203]
April 17	ACD had completed writing *The Adventure of Wisteria Lodge*. [202]
Easter	Innes Doyle spent Easter with ACD and Jean at Windlesham, Crowborough, Sussex. [124]
May	*The Grey Dress* published in *The Flag*. [6,196]
n.d.	ACD received the LL.D. from the University of Edinburgh. [7] (*5)
May 2	ACD attended the Reader's Pension Fund dinner. [608]

1908

May 16	It was advertised that a cricket match between Conan Doyle's XI and East Grinstead would be played on 4 August at East Grinstead. [822] {Note: this is possibly the match played on 12 August 1908, MCC and East Grinstead.}
May 20	Innes Doyle played cricket for MCC against Christ's Hospital at Horsham [56] at Christ's Hospital Ground, Horsham, he scored 11, MCC won. [235]
May 22	ACD and Jean were summoned, among others, to attend their Majesties the King and Queen at court at Buckingham Palace, London. (It is unclear if they attended). [1389]
May	Late May William Gillette visited ACD at Windlesham. [1030]
May 28	ACD played cricket for MCC & Ground against Royal Academy of Arts at Lord's; he scored 6 and took 4 wickets and 1 catch, MCC won. [56,235,1390]
May 30	ACD consented to act as patron of the Referees' Union. [1970]
June	ACD became a director of Cranston's Hotels Company. [202]
June 1	ACD played cricket for the Blue Mantles against Lewes Priory at the Dripping Pan, Lewes he scored 14 and took 2 wickets, Lewes Priory won. [791]
June 2	ACD supported the daylight saving bill. [1391]
June 5	ACD played cricket for Tunbridge Wells against Fulham at the Nevill Ground, Tunbridge Wells, he scored 46 not out, Tunbridge Wells won. [820]
June 13	ACD & Jean performed the opening ceremony of the new Salvation Hall, Whitehill, Crowborough, ACD made a speech to those gathered. [821]
June 15	ACD played cricket for MCC against Ardingly College at Ardingly College Ground, Haywards Heath, he scored zero, match drawn. [56]
June 16	Evidence given by ACD to the Select Committee of the House of Commons in support of the daylight saving bill. [6,7,1392]
June 17	ACD played cricket for MCC against St. John's College, Hurstpierpoint at Hurstpierpoint College Ground, he scored 9, MCC won. [56]
June 18	ACD played cricket for MCC against Brighton College at Brighton College Ground, he scored 14 and took 5 wickets, MCC won. [56]
June 20	ACD attended a Garden Party at Windsor Castle. [2030]
June 20	Innes played cricket for MCC against Royal Military College Sandhurst at Royal Military College Ground, Camberley, he scored 2, Royal Military College Sandhurst won, E.W. Hornung also played for MCC scoring 1. [235]
June 23	ACD presided at the dinner of the Incogniti Cricket Club at the Grand Hotel, Trafalgar Square, London. [2029]
June 23	ACD was elected a Director of Cranston's Hotels Company Ltd. at the annual general meeting held in Edinburgh. [609]
June 24	ACD and Jean attended the annual soirée of the Royal Academy at Burlington House, London. [2031]
June 24	ACD and Jean attended a dinner given by The Duke of Sutherland to the Tariff Commission at Stafford House, St. James's, London. [1393]
June 28	ACD chaired a Men's Meeting in conjunction with the National Purity Crusade at the Crowborough Wesleyan Chapel, Crowborough. [823]
June 30	ACD at Windlesham. [203]
June 30	ACD played cricket for Blue Mantles against Mr F.H. Gresson's XI at the Nevill Ground, Tunbridge Wells, he scored 1 and took 1 wicket. [864]
July	ACD at Windlesham. [203]
July 1	ACD played cricket for MCC against Tonbridge School at Tonbridge School Ground, he scored 40 not out, MCC won. [56,235]
July 1	It was reported in the *Daily Express* on 1 July that ACD was amongst three people believed to have been defrauded by Francis R. Crawford. [1030]
July 2	ACD and Jean attended a lunch reception held by Lady Henderson at 18 Arlington Street, London. [1394]
July 3	ACD visited the Duchess of Sutherland. [203]
July 4	ACD played cricket for Tunbridge Wells against Middlesex Hospital at the Nevill Ground, Tunbridge Wells, he scored 5. [865]

1908

July 9	ACD played cricket for MCC against Egypt and The Sudan at Lord's, he scored 13, Egypt and The Sudan won [56], he did not bat in the second innings, A.H. Wood played for MCC, he scored 5. [235]
July 10	ACD and Jean attended the Eton and Harrow cricket match at Lord's. [1395]
July 14	Mr H. Playfer won the Conan Doyle Cup at Bisley. [1396]
July 15	ACD played cricket for MCC against The Mote at Yalding, he scored 1, The Mote won [56] played at Mote Park, Maidstone, A.H. Wood played for MCC, he scored 2 and took 2 wickets and 2 catches. [235]
July 16	ACD played cricket for the Authors against the Actors at Lord's, match abandoned (rain), ACD did not bat, match drawn [56,235] A.H. Wood played for the Authors but did not bat. [235]
July 21	ACD as a director attended the seventh annual general meeting of Raphael Tuck & Sons (Ltd.) at Salisbury House, Finsbury Circus. [1397]
July 21	ACD played cricket for Blue Mantles against Old Eastbournians at the Nevill Ground, Tunbridge Wells, he scored 6 and took 2 wickets, Old Eastbournians won. [866]
July 23	ACD played cricket for Sussex Martlets against Brook House at West Hoathly, he scored 9, the result is unknown. [1176]
July 24	ACD at the Olympic games as a special correspondent for the *Daily Mail*. [10,14,215]
July 25	*A Heroic Roman. How Dorando failed to seize the Laurel* published in the *Daily Mail*. [6,198]
July 28	ACD played cricket for Blue Mantles against Upper Tooting at the Nevill Ground, Tunbridge Wells, he scored 14, Blue Mantles won. [867]
July	At the *Daily Mail* Office in London, ACD made a speech and presented a cheque for £308 and a gold cigarette case to the Olympic Marathon runner Dorando Pietri. [6] (*2)
July 31	At the *Daily Mail* Office in London, Jean presented Dorando with a gold cigarette case and a cheque for £308 10s [202] £308 and ACD also added a few words of congratulations. [1398] (*2)
August	*The Silver Mirror* published in *The Strand Magazine*. [6,194,195,196,198]
August	*The Undoing of Archibald A Composite Novelette by Fifty Popular Novelist*, including ACD published in *The Strand Magazine*. [6,196,198]
August 7	ACD played cricket for his own team, A. Conan Doyle & Crowborough & District against Heron's Ghyll at Heron's Ghyll House, Heron's Ghyll, near Crowborough, he scored 42, ACD's team won. [868]
August 12	ACD played cricket for MCC against East Grinstead at East Grinstead, he scored 4 and took 1 catch, match drawn [56] at East Grinstead Sports Club Ground, Innes also played for MCC and scored 3 and took 1 catch. [235]
August 15	*The Singular Experience of Mr. J. Scott Eccles* published in *Collier's The National Weekly*. [198]
August 15	ACD played cricket for Blue Mantles against Mr J.R. Hope's XI at the Nevill Ground, Tunbridge Wells, he scored 4 not out and took 1 wicket. [869]
August 18	ACD at Windlesham. [870]
August 25	ACD at Windlesham. [884]
September	*The Adventure of Wisteria Lodge Pt. 1 The Singular Experience of Mr. John Scott Eccles* published in *The Strand Magazine*. [6,194,195,196,198,202,203]
September 2	It was reported in the *Daily Express* on 2 September that ACD & Jean had recently been staying in Worthing, Sussex but were now headed for Scotland. [1030]
September 15	ACD was re-elected as a Vice-President of the Crowborough Rifle Club at the Annual General Meeting held at the Bricklayers Arms, Crowborough. [871]
September 24	*Round the Fire Stories* published by Smith, Elder & Co., London. [6]
October	*The Adventure of Wisteria Lodge Pt. 2 The Tiger of San Pedro* published in *The Strand Magazine*. [6,194,195,196,198,202]
October 14	ACD at Windlesham. [203]

1908

October 14	"Conan Doyle & Gibbon", ACD lectured on the Great Historian to the Crowborough Literary Society. [6,203]
October 15	ACD visited Innes probably at Camberley. [203]
October 19	ACD attended a complimentary and farewell dinner given to Jam of Nawanaga at the Guildhall, Cambridge, and ACD also proposed the toast [610], to cricketer Kumar Shri Ranjitsinhji, known as Ranji. [1030]
October 20	ACD and Lady Conan Doyle gave an embroidered table centre as a present to Mr L. Fane Gladwin and Miss E.V. Lindsay-Hogg at their wedding held at St. Peter's, Eaton Square, London. [611]
October 20	ACD at Windlesham. [203]
November	ACD at Windlesham. [18]
November	Among others ACD, Anthony Hope Hawkins and H. Rider Haggard were members of the general council of the Authors' Club. [1030]
November 13	*A Pot of Caviare* performed at the Jersey Opera House on 13 and 14 November. [6]
November 16	ACD was patron of the Wolseley-Siddeley Car Company. [1399]
November 19	ACD chaired the annual bazaar and concert on behalf of the Tunbridge Wells Cripples' Branch of Dr Barnardo's Homes at the Great Hall, Tunbridge Wells, Jean also attended. [1400]
November 24	ACD presided at the 18th annual smoking concert arranged by the students of the Middlesex Hospital in aid of the cancer wards. [11401]
November 25	ACD and Jean left England for a short stay in the south of France. [1402]
December	*The Bruce-Partington Plans* published in *The Strand Magazine*. [6,194,195,196,198,202]
December 11	It was reported that ACD and Jean had been staying a few days at the Metropole, Monte Carlo. [2001]
Christmas	Innes Doyle and Kingsley Conan Doyle at Windlesham, Crowborough, Sussex and Mary Conan Doyle spent Christmas in Dresden. [124,202]

1909

n.d.	ACD became President of the Divorce Law Reform Union until 1919. [6,11,14,15,203,215]
n.d.	*Divorce Law Reform: An Essay* published by the Divorce Reform Union. [6]
n.d.	ACD took up campaign against Belgian oppression in the Congo. [99]
n.d.	ACD was writing *The Crime of the Congo*. [99]
January 3	Death of Nelson Foley husband Jane (Ida) [68,200,202,203] in London, he died of tuberculosis. [124]
January 9	ACD was part of the Churton Collins Memorial Fund. [1403]
January 10	ACD underwent an operation at his home Windlesham for a painful but not serious intestinal affection. [202,1404] (*3)
January	ACD became seriously ill with an intestinal blockage [15,20,202,203] which called for an operation on January 11 [6,20] or January 10 [6,14] (suffering from haemorrhoids) [124], the operation was performed at Windlesham. [6,14,202] (*3)
January	ACD purchased his neighbours land for £1,400. [202,203]{Note: Windlesham Cottage was built on this land.}
January 11	ACD passed a restless and painful night after his operation. [1405]
January 11	ACD underwent an operation at his home Windlesham, Crowborough. [138] (*3)
January 12	ACD had a better night, his condition was improving. [1406]
January 13	ACD passed a restless night, but his temperature and pulse were good. [1407]
January 14	ACD passed a better night and is doing well after a recent operation at home. [612]
January 15	ACD had a better night and was doing well. [1408]
January 17	ACD was doing well, having passed through the crisis of his illness. [1409]
January 20	ACD was convalescing and was able to leave his room for an hour. [1410]

1909

January 31	ACD had a small supplementary operation carried out at Windlesham. [202,203]
n.d.	During late January or early February after his illness and operation, ACD updated his will that he had first made in January 1900. [1030]
February 1	ACD at Windlesham. [203]
February 2	Oscar Slater was held at Tombs Prison, New York awaiting extradition proceedings. [321]
February 21	In Glasgow Oscar Slater was charged with the murder of Miss Marion Gilchrist. [1411]
February 22	It was announced that ACD had accepted the presidency of the Penzance Arcadians Amateur Dramatic Society. [1771]
n.d.	ACD visited the Poldhu Hotel, Mullion, Cornwall. [62] (*5)
February	After an operation ACD recuperated in Cornwall [52] some time after the operation ACD stayed at a hotel near Mullion on the Lizard. [14] (*5)
March	ACD and Jean visited Cornwall. [3] (*5)
March	*Shakespeare's Expostulation* (poem) published in *The Cornhill Magazine*. [6,196,198]
March	ACD at Windlesham. [203]
March 1	The Poe Centenary, ACD made a speech in memory of Edgar Allen Poe at the Whitehall Rooms, Hotel Metropole, London [3,6,31,203,1972] Kingsley Conan Doyle also attended. [1412] (*2)
March 1	ACD presided at the Edgar Allan Poe Centenary dinner. [613] (*2)
n.d.	Birth of Denis Percy Stewart Conan Doyle, son of ACD and Jean. [99] (*2)
March 17	Birth of Denis Percy Stewart Conan Doyle, son of ACD and Jean at Windlesham, Crowborough, Sussex [3,16,17,68,124,200,202,203,215] born on St. Patrick's Day at about 6p.m. [140] (*2)
March 26	ACD presented the prizes at the De La Warr Golf Club, Crowborough for the March medal competition. [824]
March 26	ACD attended a lecture and demonstration on physical education by J.P. Müller. [2051]
April	*By the North Sea* published in *The Press Album*. [6,198]
April	ACD at Windlesham. [203]
April	*Bendy's Sermon* (poem) published in *The Strand Magazine*. [6,194,195,196,198]
April 15	Denis Percy Stewart Conan Doyle baptized at All Saints Church, Crowborough. [68,200,327]
April 20	ACD attended a meeting in support of the Daylight Saving Bill held at the Guildhall, London. [614]
Easter	Kingsley Conan Doyle visited Mary Conan Doyle at Dresden. [124,202]
May	ACD at Windlesham. [203]
May	ACD was elected onto the committee of Beacon Golf Club, Crowborough. [825]
May 1	It was reported that Lady Conan Doyle sent a floral tribute to the funeral of Colonel Onslow at St. John's, Withyham, Sussex. [615]
May 3	The trial of Oscar Slater started at the Edinburgh Court. [4,30,215]
May 4	It was reported that ACD and Jean had arrived at the Berkeley Hotel, Piccadilly where they will stay for a fortnight. [2002]
May 6	Oscar Slater sentenced to death, to be hanged on Thursday 27 May. [30]
May 19	ACD at Windlesham. [203]
May 22	ACD attended the memorial service for George Meredith at Westminster Abbey, London. [1413,1972]
May 25	Oscar Slater reprieved and sentenced to penal servitude for life, the sentence served at Peterhead Prison. [4,14,30]
May 26	ACD claimed to have found a dinosaur footprint at Crowborough. [38]
May 29	ACD, A.H. Wood, O. Scott and E.G. Jones all tied in the Foursomes Golf Competition at Crowborough Beacon Golf Club, they all scored 4 down. [1965]

1909

May 29	Innes played cricket for MCC against Royal Military College Sandhurst at Royal Military Academy Ground, Camberley, he scored 6 and took 1 catch, match drawn. [235]
June	ACD at Windlesham. [203]
June	*A Discord. Being A Break In A Duet* published in *Nash's Magazine*. [6]
June	ACD played in the Whitsuntide Golf Competition at Crowborough Beacon Golf Club, he won this competition. Mr H. Goldfinch came second and Mr A. Gurney Champion came third. [1414]
June 8	The Japan Society gave a garden party in the afternoon in the grounds of the Royal Botanic Society at Regent's Park, London to meet the Prince and Princess Nashimoto. ACD and Jean were among nearly a thousand guests. [797]
June 10	ACD at the Hotel Metropole, London. [203]
June 11	ACD at the Adelphi Hotel, Liverpool. [203]
June 11	*The Fires of Fate*, a play by ACD adapted from *The Tragedy of the Korosko*, performed at the Shakespeare Theatre, Liverpool, on 11 & 12 June. [6,99,202,203]
Summer	ACD met Edmund Dene Morel at a London hotel to discuss the Congo. [202,215]
June 15	Innes Doyle took Constance (Connie) to Lord's, the first night of *The Fires of Fate* at the Lyric Theatre, London and then supper with ACD at the Metropole. [124]
June 15	*The Fires of Fate*, a play by ACD adapted from *The Tragedy of the Korosko*, opened at the Lyric Theatre, London [1415] it ran from 15 June-8 October. [6,99,203]
June 15	ACD made a speech in honour of Mr Ernest H. Shackleton, the British Antarctic Explorer at the Royal Societies Club, London. [6,202]
June 17	In the King's Bench Division, before Mr Justice Channell, Mr Jocelyn Brandon, of Messrs. Brandon and Nicholson, solicitors, sued Mr William Herbert Manning, as representative of the Princess's Theatre Syndicate Limited, to recover £190, balance of £210, stated to be the costs for procuring an agreement for a lease of the Princess's, Oxford Street. It was stated that the sum of £1,000 had been paid as deposit towards the cost of the lease by Sir A. Conan Doyle, but that amount had been forfeited. [253]
June 20	ACD at Windlesham. [1834]
June 23	It was announced that ACD would attend and speak at the annual general meeting of the Research Defence Society at the house of the Royal Society of Medicine, 20 Hanover Square, London on 25 June. [1416]
June 25	ACD attended and spoke at the annual general meeting of the Research Defence Society. [2105]
July 8	ACD attended a dinner held at the Prince's Restaurant, Piccadilly, London, to celebrate the Jubilee of the National Rifle Association. [1417]
July 20	ACD spoke at a meeting arranged by the Imperial Sunday Alliance at the Kings Hall, Holborn Restaurant, London. [1418]
Summer	Mary Conan Doyle spent a fortnight with Aunt Juey, (Julia Pocock). [124]
August	Mary Conan Doyle, Kingsley Conan Doyle and Aunt Juey (Julia Pocock) took a holiday at Swanage, Dorset. [124]
August	ACD helped a Torquay girl locate her fiancé. [4]
August	*The Lord of Falconbridge. A Legend of the Ring* published in *The Strand Magazine*. [6,194,195,196,198]
August 12	*Fires of Fate* transferred from the Lyric Theatre to the Haymarket Theatre from 12 August until the end of the month, returning to the Lyric for performances from 6 September to 9 October. [1030,1419]
August 18	Mary Conan Doyle and Kingsley Conan Doyle travelled to Scotland and stayed with their friend Dorothy Kirkwood near Largs. [124]

1909

August 18	ACD opened a sale of work held at Christ Church Schoolroom, Crowborough. [616]
August 20-30	The play *Fires of Fate* performed at the Haymarket Theatre, London. [1420]
August 20	ACD made a speech held at Crowborough on the "Congo Atrocities". [6]
August 25	ACD at Windlesham. [18]
August 27	ACD at Windlesham. [99]
August	ACD contributed ten shillings and sixpence to the Captain Webb Fund under the auspices of the Amateur Swimming Association. [1966]
September	*Some Recollections of Sport* published in *The Strand Magazine*. [6,194,195,196,198]
September 6	The play *Fires of Fate* returned to the Lyric Theatre, London. [1421]
September 11	It was reported that ACD and Jean left Southampton on board the R.H.S. *Dunottar Castle* for the west Mediterranean, visiting Portugal, Spain and Morocco. [1422]
September 24	It was announced that Sir Arthur and Lady Conan Doyle had become Vice-Presidents of the Tunbridge Wells School of Music. [617]
n.d.	*The Crime of the Congo* published. [99,180]
October	*The Crime of the Congo* published by Hutchinson & Co., London. [6,124,202]
October	Clementine Churchill, wife of Winston Churchill, was staying at the Crest Hotel, Crowborough; during her stay she visited Lady Conan Doyle at Windlesham. [249]
October 2	ACD at Windlesham. [18]
October 4	ACD at Windlesham. [884]
October 5	A reporter from the *Daily Express* visited ACD at Windlesham, the purpose of the visit was to interview ACD about the situation in the Congo. [1030]
October 8	It was announced that ACD & Jean had returned to Crowborough after making a tour through France, Spain, Portugal and Morocco. [795]
October 8	*Fires of Fate* ended its run at the Lyric Theatre, London. [203]
October 9	*Fires of Fate* ended its run at the Lyric Theatre, London. [1423]
October 12	ACD spoke at a meeting held at the Mansion House, London to consider steps to provide funds for the British Antarctic Expedition, Captain Scott also spoke. [202,1424]
October 15	ACD at Windlesham. [1425]
October 29	ACD made a speech held at Crowborough called "The Congo Iniquities". [6]
October 29	ACD lectured on the Congo held in London. [4]
October 29	ACD made a speech held at Crowborough called "The Congo Iniquities" [6] at the Croft Road Lecture Hall. [826]
October 31	ACD spoke at the Whitefields Tabernacle, London about the Congo [618], ACD gave an address "The Crime of the Congo". [1144]
November	ACD was president of the newly formed Brighton and Sussex Branch of the Research Defence Society. [2032]
November	ACD at Windlesham. [203]
November 1	ACD at Windlesham. [1425]
November 3	ACD at Windlesham. [1425]
November 7	ACD at Windlesham. [1426]
November 8	ACD with E.D. Morel made a speech, "The Congo Reform Bill," at Newcastle Town Hall, Newcastle-upon-Tyne. [6,1427]
November	ACD purchased shares in Wall & Co. who had designed the Autowheel. [203]
November 10	ACD attended a meeting of the executive committee of the Congo Reform Association held at the Victoria Hotel, Northumberland Avenue, London. [2003]
November 12	ACD at Windlesham. [18]
November 18	ACD with E.D. Morel made a speech at Plymouth Guildhall, titled "The Congo Reform Bill". [6]

1909

November 18	ACD with E.D. Morel spoke at a Town Meeting at Plymouth Guildhall, titled "The Congo Atrocity", the meeting was chaired by John Yeo, J.P. Mayor of Plymouth. [157]
November 19	ACD made a speech on the Congo held at the Albert Hall, London [4,215] Jean also attended [1428]
November 20	ACD at Windlesham. [18]
November 23	ACD with E.D. Morel spoke at Hull Artillery Hall, Hull titled "The Congo Reform Bill". [6]
November 23	ACD with E.D. Morel spoke in Hull about the Congo question, the meeting was presided by the Bishop of Hull. [158]
November 24	ACD with E.D. Morel made a speech at Liverpool Sun Hall, Liverpool titled "The Congo Reform Bill". [6,1429]
November 25	ACD with E.D. Morel made a speech at Edinburgh Synod Hall, Edinburgh titled "The Congo Reform Bill". [6]
November 26	ACD with E.D. Morel made a speech at Manchester Town Hall titled "The Congo Reform Bill". [6]
November 29	ACD at Windlesham. [18]
November 30	ACD at Windlesham. [203]
December	*The Homecoming* published in *The Strand Magazine*. [6,194,195,196,198]
December 1	It was announced that ACD and Lord Cromer would be among the speakers at the public meeting held under the auspices of the Brighton and Sussex Branch of the Research Society at the Royal Pavilion, Brighton on 13 December. [2033]
December 6	*The Fires of Fate* opened in Chicago. [203]
December 9	ACD was invited to referee the forthcoming world heavy weight-boxing contest between Jim Jeffries and the coloured boxer Jack Johnson in America, ACD refused the invitation. [3,6,10,14,99]
December	ACD and Jean stayed at the Hotel Metropole, Brighton. [2034]
December 12	ACD lectured on the Congo held in Brighton [4,203] spoke on the Congo Question held at the Dome Mission, Brighton. [2034]
December 13	ACD was among the speakers at the public meeting of the Brighton and Sussex Branch of the Research Society at the Royal Pavilion, Brighton, Jean also attended. [2034]
December 17	Mary Conan Doyle arrived in London from Dresden. [124]
December 18	ACD and Jean at the Hotel Metro Metropole, Brighton. [2035]
December 18	Mary Conan Doyle visited Kingsley Conan Doyle at Eton. [124]
December 19	Mary Conan Doyle spent the evening with the Storrs' at Hindhead. [124]
December	ACD at Windlesham. [203]
December 21	Mary Conan Doyle had lunch with ACD; they then attended a rehearsal of *The House of Temperley*. [124]
December 22	Mary Conan Doyle attended a dress rehearsal of *Rodney Stone* at the Adelphi; Innes Doyle had just finished at the Staff College in Camberley and saw part of the rehearsal before going to Windlesham. [124]
December	ACD stayed at the Piccadilly Hotel, Piccadilly and Regent Street, London, W. [1430]
December	Mary Conan Doyle, Kingsley Conan Doyle and Innes Doyle spent part of Christmas at Windlesham. [124]
December 27	*The House of Temperley* opened at the Adelphi, London, ACD, Mary Conan Doyle and Innes Doyle attended. [124,202,1431]
December 28	*The Fires of Fate* opened in New York and ran for three weeks [203] at the Liberty Theatre from 28 December-15 January 1910. [6]
December 28	Mary Conan Doyle and Innes Doyle at Windlesham. [124]
December 30	Mary Conan Doyle and Innes Doyle at Windlesham. [124]
December 31	Innes Doyle attended a New Year's party at the Piccadilly Hotel given by Stratten and Clara Boulnois. [124]
December 31	Mary Conan Doyle attended a dance given by a Mrs Chalk. [124]

1910

n.d.	*A Question of Diplomacy* performed at the Marlborough Theatre, Holloway. [6,99]
n.d.	ACD had garden writing hut erected at Windlesham. [89]
n.d.	Birth of Anna Charlotte Andersen, future wife of Adrian Conan Doyle. [1016]
January 12	ACD read from his works to the Crowborough Literary Association [6] at the Croft Road Lecture Hall. [827]
January 20	Mary and Kingsley were at Windlesham. [124]
January 21	Mary celebrated her twenty-first birthday early at Windlesham. [124]
January	ACD trying to sell Undershaw. [124]
January 28	Mary Conan Doyle's twenty-first birthday. [124]
January 29	ACD and Jean were the guests of the New Vagabond Club at a dinner at the Hotel Cecil, Strand, London. [85,1432]
February	ACD at Windlesham. [18]
February 2	ACD with J.M. Barrie and E.W. Hornung appeared before Mr Justice Warrington in connection with a dispute concerning their mutual theatrical agent Addison Bright. [1030]
February 11	*The House of Temperley* was performed at the Adelphi Theatre, London before an exclusive audience of the London Territorial Force, there were forty officers and 1,400 men, Lord Esher paid £300 to hire the theatre. [202]
February 11	From 11 February–28 May, *The House of Temperley* a melodrama of the Ring by ACD was performed at the Adelphi Theatre, London [6,31] Royal Adelphi Theatre, Strand, London. [99]
February 11	ACD and J.M. Barrie attended a performance of *The House of Temperley* at the Adelphi Theatre, London, [1433] the first night. [6]
February 14	ACD at Windlesham. [884]
February 19	ACD and Jean attended a reception held by the Hon. Ivor and Mrs Guest at Wimbourne House. [1434]
February 27	ACD read a paper "Responsible and Irresponsible Criminals" at a meeting of Our Society (Crimes Club). [77]
March 7	From March 7 to 21 ACD and Jean registered at the Poldhu Hotel, Mullion, Cornwall for a two-week holiday. [59] (*5)
March	ACD and Jean spent some time at Mullion, Cornwall. [36,202,203] (*5)
March 17	ACD at The Poldhu Hotel, Mullion, Cornwall. [2053]
March	ACD was a member of the Brighton Branch of the Research Defence Society. [2052]
March 25	ACD took the chair at a concert held at the Oddfellows Hall, Crowborough to raise funds for the Crowborough Silver Prize Band. [828]
March 29	ACD at Windlesham. [884]
April	ACD was appointed as a member of the Council of the Aerial League of the British Empire. [1435]
n.d.	ACD became interested in the Oscar Slater case. [99] (*4)
April	ACD became interested in the Oscar Slater case. [4,14] (*4)
April 6	ACD at Windlesham. [203]
April 10	ACD at Windlesham. [884]
April 12	ACD at Windlesham. [18]
April 19	From 19 April to 9 May *A Pot of Caviare* a play in one act by ACD was performed at the Adelphi Theatre, London. [6,31]
April 21	ACD at the Hotel Metropole, London. [203]
April 29	It was announced in *The Times* that a charity matinee in aid of the Charing Cross Hospital Charity was being organised for Thursday June 23 at the Adelphi Theatre, London, it would include *A Japanese Revenge,* a dramatization of a short story by ACD, probably *A Pot of Caviare*. [1436] {Note: no reports have been located to confirm that it was performed.}
April 30	ACD and his wife visited Pevensey Castle, Sussex to view further excavations made by the Sussex Archaeological Society. [1145]
May	ACD had lunch with President T. Roosevelt. [3,4]

1910

May	ACD at Windlesham. [203]
May 2	It was announced that ACD would attended the 120th anniversary dinner of the Royal Literary Fund at the Whitehall Rooms, Hotel Metropole, London on 5 May. [1437] {Note: reports of this dinner do not mention ACD as attending.}
May 3	ACD made a speech titled "Literature" at a complimentary luncheon at Royal Societies Club, St. James's Street, on the return of Commander Peary from the North Pole. [6,41,108,202,203,1438]
May 10	ACD at Windlesham. [18]
May 24	ACD and Owen Seaman (editor of *Punch*) among others had lunch at the London home of Arthur Lee (M.P. for Fareham) with Mr Roosevelt. [1030]
May 28	*The House of Temperley* closed at the Adelphi Theatre, London. [6,203]
May 30	ACD and Jean attended a reception at the Ritz Hotel, London given by Sir George Reid and Lady Reid in honour of Mr and Mrs Roosevelt. [1439]
May 31	ACD attended a reception for Mr Roosevelt at the Guildhall, London. [2076]
May 31	Late afternoon ACD attended a meeting of the Church of England Waifs' and Strays Society at St. Paul's Chapter House. [1440]
June	Early June ACD played golf at Crowborough Beacon Golf Club for the monthly medal, he lost to Mr G.S. Whitfield and Mr E. White. [1441]
June 1	ACD played cricket for the Authors against the Publishers at Lord's, he scored 10 and 24 and took 1 wicket, the Authors won [56] or match drawn. [235]
June 4	ACD attended the first night performance of *The Speckled Band*, a play in three acts at the Adelphi Theatre London. [31,99,1442] (*2)
June 4	*The Speckled Band* an adventure in three acts by ACD was performed at the Adelphi Theatre, London [6,203,215] for 169 performances [6] H.A. Saintsbury played Sherlock Holmes. [184] (*2)
June 5	ACD at the Hotel Metropole, London. [203]
June 9	George Newnes, the founder of *The Strand Magazine* died at his home Hollerday House at Lynton, North Devon. [189]
June 12	J.M. Barrie visited Windlesham, Crowborough. [123]
June 13	Funeral of Sir George Newnes at Lynton, Devon. [619]
June 13	ACD played cricket for MCC against Ardingly College at Ardingly College Ground, Haywards Heath, he scored 18, MCC won. [235]
June 13	ACD played cricket for Sussex Martlets against Mr Gresson's XI at The Grange, Church Road, Crowborough he scored 41 and took 1 catch, Sussex Martlets won. [792]
June 15	ACD played cricket for MCC against St. John's College at Hurstpierpoint College Ground, he scored 11 and took 5 wickets, match drawn. [235]
June 16	ACD played cricket for MCC against Brighton College at Brighton College Ground, he scored 39, MCC won. [235]
June 18	Crowborough Beacon Golf Club held the Lord Brassey Prize, ACD played with Mr T.S. Whitfield and tied with Colonel Rumsey and Mr H.R.B. Abbey at 2 holes up. On playing off the tie was won by ACD and Mr T.S. Whitfield. [829,1443]
June 20	ACD played cricket on 20 & 21 for Blue Mantles against Warwickshire Gentlemen at Tunbridge Wells; he scored 2 and 7 and took 1 wicket [620] the Warwickshire Gentlemen won. [1774]
June 22	ACD and Jean were staying at the Old Ship Hotel, Brighton. [2036]
June 24	Innes visited ACD at the Metropole, London and attended a performance of *The Speckled Band* at the Adelphi, had dinner with ACD, Jean, Stuart Leckie, P. Trevor, E.D. Morel and Roger Casement. [124] (*2)
June 24	ACD invited Edmund Morel and Roger Casement to join him, Jean and Stewart Leckie (Jean's brother) for dinner at the Metropole and afterwards attend the play *The Speckled Band* at the Adelphi. [215] (*2)
June 25	Innes attended the play *Hullo London*, a skit on *The House of Temperley*, at the Empire Theatre, London. [124]

1910

June 29	ACD played cricket for MCC against Eton College at Agar's Plough, Eton College, he scored 5 and did not bat in second innings, match drawn. [235]
June 30	ACD attended and spoke at the annual meeting of the London Library at St. James's Square, London. [1444]
July	ACD at Windlesham. [203]
July	ACD donated £100 to the Morel National Testimonial, Jean donated £10. [1445]
July 6	ACD played cricket for the Blue Mantles against Lewes Priory at the Dripping Pan, Lewes he scored zero, Lewes Priory won. [793]
July 8	Innes attended the Eton and Windsor match with ACD, Jean, Kingsley plus Willie, Connie and Oscar Hornung. [124]
July 13	ACD attended and spoke at a dinner of the National Defence Association held at the Whitehall Rooms, London. [1446]
July 22	Charles J.G. Bourhill, M.B., Ch.B. was awarded the Conan Doyle Prize at Edinburgh University. [1447]
July 25	Mary Conan Doyle left Dresden. [124]
July 27	ACD as a director attended the ninth annual general meeting of Raphael Tuck & Sons (Ltd.) at Salisbury House, Finsbury Circus. [1448]
August	*1902-1909* (poem) published in *The Rifleman*. [6,198]
August	*The Terror of Blue John Gap* published in *The Strand Magazine*. [6,194,195,196,198,202]
August 4	ACD stayed at the Beach Hotel, Littlehampton, Sussex. [203]
August 4	ACD visited Arundel Castle, Sussex. [203]
August 5	ACD at the Beach Hotel, Littlehampton. [202]
August 8	*The Speckled Band* transferred from the Adelphi Theatre, London to the Globe. London. [6,31]
August 11	Mary Conan Doyle and Dorothy Kirkwood arrived back in London from Dresden; Kingsley Conan Doyle met them at the station. After attending a performance of *The Speckled Band*, the group plus Aunt Juey (Julia Pocock) left for a holiday in Seaview, the Isle of Wight. [124]
August	ACD played cricket on two days for Sussex Martlets against Littlehampton at Littlehampton, he scored zero and 1, and took 5 wickets in the first innings and 6 wickets in the second innings, Sussex Martlets won. [2037]
August 12	ACD played cricket on 12 & 13 for MCC against Littlehampton at the Sportsfield, Littlehampton; he scored 13 and 18, MCC won. [235]
August 16	ACD played cricket for Littlehampton against Bellevue at Littlehampton, he scored 1 and took 3 wickets, Littlehampton won. [2042]
August 17	ACD played cricket for Littlehampton against Standard Athletic Club (Paris) at Littlehampton, he scored 3 and took 1 wicket, Standard won. [2095]
August 30	ACD played cricket on 30 & 31 for Blue Mantles against Madcaps at Tunbridge Wells, he scored 1 and took 2 wickets, Madcaps won. [2096]
September	ACD at Windlesham. [203]
September	*The Marriage of the Brigadier* published in *The Strand Magazine*. [6,194,195,196,198,202]
September 1	ACD and Jean attended the first night performance of *Henry VIII* starring Herbert Tree at His Majesty's Theatre, London. [1030]
September 19	It was reported that ACD had accepted the presidency of the Divorce Law Reform Union. [621]
September 19	ACD attended a performance of *The Speckled Band* starring O.P. Heggie as Holmes at the Theatre Royal, Brighton. [2038]
September 28	It was reported that ACD and Jean were at the Old Ship, Brighton. [2039]
October	ACD made captain of Crowborough Beacon Golf Club for one year. [37,125]
October 3	ACD made an introductory address speech "The Romance of Medicine" at St. Mary's Hospital Medical School, Paddington, London [6,203] he probably attended the annual dinner in the evening at the Grand Hotel, Prince's Restaurant. [1449]

1910

October 4	ACD and Jean attended a performance of *Elektra* at the Royal Opera House, Covent Garden, London. [1030]
October 4	It was announced that ACD would attended a reception to Mme Sarah Bernhardt at the Holborn Restaurant, London on 7 October. [1450] {Note: the report of the event does not mention ACD as attending.}
October 4	Kingsley Conan Doyle went to Lausanne, Switzerland. [203] (*2)
October 5	Kingsley Conan Doyle left England to study in Lausanne, Switzerland. [124] (*2)
October 5	Mary Conan Doyle renewed her studies in London. [203]
October 5	It was announced that between 15 and 18 October ACD would be a speaker at the annual general meeting of the Liberal-Christian League at City Temple and King's Weigh House Church. [1451] {Note: this is probably the speech made on 20 October.}
October	ACD gave a speech at a dinner given by the Anti-Slavery and Aborigines' Protection Society in London. [202] (*3)
October 6	ACD and Jean attended a luncheon to Mr Booker Washington at the Whitehall Rooms, held by the Anti-Slavery and Aborigines Protection Society. [1452] (*3)
October 6	ACD spoke at a lunch given to Dr Booker Washington. [203] (*3)
October	ACD's presentation *The Romance of Medicine* printed in full in the *Saint Mary's Hospital Gazette*. [234]
October	A condensed version of *The Romance of Medicine* was published in *Lancet*. [234]
October 8	*The Romance of Medicine* published in *Lancet*. [196]
October 10	*The Speckled Band* closed at the Globe, it ran for 169 performances. [215] (*2)
October 16	"Talk on Books", address by ACD to the Crowborough P.S.A. [6]
October 17	ACD at Windlesham. [203]
October	ACD attended the trial of Dr Crippen in London. [3,202] (*2)
October 18	ACD was a Vice-President of the National Society for the Prevention of Adulteration and Food Sophistication. [1453]
October 18	ACD attended the trial of Dr Hawley Harvey Crippen at the Central Criminal Court at the Old Bailey, London. [163,203] (*2)
October	ACD delivered a lecture on Morel at the City Temple, Holborn Viaduct, London. [202] (*2)
October 20	ACD made a speech "Mr Morel and the Congo" at the Liberal Christian League's autumn assembly [6] at the City Temple Church. [203] (*2)
October	ACD made President of Crowborough Gymnasium Club. [6]
October 22	It was reported that ACD had accepted the Presidency of the Crowborough Gymnasium Club. [622]
October 29	*The Speckled Band* closed at the Globe. [1454] (*2)
October 29	ACD spoke about Shakespeare. [203] (*2)
October 31	As Chairman of the Authors' Club ACD made an address on Shakespeare. [623] (*2)
November	*The Last Galley* published in *The London Magazine*. [6,196,198,202]
November	ACD at Windlesham. [203]
November	*Through the Mists I. The Coming of the Huns* published in *Scribner's Magazine*. [6,198]
n.d.	Birth of Adrian Malcolm Conan Doyle, son of ACD and Jean. [99,202] (*2)
November 19	Birth of Adrian Malcolm Conan Doyle, son of ACD and Jean, born at Windlesham, Crowborough, Sussex. [3,16,17,68,124,200,203,215] (*2)
November 21	*The Speckled Band* opened in New York, it only ran for thirty-two performances. [6,203]
November 23	Dr Hawley Harvey Crippen hanged [163] at Pentonville Prison, London; the hangman was John Ellis. [169]
December	ACD won the monthly golf medal at Crowborough Beacon Golf Club, he beat Mr W.A.D. Evanson. [1455] (*2)

1910

December 10	ACD won the monthly golf medal at Crowborough Beacon Golf Club. [2077] (*2)
December	*The Last of the Legions* published in *The London Magazine* as *The Passing of the Legions*. [6,196,198,202]
December	*Through the Mists II. First Cargo "Ex ovo omnia"* published in *Scribner's Magazine*. [6,198]
December	*The Adventure of the Devil's Foot* published in *The Strand Magazine*. [6,194,195,196,198]
n.d.	ACD declares for Irish Home Rule, under the influence of Sir Roger Casement. [6,11] (*3)
December	ACD at Windlesham. [203]
n.d.	Innes Doyle became engaged to Clara Schwensen from Copenhagen, Denmark. [124,203,215] (*2)
December	Innes became engaged to a young Dane, Clara Schwensen. [203] (*2)
December 19	The forthcoming marriage of Major Innes Hay Doyle, Royal Field Artillery, and Deputy Assistant Adjutant General, Western Command to Clara, youngest daughter of Reinhold Schwensen of Copenhagen, was announced. [1456]
Christmas	Innes Doyle spent Christmas with the Mam at Masongill, Yorkshire. [124]
December 30	ACD at Windlesham, Crowborough. [18]

1911

n.d.	ACD won the Authors' Club billiards handicap trophy. [1973]
n.d.	Lady Jean Conan Doyle made captain of the ladies section of Crowborough Beacon Golf Club for one year. [37]
n.d.	ACD resigned for the second time from the Phoenix Lodge No. 257, (110 High Street, Portsmouth. [68,200]
n.d.	ACD demitted from the Phoenix Lodge 257, Southsea, Hampshire. [97]
January	*Through the Mist III. The Red Star* published in *Scribner's Magazine*. [6,198]
January 2	Adrian Malcolm Conan Doyle baptized at All Saints Church, Crowborough. [68,200,327]
January 11	ACD was at Windlesham. [884]
January 16	ACD was at Windlesham. [884]
n.d.	*The Speckled Band*, a play by ACD performed at the Strand Theatre, London. [99] (*2)
February 6	The play *The Speckled Band* opened at the Strand Theatre, London for 21 performances, [6] the play then toured until the early 1920s. [184] (*2)
February 13	Colonel Percy Fawcett delivered a lecture to the Royal Geographical Society about his recent expeditions to Bolivia [1457], ACD attended. [202]
February 15	ACD at Windlesham. [18]
February 24	ACD spoke in support of the Charles Dickens stamp held at the Mansion House, London. [1458]
February 25	ACD was elected president of the Amateur Field Event Association at the Annual General Meeting held in London. [1793]
February 27	ACD spoke at a reception in aid of the Waifs and Strays Society held at 3 Grosvenor Place, London. [1459]
March	ACD at the Hotel Metropole, London W.C. [18]
March	*The Contest* published in *Pearson's Magazine*. [6,196,198]
March	*The Red Circle* published in *The Strand Magazine* in March and April. [6,194,195,196,198]
March	Jean was the hostess, ACD was the chairman and Mrs E. Thompson was the guest at the March dinner of the New Vagabond Club. [1044]
March 4	ACD played golf for Crowborough Beacon Golf Club against The Royal Eastbourne Club at Eastbourne, Eastbourne won by five matches to two, ACD lost his match against Mr J. Hall Hedley. [1460]
March 5	*An Iconoclast* published in the *Associated Sunday Magazines*. [6,198]
March 16	*Songs of the Road* published by Smith, Elder & Co., London. [6,202]

1911

April	*A Career as a Medical Man* published in *Great Thoughts*. [198]
April	*The Blighting of Sharkey* published in *Pearson's Magazine*. [6,196,198,202]
April	ACD at the Royal Bath Hotel, Bournemouth. [203]
April 2	At the time that the 1911 census was being taken ACD, Jean with sons Denis and Adrian, with Mary Jakeman (lady's maid) and Catherine Money (nurse) were staying at Royal Bath Hotel, Bath Road, Bournemouth. [252]
April 2	At the time that the 1911 census was being taken Alfred Wood and his sister Emily Wood were living at Rookwood, Southview, Crowborough. [252]
April 2	At the time of the 1911 census Charles Cyril Angel and his wife Bryan Mary (Dodo) with two servants were living at 5 Annington Road, Muswell Hill North, Hornsey, Middlesex. [252]
April 26	*The Last Galley* published by Smith, Elder & Co., London. [6,202]
April 28	ACD attended a complimentary dinner at the Trocadero Restaurant, London held by the Institution of Municipal and County Engineers in honour of Mr Henry Percy Boulnois. [1461]
May 1	ACD attended the inaugural meeting of the Anglo-German Friendship Society held at the Mansion House, London. [1462]
May 5	ACD at Windlesham. [203]
May 12	ACD attended a demonstration of flying for military purposes held at Hendon Aerodrome. [1463]
May 12	ACD attended the opening of the Festival of Empire at the Crystal Palace. [1030]
May 23	ACD attended the Pilgrims' Dinner at the Savoy Hotel, London. [1464]
May 25	It was announced that ACD would presided over a Drawing room meeting of the Divorce Law Reform Union at Hayter House, Cheniston-gardens Studios, London today (May 25). [1465] {Note: no report of this meeting has been located.}
May	ACD went up in a biplane at Hendon. [202] (*2)
May 25	ACD took an excursion in a bi-plane at Hendon. [10,14,98] (*2)
May 27	ACD played cricket for Sussex Martlets against Lewes Priory at the Dripping Pan, Lewes, he did not bat in the first innings but scored 41 not out in the second innings, match drawn, A.H. Wood played for Sussex Martlets, he did not bat in the first innings but scored 6 in the second innings and took 3 catches [235,830] Sussex Martlets won. [830]
May 27	It was reported that ACD and Jean were staying at the Queen's Hotel, Cheltenham. [624]
May 29	ACD attended a luncheon in honour of Mr E.D. Morel at the Whitehall Rooms, London. [1466]
Spring	In the spring ACD visited Worthing, Sussex and played a game of golf at the Cissbury course with Sydney Roberts. [1030]
June 3	ACD played cricket for Sussex Martlets against Eastbourne College at Eastbourne College Ground, Eastbourne, he scored 3 and 1 and took 3 wickets and 1 catch, match drawn, A.H. Wood played for Sussex Martlets, he scored 10 and 2. [235]
June 8	ACD played cricket for Sussex Martlets against F.H. Gresson's XI at Wolfe Recreation Ground, Crowborough, he scored zero and took 2 wickets, F.H. Gresson's XI won, A.H. Wood played for Sussex Martlets, he scored 13 and took 1 catch. [235]
June 10	ACD played cricket for Sussex Martlets against Westminster School at Vincent Square, Westminster, he scored 37 and took 3 wickets, match drawn, A.H. Wood played for Sussex Martlets, he scored 50 and took 2 wickets and 1 catch. [235]
June 12	ACD at Windlesham. [884]
June 15	ACD played cricket for MCC against Ardingly College at Ardingly College Ground, Haywards Heath, he scored 44 and took 2 wickets, match drawn. [235]

1911

June 27	ACD at the annual general meeting of Cranston's Hotels Company held in Edinburgh as one of the directors, he made a statement regarding his position in the company. [85,202]
June	Late June ACD and Jean stayed at the Golden Lion, Rheims on route to take part in the Prince Henry Anglo-German motor car competition. [22]
July	*Giant Maximin* published in *The Literary Pageant*. [6,196,198]
July 4	ACD and Jean took part in the Prince Henry motor tour, between 4 and 20 [124] from Hamburg to London [99] he was driving a 20 horse-powered Dietrich-Lorraine; this was an Anglo-German motor race won by the British, [3] 16 horse-powered. [10,202,203]
July 4	ACD took part in The Prince Henry of Prussia Cup from 4 July to 18 July, started from Homburg, 5th Cologne, 6th Munster, 7th Bremerhaven, 8th at sea, 9th Southampton, 10th Leamington, 11th Harrogate, 12th Newcastle, 13th Edinburgh, 14th Edinburgh, 15th Windermere, 16th Cheltenham, 17th Cheltenham, 18th London and 19th a banquet in London [203]. {Note: these appear to be provisional dates only.}
July 4	Participants in the Prince Henry Motor tour assembled at Homburg. [884,1153]
July 5	The Prince Henry tour left Homburg for Cologne [215,1467] via Königstein, Weilmünster, Leun, Weilburg, Limburg, Montabaur, Coblenz, Andernach, Remagen, Bonn and Cologne, 151 miles travelled. [884]
July 5	The Prince Henry tour arrived in Cologne. [1467]
July 6	The Prince Henry tour left Cologne for Munster [1153] via Opladen, Düsseldorf, Uerdingen, Moers, Rheinberg, Wesel, Herne and Munster, 137 miles travelled. [884]
July 6	The Prince Henry tour arrived in Munster. [1153]
July 7	The Prince Henry tour left Munster for Bremerhaven [1153] via Greven, Osnabrück, Lemförde, Diepholz, Bassum, Bremen, Lesum and Bremerhaven, 140 miles travelled. [884]
July 7	The Prince Henry tour arrived in Bremerhaven where the cars were shipped on board the North-German Lloyd liner *Grosser Kurfuerst* for England. [1468]
July	ACD on board the Norddeutscher Lloyd, Bremen (Dampfer, "Gross Kurfurst"). [18]
July 8	The Prince Henry tour at sea on board the *Grosser Kurfuerst* from Bremerhaven to Southampton. [884,1469]
July 8	The following report was published in the *Sussex Agricultural Express* on Friday 14 July: "The members of the Crowborough Beacon (Ladies' Section) of the Golf Club competed on Saturday for a prize presented by Lady Conan Doyle (the captain). The competition was of the eclectic character, Miss Barrow was the winner with a net score of 77, and secured the handsome silver cup presented by the popular lady captain, Lady Conan Doyle." [831] {Note: the Saturday mentioned in the report would have been 8 July, but at this time Lady Conan Doyle was with ACD taking part in the Prince Henry tour.}
July 9	The Prince Henry tour arrived in Southampton. [1470]
July 10	The Prince Henry tour left Southampton for Leamington [1471] via Winchester, Whitchurch, Newbury, East Iisley, Abingdon, Oxford, Woodstock, Shipston, Stratford-on-Avon, Warwick and Leamington, 113 miles travelled. [884]
July 10	The Prince Henry tour arrived in Leamington. [1471]
July 11	The Prince Henry tour left Leamington for Harrogate [1472] via Rugby, Lutterworth, Leicester, Loughborough, Nottingham, Mansfield, Worksop, Tickhill, Doncaster, Ferrybridge, Aberford, Wetherby and Harrogate, 147 miles travelled. [884]
July 11	The Prince Henry tour arrived in Harrogate. [1472]
July 12	The Prince Henry tour left Harrogate for Newcastle [1473] via Ripon, Thirsk, Helmsley, Easingwold, Northallerton, Darlington, Neville's Cross, Chester-le-Street and Newcastle, 129 miles travelled. [884]
July 12	The Prince Henry tour arrived in Newcastle. [1473]

1911

July 13	The Prince Henry tour left Newcastle for Edinburgh [1474] via Morpeth, Alnwick, Belford, Berwick, Dunbar and Edinburgh, 121 miles travelled. [884]
July 13	The Prince Henry tour arrived in Edinburgh. [1474]
July 14	The Prince Henry tour had a rest day in Edinburgh. [884,1153]
July 15	The Prince Henry tour left Edinburgh for Windermere [1475] via Leadburn, Romannobridge, Moffat, Lockerbie, Ecclefechan, Gretna Green, Carlisle, Bothel, Castle Inn, Keswick and Windermere, 146 miles travelled. [884]
July 15	The Prince Henry tour arrived in Windermere. [1475]
July 16	The Prince Henry tour in Windermere [1476]
July 17	The Prince Henry tour left Windermere for Shrewsbury [1477] via Kendal, Lancaster, Preston, Ormskirk, Knowsley Park, Prescot, Warrington, Tarporley, Whitchurch, Wem and Shrewsbury, 144 miles travelled. [884]
July 17	Innes Doyle, Caroline (Lottie) and Leslie Oldham with their daughter Claire drove from Chester to Tarporley in the hope of seeing ACD on the Prince Henry route, but missed him. [124]
July 17	The Prince Henry tour arrived in Shrewsbury. [1477]
July 18	The Prince Henry tour left Shrewsbury for Cheltenham [1478] via Church Stretton, Craven Arms, Ludlow, Leominster, Peterstow, Ross, Monmouth, Chepstow and Cheltenham, 130 miles travelled. [88]
July 18	The Prince Henry tour arrived in Cheltenham. [1478]
July 19	The Prince Henry tour left Cheltenham for London [1479] via Gloucester, Nailsworth, Badminton, Chippenham, Marlborough, Newbury, Windsor Park, Staines Bridge, Richmond Park and London, 158 miles travelled. [884]
July 19	The Prince Henry tour arrived in London [1479] 1516 was the total miles travelled. [88]
July 20	All the Prince Henry tour participants paraded their cars at Brooklands, in the evening they attended a banquet at the Royal Automobile Club in London, the toast of the competitors was proposed by the Duke of Teck, and replied to by Dr J. von Meister and Sir Arthur Conan Doyle. [1154] (*3)
July 20	All the competitors of the Prince Henry Tour paraded at Brooklands. [1479] (*3)
July 20	In the evening, ACD attended a banquet at the Royal Automobile Club, London for those who took part in The Prince Henry of Prussia Cup. [215,1480]
July 20	ACD could not attend the tenth annual general meeting of Raphael Tuck & Sons (Ltd.) as he was still taking part in the Prince Henry Cup, which had been extended by one day. [1480]
July 21	ACD and other competitors gathered at Brooklands for a final event. [215] (*3)
July 22	It was reported that ACD and Jean were staying at the Queen's Hotel, Cheltenham. [625] {Note: this was probably 18 July during the Prince Henry motor tour.}
July	ACD at Windlesham. [203]
July	Count Carmer visited ACD at Windlesham, Carmer was the German observer in ACD's car during the Prince Henry of Prussia Cup. [203,1030]
July 24	ACD at Windlesham. [884]
July 25	ACD attended the wedding reception of Miss Dina Zangwill, sister of Israel Zangwill, to O.F. Horn at the Portman Rooms, Baker Street, London. [101]
July 29	Innes Doyle, Jane (Ida) Foley, ACD and Jean left Harwich for Copenhagen. [124]
August	*One Crowded Hour* published in *The Strand Magazine*. [6,194,195,196.198]
August 1	Innes Doyle, Jane (Ida) Foley, ACD and Jean arrived in Copenhagen. [124]
August 1	ACD and Jean visited the English Envoy Sir William Connyngham Greene in Copenhagen and then took an automobile tour of Copenhagen, ACD had requested a visit to Hvidøre, a small palace to the north of Copenhagen. Queen Alexandra, former Danish princess, and her sister Empress Dagmar of Russia had bought the palace in 1906 as a summer house. [2055]

1911

August 2	Innes Doyle married Danish girl, Miss Clara Schwensen in Copenhagen [16,68,124,200,202,203] (*2) at Holmens Kirke, Copenhagen, [1481] after a short honeymoon on Sjaelland they rented a house, Greenfield, near Chester [124], ACD was best man at the wedding. [1030] Married Danish pianist and opera singer Ida Claudia Clara Schwensen, the wedding took place at 4p.m. and the famous Danish Dean Fenger officiated. After the wedding they left for a short honeymoon at Elsinore, Sjælland. [2055]
August 16	ACD played cricket for Sussex Martlets against G.M. Maryon-Wilson's XI at Searles, Fletching, he scored 1 and took 5 wickets, match drawn. [235]
August 22	ACD played cricket for the Authors against the Publishers at Lord's, he scored 14 and took 2 wickets, match drawn. [56,71,235,1482]
Autumn	Kingsley Conan Doyle enrolled as a medical student at St. Mary's Hospital, Paddington, London. [180]
September	*What Reform is Most Needed?* published in *The Strand Magazine*. [6,194,195,196,198]
September	Kingsley Conan Doyle passed the preliminary examination in general education at Eton. [234]
September 18	ACD at Windlesham. [1483]
September 19	ACD at Windlesham. [18,178]
n.d.	ACD declares in favour of Home Rule for Ireland (this was granted in 1914) [163] (*3) influenced by Sir Roger Casement. [99]
September 22	ACD announced his conversion to Home Rule in a letter to the *Belfast Evening Telegraph* and *The Times*. [6,203]
September 27	ACD at Windlesham. [18]
September 26	*Why He Is Now In Favour Of Home Rule* published by Liberal Federation Department. [6,198]
October	ACD was writing *The Lost World* from October to December. [6,202]
October 2	Kingsley Conan Doyle entered St. Mary's Hospital School, London. [234]
October 4	Death of Dr Joseph Bell (1837-1911) the original of Sherlock Holmes. [6,31,1484,2010] (*2)
October	Death of Joseph Bell. [202] (*2)
November	ACD at Windlesham. [18]
November 2	ACD at Windlesham. [203]
November 2	ACD working on *The Lost World*. [203]
November 12	ACD read a paper "The Oscar Slater Case" at a meeting of Our Society (Crimes Club). [77]
November 14	ACD attended a complimentary dinner held at the Connaught Rooms, Great Queen Street, London in honour of Mr H.H. Hilton in commemoration of his victories in the British and American Amateur Golf Championships. [1485]
November 19	A letter from ACD speaks of his "fossil find" of an Iguanodon footprint near Windlesham. [38]
November	Charles Dawson visited ACD at Windlesham. [202] (*2)
November 21	Charles Dawson visited ACD at Windlesham, says fossil is a concretion of iron and sand. [38] (*2)
November	Kingsley started at St. Mary's Hospital. [202]
November 22	Kingsley enlisted into the Royal Army Medical Corps and served as a private with the 1st/1st City of London Field Ambulance as a driver. [200]
December	*The Disappearance of Lady Frances Carfax* published in *The Strand Magazine*. [6,194,195,196,198]
December	ACD at Windlesham. [18]
December 3	ACD at Windlesham. [203]
December	ACD completed writing *The Lost World*. [203]
December 8	ACD and Jean attended a dinner of the Incorporated Society of Authors "in honour of the Copyright Bill" held at the Criterion Restaurant. [1486]

1912

n.d.	ACD won the Authors' Club billiards handicap trophy. [1973]
n.d.	Kingsley Conan Doyle passed the Conjoint Board examinations in Chemistry, Physics and Biology. [234]
n.d.	The Council of the British Medical Association held their annual Conference at Windlesham. [3,14]
n.d.	ACD purchased Lock's Farm, Hurtis Hill, Crowborough, and later renamed Fey House. [55,68,200]
January	ACD at Windlesham. [18]
January 22	ACD presided at a dinner given to the editor of the *Cornhill Magazine*. [2054]
February	ACD declared himself in favour of Home Rule for Ireland. [3] (*3)
February 7	Captain A.H. Wood (commanding the company) was in the chair at the annual prize distribution and concert in connection with "G" Company (Cinque Ports) Royal Sussex at the Oddfellows Hall, Crowborough, ACD attended and Jean distributed the prizes. [832]
n.d.	ACD allied himself with the Divorce Reform Union. [3]
March 3	ACD at the Grand Hotel, Lyndhurst, New Forest, Hampshire. [18]
March 21	ACD presided at a dinner given at Trocadero, Shaftsbury Avenue, London by the Liberal Colonial Club, the question of Home Rule problem was discussed, his wife Jean also attended. [1151,1152]
March	*The Lost World* published in *Associated Sunday Magazines* from 24 March to 21 July. [198]
March	ACD at Windlesham. [18]
April	*Religio Medici* (poem) published in *Current Literature*. [198]
April	*The Lost World* published in *The Strand Magazine* from April to November. [6,99,180,194,195,196,198,203]
April	ACD at Windlesham. [203]
April 2	ACD at Windlesham. [18,99]
April 23	ACD spoke at the annual general meeting of the Anti-Slavery and Aborigines Protection Society held at Westminster Palace Hotel, London. [1487]
April 30	*Ragtime!* (poem excerpt) – Souvenir Programme of the Matinee held at the London Hippodrome published in *The Daily Telegraph*. [6,198,203]
May	ACD took an interest in the Oscar Slater case. [202] (*4)
May	ACD began work on the booklet *The Case of Oscar Slater*. [6]
May 12	Anthony Hope Hawkins visited Windlesham [123] (better known as Anthony Hope, author of *The Prisoner of Zenda*).
May 25	ACD played cricket for Sussex Martlets against Lewes Priory at Lewes he scored 12, Sussex Martlets won [794] at the Stanley Turner Ground, Lewes, A.H. Wood played for Sussex Martlets, he scored 4. [235]
Summer	ACD and family at Eastbourne on a summer holiday. [190]
June	ACD at Windlesham. [18]
June 7	ACD played cricket for Blue Mantles against I Zingari at Tunbridge Wells, heavy rain allowed only 30 minutes of play. [2097]
June 10	ACD played cricket for MCC against Ardingly College at the College Ground, Ardingly, MCC won. [1177]
June 12	ACD attended an exhibition of boxing given by the Tunbridge Wells School of Arms at the Oddfellows' Hall, Crowborough. [626]
June 17	ACD played cricket for Sussex Martlets against Eastbourne at The Saffrons, Eastbourne, he scored 14, the result is unknown. [2098]
June 24	ACD made a speech titled "Blood Brotherhood" at the annual banquet of the Pilgrims Club held at the Savoy Hotel, London [4,6,97,108,1488] the dinner celebrated the tenth anniversary of the Pilgrims Club. [255]
June 28	Death of Kate Foley, ACD's maternal aunt, of carcinoma of the stomach and exhaustion, in the Mater Misericordiae Hospital, Brisbane under the care of the Irish Sisters of Mercy. [1014]
June 29	Kate Foley was buried at Toowong cemetery, Brisbane, Australia; the funeral was conducted by Fr. J. O'Leary. [1014]

1912

July	J.M. Barrie visited Windlesham. [202]
July	ACD at Windlesham. [203]
July 10	ACD played cricket for Mr F.H. Gresson's XI against Mayfield at The Grange, Church Road, Crowborough, he scored zero and took 1 wicket, Mayfield won [627] at Wellbrook Ground, Mayfield. [235]
July 11	ACD played cricket for MCC against Royal Academy of Arts at Lord's, he scored zero and took 5 wickets, match drawn. [235]
July 15	ACD at Windlesham. [18]
July	ACD at the Princes Hotel, Brighton, Sussex. [18]
July 16	At the annual meeting of the Association for the Oral Instruction of the Deaf and Dumb held at the Carlton Rooms, Baker Street, London, ACD moved the adoption of the report [6,7] held at the Portman Rooms. [1489]
July 23	ACD as a director attended the eleventh annual general meeting of Raphael Tuck & Sons (Ltd.) at Salisbury House, Finsbury Circus. [1490]
July 29	ACD at Windlesham. [18]
July 29	ACD played cricket for Blue Mantles against Mr F.W. Gresson's XI at The Grange, Church Road, Crowborough; he scored 17, Gresson's XI won [628], at the Wolfe Recreation Ground, Crowborough. [235]
July 30	ACD played cricket for the Blue Mantles against West Kent at the Nevill Ground, Tunbridge Wells, he scored 4; the game was abandoned owing to rain [629], match drawn. [235]
August	ACD at Windlesham. [203]
August	*The Speckled Band* (a play) published by Samuel French, London. [6]
August	ACD took an interest in the case of Oscar Slater, a German Jew accused of murder in Scotland. [3] (*4)
n.d.	ACD was in charge of the national committee preparing the British team for the Berlin Olympic Games in 1916. [3,10,14,203] {Note: these were not held owing to the war.}
August 2	ACD played cricket for Sussex Martlets against Harrow Blues at the County Ground, Hove, he scored 51 and took 1 wicket, the match was drawn. [2099]
August 5	ACD at Windlesham. [18]
August 9	ACD played cricket for the Manx Cats against Crowborough Crocks at the Nevill Ground, Tunbridge Wells, he scored 12, Manx Cats won. [235,630]
n.d.	*The Case of Oscar Slater* published. [99] (*5)
Summer	*The Case of Oscar Slater* published. [180] (*5)
August	*The Case of Oscar Slater* published by Hodder & Stoughton. [202] (*5)
August 19	*The Case of Oscar Slater* published by Hodder & Stoughton, London. [6] (*5)
August 19	ACD played cricket for MCC against Hampstead at Lord's, he scored 6 and took 2 wickets. [235]
August 21	*The Case of Oscar Slater* published by Hodder & Stoughton, London. [31,1491] (*5)
August 21	ACD played cricket for the Authors against the Publishers at Lord's [202] he scored 6, match drawn [235] the match was abandoned due to rain. [56]
August 23	ACD at the Hotel Metropole, London. [884]
August 30	*The Terror of Blue John Gap* privately published in book form. [46]
Autumn	ACD was writing *The Poison Belt*. [6]
September	ACD spent some time at Le Touquet, France. [190,202,203]
October	ACD at Windlesham. [18]
October 5	ACD was staying at the Hotel Metropole, London. [99]
October 15	*The Lost World* published by Hodder & Stoughton, London. [6,99,202,203]
November	ACD at Windlesham. [203]
November 2	Kingsley volunteered for the Army Medical Corps and was assigned to be an ambulance driver. [203]
n.d.	ACD gave a speech on Meredith. [203] {Note: probably on 4 November.}

1912

November 4	ACD attended the 73rd anniversary festival dinner of the Newsvendors' Benevolent Institute held at De Keyser's Royal Hotel, London [1492], ACD also spoke. [631]
November 6	ACD made a speech "France as a Holiday Ground" at the Franco-British Travel Union dinner at the Café Royal on the need for a channel tunnel. [6,203,1492]
November 6	*La Maison de Temperley* (*The House of Temperley*) was staged at Théâtre Sarah Bernhardt, Paris. [1030]
November 7	ACD made a speech at the Savoy Hotel, London in honour of J.P. Muller, the inventor of a system of physical culture. [6,1493]
n.d.	ACD gave a speech on athletics. [203] {Note: probably on 7 November.}
November 23	ACD had been suffering from a rotten cold while writing *The Poison Belt* at Windlesham. [203]
November 23	ACD had written 20,000 or two-thirds of *The Poison Belt*. [202]
November 25	Death of Colin McLean, he was first mate on the *Hope*. [632]
December	*The Fall of Lord Barrymore* published in *The Strand Magazine*. [6,194,195,196,198]
December 1	ACD at Windlesham. [1834]
December 4	ACD at Windlesham. [884]
December 6	At a meeting arranged by the Irish Protestant Committee held at the Memorial Hall, Farringdon Street, London, ACD explained his conversion to home rule. [6]
December 12	Birth of Lena Jean Conan Doyle, daughter of ACD and Jean. [215] (*3)
n.d.	Birth of Lena Jean Annette Conan Doyle, daughter of ACD and Jean. [99] (*3)
December 21	Birth of Lena Jean Annette Conan Doyle, daughter of ACD and Jean. Later Air Commandant Dame Lena Jean Conan Doyle, Lady Bromet at Windlesham, Crowborough, Sussex. [3,16,17,68,124,200,202,203,215] (*3)
December 23	ACD at Windlesham. [203]
December 30	ACD was foreman of the jury at an inquest at Crowborough [633], held at Beacon Court, Crowborough on the body of Captain Gordon Campbell Blair of the Royal Welsh Fusiliers aged 29 years, who died on the morning of Boxing Day. The jury returned a verdict that death was due to natural causes. [872]

1913

n.d.	Kingsley Conan Doyle passed his examinations in Practical Pharmacy. [234] (*2)
January 10	Kingsley passed his Pharmacy exam with 80% result. [124] (*2)
January 27	It was announced that ACD was a subscriber for a national memorial to Field-Marshall Sir George White. [634]
January 28	ACD completed writing *The Poison Belt*. [202] (*2)
January 29	ACD attended the annual prize distribution of "G" Company 5th (C.P.) Royal Sussex Regiment at the Oddfellows' Hall, Crowborough, Captain A.H. Wood presided. [635]
January 30	Lieutenant Lushing landed his naval bi-plane at Treblers Farm, Jarvis Brook due to bad weather; he was flying from Portsmouth to Sheerness. Sir Arthur and Lady Conan Doyle, among others, watched the plane take off the following morning. [636]
February	ACD at Windlesham. [203]
February	*Great Britain and the Next War* published in *The Fortnightly Review*. [6,99,196,198,202,203]
February	ACD completed writing *The Poison Belt*. [203] (*2)
February	ACD and Jean stayed at the Metropole, London so that he could take part in the Amateur Billiards Championship. [124]
February	ACD took part in the Amateur Billiard Championship [124]; he reached the third stage of the Amateur Billiards Championship. [3,31,202,203] (*2)

1913

February 7	ACD played a heat of billiards, 1,000 up against Mr G.W.S. Willins, in the second round of the qualifying competition of the Billiards Association Amateur Championship held at Messrs. Orme and Son's Hall in Soho Square, London. The result was a victory for ACD by 60 points. [1494] (*2)
February 11	Innes Doyle and the family motored from Windlesham to Brighton except for ACD, who autowheeled and had an accident on the tramlines near the Barracks, Lewes Road, Brighton, but continued on for lunch at the Metropole, Brighton. [124,202]
February 12	ACD made a speech on "Scott, Baden-Powell and Scouting" and opened a Boy Scouts Bazaar at Crowborough, Sussex. [6,124,202]
February 14	ACD presided at a dinner given by the New Vagabond Club at the Connaught Rooms, London Jean also attended. [1495]
February 15	ACD played in the first heat in the third round of the Billiard Association Amateur Championship at Messrs. Orme and Son's Hall, Soho Square, London. ACD he was beaten by Mr H. Evens by 376 points. [1495]
March	*The Poison Belt* published in *The Strand Magazine* from March to July. [6,99,194,195,196,198]
n.d.	ACD was campaigning for a channel tunnel. [99] (*2)
March	ACD campaigned for a channel tunnel. [18] (*2)
March	ACD at Windlesham. [203]
March 10	ACD at the Athenaeum Club, London. [18]
March 13	*The Daily Express* on 13 March announced that ACD was heavily involved in the formation of a committee to take control of the financing required for Britain's participation in the 1916 Olympic Games in Berlin, it was also stated that he would remain active within the committee for at least one further year. [1030]
March 22	ACD at Windlesham. [18]
March	Gold hunt on Crowborough golf-links organized by ACD for six half sovereigns. [6,203] (*3)
March 22	ACD arranged a gold hunt for six gold sovereigns for the Scouts of the 1st Crowborough Troup on Crowborough Common and golf course. Afterwards ACD and Jean invited the scouts into Windlesham and then on to the Church Hall Room where ACD treated them to tea. [833] (*3)
March 24	On Easter Monday ACD arranged a gold hunt for six gold sovereigns for the Scouts of the 1st Crowborough Troup on Crowborough Common and golf course. Afterwards ACD and Jean invited the scouts into Windlesham and then on to the Church Hall, South Street where ACD treated them to tea. [329] (*3)
March 29	*The Golden Dog* (poem) published in the *Crowborough Weekly*. [198]
April	*Arthur Conan Doyle. A Study of a Man and His Books* by A. St. John Adcock published in *The Strand Magazine*, New York. [198]
April 1	ACD at the Athenaeum Club, London. [18]
April	ACD at Windlesham. [18]
April 8	Lena Jean Conan Doyle baptized at All Saints Church, Crowborough. [68,200,327]
April 9	ACD attended a banquet of the City Liberal Club (probably Reading). [2078]
April 10	ACD lost the final of the Authors' Club Billiards Handicap to Charles Igglesden. [2100]
April 11	The pavilion of the Nevill Cricket Ground at Tunbridge Wells was burnt down, possibly by militant suffragists. [1496]
April	William John Burns, American detective, visited ACD at Windlesham. [3,51,202] (*2)
April 13	W.J. Burns of the Burns' Detective Agency visited Windlesham. [123] (*2)
April 22	ACD's collie dog Roy vindicated of killing sheep. [6,14,31,202]

1913

April 28	Speech "Sir Arthur Conan Doyle on the Outrages" by ACD at a meeting of the National League for Opposing Women Suffrage, held in Tunbridge Wells [6,202] the meeting was protesting against the burning of the pavilion at the Nevill Cricket Ground. [1497]
April 29	ACD denounced the suffragettes at a meeting which he spoke in Wells, Somerset. [256]
May 1	It was reported that ACD was to sell part of his collection of rare coins at auction to be held at Sotheby's, London on 9 May. [637] {Note: no further details have been located.}
May 5	ACD at Windlesham. [18]
May 7	ACD chaired the 99th Anniversary dinner of the Artists' General Benevolent Institution held at the Whitehall Rooms, Hotel Metropole, London. [1498]
May 8	ACD and Jean attended the trial of a conspiracy charge against various Suffragettes at Bow Street, London. [638]
May 15	ACD at Windlesham. [18]
May 19	*The Daily Express* on 19 May reported that ACD had been ordered by his doctor to take a holiday, and suggested the Mediterranean. [1030]
May 21	ACD and Jean left England for a sea cruise in the Mediterranean. [639]
May	ACD and Jean embarked on an extended holiday. [202]
May	ACD and Jean on The Riviera visited Mentone, Nice, Grasse, Cannes, Beaulieu and Monaco. [203]
May 23	ACD sailed from Marseilles for Port Said. [606]
May 24	ACD was elected patron of the Referees' Union at their conference held at the Imperial Hotel, London. [1967]
May	Pillar-box outside Windlesham had vitriol poured into letter slot by suffragettes. [6,202] (*2)
May 25	The pillar-box outside Windlesham had a black fluid poured into it, possibly by members of the suffragist movement. [1499] (*2)
May 27	ACD and Jean arrived in Port Said, on the return trip they spent a week in Greece, a few days in Rome and a week in Mürren, Switzerland. [202]
June 12	ACD planned to be in Athens and Patras. [606]
June 13	ACD planned to be in Brindisi. [606]
June 14	ACD planned to be in Rome. [606]
June 15-17	ACD probably in Rome. [606]
June 19	ACD planned to be in Interlaken. [606]
n.d.	Birth of John Reinhold Innes son of Innes and Clara Doyle. [202] (*2)
June 24	Birth of John Reinhold Innes, son of Innes and Clara Doyle [16,68,200] born at Greenfield, Chester. [72,88,124] (*2)
July	*The Greatest Mystery of the Sea: The "Marie Celeste"* by ACD and others published in *The Strand Magazine*. [198]
July 4	ACD at Windlesham. [18]
July 9	ACD subscribed to *The Times* Crystal Palace fund by paying £5. [1500]
July 20	104 guests from the BMA Congress, Brighton at Windlesham. [6,7,202]
July 24	John Reinhold Innes Doyle baptised; ACD was godfather and Dodo godmother. [124]
July	ACD was close to completing *The Dying Detective*, manuscript dated 27 July 1913. [202]
August	ACD subscribed to the Great Britain and the Olympic Games fund by paying £25. [1501]
August 12	ACD at Windlesham. [18]
n.d.	*The Poison Belt* published. [99] (*2)
August 13	*The Poison Belt* published by Hodder & Stoughton, London. [6] (*2)
August	In mid-August ACD took his family for a holiday at Frinton-on-Sea, Essex. [202] (*2)
August 26	ACD and family on holiday at Tudor Lodge, Bagland Road, Frinton, Essex. [18,190] (*2)

1913

August 28	ACD and family on holiday at Tudor Lodge, Frinton, Essex. [203]
September	ACD at Windlesham. [18]
September	*"Borrow"-ed Scenes* published in *Pall Mall Magazine*. [198]
September	*Borrowed Scenes* published in the *Harper's Bazaar*. [6,196,198,202]
September	*How it Happened* published in *The Strand Magazine*. [6,194,195,196,198,202]
September 11	ACD at Windlesham. [1502]
September 17	It was announced that *The House of Temperley* film would be shown at a private performance at the West End Cinema, Coventry Street, London on 19 September. [1503]
September 19	A private performance of *The House of Temperley* film was shown at the West End Cinema, London, ACD was a guest. [1980]
September 20	ACD presided at a luncheon at the Piccadilly Hotel, London on the occasion of the first production of a film of his novel *The House of Temperley*. [640]]
October	ACD at Windlesham. [203]
October 10	ACD at Windlesham. [18]
October 10	It was announced that ACD would chair a lecture on "Captain Scott's" Expedition on 24 October at the Great Hall, Tunbridge Wells. [873] {Note: this lecture actually took place on 17 October.}
October	ACD contributed £10 to the British-American Peace Centenary appeal. [1504]
October 17	ACD presided at Commander Evans' lecture at the Great Hall, Tunbridge Wells. [641]
October 19	ACD received a letter from Felix de Halpert asking him to go to Warsaw to prevent a miscarriage of justice [4] ACD did not take up the case. [163]
November	*The Horror of the Heights* published in *The Strand Magazine*. [6,98,194,195,196,198,202]
November 3	*The House of Temperley* opened at the West End Cinema, Coventry Street, London. [1505]
November 3	ACD attended a banquet at King's Hall, Holborn Restaurant, London to celebrate the 50th anniversary of the foundation of the Football Association. [1506,1936]
November 6	ACD attended a banquet held by the British Olympic Council at Hotel Dieudonné. [1507]
November 18	It was reported that among others ACD and Jean had given their patronage to the Duke of Westminster's Olympic Fund. It is unclear if ACD and Jean attended a special matinee in aid of the Olympic Fund held at the London Opera House on 18 November. [1508]
November 19	ACD and Jean were staying at the Metropole Hotel, London. [1509]
November 22	*The Adventure of the Dying Detective* published in *Collier's The National Weekly*. [198]
November 23	A causerie on the Edalji and Oscar Slater cases at Our Society (Crimes Club) opened by ACD. [77]
November 27	ACD at Windlesham. [18]
November 27	ACD and Jean attended an evening dinner of the Society of Authors. [1510]
December	*The Adventure of the Dying Detective* published in *The Strand Magazine*. [6,194,195,196,198,202]
December 2	*Divorce. Reform of the Law Needed* published in *The Morning Post*. [6,198]
December 6	ACD attended a weekend party at Knole, the Kent seat of Lord Sackville. [202,203,1511]
December 8	ACD at Windlesham. [18]
December 8	ACD attended the Bombardier Wells v Georges Carpentier boxing match at the National Sporting Club, Covent Garden, London; Wells was knocked out in the first round. [1512]
December 9	*Divorce Law Reform. Sir Arthur Conan Doyle in Reply* published in *The Morning Post*. [198]

1913

December 10	ACD attended a banquet at the Savoy Hotel, London in honour of M. Anatole France, the great French writer, also present were Maurice Hewlett, Rudyard Kipling, Sir James Barrie and Bernard Shaw among others. [642]
December	ACD at Windlesham. [203]
December 23	ACD at Windlesham. [18]

1914

n.d.	Kingsley Conan Doyle passed his examinations in Anatomy and Physiology. [234]
Early 1914	ACD began writing *The Valley of Fear*. [6]
January 12	ACD presided at a dinner of the Authors' Club. [643]
January 17	Kingsley Conan Doyle and Dorothy Kirkwood joined Innes Doyle at Windlesham, Crowborough, Sussex. [124,202]
January 30	It was reported that Sir Arthur and Lady Conan Doyle had returned to the Hotel Metropole, London from Crowborough. [644]
January 31	ACD at Windlesham. [1834]
February	The film of *The Musgrave Ritual* presented for the first time at the Marble Arch Electric Palace. [1513]
February	ACD made a speech at the opening of the drill hall at Crowborough of "G" Company, 5th (Cinque Ports) Battalion Royal Sussex Regiment. [106] (*2)
February	ACD made a speech "A Mere Dream" at the opening of the drill hall of the "G" Crowborough Company of the 5th Battalion Royal Sussex. [6] (*2)
February	ACD at Windlesham. [203]
February 3	*The Speckled Band* opened in Chicago and played for sixty-three performances. [203]
February 4	ACD accompanied by Jean took part in the opening of the drill hall by Major-General Turner at Crowborough. [645]
February 6	ACD made a speech on the treatment of Portuguese Political Prisoners at a meeting of the British National Protest and the Howard Association at the Westminster Palace Hotel. [6]
February 8	ACD made a speech on Divorce Law Reform at the Ethical Church, 46 Queens Road, Bayswater, London. [6,1514]
February 26	ACD and Jean stayed at the Hotel Metropole, London. [202]
February 26	ACD made a speech at the Canon Street Hotel on a submarine railway between England and France at a meeting arranged by the House of Commons Channel Tunnel Committee. [6,202]
March	ACD at Windlesham. [203]
March 5	ACD made a speech at Westminster Palace Hotel in support of the government bill to prevent the import of skins and plumage for millinery purposes at the annual meeting of the Royal Society for the Protection of Birds, (RSPB). [6]
March 11	ACD played billiards against Major Fleming in the B.C.C. Amateur Championship at Great Windmill Street, London, in which Major Fleming won. [984]
March 14	Lord Northcliffe spent the weekend at Crowborough and played golf with ACD at Crowborough Beacon Golf Club. [646]
March 21	*The Speckled Band* closed in Chicago after sixty-three performances. [203]
March 23	A representative from the *Daily Mail* spoke with ACD on the Oscar Slater case, the article was published in the newspaper the following day. [1030]
March 25	Jean Conan Doyle attended a fashion show held at the Royal Albert Hall, London. [1515]
March 28	ACD signed the lease for Quarry Hill Farm, Crowborough, a three and a-half-acre farm and goat shed owned by Frank Humphry, the rent was £25 per year, payable on the four usual quarter days, ACD had the option to purchase the farm for £2500 and could occupy the farm as from 29 September 1914. [2028] {Note: probably known locally as Lock's Farm and later as Fey House}.

1914

March 31	ACD and Jean attended the annual dinner of the Institute of Lecturers at the Hotel Cecil, London. [647]
April 3	ACD found himself on a charge of plagiarism. The French writer Joseph Henri Honoré Boex, known as J.H. Rosny aîné, it was alleged that ACD's book *The Poison Belt* had been assisted by his work *La Force Mystérieuse*, no further action was taken. [1030,1768]
April 3	ACD at Windlesham. [18]
April 4	Innes and Clara Doyle were staying with Willie and Connie Hornung in London for a dinner party, Stanley Baldwin (later to be prime minister) and his wife also attended. [124]
April 16	It was reported that ACD had subscribed to the National Institute for the Blind Fund by paying £5. [648]
April 21	ACD probably completed writing *Danger! Being the Log of Captain John Sirius*. [2028]
n.d.	ACD played golf at Crowborough Beacon Golf Club in the Spring Meeting Vice-Presidents Cup. [649]
April	ACD completed writing *The Valley of Fear* [6] towards the end of April. [202]
May	Mr C. Igglesden M.P. won the Billiard Handicap at the Authors' Club by beating ACD in the final. [874]
May	ACD at Windlesham. [18]
May 9	Innes and Kingsley were at Windlesham, Crowborough and Malcolm Leckie was with his parents at Monkstown, Crowborough. [124]
May 11	ACD at Windlesham. [884]
May 15	Innes, Clare and John visited Denmark. [124]
May	ACD and Jean sailed on board the White Star liner *Olympic* (sister ship of the *Titanic*) for America. [15] (*3)
May 20	ACD and Jean sailed on board the White Star line RMS *Olympic* for America. [203,215] (*3)
May 20	ACD and Jean with the maid, Mary Jakeman, left Southampton on the RMS *Olympic* for tour of America and Canada. [13,19,96,202,242,1797] (*3)
May 20	ACD visited America and Canada from 20 May to 3 July, visiting Pittsburgh, Cleveland, Cincinnati, Toledo, St. Louis, Kansas City, Winnipeg, New York, Philadelphia, Boston, Yale, Rochester, Buffalo, Toronto, Detroit, Chicago, Albany, Montreal, the Great Lakes, Edmonton, Jasper Park and Fort William. [99]
May 23	ACD arrived in New York on board the RMS *Olympic*. [111] (*4)
May 27	ACD arrived in New York on board the RMS *Olympic*. [19,110,215,1798] (*4)
May 27	ACD, Jean and companion Mary Jakeman from Crowborough arrived in New York on board the RMS *Olympic*. [96,202,1516] (*4)
May 27	ACD and Jean arrived in New York; they stayed at the Hotel Plaza [3,10,13,14,15,203] (*4) Plaza Hotel [202]
May 27	ACD toured America and Canada from 27 May until 4 July. [68]
May 28	ACD visited the Tombs prison with Burns' detectives. [13]
May 28	Innes left Denmark and returned to England. [124]
May 28	ACD guest of Honour at the Dinner of the Pilgrims of the United States held at the Whitehall Club, New York. [6,13,1516,1799]
May 28	ACD attended the theatre to see *A Scrap of Paper* starring John Drew and Ethel Barrymore. [3,13]
May 29	ACD visited City Hall with Lieutenant William Kennel, met Mayor Mitchel. [13]
May 29	ACD attended private dinner for 14 guests at the home of Mrs Josephine Palmer Knapp at 247 Fifth Avenue, [13] the Mrs Joseph Palmer Knapp at the time was Elizabeth Laing Knapp. [142]
May 30	ACD visited Sing Sing prison with William J. Burns and was disgusted with the conditions [6,13] he was locked in a cell for five minutes; he then lunched with Warden Clancy and Burns. [1517,1800]

1914

May 30	ACD watched a baseball game between New York and Philadelphia Athletics [13] at the Polo Grounds, New York. [333]
May 31	ACD visited Coney Island Police Station. [13]
May 31	ACD had lunch with William S. Kenny at his home Shore Acres [1801] in Bay Ridge [13] dinner at Hotel Shelburne, Brighton Beach before visiting Coney Island as guest of William J. Burns [13,1801] he also visited Coney Island Police Station and the Brighton Casino. [1801]
June 1	ACD attended funeral of John L. Griffiths; late U.S. Consul General based in London. [13]
June 1	ACD attended a conference with F. Ray Comstock and Percival Wilde and discussed Wilde's dramatisation of *How It Happened*. [13]
June 1	ACD attended opening of Plaza Summer Garden and Air Terrace. [13]
Early June	ACD left New York for Canada. [110] (*3)
June 2	ACD left New York for Canada. [13,202,215] (*3)
June 2	ACD arrived at mid-day in a private car attached to No. 3, the fast mail train operated by the Grand Trunk Railroad, and stopped briefly at Union Station, Broadway, Albany on his way to Lake George. [815]
June 2	ACD accompanied by his wife, H.L. Clarkson of the Canadian Grand Trunk Railway and a few friends, arrived at the Fort William Henry Hotel, Lake George during the afternoon [816] arrived at 1:40 in the afternoon. [1175]
June 3	ACD left New York for Canada. [111] (*3)
June 3	In the morning ACD, Jean and friends left Fort William Henry Hotel, Lake George by steamer for Fort Ticonderoga on their way to Montreal [816,1175] or left by car at 12 o'clock for Montreal with Mr Charlton and Mr Heard; passing Glen Falls and Lake Champlain, arrived late at Montreal at about 9:30 where they were met by Mr Doble [211,215] ACD arrived in Montreal [13,14] arrived at Bonaventure Station and stayed at the Ritz Carlton Hotel, Sherbrooke Street. [2011]
June 4	Jean took lunch with Mrs Doble at the Windsor Hotel, then onto the gallery at the Montreal Canadian Club where ACD was being entertained to lunch. [211]
June 4	ACD made an address on "The Future of Canadian Literature" at the Canadian Club, Montreal, [6,13,19,211] he also lectured in Winnipeg, Edmonton and Ottawa. [19]
June 4	In the evening ACD and Jean toured the city in a car with Mr Charlton, at about 9:30 they boarded the train for Sarnia. [211]
June 5	The train bound for Sarnia stopped at London where ACD was interviewed, they then continued their journey and arrived at Sarnia Wharf and boarded the SS *Harmonic*, leaving Sarnia at about 3:30. [13,211]
June 6	ACD & Jean travelled on the Great Lakes on board the SS Harmonic, they stopped at Sault Ste. Marie where they were taken by car to see a school where Indian children were taught [211] where he visited the Algoma Indian School. [13]
June 7	ACD & Jean arrived at Fort William where they boarded a special train for Winnipeg. [13,211]
June 8	ACD & Jean arrived in Winnipeg at 8 o'clock, they were taken to the Union Hotel for breakfast, ACD was interviewed and spoke at the Winnipeg Canadian Club, after lunch they were taken around the city by car, arriving back at the train at 5:30 where they dined and slept.[13,211]
June 9	ACD & Jean left Winnipeg by train for Edmonton, arriving at 10 o'clock where they were met by Colonel and Mrs Rogers. [211]
June 9	ACD & Jean arrived at Edmonton late in the evening and stayed at the King Edward Hotel. [13]
June 10	Jean did some shopping in Edmonton in the morning, after lunch ACD and Jean were driven around the town, ACD was interviewed followed by a late afternoon address to the Edmonton Canadian Club. [13,211]
June 10-11	ACD & Jean travelled over night from Edmonton to Jasper. [211]

1914

June 11	From June 11 to 19, ACD took a restful break in Jasper Park. [13]
June 11	ACD & Jean arrived at 8 o'clock in the morning at Jasper Park, they stayed with Colonel Maynard Rogers, (Superintendent of Jasper Park), at his house, late afternoon ACD & Jean were driven to Pyramid Lake with Colonel Rogers, Mr Lett, of the Grand Trunk Pacific Railway and Beatrice niece of Mrs Rogers. [211]
June 12	ACD, Jean and a group of 6 including Colonel Rogers, Mr Lett and Mary Jakeman (Jeans maid/companion) left at 10:30 on horseback for a ride to an un-named canyon. [211]
June 13	ACD & Jean spent a leisurely morning at Jasper Park, at 3:30 their group, Colonel Rogers, Mrs Rogers and Mr Lett went off in a chaise and on horses to Lake Patricia, at 8 o'clock they all had supper by the lake, then returned to the house arriving at 9.40. [211]
June 14	Jean spent a leisurely morning at Jasper Park, ACD and Mr Lett went up to a hill nearby to see a proposed site for a hotel and to mark out a golf course. [211]
n.d.	ACD owned land in or near Fort William, Ontario, Canada. [200]
June 14	It was announced that ACD had purchased a property at 1016 Victoria Avenue, Fort William, Canada for the sum of about $20,000. [790]
June 14	ACD hit first ball at a baseball game between Jasper and Edson. [333] (*3)
June	ACD appeared as a cameo in the film *Our Mutual Girl* in movie number 22 (15 June) and in movie number 23 (22 June), this was a series of 52 silent films. [1181]
June 15	ACD, Jean, Mr Lett, Colonel and Mrs Rogers, and Beatrice left Jasper Park at 9:30 to drive in a rig and then on horseback to Medicine Lake, arriving at 6:30 where they slept overnight in a tepee. [211]
June 15-16	ACD and group camping overnight in Jasper Park. [211]
June 16	ACD, Jean and the others left the camp at 12 o'clock and arrived at the Canyon at 6.30 and spent the night in a log cabin. [211]
June 17	ACD, Jean and the group left the camp at 9.30 and arrived at Jasper at 11:30, saw a baseball game at Jasper, ACD hit off the first ball. [211] (*3)
June 18	ACD wrote *The Athabasca Trail* [13,202] during his visit to Jasper National Park. [111]
June 18	ACD visited Tête Jaune Cache. [13,202]
June 18	ACD, Jean with Colonel and Mrs Rogers with their two daughters, Mr Lett, Mr M.P. NcCall, Beatrice and celebrated Ottawa photographer, Mr William James Topley, left Jasper by train 10:30 to go into British Columbia to see Mount Robson, then passing Yellow Head Lake and Moose River, arriving back in Jasper at 9 o'clock, ACD laid the foundation stone of the Methodist-Presbyterian Church and gave a speech. [211]
June 19	ACD pitched the first ball in a baseball game at Jasper between Jasper and Edson. [13] (*3)
June 19	ACD & Jean left Jasper Park at 9:15 for Winnipeg. [211]
June 20	On board the train for Winnipeg. [211]
June 21	ACD returned to Winnipeg. [13]
June 21	Arrived in Winnipeg at 1 o'clock and stayed at Fort Garry Hotel, in the evening ACD and Jean were the guests of the Lieutenant Governors. [211]
June 21-22	ACD at Winnipeg. [203]
June 22	In the morning Jean did some shopping at Eatons, in the afternoon Mr Lett took ACD and Jean to the cinema where there was a film of ACD and Jean being shown. [211]
June 23	Mr Lett and his wife drove ACD and Jean round Winnipeg. [211]
June 23	ACD left Winnipeg at 10:30 in the evening for Fort William [211] for Algonquin Park. [13]
June 24	Arrived at Fort William at 1:30, where ACD purchased a plot of land with a small wooden house on it. Got back on the train at 6:30 for a meal and slept on the train that remained in the station overnight. [211,215]

1914

June 25	ACD & Jean left Fort William by train [211] instead of taking a steamer across the Great Lakes, ACD & Jean took a train courtesy of the Canadian Pacific Railway and travelled along the north shore of Lake Superior to Algonquin Provincial Park in Ontario where they spent three days. The journey continued on from Algonquin Park to Toronto, then around Lake Ontario to Niagara Falls [13]
June 26-28	ACD and Jean at Algonquin Park. [211]
June 29	ACD and Jean left Algonquin Park for Toronto at 4:30 and then onto Niagara, arriving at 8 o'clock. [211]
June 30	ACD visited Niagara Falls [13,211] left in the afternoon at 3:30 and returned to Montreal. [211]
June	ACD sailed for England. [15] (*4)
July	*Danger! A Story of England's Peril* published in *The Strand Magazine*. [99]
July	*Danger! Being the Log of Captain Sirius* published in *The Strand Magazine*. [6,194,195,196,198]
July	*What Naval Experts Think* published in *The Strand Magazine*. [6,196,198]
July 1	ACD left Montreal for Ottawa [211] and arrived at Ottawa's Grand Central Station in the evening, he spent the rest of evening at Government House as guest of Lieutenant-Governor Sir Douglas Cameron. [13]
July 2	*The Athabasca Trail* published in the *Montreal Gazette*. [198]
July 2	ACD made an address to the Ottawa Canadian Club at Chateau Laurier. [13]
July 2	ACD left Ottawa for Montreal. [211]
July 3	ACD returned to Montreal. [13]
July 3	ACD in Montreal. [211]
July 3	ACD and Jean left America for England. [124] (*4)
July 3	ACD and Jean on board the SS *Megantic*. [111,202]
July 4	ACD sailed for Liverpool aboard SS *Megantic*. [13,1518] (*4)
July 4	ACD sailed from Montreal for England. [111] (*4)
July 5	ACD at sea on board the SS *Megantic*. [215]
July	ACD arrived back in England. [3,14] (*3)
July	ACD arrived in Liverpool on board the SS *Megantic*. [92,96] (*2)
July 9	ACD & Jean attended the wedding of Miss Ivy Verrall and Mr B.H. Fleming at Southover Church, Lewes. [834]
July 10	*The King of the Foxes* published as *Pulled Up* in *Top Notch Magazine* (USA). [808]
July 11	ACD arrived in Liverpool on board the White Star Liner *Megantic* from New York. [650] (*2)
July 12	ACD arrived in England on board the White Star Liner *Megantic* from New York. [651] (*3)
July 14	ACD and Jean arrived in England on board the White Star steamer *Megantic* from Canada. [1519] (*3)
July 14	ACD and Jean were present at the Earl of Dysart's garden party at Ham House, Richmond. [652]
July 14	ACD at Windlesham. [18]
July 19	ACD arrived home from the tour of America and Canada. [203]
July 28	ACD as a director attended the 13th annual general ordinary meeting of Raphael Tuck & Sons (Ltd.) at Salisbury House, Finsbury Park, London. [1520]
August	ACD at Windlesham. [99,203]
August 1	ACD at Windlesham. [18]
August	ACD was John Buchan's first choice for editing the proposed *Nelson's History of the War,* with the first 60,000-word issue then being due for completion by the end of September. He refused the offer on the grounds that he was too busy, and John Buchan eventually edited the history himself. [93]
August	The Chancellor of the Exchequer, David Lloyd George, was given the task of setting up the War Propaganda Bureau (WPB), Charles Masterman appointed as the head of the organization. [54]

1914

August 4	Outbreak of World War One. [13] ACD chaired a meeting at Oddfellows Hall, Crowborough to discuss the feasibility of forming a local company for the purpose of drill efficiency. [1,6,10,14,202,215]
August	ACD formed a home guard unit, later to become the 6th Royal Sussex Volunteer Regiment. [180] (*4)
August 4	ACD formed a local volunteer force, the Civilian National Reserve (the forerunner of the Home Guard) on the outbreak of war. [21,99] (*4)
August	Clara and John left Denmark and returned to England. [124,202]
August 4	Clara and John arrived in London [202] and travelled directly to Northumberland to be with Innes. [124]
August 6	ACD at Windlesham. [18]
August 6	ACD formed a Civilian National Reserve at Crowborough. [21] (*4)
August 6	*Civilian National Reserve* published, this a single sheet, privately printed by ACD that he distributed and put them at street corners, this was to establish a volunteer force. [6]
August 7	Major Alfred Wood, ACD's secretary, served on the Western Front and Italy between 7 August 1914 & 5 January 1918. [99]
August 18	ACD and Jean at the Hotel Metropole, London. [1521]
August 23	ACD at Windlesham. [884]
August 24	Malcolm Leckie wounded in the chest. [203]
August 25	ACD at Windlesham. [203]
August 27	*The World-War Conspiracy* published in the *Daily Chronicle*. [6,198]
n.d.	Malcolm Leckie, brother of Jean Leckie, killed in action at Mons. [180]
August 28	Death of Captain Malcolm Leckie DSO, RAMC, he died of wounds received at Frameries, near Mons, brother of Jean Leckie. [6,7,68,200,202,203,213]
August 29	ACD addressed a recruiting meeting at Hove, Sussex. [653]
August 30	ACD made a speech at Crowborough calling on men to answer Kitchener's appeal for recruits. [6]
August 30	ACD formed local home guard (*4) later replaced by official body in which he served as a private, his number being 184343, 4th Battalion, the 6th Royal Sussex Volunteer Regiment [3,6,14,55,202] or the Crowborough Company of the Sixth Royal Sussex Volunteer Regiment. [1,7,10,124,203,215]
August 30	ACD at Windlesham. [203]
September	ACD at Windlesham. [203]
n.d.	*The Valley of Fear* published in *The Strand Magazine*. [180,202] (*2)
September	*The Valley of Fear* published in *The Strand Magazine* from September 1914 to May 1915. [6,194,195,196,198] (*2)
September	*The World-War Conspiracy* published for free distribution. [6]
September	*Great Britain and the Next War* published by Small, Maynard & Company, Boston. [6]
September 2	The Prime Minster, H.H. Asquith, summoned Charles Masterman, ACD, Israel Zangwill, Arnold Bennett and others with a view that those authors' would write war propaganda books and pamphlets. [1972] (*2)
September 2	ACD and other leading writers including J.M. Barrie, Thomas Hardy and H.G. Wells were invited to Wellington House, the headquarters of the new Propaganda Bureau (WPB) in London's Buckingham Gate [202] the group also included John Masefield, G.K. Chesterton, John Galsworthy, Thomas Hardy, Rudyard Kipling and H.G. Wells, amongst others [54,203] (*2)
September 4	Kingsley saw service in Malta from 4 September to 19 March 1915. [200]
September 6	ACD at Windlesham. [18]
September 8	ACD was indisposed. [1522]
September 18	*The Devil's Doctrine* published in the *Daily Chronicle*. [6,198]
September 26	*The Great German Plot* published in the *Daily Chronicle*. [6,198]
September 27	*"The War" As Seen By Sir Arthur Conan Doyle* published in the *New York Tribune*. [198]

1914

September 28	ACD addressed a recruiting meeting at St. Leonards, Sussex [654] Jean attended, held at the Royal Concert Hall, St. Leonards. [835]
September 29	ACD suggested the use of inflatable rubber lifebelts. [18]
n.d.	*To Arms!* published. [99] (*2)
September 30	*To Arms!* published by Hodder & Stoughton, London. [6] (*2)
October	ACD at Windlesham. [18,190,203]
October	ACD made a speech at a recruiting meeting at St. Leonards. [203]
October	ACD spent two weeks at 22 Grand Parade, Eastbourne, Sussex. [18]
October 2	It was announced that ACD and Jean were staying in Eastbourne, Sussex. [655]
October 9	It was reported that ACD and Jean motored from Eastbourne to Crowborough to visit the home for Belgian refugees which Jean had established in Crowborough. [656]
October 10	The "Contemptible Little Army" published in the *Daily Chronicle*. [6,198]
October 19	ACD was among many others on the platform at a meeting under the auspices of the United Irish League of Great Britain held at the Central Hall, Westminster, London. [965]
October 20	Innes attended a performance of *Monsieur Beaucaire* starring Lewis Waller. [124]
October 26	*A Policy of Murder* published in the *Daily Chronicle*. [6,198]
November 16	ACD at Windlesham. [18]
November 18	ACD made a speech "Deeds of Gallantry. Sir Arthur Conan Doyle and the Press Censor" at Crowborough. [6]
November 23	*Madness* published in the *Daily Chronicle*. [6,198]
November 24	ACD at Windlesham. [18]
November 25	ACD made a speech "Home Defence" at the Guildhall to a meeting of the Central Association of Volunteer Training Corps. [6]
December	*The German War* published by Hodder & Stoughton, London. [6]
December	*To Arms!* published as *The War. A Statement of the British Case* in *The Strand Magazine*, New York. [6,198]
December 1	ACD at Windlesham. [18]
December 1	Innes, an adjutant and a medical officer accidentally shot by at by some gardeners in Southwick cemetery apparently practising their shooting skills. [124]
December 5	The trawler "Conan Doyle" was launched at Selby shipyard. [1779]
December 7	ACD addressed a recruiting meeting in Tunbridge Wells. [1030]
December 10	ACD spoke in support of the Central Association Volunteer Training Corps at a meeting at the National Liberal Club. [836]
December 11	It was reported that ACD addressed a recruiting meeting at the Great Hall, Tunbridge Wells, Kent. [657]
December 12	ACD at Windlesham. [203]

1914/18

n.d.	Innes John Doyle was addressing letters to his wife, Clara, at care of Miss Peerless, Yew Trees, Southview Road, Crowborough. [16]

1915

n.d.	ACD titles transferred from Smith Elder to John Murray. [99]
n.d.	Five Sherlock Holmes films released in Germany. [99]
n.d.	ACD began writing *The History of British Campaign in France*. [99]
January	ACD at Windlesham. [18]
January	*To The Rocky Mountains* published in *The Cornhill Magazine* from January to April as *Western Wanderings*. [6,196,198,202]
January	*Western Wanderings* published by George H. Doran Company, New York. [6,202]
January 2	ACD suggested the use of inflatable rubber boats for the navy. [3,14]

1915

January 21	ACD made a speech at the Connaught Rooms at a meeting to form the Holborn Battalion of the National Volunteer Home Defence Force. [6]
January 28	ACD attended a meeting of the Shareholders of the Kent Coal Concessions Group of Companies at the Canon Street Hotel, London. [658]
February	*How I "Broke Into Print" Arthur Conan Doyle* published in *The Strand Magazine*. [6,194,195,198]
February	ACD at Windlesham. [203]
February 2	ACD at Windlesham. [18]
February 11	ACD at Windlesham. [18]
February 20	ACD made a speech at Tunbridge Wells on "The Great Battles of the War". [6,203]
February	At the end of February Innes arrived in France with the 4th Army Corps with the rank of Major. [124]
March	Innes posted to the Front. [99]
March 5	It was reported that ACD was confined to bed with a chill at his home in Crowborough. [659]
March 5	ACD lectured in Bournemouth. [203]
March 10	ACD in Scotland from 10-13 March. [203]
March 11	ACD made a speech at Edinburgh on "The Great Battles of the War" [6] at the Usher Hall, Edinburgh. [660]
March 13	ACD made a speech at Glasgow on "The Great Battles of the War". [6]
March 15	ACD lectured in Middlesbrough. [203]
March 16	ACD lectured in Sunderland [203] on "The Great Battles of the War" at the Victoria Hall, Sunderland. [661]
March 18	ACD lectured in Bradford. [203]
March 18	ACD in Cheltenham to lecture. [203] {Note: probably a provisional date.}
March 20	ACD made speech at the Queen's Hall, London on "The Great Battles of the War". [6,203,1523]
March 22	ACD lectured in Harrogate [203] "The Great Battles of the War" at The Kursaal, Harrogate under the auspices of the Harrogate Literary Society. [1178]
March 23	ACD at 2 Ripon Road, Harrogate. [203]
March 23	ACD lectured in Shrewsbury. [203]
March 24	ACD arrived in Cheltenham. [203]
March 25	ACD lectured in Cheltenham, Jean joined him there, [203] on "The Great Battles of War" at the Town Hall, Cheltenham. [662]
March 26	ACD lectured in Exeter [203] on "The Great Battles of War" at the Victoria Hall, Exeter. [663]
March	ACD and Jean on a two-week holiday in Torbay, they stayed at the Grand Hotel. [27]
March 27	ACD lectured on "The Great Battles of the War" at The Pavilion, Torquay [27,203] with Colonel C.R. Burn, M.P. presiding. [159]
March 29	ACD lectured in Plymouth. [203]
March 30	Kingsley discharged. [200]
April	*The Athabasca Trail* published in *The Cornhill Magazine*. [6,196,198]
April	ACD at Windlesham for Easter. [203]
April 7	Kingsley appointed to a temporary commission as 2nd Lieutenant in the Hampshire Regiment and was posted to the 1st Battalion. [200,1764]
April 11	ACD at the Royal Pavilion Hotel, Folkestone, Kent. [18,203,1524]
April 12	ACD lecture "British Battles of War" was given at Hove Town Hall, Hove, Sussex. [1045]
April 12	ACD lectured in Brighton. [203]
April 13	ACD lectured in Liverpool. [203]
April 13	It was advertised that ACD would lecture on "The Great Battles of War" at the Philharmonic Hall, Liverpool on 14 April. [664]
April 14	ACD lectured on "Battles of War" held at the Philharmonic Hall, Liverpool. [694]

1915

April 14	ACD lectured in Chester. [203]
April 15	ACD lectured at the Chester Music Hall, Chester. [694]
April 19	ACD made a speech at Crowborough on "The Great Battles of the War". [6,203]
April 24	ACD presided at an assault-at-arms and also refereed some boxing contests held at the YMCA Recreation Hut, Crowborough. [665]
April 24	ACD at Windlesham. [884]
May 2	ACD attended the performances *Waterloo* and *The Speckled Band* at the Brixton Theatre, Brixton, he was received by a guard of honour furnished by the Streatham Volunteer Corps, he delivered a speech from the stage after *Waterloo* was performed. [2084]
May 3	ACD at the Hotel Metropole, London, W.C. [18]
May 15	ACD gave his war lecture at the Devonshire Park, Eastbourne. [838]
May 22	ACD at Windlesham. [203]
n.d.	*The Valley of Fear* published. [99] (*2)
June 3	*The Valley of Fear* published by Smith, Elder & Co., London. [6,31,202] (*2)
June	ACD was one of many patrons of the organisation called France's-day, this was formed to raise funds for the French Red Cross. [1030]
July 6	Oscar Hornung, son of Willie and Constance (Connie), killed in action at Ypres [24,68,124,200,202] (*3) Second Lieutenant Oscar Hornung of the 3rd Essex Regiment, attached to the 2nd Essex Regiment, killed in action in Flanders. [203,213,1525]
July	Oscar Hornung, a Second Lieutenant in the Essex Regiment died in action at Ypres aged 20. [215] (*3)
July	ACD at Windlesham. [203]
July 9	Innes returned home on leave, lodging in Crowborough, Alfred Wood was also on leave and stayed at Windlesham. [124]
July 15	Oscar Hornung, son of Willie and Constance (Connie) Hornung, killed in action at Ypres. [180] (*3)
July 20	ACD at Windlesham. [203]
July	ACD was a vice-patron (one of many) of the Veterans' Association. [1971]
July 26	ACD at Windlesham. [18]
July 27	ACD urged the War Office to supply some sort of body armour for the head and heart of soldiers at the front. [3,14,18,1802]
July 28	ACD as a director attended the 14th annual general meeting of Raphael Tuck & Sons (Ltd.) at Salisbury House, Finsbury Circus, London. [1526] (*2)
July	ACD's nephew, Alex (Alec) Forbes a Lieutenant in the Seaforth Highlanders was killed in action. [203] (*4)
n.d.	Death of Leslie Oldham. [202] (*3)
July 28	Major Leslie Oldham killed in action, husband of Lottie (Doyle). [16,68,124,200,203,213,1527] (*3)
July 28	Captain Leslie Oldham, husband of Caroline (Lottie), killed in action. [180] (*3)
July 29	Innes attended the funeral of Leslie Oldham near Le Touret. [124]
July 29	ACD attended the 14th Annual General Meeting of Raphael Tuck & Sons at Salisbury House, London. [666] (*2)
August 1	ACD addressed the Lancashire Fusilier Brigade at the Crowborough Camp honouring the 156th anniversary of the Battle of Minden. [667]
August	ACD at Windlesham. [203]
August 2	ACD at Windlesham. [884]
August	ACD spent some time at Eastbourne. [203]
August 30	ACD at Windlesham. [203]
September	Early September Innes posted as AA and QMG to 24th Division as temporary Lieutenant Colonel, on the borders of France and Belgium. [124]
September	Captain A.H. Wood of the "D" Crowborough Company 5th Battalion Royal Sussex Regiment was promoted to the rank of Major. [839]

1915

September 22	ACD attended the funeral of Crowborough author Mr W.D. Scull at Crowborough Cemetery; he was a member of the Crowborough Volunteer Training Corps. [668]
October	*An Outing in War-Time* published in *The Strand Magazine*. [6,99,194,195,196,198]
October 2	ACD addressed a recruiting meeting at Hastings. [669]
October 3	ACD at Windlesham. [203]
October 14	ACD at the Hotel Metropole, London, W.C. [18]
October	It was reported that ACD attended a conference of Presidents of County Committee and Regiment Commanders of County Volunteer Regiments held at the County Hall, Spring Gardens, London, but no date given. [670] {Note: the *Dublin Daily Express* published on 15 October gives the date of the conference as being held on 14 October but ACD is not mentioned in the short report.}
October 16	ACD at Windlesham. [18]
October 18	ACD at Windlesham. [203]
October 25	*The Outlook on the War* published in the *Daily Chronicle*. [6,99,198]
October 26	ACD at Windlesham. [1834]
November 27	*Stranger than Fiction* published in *Collier's The National Weekly*. [198]
December	ACD at Windlesham. [203]
December	*Stranger than Fiction* published *The Strand Magazine*. [6,194,198]
December	*Ypres* published in *The Queen's Gift Book*. [6,198]
December 1	Speech at Crowborough on "Great British Battles". [6]
December 1	ACD lectured to his Crowborough neighbours on "The Later Battles of War" at The Croft, Crowborough. [671]
December 20	*Sir John French. An Appreciation* published in the *Daily Chronicle*. [6,99,198]

1916

n.d.	ACD declares his belief in spiritualism. [99]
n.d.	*The Origin and Outbreak of War* published. [99]
January 6	ACD at Windlesham. [884]
January 8	It was announced that ACD was part of a small committee to raise funds to acquire a bronze bust representing Lewis Waller as Brutus. [1775]
January 8	*The Prisoner's Defence* published in *Collier's The National Weekly*. [198]
January 14	It was announced that Major (temporary Lt. Col.) John Francis Innes Hay Doyle, R.A. was awarded the DSO. [1528,1765]
January 15	ACD at Windlesham. [18]
January	Colonel Doyle, R.A. brother of ACD was among the officers specially mentioned in Sir John French's dispatch [875] Major (temp. Lt. Col.) J.F.I.H. Doyle, R.A. [876]
n.d.	Death of Lily Loder-Symonds, a close friend of Jean Conan Doyle. [203] (*2)
January 28	Death of Lily Loder-Symonds, a close friend of Jean Conan Doyle. [202] (*2)
February	*The Prisoner's Defence* published in *The Strand Magazine*. [6,194,195,196,198]
February 2	ACD attended a Boxing Championship as a referee or an official at the YMCA Hut, Crowborough Camp, (details from a copy of the advertising poster). [82]
February 3	ACD attended a conference of Presidents of County Committee and Regiment Commanders of County Volunteer Regiments held at the County Hall, Spring Gardens. [672]
February 5	ACD at Windlesham. [18]
February 7	ACD and Jean at the Hotel Metropole, Folkestone, Kent. [1529]
February 20	ACD made a speech at His Majesty's Theatre on "The New Army" [6], "Two Great Battles – 2nd Ypres and Loos". [1530]
February 20	Death of Second Lieutenant John Peter Hornung (Willie Hornung's nephew), killed in action. [213] (*2)
February	Death Peter Hornung, (Willie Hornung's nephew, killed in action). [124] (*2)
February 21	ACD at Windlesham. [18]

1916

February 21	In the evening ACD attended an informal dinner at the Reform Club to welcome the Russian authors. [1531]
February 22	ACD with Russian authors Korney Chukovsky and Alexey Tolstoy visited places of interest in London. [788]
February 28	ACD at Windlesham. [18,1135]
March 3	Adrian Conan Doyle nearly died of pneumonia (aged about 6). [140]
March 11	ACD contributed to *Light* from 11 March 1916 until 5 July 1930. [196]
March 15	ACD attended a smoking concert held by the Crowborough Platoon, "D" Company, 5th Battalion Sussex V.T.C. at the Badminton Hall, Crowborough. The programme was arranged by Private P.F. Forbes, ACD sang his song "The man who carries the gun" and later read from "Three Men in a Boat". [673]
March 18	ACD at Windlesham. [18]
March 24	ACD at Windlesham. [203]
March 25	ACD lectured on the battle of Loos at Brighton. [203]
March 26	ACD did a sixteen route march with rifle and equipment. [203]
March 27	ACD was in London for several important engagements. [203]
April	*The British Campaign in France and Flanders* published in *The Strand Magazine* from April 1916 until June 1917. [6,194,195,196,198]
April 7	Kingsley left England for France. [124]
April 8	Innes received the DSO from King Edward VII at Buckingham Palace. [124]
April 8	Kingsley served with the British Expeditionary Force from April 8 to 3 July 1916. [200]
April 28	The manuscript of *The Empty House* was sold at auction held at Christie's, London for £11, ACD had donated the manuscript in aid of the British Red Cross Society and the Order of the Hospital of St. John of Jerusalem in England. [1022]
April 29	ACD at Portman Lodge, Bournemouth, Dorset. [18,1135]
April 30	ACD at Windlesham. [18]
May 6	ACD at Windlesham. [18]
May 7	ACD at Windlesham. [203]
May	ACD left Newhaven on board the destroyer HMS *Zulu* for Dieppe, France. [10]
May	ACD visited the Western Front and met his brother Assistant Adjutant-General Innes Doyle of the 24th Division and son Kingsley who had interrupted his medical studies to become Acting Captain and Medical Officer with the First Hampshire Regiment. [180] (*2) Following this visit ACD travelled to Italy to inspect the country's forward military positions. [180]
May 26	ACD visited Innes, now Colonel Innes Doyle, at the Front. [124] (*2)
May 26	Sir Roger Casement, Irish patriot and British Consular official was tried for treason at the Old Bailey, London. [180]
n.d.	Innes's wife Clara and son John living at Windlesham. [14]
May 28	ACD had lunch at the General Headquarters at Montreuil. [202] (*2)
May 28	ACD left the British front in France. [124]
May 29	ACD paid a short visit to the British front in France. [1532]
May & June	ACD visited the British line in France, the Italian army and the French lines. [3,6,10]
June 1	ACD had lunch at General Headquarters at Montreuil. [10] (*2)
June 2	It was announced that ACD was a member of the Sussex Duty and Discipline Committee. [840]
June	Early June ACD was probably in Paris. [86]
June	ACD visited the French lines in the Argonne Forest. [62]
June 6	ACD was in Paris. [202]
June 13	ACD was in Paris. [884]
June 13	*A Glimpse of the British Army* published in the *Daily Chronicle* on June 13 and 15. [6,198]
June 15	Kingsley appointed Temporary Lieutenant. [200]
June 16	ACD had returned from his visit to the British front in France. [1533]

1916

June	ACD at Windlesham. [203]
June 19	ACD at Windlesham. [99]
June 20	*A Glimpse of the French Line* published in the *Daily Chronicle* on June 20 and 22. [6,198]
June 22	*In the Argonne* published in the *Daily Chronicle*. [198]
June 22	ACD and Jean attended a meeting at the Mansion House, London in aid of the Veterans' Club Association. [674]
June 27	*Under Fire on Izonzo Front* published in the *Daily Chronicle*. [6,198]
June 29	ACD at Windlesham. [99]
June 29	*Warfare in the Carnic Alps* published in the *Daily Chronicle*. [6,198]
June 29	Sir Roger Casement sentenced to death for high treason after Dublin Easter Rising. [15,215]
July	ACD at Windlesham. [203]
July 1	Kingsley seriously wounded during the Battle of the Somme and sent back to England to convalesce. [33,202,203,215] (*3)
n.d.	Kingsley was wounded at the Somme River battle and invalided out of the army; he recommenced his studies as a medical student at St. Mary's Hospital, Paddington, London. [180] (*3)
July	Kingsley wounded and sent home. [124] (*3)
July 5	ACD attended a Pilgrims Dinner in London. [675]
July 6	It was announced that ACD would speak at the Anglo-French dinner to be held in Manchester on 14 July. [1534]
July	ACD received a telegram dated 7 July informing him that Kingsley had been wounded. [99]
July 9	ACD at Windlesham. [99]
July 14	ACD spoke at an Anglo-French dinner at Manchester where he proposed the toast of "France". [2104]
July 21	ACD was enrolled as Private V184343 of the 5th Volunteer Battalion of the Royal Sussex Regiment. [21]
July 22	ACD at Windlesham. [18]
July 25	ACD at Windlesham. [18]
July 31	ACD at Windlesham. [18]
n.d.	*A Visit to Three Fronts* published. [99] (*2)
August	*A Visit to Three Fronts* published by Hodder & Stoughton, London. [6] (*2)
August 3	Sir Roger Casement was hanged at Pentonville Prison, London after the Easter rising despite ACD's appeals for clemency [4,14,15,99,169,180,202,215] (*2) the hangman was John Ellis. [169]
August 3	ACD attended the 15th annual general meeting of Raphael Tuck & Sons (Ltd.) at Salisbury House, Finsbury, London. [676]
August 4	ACD was campaigning for the use of body armour for the troops. [99]
August 13	ACD at Windlesham. [884]
August 13	Sir Roger Casement was hanged at Pentonville Prison, London. [203] (*2)
August 16	ACD again suggested some form of breastplate or body shield for soldiers. [3,15]
August 16	Alec Forbes wounded. [1535]
August	Death of Alex or Alec Forbes, Jean Conan Doyle's nephew, killed in action. [124,203] (*4)
August 17	Death of Lieutenant Alec Forbes of the Seaforth Highlanders aged 22. [1535] (*4)
August 22	ACD at Windlesham. [203]
August 23	ACD was in London to see the Minister of Munitions. [203]
August 29	ACD at Windlesham. [203]
September 1	ACD at Windlesham. [18]
September 3	Death of Captain Alec Forbes, killed in action. [213] (*4)
September 19	ACD attended a meeting at Eastbourne to establish a spiritualistic society in the town, he contributed to the funds. [1839]

1916

September 20	ACD was present at the presentation of the Freedom of Eastbourne to the Duke of Devonshire. [677]
October 4	ACD at Windlesham. [203]
October 7	ACD took part in the volunteer range rifle shoot at Crowborough, he came third. [678]
October	Innes took Mary, Kingsley, Percy Foley, Lottie and Claire Oldham to the theatre to see *A Little Bit of Fluff*. [124]
October 21	The psychic magazine *Light* carries ACD's announcement of his full conversion to spiritualism. [3]
October 22	Kingsley posted to the 3rd Reserve Battalion. [200]
October 29	ACD at Windlesham. [18,179]
November	During November ACD lectured in Folkestone, Brixton, Liverpool, Chester, Leicester and Crowborough. [203]
November 4	*A New Revelation. Spiritualism and Religion* published in *Light*. [6,29,198]
November 4	ACD made public his conversion to spiritualism [6,17,20,29,202] or psychic religion. [14]
November 10	ACD presided at the annual public meeting of the Royal Surgical Aid Society at the Town Hall, Tunbridge Wells. [679]
November 14	Death of Emily (Nem) Hawkins, sister of Louise and John (Jack) [33,124,200] at Greenville House, Boutport Street, Barnstable. [680]
November 20	ACD and Jean attended a reception held by the Crowborough Branch of the Victoria League to welcome the Canadians to the Crowborough Camp held at the YMCA Waterloo Hut. [681]
November 23	*The British Campaign in France and Flanders* published in *The Strand Magazine*, November 23 1916 – 23 January 1929. [99]
November 23	*The British Campaign in France and Flanders Vol. 1* published by Hodder & Stoughton, London. [6]
n.d.	ACD visited HM Factory Gretna. [328] (*3)
November	ACD visited an arms factory in Gretna. [202] (*3)
December	At Windlesham ACD and Jean entertained some Canadian Army Officers who were based in Crowborough. [1129]
December 2	*Spiritualism and Religion* published in *Light*. [6,198]
December	ACD was willing to stand for the parliamentary vacancy of Edinburgh and St. Andrews Universities [203,1536] late December he withdrew from the contest. [6,202,203]
December	ACD had a sitting with Vout Peters. [124]
n.d.	ACD's mother left Masongill and moved to Bowshot Cottage near West Grinstead Park, the home of Connie and Willie Hornung. [14,68,200] (*2)
December 20	ACD at Windlesham. [203]

1917

n.d.	ACD won the Authors' Club billiards handicap trophy. [1973]
n.d.	ACD speaks publicly on spiritualism for the first time. [99]
January 6	It was advertised that ACD would lecture on "Science, Spiritualism and Religion on 22 February (subject to his future engagements) at the London Spiritualist Alliance in the Salon of the Royal Society of British Artists, Suffolk Street, Pall Mall, London. [1840] ACD found it impossible to speak on this date so his lecture was cancelled. [1841]
January 28	Kingsley posted to the 3rd Infantry Base Depot and re-joined the British Expeditionary Force. [200]
n.d.	Early 1917 Kingsley returned to the front. [124]
n.d.	ACD in France where he visited Innes, who was Assistant Adjutant-General with the British III Corps. [180]
February	ACD was invited with Major Albert Stern, chairman of the tank supply committee, to lunch by the Prime Minister. [202] (*2)
February 7	ACD had lunch with David Lloyd George and Colonel Stern. [70] (*2)

1917

February 8	ACD at Windlesham. [18]
February 10	ACD and Jean entertained 130 Canadian officers at Windlesham. [124]
n.d.	ACD entertained 130 officers from the Canadian Engineers who were based in Crowborough. [202]
February 12	ACD probably visited Sir Douglas Haig in France. [203]
February 14	Kingsley was posted to the 1st Battalion. [200]
February 15	ACD at Windlesham. [18]
February 16	It was reported that ACD had given part of his manuscript of *The Adventures of Sherlock Holmes* for the Red Cross Sale at Christie's. [877]
February 24	ACD was a judge at the Novices' Boxing Championships held at the YMCA Recreation Hut at Crowborough Camp. [878]
Spring	Innes made a brief visit to Crowborough to settle in his wife and son at Windlesham Cottage. [202]
March	ACD at Windlesham. [18]
March 7	ACD at Windlesham and probably completed writing *His Last Bow*. [2102]
March 22	ACD made an address at a meeting of the London Spiritualist Alliance titled "Is Spiritualism of the Devil". [6]
March 24	It was announced that ACD would preside at a lecture by Mr Curtin at Crowborough Camp (Canadian Soldiers) on 25 March. [1537] {Note: no report of this lecture located.}
March	ACD visited Downing Street for breakfast. [202] (*2)
March	ACD donated £10 to *Light* Advertisement Compensation Fund. [1842]
April	ACD invited by the Prime Minister, Mr Lloyd George, to breakfast at 10, Downing Street, London [2,3,10,15,52,215] (*2) ACD stayed at the Berkeley Hotel. [215]
April 4	ACD donated the manuscript of *The Six Napoleons* to be auctions in aid of the British Red Cross Society and the Order of the Hospital of St. John of Jerusalem in England, they were auctioned at Christie, Manson & Woods in London, it sold for £11: and 6p, the manuscripts of *The Abbey Grange* and *The Three Students* were also included in the auction. [1027]
April 12	ACD attended a dinner at the Pilgrims Club at the Savoy Hotel. [1538]
April 14	ACD at Windlesham. [1834]
April 18	ACD at Windlesham. [18]
April 19	*Supremacy of the British Soldier* published in the *Daily Chronicle*. [198]
April 20	ACD attended the 70th birthday celebrations of Major Sir Claude Champion de Crespigny held at the Sports Club, St. James's Square, London. [682]
April 25	ACD made a speech "Farmers and the Red Cross" to the Crowborough branch of the British Farmer's Red Cross [6], ACD opened a Gift Sale promoted by Crowborough, Jarvis Brook and District Branch of the British Farmers' Red Cross Fund held at the Badminton Hall, Croft Road, Crowborough. He also commenced the auction, the prize draw for a pony was conducted by Miss Doyle as Lady Conan Doyle was indisposed. [802]
April 29	ACD at Windlesham. [18]
May 9	ACD at Windlesham. [203]
May	Late May ACD and Jean took a holiday in Harrogate. [202]
May	During his visit to Harrogate ACD visited Lord Furness's Hospital. [1030]
May 25	ACD and Jean at Harrogate. [1539]
May 25	ACD and Jean attended a meeting in the Council Chamber, Harrogate where ACD addressed the gathering. [1179]
May 26	ACD at Hotel Majestic, Harrogate. [2102]
May 31	ACD at Hotel Majestic, Harrogate. [2102]
June	ACD at Windlesham. [18]
June	The Mam moved from Masongill to Bowshot Cottage, West Grinstead, West Sussex. [203] (*2)
June 10	ACD at Windlesham. [203]
June 13	ACD at Windlesham. [1540]

1917

June 16	ACD attended the Conference of Territorial Volunteers Association. [879]
June 23	*The Guards Came Through* (poem) published in *The Times*. [6,198,1541]
June 25	ACD at Windlesham. [2102]
July	*Is Sir Oliver Lodge Right?-"Yes"* published in *The Strand Magazine*. [6,194,195,198]
July	ACD at Windlesham. [18]
July 5	*The British Campaign in France and Flanders Vol.2* published by Hodder & Stoughton. [6]
July 20	Kingsley appointed Acting Captain. [200]
July 26	ACD presided at a meeting to discuss the Divorce Law Reform. [1542]
July 27	*The Guns in Sussex* (poem) published in *The Times*. [6,198,1542]
August	*What will England be like in 1930?* published in *The Strand Magazine*. [6,194,195,196,198]
August	ACD at Windlesham. [203]
August 6	ACD spent the Bank Holiday in camp at Lewes Race Stand as a private in the Sussex Volunteer Regiment. [683]
August 7	Kingsley in France. [203]
August 8	Kingsley posted to the 11th Battalion. [200]
August 21	ACD at Windlesham. [18]
August 23	Kingsley in France. [203]
August 25	ACD at Windlesham. [18]
August 31	ACD at Windlesham. [1543]
September	*His Last Bow* published in *The Strand Magazine*. [6,194,195,196,198,202]
September	It was reported in the *Daily Mirror* on 1 September that ACD had been camping with his battalion in the heart of Sussex. [1030] {Note: this might be a late report as ACD did camp on 6 August at Lewes.}
September 1	It was advertised that ACD would deliver an address before the London Spiritualist Alliance at the Salon of the Royal Society of British Artists, Suffolk Street, Pall Mall, London on 25 October titled "The New Revelation." [1843]
September 5	ACD attended the 16th annual meeting of Raphael Tuck & Sons, Ltd. at Salisbury House, Finsbury, London. [684]
September 6	ACD at Windlesham. [18]
September	ACD donated £2:2s to the proposed testimonial to Mr Alfred Vout Peters (the Peters Testimonial Fund). [1844]
September 10	ACD at Windlesham. [1544]
September 21	ACD at Windlesham. [203]
October	Innes returned home on leave. [124]
October 6	Kingsley in France. [203]
October 6	ACD travelled to Bradford. [203]
October 7	Kingsley in France. [203]
October 7	Lecture by ACD "The New Revelation" at the Eastbrook Wesleyan Mission in Bradford. [4,29,203]
October	ACD made a speech at Manchester on Divorce Law Reform. [6] (*3)
October 8	ACD gave a talk on Divorce Reform at the Free Trade Hall, Manchester. [29,203] (*3)
October 15	ACD attended a divorce reform meeting held in Manchester. [685] {Note: this is probably referring to the talk held on 8 October.} (*3)
October 22	*His Last Bow* published by John Murray, London. [6,31]
October 24	ACD at Windlesham. [203]
October 25	Lecture by ACD "The New Revelation" before the London Spiritualist Alliance at the Salon of the British Artists Gallery, Suffolk Street, Pall Mall, London with Sir Oliver Lodge presiding. [4,6,15,20,29,180,203,215,1545,1845]
October 28	ACD at Windlesham. [203]
October 28	*Phenomena and Religion of Spiritualism. A New Revelation* published in *The Sunday Times*. [6,198]
October 30	ACD at Windlesham. [884]

1917

October 31	ACD at Windlesham. [18]
November	Birth of Francis Kingsley Doyle, son of Innes and Clara. [202] (*2)
November 1	Birth of Francis Kingsley Doyle, second son of Innes and Clara, born at Crowborough [16,68,124,200,203] (*2), at Beacon Gardens, Crowborough. [880]
November 4	ACD at Windlesham. [18]
November 10	*The New Revelation* published on 10, 17 and 24 November in *Light*. [6,29,198]
November 11	Kingsley in France. [203]
November 14	ACD at Windlesham. [203]
November 14	Death of Emily (Nem) Hawkins at Barnstable, Devon. [124]
November 29	ACD made a speech "Sir A. Conan Doyle and Divorce Law" at Birmingham, given as President of the Divorce Law Reform Union. [6,203]
December	*Some Personalia about Mr. Sherlock Holmes* published in *The Strand Magazine*. [6,195,196,198,203]
December 3	Kingsley in France. [203]
December 5	ACD made an address "The New Revelation" at the London residence of Lord and Lady Glenconner, 34 Queen Anne's Gate. [1846]
December 8	ACD at Windlesham. [884]
December 10	Kingsley relinquished his acting rank of Captain and left the British Expeditionary Force. [200]

1918

n.d.	*At the Waters of Strife: Some Little Verses* by Bryan Mary Angell (ACD's sister) published by Gay and Hancock Ltd. [photo copy in the collection of Brian W. Pugh]
n.d.	ACD visited HM Factory Gretna, a munitions factory near Gretna, Scotland. [95] (*3)
January	*The New Revelation* published in the *Metropolitan Magazine*. [6,180,198]
January	For part of January and February, Kingsley enrolled at St. Mary's Hospital Medical School. [200]
January 1	It was announced that Lt. Col. John Francis Innes Hay Doyle, DSO, R.A. would be awarded the CMG. [1546,1766]
January 3	Francis Kingsley Doyle baptised at St. John's Church, Eastbourne, present were Innes and Clara, Kingsley (the English godfather) and Steffen Møhl (the Danish godfather and Clara's nephew), the Mam, ACD, Jean, Mary, Denis, Adrian, Jean (Lena), Lottie and Claire Oldham, Connie Hornung, Ida and Pabby Foley (Innes II, Ida's younger son), Branford Angell and Clara Boulnois. [124]
n.d.	Lt. Col. John Francis Innes Hay Doyle was awarded the Distinguished Order of St. Michael and St. George (CMG) by the King at Buckingham Palace. [203] (*2)
January 9	Innes received the CMG from King Edward VII at Buckingham Palace. [124] (*2)
January 10	Innes left England for France. [124]
January 14	ACD at Windlesham. [18]
January 16	ACD at Windlesham. [18]
January 16	ACD donated £10 to *Light* Maintenance Fund. [1847]
January 22	ACD at Windlesham. [203]
January 25	Kingsley resigned his Commission and was granted the honorary rank of Lieutenant. [200]
February 6	ACD at Windlesham. [18]
February 7	ACD attended the opening of the Chevrons Club. [1547]
February 8	ACD at Windlesham. [18]
February 27	Driver Rupert Mar gave a vocal and dramatic recital at Christ Church Schools, Crowborough for the V.A.D. Hospital. Lady Conan Doyle paid for the admission of wounded soldiers to the recital. [686]
March	ACD at Windlesham. [18]

1918

March 6	A whist drive took place at the Oddfellows' Hall, Crowborough, ACD was a subscriber to the Whist Drive Funds donating £1. [687]
March 7	ACD at Windlesham. [203]
March 13	It was announced that ACD would speak at a conference on "Marriage and Parenthood: Their Ideals and Dangers" on 20 March to be held at Caxton Hall, Westminster, London. [1548] {Note: no report of this conference located.}
March 25	Kingsley transferred from St. Mary's Hospital to the Medical School at St. Thomas's Hospital. [124,200]
April	*Three of Them: I. A Chat about Children, Snakes and Zebus* published in *The Strand Magazine*. [6,194,195,196,198]
April	*Three of Them: II. About Cricket* published in *The Strand Magazine*. [6,194,195,196,198]
April 9	*The British Campaign in France and Flanders Vol. 3* published by Hodder & Stoughton. [6]
April 11	ACD spoke on the Divorce Law Reform at the Lyceum Club, London. [1549]
April 16	ACD at Windlesham. [18]
April 22-23	The manuscripts of *The Dancing Men*, *The White Company* and *The Norwood Builder* donated by ACD were sold at Christie's auction in aid of the British Red Cross Society and the Order of the Hospital of St. John of Jerusalem. [2027]
n.d.	*The New Revelation* published. [99] (*3)
April 29	*The New Revelation* published by Hodder & Stoughton, London. [6] (*3)
April 29	ACD attended a war time birthday party held by Sir Claude Champion de Crespigny at the National Sporting Club, London. [688]
May	ACD donated £20 to Light Sustentation Fund. [1848]
May	*The Battle of the Somme* published in *The Strand Magazine* in May and June. [6,194,195,196,198]
May	Kingsley left the army. [33]
May 2	ACD at Windlesham. [1550]
May 5	ACD narrated some of his experiences at the various fronts at a meeting of Our Society (Crimes Club). [77]
May 24	ACD at Windlesham. [18]
June	*The New Revelation* published. [215] (*3)
June 20	The Hull trawler *Conan Doyle* was in action against an enemy submarine. [689]
June 25	ACD at Windlesham. [18]
July	*Three of Them: III. Speculations* published in *The Strand Magazine*. [6,194,195,196,198]
July 7	ACD spoke at the Spiritualists' National Union at Sheffield. [690]
July 12	It was announced that a Red Cross Sale in aid of the British Farmers Red Cross Fund would be held on 31 July, ACD among others promised his active support. [691] {Note: no report of this event located.}
July 12	ACD at Windlesham. [18]
July	Father Barry-Doyle a cousin of ACD visited Windlesham. [203]
July 27	ACD at Windlesham. [203]
August	*Three of Them: IV. The Leather Skin Tribe* published in *The Strand Magazine*. [6,194,195,196,198]
August 19	Colonel Packe took tea at Windlesham. [203]
August 20	ACD at Windlesham. [203]
August 30	ACD at 6 Clarence Parade, Southsea. [203]
Summer	ACD toured the south of England lecturing on spiritualism. [4]
September 2	ACD in Southsea. [203]
September 6	ACD lectured in Portsmouth. [203]
September 12	ACD lectured in Bournemouth. [203]
September 15	ACD in Southsea. [203]
September 21	ACD returned to Windlesham. [203]

1918

September 24	ACD attended an ordinary general meeting of Raphael Tuck & Sons (Ltd.) at Salisbury House, London Wall, London. [692]
n.d.	At the request of the Australian High Command ACD inspected the Anzac positions on the Somme River. [180,203] (*5)
September	ACD visited and addressed the Australians at the front. [2,3,6] (*5)
September 26	ACD visited and addressed the Australians at the front. [10] (*5)
September 29	ACD visited the Western Front to watch his brother's Third British Army Corps team up with the American 27th and 30th Divisions in an attack on the Hindenburg Line. [110,215, 247]
October	ACD visited and addressed the Australians at the front. [4] (*5)
October 1	ACD visited the Australian front. [1551] (*5)
October	ACD attended the Redhill Volunteer review. [203]
October	Father Barry-Doyle visited Windlesham. [203]
October	ACD made a speech "Death and the Hereafter" held in Brighton, Sussex. [6,28,203]
October	*The Battle of Arras* published in *The Strand Magazine*, October & November. [6,194,195,196,198]
October 3	*The Rent in the Line (Breaking the Hindenburg Line)* published in *The Times*. [6,198]
October 5	ACD lectured in Wimbledon. [203]
October 6	ACD at Windlesham. [18]
October 10	ACD attended a luncheon given by Viscount Northcliffe at Printing House Square, London. [1552]
October 11	ACD at Windlesham. [884]
October	ACD toured the Midlands lecturing on spiritualism. [4]
October 13	ACD completed six lectures in seven days in the Midlands. [203]
October 23	ACD lectured on "Death and the Hereafter" at the Oddfellows Hall, Brighton. [1849]
October 27	Lecture by ACD on spiritualism in Leeds Town Hall [4,87] "Death and Afterwards." [1850]
October 28	Death of son Kingsley Conan Doyle, he died of pneumonia [7,16,33,68,124,200,202] septic pneumonia. [1553] (*2)
October 28	Death of Kingsley Conan Doyle, he died in the pan-European influenza epidemic [3,14,99,180,203,215,1554] at St. Thomas's Hospital. [124,215] (*2)
October 28	ACD lectured on "Death and Afterwards" at the Mechanics Large Hall, Nottingham [693,1850]
October	ACD lecturing in Nottingham. [124]
October 29	Lecture by ACD on spiritualism at the Mechanics Institution, Nottingham. [3,4,87]
October 30	ACD lectured in Nottingham. [202]
October	ACD at the Grosvenor Hotel, London. [203]
November	Mary Conan Doyle, ACD's daughter was at 9 St. Mary's House, London. [203]
November	ACD donated £10 to the London Spiritualist Alliance. [1851]
November	*The Battle of Messines* published in *The Strand Magazine*. [6,194,195,196,198]
November 1	Kingsley was buried next to Louise at St. Luke's Church, Grayshott. [202,203]
November 5	*Life After Death [A Form Letter]* published in the *Daily Chronicle*. [6,198]
November 9	ACD at Windlesham. [18]
November 11	The armistice with Germany and the allies was signed. [1835]
November 12	ACD planned a lecture tour in Scotland, including Aberdeen and Dundee. [203] {Note: this did not take place as far as can be made out.}
November 13	ACD at Windlesham. [203]
November 29	ACD spoke on Divorce Law Reform at Caxton Hall, Westminster, London. [1555]
December	*Life After Death [A Form Letter]* privately published. [6]
December	*Three of Them: V. About Naughtiness and Frogs and Historical Pictures* published in *The Strand Magazine*. [6,194,195,196,198]

1918

December 4	*Danger! And Other Stories* published by John Murray, London. [6]
Christmas	Clara Doyle and Innes spent Christmas at Windlesham. [16]

1919

n.d.	ACD travelled to Belfast, Ireland to attend a series of séances with the Goligher family and Dr J.W. Crawford, [1018] or the Gollgher family and Dr W.J. Crawford. [1019] {Note: other than the two sources, 1018 & 1019, no other records of this visit have been located.}
n.d.	Death of Selina Leckie, mother of Jean. [202]
January	*The Battle of Cambrai* published in *The Strand Magazine*. [6,194,195,196,198]
January	ACD donated £10 to *Light* Sustentation Fund. [1852]
January 12	ACD gave a lecture on spiritualism at Hastings, Sussex, (*2) ACD and his wife afterwards had dinner with Sir Henry Rider Haggard and his wife at the latter's home, North Lodge in St. Leonards, a suburb of Hastings. [64,202]
January 12	ACD addressed a Brotherhood meeting at Hastings Congregational Church on "Life after Death." [695] (*2)
January	ACD lectured on spiritualism at Walsall. [28]
January 16	ACD lectured on spiritualism at Birmingham [20] at the invitation of the Birmingham Spiritualist Church ACD lectured on "Death and the Hereafter" at the Town Hall, Birmingham. [1853]
January 22	*The Volunteer* (poem) published in the *Daily Express*. [6]
January 27	ACD made a speech "Exploits of the Anzacs" at an Australian Day luncheon of the Australian and New Zealand Luncheon Club at the Connaught Rooms, Great Queen Street, London. [6,1556]
January 30	ACD at Windlesham. [203]
February	*The Battle of Cambrai: The Second Phase* published in *The Strand Magazine*. [195,196]
February	ACD at Windlesham. [18]
February 8	ACD's forthcoming engagements were published: 13 February at Cheltenham and 14 February at Cardiff, the address at both venues would be "The New Revelation." [1854]
February 12	W. Addy the Skipper of the S.T. *Conan Doyle* was awarded the D.S.C., Seaman David Slater and Boatswain George Boyes were awarded the D.S.M., mentioned in the "London Gazette" were Deck Hand John A. Bennett, W.T.O. Harry S. Robinson, Mate Frederick E. Sharp and Chief Engineer Francis J. Wright, the remainder of the crew received smaller monetary awards. [696]
February 13	ACD gave a lecture "Death and the Hereafter" at the Supper Room, Town Hall, Cheltenham. [697]
February 15	It was reported that ACD was staying at the Queen's Hotel, Cheltenham. [698]
February	ACD and Jean witnessed a séance in South Wales. [20,202]
February 15	ACD and Jean attended a séance in Cardiff [6,1855], ACD, Jean, the Chief Constable, the Deputy Chief Constable and others attended a séance at the residence of Mr Walter H. Wall, Hillcrest, Penylan, Cardiff; the medium was Mr Tom Thomas. [699] (*2)
February 15	ACD and Jean attended a séance at the residence of Mr Walter Wall in Cardiff, Wales [1080], held at the residence known as Hillcrest at Penylan, Cardiff, the medium was Mr Tom Thomas, there were about 20 persons present including Mr Leo Joseph, J.P., Mr David Williams, OBE (Chief Constable) and Superintendent Harrison. [1114] (*2)
February 16	ACD lectured on "Death and the Hereafter" at the Theatre Royal, Merthyr Tydfil, Wales. [700,1135,1855]
n.d.	Innes Doyle died from pneumonia following the Armistice, with the rank of Brigadier General. [99] (*4)
February 19	Death of Colonel (Brevet) John Francis Innes Hay Doyle DSO, CMG, acting as Brigadier-General (brother of ACD) at Halle, Belgium, he died of pneumonia. [1557] (*4)

1919

February 19	Death of Brigadier General John Francis Innes Hay Doyle. [213] (*4)
February 19	Death of Innes Doyle (brother of ACD) [203] he died during the pan-European influenza epidemic [180,215] he died in Belgium [124,215] he died of pneumonia. [16,68,200,202] (*4)
March	*Life After Death* an interview with ACD by Haden Church published in *The Strand Magazine*. [6,194,195,198]
March 4	ACD attended a meeting at the Oddfellows Hall, Crowborough to elect a committee for a War Memorial. [701]
March 11	It was announced that Lieutenant-Colonel (temporary Brigadier-General) John Francis Innes Hay Doyle, CMG, DSO, Royal Artillery had been awarded the Légion d'Honneur Croix de Commandeur. [1767]
March 17	ACD gave a lecture tour in South Wales. [20]
March 22	ACD's forthcoming engagements were published: 2 April at Darlington, 3 April at the Town Hall, Gateshead-on-Tyne, 4 April at the Usher Hall, Edinburgh, 6 April at St. Andrews Hall, Glasgow and 9 April at Philharmonic Hall, Liverpool. [1856]
March 27	ACD and others attended a séance by the 'medium in the mask' at an unnamed flat of P.T. Selbit in West London [1030] under the auspices of the *Sunday Express*. [1857]
March 29	It was advertised that ACD would lecture on "Death and the Hereafter" on 4 April at Usher Hall, Edinburgh. [1159]
March 31	*The British Campaign in France and Flanders Vol. 4* published by Hodder & Stoughton. [6]
April	Lecture by ACD "Death and the Hereafter" in Edinburgh and Glasgow, Scotland. [6,20,28]
April 4	ACD lectured on "Death and the Hereafter" at Usher Hall, Edinburgh, ACD was accompanied by Jean [1160] before an audience of over 3,000. [1858]
April	ACD lectured at St. Andrew's Hall, Glasgow. [1135] (*2)
April 6	ACD lectured at St. Andrew's Hall, Glasgow to an audience of about 5,000. [1858] (*2)
April 9	ACD lectured on "Death and the Hereafter" in Liverpool. [1161]
April 16	ACD donated £25 to the Crowborough and District War Memorial Fund. [702]
April 19	ACD took part in the "Verrall" Cup at Crowborough Beacon Golf Club, Crowborough, he came fifth. [703]
April 27	ACD spoke at the National Memorial Service for the Fallen of the War held at the Royal Albert Hall, London [1558] organised by the Spiritualists' National Union. [215]
May	ACD made a speech at the National Memorial Service for the Fallen in the War, Royal Albert Hall, under the auspices of the Spiritualists' National Union Ltd. [6]
May	*The Vital Message* published in *Nash's-Pall Mall Magazine,* May–August and October. [6,198]
May 7	ACD at Windlesham. [203]
May 14	ACD at Windlesham. [203]
May 14	ACD lectured in Crowborough [203] on "Death and the Hereafter" at the Oddfellows Hall, Crowborough. [704]
May	ACD lectured in Doncaster, Huddersfield, Manchester, Leicester, Northampton, Portsmouth, Worcester and Glasgow. [20,28]
May 25	ACD started a lecture tour that included Doncaster, Huddersfield, Manchester, Rochdale and Crewe. [203]
June	ACD met Houdini at Brighton, Sussex. [26]
June 7	It was announced that ACD would lecture on 9 July at Eastbourne, 10 July at Brighton and 11 July at Worthing. [1859]
June 12	ACD at Windlesham. [203]
June 15	Lecture by ACD "Death and the Hereafter" held at The Queen's Hall, London. [6,28,203,1135,1559]

1919

June 21	ACD at Windlesham. [203]
June 22	Lecture by ACD "Death and the Hereafter" held at The Queen's Hall, London. [6,28,203,1135,1560]
June 24	ACD at Windlesham. [2053]
June 28	It was advertised in *The Times* that on 29 June ACD would lecture at The Queen's Hall, London, "Death and the Hereafter". [1561]
June 29	Lecture by ACD "Death and the Hereafter" held at The Queen's Hall, London. [6,28,203,1135]
July 3	ACD at Windlesham. [2053]
July 4	ACD at Windlesham. [18]
July 9	ACD at Windlesham. [1562]
July 9	Lecture by ACD on spiritualism at Eastbourne Town Hall, Sussex. [28,203]
July 10	Lecture by ACD on spiritualism at Hove Town Hall, Sussex [28] or Brighton [203], ACD addressed the Brighton Spiritualist Brotherhood at Hove Town Hall. [1081]
July 11	Lecture by ACD on spiritualism at the Connaught Hall, Worthing, Sussex. [28,202,203]
July 15	ACD at Windlesham. [18]
August	*The Vital Message* published. [215]
August	*A Full Report of a Lecture on Spiritualism* at Worthing on 11 July published in *The Worthing Gazette*. [46]
August 11	ACD at Windlesham. [18]
September	ACD at Windlesham. [203]
September 5	*The British Campaign in France and Flanders Vol. 5* published by Hodder & Stoughton. [6]
September 6	It was announced that ACD would lecture on 6 September at Southsea and on 12 September at the Winter Gardens, Bournemouth. [1860]
September 6	ACD lectured in Portsmouth on "Death and the Hereafter" [881], at Portsmouth Town Hall or Portland Hall [1135] at Town Hall, Portsmouth. [1861]
September 7	Lecture by ACD on spiritualism at Portsmouth. [15]
September 7	ACD and his wife attended a séance given by Evan Powell, an amateur medium, in his hotel room. [20,100]
September 8	ACD and his wife attended a second séance given by Evan Powell in his hotel room. [100]
September 12	ACD lectured at the Winter Gardens, Bournemouth on "Death and the Hereafter". [1135,1861]
September 23	ACD as a director attended the eighteenth annual general meeting of Raphael Tuck & Sons (Ltd.) at Salisbury House, Finsbury Circus. [1563]
September 25	ACD discharged from the 5th Volunteer Battalion of the Royal Sussex Regiment. [21]
September 27	It was announced that ACD would lecture on 13 October at Northampton, 14 October at Leamington, 16 October at Hanley, 17 October at Worcester and on 12 and 13 November at Aberdeen. [1862]
October 4	It was advertised that ACD would lecture at the Town Hall, Northampton on 13 October. [2079]
October 5	ACD attended a meeting of like-minded people in Wimbledon [1030], gave a lecture at King's Palace Picture Theatre, Wimbledon. [1135,1863]
October 11	It was announced that ACD would lecture on 16 October at Wolverhampton instead of Hanley. [1863]
October 13	ACD lectured on spiritualism at the Town Hall, Northampton [1136] on "Death and the Hereafter" for the Northampton Spiritualist Society. [2080]
October 14	ACD lectured on "Death and the Hereafter" at the Town Hall, Leamington. [1137]
October 16	Lecture by ACD on spiritualism "Our Reply to the Cleric" at Wolverhampton. [6]
October	ACD gave an address on spiritualism at Worcester Cathedral. [20]

1919

October 17	Lecture by ACD on spiritualism at Worcester. [6]
October 19	Lecture by ACD on spiritualism "Our Reply to the Cleric" at the Palace Theatre, Leicester. [6,1864]
November 1	ACD at Windlesham. [203]
November	*The Vital Message* published. [202] (*2)
November 4	*The Vital Message* published by Hodder & Stoughton, London. [6] (*2)
November 11	ACD arrived in Aberdeen. [705]
November 12	ACD lectured on "Death and the Hereafter" at the Music Hall, Aberdeen. [706]
November 13	ACD lectured on "The New Revelation or Death and the Hereafter" at Gilfillan Memorial Hall, Dundee. [707]
November 24	Mary Louise Conan Doyle (ACD's daughter) with companion Cynthia Colonna sailed from Glasgow on board the *Columbia* for America. [242]
November 26	ACD made an address on spiritualism titled "The Material Side of the Psychic Movement" at St. Mary's Hospital at the invitation of St. Mary's Hospital Medical Society. [234]
November 30	ACD read a paper "The Psychic in Crime" at a meeting of Our Society (Crimes Club). [77]
December	*The Law of the Ghost* published in *The Strand Magazine* as *The Uncharted Coast – I. The Law of the Ghost*. [6,194,195,196,198]
December 2	ACD lectured on spiritualism at Merthyr Tydfil [708], he was accompanied by Jean. [1082]
December 4	Mary Louise Conan Doyle (ACD's daughter) with companion Cynthia Colonna arrived in New York on board the *Columbia;* they were visiting William Pettigrew at Bittenhouse, Pebble Beach. [96]
December	Mary (ACD's daughter) was at the Delmonte Hotel, Delmonte, California. [203]
December 6	ACD concluded his visit to Merthyr Tydfil. [2004]
December 9	ACD at Windlesham. [18]
December 13	ACD at Windlesham. [18]
December 16	*The Guards Came Through and Other Poems* published by John Murray, London. [6]
December 19	Mary was at the Delmonte Hotel, Delmonte, California. [203]
December 20	ACD at Windlesham. [203]
December 29	ACD at Windlesham. [18]

1920

January	*Our Reply to The Cleric* published by The Spiritualists' National Union. [6]
January	*A New Light on Old Crimes* published in *The Strand Magazine* as *The Uncharted Coast II. A New Light on Old Crimes*. [6,194,195,196,198]
January	ACD at Windlesham. [203]
January 1	ACD at Windlesham. [1564]
January 11	ACD at Windlesham. [884]
January 18	ACD at Windlesham. [884]
January 19	ACD lectured in Southport. [1138]
n.d.	ACD addressed a spiritualist meeting in Southport. [709]
January 20	ACD at the Hotel Metropole, Blackpool. [18]
January 22	ACD lectured on "Death and the Hereafter" at the Public Hall, Preston [1139] to an audience of about 2,000. [1866]
January 23	*The British Campaign in France and Flanders Vol. 6* published by Hodder & Stoughton. [6]
January	ACD donated £21 to *Light* Sustentation Fund. [1865]
February	ACD at Windlesham. [203]
n.d.	ACD sent an inscribed silver cigarette case to Mr William Addy, D.S.C., captain of the Hull trawler *Conan Doyle*. [710]
February 5	ACD at Windlesham. [18]

1920

February 7	It was advertised that ACD would lecture at the Large Town Hall, Reading on 9 March. [2081]
February 10	ACD at Windlesham. [18]
February 14	It was announced that ACD would lecture at Durham on 16 February where he would be the guest of Bishop Welldon, 17 February at Harrogate and on 18 February at Hanley. [1867]
February 15	ACD in Durham, to lecture in Durham, Harrogate and Hawley. [203]
n.d.	ACD addressed a spiritualist meeting at the Deanery, Durham. [711] (*3)
February 16	ACD delivered an address at The Deanery of Durham, he was invited by Bishop Welldon who presided. [1135] (*3)
February 17	ACD lectured at The Deanery, Durham. [1868]{Note: the report on this lecture states the date as 17, this is incorrect as it was held on 16.} (*3)
February 17	ACD gave a spiritualist lecture at the Spiritualist Church, Hanley, Stoke-on-Trent. [1031]
February 18	ACD lectured on "Life After Death" at the Royal Hall, Harrogate. [1140]
February	ACD at the Grosvenor Hotel, London. [203]
February 21	ACD and Jean attended the final of the Amateur Billiards Championship, ACD presented the cup to the winner Sidney H. Fry and Jean presented a souvenir to the ruuner-up W.B. Marshall. [1976] {Note: this was held at Thurston's Grand Hall, Leicester Square, London.}
February 28	It was announced that ACD would lecture on "My Experiences" at Battersea Town Hall on 30 March. [1869]
n.d.	ACD met Harry Houdini [99,215] in Plymouth. [180]
March	ACD first met Houdini. [15]
March	ACD at Windlesham. [203]
March 6	It was announced that ACD would lecture at Town Hall, Reading on 9 March. [1870
March 9	ACD lectured in Reading [203] on "Death and the Hereafter" at the Large Town Hall, Reading for the Reading Spiritualist Mission, ACD was accompanied by his wife. [2082]
March	Spiritualism debate between ACD and Joseph MacCabe at the Queen's Hall, London. [202] (*3)
March 11	Spiritualism debate between ACD and Joseph McCabe at the Queen's Hall, Langham Place, London, the chairman was Sir Edward Marshall-Hall, K.C. [6,15,20,203,215,1135,1565] (*3)
March 13	It was announced that ACD was a member of the council of the London Spiritualist Alliance Ltd. [1871]
March 20	ACD at Crowborough Beacon Golf Club, Crowborough. [203]
March 27	It was announced that ACD would lecture at East Ham on 7 April and Lewisham on 8 April. [1872]
March 29	ACD at Windlesham. [18]
March 30	ACD addressed a meeting on "My Experiences" held at Battersea Town Hall. [1873]
March 30	ACD lectured in West London. [203]
March 31	ACD lectured in West London. [203]
March 31	ACD addressed a meeting at the anniversary celebrations of modern spiritualism held at the Queen's Hall, London [1135] to celebrate the anniversary of Modern Spiritualism at the Queen's Hall, Langham Place, London. [1873]
April 3	It was announced that ACD would lecture at Colston Hall, Bristol on 20 April, Assembly Rooms, Bath on 21 April and Swindon Swimming Baths on 22 April. [1874]
April 5	ACD organised a "Treasure Hunt" for the 1st Crowborough Troup of Boy Scouts on Crowborough Common. [712]
April 7	ACD lectured at East Ham Town Hall. [713,1875]
April 7	ACD lectured in East London. [203]

1920

April 8	ACD lectured in Lewisham. [1875]
April 8	ACD lectured in East London. [203]
April	ACD made a speech at the Queen's Hall to commemorate the anniversary of modern spiritualism. [6]
April 9	It was announced that 'picture play-goers that they will shortly see ACD's daughter Mary "in the pictures."' She was at the time in Los Angeles doing film work for production in England. [1083]
April	ACD wrote a letter to Houdini [45] who was performing at the Hippodrome, Brighton from 12-17 April [1133] and invited him for lunch at Windlesham. [45]
April	Houdini had lunch at Windlesham. [15,203] (*3)
April	ACD entertained Houdini and Bernard Ernst at Windlesham, Crowborough. [100] (*3)
April 14	ACD and Houdini had lunch at Windlesham, Crowborough. [45,202,215] (*3)
April	ACD met Houdini after watching his act at Portsmouth. [15,20] {Note: Houdini was performing at the Hippodrome, Portsmouth from 19-24 April.} [1133]
April 20	ACD lectured in the West of England for a week. [203]
April 20	ACD lectured on "Death and the Hereafter" at Colston Hall, Bristol. [714]
April 25	ACD, Houdini with his wife Bess and their niece Julia Sawyer, attended a séance with Mrs Annie Brittain. [100]
May	*The Shadows on the Screen* published in *The Strand Magazine* as *The Uncharted Coast-III. Shadows on the Screen.* [6,194,195,196,198]
May	*The Night Patrol* (poem) published in *The Student*. [6,198]
May 1	It was announced that ACD would address the blind soldiers at St. Dunstan's on 3 May. [1876] {Note: no report has been located for this address.}
May 8	It was announced that ACD would lecture in Croydon on 10 May. [1877]
May 10	Lecture by ACD on spiritualism at Croydon [6] on "Death and the Hereafter" at the Adult School, Park Lane, Croydon. [1878]
May 14	It was announced that ACD would referee the Billiards Amateur Flying Handicap at Burroughes Hall, St. James's Street on 17 May; St. Dunstan's Day. [841]
May 17	ACD was the referee at the Amateur Flying Handicap billiard competition at the Burroughes Hall, St. James's Street, London. [1566]
May 23	ACD and Jean attended a meeting of the Society for the Study of Supernormal [715] held at the College of Psychic Science, London. [1968]
June	ACD at Windlesham. [18]
June 7	ACD at Windlesham. [1567]
June 15	ACD attended an address by Revd. Vale Owen at St. Paul's, Covent Garden, London, and in the evening attended a reception at the Rectory with Jean. [1879]
June 22	ACD attended an inquiry at County Hall, Lewes, Sussex regarding an application by East Sussex County Council to borrow £1,700 for the purchase of land at Crowborough to build an Isolation Hospital, ACD with others opposed the purchase. [716]
June	ACD became interested in the Cottingley fairy photographs. [14] (*2)
June 22	ACD greatly interested in the fairy photographs. [215] (*2)
June 26	It was announced that ACD would make an address at a Garden Part at Garden House, Upper Drive, Hove on 7 July and on 8 July he would speak at a mass meeting at Hove Town Hall. [1879]
June 30	ACD wrote separate letters to Arthur Wright and his daughter Elsie about his interest in the fairies. [215]
July 8	Lecture by ACD on spiritualism at Hove [6] at the anniversary gathering of the Brighton Brotherhood at Hove Town Hall. [1880]
July	Lecture by ACD "Death and the Hereafter" at the Town Hall, Torquay. [27]
July	The film *Rodney Stone* was part filmed at Lindfield, Surrey, directed by Mr Percy Nash. [842]

1920

July 28	ACD at the Grosvenor Hotel, London, S.W.1. [18]
July 29	Lecture by ACD "Speech with the Dead" at the Holborn Restaurant. [6]
July 29	ACD and Jean attended a farewell lunch in the Holborn Restaurant, London prior to their departure for Australia and New Zealand. [6,215,1135,1568] (*3)
July 29	ACD and Jean were the guests of honour at a Luncheon given by the Spiritualists of the United Kingdom in the Royal Venetian Chamber of the Holborn Restaurant, Kingsway, London just two weeks before their departure for Australia [1123,1135], Masters Denis and Malcolm and Miss Jean Conan Doyle were present among the guests. [1135,1881] (*3)
July	ACD and Jean attended a banquet given by Spiritualists of the United Kingdom before their departure for Australia [99] at the Holborn Restaurant, London. [203] (*3)
July 30	ACD sailed for Australia with the family on board the SS *Naldera*. [6] (*2)
August	*The Sideric Pendulum* published in *The Strand Magazine*. [6,194,195,196,198]
August	ACD paid Elsie Wright and Frances Griffiths £20 in bonds. [215]
August 4	ACD gave a lecture at the Hippodrome, Exeter, Devon titled "Death and the Hereafter". The lecture was presided by Mr F.T. Blake of Bournemouth, President of the Southern Counties Union of Spiritualists. [167,1135]
August 5	ACD gave a lecture at the New Town Hall, Torquay, Devon titled "Death and the Hereafter". The lecture was presided over by Mr H.P. Rabbich of Paignton. [168]
August 10	ACD at Windlesham. [203]
August 11	ACD as a director attended the nineteenth annual general meeting of Raphael Tuck & Sons (Ltd.) at Winchester House, Old Broad Street, E.C. [1569]
August 13	ACD sailed for Australia [6,10,20] on board the *Naldera* [22,202,203,215,1135] (*2) with ACD were his wife Jean, Denis, Malcolm, Jean [242] with Mary Jakeman the maid and Major Wood. [22,783]
n.d.	SS *Naldera* docked at Gibraltar where ACD spent an hour on shore. [22]
August 19	ACD on board the SS *Naldera* sailing past the eastern Spanish coast. [22]
August 19	ACD on board the SS *Naldera* near Barcelona. [203]
n.d.	ACD disembarked for a short visit to Marseilles. [22]
August	ACD gave a lecture on spiritualism to the first class passengers on board the *Naldera* south of Crete. [18] (*3)
August	ACD on board the SS *Naldera* approaching Port Said. [203]
August	ACD addressed 250 first class passengers on board the SS *Naldera* [203] or 200 first class passengers. [22,215] (*3)
August 24	ACD on board the SS *Naldera*, he addressed 280 first class passengers [1135,1882] (*3) it was planned that he would address the second class passengers on 27 August. [1882]
August	ACD gave a lecture on spiritualism to the second class passengers [22] and ships officers on board the SS *Naldera* [203] in the Red Sea. [18] (*2)
August 27	ACD on board the SS *Naldera*, he addressed the second class passengers. [1135] (*2)
August 27	*Spiritualism and Rationalism* published by Hodder & Stoughton Ltd., London. [6]
August 29	ACD on board the SS *Naldera* approaching Aden. [203]
September 1	ACD on board the SS *Naldera* approaching Bombay. [18]
September 2	ACD on board the SS *Naldera* approaching India. [203]
n.d.	ACD disembarked in India and lunched at the Taj Mahal Hotel. [22]
September	*The Hydesville Episode* also known as *The Rift in the Veil*, published in *The Strand Magazine* as *The Uncharted Coast – IV. An Old Story Retold*. [6,194,195,196,198]
n.d.	ACD disembarked at Colombo and stayed at the Galle Face Hotel. [22]
September 7	ACD on board the SS *Naldera*. [203]
n.d.	ACD visited Australia and New Zealand to promote his beliefs in spiritualism. [99,180]

1920

September 17	ACD on board the SS *Naldera* heading for Perth. [203]
September 17	ACD Jean, Denis, Adrian, Lena Jean, Major A.H. Wood (ACD's secretary) and Mary Jakeman (Jean's maid) arrived in Fremantle, Perth, Western Australia [246] (*3) on board the *Naldera*. [288]
September 17	ACD toured Australia from 17 September until 11 February 1921. [68]
September 17	ACD arrived with his family at Fremantle for a tour of South Australia, visiting Perth, Adelaide, Melbourne and Sydney [6,20,22,202] (*3) ACD then travelled on his own to New Zealand and visited Auckland, Wellington, Christchurch and Dunedin. [6]
September 17	ACD visited Perth. [203]
September 18	ACD probably left Perth. [203]
September 18	ACD arrived with his family at Fremantle for a tour of Australia. [6] (*3)
September 21	ACD arrived with his family in Adelaide from Fremantle and stayed at the Grand Central Hotel, [22,203,289] they were welcomed by a letter from the Prime Minister William Morris (Billy) Hughes. [22,783]
n.d.	ACD visited the vineyards and wine plant of a local firm. [22] (*2)
September 22	ACD & Jean visited Penfolds Winery, Magill, Adelaide, South Australia. [782,783] (*2)
September 23	A journalist brought Mr T.P. Bellchambers to meet ACD at his hotel. [22]
September 23	ACD dined with Dr Archibald Watson and Dr William Anstey Giles. [783]
September 24	ACD visited the South Australian Museum in Adelaide, he possibly also visited the Art Gallery. [783]
September 24	ACD lunched with the governor of South Australia, Sir Archibald Weigall. [203,783]
September 25	ACD in Adelaide for his first lecture before an audience of around 2,000 at the Town Hall, Adelaide. [215]
September 25	First lecture by ACD "The Human Argument" at Adelaide Town Hall [6,20,22,203,278] also known as "Death and the Hereafter" [290,783]
September	ACD donated £10:10s to the late Dr W.J. Crawford fund for the benefit of his widow and family. [1883]
September 26	ACD at the Grand Central Hotel, Adelaide. [203]
September 27	Second lecture by ACD "The Religious Argument" at Adelaide Town Hall. [203,278,290,783,1570]
September 28	Third lecture by ACD "Pictures of Psychic Phenomena" at Adelaide Town Hall. [22,203,291,783]
September 29	ACD visited the Humbug Scrub nature reserve owned by Mr T.P. Bellchambers, [292] the party also included his sons Denis and Adrian, plus Edgar Ravenswood Waite, Ernest Whitington (Editor of *The Register*), William G (or S.) Smith (photographer) Evan Kyffin & Massie Thomas (*The Register*), Dr William Monro Anderson of Japan, Major Wood, Thomas Paine Bellchambers and his wife Eliza Mary. [783]
September 30	ACD stayed at Gibson's Grand Central Hotel, Adelaide. [146]
September 30	A matinee lecture "Pictures of Psychic Phenomena" by ACD at Adelaide Town Hall, [279,292] a 2.30 matinee was a repeat of the 28 September lecture. [783]
September 30	In the evening ACD left Adelaide for Melbourne [203,279] by express train [292] on the Melbourne Express. [783]
October 1	ACD arrived in Melbourne and stayed at the Menzies Hotel. [203,293]
n.d.	ACD stayed at the Menzies Hotel for a few days before moving to a flat at the Grand Hotel. [22]
October 2	A preliminary announcement appeared in *The Times* for the sale of Undershaw, Hindhead. [1571]
n.d.	ACD watched the final tie of the Victorian football cup at Melbourne. [22] (*2)
October 2	ACD watched the final tie of the Victorian football cup match at Melbourne Ground between Richmond and Collingwood that was won by Richmond [784], Australian Rules football cup match at the Melbourne Cricket Ground, Melbourne. [1004] (*2)

1920

October 5	Lecture by ACD "The Human Argument" at The Playhouse, Melbourne. [22,294]
October 5	Lecture by ACD on spiritualism at The Playhouse, Melbourne. [6]
October 6	ACD made a speech "The Man in the Street" at a British Empire League Luncheon at the Menzies Hotel, Victoria. [6,295]
October 7	Lecture by ACD "The Religious Argument" at the Playhouse, Melbourne. [203,296]
October 8	ACD was the guest of the Federal Ministers luncheon at Parliament House, Melbourne. [301]
October 8	ACD attended a séance with Mrs Hunter. [22]
October 9	It was announced that Undershaw would be sold at auction on 30 November. [1788] {Note: no further details of the auction have been located.}
October 9	ACD gave a lecture "Death and the Hereafter" at the Playhouse, Melbourne. [297]
October 10	ACD addressed the members of the Spiritualistic Churches & Lyceums at the Masonic Hall, Collins Street, Melbourne. [298]
October 11	ACD gave a lecture "Pictures of Psychic Phenomena" at the Playhouse, Melbourne. [297]
October 11	It was announced that ACD would lecture at Geelong on 14 October and Bendigo on 18 October. [297]
October 13	Lecture by ACD in the small town of Geelong. [22]
October 13	Lecture by ACD in Bendigo. [22]
October 14	ACD visited and descended the Unity Mine at Bendigo. [22]
October 14	ACD gave a lecture in Geelong. [297]
October 14	ACD attended a Spiritualist service at the Auditorium, Adelaide. [22]
October 15	Branford Bryan Angell who was listed as a tea planter left the Port of London on board the SS *Nagoya* for Calcutta, India. [1837]
n.d.	ACD had a séance with Mrs Knight MacLellan in Melbourne. [22]
October 16	ACD gave a lecture "Pictures of Psychic Phenomena" at the Playhouse, Melbourne. [297]
October 18	ACD guest of the Hon. Agar Wynne at Nerrin-Nerrin, Western Victoria. [22]
October 18	ACD gave a lecture in Bendigo [297] 'Death and the Hereafter' at the Masonic Hall, Bedigo. [785]
October 21	ACD at the Grand Hotel Melbourne. [884]
October 30	ACD attended a luncheon given by Their Excellencies the Governor General and Lady Foster in their vice-regal rooms. [299]
November	Stoll films began production with Eille Norwood as Sherlock Holmes. [6]
November	*The Half Way House of Matter* published in *The Strand Magazine* as *The Uncharted Coast – V. The Absolute Proof*. [6,194,195,196,198,215]
November 2	ACD at the Grand Hotel, Melbourne. [300]
November 3	ACD at the Grand Hotel, Melbourne. [18]
November 6	It was announced in *The Times* that Undershaw was to be sold on 30 November. [1572]
n.d.	ACD had a sitting with the medium Charles Bailey. [22,215]
n.d.	ACD had a second sitting with Charles Bailey. [22,215]
n.d.	The medium Mrs Susanna Harris gave a private séance in ACD's hotel room. [22]
n.d.	ACD and Denis watched a cricket match between Victoria and England. [22]
November 10	A planned lecture by ACD at the Town Hall, Melbourne on 11 November was advertised. [302]
November 11	ACD gave a lecture "Pictures of Psychic Phenomena at the Town Hall, Melbourne. [303]
November 12	Lecture by ACD at the Town Hall, Melbourne. [22]
November 12	ACD left Melbourne for Sydney. [304]
November 13	ACD left Melbourne for Sydney. [20,22]

1920

November 13	ACD, arrived at Central Station, Sydney, Australia, they stayed at Petty's Hotel on York Street. [246,305]
November 13	Lady Conan Doyle was interviewed by the *Sydney Herald* in her sitting room at Petty's Hotel. [306]
November 13	Death of Clara Boulnois, the valued friend of the Doyle family. [124]
November 14	ACD took the ferry to Manly for a visit but did not get off the ferry. [246]
November 15	Lecture by ACD "The Human Argument" on spiritualism at the Town Hall, Sydney. [6,246,307]
November 16	ACD made a speech on great writers to the New South Wales Institute of Journalists at Farmers, Sydney. [6] (*2)
November 16	ACD, Jean and Major Wood were guests of honour at a luncheon hosted by the New South Wales Institute of Journalists held at Farmer's, Sydney, his talk was titled 'Great Writers I Have Known.'[246,308] (*2)
November 17	Lecture by ACD "Spiritualism: Its Religious Side" at the Town Hall, Sydney. [6]
November 17	Lecture by ACD "Spiritualism: The Religious Argument" at the Town Hall, Sydney. [246,308]
November 19	ACD at Petty's Hotel, Sydney. [309]
November 20	Lecture by ACD "Pictures of Psychic Phenomena" at the Town Hall, Sydney. [246,309] (*2)
November 20	Lecture by ACD "Spirit Photographs" at the Town Hall, Sydney. [6] (*2)
November 22	During the afternoon ACD watched the second day of the England/NSW cricket test at the Sydney Cricket Ground. [246]
November 22	Lecture by ACD "At the Front" at the Millions Club luncheon Sydney. [6]
November 22	ACD attended a luncheon at the Sydney Millions Club held at Sargent's Restaurant, Market Street, Sydney. [246,310]
November 23	Possibly on this date, ACD and family took the Manly ferry for Manly beach where they stayed for ten days at the Manly Pacific Hotel. [246]
n.d.	ACD was invited to speak at the Manly Congregational Church, though no record ACD's address there survives. [246]
n.d.	ACD visited Taronga Zoo, Mosman. [246]
November 25	ACD in Manly. [311]
November 26	ACD was at the Pacific Hotel, Manly. [786]
November 27	Lecture by ACD "Spiritualism. A Reply to Criticism" at the Town Hall, Sydney [6] or "Spiritualism: A Reply to Critics" [246] or "Pictures of Psychic Phenomena". [312]
November 28	In the morning ACD and family attended the weekly service at the Stanmore Road Spiritualist Church, 90 Stanmore Road, Stanmore, Sydney. [246]
November 28	In the afternoon ACD and family attended a farewell reception held by the Sydney Spiritualists at the Town Hall, Sydney [246] a United Spiritualist service under the auspices of the Spiritualist Church of New South Wales. [313]
November 28	ACD attended a reception at the Town Hall, Sydney. [22]
December	ACD wrote of his support of the Cottingley fairy photographs in *The Strand Magazine*. [99]
December	*Fairies Photographed – An-Epoch Making Event* published in *The Strand Magazine*. [6,194,195,196,198]
December 2	After a few more days with his family in Manly, ACD departed for New Zealand. [246]
December 2	ACD stayed at the Hotel Pacific, Manly, New South Wales, he left here for a fifteen-day tour of New Zealand that included eight lectures. [203]
December 2	ACD left Sydney for New Zealand. [257]
December 2	ACD left Sydney on board the *Maheno* for a tour of New Zealand, his family remained in Sydney. [314]
December 3	ACD left Sydney for Wellington, New Zealand. [258]
December 6	ACD arrived in Auckland, New Zealand. [259]
December 7	ACD arrived in New Zealand on board the ship *Maheno*. [81]

1920

December 7	Lecture by ACD "Beyond the Grave" before an audience of 3,000 at the Town Hall, Auckland [6] or a lecture "Death and the Hereafter". [260]
December 8	Lecture by ACD "The Spirit World. Psychic Photographs" at the Town Hall, Auckland [6] or a lecture "Pictures of Psychic Phenomena". [261]
December 10	ACD arrived in Wellington, New Zealand. [262]
December 10	A civic reception was planned at the Concert Chamber, Town Hall, Wellington to welcome ACD; this was cancelled at the wishes of ACD. [263]
December 11	ACD gave a lecture "Death and the Hereafter" at the Town Hall, Wellington. [264]
December 12	ACD attended a spiritualist service in Wellington and spoke for about twenty minutes. [265]
December 12	ACD attended a lecture by John Page at the Concert Chamber, Town Hall, Wellington. [266]
December 13	ACD gave a lecture "Pictures of Psychic Phenomena" at the Town Hall, Wellington. [267]
December 14	ACD left Wellington for Christchurch. [268]
December 15	ACD arrived in Christchurch. [269]
December 15	ACD gave a lecture "Death and the Hereafter" at Christchurch. [270]
December 16	ACD stayed at the Hotel Warners, Christchurch. [203]
December 17	ACD gave a lecture "Pictures of Psychic Phenomena" at Christchurch. [271]
December 18	ACD met the Maoris at Pa of Kaiopoi. [22]
n.d.	ACD left Christchurch for Dunedin. [22]
December 20	ACD gave a lecture "Death and the Hereafter" in Dunedin. [272]
December 21	ACD gave a lecture "Pictures of Psychic Phenomena" in Dunedin. [273]
December 24	ACD left Wellington for Melbourne on board the *Paloona*. [22,274]
December	Jean and family travelled to the Blue Mountains and stayed at the Medlow Bath Hotel. [246]
December 27	ACD returned to Melbourne from New Zealand on board the SS *Paloma*. He then travelled for eighteen hours from Melbourne to Sydney. [203]
n.d.	Death of Mary Doyle (née Foley) mother of ACD. [3,99] (*2)
December 30	Mary Doyle (nee Foley) died aged 83 [2,6,14,68,124,200,202,203,215,1573] aged 84 [16] mother of ACD [17] she died at Bowshot Cottage, West Grinstead, Sussex. [124] (*2)
December 30	Jean and family returned to Sydney from the Blue Mountains. [315]
December 31	ACD arrived in Melbourne from New Zealand; he then travelled by train to Sydney. [246]
n.d.	The Stoll Film Company of Cricklewood, London obtained the rights for a series of two-reelers, titled *The Adventures of Sherlock Holmes*, these films would star Eille Norwood as Sherlock Holmes. [184]

1921

January 3	The funeral of Mary Doyle, mother of ACD was held at Grayshott Church, Hampshire at 3 o'clock, [1574] {Note: as ACD was on tour in Australia and New Zealand, he and the family were unable to attend the funeral.}
January	ACD was part of the London Spiritualist Alliance Ltd. Council. [1884]
January 7	ACD and family travelled to Brisbane for a lecture and to meet local spiritualists. [246]
January 8	When passing through Toowoomba to Brisbane ACD intimated to a deputation of Toowoomba residents that he could not visit Toowoomba as his arrangements had already been made. [1015]
January 8	ACD arrived in Brisbane [6,280,316] and stayed at the Bellevue Hotel. [22]
January 10	ACD gave a lecture "The Human Argument" at His Majesty's Theatre, Brisbane. [281]
January 11	ACD gave a lecture "Pictures of Psychic Phenomena" at His Majesty's Theatre. Brisbane. [282]

1921

January 11	ACD laid the Stone of Dedication of Spiritual Church, Brisbane [99] which cost £10,000 [275] he was presented with a silver trowel [99,282] and then lunched with the Governor of Queensland, Sir Mathew Nathan at Government House. [22]
January 12	ACD driven by a Dr Doyle into his property for a day in the Bush. [22]
January 13	ACD gave a lecture at His Majesty's Theatre, Brisbane. [282]
January 13	ACD visited the Redbank Plains apiary in Brisbane. [6] (*2)
January 14	ACD visited the Redbank Plains apiary run by Mr H.L. Jones in Brisbane. [22,31,287] (*2)
n.d.	ACD returned from Brisbane to Sydney on board the Orient Liner *Orsova*. [22]
January 17	ACD arrived in Sydney in the morning and left in the afternoon for Medlow Bath. [285,317]
January 17	ACD stayed at the Medlow Bath Hotel, in the Blue Mountains. [22]
January 20	ACD and family travelled by car to visit the famous Jenolan Caves located in the Blue Mountains about forty five miles from Sydney. [22,246]
January 26	ACD and family left Medlow Bath and returned to Sydney. [246]
January 26	ACD arrived at Sydney. [20,22]
January 30	ACD and family attended the weekly service of the Stanmore Spiritualist Church held in the Dispensary Hall, 82-84 Enmore Road, Enmore [246,318] Stanmore Road. [22]
January	In late January or early February Mary Conan Doyle, daughter of ACD, returned to England from Los Angeles. [1084]
January 31	ACD attended a séance with the Melbourne medium Charles Bailey. [246]
February 1	ACD left Australia for England. [6,20,215] (*4)
February 1	ACD and family boarded the *Naldera* for the journey home via Melbourne, Adelaide, Fremantle and Colombo [22,246] (*4) Colombo, Suez, Port Said and Marseilles. [276,319]
February 3	ACD left Adelaide on board the SS *Naldera*. [203]
February 4	ACD left Australia on the *Naldera*. [1575] (*4)
n.d.	The *Naldera* was delayed for two days at Melbourne; ACD attended a farewell reception by the Victorian Spiritualists at Melbourne Town Hall. [22]
n.d.	The *Naldera* docked in Fremantle for a few hours, ACD lectured on spiritualism, this took place at 1p.m. as the *Naldera* would leave at 3p.m. [22]
February 11	ACD lectured on spiritualism at His Majesty's Theatre, Perth at 1p.m. [283,284,286]
February 11	ACD left Fremantle. [22]
February 11	ACD left Australia. [202] (*4)
n.d.	The *Naldera* docked in Colombo; ACD took the opportunity to visit Candy, seventy-two miles from Colombo. [22]
n.d.	The *Naldera* docked in Bombay; ACD took the opportunity to visit the city. [22]
February	ACD gave a lantern lecture on board the *Naldera*. [22]
March	*Dwellers on the Border* published in *The Strand Magazine* as *The Evidence for Fairies*. [6,194,195,196,198]
March	At the Queen's Hall, London ACD debated with Joseph McCabe. [14] (*3)
n.d.	ACD and family arrived in Marseilles and stayed at the Hotel du Louvre. [22]
March	ACD arrived in Marseilles, France, visited the battlefields of the Great War. [25,202]
March 12	ACD reached Marseilles on route from Australia to England. [717]
March	At Lyons, ACD visited the forensic scientist Edmond Locard [202] ACD noticed a photograph of a former chauffeur; this turned out to be Jules Bonnot the motor bandit and murderer. [25]
March	At the end of March in Paris, ACD lectured in French on psychic subjects [10,202] he also attended a private séance with the medium Eva C. [14]
n.d.	ACD and family arrived in Paris and stayed at the Hotel du Louvre. [22,86]

1921

March 22	Death of E.W. Hornung [14,15,68,124,200,202,1576]; ACD attended the funeral at St. Jean de Luz. [2,14]
March 23	ACD was in Paris on route from Australia to England. [718]
March 25	ACD left Paris for St. Jean de Luz. [2065]
March 28	During his stay in Paris ACD went to see the Anglo-French rugby match at Colombes, a town in the north-west suburb of Paris (ACD misspelt Colombes as Coulombes in *The Wanderings of a Spiritualist*.) [1786], ACD watched a rugby match between France and England in Paris [202], the match was played at Stade de Colombes and the result was a win for England 10-6. [1786]
n.d.	ACD and family were at Rheims where they stayed overnight. [22]
April	Lady Conan Doyle discovered her ability as a medium in trace writing. [14,15]
April 11	It was advertised that ACD would give three lectures, "Death and the Hereafter", at the Queen's Hall, London, April 11: "The Human Argument", April 12: "The Religious Argument", and April 15: General Conclusion and Lantern Slides. [1577]
April 11	Lecture by ACD "Death and the Hereafter. The New Revelation" at the Queen's Hall [6,22,1577] on "The Human Argument." [1885]
April 12	Lecture by ACD "Death and the Hereafter. The New Revelation" at the Queen's Hall [6,1578] on The Religious Argument." [1886]
April 15	Lecture by ACD "Death and the Hereafter. The New Revelation" at the Queen's Hall [6,1579] on "Summary and General Conclusion." [1886]
April 18	The Will of Mary Josephine Elizabeth Doyle published, gross value £1,223. [1580]
April 21	ACD made a speech on the occasion of Horace Leaf's lantern lectures on "Materialisation" at the Mortimer Hall. [6]
April 23	ACD at Windlesham. [884]
May	ACD was a patron of the newly formed Brighton Psychic Centre. [1887]
May	*A Remarkable Man (The Career of D.D. Home)* published in *The Strand Magazine* as *The Uncharted Coast – VI. A Worker of Wonders.* [6,194,195,196,198]
May 2	*The Crown Diamond, An Evening with Sherlock Holmes* a play in one act by ACD was performed at the Hippodrome, Bristol. [6,31]
May 7	Undershaw on the market for sale by C Bridger and Sons. [1581]
May 7	The *Portsmouth Evening News* carried a situations vacant advert for two parlour maids at Windlesham, one was temporary. [1046]
May 10	Sale of Undershaw announced [6] ACD directed Messrs. C. Bridger and Sons (Haslemere) to sell Undershaw for £4,750. [1582]
May 11	ACD at Windlesham. [884]
May 14	Sale of Undershaw announced in the *Farnham Herald*, the property sold for £4,000. [124]
May 16	*The Crown Diamond, An Evening with Sherlock Holmes* a play in one act by ACD was performed at the Coliseum, London for one week. [6,31,85,99,1583]
May 21	ACD at Windlsham. [884]
May 25	ACD at Windlesham. [1584]
May 29	*The Wanderings of a Spiritualist* published in *The Weekly Dispatch* from May 29 to July 10. [6,198]
June 5	ACD addressed a religious meeting at the Portland Hall, Southsea. [1047,1888]
June 6	ACD presided at a lecture titled "Messages From Beyond the Grave" given by Mr Ellis T. Powell held at the Town Hall, Portsmouth, Jean also attended. [1048]
June 6	The Will of E.W. Hornung published, he left £11,907 gross and £11,688 net, he left his literary works and copyrights, and the residue of the property to his wife, Mrs Constance (Connie) Hornung, sister of ACD. [1585]

1921

June 17	It was advertised that Two Lantern Lectures by E.L. Gardner would be held at the Town Hall, Tunbridge Wells, at 3p.m. on Monday 20 June, "The Coming of the Fairies" with ACD in the chair and at 8p.m. "Spirit Forms in Photography" with Sir Robert Gower, O.B.E. in the chair. [882]
June 20	ACD chaired the lecture given by E.L. Gardner "The Coming of the Fairies" held at the Town Hall, Tunbridge Wells. [1085]
June 26	ACD at Windlesham. [18]
July	Death of ACD's dog Carlo. [180]
July 1	In an advertisement for the Spiritualist Fellowship Centre, No. 2 Centre, Hendon, Sir Arthur and Lady Conan Doyle were listed as Vice-Presidents. [1778]
July 3	ACD made a speech on spiritualism at the Victoria Hall, Halifax [6] addressed the Annual Conference of the Spiritualists' National Union at Halifax. [1889]
August 17	ACD at Windlesham. [884]
August 24	ACD as a director attended the twentieth annual general meeting of Raphael Tuck & Sons (Ltd.) at Winchester House, Old Broad Street, E.C. [1586]
August 30	*The Crown Diamond, An Evening with Sherlock Holmes* a play in one act by ACD performed at the Coliseum, London for one week. [6,31]
n.d.	*The Wanderings of a Spiritualist* published. [124,180]
September 2	*The Wanderings of a Spiritualist* published by Hodder & Stoughton Ltd., London. [6]
September 8	ACD at Windlesham. [18]
n.d.	ACD at Mostyn Terrace, Eastbourne. [884]
September 22	*The Speckled Band*, a play by ACD was performed at St. James's Theatre, London. [6,99]
September 27	ACD made a speech at the Stoll Convention Dinner held at the Balmoral Ballroom of the Trocadero [31,48], ACD was one of the guests of the evening at the semi-annual Convention Dinner of the Stoll Film Company at the Trocadero Restaurant, London. [1049] (*3)
n.d.	ACD made a speech at the Stoll Convention Dinner to celebrate the Stoll films of Sherlock Holmes. [6] (*3)
September 28	The Stoll Convention Dinner was held in the Balmoral Ballroom of the Trocadero. The toast, Sherlock Holmes on the Screen, was proposed by ACD and seconded by Eille Norwood. [114,202] (*3)
September 30	ACD at Windlesham. [18]
October	James Douglas, editor of the *Sunday Express*, spent the weekend at Crowborough discussing the subject of spiritualism with ACD. [1030]
October	*The Adventure of the Mazarin Stone* published in *The Strand Magazine*. [6,31,194,195,196,198,203]
October	Lectures by ACD at Manchester on 5 October [20] and then Warrington. [6]
October 1	It was announced that ACD would lecture on 5 & 6 October at the Free Trade Hall, Manchester, October 8 at Warrington, 10 October at Congleton, near Derby, on 7 & 8 November at Nottingham, 30 November at Sheffield, 2 December at Leeds and on 19 December at the Church of England, Anerley. [1890]
October 5	ACD lectured on "The Life Beyond" at the Free Trade Hall, Manchester. [1891]
October 6	ACD lectured on "Psychic Photography" at the Free Trade Hall, Manchester. [1891]
October 8	ACD lectured at the Parr Hall, Warrington. [1891]
October 9	ACD addressed the congregation at Orford Church, Warrington, the church of the Revd. G. Vale Owen. [719]
October 13	ACD at Windlesham. [884]
November	ACD accompanied by James Douglas witnessed Mr Hope of the Crewe Circle demonstrating psychic photography. [6]

1921

November	*The Bully of Brocas Court. A Legend of the Ring* published in *The Strand Magazine*. [6,194,195,196,198]
November	ACD at the Grosvenor Hotel, London, S.W.1. [18]
November 5	ACD lectured at the Gladstone Hall, Nottingham. [720]
November 7	Lecture by ACD at Nottingham [6] lectured "Religious and Scientific Aspects" at the Albert Hall, Nottingham [721] on "The Proof of Survival." [1892]
November 8	Lecture by ACD at Nottingham [6] lectured "Recent Psychic Research" at the Albert Hall, Nottingham [722] on "The Proof of Survival." [1892]
November 9	ACD presented the winners cup to A. Peall for the second division billiards tournament at Burroughes Hall, London. [2066]
November 28	The autograph manuscript of *The Adventure of the Empty House* consisting of 47 pages sold for £2:10s at Christie's London. [1587]
November	ACD resigned as a Deputy Lieutenant of Surrey. [6] (*2)
November 29	It was announced in the *Gazette* that ACD, among others, had resigned as a Deputy Lieutenant for Surrey. [1588] (*2)
November 30	ACD lectured on "Modern Psychic Thought" at the Victoria Hall, Sheffield. [1937]
Winter	ACD's spirit guide Pheneas started to appear at séances held at Windlesham. [14] (*2)
December	*The Nightmare Room* published in *The Strand Magazine*. [6,194,195,196,198]
December 2	ACD gave a talk on spiritualism at the Albert Hall, Leeds on "Recent Psychic Research." [1780]
December 3	ACD gave a second talk on spiritualism at the Albert Hall, Leeds on "Proofs of Immortality." [966,1781]]
December 18	ACD addressed the Anerley Congregational Church, Anerley. [723,1893]
December	At the request of the Home Secretary Edward Shortt, ACD paid a surprise visit to Portland Borstal near Rochester, Kent, he was then to report his findings to Edward Short. [803]
December 26	*The Speckled Band* moved to the Royalty Theatre, London from the St. James's Theatre, London. [6]
December 27	ACD's report on his visit to Portland Borstal was published in the *Daily Telegraph* and was dated 19 December. [803]
December 30	It was announced that in view of the attacks on the Borstal Institutions the Home Secretary had asked ACD to investigate the system and make a report in order to satisfy the public on the subject. [843]

1922

n.d.	The manuscripts of *The Adventure of the Red Circle*, *The Devil's Foot*, *Lady Frances Carfax*, *The Priory School*, *The Second Stain* and *The Solitary Cyclist* were sold at auction through the Pagent Literary Agency of New York at the American Art Association in New York. [1029]
January 7	It was announced that ACD would lecture on "The New Revelation" on 10 January at the New People's Palace, Mile End Road, London under the auspices of the Jewish Spiritualist Society. It also announced that he would lecture on 17 January at Blackburn, 18 January at Bolton, 20 January at Birmingham, on 1 February at Usher Hall, Edinburgh, 6 and 9 February at St. Andrew's Hall, Glasgow and on 9 March at St. Thomas's Hospital. [1894]
January	ACD presided over a dinner for playwright Henry Arthur Jones held at the Authors' Club. [1972] (*2)
January 9	ACD made a speech "Patriotism of Modern Writers. Sir A. Conan Doyle's Criticism" at a dinner in honour of Henry Arthur Jones held at the Authors' Club. [6] (*2)
January 10	ACD made a speech at the Jewish Spiritualists Society, Mile End Road, London [20] on "The New Revelation". [1895]
January 20	ACD lectured on "Proof of Immortality" at Birmingham Town Hall under the auspices of the Birmingham Spiritualist Church. [2067]

1922

January 21	It was announced that ACD would preside at a meeting and farewell to Horace Leaf prior to his departure for Australia, to be held on 26 January at the Hall of the London Spiritualist Alliance, 6 Queen Square, London. [1895]
January 22	Six of Holmes manuscripts were sold by ACD at auction at the American Art Association in New York, they were *Lady Frances Carfax*, *The Devil's Foot*, *The Red Circle*, *The Solitary Cyclist*, *The Priory School* and *The Second Stain*. [2026]
January 26	ACD presided over a farewell meeting to Horace Leaf at 6 Queen Square, London on the occasion being the eve of the departure of Horace Leaf on a lecture tour of Australia and New Zealand. [1896]
January 31	ACD had lunch in London with Mr J.S. Daughter, head of the Forgery Department of the New York Police. [1115]
February	*The Problem of Thor Bridge* published in *The Strand Magazine* in February and March. [6,194,195,196,198,202]
February 1	ACD lectured at the Usher Hall, Edinburgh [1897] on "Life After Death". [1938]
February 5	Lecture by ACD in Edinburgh. [20]
February 5	Mr A. Vout Peters addressed a large meeting in Glasgow where ACD presided. [1898]
February 8	The *Daily Mirror* dated 8 February reported that ACD was giving a series of lectures in Glasgow which were due to end on 9 February. [1030]
February 9	Lecture by ACD at St. Andrew's Hall, Edinburgh. [20]
February 22	ACD and Jean were the host and hostess at The After Dinner Club of 1920 at the Suffolk Street Galleries, London. [1589]
Spring	Lecture by ACD at the Usher Hall, Edinburgh titled "Life After Death and Recent Psychic Research". [1]
March	*The Book I Most Enjoyed Writing* published in *The Strand Magazine*. [6,194,195,198]
March	ACD had lecturing engagements at Hove, Sussex. [1086]
March	ACD made a speech on spiritualism at Brighton. [6]
March 15	ACD and Jean were entertained by the Spiritualists of Sussex at a complimentary luncheon at the Royal Pavilion, Brighton and in the evening ACD gave a lecture at Town Hall, Hove. [1899] (*2)
March 15	ACD was entertained to a complimentary luncheon by local spiritualists in Hove, Sussex. [1087] (*2)
n.d.	ACD travelled to America, lectured on spiritualism. [99] (*3)
April 1	ACD left England aboard the *Baltic* for a lecture tour of America and Canada. [10,96,1590] (*3)
April 1	ACD, Jean, Denis, Malcolm, and Lena left Liverpool for New York on board the *Baltic*, also with them were Laura Stable, governess and Edmund Preston, tutor. [242] (*3)
April	ACD, Jean, Denis, Adrian and Jean toured America [180] lecturing in New York, Boston, Washington and Philadelphia. [100]
April 9	ACD, Jean, Denis, Adrian and Lena Jean with Mr Preston, secretary and Miss Stable, nanny, arrived in New York; they stayed at the Ambassador Hotel. [150,247] (*5)
April 9	ACD, Jean, Adrian, Denis and Jean arrived in New York aboard the White Star Liner *Baltic*. [3,6,15,20,215] (*5)
April 9	ACD, Jean and the three children arrived in New York for a tour that lasted for just over two-months [124] he arrived on board the White Star liner *Baltic* from Liverpool and was accompanied by his wife Jean, Denis (aged 13), Malcolm (aged 11) and Miss Lena Conan Doyle (aged 9). [1803] (*5)
April 9	A further lecture tour of America and Canada. Lectures in New York, Boston, Yale, New Haven (Yale), Atlantic City, Washington, Philadelphia, Buffalo, Toronto, Detroit, Toledo and Chicago. [6,215]
April 9	ACD toured America from 9 April until 24 June. [68]

1922

April 9	ACD arrived at the Port of New York on board the *Baltic* and stayed at the Ambassador Hotel. [110,202] (*5)
April 10	ACD, Lady Conan Doyle, Denis, Malcolm and Lena Jean arrived in New York on board the *Baltic*. Their contact address was at Prince George Hotel, New York, c/o Mr Lee Keedick, 437 Fifth Avenue, New York. [96] (*5)
April 10	ACD met the New York Press at the Ambassador Hotel. [247]
April	ACD attended the film *The Man Beyond* starring Houdini at the Times Square Theatre, New York. [1157]
April 11	ACD began his lectures at Carnegie Hall, New York. [20,110]
April 12	ACD delivered his first lecture at Carnegie Hall [65,215,1804]; he made nine consecutive talks on spiritualism at Carnegie Hall, New York [15] or seven consecutive talks [20,14] or six consecutive talks. [215]
April	Mr Keedick, the agent who organised ACD's lecture tour in America, arranged for ACD to see the opening baseball game of the season. This was between the New York Giants and Brooklyn. [247] (*2)
April 12	ACD attended the opening baseball game of the season between the Brooklyn Robins and the New York Giants, the Robins won with a 4-3 score. [1128] (*2)
April 13	ACD at the Academy of Music, Brooklyn. [1805]
April 14	ACD attended a séance in New York in order to test a young Italian named Pecorano. [65,247]
April 16	ACD had a sitting with a well-known amateur medium, Mr Ticknor. [20,247]
April 18	ACD at the Ambassador Hotel, New York. [884]
April 18	ACD made his second lecture at Carnegie Hall. [209,247]
April 21	ACD lectured at Carnegie Hall, New York. [212,1806]
April 22	ACD left New York for Boston [209] arrived during the afternoon. [1818]
April 23	It was announced that ACD would give a lecture at the Symphony Hall, Boston. [1818]
April 24	ACD lectured at Symphony Hall, Boston. [247]
April 25	ACD visited Mount Auburn Cemetery and the grave of Oliver Wendell Holmes and then spent some time at Harvard library. [247]
April 26	ACD was appointed Honorary President of the County Guild of Spiritualism for Sussex, Jean was Honorary Vice-President. [1900]
April 27	ACD left Boston for Washington. [247]
April 27	ACD arrived in Washington. [110]
April 30	ACD had lunch with Dr Cushman in Washington. [247]
May	ACD and family visited Niagara Falls. [247]
May 4	ACD made a speech at the American Psychical Institute & Laboratory, 40 West Fifty-street, New York. [1807]
May 5	ACD lectured at Carnegie Hall, New York. [212]
May 7	ACD lectured at Carnegie Hall, New York. [212,1808]
Early May	ACD and Jean visited Houdini at his home. [100]
May 10	ACD and Lady Conan Doyle visited Houdini at his home in New York [20,26,65,202] 278 West 113th Street. [215]
May 14	ACD left Niagara for Toronto. [247]
May 15	ACD lectured at the Massey Hall, Toronto. [337]
May 19	ACD was in Toledo for a lecture. [211]
May 20	ACD lectured on spiritualism at Toledo, Ohio and visited the medium Miss Ada Besinnet. [65]
May 21	ACD arrived in Chicago. [1809]
May 22-26	ACD was in Chicago. [211]
May 30	ACD at The Ambassador Hotel, New York. [884]
May 31	Undershaw was being advertised as being Undershaw Hotel. [1789]
June	*The Lift* published in *The Strand Magazine*. [6,194,195,196,198]
June	ACD attended the annual Society of American Magicians' banquet. [100] (*2)

1922

June 2	As the guest of honour ACD attended the annual banquet of The Society of American Magicians at the invitation of Houdini, held at the McAlpine Hotel, New York [15,41,110,202,215] (*2), American Club of Magicians. [65,247]
June 3	ACD and family at the Ambassador Hotel, New York. [247]
June 3	It was announced that ACD would be one of the speakers at the Spiritualists' National Union at Caxton Hall, London on 2 July [1901] he did not attend as he did not arrive back from America in time. [1902]
June 4	ACD visited cottage at Fordham, near New York where Edgar Allen Poe had spent the last years of his life. [31]
June 15	ACD participated in a wireless broadcasting demonstration in Atlantic City. [2068]
June 16	ACD was in Atlantic City. [799]
June 17 & 18	Houdini and his wife Bess joined ACD and his family for the weekend at the Ambassador Hotel in Atlantic City. [14,15,65,20,100,202,215]
n.d.	ACD and Jean were joined by Houdini and his wife Beth at the Ambassador Hotel, Atlantic City for a séance. [180]
June 18	ACD held a séance with Jean as the medium, in Atlantic City, New Jersey, America with Houdini. [100]
June 20	ACD at the Ambassador Hotel, New York [1982]
June 22	ACD and Houdini attended The Carroll Theatre to see Raymond Hitchcock's *Pinwell Revue* in New York [26] Houdini invited him to celebrate his twenty-eighth wedding anniversary at the theatre. [65,100,202]
June 23	ACD left America on board the *Adriatic*. [65,202] (*3)
June 24	ACD and family left America [6,14,15,20,150] on board the *Adriatic*. [110,1591,1810] (*3)
June 24	ACD and family left New York for England on board the *Adriatic*. [209,247] (*3)
June 29	ACD on board the R.M.S. *Adriatic*. [884]
July	ACD arrived back in England early July. [10] (*3)
July	ACD and his family arrived in England on board the *Adriatic*. [96] (*3)
July 2	ACD and his family arrived in Liverpool on board the Star Liner *Adriatic*. [2056] (*3)
July	*Now Then Smith!* (poem) published in *The Strand Magazine*. [6,194,195,196,198]
July 3	ACD was one of the essayists at a session of the International Congress of Spiritualists held at the South Place Institute, Finsbury, London. [1050,1902]
July 6	An advert was published in the *Portsmouth Evening News* for a housemaid at Windlesham. [1051]
July 12	*Tales of the Ring and Camp/The Croxley Master and Other Tales of the Ring and Camp* published by John Murray. [6]
July 12	*Tales of Pirates and Blue Water/The Dealings of Captain Sharkey and Other Tales of Pirates* published by John Murray, London. [6]
July 12	*Tales of Terror and Mystery/The Black Doctor and Other Tales of Terror an Mystery* published by John Murray, London, London. [6]
July 18	ACD attended a luncheon given by Sir Malcolm and Lady Morris. [1592]
July 18	ACD was one of six who sat with Frau Silbert, the Austrian medium, at the British College of Psychic Science. [1903]
July 27	*Tales of Twilight and the Unseen/The Great Keinplatz Experiment and Other Tales of Twilight and the Unseen* published by John Murray, London. [6]
July 27	*Tales of Adventure and Medical Life/The Man from Archangel and Other Tales of Adventure* published by John Murray, London. [6]
July 28	ACD at Windlesham. [884]
July 28	ACD made a donation to a number of causes totalling £1,227:10s, this was some of the profit made from his American lecture tour. [1904]
August 14	Death of Aunt Juey (Julia Pocock), soon after Mary embarked on a European tour. [124]

1922

August 18	It was reported the Sir Arthur and Lady Conan Doyle were staying at the Pier Hotel, Bognor, Sussex. [724]
September	*A Point of Contact* published in *Hearst's International.* [198]
n.d.	*The Coming of the Fairies* published. [99,180,215] (*2)
September 1	*The Coming of the Fairies* published by Hodder & Stoughton, London. [6] (*2)
September 3	*Our American Adventure* published as *The Adventures of a Spiritualist in America* in *Lloyd's Sunday News* from September 3 to 17 December. [6,198]
September 19	ACD as a director attended the twenty-first annual general meeting of Raphael Tuck & Sons (Ltd.) at Winchester House, Old Broad Street, E.C. [1593]
September 21	*The Poems of Arthur Conan Doyle – Collected Edition* published by John Murray, London. [6]
September 23	It was announced that ACD would speak at the anniversary service of the Marylebone Spiritualist Association Ltd. at the Aeolian Hall, 135 New Bond Street, London on 15 October. [1905]
September 24	ACD at Windlesham. [884]
September 27	ACD at Windlesham. [884]
September 29	ACD signed a five-year lease for a flat at 15 Buckingham Palace Mansions, London. [32] (*3)
September 30	It was announced that ACD would address a meeting at the Town Hall, Woolwich on 9 October titled "The New Revelation." [1906]
September 30	Mary and young Indian friend, Pillo, were in Florence. [124]
October	ACD owned a flat at 15 Buckingham Palace Mansions, Victoria Street, London. [68,200] (*3)
October	ACD made a speech on spiritualism at Woolwich, the leaflet *Spiritualism-Some Straight Questions and Direct Answers* was distributed at this meeting. [6]
October	ACD made an address "Spiritualism and Christianity", for the Jubilee of the Marylebone Society. [6]
October	*The Mystery of the Fox Sisters* published in *The Quarterly Transactions of the British College of Psychic Science.* [6,198]
October 9	ACD made an address "The Revelation" at the Town Hall, Woolwich under the auspices of Woolwich and Plumstead Spiritualist Society. [1907]
October 13	ACD at Windlesham. [40]
October 14	*Spiritualism-Some Straight Questions and Direct Answers* published in *Light*. [6,198]
October 15	ACD attended and addressed a meeting of the Marylebone Spiritualist Association at the Aeolian Hall, 135, New Bond Street, London [1030] on "Spiritualism and Christianity" at the fifth anniversary of the Marylebone Spiritualist Association. [1908]
November 2	*Tales of Long Ago/The Last of the Legions and Other Tales of Long Ago* published by John Murray, London. [6]
November 7	ACD made a speech on spiritualism titled "The New Revelation" at the Town Hall, Yarmouth. [164,1909]
November 8	ACD made a speech on spiritualism titled "The New Revelation" at St. Andrew's Hall, Norwich. [165,1909]
November 11	ACD performed the opening ceremony of the Ex-Service Men's Club, Eridge Road, Crowborough; it was previously the Parish Room. Among those also present were Lady Conan Doyle, Miss Mary Conan Doyle and A.H. Wood (Hon. Treasurer of the club) [725]
November 13	ACD at Windlesham. [18]
November 14	ACD attended the 194th meeting of the Society of Psychical Research at 31 Tavistock Square, London. [133]
November 19	ACD at Windlesham. [1892]
November 20	ACD and Jean were the guests of the Lyceum Club at a dinner where ACD spoke on "Spirit Photography." [726]
November 21	ACD and Jean attended the dinner of The Society of Authors, Playwrights and Composers held at the Connaught Rooms, London. [1594]

1922

November 28	ACD lectured on "Death and the Hereafter" at the Victoria Hall, Sunderland. [1939]
November	Late November ACD lectured on "Death and the Here After" at Newcastle-on-Tyne. [1910]
December	ACD at Windlesham. [18]
December	*The Centurion* published in *The Storyteller*. [6,198]
December	*Billy Bones* published in *The Strand Magazine*. [6,194,195,196,198]
December 5	ACD opened a Spiritualist bazaar at Lewisham. [1977]
December 10	ACD's spirit guide Pheneas made himself known. [15,20,202,215] (*2)
December 11	ACD & Jean gave a dinner party at the Berkeley Hotel, London. [883]
December 14	*The Case for Spirit Photography* published by Hutchinson & Co., London. [6]
December 19	ACD at Windlesham. [884]
December 21	ACD at Windlesham. [40]
December 31	ACD at Windlesham. [884]

1923

n.d.	Full scale production of the film *The Lost World* began. [41]
January	ACD at Windlesham. [18]
January 1	ACD at Windlesham. [1982]
January 6	It was advertised that ACD would lecture on "Some New Psychic Photographs" (illustrated with slides) on 11 January at the London Spiritualist Alliance, 5 Queen Street, Southampton Row, W.C.1. London. [1911]
January	ACD made an address on "Psychic Photography" before the London Spiritualist Alliance. [6] (*2)
January 11	ACD lectured on "Psychic Photography" at the London Spiritualist Alliance. [1912] (*2)
January 13	ACD at Windlesham. [884]
January 15	ACD presided at the Authors' Club Dinner. [1088]
January 25	ACD lectured at Luton. [727]
January 26	On 26 January the *Daily Mirror* reported that ACD's play, *Fires of Fate*, was to be filmed, and that casting had taken place, the cast and crew were to head for Cairo shortly. [1030]
n.d.	ACD took a flat at 15 Buckingham Palace Mansions, Buckingham Palace Road, London. [39,233] (*3)
January 31	At an auction held at the American Art Galleries, 30 East 57 Street, New York a number of manuscripts were sold, *Micah Clarke* ($360), *The Refugees* ($300), *Rodney Stone* ($275) and *The Valley of Fear* ($275). Other manuscripts at the auction were: *The Adventure of the Missing Three-Quarter*, *The Adventure of Charles Augustus Milverton*, *A Shadow Before*, *The Green Flag*, *The King of the Foxes*, *The Last Galley*, *The Leather Funnel*, *Sir Nigel*, *An Iconoclast*, *The Coming of the Huns*, and *The Fall of Lord Barrymore*. The sale produced a total of $2,340. [1595]
January 31	ACD attended the AGM of the Society of Psychical Research at 31 Tavistock Square, London. [133] (*2)
n.d.	ACD attended the annual general meeting of the Society for Psychical Research. [1913] (*2)
February	ACD at Windlesham. [18]
February	*The Cottingley Fairies. An Epilogue* published in *The Strand Magazine*. [6,194,198]
February 5	ACD at Windlesham. [2053]
February 16	It was reported that The "Windlesham" Billiards Competition had been held at Windlesham where ACD beat Colonel J.H. Bell in the final. [728]
February 20	ACD arrived at Torquay Station with his wife Jean and was interviewed by the local newspaper the *Western Morning News*. [160]

1923

February 21	Lecture by ACD "The New Revelation" at The Pavilion, Torquay [6,20,27] the Mayor of Torquay, Mr G.H. Iredale presided, Jean accompanied ACD, also attending were Evan Powell and Mr J. Rabbich. [1914]
n.d.	ACD and Jean stayed at the Victoria and Albert Hotel, Torquay. [27]
February 23	ACD gave a lecture at the Plymouth Guildhall, Plymouth titled "The New Revelation". They stayed at the Grand Hotel, Plymouth. [161] {Note: the Grand Hotel was next to Elliot Terrace on the opposite corner.}
February 23	ACD was interviewed at the Grand Hotel, Plymouth by the *Western Morning News*. [162]
February 26	ACD played billiards at the Ex-Service Men's Club, Eridge Road, Crowborough where he beat Mr Wormesly, Major A.H. Wood lost to Mr P. Playford. [729]
February 28	ACD lectured on "Christianity and Spiritualism at Fulham. [2069]
n.d	It was reported that ACD had lectured at Fulham on "Christianity and Spiritualism" [730], at Munster Wesleyan Church, Fulham. [1032]
March	*The Adventure of the Creeping Man* published in *The Strand Magazine*. [6,194,195,196,198]
March 6	ACD at Windlesham. [18]
March 8	ACD at 15 Buckingham Palace Mansion, London, S.W.1. [1982]
n.d.	*Our American Adventure* published. [99]
March 16	*Our American Adventure* published by Hodder & Stoughton Ltd., London. [6]
March 20	ACD and Jean attended a dinner of the After-Dinner Club at the Suffolk Street Galleries. [731]
March 27	ACD in London. [884]
March	ACD left England for a further lecture tour of America. [10] (*3)
March 28	ACD and family caught the train from Waterloo to Southampton to connect with their ship *Olympic* for a tour of America. [1030]
March 28	ACD and family left Southampton on board the *Olympic* [96] the end of March [202] on board the White Star liner *Olympic* for New York. [1596] (*3)
March 28	ACD, Jean, Denis, Malcolm and Jean left Southampton for New York on board the *Olympic*, also with them was Emily French, governess. [242] (*3)
April	*Haunting Dreams* by ACD and others published in *The Strand Magazine*. [6,194,195,196,198]
n.d.	ACD, Jean, Denis, Adrian and Jean toured America and Canada. [99,180] (*2)
April	ACD toured America and Canada from 3 April until 4 August. [68] (*2)
April 3	ACD and family arrived in New York [111,124] (*4) and stayed at the Biltmore Hotel. [202,248]
April 3	ACD arrived in New York for lectures in Rochester, Hydesville, Cleveland, Pittsburgh, Cincinnati, Indianapolis, Chicago, St. Louis, Kansas City, Denver, Salt Lake City and onto Los Angeles where he met Douglas Fairbanks, Mary Pickford and Jackie Coogan, then onto San Francisco, Seattle, Vancouver, Edmonton, Calgary, Winnipeg and Montreal. [6,14,20,215] (*4)
April 3	ACD arrived in New York on board the *Olympic*. [248] (*4)
April 4	ACD, Jean, Denis, Malcolm and Jean with companion Constance Emily French of Crowborough arrived in New York on board the *Olympic*. [96,202] (*4)
April 6	Lecture by ACD on spiritualism at Carnegie Hall, New York. [202,248,1811]
April 8	Lecture by ACD on spiritualism at Carnegie Hall, New York. [65,248,1812]
April 10	ACD attended a luncheon held by the Dutch Treat Club. [248]
April 13	ACD travelled to Rochester. [248]
April 14	ACD lectured at Rochester. [248]
April 14	ACD left Rochester and returned to New York. [248]
April	It was reported in *Light* that Jean had broadcasted a lecture by radio in New York. [1917
April 15	ACD with the family and others honoured W.T. Stead's memory at the memorial in his honour near Central Park, New York. [248]
April 15	Lecture by ACD on spiritualism at Carnegie Hall, New York. [248,1813]

1923

April 16	ACD left New York for Cleveland. [248] (*2)
April 16	ACD left New York. [202] (*2)
April 17	ACD was in Cleveland. [248]
April 19	ACD was in Pittsburgh where he was interviewed by a reporter from *The Pittsburgh Gazette Times* at the William Penn Hotel, Grant Street. [1155]
April 20	ACD lectured on "The Proofs of Immortality" at Carnegie Music Hall, Oakland, Pittsburgh. [1155]
April 21	It was announced that ACD would lecture at Cincinnati on 22 April, Indianapolis on 24 April, Columbus on 25 April, Chicago on 28 April and 1 May. [1915]
n.d.	ACD visited a full size replica of Columbus's ship. [248]
April	ACD was in Columbus. [248]
April 22	ACD arrived in Cincinnati and visited the local mediums. [150]
April 22	ACD gave a lecture at Emery Hall, Cincinnati. [150]
April 23	ACD travelled from Cincinnati to Indianapolis. [150]
April 23	ACD arrived in Indianapolis and stayed at the Claypool Hotel. [150]
April 23	ACD gave a lecture at the Murat Theatre, Indianapolis. [150]
April 24	ACD left Indianapolis for Chicago. [150]
April 26	ACD attended a séance by Miss Ada Besinnet at Toledo, Ohio. [65,1814]
April 28	ACD at the Orchestra Hall, Chicago [1815] lectured on "Personal Psychic Experiences" (illustrated) at 2:30. [1836]
May 1	It was advertised that ACD would lecture on "Recent Psychic Evidence" (illustrated) at the Orchestra Hall, Chicago on 1 May at 8:15. [1836]
n.d.	ACD left Chicago for St. Louis and Kansas City, Jean and family travelled to Colorado Springs. [248]
n.d.	ACD stayed at the Hotel Chase, St. Louis. [248]
n.d.	ACD lectured at the American Theatre, St. Louis. [248]
May 5	It was announced that ACD would lecture at Kansas City on 5 May, Grand Theatre, Los Angeles on 21 May, Trinity Auditorium, San Diego on 22 May, Los Angeles on 23 May and Trinity Auditorium on 28 May. [1916]
May 7	ACD arrived in Denver and stayed at the Brown Palace Hotel, Houdini was also staying at the hotel. [202]
May	ACD lectured in Denver. [65]
n.d.	ACD lectured in Colorado Springs, he stayed at the Antlers Hotel. [248]
May 8	ACD attended a performance by Houdini at the Orpheum Theatre, Denver, Colorado. [65]
May 9	ACD spent some time with Houdini. [2029]
May 9	ACD at The Brown Palace Hotel, Denver, Colorado. [1982]
May 9	ACD left Denver for Salt Lake City. [248]
May	ACD travelled from Denver to Salt Lake City via Colorado Springs and Pueblo. [248]
May 10	ACD arrived in Salt Lake City. [202]
May 10	ACD was at the Hotel Utah, Salt Lake City. [1127]
May 11	ACD arrived in Salt Lake City and gave a lecture at the Mormon Tabernacle. [110]
May 14	ACD arrived in Los Angeles and stayed at the Ambassador Hotel. [110]
n.d.	ACD with his sons visited Sid Grauman's Egyptian Theater to see the film *The Covered Wagon*. [110]
May 17	ACD took a short holiday to Catalina Island. [110,248]
May 18	ACD & family were staying at the St. Catherine Hotel, Avalon, Catalina Island. [248]
May 19	ACD returned to the Ambassador Hotel, Los Angeles. [20,248]
May 19	ACD gave a lecture in San Diego. [110]
May 20	ACD met Dr Wickland and his wife and had a long talk. [248]
May 21	ACD lectured at San Diego. [248]
May 22	ACD was back in Los Angeles. [248]

1923

May 22	ACD was given a large birthday cake at the Ambassador Hotel, Los Angeles and a specially arranged tour of Samuel Goldwyn studios. [110]
May 23	ACD at the Ambassador Hotel, Los Angeles. [1982]
May 23	ACD lectured at the Trinity Auditorium, Los Angeles. [248]
n.d.	ACD attended a meeting of the Society of Advanced Psychic Research at Altadena, approximately 15 miles from Los Angeles. [248]
May 24	ACD attended a séance with Mrs Inez Wagner. [248]
May 25	ACD visited the cinema studios where he met Douglas Fairbanks and Mary Pickford [110,248], he also met Jackie Coogan. [31,248]
May 26	ACD was entertained to lunch by the business men of Los Angeles at the City Club. [110,248]
May 27	ACD visited the Ventura oil fields near Los Angeles. [110]
May 29	ACD and his family left Los Angeles early morning for San Francisco, arriving just before midnight and stayed at the Clift Hotel. [110]
May 30	ACD spent some time exploring San Francisco [110] visited Sausalito, Tamalpais Mountain, Muir Woods and Redwood Grove. [248]
June	*Psychic Phenomena are Real* published in *The London Magazine*. [6,196,198]
June 2	Lecture by ACD on "Life in Spirit World Told by Conan Doyle" before an audience of about 3,000 at the Dreamland Auditorium, San Francisco. [6]
June 2	ACD lectured on "The Life Beyond" at the Dreamland Auditorium, San Francisco. [110]
June 5	ACD lectured in Oakland. [110]
June 6	ACD lectured in San Francisco. [110]
June 6	ACD gave his last lecture at the Dreamland Auditorium, San Francisco. [112]
June 6	ACD arrived at the San Francisco Ferry Building shortly before midnight. [112]
June 6	ACD left the San Francisco Ferry Building just after midnight, arriving at the Oakland 7th Street Pier. [112]
June 7	ACD left Oakland by train at 12:40a.m. for Portland. [112]
June 7	ACD arrived in Shasta Springs just before noon, he and the rest of the party disembarked for a few minutes to stretch their legs. [112]
June 8	ACD arrived in Portland at 7:40a.m., ACD disembarked while the rest of the party transferred to the No. 408, North Pacific train leaving for Seattle at 8:05a.m. [112]
June 8	ACD arrived at Portland for a lecture at the Portland Public Auditorium. [112]
June 8	ACD arrived at Portland. [248]
June 9	ACD attended a private séance in the morning, the rest of the day was spent sightseeing, in the evening he attended a séance with another medium by the name of Mrs M.T. Downes. [112]
June 10	ACD left Portland by train for Tacoma where he stayed at the Tacoma Hotel. [112]
June 10	ACD gave a lecture at the Scottish Cathedral, Tacoma. [112]
June 11	ACD arrived in Seattle. [112]
June 11	ACD gave a lecture at the Public Arena, Seattle. [112]
June 12	ACD and his family left Seattle. [112]
June 12	ACD left America for Canada on board the *Princess Victoria*. [248]
June 12	ACD left Seattle Harbour on board the Canadian Pacific Steamship *Princess Victoria* at approximately 9a.m. and arrived shortly after 1p.m. at Inner Harbour, Victoria, Vancouver Island, the ship remained in port for a while, long enough for ACD to give a couple of interviews and the family to do some sightseeing, they continued on the steamship to the city of Vancouver. [112]
June 12	ACD and his family arrived at Vancouver Island. [112]
June 13	ACD gave a lecture in Vancouver. [112]
June 14	ACD and party travelled from Vancouver to Victoria where they stayed at the Empress Hotel, Inner Harbour, Victoria. [112]
June 14	ACD gave a lecture in Victoria at the Capitol Theatre. [112]

1923

n.d.	ACD travelled from Vancouver to Jasper Park, where he left his family, he then continued to Edmonton and Calgary. [248]
n.d.	ACD left Calgary to return to Jasper Park via Edmonton. [248]
n.d.	ACD & family left Jasper Park for Winnipeg via Edmonton. [248]
June 17	ACD arrived in Edmonton from Jasper Park. [1833]
June 18	Lecture by ACD in Edmonton [75] on "Proofs of Immortality" at the Allen Theatre, Edmonton. [1833]
June 19	ACD travelled from Edmonton to Calgary. [248, 1833]
June 20	Lecture by ACD on "Proofs of Immortality" at the Al Temple, Calgary [75] at the Al Azhar Temple, Calgary. [1833]
July 1	ACD arrived in Winnipeg [111,215] at Union Station and stayed at the Fort Garry Hotel. [334]
July 1	ACD attended a circle for psychical research at the home of Winnipeg resident Thomas Glendenning Hamilton. [334]
July 2	ACD attended baseball match between Winnipeg Arenas and Minneapolis All-Stars at Wesley Park, Winnipeg. [334]
July 3	ACD lectured in Winnipeg, [248] at the Walker Theatre [111,334] on "Proofs of Immortality". [334]
July 4	ACD attended a séance near Winnipeg. [248,334]
July 7	ACD at Jasper. [884] {Note: date taken from a letter from ACD to *Light* dated 7 July 1923, Jasper, Alberta, Canadian Rockies and published in *Light* on 21 July 1923.}
July 8	ACD arrived in Montreal, Canada [805] at the Mount Royal Hotel. [1180]
July 10	ACD at Mount Royal Hotel, Montreal for a lecture. [806]
July 12	ACD was staying at Loon Lake House, home of Mr George Holley of Detroit. [248]
n.d.	ACD gave a lecture at Loon Lake. [248]
July	Late July early August, ACD and the family were staying at the Biltmore Hotel, New York. [248]
August	*The Forbidden Subject* published in *The Strand Magazine*. [6,194,195,196,198]
August 4	ACD left America and returned to England [6,20,65] left New York for England [111,215] on board the *Adriatic*. [202,248]
August 8	An advert was published in the *Portsmouth Evening News* for a between-maid at Windlesham. [1052]
August 9	An advert was published in the *Portsmouth Evening News* for a between-maid at Windlesham. [1053]
August 13	ACD arrived in England from America. [248] (*2)
August 13	ACD and family arrived in Liverpool on board the White Star liner *Adriatic*. [1597] (*2)
August 13	ACD arrived in London from New York. [1918]
August 15	ACD in London. [18]
August	Late August or early September ACD attended the International Congress for Spiritualism at Liege. [1089]
August 25	ACD and Jean arrived in Liege to attend the International Congress for Psychical Research. [1919]
August 26	ACD attended the International Congress for Psychical Research in Liege, in the afternoon they visited Grevignee (Grivegnée) Cemetery. [1919]
August 28	ACD attended the International Congress for Psychical Research in Liege. [1919]
September	ACD was at a rented house in the New Forest, Hampshire. [202]
October	Lady Conan Doyle donated one guinea to the Tunbridge Wells Hospital Pay Day Fund. [1090]
October	ACD's autobiography *Memories and Adventures* published in *The Strand Magazine* from October 1923 to July 1924. [6,180,194,195,196,198]

1923

October 1	*The Return of Sherlock Holmes*, a play by J.E. Terry and Arthur Rose performed at the Playhouse Theatre, Cardiff, starring Eille Norwood as Holmes. [184]
October 9	*The Return of Sherlock Holmes*, a play by J.E. Terry and Arthur Rose opened at the Princes Theatre, London, starring Eille Norwood as Holmes, this play stayed for 104 performances [99,184] ACD attended this first performance. [1598]
October 17	ACD as a director attended the twenty second annual general meeting of Raphael Tuck & Sons (Ltd.) at Winchester House, Old Broad Street, E.C., London. [1599]
October 27	It was announced that ACD would give an address in the church of St. Luke's, Queen's Road, Forest Hill on 28 October. [1920]
October 28	ACD made an address in the church of St. Luke's, Queen's Road, Forest Hill. [1921]
November 2	*Three of Them* published by John Murray, London. [6]
November 4	ACD spoke at St. Luke's Spiritualist Church, Forest Hill, London. [732]
November 4	ACD at Windlesham. [18]
November 7	ACD & Jean attended a séance at Long Acre [885], and the editor of *Light* and a few others at a house in Long Acre near Covent Garden, London. The agent for the medium was P.T. Selbit, the medium was known as 'The Medium in the Mask' in March 1919. [1030]
November 11	ACD and Jean attended the Armistice Remembrance at the Cenotaph, London and then a service at the Queen's Hall. [1922]
November 19	ACD presided at a dinner at the Authors' Club. [1923]
Early Winter	ACD attended a series of meetings at The Queen's Hall, London. [1]
December	The play *The Crown Diamond* was performed at the Coliseum, London starring Dennis Neilson-Terry. [1600]

1924

n.d.	ACD won the Authors' Club billiards handicap trophy for the fourth time. [1973]
January	ACD attended a complimentary luncheon to H.G. Siedeberg given by members of the Billiards Association and Control Club at their premises at 19 Stratford Place, London. [2101]
January	*The Adventure of the Sussex Vampire* published in *The Strand Magazine*. [6,194,195,196,198]
January 8	Lecture by ACD "Modern Psychic Knowledge" at the Royalty Theatre [6] spoke about the play *Outward Bound* (a psychic play) from the stage, Jean, Denis, Malcolm and Jean (Lena) were present. [1924]
January 13	ACD at Windlesham. [884]
January 31	ACD mounted an exhibition of the works of his father, Charles Doyle, at The Brooke Galleries, London from January 31 to February 14 [60,1601] some 50 works. [180] (*2)
February	ACD mounted an exhibition of the works of his father, Charles Doyle, at The Brooke Galleries, London. [15] (*2)
February 2	ACD in London. [884]
February	ACD at Windlesham. [18]
February	Address by ACD at a London Spiritualist Church Service at the Queen's Hall. [6,20]
February 3	ACD spoke at a spiritualist service at the Queen's Hall, Jean and Mary were present. [1925]
February 9	"Sir Adolph Tuck's 70th Birthday", a dinner celebration at the Grand Central Hotel, ACD attended as a Director of Raphael Tuck & Sons. [6]
February 10	ACD was the reader at the Queen's Hall, Ernest Oaten made the address and Horace Leaf presided. [1926]

1924

February 15	*Our Second American Adventure* published by Hodder & Stoughton Ltd., London. [6]
February 17	ACD made a reading at the Queen's Hall. [1927]
February 24	ACD gave his concluding lecture at the Queen's Hall, London. [886,1928]
February	ACD accepted the Honorary Presidency of the Executive of the Federation International des Spiritistes of Paris. [1929]
March	ACD lost a billiards match against Mr P. Walters played at the Ex-Service Men's Club Crowborough. [888]
March	*Early Psychic Experiences* published in *Pearson's Magazine*. [6,196,198]
March	ACD attended the Authors' Club dinner and proposed the toast. [887]
March 2	ACD made an address at Ardwick Picture House, Manchester. [733]
March 5	ACD at Windlesham. [884]
April	*What Comes After Death?* published in *Pearson's Magazine*. [6,196,198]
April 19	ACD laid the foundation stone on the extension to the Ex-Service Men's Club, Crowborough [844] for a new billiard room. [889]
April 22	A collection of spirit photographs loaned by ACD were exhibited at the Portsmouth Temple of Spiritualism, 73 Victoria Road South, Southsea from 22 April to 26 April. [1054]
April 24	ACD attended the Amateur Tennis Championship at the Queen's Club. [1602]
May	Lecture by ACD in Holloway and Brixton. [20]
May 3	It was announced that ACD and Jean would be the guests at Caxton Hall, Westminster on 13 May. [1929]
May 4	ACD gave a lecture at the Holloway Theatre, London. [890]
May 10	It was announced that ACD would address a mass meeting at the London District Council of the Spiritualist National Union at South Place Institute, Finsbury on 15 May. [1930]
May 13	ACD and Jean were the guests of the London Spiritualist Alliance at Caxton Hall, Westminster. [1931]
May	Address by ACD to the London District Council of the Spiritualists' National Union at the South Place Institute. [6]
May 15	ACD addressed a mass meeting of the London District Council of the Spiritualist Union at South Place Institute, Finsbury. [1931]
May 20	ACD at Windlesham. [884]
May 20	The BBC transmitted "Psychic Developments": A Wireless Lecture as Delivered by Sir Arthur Conan Doyle through the Broadcasting Station. [6,241]
May 21	ACD at the Athenaeum Club, London. [18]
May 24	It was advertised that ACD, accompanied by Jean, would lecture on "Life after Death" at the New Council Hall, United Services Club Ltd., 33 London Road, Bromley on 26 May. [1931]
May 24	ACD played golf for the Crowborough Beacon Golf Club against De La Warr (Artisan Club), he lost his game and De La Warr won. [891]
May 26	ACD accompanied by Jean lectured on "Life after Death" at Bromley. [892]
May 28	ACD assisted in a séance at a haunted house near Piccadilly, London, Horace Leaf and Revd. Vale Owen also attended. [1055]
May 30	*A London Ghost* published in the *Daily Express* as *A Talk with the "Ghost" of Lenin*. [6,198]
June	*How Watson Learned the Trick* published by Methuen & Co. in *The Book of the Queens Dolls' House*. [6]
n.d.	Death of Constance (Connie) Hornung. [202] (*4)
June 8	Death of sister Constance (Connie) Hornung in Beckenham, Kent, aged fifty-six. [16,68,124,200] (*4)
June 12	Funeral of Constance (Connie) Hornung at West Grinstead, West Sussex. [1603]
June 16	ACD at 15 Buckingham Palace Mansions, London, S.W.1. [884]
June 24	Death of sister Constance (Connie) Hornung. [203] (*4)
July 19	ACD at 15 Buckingham Palace Mansions, London, S.W.1. [40]

1924

July 23	ACD at 15 Buckingham Palace Mansions, London, S.W.1. [40]
August 11	An exhibition of "Spirit" photographs was opened at the National Spiritualist Church, Dewsbury, it comprised of 91 prints that were loaned by ACD. [1782]
August 24	*How Watson Learned the Trick* published in *The New York Times*. [6,198]
August 27	ACD at The Okefield, Lyndhurst, Hampshire. [884
September 18	*Memories and Adventures* published by Hodder & Stoughton Ltd., London. [6]
September 22	ACD at Windlesham. [40]
September 25	ACD at 15 Buckingham Palace Mansions, London. [18]
September 30	ACD at Windlesham. [40]
October	*Edward Irving and the Voices* published in *The Quarterly Transactions of the British College of Psychic Science*. [6,198]
October	ACD was writing *The Land of Mist*. [6]
October 1	ACD at Windlesham. [40]
October 12	ACD at Windlesham. [40]
October 15	ACD addressed the Ilford Psychical Research Society on the occasion of the opening of their new hall in Clement Road, Jean and Jean (Lena) attended. [1932]
October 25	ACD at Windlesham. [18]
October 25	*The Adventure of the Three Garridebs* published in *Collier's The National Weekly*. [198]
October 28	ACD as a director attended the twenty-third annual general meeting of Raphael Tuck & Sons (Ltd.) at Winchester House, Old Broad Street, E.C., Lady Conan Doyle also attended. [1604]
October 30	ACD attended a lecture by H. Denis Bradley at the Steinway Hall held by the London Spiritualist Alliance, ACD moved a vote of thanks to the lecturer. [1933]
November 5	ACD was among the guests at the luncheon at the Stationers' Hall to celebrate the bi-centenary of Messrs. Longman. [893]
November 7	It was announced that a Psychic Lecture Week would be held at the Town Hall, Tunbridge Wells from 13 November to 18 November, and that ACD would take the chair on 13 November. [894]
November 8	*The Adventure of the Illustrious Client* published in *Collier's The National Weekly*. [198]
November 9	Address by ACD "Simplicity in Religion. Sir A. Conan Doyle on the Brotherhood of Man" to the Marylebone Spiritualist Association at the Queen's Hall, London. [6]
November 13	ACD chaired the meeting at the Town Hall, Tunbridge Wells on the first evening of the Psychic Lecture Week. [895]
November 25	ACD at Windlesham. [884]
November 25	Lecture by ACD on spirit photography at Surbiton [6] at the Assembly Rooms, Surbiton under the auspices of the Kingston Spiritualist Society. [1934]
November 27	ACD made a speech "A Breach of Liberty. Sir A. Conan Doyle Defends Spiritualists" at the Dome, Brighton. [6]
December	*How Our Novelists Write Their Books* published in *The Strand Magazine*. [6,194,195,196,198]
December 6	It was announced that the Revd. George Vale Owen would give a lecture, with ACD presiding, at County Hall, Spring Gardens (Admiralty Arch) on 7 December. [1935]
December 7	ACD made an address at a Spiritualist Service held at County Hall, Spring Gardens, London [1030] ACD presided. [1936]
December 10	ACD at 15 Buckingham Palace Mansions, London, S.W.1. [40]
December 14	ACD made an address "Sir A. Conan Doyle and His Spiritual Guide" delivered at the Spiritualists Community Service at County Hall, Admiralty Arch, London. [6]
December 14	ACD lectured at the London Spiritualist Church. [2070]

1924

December 15	It was reported that ACD had purchased, through a second party, No. 244, West Seventieth Street, New York, the house where Mr J.B. Elwell was murdered under mysterious circumstances on 11 June 1920, the object of ACD was to make a spirit test. [734]
December 16	ACD at 15 Buckingham Palace Mansions, London. [18]
December 20	ACD at Villa Berna, Grindelwald, Switzerland. [40]
December 23	It was reported that Mary Conan Doyle had formed the Scolia Quartette. [735]
December	ACD's daughter, Mary Conan Doyle, with the Scolia Quartette performed at the Lyceum Club for the American Circle. [1091]
December	ACD took a short break at Villa Berna, Grindelwald, Switzerland. [202]
December 27	By the 27 December ACD had arrived at Grindelwald. [1605]
December 28	ACD at Villa Berna, Grindelwald, Switzerland. [40]
December 29	ACD at Chálet Berna, Grindelwald. [1606]

1925

n.d.	*The Lost World* made into a film. [99]
January	*The Adventure of the Three Garridebs* published in *The Strand Magazine*. [6,194,195,196,198]
n.d.	ACD was proposed as a candidate for the Rectorship of St. Andrews University, Edinburgh, together with: John Buchan, John Galsworthy, Fridjof Nansen and George Bernard Shaw, the students elected Nansen. [94]
January	ACD returned to England from a short break in Switzerland. [202]
January	ACD donated £10 to the St. Paul's Cathedral Fund. [1607]
January 18	ACD left Grindelwald. [884]
January	ACD opened a psychic bookshop in Victoria Street, London. [4,15,99,180,202,215] (*4)
January 19	ACD at Windlesham. [1834]
January 20	ACD made an address "Messages from Lord Northcliffe" given by ACD at the Queen's Hall, London [6], attended the Spiritualist Séance at the Queen's Hall, London. [1023]
January 21	ACD presented his inaugural speech as president of the London Spiritualist Association. [40]
January 23	ACD at Windlesham. [884]
January 28	The original manuscripts of *The Solitary Cyclist*, *The Dancing Men* and *The Priory School* were sold at auction in London for £66, *Sir Nigel* sold for £30. [736]
February	It was reported that ACD was among those attending the banquet of the Pilgrim Society to bid farewell to Mr F.B. Kellogg, the retiring American Ambassador. [896]
February	*The Adventure of the Illustrious Client* published in *The Strand Magazine* in February and March. [6,194,195,196,198,202]
February 1	It was advertised that the film *The Lost World*, a First National Picture, was scheduled to go into the Astor Theatre, New York on February 8. [1783]
February 2	After three years of tests and production, *The Lost World* was finally completed. [1109]
February 4	ACD was elected President of the Ex-Service Men's Club, Crowborough. [1024]
February 7	*The Story of Swedenborg* published in *Light* on 7 and 14 February. [6,198]
February 8	The First National Picture, *The Lost World*, was presented for the first time at the Astor Theatre, New York. [1784]
February 9	ACD and Jean opened The Psychic Bookshop and Library at 2 Victoria Street, London [32,68,200] (*4) near Westminster Abbey. [241]
February 15	*The Lost World* film premiered at the Astor Theatre, New York. [41]
February 21	*First Developments in America* published in *Light*. [6,198]
February 22	ACD made an address at the Spiritualist Community Service. [6]
February 24	ACD completed writing *The Land of Mist*. [6,20,202]

1925

February 28	*The Prophet of the New Revelation* published in *Light* on 28 February, 7 and 14 March. [6,198]
February 28	It was announced that ACD would lecture at the Indian National Council of the YMCA's at 112 Gower Street, London on "Psychic Experiences" on 29 February. [1608] {Note: no report of this lecture located.}
March	ACD became interested in the Norman Thorne murder case at Blackness, Crowborough, [55] (*2) {Note: this became known as the chicken run murder.}
March 3	The film of *The Lost World* was shown at The Palace, London. [1609]
March 6	An advert was published for a lady cook at Undershaw Hotel. [1790]
March 8	ACD made an address given at the Aeolian Hall. [6]
March 11	The trial of Norman Thorne opened at Lewes Assizes. [338]
March 16	Norman Thorne found guilty of murder and sentenced to death. [338]
March 19	*The Land of Mist* published by Hutchinson & Co., Ltd., London. [6]
March 21	*The Eddy Brothers and the Holmeses* published in *Light* from March 21 to 18 April. [6,198]
March 26	ACD at Windlesham. [40]
March	Lady Conan Doyle offered a silver cup for the winner of the billiards competition to take place at Windlesham, entries to Major A.H. Wood before 28 March. [332]
April 6	*The Lost World* became one of the first movies to be screened in an aeroplane, this during a 30-minute Imperial Airways Flight from London to Paris. [1109,1785] {Note: the first in-flight movie was a promotional film *Howdy Chicago!* shown in the Santa Maria hydroplane above Chicago in 1921 during the Chicago Pageant of Progress.} [1109,1785]
April 7	*The Lost World* became the first film to be shown in an airplane, it was shown to 12 passengers leaving Croydon Aerodrome, the plane flew round in a large circle for nearly 1 hour. [41,1610]
April	ACD wrote to the press on his feelings of Norman Thorne being found guilty on circumstantial evidence. [6]
April 22	Norman Thorne was hanged at Wandsworth Prison, London by Thomas Pierrepoint. [169]
April 28	ACD lectured on "Proofs of Immortality" for the Practical Psychology Club held at Church House, Westminster, London. [1611]
May	ACD became interested in the Norman Thorne case. [202] (*2)
May	ACD made an address on "The Case of Lester Coltman" at the Spiritualist Community Service. [6]
May 9	ACD and Jean took the ferry SS *Graphic* from Liverpool to Belfast. [92,139]
May 10	ACD and Jean arrived in Belfast from Liverpool on board the SS *Graphic* and stayed at the Midland Hotel, York Street, Belfast [139] or the Midland Station Hotel, Belfast, Northern Ireland [18], they arrived in the morning at Donegall Quay, Belfast after an overnight sailing from Liverpool on board the SS *Graphic*. [1017]
May 10	ACD & Jean met a number of members of the Psychic Research Society in Belfast and attended a séance in the evening, [818] the séance may have been at the home of Henry Berrington and his wife in Donaghadee, Co. Down, Berrington was a prominent local spiritualist or at St. George's Hall, High Street, Belfast. [1017]
May 11	ACD was at the Midland Station Hotel, Belfast. [139]
May 11	ACD spent the day at the Giant's Causeway, Ireland. [817]
May 12	ACD gave a talk to the Belfast Rotary Club at its luncheon in Ye Olde Castle Restaurant, Castle Place, Belfast. [139,170,171,172]
May 13	Lecture by ACD "The New Revelation" at the Ulster Hall, Belfast [6] Revd. Canon R.W. Seaver, MA, BD presided. [173,174,176]
May 14	ACD sat alongside Mr Justice Brown as a guest in the King's Bench NI Division. [819]

1925

May 14	Lecture by ACD "Proofs of Immortality" at the Ulster Hall, Belfast [6] Mr Joseph Irwin, President of the Belfast Association of Spiritualists, presided. [175,177]
May 15	It is highly probable that ACD & Jean returned to England, leaving at 9p.m. from Donegall Quay, Belfast on board the SS *Graphic*. [1017]
May 20	It was announced by the *Daily Express* of 20 May that ACD and Sybil Margaret Thomas, Viscountess Rhonda, were to open a psychic exhibition at Caxton Hall in Westminster on that very day. [1030]
n.d.	Death of Jane (Hawkins) Doyle. [202] (*3)
May 25	Death of Jane Henrietta (Hawkins) Doyle. [68] (*3)
May 27	Death of Jane Henrietta (Hawkins) Doyle, she was buried with James. [124,200] (*3)
June 5	ACD was at the Grand Hotel, Lyndhurst. [2040]
June 8	It was reported that ACD who was on a motor tour stopped at the Grand Pump Room Hotel, Bath. [1110]
June 12	*The Lost World* film premiered at the New Gallery Cinema, Regent Street, London [41,1105], at The New Gallery Kinema, Regent Street, London. [1030]
June 18	The gala performance of *The Lost World* was shown at Sid Grauman's Million Dollar Theater, Lost Angeles, America. [1109]
June 19	*The Lost World* film was shown at a matinee performance in aid of the British Museum Fund for the Exploration of South Africa [41] held at the New Gallery Cinema, Regent Street, London. [1785]
June 24	*The Lost World* film closed at the New Gallery Cinema, Regent Street, London. [1106]
June 26	It was reported that ACD was a visitor at Wells, Somerset last week. [1111]
n.d.	*The Land of Mist* published in *The Strand Magazine*. [180] (*2)
July	*The Land of Mist or the Quest of Edward Malone* published in *The Strand Magazine* from July 1925 to March 1926. [6,194,195,196,198] (*2)
July 4	ACD at 15 Buckingham Palace Mansions, London, S.W.1. [1834]
July 5	ACD spoke on "The Early Christian Church and Spiritualism" at the annual conference of the National Union of Spiritualist at the Empire Theatre, Bristol. [737]
July	ACD had the Psychic Bookshop expanded to include a museum in the basement. [1030]
July 24	ACD opened the Psychic Museum in Victoria Street, London. [1612] (*2)
July 25	ACD opened a Psychic Museum in the basement of the bookshop. [32] (*2)
Summer	ACD opened the spiritualist bookshop at 2 Victoria Street, London. [14] (*4)
August	ACD made an address "Spiritual Communion in the Home Circle" at the Spiritualist Community Service. [6]
August 28	It was reported that ACD & Jean were spending a holiday in the New Forest. [897]
August 29	ACD opened his psychic bookshop in London. [20] (*4)
n.d.	*The Early Christian Church and Modern Spiritualism* published by the Psychic Bookshop and Library, London. [6,99]
September 1	ACD at Windlesham. [40]
September 4	ACD at Windlesham. [18]
September 5	ACD at The Psychic Bookshop and Library, Abbey House, Victoria Street, Westminster, London, S.W. [40]
September 5	ACD and Jean arrived at the Hotel Regina, Paris. [86]
September 5	ACD arrived in Paris. [2071]
n.d.	ACD attended and was chairman at a meeting of the International Spiritualist Congress in Paris, France. [99,180,202] (*2)
September 5	ACD lectured and presided over The Congress of the International Spiritualist Federation in Paris [20] 6 or 11 September. [46] (*2)
September 6	ACD was present at the first morning sitting of the Spiritualist Conference in Paris. [2072]

1925

September 6	ACD was the principle speaker at a meeting of the Spiritualist Congress in Paris [1056], in the hall of the Société des Savantes [1030], in a lecture room located in the Rue Copernic. [86]
September 7	ACD at Hotel Regina, Paris. [40]
September 7	ACD gave his first lecture in French in the hall of Sociétés Savantes in Rue Danton, Paris. [86]
September 8	ACD attended a performance of a Sherlock Holmes play at the Theatre Albert, Paris. [86]
September 10	It was announced that ACD would exhibit some remarkable spiritualistic photographs at the Salle Wagram, Paris. [2073]
September 11	ACD gave a second lecture in French on spiritualism at the Salle Wagram, Paris. [86]
September 11	It was reported that ACD had taken for the season the deer forest of Glenforsa, Aros, Isle of Mull from Colonel Greenhill-Gardyne. [1092]
September 12	ACD gave a lecture at the International Spiritualist Conference in Paris. [898]
September 13	ACD gave a lecture on Spirit Photography at the Salle Wagram, Paris. [1030]
September 17	ACD at Windlesham. [40]
September 18	Branford Bryan Angell who was listed as a planter left the Port of London on board the SS *Rawalpindi* for Calcutta, India, his last address given was Dunkerton Rectory, Bath. [1837]
September 20	ACD at Windlesham. [40]
September 23	ACD at Windlesham. [40]
October 4	ACD gave a speech "Conan Doyle on the Others. Fellow Authors Criticised. What He Thinks of Their Articles" at the Grotrian Hall. [6]
October 7	ACD at Windlesham. [40]
October 9	ACD at Windlesham. [40]
October 13	ACD at Windlesham. [40]
October 15	ACD arrived in Pulboro (probably Pulborough, West Sussex). [40]
October	In mid-October ACD was staying at his flat at Buckingham Palace Mansions, London. [1030]
October	ACD attended a concert by the Scolia Folk Song Quartette, which included daughter Mary, at the Aeolian Hall, New Bond Street, London. [202]
October 23	Mary arranged the music, pianist for the Scolia Folk-song Quartette at the Aeolian Hall, New Bond Street, London [124] Scolia Folk Song Quartet. [1613]
October 23	An advert was published in the *Portsmouth Evening News* for a cook and a house-parlour maid at Windlesham. [1057]
October 24	An advert was published in the *Portsmouth Evening News* for a cook and a house-parlour maid at Windlesham. [1058]
October 24	ACD organised hunt for three snakes that had escaped from his private collection, he omitted to say that the snakes were stuffed. 16 Scouts set off on the hunt, after the snakes had been found ACD presented the successful searchers with a valuable book each. He then entertained all 16 to tea at Messrs. Mockett's Café, after tea Jean entertained the boys at The Crowborough Picture Palace, Croft Road, Crowborough. [330]
October 25	ACD at Windlesham. [40]
October 27	ACD as a director attended the twenty-fourth annual general meeting of Raphael Tuck & Sons (Ltd.) at Winchester House, Old Broad Street, E.C. [1614]
n.d.	ACD purchased a country house, Bignell Wood, Wittensford Bridge near Minstead in the New Forest, Hampshire. [3,14,15,180,202] (*3)
October	ACD purchased a derelict cottage at Bignell Wood near Brockenhurst in the New Forest. [42,68,200] (*3)
October 27	ACD purchased Bignell Wood in the New Forest, Hampshire. [232] (*3)
November 7	It was announced that ACD would be with others taking part in a mass telepathy broadcast on the BBC at 10:30p.m. on 12 November. [1113] {Note: no reports have been located that this took place.}

1925

November	*Psychic Experiences* published by G.P. Putman's Sons, London. [6]
November 8	ACD address "Spiritualists and Fallen" given at the Spiritualist Armistice Sunday Service of Remembrance at the Queen's Hall [1108], Queen's Hall, Langham Place, London. [1059]
November 11	ACD presided at a Re-union Concert for all ex-Service men held at the Ex-Service Men's Club, Crowborough. [331]
November 13	An advert for staff was published in the *Sevenoaks Chronicle & Kentish Advertiser* for a houseman at Windlesham. [1093]
November 17	ACD address "Mediums and the Law" at the Grotrian Hall (late Steinway Hall) as chairman of the meeting. [6]
November 20	Mary held a similar concert to that held on 23 October but this time in lecture form at the Regent Street Polytechnic, London. [124]
November 20	ACD at Windlesham. [884]
December 5	ACD gave a speech at the 68th annual dinner of the Savage Club at the Victoria Hotel. [6,31,202,1615]
December 10	ACD at Windlesham. [884]
December 15	ACD at 15 Buckingham Palace Mansions, London, S.W.1. [40]

1926

n.d.	*The Land of Mist* published. [99]
January 3	ACD gave a speech "The State of Spiritualism in 1925" at the Spiritualist Community Service. [6]
January 7	ACD at 15 Buckingham Palace Mansions, London, S.W.1. [40]
January 9	The annual general meeting of the Portsmouth Literary and Philosophical Society was held at the Ashburton Hall, Southsea where ACD was appointed a Vice-President. [1060]
January 13	ACD gave a speech "On The Outlook For 1926" at the Spiritualist Community Service. [6]
January 16	ACD made an address at the opening of new premises for the London Spiritualist Alliance at Queensberry Place, South Kensington. [6] (*2)
January 21	ACD addressed the London Spiritualist Alliance at a housewarming at their new premises at 16 Queensberry Place, South Kensington, London. [2110] (*2)
January 22	ACD at 15 Buckingham Palace Mansions, London, S.W.1. [40]
January 26	ACD at 15 Buckingham Palace Mansions, London, S.W.1. [40]
January 26	Death of Mrs Isabella Ann Claxton, eldest daughter of Mr Patrick Comrie Leckie and sister of Mr J.B. Leckie, aged 82, at Sunnyhaven, Rusthall Park, Tunbridge Wells. [900]
January	It was reported that ACD was among those present at the Savoy in honour of the centenary of Brillat Savarin. [899] (*2)
January 27	ACD attended a lunch event at the Savoy Hotel, London to commemorate the centenary of the death of French lawyer Jean Anthelme Brillat-Savrin who had found fame as a gastronome. [1030] (*2)
January 30	The funeral of Mrs Isabella Ann Claxton of Sunnyhaven, Rusthall Park, Rusthall, Tunbridge Wells took place at the Borough Cemetery, Tunbridge Wells. The mourners included Mr Leckie (brother), Sir Arthur and Lady Conan Doyle (niece) with their two sons and daughter and Major Wood. [901]
February 1	ACD at Windlesham. [884]
February 2	ACD at Windlesham. [40]
February	ACD was part of the Grand Council of the British Film Institute [1616], British Empire Film Institute that was established at Abbey House, Victoria Street, S.W.1. [1061]
February 4	*The Lost World* was shown on an aeroplane of the German Air Service Company during a flight over Berlin. [1109,1785]
February 6	ACD at 15 Buckingham Palace Mansions, London, S.W.1. [40]
February 12	ACD at Windlesham. [40]

1926

February 18	ACD attended the British Industries Fair at the White City where he had a long chat with King George V and Queen Mary. [1033]
February 19	ACD at 15 Buckingham Palace Mansions, London, S.W.1. [40]
February 24	ACD made an address on "The Future of Life" at the People's Palace, Mile End Road, London. [6]
February 26	It was reported that ACD & Jean had accepted invitations to attend the annual dinner of the Society of Authors to be held on 18 March. [902]
February 26	It was announced that ACD and Jean would attend the annual dinner of the Society of Authors, Playwrights and Composers in March. [738]
March 7	ACD made an address "What Spiritualism gives the World" at the Aeolian Hall. [6]
March 8	ACD at Buckingham Palace Mansions, London. [884]
March 9	Lady Conan Doyle presented the winners' cup of the Amateur Billiards Championship at the Palace Hotel, Bloomsbury Street, London [1617] the winner J. Earlam of Liverpool beat J. Helyer (or Heyler) of Middlesborough. [1827]
n.d.	Death of John Buchan a whaler on board the Hope at the same time as ACD's voyage. [739]
March 17	ACD was elected as President of the Ex-Service Men's Club, Crowborough. [903]
March 18	It was announced that the Society of Authors, Playwrights, and Composers would hold their annual dinner at Hyde Park Hotel, London today at 8p.m. [1119]
March 19	ACD & Jean attended the annual dinner of the Society of Authors. [904] {Note: this report appears to give the wrong day/date.}
March	The Will of Mrs Isabella Ann Claxton was proved at the gross value of £17,048 with net personalty £13,412. She left to Patrick Stewart Leckie (nephew) £200, Jean Conan Doyle (niece), James Blyth Leckie (brother), Jean (Lena) Conan Doyle, Denis Conan Doyle £500 each. Her residence to Patrick Stewart Leckie, the residue of her property to her nieces Sarah Mildred Forbes, Jean Conan Doyle, Patrick Stewart Leckie and Patrick Leckie Forbes in equal shares [905], and £500 to Adrian Malcolm Conan Doyle [906].
March 24	ACD made an address at the opening of the Worthing Spiritualist Church [6], ACD opened the Worthing Spiritualist Mission Church, Grafton Road, Worthing, Sussex [1034], the cost to build this new church was nearly £1,500 and had a seating capacity for 200. [1035]
March 25	ACD probably attended a reception at the Hyde Park Hotel, London to meet Major and Mrs Court Treatt. [1120] {Note: he was invited but it is unclear if he did actually attend.}
March 27	ACD organised a treasure hunt in Crowborough for the scouts. [907]
April 7	ACD made an address "The Psychic Movement" at the Queen's Hall. [6]
April 9	ACD made an address "My Psychic Experiences" at the Queen's Hall. [6]
April 10	ACD at the Athenaeum Club, London. [18]
April 21	ACD at 15 Buckingham Palace Mansions, London, S.W.1. [18]
April 25	ACD addressed a meeting of the Spiritualist community at the Grotrian Hall, London. [1062]
April 28	ACD and Mr J.B. Leckie attended the presentation of the cup and trophy in connection with the first and second divisions of the Crowborough & District Billiard League and the Championship Cup of the Ex-Service Men's Club, held at the Ex-Service Men's Club, Crowborough. [908]
May	ACD donated £5 to the National Police Fund. [1618]
May 2	ACD at Windlesham. [40]
n.d.	*The History of Spiritualism* published. [99,180] (*2)
June	*The History of Spiritualism Vol. 1 and Vol. 2* published by Cassell and Company Ltd, London, this was written by ACD in collaboration with Leslie Curnow. [6] (*2)

1926

June 9	ACD at Windlesham. [884]
June 10	ACD at 15 Buckingham Palace Mansions, London, S.W.1. [18]
June 24	ACD attended a private viewing of a new film *Fake Spiritualism Exposed* at the Marble Arch Pavilion, London, he also spoke at the end of the film. [910,1063]
June 28	ACD made an address on spiritualism at the Everyman Theatre, Hampstead. [6]
June 30	ACD, Lord Sackville, Mr & Mrs Rudyard Kipling were present at the Royal Academy Soirée. [909]
July 3	Sir Adolph Tuck died at his home at 29, Park Crescent, Portland Place, London. [911]
July 3	ACD at Windlesham. [1064]
July 6	Sir Adolph Tuck was buried at the Jewish Cemetery, Willesden, London. [912]
July 14	Mr J.T. Evens beat ACD in the final heat of the Wright Cup Handicap promoted by the Billiards Control Club; Mr Evens scored 250 points, ACD 152 points. [85]
August	ACD at the Athenaeum Club, London. [18]
August	ACD at Lyndhurst, Hampshire. [18]
September 14	ACD at Bignell Wood, Minstead, Lyndhurst, Hampshire. [40]
September 18	*The Adventure of the Three Gables* published in *Liberty*. [198]
September 28	At the annual general meeting of the Crowborough & District Billiards League held at the Constitutional Club, Crowborough ACD was elected as a Vice-President. [913]
September 30	ACD at Bignell Wood, Minstead, Lyndhurst, Hampshire. [2053]
October	*The Adventure of the Three Gables* published in *The Strand Magazine*. [6,194,195,198]
October 4	ACD was among the speakers at Ye Olde Cheshire Cheese, Fleet Street, London, the toast of "Dr Johnson" was proposed by ACD. [1121]
October 6	ACD gave a speech of introduction at a bazaar at Waterloo Hall, Crowborough on behalf of the Crowborough Cottage Hospital. [6]
October 11	ACD at 15 Buckingham Palace Mansions, London. [2053]
October 16	*The Adventure of the Blanched Soldier* published in *Liberty*. [198]
October 20	Jean assisted by ACD opened the Grand Bazaar in aid of the Portsmouth Temple of Spiritualism, 73 Victoria Road, Southsea held at Kingsley Hall, Fawcett Road, Southsea. [1036]
October 22	ACD gave a lantern lecture titled "The Unseen World" held at the Guildhall, Portsmouth. [1065]
October 24	ACD spoke at a meeting of the Brotherhood at the Wesley Church, Arundel Street, Portsmouth. [1066]
October 27	ACD as a director attended the twenty-fifth annual general meeting of Raphael Tuck & Sons (Ltd.) at Winchester House, Old Broad Street, E.C. [1619]
October 30	ACD laid the foundation stone at the Rochester Square Spiritualist Temple, Rochester Square (off Camden Road), London, NW1 9RY; he also donated £500 towards the building of the temple. [230]
October 31	Death of Harry Houdini [15,215] at 1:26p.m. [65]
November	*The Adventure of the Blanched Soldier* published in *The Strand Magazine*. [6,194,195,196,198]
November	ACD donated a drawing of John Doyle drawn by Henry Edward Doyle to the National Portrait Gallery. [1620]
November	ACD at 15 Buckingham Palace Mansions, London, S.W.1. [18]
November 1	ACD lectured the scientists at St. Catherine's John Ray Society, Cambridge. [1130]
November 4	ACD at Abbey House, 2 Victoria Street, London, S.W.1. [1067]
November 11	ACD made an Armistice Day address at the Albert Hall, London. [20]
November 12	ACD at Bignell Wood, Minstead, Lyndhurst, Hampshire. [884]
November 14	ACD was the principle speaker at the Spiritualist Service of Remembrance at the Albert Hall, London. [914]
November 19	ACD at Bignell Wood, Minstead, Lyndhurst, Hampshire. [18]

1926

November 27	*The Adventure of the Lion's Mane* published in *Liberty*. [198]
December	*The Adventure of the Lion's Mane* published in *The Strand Magazine*. [6,194,195,196,198]
December	ACD presented a drawing of John Doyle by Henry Edward Doyle to the National Portrait Gallery. [1068]
December 14	ACD at The Psychic Bookshop, Library and Museum, 2 Victoria Street, Westminster, London, S.W.1, [884]
December 16	ACD at The Psychic Bookshop, Library and Museum, 2 Victoria Street, Westminster, London, S.W.1. [18]
December 18	*The Adventure of the Retired Colourman* published in *Liberty*. [198]
December 28	In the will of Sir Adolf Tuck ACD was left £50. [1621]
December 31	Denis & Adrian attended a New Year's Eve Carnival Dance at Moorside Dormy House, Crowborough. [915]

1927

n.d.	*Spiritualism* published by the Psychic Bookshop, London for distribution at lectures given by ACD. [6]
n.d.	ACD filmed talking at Windlesham. [7] (*2)
January	*The Adventure of the Retired Colourman* published in *The Strand Magazine*. [6,194,195,196,198]
January 5	Denis & Adrian attended The "Grange" Ball at The Grange, Church Road, Crowborough held by Mr & Mrs F.H. Gresson in aid of the Crowborough Cottage Hospital. [916]
January 22	*The Adventure of the Veiled Lodger* published in *Liberty*. [198]
February	*The Adventure of the Veiled Lodger* published in *The Strand Magazine*. [6,194,195,196,198]
February 1	*The British Army in Italy* published in *The Fortnightly Review*. [6,99,198]
February 6	ACD attended a meeting of Our Society (Crimes Club). [77]
February 8	ACD was summoned at Hurst Springs, Sussex Petty Sessions in respect of two dogs, an Airedale and an Irish terrier, worrying sheep in a field at Rotherfield on 26 January. An order was made for the dogs to be kept under proper control [740], at Mark Cross Court for failing to keep two alleged dangerous dogs under proper control at Crowborough on 28 January, it was claimed that they had been chasing sheep. An order was made for the dogs to be kept under proper control and ACD to pay the costs. [917]
n.d.	Death of Bryan Mary (Dodo) Angell. [202] (*3)
February	Death of sister Bryan Mary (Dodo) Angell. [16] (*3)
February 8	Death of Bryan Mary (Dodo) [68,200,203] in hospital at Paulton, Somerset, wife of Charles Cyril Angell. [124] (*3)
February 14	ACD at Windlesham. [18]
February 24	ACD was re-elected as President of the Ex-Service Men's Club, Crowborough. [918]
February 25	ACD attended the British Industries Fair at the White City, London as the representative of Raphael Tuck, it was in this capacity that he met King George V and Queen Mary. [1030]
March	*The Sherlock Holmes Competition-Mr. Sherlock Holmes to his Readers* published in *The Strand Magazine*. [6,99,194,195,196,198]
March 1	ACD presided at the annual dinner of the British College of Psychic Science. [919]
March 5	*The Adventure of Shoscombe Old Place* published in *Liberty*. [198]
March 14	ACD & Jean attended the annual Ladies Banquet of the Authors' Club. [920]
March 20	ACD made an address to the Marylebone Spiritualist Association at the Aeolian Hall. [6]
n.d.	*Pheneas Speaks* published. [180,202] (*2)
March 21	*Pheneas Speaks* published by The Psychic Press, London. [6,20] (*2)

1927

March 21	ACD attended the showing of the new German film *Metropolis* at the Marble Arch Pavilion, also attending were Sir Oliver Lodge, Mr Derwent Hall Caine and Mr H.G. Wells. [2074]
March 21	It was announced that The Scotia Folk Song Quartet would give a concert with lecture by Miss Mary Conan at the Faculty of Arts Gallery on 24 March at 8:30. [1622] {Note: no report located.}
March 30	ACD at Buckingham Palace Mansions, London. [884]
April	*The Adventure of Shoscombe Old Place* published in *The Strand Magazine*. [6,31,194,195,196,198]
April 5	ACD at Bignell Wood, Minstead, Lyndhurst, Hampshire. [884]
April 14	It was reported that ACD and Jean were spending a quiet holiday at the Imperial Hotel, Exmouth. [741]
April 23	ACD laid the foundation stone at The Kingston Spiritualist Church. [43] (*2)
April 24	ACD laid the foundation stone of a new Spiritualist Church in Kingston. [1030] (*2)
April 24	ACD at 15 Buckingham Palace Mansions, London. [884]
April 26	Debate at the Cambridge Union between ACD and Mr J.B.S. Haldene. [6]
April 27	ACD spoke at the dedication of a new Spiritualist Church in Southwark Bridge Road, London. [1030]
May	The manuscript of *The Maracot Deep* completed [99] original title was *The Fabricius Deep*. [6,202]
May 1	*Some Curious Personal Experiences* published in *The Weekly Dispatch* as *Ghosts I Have Seen – I. The Spectral Friars*. [6,198]
May 10	ACD spoke at Southampton. [1983]
May 15	ACD made an address "The Etheric Body" at the Spiritualist Community Service, the Grotrian Hall. [6]
May 31	ACD made an address at a public meeting at The New Spiritualist Church, Surbiton. [43]
June	*The Sherlock Holmes Prize Competition-How I made my list* published in *The Strand Magazine*. [6,195,196,198]
June 1	ACD presided over a meeting at the Psychical Research Laboratory, Kensington. [742]
June 7	ACD at Bignell Wood, Minstead, Lyndhurst, Hampshire. [40]
June 16	A reporter visited and interviewed ACD at Windlesham. [1030]
n.d.	*The Case-Book of Sherlock Holmes* published. [99]
June 16	*The Case-Book of Sherlock Holmes* published by John Murray, London. [6,202]
June 18	ACD at Windlesham. [241]
July	*W.G. Grace-A Memory* published in *The Strand Magazine*. [6,194,195,196,198]
July 3	ACD made an address "Survival and Communication" at the Spiritualist Community Service at the Grotrian Hall, Wigmore Street, London [6] or "Our Life After Death". [1623]
July 26	It was announced that ACD intended to attend a dinner of the Pilgrims to be held at the Victoria Hotel, London. [1624] {Note: no report located.}
July	*Houdini the Enigma* published in *The Strand Magazine*. [202] (*2)
August	*The Riddle of Houdini* published in *The Strand Magazine* in August and September as *Houdini the Enigma*. [6,194,195,196,198] (*2)
August	ACD at Bignell Wood, Minstead, Lyndhurst. [18]
August 4	*The Ghost of the Moat* published in the *Daily Express*. [6,198]
August 7	ACD made an address on the return of literary men through mediums at the Spiritualist Community Service at the Grotrian Hall. [6]
August	ACD donated $500 for the erection of a boulder to stand as a monument to spiritualism in the grounds of the Plymouth Spiritualist Church in Rochester, New York. The boulder to be placed on the site close to the Rochester home of the Fox sisters. [1625]
August	Late August ACD donated £5 to the Boy Scouts London Appeal. [1626]

1927

September 4	ACD made an address at Spiritualist Community Service at the Grotrian Hall. [6]
October	The film *Brigadier Gerard* starring Rul La Rocque was shown at the Capitol, Haymarket, London. [1627]
October	ACD at Bignell Wood, Minstead, Lyndhurst. [18]
October	ACD attended a conference of many faiths at the City Temple, ACD (Spiritualist), Anagarika Dharmapala (Buddhist), Dr F.W. Norwood (Protestant), Dr Annie Beasant (Theosophist), Revd. A. Green (Jew), Dr A.D. Jilla (Mohammedan), Revd. Theodore Smith (Zoroastrian), Mr S.N. Silk (Hindu) and Mr K.N. Das Gupta, the organiser of the meeting, addressed the meeting on what Christianity means in different faiths. [1828]
October	ACD made an address at Spiritualist Community Service at the Grotrian Hall. [6]
October	*The Maracot Deep* published in *The Strand Magazine* from October 1927 to February 1928 [6,194,195,198,202] October 1927 to May 1929. [196]
October 26	ACD as a director attended the twenty-sixth annual general meeting of Raphael Tuck & Sons (Ltd.) at Raphael House, Moorfields, London, E.C. [1628]
November	ACD at Windlesham. [18]
November 8	The secretary of state for Scotland authorised the release of Oscar Slater. [1127]
November 11	It was announced that ACD & Jean would attend the annual dinner of the Society of Authors at the Hyde Park Hotel, London on 30 November. [921] {Note: no reports of this dinner located.}
November 11	It was announced that ACD would speak at the Spiritualist Service of Remembrance at the Royal Albert Hall, London on Armistice Sunday 13 November. [986]
November 13	ACD spoke at the Spiritualist Service of Remembrance at the Royal Albert Hall, London. [987]
November 13	ACD made an Armistice Sunday address at the Grotrian Hall. [6]
November 13	ACD attended a meeting of Our Society (Crimes Club). [77]
n.d.	Oscar Slater released from prison. [99,203] (*3)
November 14	Oscar Slater released from Peterhead Prison. [4,6,15,202] (*3)
November 15	Oscar Slater released from Peterhead Prison. [31,215] (*3)
November 16	ACD attended and spoke at a luncheon of the Association of American Correspondents at the Savoy Hotel, London. [1122]
November 18	It was announced that ACD would distribute the prizes to the successful students of the Tunbridge Wells Technical Institute and School of Arts at the Town Hall, Tunbridge Wells on 6 December. [922]
November	Late November ACD attended and spoke at a dinner held at the Connaught Rooms in honour of the 70th birthday of Mr Gustave Tuck. [1094]
December	*The Alleged Posthumous Writings of Known Authors* published in *The Fortnightly Review*. [6,198]
December	*The Great Characters of Fiction: "Which Should I Most Like to have Created?"* published in *The Strand Magazine*. [6,194,195,198]
December 6	ACD gave a speech on literature at the annual prize giving of the Technical Institute at the Town Hall, Tunbridge Wells. [6]

1928

January	The cellar beneath the Psychic Museum was damaged by flooding. [1030]
January	ACD attended the funeral of Thomas Hardy at Westminster Abbey. [1972]
January 25	ACD made an address to the London Spiritualist Alliance at Kensington Town Hall. [6]
February	*A Word of Warning* published by The Psychic Press, London. [6]
February	*What Does Spiritualism Actually Teach and Stand For?* published by the Psychic Bookshop, London. [6]
February	ACD joined the staff of the *Sunday Express* as a weekly contributor. [1030]
February 5	ACD at Windlesham. [40]

1928

February 15	ACD took part in an exhibition billiards match at the Ex-Service Men's Club, Crowborough. [923]
February 16	ACD at Windlesham. [40]
February 18	ACD at Windlesham. [884]
February 22	ACD at The Psychic Bookshop and Library, Abbey House, Victoria Street, London, S.W. [40]
February 22	ACD was re-elected President of the Ex-Service Men's Club, Crowborough. [924]
February 24	ACD at Windlesham. [884]
February 24	ACD at 15 Buckingham Palace Mansions, S.W.1. [40]
February 25	*When the World Screamed* published in *Liberty* on 25 February and 3 March. [198]
February 26	ACD at Windlesham. [40]
March 25	ACD made an address on "The Use of Spiritualism" at the Grotrian Hall [6,31], William Gillette shared the platform with ACD but did not speak. [1030]
April	ACD made an address on "The White Ant" (by Maeterlinck) at the Grotrian Hall. [6]
April	*A Strange Prophet* published in *The Quarterly Transactions of the British College of Psychic Science* as *Thomas Lake Harris: A Strange Prophet*. [6,198]
April	*When the World Screamed* published in *The Strand Magazine* in April and May. [6,194,195,196,198,202]
May	*Blood Sports – Should They Be Abolished?* by ACD and others published in *The Strand Magazine*. [6,195,196,198]
May 6	ACD made an address at the Aeolian Hall. [6]
n.d.	ACD purchased a picture painted under psychic influence by Captain Will Longstaff. [743]
May 8	ACD and Jean attended the 88th annual dinner of the Newspaper Society at the Hotel Cecil, London. [1978]
May 20	ACD made an address at the Grotrian Hall. [6]
June	*Notes from a Strange Mailbag – The Dreamers* published in *The Strand Magazine*. [6,194,195,196,198]
June 8	ACD attended the appeal by Oscar Slater at the Scottish Court of Criminal Appeal, Edinburgh. [744]
June 11	ACD had a meeting with Oscar Slater in London. [1030,1984]
June 13	ACD was interviewed at Cadnam, near Southampton [1979] interviewed by a Press representative. [1984]
June 18	In the Will of Mr Clare Verus Pontifex, ACD was left his Alfred Russell Wallace Collection. [1629]
June 24	ACD made an address "Where Are the Dead?" at the Grotrian Hall. [6]
June 27	ACD was invited to the reception held by the President and Council of the Royal Academy of Arts at Burlington House. [1095]
July 5	Lecture by ACD on "Psychic Experiences" at the Waterloo Hut, Crowborough. [76]
July 9	ACD again attended the appeal by Oscar Slater at the Scottish Court of Criminal Appeal, Edinburgh. [745]
July 10	ACD attended the appeal by Oscar Slater at the Scottish Court of Criminal Appeal, Edinburgh. [1985]
July 11	ACD and Jean performed the opening ceremony of the new premises of the Scottish Psychical Society at 22 Stafford Street, Edinburgh. [746]
July 15	ACD made an address at the Spiritualist Community Service at the Grotrian Hall. [6]
July	Oscar Slater's sentence quashed. [202] (*4)
July 18	Oscar Slater's sentence quashed. [14] (*4)
July 20	Oscar Slater's sentence quashed. [2,4,31] (*4)
July 21	Oscar Slater's sentence was quashed by the Scottish Court of Criminal Appeal. [1030] (*4)

1928

July 24	ACD gave evidence as the president of the London Spiritualist Alliance at the trial of Miss Mercy Phillimore at Westminster Police Court, as did Sir Oliver Lodge. [1630]
July 25	ACD at 15 Buckingham Palace Mansions, London, S.W. [1631]
July 25	ACD presided at a meeting of the Council of the London Spiritualist Alliance where it was decided not to appeal against the decision in the recent fortune-telling case at Westminster Police Court. [747]
July	Late July it was reported by the *Daily Express* on 31 July that ACD had taken part in a séance at Beaulieu Abbey. [1030]
September	ACD at 15 Buckingham Palace Mansions, London, S.W. [18]
September 5	ACD at Bignell Wood, Minstead, Lyndhurst, Hampshire. [40]
September 9	ACD gave a demonstration of psychic pictures at the International Spiritualist Congress at Queen's Hall, London. [A copy of the invitation in the author's collection]
September 10	ACD at 15 Buckingham Palace Mansions, London, S.W.1. [40]
September 10	From 10 to 13 September ACD attended the Triennial Congress of the International Federation of Spiritualists at Queen's Gate Hall, South Kensington [748]; he spoke at the session on 13 September. [749]
September 12	ACD at 15 Buckingham Palace Mansions, London, S.W.1. [40]
September 14	ACD at 15 Buckingham Palace Mansions, S.W.1. [40]
September 25	ACD at 15 Buckingham Palace Mansions, London, S.W.1. [2053]
September 25	Sir Arthur and Lady Conan Doyle attended the wedding of Major J.R. Wynter and Miss V. Yates at St. Margaret's Church, Westminster. [1632]
September 30	ACD gave an interview on how clairvoyants could assist in the solving of crime. [1030]
October	*Can We Speak with the Dead?* published in *The London Magazine*. [6,196,198]
October	*The Story of Spedegue's Dropper* published in *The Strand Magazine*. [6,194,195,196,198,202]
October	ACD was filmed talking at Windlesham. [44,215] (*2)
October 4	ACD at 15 Buckingham Palace Mansions, S.W.1. [40]
October	A farewell banquet given by the Spiritualists of the United Kingdom. [99] (*2)
October 10	Farewell luncheon given by Spiritualists of the United Kingdom at the Holborn Restaurant, before ACD and Jean left for lecture tour of South Africa. [6] (*2)
n.d.	*The Complete Sherlock Holmes* published. [99]
October 15	*The Complete Sherlock Holmes Short Stories* published by John Murray, London. [6]
October 18	ACD as a director attended the twenty-seventh annual general meeting of Raphael Tuck & Sons (Ltd.) at Raphael House, Moorfields, London, E.C. [1633]
October 20	ACD at the Psychic Book Shop. [884]
October 26	ACD and family sailed from Southampton for South Africa [750] on board the *Winsor Castle* for Cape Town, South Africa. [137]
November	*The British Campaigns in Europe 1914-1918* published by Geoffrey Bles. [6]
November	ACD and his family left England for South Africa. [14,15,215]
n.d.	ACD toured South Africa, Kenya and Rhodesia with the whole family to lecture on spiritualism. [6] (*3)
n.d.	ACD and his family toured South Africa promoting the case of spiritualism [124,180] ACD launched a five-month tour of South Africa. [99] (*3)
n.d.	The *Windsor Castle* docked in Madeira, ACD, Jean and Billy (Jean) took in the sites while Denis and Adrian went off to Funchal. [74]
n.d.	The *Windsor Castle* passed the Canary Islands. [74]
November 1	ACD on board the *Windsor Castle* passed close Cape de Verde. [74]
November 12	ACD and his family toured South Africa, Rhodesia and Kenya from 12 November 1928 until 18 March 1929. [68] (*3)
November 12	ACD arrived in Cape Town, South Africa and stayed at the Mount Nelson Hotel. [74,215] (*2)

1928

November 12	ACD arrived aboard the *Windsor Castle* in South Africa, [6,20] (*2) he visited Port Elizabeth, Bloemfontein, Durban, Johannesburg and Pretoria, then the Khami Ruins, the Matoppo Hills, Victoria Falls, Bulawayo, Salisbury, the Great Lakes, Kampala and Nairobi, he started for home on 13 March 1929. [6]
November 13	ACD made a broadcast on radio from Cape Town. [74]
November 21	Lecture by ACD at City Hall, Cape Town [74] lectured on "Life After Death in the Third Sphere" at the City Hall, Cape Town. [6]
November 23	ACD attended a séance with the medium Mrs Kempton in the sitting room of the Mount Nelson Hotel, Cape Town. [74]
November 23	ACD lectured in Stellenbosch, a town approximately 31 miles East of Cape Town. [74]
November 24	ACD visited the two Houses of Parliament and library in Cape Town. [74]
November 25	ACD attended a spiritualist service at the Town Hall, Cape Town. [74]
November 26	ACD gave a photographic lecture at the Town Hall, Cape Town. [74]
November 27	Lecture by ACD "The Wonders of Psychic Knowledge" at the City Hall, Cape Town. [6]
November 27	ACD left Cape Town for Port Elizabeth on board the *Armadale Castle*. [6,74]
November 29	ACD arrived in Port Elizabeth and stayed at the Humewood Hotel. [74]
November 29	Lecture by ACD at the Opera House, Port Elizabeth. [74]
November 30	ACD exploring the beauties of Port Elizabeth, late evening travelled to Bloemfontein. [74]
December 1	ACD arrived in Bloemfontein and stayed in Polley's Hotel. [74]
December 2	ACD visited many sites around Bloemfontein [74], including a visit to the Ramblers Ground in South Africa where the Langman Hospital had been located during the Boer War. [1030]
December 5	ACD left Bloemfontein for Natal. [74]
December 6	ACD arrived in Natal early morning and stayed at the Imperial Hotel. [74]
December 6	Lecture by ACD at the Town Hall, Natal. [74]
December 7	ACD travelled to Durban and stayed at the Marine Hotel. [74]
December 8	Adrian visited Johannesburg. [74]
December 8	ACD had a sitting with Mrs Kelland. [74]
December	Lecture by ACD in Durban. [74]
December 13	ACD left Durban for Johannesburg. [74]
December 14	ACD arrived in Johannesburg and stayed at the Carlton Hotel. [74]
December 16	Lecture by ACD "No Change in Death" at the Orpheum Theatre, Johannesburg. [6,74]
December 18	ACD made an address on spiritualism at the Rotary Club, Johannesburg. [6]
December 19	ACD made a second lecture in Johannesburg. [74]
December 20	Lecture by ACD "The Marvels of Psychic Knowledge" at the Standard Theatre, Johannesburg. [6]
December 21	ACD a guest at the Country Club, Johannesburg. [74]
December 22	The World's largest sailing ship *København* (*Copenhagen*) is last heard from. Sixty seamen, fifty five of whom were boys disappeared and were never seen again. ACD and Jean were later consulted about this. [2055]
December 23	ACD left Johannesburg for Pretoria and stayed at the Carlton Hotel. [74]
December 23	Lecture by ACD in Pretoria. [74]
December 23	ACD returned to Johannesburg. [74]
December 30	ACD made a third lecture in Johannesburg. [74]
December 30	Lecture by ACD "Photos of Fairies" at the Orpheum Theatre, Johannesburg. [6]
December 31	ACD saw in the New Year at the Country Club, Johannesburg. [74,202]

1929

n.d.	Birth of Robert Foley son of Percy (Michael) and Barbara Foley. [124]
n.d.	Death of Constance Amelia Monica (Connie) Hornung. [202] (*4)
January	*The Disintegration Machine* published in *The Strand Magazine*. [6,194,195,196,198,202]

1929

n.d.	Adrian and Denis purchased a Mercedes-Benz SSK sports car, which they both raced. [124]
January 1	ACD visited Dr Erasmus Ellis, Mrs Ellis and General Tanner. [74]
January 4	ACD visited the Robinson gold mine. [74]
January 5	ACD and Denis investigated the criminal slums of Johannesburg. [74]
January 6	ACD made an address at the Spiritualist Divine Service at the Orpheum Theatre, Johannesburg. [6]
January 6	ACD attended a spiritualist service in Johannesburg. [74]
January	ACD visited the Premier Diamond Mine. [74]
January	ACD had an attack of gastro-enteritis, he was ill for three days. [74]
January	ACD left Johannesburg for Bulawayo via Mafeking. [74]
January 12	ACD left Johannesburg. [6]
January 13	ACD visited the Khami Ruins. [74]
January 13	ACD visited the grave of Cecil Rhodes at the Matoppo Hills, 27 miles from Bulawayo. [74]
January 14	ACD stayed at the Grand Hotel, Bulawayo. [74,99]
January 14	ACD left Bulawayo for the Victoria Falls. [74]
January 15	15 & 16 January, ACD visited the Victoria Falls and surrounding area. [74]
January 20	ACD arrived back in Bulawayo for an evening lecture. [74]
January 20	ACD gave a speech "Life as it is Beyond the Veil" at the Palace Theatre, Bulawayo. [6]
January	ACD visited the farm of Mr Harding Forrester. [74]
January 22	ACD at Bulawayo, Rhodesia. [99]
January 23	ACD travelled from Bulawayo to Salisbury. [74]
January 29	ACD arrived in Salisbury. [163]
January	ACD stayed at Meikle's Hotel, Salisbury. [74]
January	ACD visited the home of Judge McIlwaine near Salisbury. [74]
January	ACD spoke to the Salisbury Psychic Society. [74]
January	Lecture by ACD in Salisbury. [74]
January	ACD left Salisbury. [74]
January	ACD arrived in Beira and stayed at the Savoy Hotel. [74]
January	During January & February ACD was on board the *Karoa* travelling to Mombasa. [74]
January	ACD gave a speech about the Psychic Question while on board the *Karoa* on route for Mombasa. [74]
February 7	ACD arrived early afternoon in Mombasa. [74]
February 7	ACD travelled on the Uganda Railway from Mombasa to Nairobi. [74]
February	ACD arrived in Nairobi and stayed at the Norfolk Hotel. [74]
February 8	Branford Bryan Angell who was listed as a planter left the Port of London on board the SS *Naldera* for Bombay, India. [1837]
February 12	ACD, Denis and Adrian enjoyed a day's sport at the Athi Plains, near Nairobi. [74]
February 14	ACD, Jean and Billy (Jean) visited a game reserve of Mr Henry Tarlton six miles from Nairobi. [74]
February 15	ACD arrived in Nairobi. [6]
February	ACD with Denis lectured in Nairobi. [74]
February 17	Lecture by ACD "My Psychic Experiences" at the Theatre Royal, Nairobi. [6]
February 18	ACD at Windlesham. [40] {Note: ACD was still in South Africa when this letter was dated.}
February 19	Lecture by ACD "The Wonders of Psychic Knowledge" at the Theatre Royal, Nairobi. [6]
February 22	ACD in Nairobi. [18]
February 23	ACD, Denis and Adrian visited a farm owned by Mr Edgley. [74]
February 26	ACD left Nairobi for Lake Victoria Nyanza. [74]
February 26	ACD stayed overnight at Nakuru. [74]
February 27	ACD travelled from Nakuru to Kisumu. [74]

1929

February 28	ACD on board the steamer *Usoga* travelling around Lake Victoria Nyanza. [74]
March 4	ACD made a speech on his university career at a dinner at the Grand Hotel, Nairobi [6] or Hotel Avenue. [31]
March 9	ACD arrived back in Kisumu. [74]
March 10	ACD arrived back in Nairobi at the Norfolk Hotel. [74]
March	Lecture by ACD in Nairobi. [74]
March 12	Lecture by ACD on the Cottingley Fairies at the Theatre Royal, Nairobi. [6]
March 13	ACD left South Africa. [6,20]
March 13	ACD left Nairobi [74] travelled to Mombasa. [1974]
March	ACD arrived in Mombasa and stayed at the Manor Hotel. [74]
March	ACD lectured in Mombasa. [74]
March 15	ACD left South Africa for England. [1030]
March 16	ACD left Mombasa on board the *Modasa*. [74] (*2)
March 21	ACD in Aden. [18]
March 22	ACD saw the barren rocks of Aden. [74]
March 23	ACD sailed past the Twelve Apostle Rocks. [74]
March 24	ACD left Mombasa. [6] (*2)
March 24	The *Modasa* docked at Port Soudan. [74]
March	ACD and Jean travelled by train to Suakim. [74]
March	ACD returned to Port Soudan after visiting Suakim and continued on board the *Modasa* for Cairo. [74]
March	ACD arrived at Suez. [74]
March 29	ACD travelled by car to Cairo and stayed at the Mena Hotel. [74]
March	ACD visited the Pyramids and the Sphinx. [74]
March	ACD gave a lecture on spiritualism on board the *Modasa*. [74]
April	ACD made a short stop at Malta. [74]
April	*The Lord of the Dark Face* I. *The Dangers of the Deep* published in *The Strand Magazine* in April and May. [6,194,195,198]
April 6	ACD and family arrived in Marseilles on route for England from South Africa. [751]
n.d.	ACD and his family were staying in Paris on route for England from South Africa. [752]
April	In early April ACD was back in England. [202]
n.d.	ACD and Jean among others welcomed home MCC cricket team on their return from Australia. [753]
Spring	ACD and Lady Conan Doyle returned to England. [3]
May	*The Lord of the Dark Face* II. *The Crisis* published in *The Strand Magazine*. [6,194,195,198]
May 5	ACD attended a meeting of Our Society (Crimes Club). [77]
May 22	ACD celebrated his 70th birthday at Bignell Wood. [215] (*2)
May 22	ACD observed his birthday at Windlesham, taking a drive over the South Downs and a round of golf at Crowborough Beacon Golf Course. In the evening he travelled to London with Jean to dine and attend the theatre. [1126] (*2)
May	*An Open Letter to Those of My Generation* published by The Psychic Press. [202] (*2)
May 22	*An Open Letter to Those of My Generation* published by The Psychic Press, London. [6] (*2)
May 23	ACD addressed a meeting of spiritualists at Queen's Gate Hall, Kensington, London. [925]
May 26	ACD made an address on his African tour at the Spiritualist Community Service, held at the Grotrian Hall. [6]
June	ACD at Bignell Wood, Minstead, Lyndhurst. [18]
June	ACD at Windlesham. [18]
June 10	ACD and Jean were attended a garden party held in Albany, Piccadilly, London. [1634]

1929

June 16	Adrian was caught speeding in Crowborough. [845]
June 18	ACD at 15 Buckingham Palace Mansions, London, S.W.1. [18]
June 20	ACD at 15 Buckingham Palace Mansions, London, S.W.1. [884]
June 26	*The Conan Doyle Stories* published by John Murray, London. [6]
June 26	ACD was invited to attend the annual soirée of the Royal Academy held at the Academy. [1635]
June 27	It was reported that many crack drivers were practising at Brooklands for the Brooklands Automobile Racing Club (BARC) Six Hour race, Adrian Conan Doyle was among those practising in his Frazer Nash, the race was due to be held on Saturday 29 June. [2017]
June 29	It was reported that Adrian Conan Doyle, with Dick Nash as his co-driver, raced the Frazer Nash with a supercharged Anzani engine at the BARC Six Hour race at Brooklands. After over five hours racing it retired with ignition problems. [2018]
July 9	At Mark Cross Petty Sessions Adrian pleaded guilty to driving a motor car at a speed exceeding 20 miles an hour at Crowborough on June 16, and was fined £5 and costs. P.C. William Harris said the defendant was travelling at between 40 and 45 miles an hour. [846] (*2)
n.d.	ACD's son was fined £5 at the magistrates at Mark Cross, Sussex for speeding. [754] {Note: the son is unnamed in the report.} (*2)
July 13	ACD at Windlesham. [18]
n.d.	ACD visited Groombridge Place with Dr and Mrs Wickland. [20]
n.d.	*The Maracot Deep* published. [99] (*3)
July	*The Maracot Deep and Other Stories* published. [202] (*3)
July 29	*The Maracot Deep and Other Stories* published by John Murray, London. [6] (*3)
August 5	Adrian & Denis attended a carnival dance at the Village Hall, Maresfield, Sussex, it was held in aid of the Recreation Ground Fund. [847]
August	Fire damaged Bignell Wood, Minstead. [6,14,15,20,215] (*2)
August 15	Bignell Wood gutted by fire, [68,200,202,1636] (*2) Lady Conan Doyle, Denis, Malcolm and Jean were at home at the time, ACD was taking his usual morning stroll in the forest. [1636]
August 16	ACD at Bignell Wood, Minstead, Lyndhurst, Hampshire. [18]
August 23	On August 23 & 24 ACD stayed at the home of Sir James Barrie in Cheltenham. [2]
September	*Our African Winter* published by John Murray. [202] (*2)
September 9	*Our African Winter* published by John Murray, London. [6] (*2)
September 14	*The Complete Sherlock Holmes Long Stories* published by John Murray, London. [6]
Autumn	M. Paul Forthunay of France (the Continental Editor of the *International Psychic Gazette*) visited ACD at Bignell Wood. [1]
September 28	Adrian Conan Doyle driving a supercharged Anzani Frazer Nash ('The Slug') won the 2000cc racing car event and received the Crawshay Challenge Trophy for the best time by a Kent & Sussex Club member at the Lewes Speed Trials. [134]
October	*The Roman Catholic Church-A Rejoinder* published by The Psychic Press, London. [6,99]
October	*The Death Voyage: The Kaiser And His Fleet* published in *The Strand Magazine*. [6,194,195,196,198]
October 7	ACD presided at the Authors' Club. [2057]
October 8	ACD as a director attended the twenty-eighth annual general meeting of Raphael Tuck & Sons (Ltd.) at Raphael House, Moorfields, London, E.C. [1637]
n.d.	Denis was at Gonville and Caius College, Cambridge reading medicine. [202]
n.d.	ACD toured Scandinavia and Holland. [99] (*4)

1929

October	ACD toured the Netherlands, Denmark, Sweden and Norway during October and November. [68,124] (*4)
October	ACD toured the capitals of Europe and lectured on spiritualism, he visited The Hague, Copenhagen, Stockholm and Oslo. [2,10,14,15,20,215] (*4)
October 10	ACD toured the Netherlands and Scandinavia. [202] (*4)
October 10	ACD, Lady Conan Doyle and their friends Mr and Mrs Ashton Jonson sailed from Harwich to the Hook of Holland. [2041]
October 11	ACD, Lady Conan Doyle with Mr and Mrs Jonson arrived in The Hague at 7:40a.m. and stayed at Hotel des Indes. [2041] (*2)
October 12	ACD arrived at The Hague. [755] (*2)
October 12	ACD at the Hotel des Indes, La Hague, Holland. [884]
October 12	ACD, Lady Conan Doyle, Mr and Mrs Jonson went to the zoo, met Mr Van Bylandt, they were driven round the town by a Dutch lady spiritualist, and visited the seaside. [2041]
October 13	ACD visited Verdun. [2041]
October 14	ACD, Lady Conan Doyle, Mr and Mrs Jonson went to the seaside suburb Scheveningen in the morning. [2041]
October 15	ACD gave an 8p.m. lecture "Het leven na den dood" ("Life after Death") at the great hall of the Dierentuin (the Zoo) in The Hague, arranged by the Nederlansche Vereeniging van Spiritisten "Harmonia". [2041]
October 16	ACD visited Musee Moritz (Mauritshuis), The Hague. A formal welcome dinner for ACD, his wife and the Jonsons, arranged by the Committee of Twenty-Five. [2041]
October 17	ACD gave a lecture for the English-Holland Society at the Colonial Museum, Amsterdam. [2041]
October 18	ACD gave a lecture "Het leven na den dood" ("Life after Death") at Gebouw voor Kunsten en Wetenschappen, Rotterdam, arranged by the Rotterdamsche Vereeniging van Spiritisten, Rotterdam "Harmonia". [2041]
October 19	ACD complained of feeling unwell. [202]
October 19	ACD, Lady Conan Doyle, Mr and Mrs Jonson travelled by train to Hamburg where they stayed at Hotel Atlantic. [2041]
October 20	ACD, Lady Conan Doyle, Mr and Mrs Jonson went to Karl Hagenbesk's Zoo. [2041]
October 21	ACD, Lady Conan Doyle, Mr and Mrs Jonson left Hamburg at 8:30a.m. by train to Warnemunde and then by ferry to Gjedser, Denmark. [2041]
October 21	ACD, Lady Conan Doyle, Mr and Mrs Jonson travelled by train from Gjedser, Denmark and arrived at Copenhagen, Denmark in the evening. They stayed at Hotel d'Angleterre. [2041]
October 21	ACD arrived in Copenhagen and stayed at Hotel Angleterre, ACD again feeling unwell [202] ACD, Lady Conan Doyle, Mr and Mrs Ashton Jonson arrived in Copenhagen. [2055]
October 22	A reception was held for ACD and Lady Conan Doyle. [2055]
October 23	ACD gave a lecture at Idrætshuset, Copenhagen [2041] lecture on spiritualism "Livet efter døden" ("Life after Death") to a full house, tickets were sold out quickly. [2055]
October 24	At 4:15p.m. ACD talked about spiritualism on Danish radio [2041] about *Our African Winter*, after he had finished *The New Revelation* was read in a Danish translation. [2055]
October 24	A reception for ACD was held at Hotel d'Angleterre. [2041]
October 25	ACD gave a lecture at Odd Fellowpalæet, Copenhagen. [2041,2055]
October 25	ACD was at Hotel Angleterre, Copenhagen [31] or Hotel D'Angleterre. [884]
n.d.	Peter Vilhelm von Schwanenflügel sent a letter to Lady Conan Doyle during her stay in Copenhagen asking for assistance to contact the boys from the missing sailing ship *Københavin*. Vilhelm von Schwanenflügel had a son on the ship. [2055]
October 26	ACD was in Stockholm. [202]

1929

October 26	ACD and Ashton Jonson went to see the film *The Hound of the Baskervilles* during the afternoon. The audience all rose and the orchestra played "God Save the King". [2041]
October 26	ACD, Lady Conan Doyle, Mr and Mrs Jonson left Copenhagen at 8p.m. by train. [2041]
October 27	ACD, Lady Conan Doyle, Mr and Mrs Jonson arrived in Stockholm by train at 8:50a.m. from Copenhagen they stayed at Grand Hôtel. [2041]
October 27	On October 27 or 28 a reception was held at the British Embassy, Stockholm, among the other guests was the famous Swedish actor Gösta Ekman. [2041]
October 27	ACD gave a lecture, "Livet efter döden" ("Life after Death") at 8p.m. at Konserthuset, Stockholm. [2041]
October 28	ACD at Grand Hotel, Stockholm. [2055]
October 29	ACD and Lady Conan Doyle attended a luncheon with the Stockholm Spiritualist Society. [2041]
October 29	ACD and Lady Conan Doyle saw the play "Männen vid fronten" ("Journey's End") at Oscarsteatern, (Oscar Theatre). [2041]
October 29	Painter Vilhelm von Schanenflügel received a letter from ACD, sent from the Grand Hotel, Stockholm, ACD answered on behalf of Lady Conan Doyle and promises to do his best to help when he is back in London. [2055]
October 30	From 9:40p.m. to 10:00p.m. ACD talked on Swedish radio. [2041]
October 31	ACD sightseeing in Saltsjöbaden. [2041]
October 31	ACD was in Oslo. [202]
October 31	ACD gave a lecture, "Den psykiska forskningens resultat" ("The Results of the Psychic Research") at 8p.m. at Konserthuset, Stockholm. [2041]
November 1	ACD, Lady Conan Doyle, Mr and Mrs Jonson arrived in Christiana (Oslo), Norway. [2041]
November	ACD was at the Grand Hotel, Oslo 1-4 November. [884]
November 3	ACD gave a lecture, "Livet efter dødene" ("Life after Death") at 8p.m. in Aulaen, Christiana (Oslo). [2041]
November 4	ACD gave a lecture, "Den psykiske forsknings resultater" ("The Results of the Psychic Research") at 5p.m. in Aulaen, Christiania (Oslo). [2041]
November 4	ACD, Lady Conan Doyle, Mr and Mrs Jonson left Christiania (Oslo) in the evening. [2041]
November 5	ACD, Lady Conan Doyle, Mr and Mrs Jonson arrived in Hamburg in the evening and stayed at Hotel Atlantic. [2041]
November 7	ACD arrived in Dover and then travelled by train to Victoria Station, then by wheelchair to Buckingham Palace Mansions. [202]
November	ACD confined to bed at Windlesham through over work. [85]
n.d.	ACD had his first heart attack. [99]
November 10	ACD returned home exhausted. [14]
November 10	ACD managed to speak at the Armistice Day ceremony at the Albert Hall, London and then in the evening at the Spiritualist Remembrance Service at Queen's Hall, London. [1,2,14,15,202,215,2058]
November 11	Mr Jonson who was with ACD in Copenhagen sends a letter on the behalf of ACD to Vilhelm von Schwanenflügel, stating that the famous psychometrist, Frau Lotte Plaat had examined a hat and a letter from two of the boys from the missing sailing ship København, she had seen the boys drowned and floating in the water and that they would never be found. [2055]
November 13	The manuscript of *The Adventure of the Speckled Band* containing 32 pages, sold for £235 at Sotheby's, London. [1638]
November 20	ACD confined to his bed at Windlesham suffering from over work. [85,1639]
November 20	Funeral of Mrs Nora Cicely Lindsay-Hogg at Rotherfield Parish Church, ACD, Jean and family sent a wreath but did not attend. [1096]
November 29	ACD at Buckingham Palace Mansions, S.W.1. [40]

1930

n.d.	*The Crowborough Edition* published by Doubleday, Doran & Company, Inc., New York, comprising 24 volumes limited to 760 sets with the first volume signed by the author. [6]
n.d.	Death of Branford Bryan Angell, son of Charles and Bryan (Dodo) Mary Angell in Australia. [68,124] (*3)
n.d.	ACD lent Adrian £500 to buy a Frazer-Nash, known as 'The Slug'. [202]
January	*[A Form Letter]* privately printed by ACD. [6]
January 7	ACD at Windlesham. [884]
January 10	ACD at Windlesham. [18]
January 15	At 15 Buckingham Palace Mansions ACD sat for his bust being sculptured by Jo Davidson. [2109]
January	ACD resigned from the Society for Psychical Research after thirty-six years. [14,215] (*3)
January 22	ACD resigned from the Society of Psychical Research after being a member for thirty-six years. [133] (*3)
January 24	Branford Bryan Angell who was listed as a planter left the Port of London on Board the R.M.S. *Mongolia* for Colombo, his last address given was 8 Park Avenue, Dover. [1837]
January 28	ACD was re-elected as a Vice-President of the Portsmouth Literary and Philosophical Society. [1069]
January 30	ACD at Bignell Wood. [884]
February	*[A Second Form Letter]* privately printed by ACD. [6]
February	The condition of ACD, who had been confined to his bedroom for 10 weeks owing to heart trouble, his condition was 'very fair'. [1640]
February 10	ACD consulted a heart specialist in London and was ordered to take a complete rest for three months; he had already been indisposed for ten weeks. [756]
February	In the Inter-collegiate Competition, Caius beat St. John's by 58 points to 46. In putting the weight competition, Denis Conan Doyle came second. [1641]
March	ACD resigned from the Society for Psychical Research after thirty-six years. [2,6] (*3)
March	Adrian and Denis raced the Frazer Nash ('The Slug') in the Cambridge Speed Trials coming third. [202]
March	Denis left his course at Cambridge. [202]
March 22	Denis and Adrian Conan Doyle took part in the first meeting of the Southport Motor Club races held on Ainsdale Sands, Southport, Merseyside. [1821]
March 24	Adrian Conan Doyle did not appear at St. Ives (Hunts) Police Court to answer a summons for dangerous driving a car at Fenstanton, he was travelling at 35 to 40 miles an hour where the speed limit is 30 miles an hour, he was fined £3. [757]
March 27	ACD at Windlesham. [18]
April 4	ACD at 15 Buckingham Palace Mansions, London, S.W.1. [884]
May 5	ACD drew up his will. [124]
May 6	ACD drew up his will. [Date taken from copy of the Will]
May 9	ACD at Windlesham. [40]
May 14	ACD recorded a talk for a gramophone record titled 'A Chat with Conan Doyle'. [789]
May 17	Adrian Conan Doyle won the 1500cc and the unlimited racing group (the fastest time of the day for which he won the Clayton Cup and replica cup) driving the Frazer Nash at the Lewes Speed Trials, Sussex [134] Denis driving the Anzani Frazer Nash ('The Slug') came second in the 2-litre class at the same meeting. [134]
May 23	ACD at Windlesham. [40]
May 24	ACD at Windlesham. [40]
May 27	ACD at Windlesham. [1642]
June 7	ACD at Windlesham. [884]

1930

June 8	Death of Patrick Stewart Leckie in a nursing home at Folkestone, Kent [1643] brother of Jean Leckie, following a fall down a flight of stairs at the Royal Pavilion Hotel, Folkestone, Kent. [812]
June 10	The inquest into the death of Patrick Stewart Leckie returned the verdict of death from a fractured skull. He died at a Folkestone Nursing Home in Kent following a fall downstairs at a Folkestone Hotel [813] ACD gave evidence. [2044,2059]
June 12	Funeral of Patrick Stewart Leckie at the Municipal Cemetery, Tunbridge Wells, Kent [1643], principal mourners were Mr J.B. Leckie, Lady Conan Doyle, Mrs Forbes, Mr Richard Leckie, Miss Leckie, Mr J.B. Forbes, Denis & Adrian Conan Doyle, ACD was unable to attend due to his health. [926]
June 17	ACD, Jean and Denis attended the wedding of Miss Jean Lindsey Cowan and Mr John Barnes at Maresfield Parish Church, Maresfield, Sussex. [927]
June 18	ACD's criminological library, 115 books and pamphlets ranging in date from 1705 to the present day, were sold in one lot for £95 at Sotheby's London. [1644]
n.d.	ACD's last book *The Edge of the Unknown* published. [99,180,202] (*2)
June 24	*The Edge of the Unknown* published by John Murray, London. [6] (*2)
June 28	Adrian came fourth in the 1500cc racing car event in the Frazer Nash ('The Slug') at Lewes Speed Trials. [134]
July 1	ACD made a speech while leading a deputation to the Home Secretary in the cause of spiritualism. [1,2,6,14,15,202,215,238]
July 1	Adrian came third in his Frazer Nash in a hill climb competition [928,2060] in connection with the Brighton Motor Rally and Gala Week. [1097]
July	ACD resigned as President of the London Spiritualist Alliance a few days before his death. [239]
July 4	ACD at Windlesham. [18]
July 6	ACD suffered a heart attack. [14]
July 7	Death of ACD at Windlesham at 08:17hrs [90] at 08:30hrs. [3,4,11,14,99] at 9:15hrs [202,2061] at 09:30hrs. [2,215] (*2)
July 7	Death of ACD at Windlesham. [1,7,15,68,124,180,200,203,1645] (*2)
July 8	Death of ACD at Windlesham. [20,15] (*6)
July 11	Garden funeral and burial at Windlesham, [1,3,7,15,99,215] the service was conducted by the Revd. Drayton Thomas and the Revd. Charles Cyril Angell [1,124,202] the chief mourners were Lady Conan Doyle, Adrian Conan Doyle, Jean (Lena)Conan Doyle, Mary Conan Doyle, Mrs Foley, Mrs Oldham, Miss Oldham, Mr John Doyle and Mr Francis Doyle, Denis Conan Doyle was unable to attend owing to indisposition [1646] Mr J.B. Leckie (father-in-law), Mrs L. Oldham & Mrs I. Foley (sisters), Mrs Forbes (sister-in-law), Mr & Mrs P. Foley (nephew & niece), Mr Leckie Forbes (nephew), Miss C. Oldham (niece), Miss Hollands (secretary) and Major A.H. Wood. The coffin plate read: "Sir Arthur Conan Doyle, M.D., LL.D born 22nd May 1859; died 7th July 1930. There is no death". [929]

The coffin arriving for the funeral service in the garden of Windlesham

Pallbearers with ACD's coffin approaching the grave.

Sir Arthur's writing hut and floral tributes prior to his funeral July 1930

Sir Arthur's writing hut, on the right hand side is the oaken grave marker.

Mourners at ACD's funeral

On the left is the original oak grave marker that was at Windlesham, Crowborough, ACD was buried in his garden, at a spot next to his writing hut under a copper beech behind Windlesham Cottage, this became known to the family as the Sanctum. [124,180] On the right is Jean Conan Doyles original oak grave marker that was also at Windlesham, Crowborough.

Other Dates Of Interest After The Death Of Sir Arthur Conan Doyle

1930

July 13	Memorial service organised by the Marylebone Spiritualist Association to ACD was held at the Albert Hall, London [124,180,215] with a congregation of eight thousand [6,14,20] six thousand [15,202,203], on the platform were Lady Conan Doyle, with a vacant chair on her right labelled "Sir Arthur Conan Doyle", Mr Denis Conan Doyle, Mr Adrian Conan Doyle, Miss Mary Conan Doyle, Miss Jean Conan Doyle, and Mrs Estelle Roberts. Mr George Craze presided [1647] some 10,000 people attended. [233]
August	*The Parish Magazine* published in *The Strand Magazine*. [6,194,195,196,198]
August 9	Jean was at Windlesham. [40]
August 16	*The Last Resource* published in *Liberty*. [198]
August 23	*The End of Devil Hawker* published in the *Saturday Evening Post*. [198]
September	*The Passing of Conan Doyle* by Greenhough Smith published in *The Strand Magazine*. [198]
September	*A Scandal in Bohemia* republished in *The Strand Magazine*. [6,194,195]
September 19	It was announced that the will of Mr Patrick Stewart Leckie who died on 8 June had been proved. In it he left his estate of the gross value of £45,829 with net personalty £45,056. He left £500 each to Denis, Malcolm & Jean (Lena) Conan Doyle and Major A.H. Wood with the residue of the property shared between his sisters Jean Conan Doyle & Sara Mildred Forbes. [930]
September 20	Adrian raced the Frazer Nash ('The Slug') at the Lewes Speed Trials coming second in the 1500cc, 2000cc and the unlimited classes. [134]
September 20	Jean was in Southampton. [931]
October	*Some Letters of Conan Doyle* published in *The Strand Magazine*. [194,195,196,198]
October 18	Denis formally opened a new Christian Spiritualist Church at Philadelphia, Co. Durham. [1648] (*2)
October 19	Denis formally opened a new Christian Spiritual Church at Philadelphia, County Durham, he deputised for his mother who was unable to attend owing to illness. [932] (*2)
November	*The End of Devil Hawker* published in *The Strand Magazine*. [6,99,194,195,196,198]
November 3	Death of Clara Doyle, widow of Innes Doyle, at Holywell, Cliff Road, Eastbourne, Sussex. [68,124,200]
December	*The Last Resource* published in *The Strand Magazine*. [6,194,195,196,198]
December 2	Denis Conan Doyle attended the annual Police and Observer Corps Ball held at the Drill Hall, Horsham. [2043]
December	Denis Conan Doyle attended the Cambridge University Quinquaginta Dance Club Ball held at the Masonic Hall, Cambridge. [1829]
December 15	Jean was elected vice-president of the Crowborough & District Cricket League at the annual general meeting held at the Railway Hotel, Jarvis Brook, Crowborough. [933]

1931

January 11	Lady Conan Doyle and Denis attended a meeting of spiritualist at the Fortune Theatre, London. [934]
January 18	Denis presided at a spiritualist meeting at the Fortune Theatre, London, he introduced Mrs Meurig Morris as "a connecting box between two worlds speaking through her guide 'Power'". [758]
February 9	Denis was among the guests of honour at a dinner given by the Psychical Research Circle at the Lyceum Club, London. [935]
February 19	Denis gave a lecture "Spiritualism" at Albert Road Co-operative Hall, Southsea. [1070]
February	Jean donated £20 for the Conan Doyle Room at Portsmouth Hostel for Boys. [1071]

1931

February 21	At the speed trials of the Cambridge University Automobile Club at Branches Park near Newmarket, Denis finished third in the 1500cc class driving the 1496cc 'Slug' Frazer Nash. [250]
February 28	Denis addressed a large meeting at the Dome, Brighton under the auspices of Brighton Spiritualist Church, Jean sat by her son on the platform but did not address the meeting. [936]
May 2	At the Lewes Speed Trials held on the Race Hill, Lewes, Adrian came third in the racing cars up to 2000cc in his Frazer Nash 1496cc [848] he also race the 6-litre Nazzaro but was unplaced. [134]
May 13	Probate granted on the Will of ACD [date from copy of the Will] probate granted on the Will of ACD. [1649]
May 26	Denis spoke for the case of spiritualism held at Horam Road Men's Christian Society (YMCA), Horam, Sussex. [849]
May 26	At Lewes Police Court Adrian was summoned for using an unlicensed motor car on the highway on 2 May, he was fined 5 shillings. [850]
May/June	The oak grave marker was erected over ACD's grave. [2062]
June 8	It was announced that Adrian had become engaged to Miss Margaret Bridges of Belleisle, County Fermanach (now Fermanagh), Ireland. [759]
June 16	Branford Bryan Angell sailed on board the *Port Caroline* from the Port of London for Australia [242] he was listed as a wool merchant leaving for Melbourne, his last address given was the Strand Palace Hotel, London. [1837]
June 27	Denis driving the Austro-Daimler won the unlimited super sports car event. Adrian driving the Frazer Nash won the 1500cc & the unlimited racing group (the fastest time of the day) at the Lewes Speed Trials, Sussex [134]; Denis won the Super Sports Car Unlimited Group in a T.T. Austro-Daimler 2933cc and came third in the Handicap Class in the T.T. Austro-Daimler 2993cc. Adrian won the Racing Car 1500cc Group the Racing Car Unlimited Group in the Frazer Nash 'Slug' 1496cc, he was presented with the Normanhurst Challenge Cup and Replica for the fastest time in the racing classes for members only. [851]
July 17	Denis raced his 3-litre Austro Daimler at Skegness Sand Races [963], Adrian driving the Frazer-Nash, 'The Slug 1', came second in the Racing or Sports Car up to 2 litres, Denis driving the 3-litre Austro-Daimler came third in the Sports Cars-Unlimited Class, he also came second in the Unlimited Sports (four lap scratch) race in the 3-litre Austro-Daimler. [995]
July 25	Adrian raced his Frazer Nash ('The Slug') at Brooklands. [963]
August 11	Denis and Adrian crashed their car in the Banbury Road, Oxford, there were no injuries. [760]
September	Denis attended and spoke at the World Congress of Spiritualism at The Hague. [2063]
September 19	Adrian raced his Frazer Nash ('The Slug') at the Lewes speed trials, he was unplaced. [963]
October 8	Jean and her sons, Adrian and Denis, attended the wedding of Mr G.H. Ferguson and Miss Gower at St. James's, Spanish Place [1650], Jean with sons Denis & Adrian and daughter Jean attended the wedding of Mr George Hamilton Ferguson and Dorothy Vaughan Gower at St. James' Church, Spanish Place, London and the reception at the Park Lane Hotel, London. [937]
October 24	Conan Doyle [possibly Jean (Lena)] played hockey for Tunbridge Wells Ladies (Nevill) "A" team against Hamilton House at the Nevill Ground, Tunbridge Wells, the result was a draw. [949]
November 17	Denis gave a talk on spiritualism at the Union Church Young Peoples Society, Heathfield, Sussex; he was accompanied by his brother Adrian. [852]
November 21	Conan Doyle [possibly Jean (Lena)] played hockey for Tunbridge Wells against Old Palace, Mayfield at Mayfield, Tunbridge Wells won 6-2. [950]
December 7	Conan Doyle [possibly Jean (Lena)] played hockey for Tunbridge Wells against Uckfield at Uckfield, Tunbridge Wells won 7-2. [951]

1932

n.d.	Early 1932 the Psychic Bookshop, Library and Museum closed. [241]
January 9	Conan Doyle [possibly Jean (Lena)] played hockey for Tunbridge Wells (Nevill) against Tonbridge at the Nevill Ground, Tunbridge Wells, Tonbridge won 2-0. [952]
January 14	Denis attended the funeral of Sir Henry Cowan at Maresfield Parish Church, Maresfield, Sussex, Jean sent a floral tribute but did not attend. [853]
February 6	Conan Doyle [possibly Jean (Lena)] played hockey for Tunbridge Wells (Nevill) against Sevenoaks at the Nevill Ground, Tunbridge Wells, Tunbridge Wells won 2-1. [953]
February 22	Conan Doyle [possibly Jean (Lena)] played hockey for Tunbridge Wells (Nevill) against Uckfield at the Nevill Ground, Tunbridge Wells won 3-1. [954]
March 17	Conan Doyle [possibly Jean (Lena)] played hockey for Tunbridge Wells (Nevill) against Benenden, Tunbridge Wells won 6-1 and Conan Doyle scored a goal. [955]
March	Adrian took part in the Varsity Hill Club Climb held by Oxford and Cambridge clubs on the Eynsham-By-Pass, a new road not fully completed, he was unplaced in the Super Sports Unlimited Class driving the Austro-Daimler. [998]
March 23	Jean visited the Great Hall Cinema, Tunbridge Wells to see *The Hound of the Baskervilles* film starring Robert Rendel as Sherlock Holmes. [938]
April 11	Jean was among the witnesses in libel action brought by Mrs Louisa Ann Meurig Morris, a Spiritualist medium, against Associated Newspapers Ltd [761], witness at the King's Bench Division. [1072]
May 2	Sir Gilbert Parker spoke at the unveiling of a tablet to the memory of Sir Arthur Conan Doyle in the library of the Authors' Club, Whitehall Court, London, Lord Gorell, chairman of the Authors' Club performed the unveiling. [762,1972]
June 18	Denis driving the Mercedes Benz SSK won the unlimited super sports car group at the Lewes Speed Trials, Sussex [134] and Adrian came third in the Racing Cars up to 1500cc in the Frazer Nash ('The Slug') and second in the Racing Cars up to 2000cc in the Frazer Nash ('The Slug'). [854]
June 25	Denis driving a Mercedes Benz in the 3 mile unlimited race at Birkdale Sands, Southport. [1163]
July 11	Colonel F.A. Wilson, a member of the British College of Psychic Science, collapsed and died during a talk at the Fortune Theatre, London, Lady Conan Doyle was in the audience. [763]
July 19	Death of Revd. Dr John Lamond in London, he was a prominent member of the Society for Psychical Research and wrote *Arthur Conan Doyle: A Memoir* that was published in 1931 by John Murray. [764]
August 1	Denis & Adrian attended an evening dance at the Village Hall, Maresfield held by Mr & Mrs Cowan. [855]
August 13	Denis was unplaced in the 100 mile handicap in the Mercedes Benz at Birkdale Sands, Southport. [1163]
September	Death of John Lamb aged 80, he served as a steward on the *Hope*, ACD was a surgeon on the *Hope* in 1880. [1651]
October 29	Conan Doyle [possibly Jean (Lena)] played hockey for Tunbridge Wells (Nevill) "A" team against St. Clair at the Nevill Ground, Tunbridge Wells, Tunbridge Wells won 7-2 and Conan Doyle scored a goal. [956]
October	The Finance Committee and the Roads Works and Drainage Committee, Portsmouth named a road commemorating ACD, Doyle Avenue. [1073]
October 29	Adrian raced at Brooklands. [967]
November	Denis spoke about spiritualism at a Wigan meeting under the auspices of the Youth and Survival League. [939]
November 5	Conan Doyle [possibly Jean (Lena)] played hockey for Tunbridge Wells (Nevill) against Worthing at the Nevill Ground, Worthing won 8-5 and Conan Doyle scored a goal. [957]

1932

November 10	Conan Doyle [possibly Jean (Lena)] played hockey for Tunbridge Wells (Nevill) against Pilgrims, Pilgrims won 5-4 and Conan Doyle scored a goal. [958]
December 8	William Latter, chauffeur for Lady Conan Doyle, was driving a car belonging to Jean was involved in a minor collision with a car owned by Major Gus Larnach-Nevill and driven by Mr Pullen [940] it appears that Mr Pullen skidded on ice near the Blue Anchor, Beacon Road, Crowborough into the back of Jean's car. [941]
December 19	The funeral of Mr George Pentecost took place at the Forest Fold Chapel, Lady Conan Doyle did not attend but sent a floral tribute. [1098]

1933

n.d.	Birth of Peter Foley son of Percy (Michael) and Barbara Foley. [124]
February 6	Conan Doyle [possibly Jean (Lena)] played hockey for Tunbridge Wells against Hildenborough at the Nevill Ground, Tunbridge Wells, Tunbridge Wells won 7-1 and Conan Doyle scored 2 goals. [959]
February 16	Conan Doyle [possibly Jean (Lena)] played hockey for Tunbridge Wells against Oxted at the Nevill Ground, Tunbridge Wells, Tunbridge Wells won 9-1 and Conan Doyle scored a goal. [960]
February 25	It was reported that Lady Conan Doyle was staying at the Empire Hotel, Bath. [765]
March 8	Death of The Right Reverend Monsignor Richard Barry-Doyle. [69]
May 2	Denis attended a cocktail party in aid of Disabled Officers' Garden Homes at Mulberry House, Smith Square. [1652]
May 9	Denis attended the annual dinner of the British Homoeopathic Association at the Grosvenor House, London. [1653]
May 13	Denis driving the Mercedes Benz SSK won the unlimited super sports car group at the Lewes Speed Trials, Sussex [134,856]
June 20	Jean was at Windlesham. [40]
June 23	Jean was at Windlesham. [40]
June 24	Denis took part in the Unlimited Super Sports Car Race in the Mercedes-Benz and came third, the event was held by the Kent & Sussex Light Car Club at the Race Hill, Lewes, Sussex. [999]
August 12	The Southport Motor Racing Club held a race meeting at Birkdale Sands, Southport. In the Southport 100 mile race Adrian raced the 1,993cc Delage 8, he retired after 3 laps with an engine problem; Denis raced the 6,740cc Mercedes-Benz S., he retired after 28 laps owing to a burst tyre. [996]
September 9	Denis came second in the Super Sports Car Group in the Mercedes Benz at Lewes Speed Trials. [857]
November 4	Conan Doyle [possibly Jean (Lena)] played hockey for Tunbridge Wells Nevill Ladies XI against Old Palace, Mayfield at Mayfield, Old Palace won 6-0. [961]
n.d.	Death of Branford Bryan Angell son of Charles and Bryan Mary (Dodo) Angell. [202] (*3)
November 20	Death of Branford Bryan Angell son of Charles and Bryan Mary (Dodo) Angell, committed suicide by jumping off Sydney Harbour Bridge, Australia. [136,200,1654] (*3)

1934

n.d.	*The Field Bazaar* privately printed by The Athenaeum Press, limited to 100 copies. [6]
January 20	Conan Doyle [possibly Jean (Lena)] played hockey for Tunbridge Wells (Nevill) against Worthing at Worthing, Worthing won 6-1. [962]
March 2	It was announced that the manuscripts of *The Speckled Band* and *The Golden Pince-Nez* were due to be sold at auction at Sotheby's, London on 26-27 March. [1655]

1934

March 9	It was reported that L.G. Stanger-Leathes, proprietor of a private hotel, Undershaw, had filed for bankruptcy at Guildford Court. [1791]
April 11	Adrian attended a reception at the Café Royal. [1656]
April 28	At a séance held by Noah Zerdin at the Aeolian Hall, New Bond Street, London before a capacity audience of 560, ACD was one of 44 people heard speaking from the 'other side'. [789]
May 2	It was announced that Undershaw would be sold at auction on 31 May. [1192] {Note: no further details of the sale located. It appears that it was sold and continued as a hotel, advertising as such until 2005.}
May 25	Under the auspices of the Cosham Spiritualist Church, Denis gave a lecture "A Talk on Survival" at the Trades' Hall, Southampton Road, Cosham. [1074]
August	Denis driving the Mercedes-Benz raced at Skerries Circuit near Dublin, Ireland but was unplaced, the meeting was held by the Leinster Motor Cycle and Car Club. [1000]

1935

n.d.	Adrian and Denis purchased a second Mercedes-Benz similar to the SSK. [124]
January 14	Death of Herbert Greenhough Smith. [1657]
January 21	Jean and son Denis attended the funeral of Lady Caillard at The Belfry, West Halkin Street, London and then at the Golders Green Crematorium. [766]
January 28	Lady Conan Doyle at Windlesham. [767]
January 29	Death of Walter Paget aged 72. [1658]
April 11	Jean was at Windlesham. [942]
April 16	Adrian appeared at Clerkenwell court for exceeding the 30 mile an hour speed limit. [768]
August 9	Denis attended the funeral of Lady Winifrede Cowan at Maresfield Parish Church, Maresfield, Sussex, Denis, Adrian and Jean (Lena) sent a wreath as did Lady Conan Doyle. [858]
December 8	Denis lectured on "The After Life" held at the Regent Theatre, Chelmsford under the auspices of the Chelmsford Spiritualists' Society. [769]

1936

n.d.	Denis purchased a 1936 Mercedes-Benz 500K Special Roadster for Princess Mdivani. [201]
January	Denis at Windlesham. [1659]
February 18	Lady Conan Doyle was ill at Windlesham after undergoing two major operations in the past week for internal trouble. [1660]
February 28	Lady Conan Doyle still unwell. [1661]
March 8	The health of Lady Conan Doyle was fairly satisfactory. [1662]
April 25	Adrian came fifth in the 50 mile handicap at Southport Motor Club's first speed meeting of the season driving the Mercedes Benz owned by Princess Nina Mdivani who was a spectator, Denis won the straight mile for cars up to 1,500cc in the Mercedes-Benz S.S.K. [992]
April 26	Death of Arthur Twidle aged 71. [1663]
June 4	The engagement was announced of Denis Percy Stewart Conan Doyle and Princess Nina Mdivani, daughter of the late Highness Prince Zachary Mdivani and Princess Elizabeth Mdivani. [1664]
June 17	Death of James Blythe Leckie in his 94th year at Monkstown, Crowborough, father of Jean Leckie. [1665]
June	Adrian drove the Bugatti at Bangor in the County Down Trophy Race and was placed seventh. [1001] (*2)
June 20	Adrian drove the Bugatti at Bangor in the County Down Trophy Race and was placed seventh. [1986] (*2)

1936

June 22	James Blythe Leckie was buried at the Borough Cemetery, Tunbridge Wells, chief mourners were Mr P. Leckie Forbes & Mr John Doyle (grandsons), Miss Jean Conan Doyle (granddaughter), floral tributes were sent by Lady Conan Doyle, Denis & Adrian. [943]
July 2	It was announced that Adrian had become engaged to Miss Rita Cooper, the popular West End musical comedy actress, from Skegness. [770]
July 18	Competing in the Leinster Trophy car race near Dublin Denis crashed his Mercedes Benz, Adrian stopped his Bugatti to help Denis whose head & chest were injured. The fiancées of the two men, Princess Nina Mdivani and Miss Rita Cooper were sheltering in a tent owing to heavy rain. [944]
August 8	Denis raced the 1½ litre Bugatti at a meeting of Southport Motor Racing Club at Birkdale Sands, Southport in the straight mile car race and came second, he also raced in the 100 mile race but retired with an engine problem. [997]
August 18	Denis married Princess Nina Mdivani [68,200] at the Register Office, Bridgend, Glamorgan. [124,1666] (*2)
August 18	Denis married Princess Nina Mdivani, they motored from St. Donat's Castle, Glamorgan, the ceremony took place at Bridgend Registry Office [771], and the witnesses included Adrian Conan Doyle, Miss Jean Conan Doyle and the Marquis de Amodio. [772] (*2)
August 20	Adrian entered the Bugatti owned by Princess Mdivani, in the Junior Car Club International 200 miles race to be held at Donnington on 29 August [1667]. The race did take place, but it appears that Adrian did not arrive to take part in the race. [214]
August 21	It was reported that Lady Conan Doyle was staying in Cliftonville, Kent for a few days. [945]
August 29	Adrian entered the Bugatti in The Junior Car Club ninth 200-mile run off at Donington Park; he did not compete owing to gear-box and timing problems with the car. [1002]
September	Adrian took part in the Southport Sand-Racing Club Meeting held on Southport Sands, he won the 1½ litre straight mile in the Bugatti. [1003]
November	Jean was among the subscribers to the fund for a new vicarage at the Parish Church, Jarvis Brook. [1099]
December	Denis donated £3:3s to the King George V National Memorial Fund. [1668]

1937

January 6	Denis and his wife Nina sailed from Southampton on board the *Aquitania* for America. [96]
January 13	Denis and his wife Nina arrived in New York. [1816] (*2)
January 14	Denis and his wife Nina arrived in New York. [96] (*2)
May 12	Anna Charlotte Andersen (future wife of Adrian) visited London to see the coronation of King George VI, in the evening she went to a party where she met Adrian for the first time. It is said that Adrian proposed to her a few days after the party. [1181]
May 15	Adrian entered the GP Delage in the XII Grand Prix Des Frontiéres at Chimay, Belgium but did not race. [993]
May 22	Miss Rita Cooper, the actress and fiancée of Adrian was rushed to St. Pancras, London after being taken ill. [946]
May 30	Adrian entered the Avus Grand Prix in Berlin but did not compete as his car was not ready [1669], he entered the GP Delage in the VI Internationales Avus Rennen at Berlin, Germany but did not race. [993]
June 7	Denis and Nina attended a cocktail party at the Dorchester, London. [1670]
June 19	Adrian driving a Bugatti finished fourth in the Ulster Trophy held at Ballyclare, Antrim, Northern Ireland [105] driving a 1497 Bugatti S [277] he won a replica trophy and £10. [1975]
June 27	Adrian entered the GP Delage in the XIII Grand Prix De Picardie at Peronne, France but did not race. [993]

1937

July 1	Death of Jane Adelaide Rose (Ida) Foley [203] died at The Horns, Hankham, Westham, Sussex, widow of Nelson Foley. [68,124,200,1671] (*2)
July 5	Jane Adelaide Rose (Ida) Foley buried at St. Mary's Church, Westham, Pevensey, Sussex [1671], the Revd. H. Graham officiated and the Revd. H. Angel read the lesson; among the mourners were Major & Mrs Foley (son & daughter-in-law), Mr Innes Foley (son), Mr Nelson Foley (step-brother), Mr John Doyle & Mr Francis Doyle (nephews) and Miss Doyle. [859]
July 17	Adrian raced the Bugatti in the International Leinster Trophy and came tenth. [1987]
September 30	Death of Charles Cyril Angell. [68,124,200]

1938

May 23	Adrian married Anna Charlotte Andersen [68,200] at All Saints Church, Minstead, Hampshire [124], the Revd. H. Horton officiated; the bride was given away by Mr Innes Foley (cousin of the bridegroom), Denis was best man, the reception was held at Cuffnells, Lyndhurst. Jean, Jean (Lena), Mary, Francis Doyle, Mrs Innes Foley and Marquis Julio de Amodio attended. [947]
May 25	Adrian and Anna left England for a 3-month honeymoon in the Cameroons. [1181]
n.d.	Mary Conan Doyle playing the piano with Ambrose John playing the violin won a medal at the Twickenham and Richmond Music Festival, they came first in the section for violin and piano. [124]
August 12	It was announced that four hairy frogs were on show at London Zoo; Adrian had brought them back from Africa where he had been on honeymoon. [773]
September	Jean sent a cheque to the Billiards Association to buy new billiard balls and cues to be chosen by the Association. [1100]
n.d.	Jean (Lena) joined the Royal Air Force. [203]
September	Jean (Lena) joined up as a driver in the ATS RAF Company. [124]
September	Jean (Lena) joined No. 46 (County of Sussex) ATS, RAF Company, enlisting as aircraftswoman, second class. [193,1193]
October 26	Tiko, the pet python of Adrian disappeared from the Chelsea flat where Adrian was living. [1672]
October 31	Tiko, the pet python of Adrian was found hiding in the chimney of the Chelsea flat. [1672]

1939

n.d.	Death of Jane Adelaide Rose (Ida) Foley. [202] (*2)
July 21	An advert for sale was published, a '1937 Fiat 6.7H.P. Convertible Coupe, grey, red upholstery, exceptionally good engine; £60 – A. Conan Doyle, Windlesham, Crowborough.' [1101]
October 1	Denis & Nina arrived in New York on board the *Saturnia* sailing from Genova. [96]
October 10	Frederick Thomas Holden, houseman, formerly employed at Windlesham, was charged with stealing a gold cigarette case marked "A.A." in one corner and also one sovereign, both the property of Mrs Anna Conan Doyle. He was bound over for one year under the care of the Probation Officer. [774]

1940

March	Jean (Lena) was commissioned in the Woman's Auxiliary Air Force (the predecessor of the Women's Royal Air Force) as Assistant Section Officer. [1193]
April 3	Miss J.L.A. Conan Doyle appointed Assistant Section Officer in the Womans Auxiliary Air Force. [1673]
June 17	Lady Conan Doyle moved from Windlesham. [42]
n.d.	Death of Lady Conan Doyle. [202,203]

1940

June 27	Death of Lady Conan Doyle [6,68,124,180,200] at 20 Devonshire Place, London, (certified copy of an entry of death) at The London Clinic. [1674]
July 1	Funeral of Lady Conan Doyle at Windlesham [1675] she was buried beside ACD at Windlesham [124], the Revd. Maurice Eliot officiated, those present included Mr & Mrs Adrian Conan Doyle (son & daughter-in-law), Miss Jean Conan Doyle (daughter), Miss Mary Conan Doyle (step daughter), Mr E.J. Goacher (head gardener at Windlesham & Mrs Goacher, Mr W. Latter (chauffeur), & Mrs Latter and Mr B. Jacques (former employee). Denis was with his wife in San Francisco and latterly been in poor health did not attend. [948]
August 22	Death of Sir Oliver Lodge aged 89. [1676]

1941

n.d.	Windlesham was requisitioned for the war effort. [124]
April 19	Death of Major Alfred Herbert Wood one time secretary to ACD [107,109,235] died at the Royal Pier Hotel, Sussex Terrace, Southsea. [107]
April 23	The Funeral service of Major Alfred Herbert Wood was held at St. James's Church, Southsea followed by his interment at Highland Road Cemetery, Southsea [107], the funeral service was held at St. Jude's Church, Southsea. [1075]
April 28	The will of Lady Conan Doyle was published [6] she left £39,896 net, gross value £47,302. [1677]
n.d.	Death of Caroline (Lottie) Mary Burton (Doyle) Oldham. [202]
May 3	Death of Caroline (Lottie) Mary Burton (Doyle) Oldham, [203] died at The Wickham Nursing Home, Lewes, Sussex. [68,124,200]

1942

January	Between January 25 and February 5 Denis Conan Doyle lectured "Will This War End Christianity" at Barrington Town-Warming Lectures, Barrington, Illinois, USA. [810]
February 1	Jean Conan Doyle was promoted from Section Officer to temporary Flight Officer in the WAAF. [1182]
n.d.	Death of Francis Kingsley Doyle (son of Innes Doyle). [202] (*2)
May 30	Death of Francis Kingsley Doyle, (son of Innes Doyle) [16] killed in action of during the night of 29/30 May [68,124,200], Flying Officer Francis Kingsley Doyle. [213] (*2)
December 17	Death of Peter McKenzie aged 88; he was a whaler on board the *Hope* at the same time that ACD was on the voyage. [775]

1943

July 7	Adrian called up for service in the Royal Navy as an ordinary seaman on HMS *Collingwood*. [124]
October 13	Adrian released from the navy on compassionate grounds for five months. [124]
n.d.	Jean Conan Doyle served throughout the Second World War in various postings in England and Northern Ireland from 1943-1945. [1193]

1944

March	Adrian served with the navy from March 12 until April 25, and then discharged. [124]
May 23	Miss Conan Doyle took part in the annual meeting of the Church of Ireland Moral Welfare Association at the Clarence Place Manor Hall, Belfast. [1988]
July 1	Jean Conan Doyle was promoted to temporary Squadron Officer in the WAAF. [1183]

1945

May 7 — It was announced that Squadron Officer Conan Doyle, W.A.A.F. Staff Officer, Northern Ireland would take the salute of the march past of the Girls Training Corps at the City Hall, Belfast on 13 May. [1989] {Note: no further reports of this event have been located.}

1946

June 24/25/26 — A three day auction of surplus, superior furniture and effects at Windlesham these were auctioned by order of the Executors of the late Sir Arthur Conan Doyle. [148]

1947

June 19 — Jean Conan Doyle, Acting Wing Officer, was granted a short-service commission as a Flight Officer in the WAAF, G Branch, with seniority from 26 September 1943. [1184,1185]

July — ACD manuscript found in vault of Crowborough Westminster Bank as Denis was searching for other documents. This was the one-act play titled *The Crown Diamond*, which had been placed in the bank in 1922. [6,31]

n.d. — Jean Conan Doyle was a W.R.A.F. Staff Officer at H.Q. British Air Forces of Occupation, Germany. [1678]

n.d. — Jean Conan Doyle joined the British forces of occupation at Buckeburg air headquarters. [1193]

July — Jean Conan Doyle was Wing-Officer and left her Staff Officer's post at 28 Group H.Q. for Germany. [776]

July 12 — It was reported in *The Times* that several writings of ACD had been found among manuscripts in a cardboard hatbox, which ACD had placed in a bank at Crowborough in 1922. The manuscripts included a one-act play titled *The Crown Diamond*, plus other papers. [1679]

August 15 — It was reported that Adrian was selling at £475 his 1938 model Austin Ten (registered October 1937), owner and chauffeur driven only. [777]

October 3 — It was announced that the remaining furniture and effects of Windlesham were to be sold by auction at Windlesham on 17 October on the instructions of Denis. [860]

1948

n.d. — Acting Wing Officer Jean L.A. Conan Doyle appointed an OBE (Military Division) in the 1948 New Years Honours List. [1186,1193,1680]

n.d. — Death of William (Bill) Foley son of Percy (Michael) and Barbara Foley. [124]

January 3 — Death of Oscar Slater aged 75. [90] (*3)

January 31 — Death of Oscar Slater aged 76. [91,1681] (*3)

February 3 — Death of Oscar Slater aged 75. [18] (*3)

March — It was announced that Adrian would be selling a collection of mediaeval locks that he inherited from his father, the collection would be sold at Sotheby's, London. [778]

March 9 — It was announced that Adrian M. Conan would be selling a collection of armour and weapons at Sotheby & Co., London on 12 March. [1981] {Note: no report of the sale have been located.}

December 20 — Wing Officer J.L.A. Conan Doyle OBE promoted to Acting Group Officer. [1682]

December — Late December or early January Adrian had taken up residence in Tangier. [124]

1949

n.d. — Jean Conan Doyle received the AE (Air Efficiency Award). [193,1193]

February 1 — Jean Conan Doyle was granted a permanent commission as a Wing Officer in the secretarial branch in the Woman's Royal Air Force (WRAF). [1187]

1949

April 22	A stone plaque in memory of Sir Arthur Conan Doyle was unveiled at 11 Picardy Place, Edinburgh, his birthplace. Major John Doyle, a nephew of ACD represented the family [1683] it was unveiled by Sir Andrew Murray; Lord Provost of Edinburgh. [779]
October 7	It was reported that Windlesham could become a hostel. [1104]

1950

February 6	Group Officer L.A. Conan Doyle promoted to Staff Officer at Headquarters, Technical Training Command. [1684]
October 22	Adrian and Anna sailed from Mahé, Seychelle Islands with F.A. Mitchell-Hedges for a two month expedition to the Indian Ocean in search of sea monsters. [780]
November 5	Jean was at the Officers' Mess, Royal Air Force, Brampton, Huntingdon. [1685]

1951

n.d.	Windlesham sold. [124]
February 12	The manuscripts of *The Casebook of Sherlock Holmes* in three quarto pages sold for £100 at Sotheby's, London. [1686]
March 15	Group Officer Conan Doyle from H.Q. Technical Training Command attended an exhibition of handiwork by airmen and airwomen of Melksham and six other stations in No. 24 Group, the exhibition was held at R.A.F. Station, Melksham, Wiltshire. [2009]
May 21	Jean and Denis opened The Sherlock Holmes Exhibition at Abbey House, Baker Street, London, Mary also attended. [124,1687]
July 13	It was announced that Windlesham would be sold at auction in July 20 at the sale to be held at The Castle Hotel, Tunbridge Wells, the house was listed as "containing 7 principle bedrooms, 2 dressing rooms, 5 bathrooms, 4 reception rooms, 5 staff rooms, usual offices. Mains services, central heating. The grounds extend in all to about 1 acre. The property is held on lease by the Ministry of Works at a rental of £500 per annum and offers a first class investment". [861]
October	Group Officer J.L.A. Conan Doyle was appointed as Deputy Director (Personnel) of The Woman's Royal Air Force. [1688]
October 29	Denis and Adrian were joint executors of the Conan Doyle estate. [124]
November 22	St. Marylebone Borough Council agreed to sell the reproduction of Sherlock Holmes room that was on display as a Festival of Britain Exhibition to Mrs Adrian Conan Doyle. [968]

1952

n.d.	*Heaven Has Claws* by Adrian Conan Doyle published. [124]
January 1	Jean Conan Doyle was promoted to Group Officer in WRAF. [1188]
February 19	Anna Conan Doyle sailed from Southampton on board the SS *America* for New York. [96]
February 20	Mrs Adrian Conan Doyle left Southampton on board the *America* for New York to supervise the arrangements for a tour extending over two years to be made by the Sherlock Holmes exhibition [1107], she was listed as a housewife aged 41; her last address in the UK was 18 Woburn Square, London, W.C.1. [137]
February 26	Anna Conan Doyle arrived in New York on board the SS *America*, her destination was the Biltmore Hotel, New York. [96]
March 12	Adrian on board the *America* left Southampton for New York, he was listed as an explorer aged 51; his last address in the UK was Flat 6, 56 Curzon Street, London, W.1. [137]
March 19	Adrian arrived in New York on board the SS *America*, his destination was the Gladstone Hotel, New York. [96]

1953

January 21	The ballet, *The Great Detective* performed at Sadler's Wells Theatre, London. [1689]
January 29	It was announced that Lieutenant-Colonel J.R.I. Doyle had become engaged to Miss Ann Ruml, the marriage will take place in Paris. John Reinhold Innes Doyle, the Kings Own Yorkshire Light Infantry, son of Brigadier-General and Mrs J.F.I.H. Doyle, Ann Ruml daughter of Mr and Mrs Beardsley Ruml of 213 East 62nd Street, New York City. [1690]
February 10	Denis and Nina were staying at the Trianon Palace Hotel, Versailles. [124]
April 18	John Doyle married Ann Ruml in Paris, Denis Conan Doyle was best man, and the reception was held at the Hotel Ritz. [124]
June 17	Death of George Edalji. [18,189]
November 22	Denis and Nina were staying at the Hotel Royal Danieli in Venice, both being rather unwell. [124]

1954

April 21	Group Officer J.L.A. Conan Doyle appointed an Inspector of The W.R.A.F. [1691]

1955

n.d.	Birth of Charles Foley son of Innes and Ruth Foley. [124]
n.d.	Birth of Catherine Ruml Doyle daughter of John and Ann Doyle. [202] (*2)
January 1	Birth of Catherine Ruml Doyle daughter of John and Ann Doyle. [124] (*2)
n.d.	Death of Denis Conan Doyle. [202,203] (*2)
March 9	Death of Denis Conan Doyle after a heart attack at a hotel near Mysore, aged forty-three [6,68,200,1692] aged forty-five. [16,124] (*2)
March 16	Adrian's address was 3 Quai Turrettini, Geneva, Switzerland. [1693]
n.d.	Windlesham was put up for sale. [202]
June	Windlesham estate sale announced. [6] (*3)
June 24	The sale of Windlesham was announced. [126] (*3)
June 25	Windlesham estate sale announced, Messrs. Charles J. Parris of Crowborough were the appointed agents for the sale of the property. [1694] (*3)
July	Exhumation of remains of ACD and Lady Conan Doyle from Crowborough. [6] (*2)
July 1	Exhumation of remains of ACD and Lady Jean Conan Doyle from Windlesham, Crowborough. [147] (*2)
July 7	The remains of Sir Arthur Conan Doyle and his second wife, Lady Conan Doyle, were reinterred at Minstead Church in the New Forest, [68,124,180,200] the Revd. T.R. Fraser Bowen conducted the burial service in the presence of Miss Mary Conan Doyle, daughter of ACD and his first wife, and Group Officer Jean Conan Doyle, W.R.A.F., daughter of ACD and his second wife. [135,1695]

1956

February 28	At the Royal Horticultural Society's Show a first class certificate was awarded to cymbidium "Windlesham variety. Memoria Denis Conan Doyle". Blush-Pink with crimson markings on lip, shown by McBean's Orchids Ltd. [1696]
March 26	It was announced that Group Officer J.L.A. Conan Doyle had been appointed Commanding Officer, R.A.F Station Hawkinge, Kent with effect from June 1. [1697]
April	Jean unveiled a plaque in Aston where ACD once lived, Mary also attended. [124] (*2)
April 14	Miss Jean Conan Doyle and Miss Mary Conan Doyle attended the unveiling of the plaque marking the house where ACD once lived at Clifton House, Aston Road North, Birmingham, the ceremony was performed by the Deputy Mayor, Alderman J.R. Balmer. [2075] (*2)
July	Windlesham still for sale. [1698]

1957

February 11	Group Officer J. Conan Doyle, C.O. R.A.F. Hawkinge, Kent presented the trophy and prizes at the Woman's Services Rifle match at Uxbridge. [1699]
March 9	A memorial service for Denis P.S. Conan Doyle was held at the British Embassy church in Paris. [1700]
May 30	Adrian raced the Ferrari 500 TRC at St. Etienne, France in the two hour race; he had an accident and did not finish the race. [994]
June 9	Adrian entered the Ferrari 500 TRC at the GP des Frontiéres, held at Chimay, Belgium, he did not race. [994]
August 11	Adrian entered the Ferrari 500 TRC at the GP Sverige, held at Kristianstad, Sweden, he did not race. [994]
September	Adrian claimed that Denis's estate owed him and his sister Jean $189,000. [202] (*3)

1958

April 27	Adrian raced the Ferrari 500 TRC at the GP Napoli held at Posillipo, Italy, he finished ninth. [994]
May 15	Adrian raced the Ferrari 500 TRC at Aspern, Austria, result unknown. [994]
July	*The Crown Diamond* privately printed by Baskerette Press, New York. [6]
October 8	Lawsuit by Adrian against Princess Mdivani, his sister in-in-law, for $189,000 (about £67,000 at the time). [1701] (*3)
October	Lawsuit by Adrian against his sister-in-law Nina Mdivani for £67,000. [6] (*3)

1959

February	Group Officer J.L.A. Conan Doyle was appointed Inspector of the Woman's Royal Air Force, a post that she held from April 1954 to June 1956. [1702]
May 20	Group Officer J. Conan Doyle attended a dinner at the Savoy Hotel, London held by the Sherlock Holmes Society of London. [1703]
May 21	A dinner in honour of the centenary of the birth of ACD was held at the Authors' Club, London. [1704]
June 26	Adrian at 3 Quai Turrettini, Geneva, Switzerland. [2053]
July 25	Adrian at 3 Quai Turrettini, Geneva, Switzerland. [2053]
December	Acquisition by the National Portrait Gallery of a painting of ACD. [6]

1960

March 23	It was announced that Group Officer J.L.A. Conan Doyle had been appointed Deputy Director, Woman's Royal Air Force with effect from April 1. [1705]
April 28	Adrian was sued by his sister-in-law, Mrs Nina Mdivani Harwood, for $40,300 (about £14,390 at the time). [1706]
November	*Tales of Love and Hate* by Adrian Conan Doyle published. [1707]

1962

April 3	It was announced that Group Officer Jean Conan Doyle was appointed Command W.R.A.F. Administrative Officer, Technical Training Command as from May 7. [1708]
November 14	It was announced that Group Officer Jean Conan Doyle was to become Director of the Woman's Royal Air Force, with the rank of Air Commandant. [1709]

1963

n.d.	Birth of Richard John Francis Doyle son of John Reinhold and Ann Doyle. [202] (*2)
January	*Strange Studies from Life* published by The Candlelight Press, New York. [6]
n.d.	Jean Conan Doyle who was appointed OBE in 1948 advanced to DBE in 1963. [193,1193]
n.d.	Jean Conan Doyle appointed as Director of the Woman's Royal Air Force with the rank of Air Commandant, DBE. [124,202]

1963

April 1	Jean Conan Doyle was promoted to Air Commandant, the highest rank in the WRAF. [1189,1193]
April 1	Air Commandant Jean Conan Doyle took up her duties as Director of the W.R.A.F. [1710]
April 26	The Duchess of Gloucester, Air Chief Commandant Woman's Royal Air Force, visited the Royal Air Force Station at Sopley; Air Commandant J.L.A. Conan Doyle was in attendance. [1711]
April 29	Jean Conan Doyle was appointed an honorary Aide-de-Camp to Queen Elizabeth II, serving until 1966. [1190,1193]
May	The Queen approved the appointment of Air Commandant Conan Doyle, W.R.A.F. as Honorary Aide-de-Camp to Her Majesty with effect from April 29 [1712]
n.d.	In the 1963 Birthday Honours, Jean Conan Doyle was elevated to Dame Commander of the British Empire (DBE, Military Division). [1191,1193]
n.d.	Death of Ann Doyle, wife of John Doyle. [124,200]
June 27	Death of Ann (Ruml) Doyle first wife of John Reinhold Innes Doyle. [1713]
October 26	The Director of the Woman's Royal Air Force, Air Commandant Dame Jean Conan Doyle welcomed the guests at the annual reunion of the Woman's Royal Air Force Officers' Association held at the Royal Aero and Lansdown Club, Fitzmaurice Place, London. [1714]
November	*Lone Dhow* by Adrian Conan Doyle published. [1715]
November 6	Air Commandant Dame Jean Conan Doyle, Director of the Woman's Royal Air Force, left by air for Singapore to visit W.R.A.F. units of the Far East Air Force, she was due to return on November 22. [1716]
December 12	Dame Jean Conan Doyle attended a dinner and dance held by the Danish Club at the Dorchester Hotel, London. [1717]

1964

January 1	The engagement was announced between John Reinhold Innes Doyle of 2 Queens Gate, London, SW7, son of Brigadier-General and Mrs J.F.I.H. Doyle and Angela, youngest daughter of Mr and Mrs G. Firmstone-Williams of 72 Cadogan Square, London, SW1. [1718]
February 7	Dame Jean Conan Doyle attended a reception at the Connaught Rooms, London. [1719]
February 28	Dame Jean Conan Doyle attended a dinner at the Officers' Mess, R.A.F. Uxbridge. [1720]
March 4	Air Commandant Dame Jean Conan Doyle attended a meeting of the Franco-British Society at 66 Portland Place, London. [1721]
March 20	John Doyle married Angela Firmstone-Williams [124] at Holy Trinity, Brompton. [1722]
July 22	Air Commandant Dame Jean Conan Doyle attended a garden party at Amport House, Andover. [1723]
October 30	Air Commandant Dame Jean Conan Doyle attended the annual reunion of the Woman's Royal Air Force Officer's Association held at the Royal Aero and Lansdowne Club. [1724]
December 7	Air Commandant Dame Jean Conan Doyle, Director of the W.R.A.F left Gatwick airport to visit the W.R.A.F. in Germany. [1725]
December 18	The manuscript of *The Adventure of the Greek Interpreter* sold for £4,500 at a sale at Christie's London. [1726]

1965

February 10	Dame Jean Conan Doyle attended the Memorial Service for Marshall of the R.A.F. Lord Trenchard in the Royal Air Force Chapel, Westminster Abbey, London. [1727]
February 19	Dame Jean Conan Doyle attended a dinner at the Officers' Mess, R.A.F. Uxbridge. [1728]

1965

May 12	Dame Jean Conan Doyle attended a reception on HMS *President*, London. [1729]
n.d.	Jean Conan Doyle married Air Vice-Marshall Sir Geoffrey Bromet. [202] (*2)
June 11	Jean Conan Doyle married Air Vice-Marshall Sir Geoffrey Bromet [68,200] (*2) at St. Clement Danes Church, Strand, London [16,124] the bride was given away by her brother Adrian Conan Doyle and Michael Pooley (grandson of the bridegroom) was best man. [1730]
August 3	Richard John Francis Doyle born, son of John and Angela Doyle. [3,124] (*2)
October 4	Dame Jean Conan Doyle attended the annual Woman of the Year Luncheon at the Savoy Hotel, London. [1731]
October 23	Dame Jean Conan Doyle attended and received the guests at the annual reunion of the W.R.A.F. Officers' Association held at the Royal Aero and Lansdown Club. [1732]
November 11	Dame Jean Conan Doyle attended a dinner given by the Air Force Board at Headquarters, Fighter Command, Bentley Priory. [1733]

1966

April 28	The manuscript of *The Lion's Mane* was sold at an auction held at Christie's, London. [1025]
May 11	Jean Conan Doyle retired from the WRAF. [1192,1193] (*2)

1967

July 21	Death of Basil Rathbone aged 75 in New York (b. 13 June 1892). [1734]

1968

n.d.	Jean Conan Doyle retired from the Royal Air Force. [203] (*2)
n.d.	Jean Conan Doyle was a governor of the Royal Star and Garter Home from 1968 until 1972. [193,1193]

1969

January 28	Mary Conan Doyle celebrated her eightieth birthday at Whitley Ridge, Brockenhurst, Hampshire. [124]
June	11 Picardy Place, Edinburgh was demolished. [124]

1970

n.d.	Jean Conan Doyle was a member of the council of the Officers' Pension Society from 1970 until 1975, she was vice-president from 1981 until 1988. [193,1193]
n.d.	Death of Adrian Conan Doyle. [202,203] (*3)
June	Death of Adrian Conan Doyle (his ashes were placed on the battlements at Lucens. [124] (*3)
June 3	Death of Adrian Conan Doyle [16,68,124,200,1817] aged 59. [1735] (*3)

1971

n.d.	Mrs Nina Harwood (Mdivani) took High Court action to prevent the sale by a Swiss trustee of literary, film and television rights. [6]

1972

April 21	The manuscript of *The Adventure of Black Peter* sold for $4,700 (£1,800) in New York. [1736]

1974

April 24	Air Commandant Dame Jean Conan Doyle attended the memorial service for Air Marshall Sir George Gun at St. Clement Danes, Strand. [1737]

1975

n.d.	Jean Conan Doyle was a member of the committee of the Not Forgotten Association from 1975 until 1991, she was president from 1981 until 1991. [193,1193]
February 21	Air Commandant Dame Jean Conan Doyle attended the service for Air Marshall Sir Walter Pretty at St. Clement Danes, Strand. [1738]
May 9	Air Commandant Dame Jean Conan Doyle the service for Air Chief Marshall Sir Donald Evans at St. Clement Danes, Strand. [1739]
May 27	Death of Angela (Firmstone-Williams) Doyle second wife of John Reinhold Innes Doyle. [1740]

1976

n.d.	Death of Percy Fitzgerald (Michael) Foley, son of Nelson and Jane (Ida) Foley. [124,202]
n.d.	Death of Mary Louise Conan Doyle. [203] (*2)
June 12	Death of Mary Louise Conan Doyle, eldest daughter of ACD [68,200] (*2) aged 87 [1741] aged eighty-seven and half [124] at 37 Copthall Gardens, Twickenham. [33]
June 16	Funeral of Mary Louise Conan Doyle at Southampton, Hampshire. [124]
November	Will of Mary Louise Conan Doyle published [6] £12,972 net. [1742]

1979

February 7	Jean at Home Green, Littlestone-on-Sea, New Romney, Kent. [2053]

1980

October 10	Air Commandant Dame Jean Conan Doyle attended a reception held at the Royal Air Force Club, London. [1743]

1981

April 29	The manuscript of *The Problem of Thor Bridge* sold for £13,000 at Christie's London. [1744]

1983

May 20	Death of Innes Cliffe Foley son of Nelson and Jane (Ida) Foley. [124]
August 2	Air Vice-Marshall Sir Geoffrey Bromet and Air Commandant Dame Jean Conan Doyle attended the annual garden party of "The Not-Forgotten" Association held in the grounds of Buckingham Palace. [1745]
November 16	Death of Sir Geoffrey Bromet, husband of Jean Conan Doyle, [68,124,200,202] aged 92 [1746] his ashes were buried at Minstead Church. [68]

1984

July 31	Air Commandant Dame Jean Conan Doyle attended the annual garden party of "The Not-Forgotten" Association held in the grounds of Buckingham Palace. [1747]
October 25	Dame Jean Conan Doyle attended a service of thanksgiving for the life of Lord Gore-Booth at St. Margaret's, Westminster. [1748]

1985

July 30	As the President of the "Not-Forgotten" Association, Air Commandant Dame Jean Conan Doyle attended the association's annual garden party in the grounds of Buckingham Palace. [1749]

1986

May 29	The manuscript of *A Regimental Scandal* was sold at an auction held at Christie's, London. [1026]

1986
July 22　　　Air Commandant Dame Jean Conan Doyle attended the annual garden party of "The Not-Forgotten" Association held in the grounds of Buckingham Palace. [1750]

1987
February 6　　Air Commandant Dame Jean Conan Doyle attended the memorial service for Air Marshall Sir Victor Goddard at St. Clement Danes, Strand, London. [969]

February 19　 Death of Nina Mdivani (Mrs Nina Harwood), widow of Denis Conan Doyle. [68,72,124,200] (*2) in Tiflis, Georgia (now known as Tbilisi). [964]

March　　　　Death of Nina Mdivani. [202] (*2)

March 3　　　Funeral of Nina Mdivani (Mrs Nina Harwood), widow of Denis Conan Doyle and Anthony Harwood held at Brampton Oratory, London followed by a private cremation. [964]

n.d.　　　　　Death of John Reinhold Innes Doyle son of Innes and Clara Doyle. [202] (*2)

May 2　　　　Death of John Reinhold Innes Doyle, son of Innes and Clara Doyle [16, 68,72,124,200] aged seventy-three. [124] (*2)

July 28　　　 As the President of "The Not-Forgotten" Association, Air Commandant Dame Jean Conan Doyle attended the association's annual garden party in the grounds of Buckingham Palace. [1751]

1988
August 2　　　Air Commandant Dame Jean Conan Doyle attended the annual "Not Forgotten" Association garden party held in the gardens of Buckingham Palace, London. [970]

1989
April 20　　　Air Commandant Dame Jean Conan Doyle attended a service of thanksgiving for the life and work of Field Marshall Lord Harding of Petherton at Westminster Abbey. [1752]

August 1　　　Air Commandant Dame Jean Conan Doyle attended the annual "Not Forgotten" Association garden party held in the gardens of Buckingham Palace, London. [971]

1990
n.d.　　　　　Death of Anna Conan Doyle widow of Adrian Conan Doyle. [202] (*3)

December　　 Death of Anna Charlotte Conan Doyle widow of Adrian Conan Doyle in Geneva. [68,124,200] (*3)

1991
January 23　　Death of Anna Conan Doyle widow of Adrian Conan Doyle in Geneva, (*3) her ashes were interred near those of Adrian on the battlements of Lucens Castle. [1181]

July 31　　　 Air Commandant Dame Jean Conan Doyle attended the annual "Not Forgotten" Association garden party held in the grounds of Buckingham Palace, London. [972]

September 24　Air Commandant Dame Jean Conan Doyle retired as Lady President of the "Not Forgotten" Association. [973]

1992
January 10　　Dame Jean Conan Doyle attended and was among other speakers at the 40th Anniversary Dinner of the Sherlock Holmes Society of London at the Langham Hilton Hotel, London. [974]

March 6　　　Air Commandant Dame Jean Conan Doyle attended a service of thanksgiving for the life of Sir Alasdair Steedman at St. Clement Danes. [1753]

1992

September 20 Dame Jean Conan Doyle, among many others, attended the Battle of Britain Service of Thanksgiving and Rededication at Westminster Abbey. [1776]

1993

March 3 Air Commandant Dame Jean Conan Doyle attended a service of thanksgiving for the life of Sir Hugh Wontner held at St. Clement Danes, Strand, London. [1754]

June 3 Air Commandant Dame Jean Conan Doyle attended a service of thanksgiving for the life of Marshall of the RAF, Lord Elworthy, KG at St. Clement Danes. [1755]

1994

May 22 Dame Jean Conan Doyle unveiled the plaque at 2 Upper Wimpole Street, London. [1756]

September 18 Dame Jean Conan Doyle, among many others, attended the Battle of Britain Service of Thanksgiving and Rededication at Westminster Abbey. [1777]

November 10 Air Commandant Dame Jean Conan Doyle attended a memorial service for Miss Anne Shelton at Corpus Christi, Covent Garden. [1757]

1995

November 29 Air Commandant Dame Jean Conan Doyle attended a memorial service for Mr Jeremy Brett at St. Martins-in-the Fields. [1758]

1996

February Death of Claire Oldham, daughter of Leslie and Caroline (Lottie) Oldham. [68,124,200]

1997

n.d. Death of Dame Jean Conan Doyle. [202,203] (*2)

November 18 Death of Dame Jean Conan Doyle (*2) aged almost eighty-five. [68,124,200,1759]

1998

January 17 Will of Dame Jean Conan Doyle published. [1760]

January 29 Memorial service for Dame Jean Conan Doyle held at St. Clement Danes, Strand, London. [1761]

A SERVICE
OF THANKSGIVING

for the Life of
DAME JEAN CONAN DOYLE, DBE, AE
1912 – 1997

ST CLEMENT DANES CHURCH
STRAND

Thursday, 29th January, 1998
12 noon

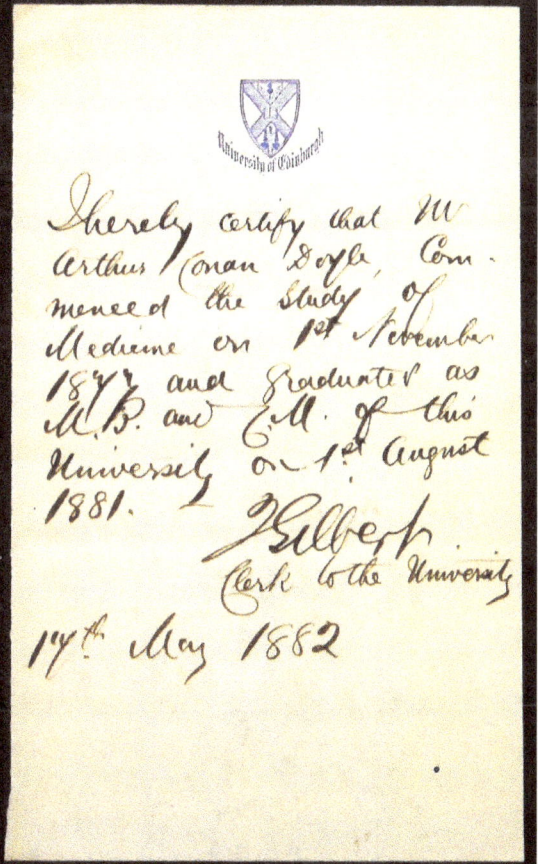

Arthur Conan Doyle graduating 1881 and certificate of graduation.

Arthur Conan Doyle leaving St. Giles Cathedral, Edinburgh after receiving the LL.D.
7 April 1905

Arthur Conan Doyle 1894

Family group at
Nielsen Park, Sydney. Australia, 1920

6th Royal Sussex Volunteer Regiment, 1914
Arthur Conan Doyle second from the left.

Arthur Conan Doyle with German observer (Count Carmer)
to his left during the Prince Henry Tour in 1911

Arthur Conan Doyle and his wife at log cabin in Jasper Park, 1914

Arthur Conan Doyle and family at Blue Mountains, Australia, 1921

Arthur Conan Doyle and his children, May 1922
Left to Right: Denis, ACD, Adrian and Lena Jean

Arthur Conan Doyle and family probably in USA

Arthur Conan Doyle and his wife in Stockholm, Sweden, 1929

Denis and Anna Andersen at their wedding

An Arctic Voyage in 1880

n.d.	ACD served in the capacity of surgeon for seven months on board the whaling ship *Hope* of Peterhead. [99,180] (*4)
February 27	ACD signed on as ship's surgeon on the Greenland whaler *Hope*. [144,202] (*4)
February 28	ACD set sail from Peterhead on board the Greenland whaler *Hope*. [99,144,202,215]
February 28	ACD served as ship's surgeon on the Greenland whaler *Hope* of Peterhead for seven months [2,7,10,14,15] (*4) February to September. [11,68,200]
February 28	ACD sailed at 2 o'clock on board the *Hope* for Shetland. [336]
March	ACD served as ship's surgeon on the Greenland whaler *Hope* of Peterhead for six months. [5] (*4)
February	ACD in Lerwick, Scotland. [203]
February 29	*Hope* arrived in Lerwick at 7:30p.m. [336] {Note: this entry in the Log is dated Sunday March 1, an error by ACD as 1880 was a leap year, so he arrived on Sunday 29 February.} (*2)
March 1	*Hope* in Lerwick harbour. [336]
March 2	*Hope* in Lerwick harbour. [336]
March 3	ACD and Captain Gray went ashore at Lerwick and enlisted the Shetland hands at George Reid Tait's, the draper, clothier and shipping agent. [336]
March 4	ACD went ashore at Lerwick went to the Queen's Hotel and the Commercial Hotel. [336]
March 5	ACD and Captain Gray went ashore for dinner with George Tait after playing billiards at the Queen's Hotel. [336]
March 6	ACD did nothing all day as it was raining and blowing hard. [336]
March 7	The engineer of the *Windward* had crushed his two forefingers yesterday, and ACD dressed them before breakfast. [336]
March 8	ACD went ashore with Captain Gray and watched a football match between Orkney and Shetland. They met the Captains of *Jan Mayen*, *Nova Zembla* and *Erik*; they all went to the Queen's Hotel after the match. [336]
March 8	ACD wrote a letter to his mother thanking her for her letters, parcels and updating her on his news. [336]
March 9	ACD arrived at Lerwick on board the *Hope* in the Shetland Islands. [202] (*2)
March 9	ACD went ashore with Captain Gray. [336]
March 10	A north wind prevented the *Hope* sailing, went ashore in the evening and played billiards. [336]
March 10	ACD left Lerwick on the Shetland Islands. [202,203] (*2)
March 11	*Hope* left Lerwick about one o'clock and came to anchorage about seven in a little inlet. [336] (*2)
March 12	*Hope* was still anchored owing to a high gale. [336]
March 13	*Hope* left its anchorage and set sail in high winds and heavy rain. [336]
March 14	*Hope* all day under steam and sail. [336]
March 15	*Hope* first under steam and sail, and then under sail alone. [336]
March 15	ACD sighted the first seal. [99] (*2)
March 16	*Hope* still under sail. [336]
March 16	ACD reached the ice. [203] (*2)
March 17	*Hope* under steam and first encountered ice (*2), ACD spent the morning up the crow's nest. [336]
March 18	*Hope* north of Jan Mayen, ACD and crew saw their first seal, a bladdernose. [336] (*2)
March 19	*Hope* travelling through thick haze and drizzle. [336]
March 20	About a couple of hundred seals visible from the crow's nest. [336] (*2)
March 20	ACD saw his first real pack of seals. [203] (*2)
March 21	*Hope* had to lay to all day owing to thick haze. [336]
March 22	The fog lasted all day so the *Hope* had to lay to. [336]
March 23	*Hope* under steam, blowing a gale all day. [336]

March 24	The crew of the *Hope* sighted an enormous pack of seals. [336]
March 25	*Hope* took up her position, mounting boats and cleaning guns. [336]
March 26	ACD saw the young seals suckling, hurt his hand boxing with Stewart, stuffed old Keith's tooth and cured young Keith's collywobbles. [336]
March 27	*Hope* was steaming a little, rifles were issued, Haggie Milne health improving. [336]
March 28	Haggie Milne taken ill again, ACD had dinner on board the *Eclipse*. [336]
March 29	Thick day with a driving snow. [336]
March 30	Nothing much doing, the *Windward* came alongside the *Hope* and Captain Murray came aboard, ACD sparred with Colin and Stewart. [336]
March 31	Very little doing all day, a heavy swell had set in. [336]
April 1	The swell continued and the *Hope* steamed for a while. [336]
April 2	The swell was still on. [336]
April 3	ACD took part in the first seal hunt. [99,202,203,215] (*2)
April 3	Hunting started on 3 April [202] (*2), during the hunting season ACD fell into the water and was then nicknamed 'the great northern diver' by Captain John Gray of the *Hope*, the total catch by the Hope was 2 Greenland whales and 3,614 seals, ACD own 'game bag' was 55 seals. [99,202]
April 3	The swell was still on, while getting over the ships side ACD, fell in the sea, he succeeded in killing a couple seals, and the crew took 760 seals. [336]
April 4	ACD was working on the pack ice all day and fell into the sea three times, the crew took about 460 seals. [366]
April 5	ACD working again, he fell into the sea yet again (*2), after he had killed a seal, the crew took about 400 seals. [336] {Note: this entry is dated Monday 6 April in the Log, but the 5 April was a Monday.}
April 5	ACD nearly lost his life when he fell from a large piece of ice. [203,215] (*2)
April 6	ACD shot an eleven-foot long sea elephant. [203]
April 6	ACD working on the pack ice, although he did not fall into the sea, the Captain called him "the Great Northern Diver." ACD shot two large bladdernoses, also called Sea Elephants. The crew took 270 young and 58 old seals. [336]
April 7	ACD off Jan Mayen's Island in the Arctic Circle. [203,215] (*2)
April 7	A poor day, very few seals about, only 133 taken. Crew member Andrew Haggie Milne seriously ill. [336]
April 8	The *Active* collected letters from the *Hope*, only about 30 seals taken, gale in the evening. [336]
April 9	The gale continued with a heavy swell, ACD did nothing but sleep and write up his log. [336]
April 10	Andrew Milne almost beyond help, gale and heavy swell continued. [336]
April 11	Andrew Milne died, about 60 seals were taken. [336]
April 12	Andrew Milne buried at sea, about 60 seals were taken. [336]
April 13	*Hope* had to lay to all day owing to the continuing gale, ACD did some fine boxing, no seals taken. [336]
April 14	About 80 seals taken, making the total to about 2450, ACD stood at the forecastle all day reporting progress. [336]
April 15	Beautiful fine day only about 46 seals taken, ACD assisted in shooting 2 bladdernoses. [336]
April 16	*Hope* was steaming northwest to locate seals, only took half a dozen. [336]
April 17	*Hope* was steaming south, only took half a dozen seals. [336]
April 18	A snowy drizzly day, ACD shot a seal in the morning, in the evening he attended a Methodist meeting. [336]
April 19	*Hope* was steaming north, the crew got a few bladdernoses. [336]
April 20	*Hope* was steaming northeast. [336]
April 21	Heavy cross sea and swell, nothing to do. [336]
April 22	Heavy swell still on, took 13 seals of which ACD shot 2, he claims to have shot about 15 in all. [336]
April 23	A total of 36 seals were taken, of which ACD took 11, making 26 in all. [336]

April 24	*Hope* was steaming northwest, picked up 17 young seals, no shooting today, ACD sparred in the morning. [336]
April 25	22 young seals taken, ACD shot 7 young seals, total taken by the crew so far 2502, boxed with Stewart in the evening. [336]
April 26	*Hope* was sailing north and northwest all day looking for old seals; ACD did some boxing in the evening. [336]
April 27	*Hope* was steaming north and northwest all day. [336]
April 28	*Hope* came across heavy ice. [336]
April 29	*Hope* steaming north all day. [336]
April 30	*Hope* steaming northeast. [336]
May 1	*Hope* crew took 69 seals. [336]
May 2	*Hope* steaming north in showers, heavy ice, snow and wind. [336]
May 3	The hunting boats were lowered at about 6a.m., ACD's boat took 27 seals, at 2p.m. dinner was taken and then the boats were lowered again, this time ACD's boat took 28 or so seals, total for the ship taken during the day was 540 old seals. [336]
May 4	Again the boats were lowered at 6a.m., ACD took 7 seals, total for the day was 275 old seals. [336]
May 5	*Hope* steaming northeast, the crew took 71 seals. [336]
May 6	*Hope* steaming southwest, heavy swell and no sign of seals. [336]
May 7	*Hope* sailing northeast, no sign of seals. [336]
May 8	*Hope* steaming northwest, no sign of seals. [336]
May 9	*Hope* steaming northwest, no sign of seals. [336]
May 10	*Hope* steaming north, thick rain and wind, no sign of seals. [336]
May 11	*Hope* steaming north, heavy gale, no sign of seals. [336]
May 12	A beautiful day with blue sky, no sign of seals. [336]
May 13	Seals sighted but no hunting. [336]
May 14	Boats were lowered at 9a.m.; ACD's boat took 5 seals, 119 seals taken by the crew. [336]
May 15	32 seals taken by the crew, *Hope* steaming and sailing north. [336]
May 16	*Hope* steaming north, no seals found. [336]
May 17	*Hope* steaming about 100 miles west of Spitzbergen, 6 seals taken. [336]
May 18-20	From 18 to 20 heavy gale blowing. [336]
May 21	No seals sighted. [336]
May 22	Birthday of ACD, he became of age. [336]
May 23	*Hope* sailing west. [336]
May 24	Strong winds, no seals sighted. [336]
May 25	Stronger winds, no seals sighted. [336]
May 26	Fine day but no seals sighted. [336]
May 27	No seals sighted. [336]
May 28	*Hope* steaming north and northeast, no seals sighted. [336]
May 29	No seals sighted. [336]
May 30	2 ground seals taken. [336]
May 31	No seals sighted. [336]
June 1	One bladdernose taken. [336]
June 2	*Hope* sailing west and south, no seals sighted. [336]
June 3	No seals sighted. [336]
June 4	No seals sighted. [336]
June 5	One sea elephant shot. [336] {Note: this entry is dated Saturday June 6, whereas it should be Saturday June 5.}
June 6	One narwhal taken, 2 rare ducks were shot by the captain. [336]
June 7	ACD went aboard the *Eclipse*. [336]
June 8	No seals sighted, ACD went bird shooting, he shot a roach and loon. [336]
June 9	No seals sighted, ACD went bird shooting, he took a roach and 6 snowbirds. [336]
June 10	No seals sighted, ACD shot a kittiwake, a maulie and 3 loons. [336]

June 11	Jack Williamson, crew member, suffered a terrible blow to his head, ACD stitched the wound. [336]
June 12	Crew shot a bear; ACD went aboard the *Eclipse* for dinner. [336]
June 13	*Hope* sailing west and south west. [336]
June 14	Jack Williamson doing very well. [336]
June 15	Thick fog, no seals sighted. [336]
June 16	Many narwhals seen during the evening. [336]
June 17	No seals sighted, ACD and Mathieson hunted a bear, ACD wounded the bear but it ran off. [336]
June 18	Buchan, crew member shot a bear and two cubs, no seals sighted. [336]
June 19	Many narwhals seen, but no seals. [336]
June 20	*Hope* anchored up. [336]
June 21	*Hope* anchored up. [336]
June 22	*Hope* anchored up. [336]
June 23	*Hope* steaming south and east. [336]
June 24	Hard gale blowing. [336]
June 25	Strong wind blowing, *Hope* steaming north. [336]
June 26	One Greenland whale taken. [336]
June 27	No seals sighted. [336]
June 28	No seals sighted. [336]
June 29	ACD shot a burgy, a snowbird and 5 loons, *Hope* laying to. [336]
June 30	No seals sighted, *Hope* laying to, ACD went aboard the *Eclipse*. [336]
July 1	*Hope* laying to in a thick fog, one large Narwhal taken by Colin McLean the first mate. [336]
July 2	*Hope* still laying to in a thick fog. [336]
July 3	Fog had cleared and the *Hope* was heading north and northwest. [336]
July 4	*Hope* sailing north and then south. [336]
July 5	No seals sighted. [336]
July 6	ACD went aboard the *Eclipse*, then went shooting and shot 7 loons, a roach, a kittiwake, a snowbird and a flaw rat, saw 2 Sea Swallows. [336]
July 7	*Hope* steaming south. [336]
July 8	Crew took a whale. [336]
July 9	No seals sighted. [336]
July 10	*Hope* heading north, no seals sighted. [336]
July 11	No seals sighted. [336]
July 12	ACD went aboard the *Eclipse* for dinner and then aboard the *Eira* where ACD was photographed among a distinguished group on the quarterdeck. [336]
July 13	*Hope* steaming south. [336]
July 14	*Hope* steamed and sailed south and south west, foggy all day. [336]
July 15	Thick fog all day. [336]
July 16	Still foggy, ACD went aboard the *Eclipse*. [336]
July 17	Thick fog, *Hope* steaming south and east. [336]
July 18	Heavy wind blowing. [336]
July 19	Blowing a gale all day. [336]
July 20	*Hope* steaming south and west. [336]
July 21	Thick fog again, anchored up, ACD and the captain went aboard the *Eclipse* in the evening. [336]
July 22	*Hope* still anchored owing to thick fog. [336]
July 23	*Hope* steaming south and south west, under sail at night. [336]
July 24	*Hope* steaming south west. [336]
July 25	A very clear day, *Hope* steaming west, under sail at night. [336]
July 26	*Hope* sailing west and south west. [336]
July 27	*Hope* sailing south, south west. [336]
July 28	Heavy wind, thick fog and ice everywhere. [336]
July 29	*Hope* anchored up waiting for better weather, *Hope* steamed south east later in the day when the weather cleared, but fog grew thicker, *Hope* anchored up again. [336]

July 30	*Hope* steaming south, south east, 2 bladdernose seals shot, 1 by ACD. [336]			
July 31	*Hope* steaming west, south west. [336]			
August 1	No entry in diary. [336]			
August 2	Hunted 4 bottlenose whales, but they got away. [336]			
August 3	*Hope* sailing west. [336]			
August 4	No seals sighted. [336]			
August 5	*Hope* sailing southwest. [336]			
August 6	*Hope* steaming east, southeast for Shetland. [336]			
August 7	*Hope* under steam in thick fog. [336]			
August 8	Sighted land at about 8p.m. that proved to be the north end of Faeroe Island. [336]			
August 9	Clear day with blue sky and bright sun, all hands on the lookout for land. [336]			
August 10	Land sighted, *Hope* under steam, passed Lerwick heading for Peterhead. [336]			
August 10	*Hope* returned to Scotland. [203]			
August 11	Saw Rattray Head, *Hope* less than 10 miles from Peterhead. [336]			
August 12	*Hope* arrived back in Peterhead. [144] (*2)			
August	Mid-August ACD arrived back in Peterhead on board the *Hope*. [202] (*2)			

Game Bag of the *Hope*:

	Young seals	Old seals	Other species	ACD's bag
April 3	760	57		1 old seal
April 4	450	10		
April 5	400			
April 6	270	57	6 Bladdernoses	2 Bladdernoses
April 7	133			
April 8	30			
April 9	50			
April 10	72			2 seals
April 14	80			2 seals
April 15	46		2 Bladdernoses	2 seals, 1 Bladdernose
April 16	6		1 hawk	
April 17	10	2		
April 18	10			1 seal
April 19	6			
April 22	13			2 seals
April 23	36			11 seals
April 24	17			
April 25	22			8 seals
May 1		69		
May 3		540		27 seals
May 4		275		10 seals
May 5		71		
May 14		119		
May 15		32		
May 17		6		
May 30			2 Ground Seals	
May 31			1 Flaw Rat	
June 1			1 Bladdernose	
June 2			4 Roaches, 7 Loons	
June 5			1 Bladdernose	
June 6			1 Narwhal, 2 Rare Ducks	
June 8				1 Roach, 1 Loon
June 9				1 Roach, 6 Snowbirds
June 10				1 Kittiwake, 1 Maulie, 3 Loons

June 11	1 Whiting
June 12	1 Bear
June 18	1 Bear & 2 Cubs
June 20	1 Bear
June 26	1 Greenland Whale
June 30	1 Burgomaster, 1 Snowbird, 5 Loons, 1 Flaw Rat
July 1	1 Narwhal
July 6	1 Flaw Rat, 7 Loons, 1 Roach, 1 Kittiwake, 2 Snowbirds
July 8	1 Greenland Whale
July 31	2 Bladdernoses
August 4	1 Boatswain
August 5	2 Eider Ducks

According to ACD's reckoning the whole game bag was as follows:

2 Greenland Whales	2400 Young Seals	1200 Old Seals
5 Polar Bears	2 Narwhals	12 Bladdernoses
3 Flaw Rats	1 Iceland Falcon	2 Ground Seals
2 King Eider Ducks	2 Eider Ducks	1 Boatswain
7 Roaches	23 Loons	1 Burgomaster
8 Snowbirds	3 Kittiwakes	

According to ACD his own game bag was as follows:

38 Young Seals and Young Bladders	29 Old Seals	10 Loons	3 Roaches
1 Maulies	2 Snowbirds	4 Kittiwakes	2 Flaw Rats

On close scrutiny, ACD appears to lose count of the whole game bag and that of his own.

Notes:

Roach	A small auk.
Bladdernose Seal	Also known as Sea Elephants, Elephant Seal or Hooded Seal, average size 8½ feet in length.
Flaw Rat or Floe Rat	The smallest variety of seals.
Ground Seal	A rare variety of seal, nearly as large as a Bladdernose.
Maulie	An Arctic Petrel.
Narwhal	Also known as a Sea Unicorn, medium sized toothed whale with large tusk, 11½ feet to 16½ feet in length.
Loon	Also known as the Foolish Guillemot, a diving bird.
Snowbird	Also known as Ivory Gull, completely white and 16in to 19inches long.
Kittiwake	A large gull, approximately 15inches long with a 3 foot wingspan.
Burgy	Burgomaster Gull or Glaucous Gull, a large gull 30inches long.
Sea Swallow	A variety of Arctic Tern, 12½ inches to 14 inches long.
Hawk	Probably the Iceland Hawk.
Boatswain	A type of gull

On deck of the *Eira*, 12 July 1880
From left to right are:
David Gray at the helm (Captain of *Eclipse*), Benjamin Leigh-Smith (Captain/owner of *Eira*), Arthur Conan Doyle (Surgeon on *Hope*), John Gray (Captain of *Hope*), Doctor Walker (of the *Eclipse*) and Doctor Neale (of the *Eira*), William Lofley (ice master on *Eira*) right at stern.

© Hull Maritime Museum: Hull Museum

The *Hope*
[From *The Strand Magazine*, January 1897, The Life on a Greenland Whaler]

Louise Conan Doyle

Jean Conan Doyle 1907

Mary Doyle (The Mam)

ACD Jean, Adrian, Denis, Jean behind ACD

ACD in fancy dress as a Viking
Undershaw 1898

ACD in the uniform of
a deputy Lieutenant of Surrey, 1907

ACD and son Kingsley

ACD & Jean at an Australian apiary 1921

The Langman Hospital 1900

ACD in South Africa 1900

ACD in Sri Lanka, Ceylon, 1919-1920

Jean, ACD, Jean, Denis & Adrian
at Niagara Falls 1922

ACD sitting for his bust by J.O. Davidson
at 15 Buckingham Palace Mansions, London
15 January 1930

Innes Doyle

Malcolm Leckie

Jean, ACD, Mary Pickford & Douglas Fairbanks

Denis and Nina Mdivani

James Blythe Leckie and his wife Selina
Father and mother of Jean Leckie

Adrian, Denis, Major Wood, ACD & Jean.

Windlesham, Hurtis Hill, Crowborough, East Sussex

The medal won by Denis Conan Doyle on 17 May 1930 (engraving error Dennis)

Arthur Conan Doyle with his mother at the original Fey House, Crowborough

Arthur Conan Doyle and Family at The Old Mint House, Pevensey, Sussex, c.1917

Arthur Conan Doyle at Windlesham c.1927

The following map of Conan Doyle's itinerary in 1894 appears with kind permission of Christopher Redmond and is his copyright.

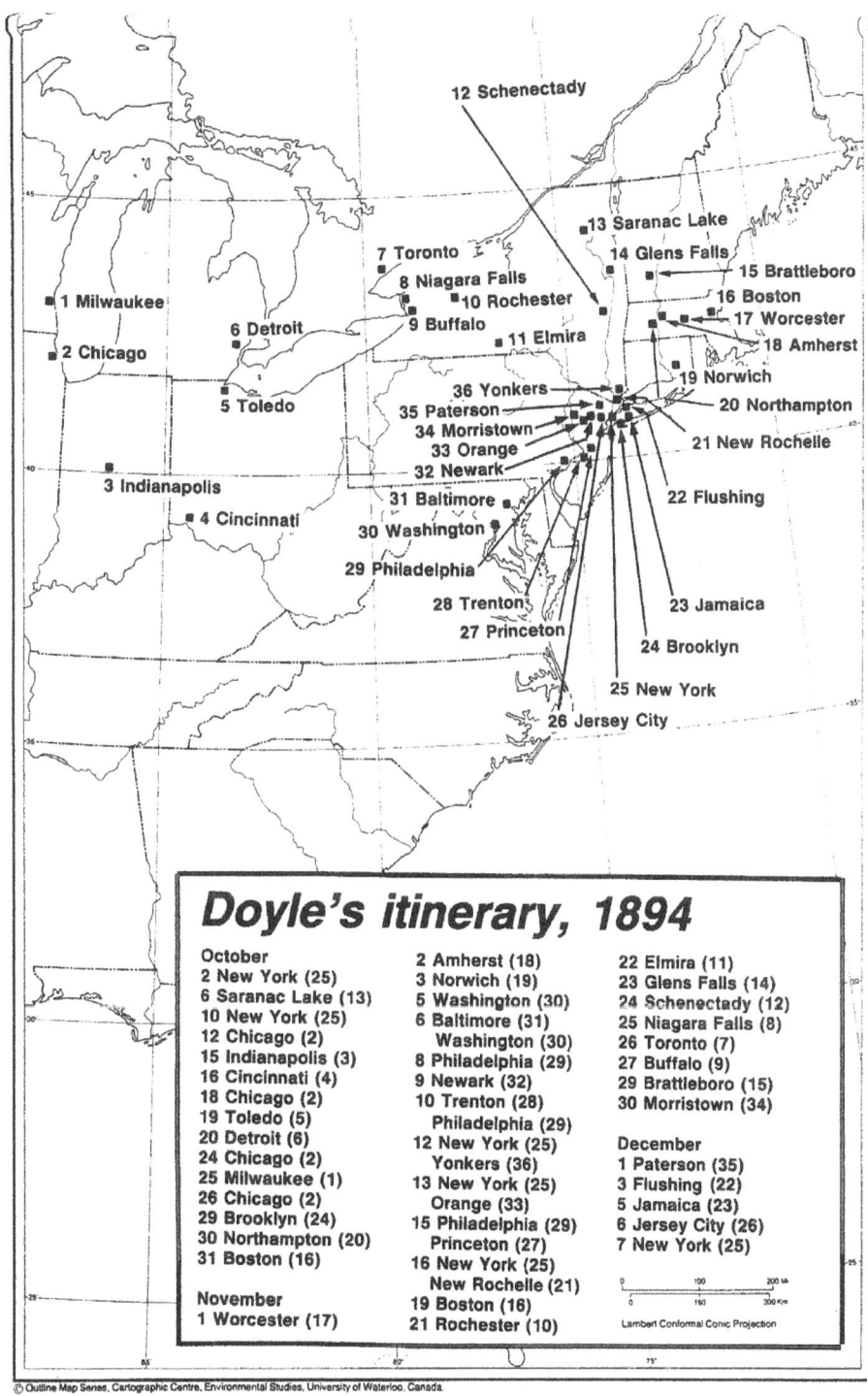

Full details of this 1894 visit can be found in the excellent book *Welcome to America, Mr. Sherlock Holmes* by Christopher Redmond, published in 1987 in Canada by Simon & Pierre Publishing Company Limited.

The following maps appear with kind permission of Alexis Barquin
© Arthur-Conan-Doyle.com

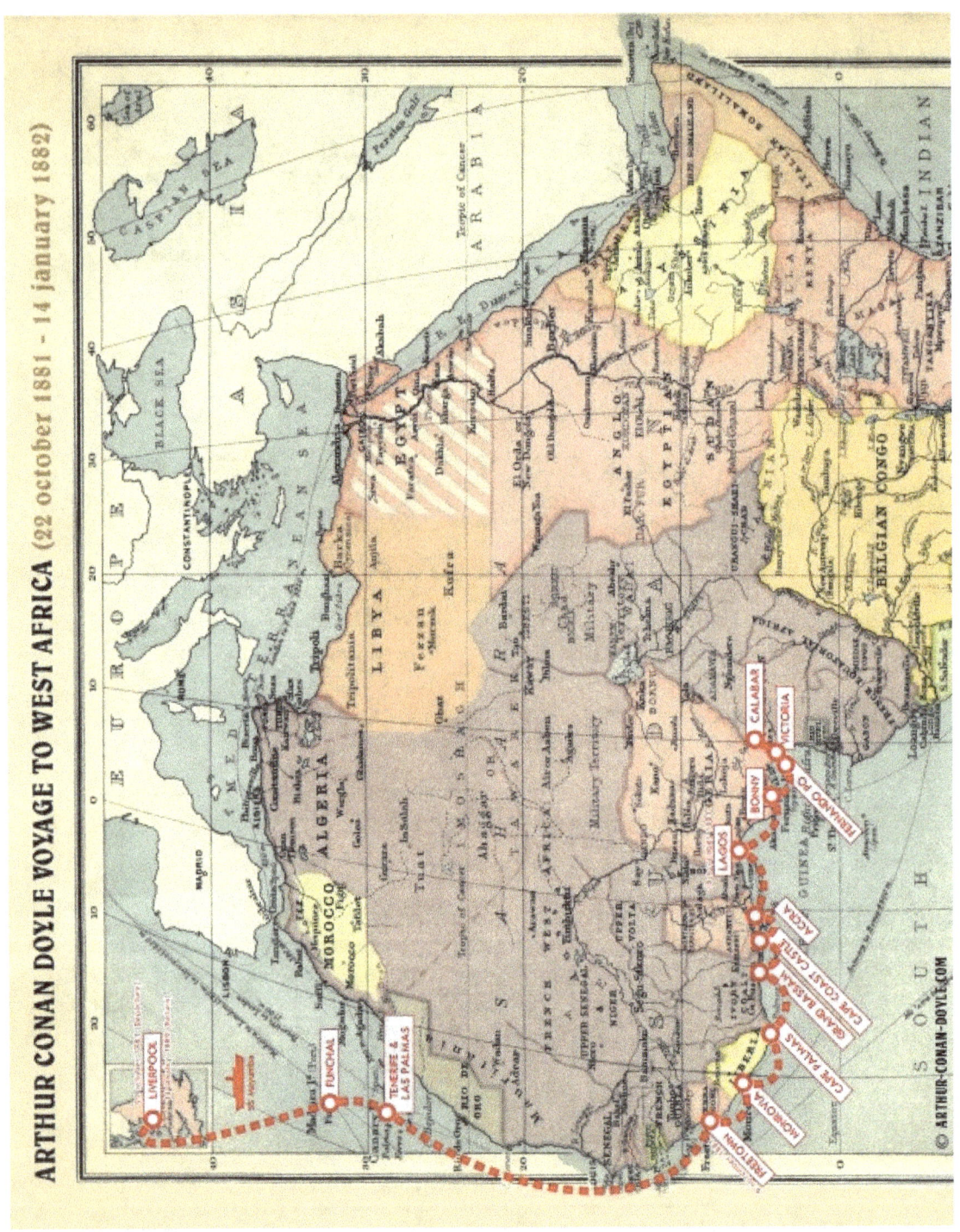

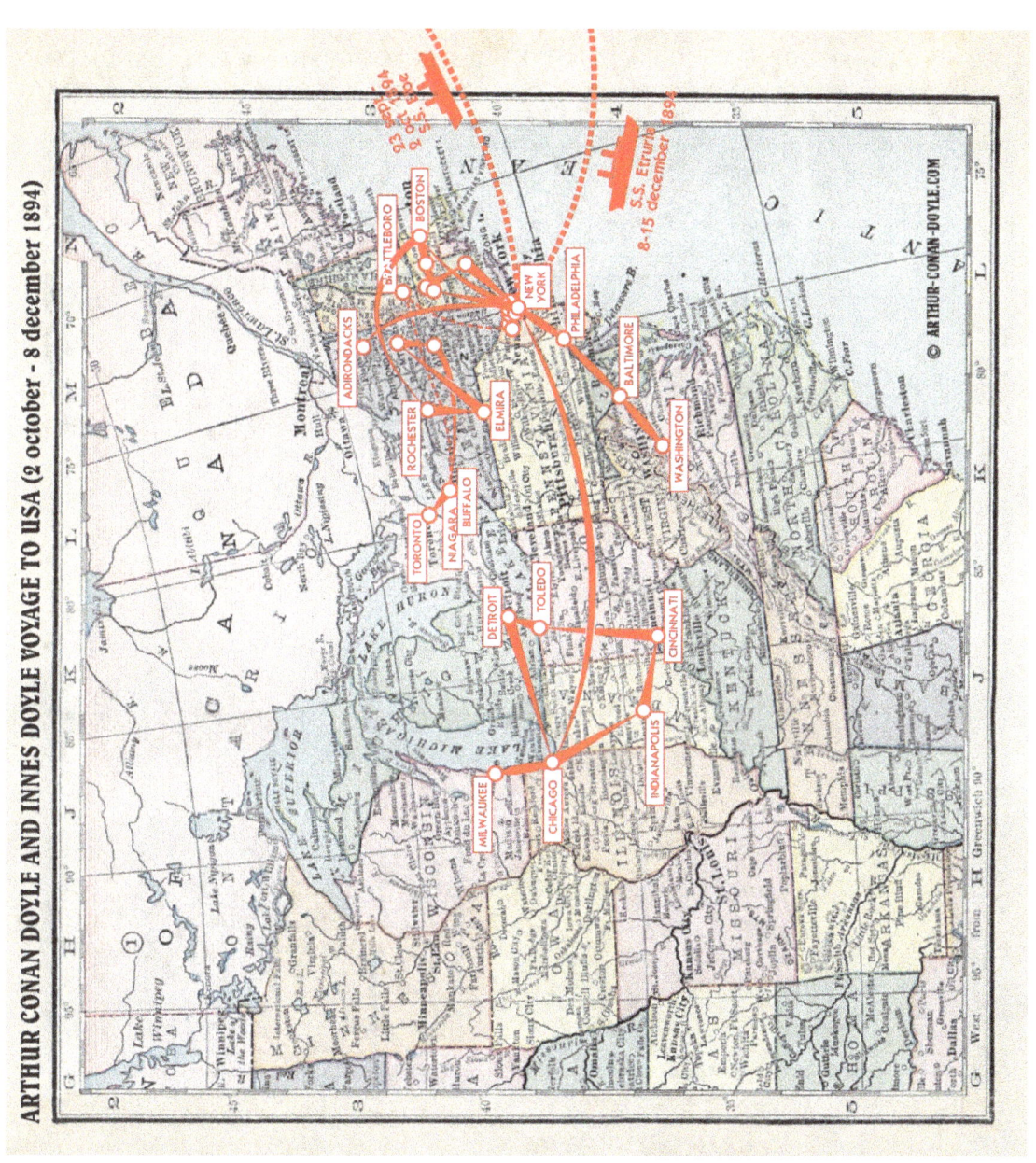

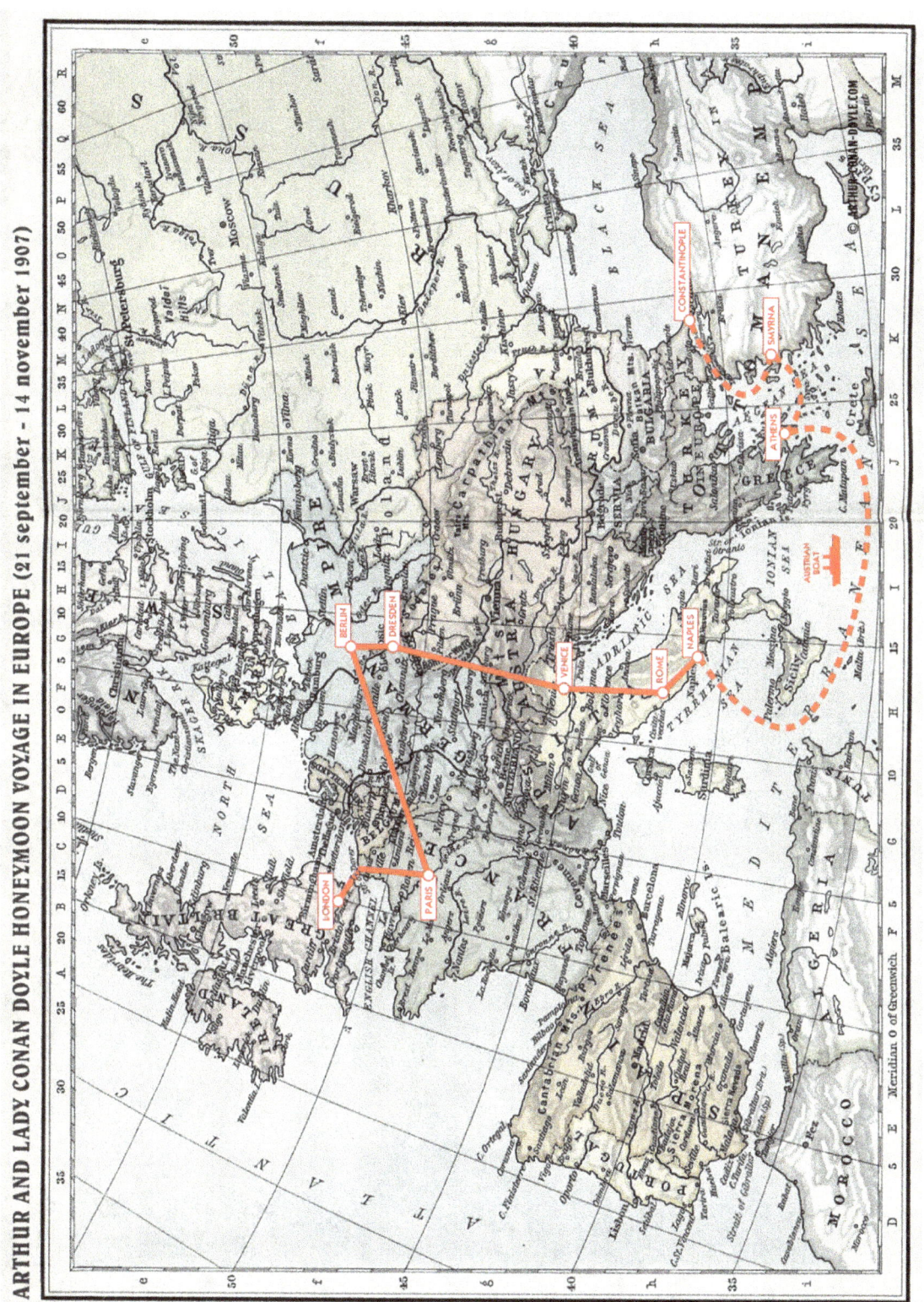

Arthur Conan Doyle and the Prince Henry of Prussia's Cup 4 – 19 July 1911

Berliner Tageblatt 3 July 1913, page 13

Prince Henry Car Tour 4 July – 19 July 1911

July 4	Participants assembled at Homburg.
July 5	Homburg to Cologne via Königstein, Weilmünster, Leun, Weilburg, Limburg, Montabaur, Coblenz, Andernach, Remagen, Bonn and Cologne, 151miles travelled.
July 6	Cologne to Munster via Opladen, Düsseldorf, Uerdingen, Moers, Rheinberg, Wesel, Herne and Munster, 137 miles travelled.
July 7	Munster to Bremerhaven via Greven, Osnabrück, Lemförde, Diepholz, Bassum, Bremen, Lesum and Bremerhaven, 140 miles travelled.
July 8	At sea on board the *Grosser Kurfuerst* from Bremerhaven to Southampton.
July 9	Arrived in Southampton.
July 10	Southampton to Leamington via Winchester, Whitchurch, Newbury, East Iisley, Abingdon, Oxford, Woodstock, Shipston, Stratford-on-Avon, Warwick and Leamington, 113 miles travelled.
July 11	Leamington to Harrogate via Rugby, Lutterworth, Leicester, Loughborough, Nottingham, Mansfield, Worksop, Tickhill, Doncaster, Ferrybridge, Aberford, Wetherby and Harrogate, 147 miles travelled.
July 12	Harrogate to Newcastle via Ripon, Thirsk, Helmsley, Easingwold, Northallerton, Darlington, Neville's Cross, Chester-le-Street and Newcastle, 129 miles travelled.
July 13	Newcastle to Edinburgh via Morpeth, Alnwick, Belford, Berwick, Dunbar and Edinburgh, 121 miles travelled.
July 14	Edinburgh rest day.
July 15	Edinburgh to Windermere via Leadburn, Romannobridge, Moffat, Lockerbie, Ecclefechan, Gretna Green, Carlisle, Bothel, Castle Inn, Keswick, and Windermere, 146 miles travelled.
July 16	Windermere, spent the day sightseeing.
July 17	Windermere to Shrewsbury via Kendal, Lancaster, Preston, Ormskirk, Knowsley Park, Prescot, Warrington, Tarporley, Whitchurch, Wem and Shrewsbury, 144 miles travelled.
July 18	Shrewsbury to Cheltenham via Church Stretton, Craven Arms, Ludlow, Leominster, Peterstow, Ross, Monmouth, Chepstow, and Cheltenham, 130 miles travelled.
July 19	Cheltenham to London via Gloucester, Nailsworth, Badminton, Chippenham, Marlborough, Newbury, Windsor Park, Staines Bridge, Richmond Park and London, 158 miles travelled, total distance travelled on the road 1516 miles.
July 20	At 12 noon the participants paraded their cars at Brooklands, in the evening they attended a banquet at the Royal Automobile Club in London, the toast of the competitors was proposed by the Duke of Teck, and replied to by Dr J. von Meister and Sir Arthur Conan Doyle.

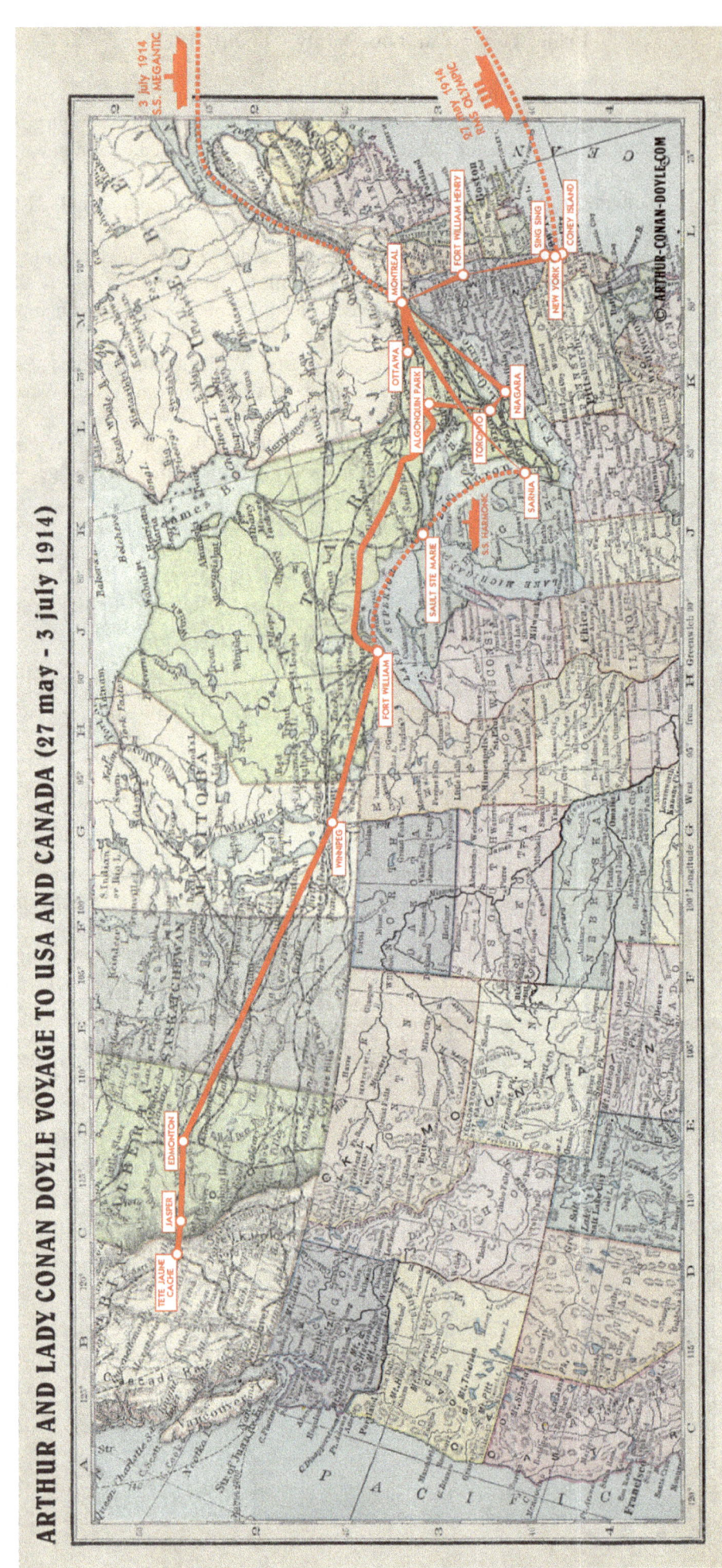

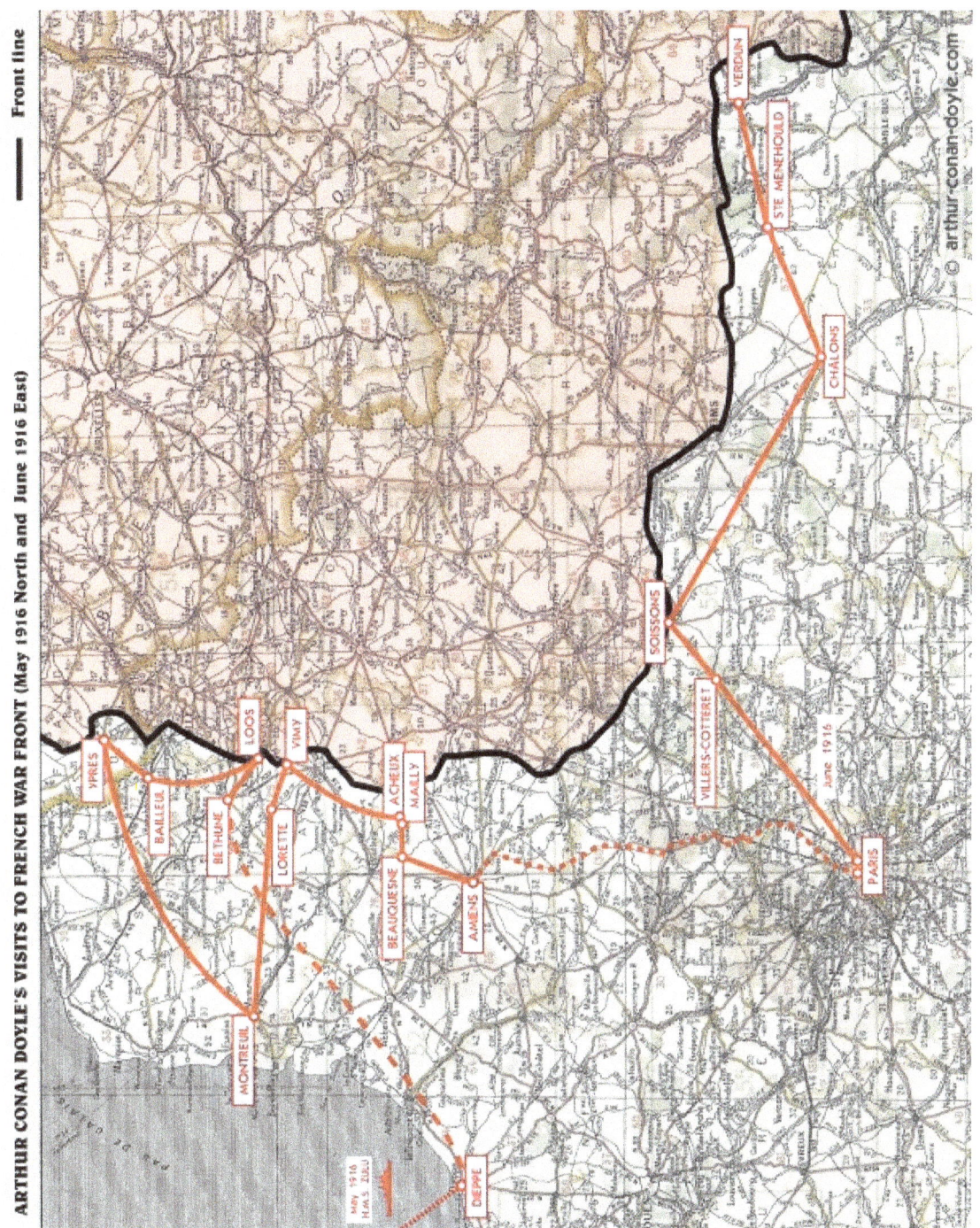

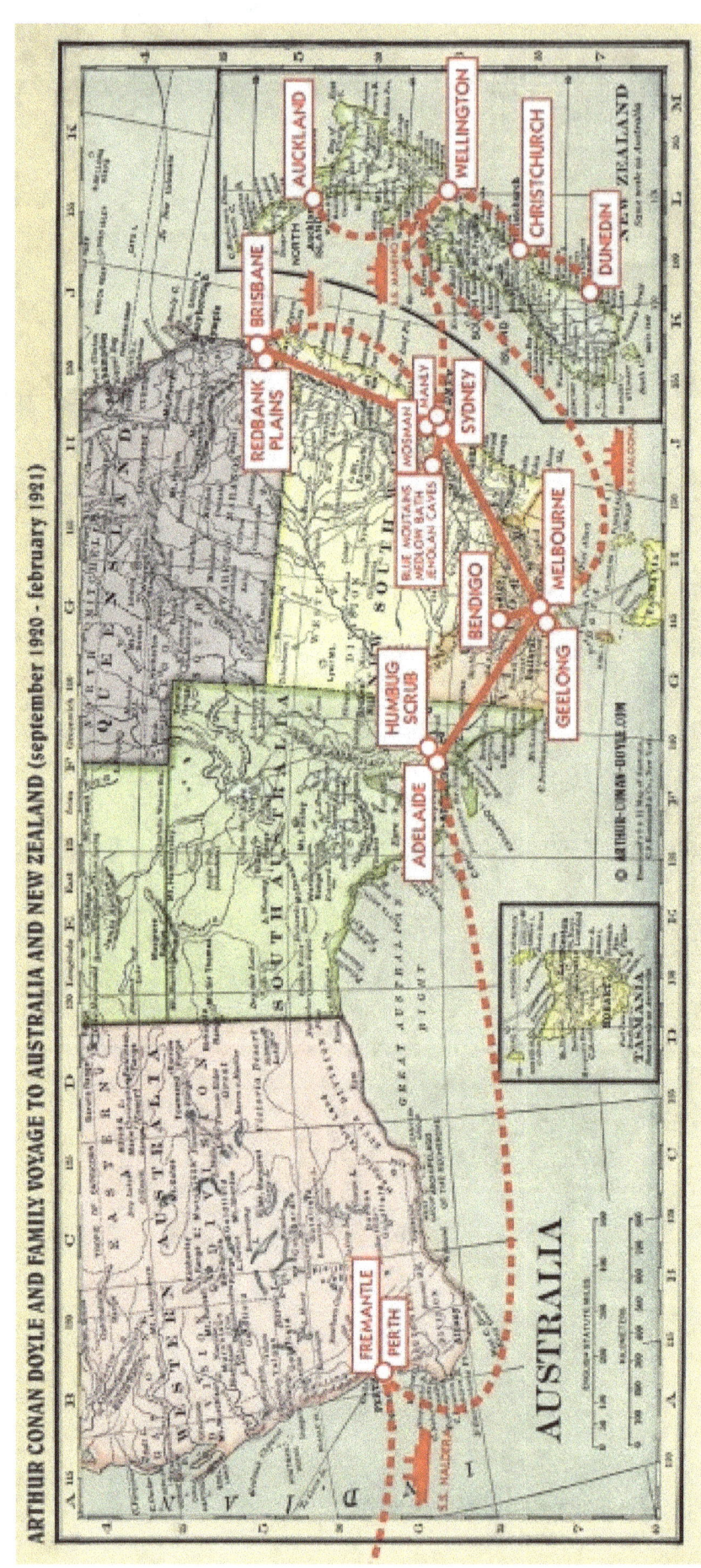

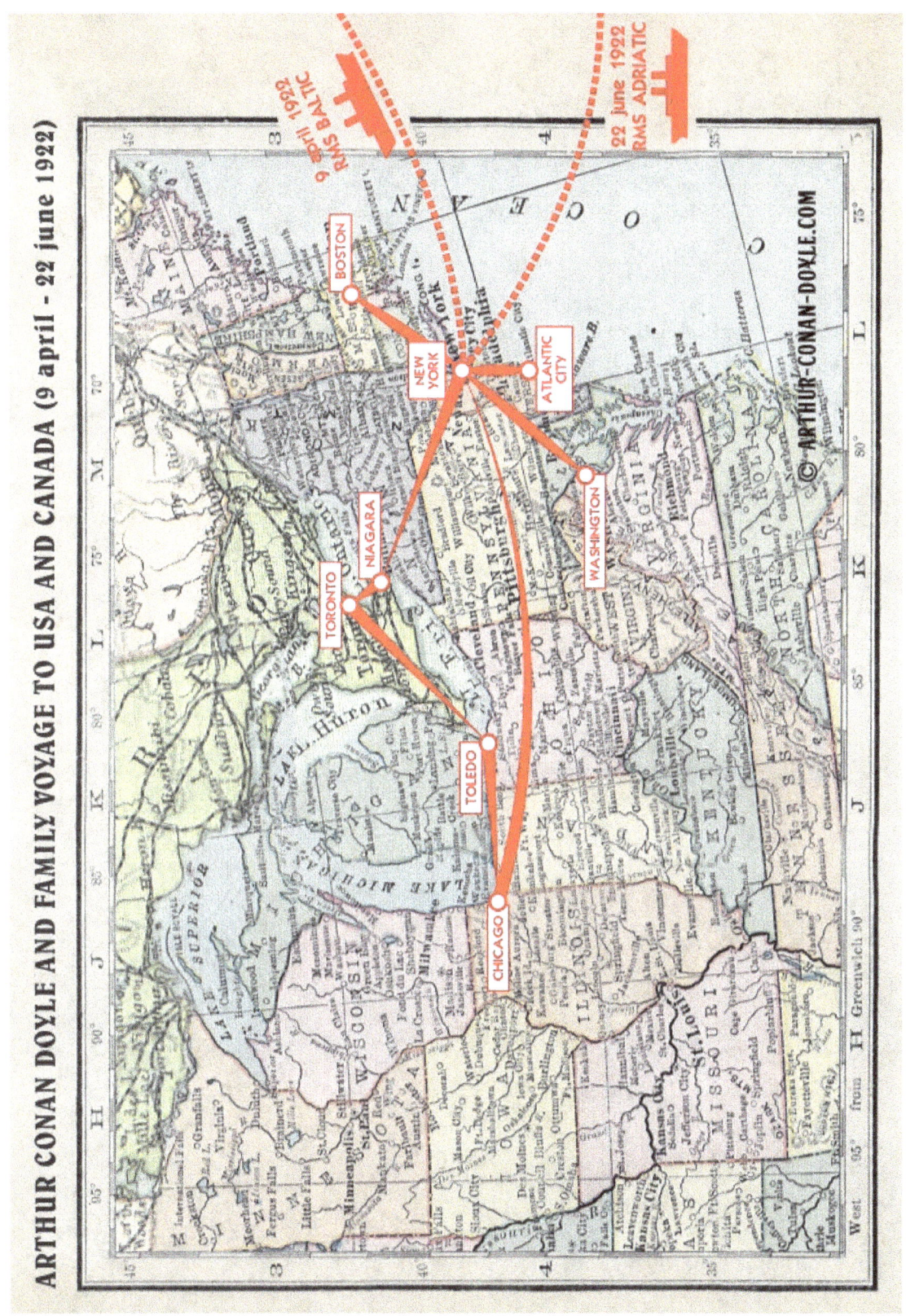

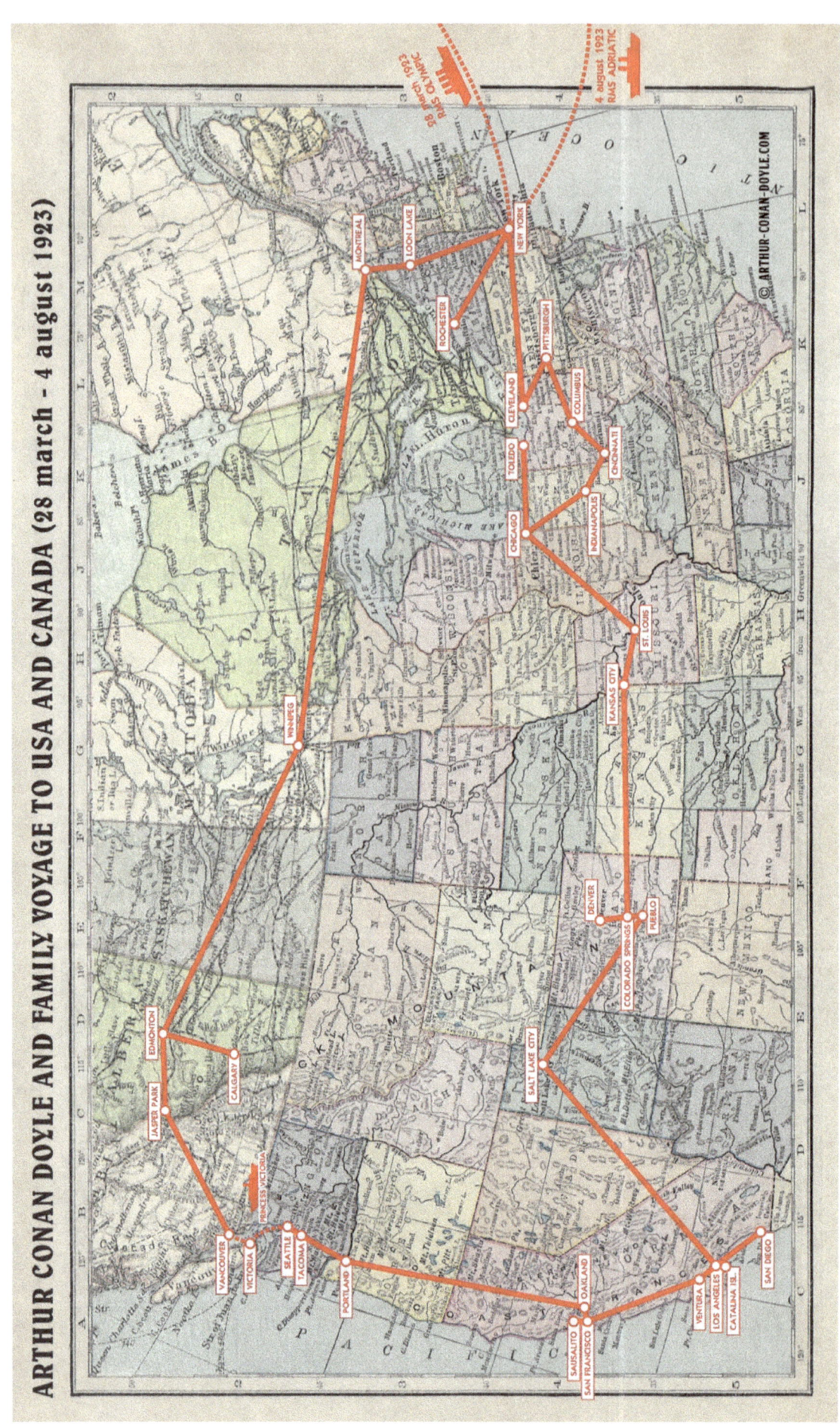

The Residences Of Arthur Conan Doyle And Family 1859-1930

11 Picardy Place, Edinburgh is located on the right of W. M. Douglas Ltd., in line with the bonnet of the white car; the plaque to the right of the front door can just be seen.

1849	Charles Altamont Doyle lodged at 27 Clyde Street, Edinburgh.
1849	Charles Altamont Doyle lodged at 8 Scotland Street, Edinburgh.
1850	Charles Altamont Doyle lodged at Abercromby Place, Edinburgh.
1851	Charles Altamont Doyle lodged at 27 Clyde Street, Edinburgh.
1852	Charles Altamont Doyle lodged at 5 Nicolson Street, Edinburgh.
1857	Charles Altamont and Mary Doyle lived at 1 South Nelson Street, Edinburgh.
1858	Charles Altamont and Mary Doyle lived at 5 Nelson Street, Edinburgh.
1859	11 Picardy Place, Edinburgh.
1861/2	3 Tower Bank, Portobello Edinburgh.
1866	Arthur Conan Doyle lived at Liberton Bank House, Edinburgh while attending Newington Academy.
1868	The Doyle family resided at 3 Sciennes Hill Place, Newington, Edinburgh.
1867	Arthur Conan Doyle a boarder at Hodder Preparatory School, Lancashire.
1870	Arthur Conan Doyle a boarder at Stonyhurst School, Lancashire.
1875	Arthur Conan Doyle a boarder at the Jesuit School in Feldkirch, Austria.
1875	The Doyle family resided at 2 Argyle Park Terrace, Edinburgh.
1877	The Doyle family resided at 23 George Square, Edinburgh.
1881	The Doyle family resided at 15 Lonsdale Terrace, Edinburgh.
1882-1917	Mary Foley Doyle residing at Masongill Cottage, Masongill, Yorkshire.
1878-1882	Arthur Conan Doyle has various positions as an assistant to doctors in Sheffield, Ruyton-XI-Towns, Birmingham and surgeons clerk to Dr Joseph Bell.
1882	In partnership for six weeks with Dr Budd at 1 Durnford Street, Plymouth and lived with Dr Budd at 6 Elliot Terrace, The Hoe, Plymouth.
1882	1 Bush Villas, Elm Grove, Southsea.
1891	23 Montague Place, Russell Square, London.
1891-1894	12 Tennison Road, South Norwood.
1896	Temporary accommodation at Grayswood/Greyswood Beeches, Haslemere.
1897	Temporary accommodation at the Moorlands Hotel, Hindhead.
1897	Undershaw, Hindhead, Surrey.
1907-1930	Windlesham, Hurtis Hill, Crowborough, Sussex.
1923-1930	15 Buckingham Palace Mansions, Buckingham Palace Road, London.
1925-1930	Some time spent at Bignell Wood, near Minstead, Hampshire.

Undershaw under construction

Undershaw, Hindhead, Surrey

Sir Arthur in the garden of Bignell Wood, Hampshire.

ACD, Jean & Jean at Davos, Switzerland

The Arthur Conan Doyle Statue at Cloke's Corner, Crowborough

Where Are They Buried?

Sir Arthur Conan Doyle
    All Saints Church, Minstead, The New Forest, Hampshire.

Jean Conan Doyle (second wife)
    All Saints Church, Minstead, The New Forest, Hampshire.

Dame Jean Conan Doyle, Lady Bromet (daughter of ACD)
    Ashes at All Saints Church, Minstead, The New Forest, Hampshire.

Denis Conan Doyle (son of ACD)
    Part of ashes at All Saints Church, Minstead, The New Forest, Hampshire.

Adrian Conan Doyle (son of ACD)
    Ashes at Lucens Castle, Switzerland.

Sir Geoffrey Bromet (husband of Dame Jean Conan Doyle, Lady Bromet)
    All Saints Church, Minstead, The New Forest, Hampshire.

Louise Conan Doyle (first wife)
    St. Luke's Church, Grayshott, near Hindhead, Surrey.

Kingsley Conan Doyle (son of ACD)
    St. Luke's Church, Grayshott, near Hindhead, Surrey.

Mary Doyle (mother of ACD)
    St. Luke's Church, Grayshott, near Hindhead, Surrey.

Emily Hawkins (mother of Louise Conan Doyle)
    St. Mary's Church, Chart Lane, Reigate, Surrey.

Jeremiah Hawkins (eldest son of Emily Hawkins)
    St. Mary's Church, Chart Lane, Reigate, Surrey.

Louisa Butt (sister of Emily Hawkins) [She was buried in the same plot as Emily and Jeremiah]
    St. Mary's Church, Chart Lane, Reigate, Surrey.

John Francis Innes Hay Doyle (brother of ACD)
    Halle Cemetery, Belgium.

Mary Conan Doyle (daughter of ACD)
    Half ashes at All Saints Church, Minstead, The New Forest Hampshire.
    Half ashes at St. Luke's Church, Grayshott, near Hindhead, Surrey.

Clara Doyle (wife of Innes)
    Langney Cemetery, Langney, Eastbourne, East Sussex.

E.W. Hornung (husband of Constance, sister of ACD)
    St. Jean de Luz Cemetery, France.

Constance (Connie) Hornung (wife of E.W. Hornung, sister of ACD)
    Shrine of Our Lady of Consolation, Park Lane, West Grinstead, West Sussex.

Bryan (Dodo) Mary Angel (wife of Charles Angel and sister of ACD)
    Dunkerton Church, near Bath, Somerset.

Charles Altamont Doyle (father of ACD)
    High Cemetery, Dumfries, Scotland.

Annette Conan Doyle (sister of ACD)
    High Cemetery, Dumfries, Scotland.

Katherine Angela Doyle (sister of ACD)
    High Cemetery, Dumfries, Scotland.

Mary Monica Doyle (sister of ACD)
    High Cemetery, Dumfries, Scotland.

Jane Adelaide Rose (Ida) Foley (widow of Nelson Foley & sister of ACD)
    St. Mary's Church, High Street, Westham, Pevensey, East Sussex.

Annette Doyle (daughter of John and Marianna Doyle)
    St. Mary's Catholic Cemetery, Harrow Road, Kensal Green, London.

Jane Isabella Doyle (wife of Henry Doyle)
    St. Mary's Catholic Cemetery, Harrow Road, Kensal Green, London.

Richard Doyle (son of John and Marianna Doyle)
    St. Mary's Catholic Cemetery, Harrow Road, Kensal Green, London.

Henry Doyle (son of John and Marianna Doyle)
    St. Mary's Catholic Cemetery, Harrow Road, Kensal Green, London.

Richard Barry-Doyle, The Right Reverend Monsignor (second cousin of ACD)
    Gilroes Cemetery (Catholic Section), Groby Road, Leicester.

John (HB) Doyle
    Norwood Cemetery, Norwood Road, Lambeth, London.

Marianne Doyle (wife of John (HB) Doyle)
    Norwood Cemetery, Norwood Road, Lambeth, London.

Francis (Frank) Doyle (son of John (HB) and Marianne Doyle)
    Norwood Cemetery, Norwood Road, Lambeth, London.

Adelaide Doyle (daughter of John (HB) and Marianne Doyle)
    Norwood Cemetery, Norwood Road, Lambeth, London.

Anna Conan Doyle (wife of Adrian Conan Doyle)
    Ashes at Lucens Castle, Switzerland.

John (Jack) Hawkins (brother of Louise Hawkins)
    Highlands Road Cemetery, Southsea, Hampshire.

Major Alfred Wood (ACD's secretary for many years) (unmarked grave)
    Highlands Road, Cemetery, Southsea, Hampshire.

Dr George Turnavine Budd (ACD worked with Budd at Plymouth for a few weeks)
    Ford Park Cemetery, Plymouth, Devon.

William Budd (son of George Turnavine & Kate Budd)
    He is buried in the same grave as George Turavine Budd
    Ford Park Cemetery, Plymouth, Devon.

Statues and Plaques Dedicated To
Sir Arthur Conan Doyle, Sherlock Holmes and Others

**Please note: Many of the plaques mentioned have been removed or lost.
So I cannot guarantee that the plaques and statues are still at the locations as listed.**

America: **Indianapolis.**

Location: The Grand Hall of Union Station, Indianapolis.
Type: Plaque to commemorate Arthur Conan Doyle's visit in October 1894.
Unveiled: 15 October 1994.

San Francisco.

Location: 2151 Sacramento Street, San Francisco, California.
Type: Plaque to commemorate Arthur Conan Doyle occupying the house.
Unveiled: Not known.

New York.

Location: 57th & 7th Avenue Subway Station, New York.
Type: Wall tile commemorating ACD performing at Carnegie Hall on 12 April 1922.
Unveiled: Unknown.

Australia: **Adelaide.**

Location: Outside Hungry Jack's which occupies part of the site of Gibson's Grand Central Hotel, Rundle Street.
Type: Plaque to commemorate Arthur Conan Doyle's visit in September 1920.
Unveiled: 1995 rededicated September 2004.

Sydney.

Location: Outside the Museum of Contemporary Art, the "Writers Walk", inserted in walkway by NSE Ministry of the Arts.
Type: Plaque to commemorate Arthur Conan Doyle's visit in 1920-21.
Unveiled: 1991.

England: **Birmingham, Staffordshire.**

Location: 63, Aston Road North, Aston, Birmingham.
Type: Plaque to Arthur Conan Doyle.
Unveiled: 14 April 1956 (this was replaced with the following plaque).

Location: 63, Aston Road North, Aston, Birmingham, Staffordshire.
Type: Plaque to Arthur Conan Doyle.
Unveiled: 29 October 1976.

Crowborough, Sussex.

Location: Windlesham Manor, Hurtis Hill, Crowborough, Sussex.
Type: Plaque to Arthur Conan Doyle at front door.
Unveiled: 1984.

Location: Terrace Montargis, Croft Road, Crowborough, Sussex.
Type: Plaque to Arthur Conan Doyle.
Unveiled: 23 May 1992.

Crowborough, Sussex.

Location: The Whitehill Centre, Whitehill, Crowborough, Sussex.
Type: Plaque on opening the centre by Dame Jean Conan Doyle.
Unveiled: 24 February 1994.

Location: Cloke's Corner, Crowborough, Sussex.
Type: Plaque to Dame Jean Conan Doyle on bench seat.
Unveiled: 1998.

Location: Cloke's Corner, Crowborough, Sussex.
Type: Plaque to Malcolm Payne on bench seat.
(First Curator of The Conan Doyle (Crowborough) Establishment).
Unveiled: 1998.

Location: Cloke's Corner, Crowborough, Sussex.
Type: Statue of Arthur Conan Doyle.
Unveiled: 14 April 2001.

Location: On each of the four main roads into Crowborough, Sussex.
Type: Town road signs.
Unveiled: 1998. Replaced by new signs in 2008.

Croydon, Surrey.

Location: 12, Tennison Road, South Norwood, Croydon.
Type: Plaque to Arthur Conan Doyle.
Unveiled: 18 May 1973.

East Dean, Near Eastbourne, Sussex.

Location: Estate Office, The Green, East Dean.
Type: Plaque stating that Sherlock Holmes retired here.
Unveiled: 2008.

Groombridge, Sussex.

Location: Groombridge Place, Groombridge, Nr. Crowborough, Sussex.
Type: Plaque to Arthur Conan Doyle.
Unveiled: 1 July 1995.

Happisburgh, Norfolk.

Location: Hill House Hotel.
Type: Plaque to commemorate Arthur Conan Doyle's visit in 1903.
Unveiled: Not known.

Location: Hill House Hotel.
Type: Plaque.
Unveiled: 15 July 2006.

Hindhead, Surrey.

Location: Undershaw Hotel, Hindhead, Surrey.
Type: Plaque to Arthur Conan Doyle in bar.
Unveiled: 6 July 1997 [this has now been removed and is in storage].

Hindhead, Surrey.

Location:	Undershaw, Hindhead, Surrey.
Type:	Plaque commemorating the home of Arthur Conan Doyle 1897-1907.
Unveiled:	9 September 2016.

Plymouth, Devon.

Location:	Durnford Street, Plymouth.
Type:	Plaque to Arthur Conan Doyle.
Unveiled:	Not known [this has been removed or stolen].

Location:	85 – 125 Durnford Street, Plymouth.
Type:	Various plaques in footpath.
Unveiled:	24 June 1991.

Location:	6 Elliot Terrace, The Hoe, Plymouth.
Type:	Plaque commemorating that Arthur Conan Doyle lodged here.
Unveiled:	9 September 2017, actually attached to wall on 7 April 2017.

Princetown, Devon.

Location:	The High Moorland Visitor Centre.
Type:	Plaque to Arthur Conan Doyle.
Unveiled:	9 June 1993.

Ipplepen, Devon.

Location:	Bridge Street, Ipplepen.
Type:	Plaque on public bench in memory of Bertram Fletcher Robinson.
Unveiled:	2009.

Kingston, Surrey.

Location:	Kingston Spiritualist Church, Villiers Road, Kingston, Surrey.
Type:	Foundation stone laid by Arthur Conan Doyle.
Laid:	23 April 1927.

London.

Location:	The Criterion Bar.
Type:	Two Plaques to Sherlock Holmes.
Unveiled:	3 January 1953 & 1981.

Location:	St. Bartholomew's Hospital.
Type:	Plaque to Sherlock Holmes.
Unveiled:	21 January 1954.

Location:	Baker Street Underground Station.
Type	Wall Tiles of Sherlock Holmes.
Unveiled:	11 April 1979.

Location:	The Abbey National, Baker Street.
Type;	Plaque to Sherlock Holmes.
Unveiled:	27 September 1978.

London.

Location:	The Abbey National, Baker Street.
Type:	Plaque to Sherlock Holmes.
Unveiled:	7 October 1985.

Location:	2, Upper Wimpole Street.
Type:	Plaque to Arthur Conan Doyle.
Unveiled:	22 May 1994.

Location:	Outside Baker Street Underground Station in Marylebone Road.
Type:	Statue of Sherlock Holmes.
Unveiled:	23 September 1999.

Location:	2, Devonshire Place.
Type:	Fanlight over front door Conan Doyle House.
Unveiled:	1993.

Location:	Rochester Square Spiritualist Temple, Rochester Square (off Camden Road) NW1 9RY.
Type:	Foundation stone laid by Arthur Conan Doyle.
Laid:	30 October 1926.

Location:	The Langham Hotel, at the entrance to the Langham's Landau Restaurant, facing All Soul's, Langham Place.
Type:	Plaque to commemorate the meeting that led to *The Sign of Four* & *The Picture of Dorian Gray* on 30 August 1889.
Unveiled:	19 March 2010.

Location:	The Sherlock Holmes Museum, Baker Street.
Type:	Plaque to 221b Baker Street and Sherlock Holmes.
Unveiled:	Not known

Location:	The Authors' Club, Whitehall Court.
Type:	Plaque to Arthur Conan Doyle.
Unveiled:	2 May 1932.

Location:	The College of Psychic Studies, 16, Queensbury Place, London, SW7 2EB.
Type:	Plaque commemorating that Arthur Conan Doyle was President of the College 1926-1930.
Unveiled:	23 January 2016.

Portsmouth, Hampshire.

Location:	Outside Debenhams, Arundel Street, Portsmouth.
Type:	Bench seat.
Unveiled:	2004.

Southsea, Hampshire.

Location:	On the site of Bush Villas, Elm Grove, Southsea, Hampshire.
Type:	Plaque to Arthur Conan Doyle.
Unveiled:	18 November 1982.

Location:	On the site of the Bush Hotel, Elm Grove, Southsea, Hampshire.
Type:	Plaque to Arthur Conan Doyle.
Unveiled:	22 June 2006 [this plaque replaced the one mentioned above.]

Southsea, Hampshire.

Location:	On the site of the Bush Hotel, Elm Grove, Southsea, Hampshire.
Type:	Plaque to Arthur Conan Doyle.
Unveiled:	22 June 2006.

Winchester, Hampshire.

Location:	Junction of Southgate Street and the High Street on the site of the Black Swan.
Type:	Plaque to commemorate the visit to the Black Swan of Holmes and Watson.
Unveiled:	22 October 2013.

Worthing, Sussex.

Location:	Worthing Spiritualist Church, Grafton Road, Worthing, Sussex.
Type:	Plaque to commemorate the opening of the church by Arthur Conan Doyle.
Unveiled:	24 March 1926.

Austria: Feldkirch.

Location:	Feldkirch Chamber of Labor in the courtyard.
Type:	Sculpture of a pen with the words "You are wonderful" at the pen tip.
Unveiled:	Not known.

France: Paris.

Location:	Hôtel du Louvre, Paris, France.
Type:	Plaque to Sherlock Holmes.
Unveiled:	10 May 1997.

Italy: Florence.

Location:	Corsellini Pipe Shop, Via Ghibellina, Florence.
Type:	Plaque to Sherlock Holmes.
Unveiled:	2000.

Sesto Fiorentino.

Location:	City Hall, Piazza Vittorio Emanuele, Sesto Fiorentino.
Type:	Bust of Sherlock Holmes.
Unveiled:	March 2002.
Relocated to:	Biblioteca Ernesto Ragionieri, 4, Piazza della Biblioteca, 50019, Sesto Fiorentino.
Unveiled:	14 May 2011.

Posillipo, Naples.

Location:	On wall in park overlooking Isola La Gailoa, Posillipo, Naples, Italy.
Type:	Plaque to commemorate Arthur Conan Doyle's visit to the Island of Gailoa in 1895.
Unveiled:	May 2004 [not yet fitted in place].

Japan: Oiwake, Karuizawa.

Location:	Oiwake, Karuizawa, Japan.
Type:	Statue of Sherlock Holmes.
Unveiled:	9 October 1988.

Russia: **Moscow.**

Location:	Smolenskaya Embankment, near the British Embassy.
Type:	Statues of Holmes and Watson.
Unveiled:	27 April 2007.

Ekaterinburg.

Location:	Greenwich Shopping Mall, Ekaterinburg.
Type:	Statues of Holmes and Watson.
Unveiled:	2016.

Scotland: **Edinburgh.**

Location:	11, Picardy Place, Edinburgh.
Type:	Plaque on wall right hand side of front door.
Unveiled:	22 April 1949.

Location:	2, Picardy Place, Edinburgh.
Type:	Plaque to Arthur Conan Doyle identifying that he lived opposite at number 11.
Unveiled:	Not known.

Location:	23, George Square, Edinburgh.
Type:	Plaque to Arthur Conan Doyle.
Unveiled:	20 November 1987.

Location:	Picardy Place, Edinburgh.
Type:	Statue of Sherlock Holmes/Plaque to Arthur Conan Doyle.
Unveiled:	24 June 1991.

Location:	Teviot Place, Edinburgh, on wall of the main entrance of the medical school.
Type:	Plaque to Arthur Conan Doyle.
Unveiled:	Not known.

Location:	The Last Drop, 74-78 Grassmarket, Edinburgh.
Plaque:	Famous Scots, Arthur Conan Doyle.
Unveiled:	Unknown.

Switzerland: **Meiringen.**

Location:	The Rossli Hotel, Meiringen, (now a pizza restaurant).
Type:	Plaque to Sherlock Holmes.
Unveiled:	November 1952.

Location:	The Reichenbach Falls, Meiringen, Switzerland.
Type:	Plaque to Sherlock Holmes at The Falls.
Unveiled:	25 June 1957, moved 2 May 1968 to the car park at the falls.

Location:	Meiringen, Switzerland.
Type:	Plaque to Arthur Conan Doyle.
Unveiled:	2 May 1968.

Location:	The Reichenbach Falls, Meiringen, Switzerland.
Type:	A star marking the site of the Holmes/Moriarty struggle.
Unveiled:	1968.

Meiringen.

Location:	The Hôtel du Sauvage.
Type:	Plaque identifying the hotel as the "Englischer Hof".
Unveiled:	1987.

Location:	The Gemmi Pass.
Type:	Plaque to Sherlock Holmes.
Unveiled:	4 May 1987.

Location:	Meiringen, Switzerland.
Type:	Statue of Sherlock Holmes.
Unveiled:	10 September 1988.

Location:	The Reichenbach Falls, Meiringen, Switzerland.
Type:	Plaque to Sherlock Holmes.
Unveiled:	2 May 1992.

Davos.

Location:	Adjacent to the sports arena.
Type:	Plaque to Arthur Conan Doyle.
Unveiled:	3 May 1968.

Location:	Villa am Stein.
Type:	Plaque to Arthur Conan Doyle, Robert Louis Stevenson and Thomas Mann.
Unveiled:	Unknown.

Lausanne.

Location:	Hôtel National.
Type:	Plaque to commemorate Dr Watson's stay at the hotel.
Unveiled:	30 October 2004.

Leukerbad.

Location:	The Gemmi Pass.
Type:	Plaque.
Unveiled:	2 May 1987.

Riffelalp.

Location:	Not known.
Type:	Plaque to commemorate Arthur Conan Doyle who stayed at the Rifflelap Resort in August 1893.
Unveiled:	19 June 2005.

Arthur Conan Doyle and Cricket

The cricket career covered the years from 1878 until 1912, he played first and second class cricket for the following teams:

First Class for Marylebone Cricket Club (MCC) 1900-1907

Second class and other teams:

Ruyton 1878	Lismore 1881
Portsmouth XI 1884	Portsmouth Borough 1884-1890
South Hampshire 1884	Theatre Royal 1885
Stonyhurst Wanderers 1885	Majilton's Gay City Company 1886
Portsmouth Cricket Club 1886-1889	South Hampshire Rovers 1886-1889
Fareham 1887	In the Ranks Dramatic Company 1888
Southsea Rovers 1889	Corinthians 1889
Hampshire Rovers 1890-1907	United Services Portsmouth 1890
Hampshire XI 1890	Norwood Club 1891-1894
Allahakbarries 1891-1903	Emeriti 1892
Idlers 1892	Dr Thomson's XI 1893
Thorpe Asylum 1894, 1897	Authors 1896-1912
Hampshire 2nd XI 1896	Haslemere 1896-1905
Eastbourne 1897	Hindhead School 1898
Dr Conan Doyle's XI 1898	Grayshott 1898-1905
Mitcham 1899	Incogniti 1899-1901
C.M. Tukes XI 1899	Marylebone Cricket Club 1899-1912
SS *Oriental* ship's eleven 1900	Gentlemen of MCC 1901-1905
Undershaw Team 1902-1905	Esher 1904
Lythe Hill 1904	Hythe Hill 1905
Cricket Golfers 1905	Blue Mantles 1908-1912
Tunbridge Wells 1908	A. Conan Doyle & Crowborough 1908
Sussex Martlets 1910-1912	Littlehampton 1910
Mr F.H. Gresson's XI 1912	Manx Cats 1912

His batting was right handed and his bowling was right arm slow. He played 10 first class matches for MCC from 1900 until 1907, his batting career for these 10 matches is that he had 18 innings, 6 not out, scored 231 runs his highest score being 43, his bowling career was 85 balls, 1 maiden, 50 runs and he took 1 wicket. His 1 wicket taken was that of W.G. Grace on 23 August 1900, Grace had scored 110, caught by W. Storer, bowled A.I. Conan Doyle. In other matches the highest runs scored in an innings by Conan Doyle was 111 on 11 May 1889 and he took 8 wickets in a match on 30 August 1899.

The team that Arthur Conan Doyle played for are named first in all entries.

1878
n.d.　　　　During July or August, played for Ruyton and took 7 wickets for 11 runs. [203]

1881
July 1　　　Lismore against the 25th Regiment. [202]
July　　　　Lismore against Cahir. [202]

1884
April　　　　Portsmouth XI against the Royal Engineers; he scored 27. [203]
April 19　　Portsmouth XI against United Services at United Services Recreation Ground, Portsmouth; he scored 11, match drawn. [235]
May 10　　　Portsmouth Borough against Southsea Rivals at North End, Portsmouth. [8]
May 15　　　Portsmouth Borough against Ordnance Survey at County Ground, Southampton; he scored 15, match drawn. [235]

1884

May 21	Portsmouth Borough against the Royal Artillery [8], at United Services Recreation Ground, Portsmouth, he scored 27 and 2, match drawn. [235]
June 10	Portsmouth Borough against Hampshire Regiment [8], at United Services Recreation Ground, Portsmouth; he scored 44 and took 1 wicket, match drawn. [235]
July 28	Portsmouth Borough against Royal Artillery at St. George's, Portsmouth; he scored 12 and took 1 catch, Portsmouth Borough won. [235]
August 20	South Hampshire against United Services Portsmouth at Hilsea, Portsmouth; he scored 22 and 11, match drawn. [235]

1885

May 9	Portsmouth Borough against Southsea Rivals at North End Cricket Ground, Portsmouth, he scored 1 and 2, match drawn. [235]
July 18	Theatre Royal against Fun of the Bristol at Governor's Green, Portsmouth, he scored 65 and took 1 wicket, Theatre Royal won. [235]
August 3	Stonyhurst Wanderers against Stonyhurst College at Stonyhurst College Ground, Clitheroe, he scored 8 not out, Stonyhurst Wanderers won [235], for Old Stonyhurst (Wanderers) against Stonyhurst College. [66,202]
August 10	Stonyhurst Wanderers against Phoenix at Phoenix Cricket Club Ground, Phoenix Park, Dublin, he scored 15, Stonyhurst Wanderers won. [235]
August 12	Played on 12 &13 for Stonyhurst Wanderers against Dublin University at College Park, Dublin, he scored 24 and took 1 catch, Stonyhurst Wanderers won [235], for Old Stonyhurst (Wanderers) against Dublin University. [66,220]
August 14	Played on 14 & 15 for Stonyhurst Wanderers against Leinster at Observatory Lane, Rathmines, Dublin, he scored zero and 10 and took 1 catch, Stonyhurst Wanderers won [235], played for Old Stonyhurst (Wanderers) against Leinster Club at Rathmines, Dublin. [66,220]

1886

May	From mid-May ACD played cricket regularly for Portsmouth Cricket Club, scoring 22, 41, 42 and 25 in successive games. [8]
May 17	Portsmouth Borough against United Services Portsmouth at United Services Ground Portsmouth, he scored 8, took 1 wicket and 1 catch, United Services Portsmouth won. [235]
May 26	Majilton's Gay City Company against United Services Portsmouth at United Services Ground, Portsmouth, he scored 8, match drawn. [235]
June 23	Portsmouth Cricket Club against Fareham at Fareham, he scored zero in both innings. [8]
July 29	Portsmouth Borough against Royal Artillery Northern Division at United Services Recreation Ground, Portsmouth, he scored 3 and took 2 wickets, Portsmouth Borough won. [235]
August 4	South Hampshire Rovers against Brixton Wanderers at Hilsea, Portsmouth, he scored 6, match drawn. [235]
August 25	Portsmouth against Royal Sussex Regiment at United Service Cricket Ground, Portsmouth, he scored 31 and took 5 wickets, Portsmouth won. [2085]
August 26	Portsmouth Borough against Fareham at Catisfield, Fareham, he scored 12 and took 5 wickets, Portsmouth Borough won. [235]
August 28	Portsmouth Borough against United Services Portsmouth at United Services Recreation Ground, Portsmouth, he scored zero and took 1 wicket, match drawn, A.H. Wood played for Portsmouth Borough, he scored 22. [235]
September 8	Portsmouth Borough against Sarisbury at Hilsea, Portsmouth, he scored 47, match drawn, A.H. Wood played for Portsmouth Borough, he scored 115, took 3 wickets and 1 catch. [235]

1887

May 25	Portsmouth Borough against Fareham at Catisfield, Fareham, he scored 2 and zero, and took 2 wickets and 1 catch, match drawn. [235]
July 13	Fareham against Ockley at Catisfield, Fareham, he scored 2 and 2 and took 1 wicket, match drawn. [235]

1888

May 24	Portsmouth Borough against Royal Artillery Hilsea at United Services Recreation Ground, Portsmouth, he scored 21, took 1 wicket and 1 catch, Portsmouth Borough won. [235]
May 27	Portsmouth Borough against Royal Artillery Gosport at United Services Recreation Ground, Portsmouth, he scored 5, Royal Artillery won. [235]
June 6	Portsmouth Borough against United Services Portsmouth at United Services Recreation Ground, Portsmouth, he scored 3 and took 2 catches, United Services Portsmouth won. [235]
June 16	Portsmouth Borough against Royal Engineers at United Services Recreation Ground, Portsmouth, he scored 49 not out and took 2 wickets, Portsmouth Borough won. [235]
June 26	Portsmouth Borough against Fareham at Hilsea, Fareham, he did not bat, Portsmouth Borough won, A.H. Wood played for Portsmouth Borough, he did not bat but took 5 wickets and 1 catch. [235]
June 28	Portsmouth Borough against Ryde at Quarr Hill, Ryde, he scored 37, Ryde won. [235]
July 6	Portsmouth Borough against Southsea Rovers at Hilsea, Portsmouth, he scored 49, Portsmouth Borough won. [235]
July 14	Portsmouth Borough against South Lancashire Regiment at United Services Recreation Ground, Portsmouth, he scored 19, Portsmouth Borough won. [235]
July 19	Portsmouth Borough against Fareham at Catisfield, Fareham, he scored 7 and zero, match drawn. [235]
July 24	Portsmouth Borough against Ordnance Survey at County Ground, Southampton, he scored 5 and 36, match drawn. [235]
August 4	Portsmouth Borough against Royal Engineers at United Services Recreation Ground, Portsmouth, he scored 29 and took 7 wickets, Royal Engineers won. [235]
August 9	South Hampshire Rovers against Ye Olde Carawan at Adhurst St. Mary, he scored zero, match drawn, A.H Wood played for South Hampshire Rovers, he scored 35 and took 4 wickets and 1 catch. [235]
August 25	Portsmouth Borough against South Lancashire Regiment at United Services Recreation Ground, Portsmouth, he scored 17 and took 8 wickets, match drawn. [235]
August 30	Portsmouth Borough against Southampton at United Services Recreation Ground, Portsmouth, he scored 4 and did not bat in second innings, match drawn. A.H. Wood played for Portsmouth Borough, he scored 7 in the first innings and did not bat in the second innings, he took 2 wickets. [235]
September 1	Portsmouth Borough against Dorset Regiment at United Services Recreation Ground, Portsmouth, he scored 20 and did not bat in second innings, match drawn. [235]
September 13	In the Ranks Dramatic Company against Border Regiment at United Services Recreation Ground, Portsmouth, he scored 82 not out and took 1 wicket, In the Ranks Dramatic Company won. [235]
September 14	Played on 14 & 15 for Portsmouth Borough against Winchester at County Ground, Southampton, he scored 13 and 32, he took 2 wickets and 1 catch, Winchester won. A.H. Wood played for Portsmouth Borough, he scored 12 and 4 and took 1 wicket. [235]

1889

April 27	Portsmouth Borough against South Lancashire Regiment at United Services Recreation Ground, Portsmouth, he scored 6 and took 1 catch, South Lancashire Regiment won. [235]
May 3	Played on the 3 & 4 for Southsea Rovers against United Services Portsmouth at United Services Recreation Ground, Portsmouth; he scored 6 and took 3 wickets, match drawn. [235]
May 11	Portsmouth Borough against Royal Artillery Southern Division at United Services Recreation Ground, Portsmouth, he scored 111 not out and did bat in second innings, Portsmouth Borough won. [235]
May 15	Portsmouth Borough against United Services Portsmouth at United Services Recreation Ground, Portsmouth, he scored 3 and took 2 wickets, United Services Portsmouth won. [235]
May 24	Played on 24 & 25 for South Hampshire Rovers against United Services Portsmouth at United Services Recreation Ground, Portsmouth; he scored 29 and 24 and took 3 catches, match drawn. [235]
May 29	Portsmouth Borough against Fareham at Catisfield, Fareham, he scored 20 not out and 25, taking 2 wickets and 1 catch, match drawn. [235]
June 1	South Hampshire Rovers against Royal Navy at United Services Recreation Ground, Portsmouth, he scored 61 and took 3 wickets, South Hampshire Rovers won, A.H. Wood played for South Hampshire Rovers, he scored 4 and took 1 wicket. [235]
June 3	Played on 3 & 4 for Corinthians against United Services Portsmouth at United Services Recreation Ground, Portsmouth, he scored 16 and did not bat in second innings and took 7 wickets and 1 catch, Corinthians won. [235]
June 14	Portsmouth Cricket Club against Southampton Cricket Club in the Hants County Cricket Challenge Cup at Hilsea. [398]
June 18	South Hampshire Rovers against Hampshire Hogs at County Ground, Southampton, he scored 5 and took 2 wickets, match drawn. [235]
June 19	Portsmouth Borough against Havant at Havant Park, Havant, he scored zero and took 1 wicket, Havant won. [235]
June 22	Portsmouth Borough against Royal Artillery Southern Division at United Services Recreation Ground, Portsmouth, he scored 14, took 3 wickets and 1 catch, match drawn. [235]
June 27	Southsea Rovers against Royal Marine Artillery at United Services Recreation Ground, Portsmouth, he scored 26 and took 1 catch, match drawn. [235]
June 29	Portsmouth Borough against Dorset Regiment at United Services Recreation Ground, Portsmouth, he scored 4 and took 6 wickets, match drawn. [235]
July 4	Portsmouth Borough against Southampton at Hilsea, Portsmouth, he scored zero and did not bat in second innings and took 6 wickets, Southampton won, A.H. Wood played for Portsmouth Borough, he scored 1 and took 1 wicket. [235]
July 9	Played on 9 & 10 for Corinthians against United Services Portsmouth at United Services Recreation Ground, Portsmouth, he scored 4 and 30, he took 1 wicket and 1 catch, match drawn. [235]
July 13	South Hampshire Rovers against United Services Portsmouth at United Services Recreation Ground, Portsmouth, he scored 1 and 4, match drawn. [235]
July 24	Portsmouth Borough against Havant at Hilsea, Portsmouth, he scored 20 and took 1 catch, Portsmouth Borough won. [235]
July 27	South Hampshire Rovers against Portsmouth Grammar School at Hilsea, Portsmouth, he scored 10 and took 1 wicket, match drawn, A.H. Wood played for Portsmouth Grammar School, he scored 44 and 19 and took 2 catches. [235]
August 6	Portsmouth Borough against Ryde at Quarr Hill, Ryde, he scored 10, and took 1 wicket and 1 catch, match drawn. [235]

1890

April 25	Played on 25 & 26 for the United Services against MCC at Portsmouth; he scored 20 and took 1 catch. [31]
May 21	Hampshire Rovers against Fareham at Hilsea, Portsmouth, he scored 8 and 11 not out, and took 7 wickets, match drawn. [235]
May 30	Played on 30 & 31 for Hampshire Rovers against United Services Portsmouth at United Services Recreation Ground, Portsmouth; he scored 22 and took 6 wickets, match drawn. [235]
June 16	Played on 16 & 17 for Hampshire Rovers against South Lancashire Regiment in Jersey, he scored 22 and 26, and took 5 wickets, Hampshire Rovers won. [235]
June 18	Hampshire Rovers against Victoria College, Jersey at the Victoria College Ground, St. Helier, Jersey, he scored 28 and took 4 wickets, match drawn. [235]
June 19	Hampshire Rovers against Jersey in Jersey, he scored 6, match drawn. [235]
July 2	Played on 2 & 3 for Portsmouth against United Services at United Services Recreation Ground, he scored 40 and 2 and took 4 wickets in the first innings and 6 wickets in the second innings, Portsmouth won. [410]
July 11	Played on 11 & 12 for Hampshire Rovers against United Services Portsmouth at United Services Recreation Ground, Portsmouth; he scored zero and 14 and took 4 wickets, United Services Portsmouth won. [235]
July 16	Played on 16 & 17 for United Services Portsmouth against Incogniti at the United Services Cricket Club, he took 1 wicket but did not bat, match drawn. [411]
August 18	Hampshire Rovers against Green Jackets at St. Cross, he scored 3, match drawn. [1969] {Note: St Cross ground at Winchester.}
August 20	Played on 20 & 21 for United Services Portsmouth against Free Foresters at United Services Recreation Ground, Portsmouth; he scored 4 and 1, and took 4 wickets and 1 catch, Free Foresters won, [235] at the United Services Cricket Club. [412]
August 22	Played on 22 & 23 for United Services Portsmouth against Crystal Palace at United Services Ground, Portsmouth, he scored 7 and 18 and took 2 wickets, match drawn. [235]
August 25	Played on 25 & 26 for United Services Portsmouth against MCC at United Services Recreation Ground, Portsmouth, he scored 20 and took 1 catch, match drawn, A.H. Wood played for United Services Portsmouth, he scored 16 and took 5 wickets. [235]
August 28	Played on 28 & 29 for Hampshire XI against Hampshire Colts at Winchester College Ground, he scored 6 and 4, and took 2 catches, Hampshire XI won, A.H. Wood played for Hampshire XI, he scored 2 and then 7 not out and took 4 wickets. [235]
September 9	United Services Portsmouth against South Hampshire at United Services Cricket Club, he scored 3 and 15, and took 1 wicket, match drawn, [235] South Hampshire won. [413]
September 15	Portsmouth Borough against Winchester at County Ground, Southampton, he scored 5 and 2, and he took 4 wickets, Winchester won, A.H. Wood played for Portsmouth Borough, he scored zero and 13 and took 1 wicket and 2 catches. [235]

1891

n.d.	Allahakbarries against Shere. [1146]
June 30	Norwood Club away at Addiscombe, he scored 22 [320] for Norwood Club against Addiscombe at Norwood Green, he scored 21, match drawn. [235]
July 1	Norwood Club at home to the Surrey Club and Ground, he scored zero [320] at Norwood Green, he scored zero, Surrey Club and Ground won. [235]
July 3	Norwood Club against Willesden at Norwood Green, he scored zero, Norwood Club won. [235]
July 4	Norwood Club against Oakleigh Wanderers at Norwood Park, he scored 15 and took 1wicket, Norwood Club won. [235]

1891

n.d.	Norwood Club against Norbury Park, he scored 32 and took 5 wickets. [320]
July 15	Norwood Club against The Erratics at Norwood Green, he scored 27 and took 2 wickets and 1 catch, Norwood Club won. [235]
July 18	Norwood Club against Hornsey at Norwood Green, he scored 2, match drawn. [235]
July 22	Norwood Club against Northbrook at Norwood Green, he scored 2, match drawn. [235]
August 1	Norwood Club against Granville (Lee) at The Cedars, Lee, he scored 2, Granville (Lee) won. [235]
August 3	Norwood Club against Willesden at Toleys Cricket Ground, Willesden, he scored 6 and took 3 wickets, match drawn. [235]
August 8	Norwood Club against Addiscombe at Sandilands, Croydon, he scored zero, match drawn. [235]
August 12	Norwood Club against Windsor Home Park at Windsor Park, Windsor, he scored 18 and took 1 catch, Norwood Club won. [235]
September 2	Norwood Club against East Dulwich at Norwood Green, he scored 33 and took 1 wicket, match drawn. [235]]

1892

May 14	Norwood Club against Croydon at Norwood Green, he scored zero and took 5 wickets, Norwood Club won. [235]
May 20	Played on 20 & 21 for Hampshire Rovers against United Services Portsmouth at United Services Recreation Ground, Portsmouth, he scored zero and 1, and took 2 wickets, Hampshire Rovers won, A.H. Wood played for Hampshire Rovers, he scored 31 and 28, he took 3 wickets and 1 catch. [235]
May 28	Norwood Club against Dulwich at Norwood Green, he scored 14 and took 1 wicket, match drawn. [235]
June 6	Norwood Club against Forest Hill at Norwood Green, he scored 48 and took 3 wickets, Norwood Club won. [235]
June 11	Norwood Club against Plaistow at Norwood Green, he scored 11, match drawn. [235]
June 18	Norwood Club against Norbury Park at J.W. Hobbs Ground, Norbury, he scored 3 and took 3 wickets, Norwood Club won. [235]
June 21	Emeriti against Beaumont College at Beaumont College Ground, Old Windsor, he scored 3 and took 4 wickets and took 1 catch, Emeriti won. [235]
June 22	Norwood Club against Croydon at Fairfield Ground, Croydon, he scored 16 and took 1 wicket and 1 catch, Norwood Club won. [235]
June 25	Norwood Club against The Grecians at Norwood Green, he scored 79, Norwood Club won. [235]
June 27	Emeriti against Hampstead at Lymington Road, Hampstead, he scored 15, match drawn. [235]
June 29	Norwood Club against Addiscombe at Sandilands, Croydon, he scored 18 and took 1 catch, Norwood Club won. [235]
July 4	Norwood Club against The Erratics at Norwood Green, he scored 25 and 19 and took 1 wicket and 1 catch, match drawn. [235]
July 6	Norwood Club against Willesden at Norwood Green, he scored 19 and took 4 wickets and 1 catch, Norwood Club won. [235]
July 7	Norwood Club against MCC at Merchant Taylors' Ground, Northwood, he scored 4 and then 1 not out, match drawn. [235]
July 8	Norwood Club against S. Ellis' XI at Norwood Green, he scored zero and took 2 wickets and 1 catch, match drawn. [235]
July 20	Norwood Club against Sutton at Cheam Road, Sutton, he scored 4 and took 5 wickets, Norwood Club won. [235]
July 30	Norwood Club against Norbury Park at Norwood Green, he scored 9, Norwood Club won. [235]

1892

August 1	Norwood Club against South Croydon at Norwood Green, he scored zero and took 7 wickets and 2 catches, Norwood Club won. [235]
August 6	Norwood Club against Dulwich College at Turney Road, Dulwich, he scored 104 not out, Norwood Club won [235] against Dulwich. [320]
August 10	Norwood Club against Roving Friars at Norwood Green, he scored 26 and took 2 wickets and 1 catch, Norwood Club won. [235]
August 13	Norwood Club against Epsom at Epsom Down, Epsom, he scored 40, match drawn. [235,320]
August 17	Norwood Club against Addiscombe at Norwood Green, he scored 29 and took 5 wickets, match drawn. [235]
September 3	Norwood Club against Granville (Lee) at Norwood Green, he scored 10, match drawn. [235]
September 6	Idlers against Norwood Club at Norwood Green, he scored 17 and took 3 wickets, match drawn. Also in the Idlers team were A.H. Wood who scored 8 and took 1 catch, Innes Doyle scored 25 and E.W. Hornung who scored 10. Jerome K. Jerome was officiating as scorer and did not play. [235] ACD was captain of The Idler team. [124]
September 7	Idlers against Norwood Club at Norwood, he scored 17 and took 4 wickets, match drawn. Also in the Idlers team were A.H. Wood who scored 8 and took 1 catch, Innes Doyle scored 25 and E.W. Hornung who scored 10. [320]

1893

n.d.	Allahakbarries against Shere. [1146]
May 22	Norwood Club against Chislehurst at Norwood Pavilion Ground, he scored 10 [320] Norwood Club won [221], at Norwood Green, he scored 10 and took 1 catch, match drawn. [235]
June 3	Norwood Club 1st team against Dulwich 1st team at Norwood Pavilion Ground, Norwood Club won [222], at Norwood Green, he scored zero. [235]
June 17	Norwood Club 1st team against Forest Hill 1st team at Norwood Pavilion Ground, Norwood Club won [223] he scored 8 and took 1 catch. [235]
June 24	Norwood Club against London & Westminster Bank at Norwood Pavilion Ground, Norwood Club won [224] at Norwood Green, he scored 3, match drawn. [235]
June 28	Norwood Club against Epsom probably at Norwood Pavilion Ground, Epsom won, he scored 38. [225]
July 3	Norwood Club against Croydon during Norwood Cricket Week, implying that the game was played at Norwood Pavilion Ground, match drawn [226] at Norwood Green, he scored zero. [235]
July 4	Norwood Club against Brixton Wanderers during Norwood Cricket Week, implying the game was played at Norwood Pavilion Ground, Norwood Club won [227] at Norwood Green, he scored 16 and took 1 catch. [235]
July 8	Norwood Club against Forest Hill at Norwood Green, he scored 37, Norwood Club won. [235]
July 15	Norwood Club 2nd team against Addiscombe 2nd team at Addiscombe Ground, Norwood Club won. [228]
July 22	Norwood Club 2nd team against Grecians 2nd team at Norwood Pavilion Ground, Norwood Club won. [229]
July 27	Dr Thomson's XI against Dr Law's XI at Thorpe Asylum Ground, St. Andrew's Norfolk, he took 8 wickets for 9 runs and scored 12, Dr Thomson's XI won. [2022]
September 9	Norwood Club against Kenley at Norwood Green, he scored zero, match drawn. [235]

1894

May 14	Norwood Club at home against the London and Westminster Bank, he scored zero. [320]

1894

n.d.	Norwood Club second eleven against the Spencer team. [320]
June 16	Norwood Club against Caterham at Norwood Green, he did not bat, Norwood Club won. [235]
July	Early July Norwood Club against Croydon during the Norwood Cricket Club week, he scored 40, Norwood Club won. [1940]
July 3	Norwood Club against Crystal Palace at Norwood in the second match of the cricket week, he scored zero and took 5 wickets, Crystal Palace won. [1941] (*3)
n.d.	Norwood Club against Crystal Palace and took 5 wickets. [320] (*3)
July 4	Norwood Club against "the well known Crystal Palace Eleven", he took 5 wickets. [448] (*3)
July 4	Norwood Club against Mitcham at Norwood, he scored 5 and took 2 wickets, Mitcham won. [1941]
July 5	Norwood Club against MCC at Merchant Taylors' Ground, Northwood, he scored 4 and zero, and took 1 wicket and 1 catch, MCC won. [235]
July 12	Norwood Club against MCC, he scored 4, MCC won. [237]
August 2	Norwood Club against Croydon, he scored 45, due to heavy rain the play was abandoned leaving the match as a draw. [1942]
August 6	Norwood Club against Gentlemen of Netherlands at Merchant Taylors' School Ground, Northwood, he scored 64 and took 2 catches, match drawn. [235]
n.d.	Norwood Club against Burlington Wanderers and scored 100. [320]
August 18	Norwood Club against Northbrook at Norwood Green, he scored 35 and took 6 wickets, Norwood Club won. [235,320]
August 25	Thorpe Asylum against Lowestoft Visitors at Thorpe Asylum, Norfolk, he scored 65, Thorpe Asylum won. [2013,2022]
August 30	Norfolk County Asylum against 1st King Dragoon Guards at Thorpe Asylum, he scored 1 and 30 and took 10 wickets all in one innings, 10 wickets for 15 runs, Norfolk County Asylum won. [2014]
September 1	Norwood Club against Granville at Norwood, he scored 20 and took 1 wicket, Granville won. [2018]
September 8	Played his last game for Norwood Club against F. Loud's XI at Norwood, ACD scored 5, Norwood Club won. [320]

1896

May 14	Hampshire Rover 2nd XI against the Army Service Corps at the Recreation Ground, Portsmouth, he scored 36, Hampshire Rovers won. [455]
May 25	Played on 25 & 26 for Hampshire Rovers against United Services Portsmouth at United Services Recreation Ground, Portsmouth; he scored 84 not out and 16 and took 2 wickets, match drawn. [235]
July 24	Played on 24 & 25 for Hampshire Rovers against United Services Portsmouth at United Services Recreation Ground, Portsmouth; he scored 44, Hampshire Rovers won. [235]
August 10	Played on 10 & 11 for Hampshire Rovers against Littlehampton at the Sportsfield, Littlehampton, he scored 17 and 7, Littlehampton won, in the Rovers team were A.H. Wood who scored 17 and 20 and took 3 wickets, and Innes Doyle who scored 7 and then 16 not out and took 2 catches. [235]
August 15	Haslemere at Lythe Park against East Lyss. [63]
August 17	Played on 17 & 18 for Hampshire Rovers against Kensington at Hilsea, Portsmouth, he scored 28 and took 2 wickets, match drawn, in the Rovers team was A.H. Wood who scored 100 and took 1 wicket. [235]
August 24	Played on 24 & 25 for Hampshire Rovers against Old Malvernians at Hilsea, Portsmouth, he scored 15 and did not bat in second innings, he took 1 wicket and 1 catch, match drawn, in the Rovers team was A.H. Wood who scored 12 and 2 and took 4 wickets. [235]
August 26	Haslemere against Godalming. [63]

1896

September 17   Authors against the Press at Lord's, he scored 101 not out and took 2 wickets, match drawn. [235,1214]

1897

May 8   Eastbourne against Thirteen Local Clubs at Eastbourne, he scored 49, Eastbourne won. [466]

June 12   Hampshire Rovers against Royal Navy at United Services Recreation Ground, Portsmouth, he scored 19, Royal Navy won. [235]

June 17   Played on 17 & 18 for Hampshire Rovers against Leighton at Leighton, Wiltshire, he scored 42 in the first innings and 9 not out in the second innings, he took 2 wickets and 2 catches. [2008]

June 19   Allahakbarries against the Artists at Broadway, Worcester. [1146]

June 24   Eastbourne against South Lynn at The Saffrons, Eastbourne, he scored 2 and took 2 wickets, South Lynn won. [1943]

July 19   Played on 19 & 20 for Eastbourne against Surrey Club & Ground at The Saffrons, Eastbourne, he scored 4, took 1 wicket and 1 catch, match drawn. [1944]

August 2   Played on 2 & 3 for Eastbourne against Plaistow at The Saffrons, Eastbourne, he scored 67, took 3 wickets and 1 catch, Eastbourne won. [1945]

August 4   Played on 4 & 5 for Eastbourne against Old Yverdonians at The Saffrons, Eastbourne, he scored 6 and took 2 wickets, Eastbourne won. [1946]

August 6   Played on 6 & 7 for Eastbourne against Uppingham Rovers at The Saffrons, Eastbourne, he scored 12 and took 1 and 5 wickets, Eastbourne won. [1947]

August 9   Played on 9 & 10 for Hampshire Rovers against Littlehampton at the Sportsfield, Littlehampton, he scored 16 and 3, and took 6 wickets, Littlehampton won, A.H. Wood scored 1 for the Rovers and took 7 wickets. [235]

August 11   Played on 11 & 12 for Eastbourne against Old Cholmellians at The Saffrons, Eastbourne, he scored 15, Eastbourne won. [1948]

August 16   Played on 16 & 17 for Eastbourne against Reigate Priory, he scored zero and 48 and took 1 wicket, drawn match. [1949]

August 18   Played on 18 & 19 for Eastbourne against Incogniti at The Saffrons, Eastbourne, he scored 4 and took 6 wickets, Eastbourne won. [235]

August 23   Played on 23 & 24 for Eastbourne against MCC at The Saffrons, Eastbourne, he scored 35 and 27, and took 1 wicket, MCC won. [235]

August 25   Played on 25 & 26 for Eastbourne against Old Malvernians at The Saffrons, Eastbourne, he scored 1 and took 1 wicket, drawn match. [1950]

August 30   Played on 30 & 31 for Eastbourne against Peripatetics at The Saffrons, Eastbourne, he scored 35 and 1, took 1 wicket, Peripatetics won. [1951]

September 9   Norfolk County Asylum against CEYMS (Church of England Young Men's Society) at The Asylum, he scored 44, The Asylum won. [2022]

1898

May 28   Grayshott against Liphook at Grayshott Hall and scored 37. [63]

May 30   Played on 30 & 31 for Hampshire Rovers against United Services Portsmouth at United Services Recreation Ground, Portsmouth; he scored 16 and 11, and took 2 wickets, match drawn. [235]

June 4   Grayshott against Lychmere at Grayshott Hall and scored 43 not out. [63]

June 11   Allahakbarries against the Artists at Broadway, Worcester, he scored 46, the Allahakbarries won. [1146]

July 6   Haslemere against Petworth at Lythe Hill Park and scored 17 and took 3 wickets. [63]

July 20   Hindhead School against Churt. [63]

July 22   Played on 22 & 23 for Hampshire Rovers against United Services Portsmouth at United Services Recreation Ground, Portsmouth, he scored 28, and there was no play on the final day, match drawn. [235]

1898

August 1	"Dr Conan Doyle's XI" against Haslemere [63] Undershaw (Dr Conan Doyle's Eleven) at Haslemere, he scored 16, Undershaw won. [1952]
August 3	Undershaw (Dr Conan Doyle's Eleven) against Mr Turle's Eleven, he scored 5, Undershaw won. [1953]
August 4	"Dr Conan Doyle's XI" against Churt [63] Undershaw (Dr Conan Doyle's Eleven) he scored 12, Undershaw won. [1954]
August 5	Undershaw (Dr Conan Doyle's Eleven) against Captain Clark's Eleven at Beacon Hill, he scored 4, match drawn. [1954]
August 15	Haslemere against Northchapel. [63]

1899

May 9	Mitcham against Surrey Colts at the Oval, he scored 6, match drawn. [1955]
May 15	Played on 15 & 16 for Incogniti against Aldershot Division at Officers Club Services Ground, Aldershot, he scored 17 and too 1 catch, match drawn. [235]
May 18	Played on 18 & 19 for Hampshire Rovers against United Services, Portsmouth at United Services Recreation Ground, Portsmouth; he scored 11 and 3, and took 2 wickets, Hampshire Rovers won. [235]
May 22	Played cricket, he scored 53 and took 10 wickets, teams unknown. [203,215]
May 24	Played on 24 & 25 for Incogniti against Uppingham at Upper Field, Uppingham School, he scored 6, match drawn. [235]
June 1	Authors against the Artists at Denmark Hill, he scored 5, the Authors won. [235]
June	Played for Incogniti on schools tour against Clifton College, Sherborne School, East Gloucester and Cheltenham College. [63]
June 3	Incogniti against Clifton College at Clifton College Close Ground, Clifton, he scored 4 and took 4 wickets, Clifton College won. [235,1148]
June 5	Played on 5 & 6 for Incogniti against Sherborne School at Sherborne School, Sherborne, he scored 7 and took 1 catch, match drawn. [235]
June 8	Incogniti against East Gloucester at Charlton Park, Gloucester, he scored 67 and took 3 wickets, Incogniti won [1117], played at East Gloucester Cricket Club Ground, Cheltenham, match drawn. [235]
June 9	Played on 9 & 10 for Incogniti against Cheltenham College at the College Ground, Cheltenham, he scored 43 and took 3 wickets, Incogniti won. [235,1118,1148]
June 11	Incogniti against Clifton, Bristol at Bristol, he scored 4 and took 4 wickets, Clifton won. [477]
June 23	C.M. Tuke's XI against Incogniti at Chiswick Park, Chiswick, he scored 15, Incogniti won. [235]
June 24	Incogniti against Blackheath at The Rectory Field, Blackheath, he scored 1 and took 2 wickets, match drawn. [235]
June 30	Allahakbarries against the Artists' at Broadway, Worcester. [481]
July 1	Grayshott against Farnham. [63]
July 5	MCC & Ground against Richmond at Richmond he zero and took 1 wicket, MCC won. [4] MCC against Richmond at Old Deer Park, Richmond, match drawn. [235]
July 19	MCC against Dorking at Cotmandene, Dorking, he scored 9 and took 3 wickets, match drawn. [235]
July 21	Played on 21 & 22 for Hampshire Rovers against United Services, Portsmouth; he scored 55 and took 1 catch, Hampshire Rovers won. [235]
July 24	Played on 24 & 25 for MCC against Wiltshire at Trowbridge Cricket Club Ground [203]; he missed the first innings but scored 6 in the second innings and took 1 catch, Wiltshire won. [235,322]
July 28	MCC against Oaklands Park at Oaklands Park Cricket Club Ground, Weybridge, he scored 53 and took 2 wickets, MCC won. [235]
July 29	Grayshott against Shottermill. [63]

1899

August	ACD held his August cricket week; he staged games against Haslemere, Grayshott and other local clubs. [202,322]
August 4	MCC against Surbiton at Surbiton, he scored 1 and took 2 wickets, Surbiton won. [235]
August 21	Incogniti against Hampshire Hogs at County Ground, Southampton, he scored 16, match drawn. [235]
August 23	Played on 23 & 24 for Incogniti against Hampshire Rovers at Hilsea, Portsmouth, he scored 89 and took 3 wickets, 1 of which was that of A.H. Wood, match drawn, A.H. Wood played for Hampshire Rovers, he scored 8 and took 1 wicket. [235]
August 25	Played on 25 & 26 for Incogniti against Bournemouth at Dean Park, Bournemouth, he scored 31 and zero and took 4 wickets in both innings, match drawn. [235]
August 30	Played on 30 & 31 for MCC & Ground against Cambridgeshire at Lord's, he took 7 wickets [63] (*2), including a hat trick [56,322,1235], MCC against Cambridgeshire, he did not bat but took 7 wickets in the first innings and 1 wicket in the second innings, match drawn. [56,235]

1900

March 9	SS *Oriental* ship's eleven against St. Vincent, Cape Verde; he took 3 wickets, ship's eleven won. [337,494]
August 8	Played on 8 & 9 for MCC against Hertfordshire at Lord's; he scored 1, match drawn. [235]
August 13	played on 13 & 14 for MCC against Buckinghamshire at Lord's; he scored 6 and took 3 wickets, MCC won. [235]
August 15	Played on 15 & 16 for MCC against Wiltshire at Lord's; he scored 34 and 3, Wiltshire won. [235,497]
August 17	Played on 17 & 18 for MCC against Cambridgeshire at Lord's; he scored 33 and 6, he took 1 wicket, match drawn. [235,1249]
August 23	Played a first class match on 23, 24 & 25 for MCC against London County at Crystal Palace Park, there was no play on the first day; he scored 4 and took the wicket of W G Grace, this being his only first class wicket, MCC won. In this match ACD made his debut in First-Class Matches. [56,71,202,235,322]
August 29	Haslemere against Northchapel at Lythe Park and scored 78. [63]
September 1	Haslemere against Petersfield at Lythe Park and took 8 wickets. [63]

1901

May 16	Played a first class match on 16, 17 & 18 for MCC against Leicestershire at Lord's [63,1260], he scored 1 and then 32 not out, MCC won. [235]
May 20	Allahakbarries against the Artists at Kensington Park [63] at St. Quintin's Park, Kensington, he scored 91 and took 8 wickets, the Allahakbarries won. [235]
May 23	Played a first class match on 23 & 24 May, for MCC against Derbyshire at Lord's the match was scheduled for 3 days but was completed in 2 days [63,1262]; he scored 28, MCC won. [235]
June 3	Played on 3 & 4 for Incogniti against Sherborne School [61,63,80,202], at Sherborne School, he scored 11 and took 4 wickets in first innings and 3 in second innings, match drawn, A.H. Wood played for Incogniti, he scored 57 and took 3 wickets. [186,235]
June 5	Played on 5 & 6 for Incogniti against Lansdown at Coombe Park, Bath [61,80] or Combe Park [63] or Lansdown Cricket Club Ground, Combe Park, Bath, he scored 5 and took 2 wickets, match drawn, A.H. Wood played for Incogniti, he scored 36 and took 2 wickets. [235]
June 7	Played on 7 & 8 for Incogniti against Cheltenham College at the College Ground, Cheltenham [61,63,80] he scored 23 and 13, he took 1 wicket, match drawn [187,235] A.H. Wood played for Incogniti, he scored 38 and 20 and took 5 wickets. [22,36]

1901

June 13	Played a first class match on 13 & 14, for MCC against London County at Lord's, the match was scheduled for 3 days but was completed in 2, he scored 21 not out and 10, London County won. [235]
June 17	Played on 17 & 18 for MCC against Minor Counties at Lord's [56], he scored 7 and 8 and took 2 wickets, Minor Counties won. [235]
June 21	Authors against the Artists in Esher [63] at New Road, Esher, he scored 2 and took 5 wickets, the Artists won. [235]
June 24	Played on 24 & 25, for MCC against the Grange Club at Lord's, he scored 4 and 1 [63,1264], Gentlemen of MCC against Grange Club, Grange won. [235]
June 26	Gentlemen of Marylebone Cricket Club against The Royal Navy at Lord's; he scored 31, The Gentlemen won. [63,235]
June 29	MCC against the Royal Military College at Camberley [63], at Royal Military Academy Ground, Camberley, he scored zero, match drawn. [235]
July 17	Hampshire Rovers against Royal Marines at Royal Marines Ground, Eastney, Southsea, he scored 10 and took 4 wickets, match drawn. [235] (*2)
July	Hampshire Rovers against R.M.A at the Officers' Ground, Portsmouth, he scored 10 and took 4 wickets, R.M.A. won. [523] (*2)
July 19	Played on 19 & 20 for Hampshire Rovers against United Services at United Services Ground, Portsmouth; he scored 24 and 25, match drawn, A.H. Wood played for Hampshire Rovers, he scored 83 and 23 and took 3 catches. [235,524]
August 9	Played on 9 & 10 for MCC against Norfolk at County Ground, Lakeham [63]; he scored 16, and took 4 wickets, match drawn. [235]
August 14	Played on 14 & 15 for MCC against Dorsetshire at Lord's, he scored 4 not out and took 1 wicket, match drawn. [63,235]
August 16	Played on 16 & 17 for MCC against Wiltshire at Lord's [63,1268], and scored 4 not out and 33, he took 1 wicket, Wiltshire won. [235]
August 23	Played on 23 & 24 for MCC against Oxfordshire at Lord's [1269], and scored 31 not out and zero, he took 2 wickets, MCC won. [235]
August 31	MCC against London Playing Fields at Lord's, he scored 53, match drawn. [63,235,1270]

1902

June	Authors against the Royal Engineers at Chatham, he took 5 wickets. [202]
June 23	Played a first class match on 23 & 24 for MCC against Derbyshire at Lord's the match was scheduled for 3 days but was completed in 2 days [1278], he scored zero and did not bat in second innings, MCC won. [235]
June 30	Authors against the Artists at Esher, Surrey, the Artists won [322] at New Road, Esher, he scored 13 and did not bat in the second innings, and took 3 wickets, match drawn. [235]
July 14	Played a first class match on 14, 15 & 16 for MCC against London County at Crystal Palace Park [1282], ACD scored 43 and zero. ACD passed his previous highest First Class score of 32, London County won. [235]
July 25	Played on 25 & 26 for the Gentlemen of Marylebone Cricket Club against Royal Engineers at Lord's and scored 1 and took 2 wickets and 1 catch, MCC won. [235,1284]
August 2	The Undershaw Team against Eashing at Haslemere, he scored 19 and took 2 wickets, Undershaw won. [2087]
August 7	The Undershaw Team against Broadwater at Broadwater, he scored 11 and took 8 wickets, Undershaw won. [2088]
August 8	The Undershaw Team against Lynchmere at Lynchmere, he scored 61 & 5 and took 5 wickets and on1 catch, Undershaw won. [2089]
August 13	Played on 13 & 14 for MCC against North Devon at North Devon Club Ground, Sandhills, Instow, he scored 5, took 2 wickets and 1 catch, match drawn, [235]

1902

August 15	Played on 15 & 16 for MCC against R.W. Sealy's XI at Golf Links Road, Westward Ho!, he scored 64 and took 3 wickets and 1 catch, MCC won. [235]
August 18	On 18 & 19 he was in MCC team to play Devon at Kelly College Ground, Tavistock, but owing to heavy rain the match appears to have been cancelled. [2090]
August 20	Played on 20 & 21 for MCC against Teignbridge at Teignbridge; he scored 1 and 31, MCC won. [235]
August 25	Played on 25 & 26 for MCC against Cornwall at Boscawen Park, Truro, Cornwall; he scored 7 and 4, and took 3 catches, MCC won. [235]
August 27	Played on 27 & 28 for MCC against Sidmouth at Belmont Grounds, Sidmouth, he scored 7 and 27, he took 1 wicket, Sidmouth won. [235]

1903

May 22	Authors against the Artists at Esher, Surrey [71], at New Road, Esher, he scored 28 and took 1 wicket, the Authors won. [235,1146]
May 23	Authors against Esher at Esher, Surrey [71], he scored 29 and Esher won. [1078,1146]
May 28	Played a first class match on 28 & 29 for MCC & Ground against Kent at Lord's [1301], the match was scheduled for 3 days but completed in 2 days, ACD scored 3 and then 16 not out, Kent won. [235]
June 5	Allahakbarries against Royal Engineers (Chatham) at Chatham, he 29 not out and took 5 wickets. [1956]
June 26	Played on 26 & 27 for MCC against 1st Army Corps at Officers Club Services Ground, Aldershot; he scored 13 and 10, and took 2 catches, 1st Army Corps won. [235]
July 4	Played a cup match for Grayshott against Blackmoor. [63]
July 6	Authors against the Artists at Frensham Hill, Farnham, he scored 25 and took 3 wickets, the Artists won. [235]
July 8	MCC against Bedford Grammar School at Bedford School Ground, he scored zero, match drawn. [235]
July 9	MCC against Bedford Modern School at Bedford Modern School Ground, he scored 15 and took 1 wicket, MCC won. [235]
July 10	MCC against Bedford County School at Bedford County School Ground, he scored 30, MCC won. [235]
July 14	MCC against Oatlands Park at Oatlands Park Cricket Club Ground, Weybridge, he scored 82, match drawn. [235]
July 18	Played a cup match for Grayshott against Linchmere [63], l'Anson Cup final at Lynchmere Cricket Ground, he scored 37, took 1 wicket and 1 catch, Grayshott won. [235]
July 20	Played on 20 & 21 for MCC against Gentlemen of Warwickshire at Warwick Cricket Club Ground; he scored 11 and 1, match drawn. [235]
July 22	Played on 22 & 23 for MCC against Leamington Town at Leamington Cricket Club Ground; he scored 1 and took 1 wicket, match drawn. [235]
July 24	MCC against Coventry and North Warwickshire at The Butts Ground, Coventry, he scored 22 not out and did not bat in second innings, he took 1 wicket and 1 catch, match drawn. [235]
July 25	MCC against Rugby Town at Rugby Town Club Ground, he scored 65 and took 1 wicket, MCC won. [235]
August 5	The Undershaw Team against Grayshott at Grayshott, he scored 23 and took 1 wicket, Undershaw won. [2091]
August 6	The Undershaw Team against Broadwater at Godalming, he scored 8 and took 3 wickets and 1 catch, Undershaw won. [2091]
August 14	Played on 14 & 15 for MCC against Sidmouth at Belmont Grounds, Sidmouth, he scored zero and 4, match drawn. [235]
August 17	Played on 17 & 18 for MCC against United Services at Devonport; he scored 3 and 35, MCC won. [235]

1903

August 19	Played on 19 & 20 for MCC against Teignbridge at Teignbridge, he scored zero, match drawn. [235]
August 21	Played on 21 & 22 for MCC against Devon at Kelly College Ground, Tavistock, Devon; he scored 8, MCC won. [235]
August 24	Played on 24 & 25 for MCC against Instow at North Devon Cricket Club Ground, Sandhills, Instow; he scored 9, MCC won [235] or North Devon at Instow. [546]
August 26	Played on 26 & 27 for MCC against R.W. Sealy's XI at Golf links Road, Westward Ho!, he scored 96 not out, match drawn. [235]

1904

n.d.	MCC against Cambridgeshire at Lord's, he took 7 wickets. [10] (*2) {Note: ACD has this wrong in his autobiography, the match actually took place on 30 & 31 August 1899.}
May 2	Played a first class match on 2, 3 & 4 for MCC against London County at Lord's [1322]; he scored 10 not out and 31, London County won. [235]
May 14	Esher against Marlborough Blues at New Road, Esher, he scored 3, match drawn, Innes Doyle also played for Esher and scored 8. [235]
May 16	Played a first class match on 16 & 17 for MCC against Kent [1323], the match was scheduled for 3 days but was completed in 2 days, he scored zero and 5 not out, MCC won. [235]
May 20	Authors against the Artists at Esher, Surrey [71] at New Road Esher, he scored 27 and took 5 wickets and 1 catch, the Authors won, also playing for the Authors were Innes Doyle who scored 15 and E.W. Hornung who cored zero. [235]
May 21	Authors' against Esher at Esher, he scored 8, Esher won. [2092]
June 21	MCC (Sir A. Conan Doyle's XI) against Hawick at Hawick he scored zero, MCC won [562] at Buccleuch Park, Hawick A.H. Wood played for MCC, he scored 54 and took 1 catch. [235]
June 22	MCC (Sir A. Conan Doyle's XI) against Gala at Galashiels, he scored 10, MCC won [563] at Mossilee, Galashiels, A.H. Wood played for MCC, he scored 58 and took 1 catch and stumped 3. [235]
June 23	MCC (Sir A. Conan Doyle's XI) against Selkirk at Philiphaugh, Selkirk he scored 35 and zero and took 1 catch, MCC won [235,564] A.H. Wood played for MCC, he scored zero and took 2 catches. [235]
June 24	Played on 24 & 25 for MCC (Sir A. Conan Doyle's XI against South of Scotland at Galashiels, he scored 8 and took 3 wickets [565], MCC won, at Mossillee, Galashiels, A.H. Wood played for MCC, he scored 56 and took 1 catch and 1 stump. [235]
July 7	MCC against Haverford College at Lord's; he scored 41 not out, and took 1 catch, Haverford College won. [325]
July 13	Lythe Hill against Marlborough Blues at Lynchmere Cricket Ground, Lynchmere, he scored 4 and took 6 wickets, Marlborough Blues won. [235]
July 19	Lythe Hill against Incogniti at Lynchmere Cricket Ground, Lynchmere, he scored 7 and zero and took 2 wickets, match drawn. [235]
August 12	Played on 12 & 13 for MCC against Devon Dumplings at County Cricket Ground, Exeter; he scored zero and 8, MCC won. [235,566]
August 15	Played on 15 & 16 for MCC against Exmouth at Exmouth; he scored zero and 32 and took 1 catch [567] at The Maer Ground, Exmouth, MCC won. [235]

1905

May 19	Authors against the Artists at New Road, Esher, he scored 24 and took 5 wickets, the Authors won, A.H. Wood played for the Authors and scored 116 and stumped 2. [235]

1905

May 26	Played on 26 & 27 for Hampshire Rovers against United Services at the Officers' Recreation Ground, Portsmouth. A.H. Wood was also in the same team, ACD scored 78 and took 2 wickets, A.H. Wood scored 34, but the result is unknown. [1041]
June 22	Gentlemen of Marylebone Cricket Club against the Royal Navy at Lord's, he scored 1 run, and took 1 catch, Gentlemen won. [235]
June 23	Played on 23 & 24 for MCC against Wiltshire; he scored 24, and took 1 catch, MCC won. [235]
June 29	Authors against the Actors at Lord's, he scored 2, the Actors won [71]; he scored 2, match drawn. [235]
July 13	Hythe Hill against Incogniti at Lynchmere Cricket Ground, Lynchmere, he scored 17 and zero, match drawn, A.H. Wood played for Hythe Hill, he scored 29 and then 34 not out, he took 1 catch [235] Incogniti won. [1957]
July 15	Haslemere against Wilts Regiment at Lythe Hill Park and took 7 wickets. [63]
July 21	Hampshire Rovers against United Services at the Officers' Recreation Ground, Portsmouth. A.H. Wood was also in the same team, ACD scored zero and A.H. Wood scored 19, but the result is unknown. [1042]
July 31	The Undershaw Team against Haslemere at Haslemere, he scored 65 and took 1 wicket, Undershaw won. [2093]
August 1	The Undershaw Team against Broadwater at Broadwater, he scored 42, Undershaw won. [2093]
August 2	Played on 2 &3 for The Undershaw Team against Frensham Hill at Frensham Hill, he scored 44 not out, Undershaw won. [2093]
August 4	Played on 4 & 5 for The Undershaw Team against Lythe Hill at Lythe Hill, he scored zero and 24, Undershaw won. [2093]
August 18	MCC against Hythe at Hythe, he scored 1, result unknown. [2094]
August 26	Played a cup match for Grayshott against Liss. [63]
August 31	Cricket Golfers against Golf Cricketers at Lord's [1346], he scored 11 and 1; he took 4 wickets, match drawn. [235]

1906

May 19	Authors against the Artists at New Road, Esher, he scored 2, the Artists won, also in the Authors team were Innes Doyle who scored 51 and E.W. Hornung who scored 1. [235]
May 26	MCC & Ground against R.M.C. (Sandhurst) at Sandhurst, he scored zero and took 1 catch, MCC & Ground won. [1959]

1907

May 13	Played a first class match on the 13, 14 & 15 for MCC against Derbyshire at Lord's, there was no play on the 14 owing to heavy rain [1375] he scored 19 and then 8 not out and took 1 catch, MCC won. This was to be ACD's last appearance in first-class matches. [235]
May 25	Hampshire Rover against United Services at United Services Ground, Portsmouth, he scored 5 and 8, drawn match. [1960]
May 31	Authors against the Artist at Esher, Surrey, he scored 36 and took 4 wickets, the Authors won [603], or for E.W. Hornung's XI against the Artists, he scored 26 took 4 wickets and 1 catch, E.W. Hornung's XI won. Also playing for E.W. Hornungs team were Innes Doyle who scored 1 and took 1 catch and E.W. Hornung scored zero. [235]
June 6	Played on 6 & 7 for MCC against Hampstead at Lord's; he scored 35 and took 1 catch, match drawn A.H. Wood played for MCC, he scored 14 and took 1 catch. [235,1961]
June 19	MCC against Egypt and The Sudan at Lord's, he scored 47, match drawn. [235]
July 12	Played on 12 & 13 for MCC & Ground against Leamington at Leamington; he scored 9 and took 3 wickets and 1 catch, MCC won [604] played at Arlington Avenue, Leamington Spa, he did not bat in the second innings. [235]

1907

July 15	MCC & Ground against Coventry & North Warwickshire at Stoke, he scored 11, MCC won [605] at Bulls Head Ground, Coventry. [235]
July 17	Played on 17 & 18 for MCC & Ground against Warwickshire Gentlemen at Warwick, in the first innings he scored 37 not out and 30 in the second innings, he also took 2 wickets, the result was a draw. [1773]
July 29	Played on 29 & 30 for MCC against Royal Navy at Lord's; he scored 36 and 43 and took 1 catch, A.H. Wood played for MCC, he scored 10 and 9 and stumped 4 [235] Royal Navy won. [1962]
August 9	Played on 9 & 10 for MCC against Wiltshire at Lord's; he scored 27 and 9, Wiltshire won. [235]
August 14	MCC against Royal Academy of Arts at Lord's, he scored 56 and took 4 wickets [235] MCC won. [1963]
August 15	Authors against the Actors at Lord's, he scored 4 and took 1 wicket, the Actors won, the Authors team included F.G. Guggisberg who scored 56, A.H. Wood zero, A.A. Milne 5, P.G. Wodehouse 1 and E.W. Hornung 7 not out. [235,1381]
August 21	MCC & Ground against London Playing Fields at Lord's, he scored 2 and took 3 wickets, match drawn. [235,1382]

1908

May 28	MCC & Ground against Royal Academy of Arts at Lord's; he scored 6 and took 4 wickets and 1 catch, MCC won. [56,235,1390]
June 1	Blue Mantles against Lewes Priory at the Dripping Pan, Lewes he scored 14 and took 2 wickets, Lewes Priory won. [791]
June 5	Tunbridge Wells against Fulham at the Nevill Ground, Tunbridge Wells, he scored 46 not out, Tunbridge Wells won. [820]
June 15	MCC against Ardingly College at Ardingly College Ground, Haywards Heath, he scored zero, match drawn. [56]
June 17	MCC against St. John's College at Hurstpierpoint, at Hurstpierpoint College Ground, he scored 9, MCC won. [56]
June 18	MCC against Brighton College at Brighton College Ground, he scored 14 and took 5 wickets, MCC won. [56]
June 30	Blue Mantles against Mr F.H. Gresson's XI at the Nevill Ground, Tunbridge Wells, he scored 1 and took 1 wicket. [864]
July 1	MCC against Tonbridge School at Tonbridge School Ground, he scored 40 not out, MCC won. [56,235]
July 4	Tunbridge Wells against Middlesex Hospital at the Nevill Ground, Tunbridge Wells, he scored 5. [865]
July 9	MCC against Egypt and The Sudan at Lord's, he scored 13, Egypt and The Sudan won [56], he did not bat in the second innings, A.H. Wood played for MCC, he scored 5. [235]
July 15	MCC against The Mote at Yalding, he scored 1, The Mote won [56] played at Mote Park, Maidstone, A.H. Wood played for MCC, he scored 2 and took 2 wickets and 2 catches. [235]
July 16	Authors against the Actors at Lord's, match abandoned (rain), ACD did not bat, match drawn [56,235] A.H. Wood played for the Authors but did not bat. [235]
July 21	Blue Mantles against Old Eastbournians at the Nevill Ground, Tunbridge Wells, he scored 6 and took 2 wickets, Old Eastbournians won. [866]
July 23	Sussex Martlets against Brook House at West Hoathly, he scored 9, result unknown. [1176]
July 28	Blue Mantles against Upper Tooting at the Nevill Ground, Tunbridge Wells, he scored 14, Blue Mantles won. [867]
August 7	A. Conan Doyle & Crowborough & District against Heron's Ghyll at Heron's Ghyll House, Heron's Ghyll, near Crowborough, he scored 42, ACD's team won. [868]
August 12	MCC against East Grinstead at East Grinstead, he scored 4 and took 1 catch [56] match drawn. [235]

1908

August 15	Blue Mantles against Mr J.R. Hope's XI at the Nevill Ground, Tunbridge Wells, he scored 4 not out and took 1 wicket. [869]

1910

June 1	Authors against the Publishers at Lord's, he scored 10 and 24 and took 1 wicket; the Authors won [56], or match drawn. [235]
June 13	MCC against Ardingly College at Ardingly College Ground, Haywards Heath, he scored 18, MCC won. [235]
June 13	Sussex Martlets against Mr Gresson's XI at The Grange, Church Road, Crowborough he scored 41 and took 1 catch, Sussex Martlets won. [792]
June 15	MCC against St. John's College at Hurstpierpoint College Ground, he scored 11 and took 5 wickets, match drawn. [235]
June 16	MCC against Brighton College at Brighton College Ground, he scored 39, MCC won. [235]
June 20	Played on 20 & 21 for the Blue Mantles against Warwickshire Gentlemen at Tunbridge Wells; he scored 2 and 7 and took 1 wicket [620] Warwickshire Gentlemen won. [1774]
June 29	MCC against Eton College at Agar's Plough, Eton College, he scored 5 and did not bat in second innings, match drawn. [235]
July 6	Blue Mantles against Lewes Priory at the Dripping Pan, Lewes he scored zero, Lewes Priory won. [793]
August	Sussex Martlets against Littlehampton over two days at Littlehampton, he scored zero and 1, and took 5 wickets in the first innings and 6 wickets in the second innings, Sussex Martlets won. [2037]
August 12	Played on 12 & 13 for MCC against Littlehampton at the Sportsfield, Littlehampton; he scored 13 and 18, MCC won. [235]
August 16	Littlehampton against Bellevue at Littlehampton, he scored 1 and took 3 wickets, Littlehampton won. [2042]
August 17	Littlehampton against Standard Athletic Club (Paris) at Littlehampton, he scored 3 and took 1 wicket, Standard won. [2095]
August 30	Played on 30 & 31 for Blue Mantles against Madcaps at Tunbridge Wells, he scored 1 and took 2 wickets, Madcaps won. [2096]

1911

May 27	Sussex Martlets against Lewes Priory at the Dripping Pan, Lewes, he did not bat in the first innings but scored 41 not out in the second innings, match drawn, A.H. Wood played for Sussex Martlets, he did not bat in the first innings but scored 6 in the second innings and took 3 catches [235,830] Sussex Martlets won. [830]
June 3	Sussex Martlets against Eastbourne College at Eastbourne College Ground, Eastbourne, he scored 3 and 1 and took 3 wickets and 1 catch, match drawn, A.H. Wood played for Sussex Martlets, he scored 10 and 2. [235]
June 8	Sussex Martlets against F.H. Gresson's XI at Wolfe Recreation Ground, Crowborough, he scored zero and took 2 wickets, F.H. Gresson's XI won, A.H. Wood played for Sussex Martlets, he scored 13 and took 1 catch. [235]
June 10	Sussex Martlets against Westminster School at Vincent Square, Westminster, he scored 37 and took 3 wickets, match drawn, A.H. Wood played for Sussex Martlets, he scored 50 and took 2 wickets and 1 catch. [235]
June 15	MCC against Ardingly College at Ardingly College Ground, Haywards Heath, he scored 44 and took 2 wickets, match drawn. [235]
August 16	Sussex Martlets against G.M. Maryon-Wilson's XI at Searles, Fletching, he scored 1 and took 5 wickets, match drawn. [235]
August 22	Authors against the Publishers at Lord's, he scored 14 and took 2 wickets, match drawn. [56,71,235,1482]

1912

May 25	Sussex Martlets against Lewes Priory at Lewes he scored 12, Sussex Martlets won [794] at the Stanley Turner Ground, Lewes, A.H. Wood played for Sussex Martlets, he scored 4. [235]
June 7	Blue Mantles against I Zingari at Nevill Ground, Tunbridge Wells, rain only allowed 30 minutes of play. [2097]
June 10	MCC against Ardingly College at The College Ground, Ardingly, MCC won. [1177]
June 17	Sussex Martlets against Eastbourne at The Saffrons, Eastbourne, he scored 14, result unknown. [2098]
July 10	Mr F.H. Gresson's XI against Mayfield at The Grange, Church Road, Crowborough, he scored zero and took 1 wicket, Mayfield won [627] at Wellbrook Ground, Mayfield. [235]
July 11	MCC against Royal Academy of Arts at Lord's, he scored zero and took 5 wickets, match drawn. [235]
July 29	Blue Mantles against Mr F.W. Gresson's XI at The Grange, Church Road, Crowborough; he scored 17, Gresson's XI won [628], at the Wolfe Recreation Ground, Crowborough. [235]
July 30	Blue Mantles against West Kent at the Nevill Ground, Tunbridge Wells, he scored 4; the game was abandoned owing to rain [629], match drawn. [235]
August 2	Sussex Martlets against Harrow Blues at the County Ground, Hove, he scored 51 and took 1 wicket, match drawn. [2099]
August 9	Manx Cats against Crowborough Crocks at the Nevill Ground, Tunbridge Wells, he scored 12, Manx Cats won. [235,630]
August 19	Played on 19 & 20 for MCC against Hampstead at Lord's; he scored 6 and took 2 wickets. [235]
August 21	Authors against the Publishers at Lord's, [202] he scored 6, match drawn [235], but the match was abandoned due to rain. [56]

"The most singular ball I have ever received."
[From *The Strand Magazine*, September 1909, Some Recollections of Sport]

Leamington v MCC 22 & 23 July 1903

Arthur Conan Doyle is standing left of doorway

Authors v Artists – 22nd May 1903
E.W. Hornung, E.V. Lucas, P.G. Wodehouse, J.C. Smith, G. Chowne, Sir A. Conan Doyle,
Hesketh Prichard, L.D. Luard, C.M.Q. Orchardson, L.C. Nightingale, A. Kinross

C. Gascoyne, Shan F. Bullock, G. Hillyard Swinstead, Reginald Bloomfield, Hon. W.J. James,
E.A. Abbey, A. Chevallier Tayler, J.M. Barrie, G.C. Ives, G. Spencer Watson,
A.B.W. Mason

The cricket team that toured Holland in 1891, ACD is seated centre.

ACD is seated in the centre, on his right is his wife Louise, on his left is his sister Connie. Behind Connie is her husband E.W. Hornung.

Arthur Conan Doyle and Portsmouth Association Football Club (PAFC)

1884

November 15	Played in goal for PAFC at North End against Hayling Island, PAFC won 5-1. [107]
December 13	Played in goal for PAFC away against Havant, PAFC won 2-0. [107]
December 27	Played in goal for PAFC at North End against Cowes, drew 2-2. [107]

1885

January 17	Played in goal for PAFC at East Hants Ground, Southsea against Mr Pares's Team, Sunflowers, PAFC lost 2-0. [107]
January 24	Played in goal for PAFC at North End against Havant, PAFC won 7-2. [107]
January 31	Played in goal for PAFC away against Chichester, PAFC lost 4-2. [107]
February 7	Played in goal for PAFC away against Hayling Island, PAFC won 3-0. [107]
February 14	Played in goal for PAFC at North End against Southsea, PAFC won 1–0. [107]
March 7	Played in goal for PAFC at North End against Fareham, drew 2-2. [107]
March 23	Played for PAFC (position unknown) away against Cowes, PAFC won 3-1. [107]
October 3	Played in goal for PAFC away against Havant, PAFC won 3-0. [107]
October 17	Played as a back for PAFC at North End against Hilsea Artillery Ramblers, PAFC won 2-0. [107]
October 24	Played as a back for PAFC away against the Argyll & Sutherland Highlanders, PAFC lost 8-0. [107]
November 7	Played as a full back for PAFC away against Chichester, PAFC won 4-1. [107]
November 14	Played in goal for PAFC at North End against Stubbington House, PAFC won 3-0. [107]
November 22	Played as a back for PAFC away against Midhurst, PAFC won 3–2. [107]
December 5	Played as a full back for PAFC at Garrison Barracks Ground against Wimborne, PAFC lost 2-1. [107]
December 9	Played as a back for PAFC at North End against Horndean, PAFC won 4–1. [107]
December 26	Played in goal for PAFC away against Fareham, PAFC won 2–0; this was a morning kick off. [107]
December 26	Played as a back for PAFC at Garrison Recreation Ground against the Worcestershire Regiment, PAFC won 3-0 this was an afternoon kick off. [107]
December 28	Played as a full back for PAFC at North End against Havant, PAFC won 6–4. [107]
December 30	Played for PAFC (position unknown) at Forton against the Royal Marines Light Infantry, PAFC won 10–0. [107]

1886

January 2	Played as a full back for PAFC at North End against Sunflowers, PAFC won 2–0. [107]
January 9	Played as a full back for PAFC at North End against Cowes, drew 2–2. [107]
January 25	ACD played as a full back for PAFC at Garrison Recreation Ground against the 93rd Regiment, PAFC lost 4–2. [107]
January (end)	Played as a full back for PAFC at North End against Hilsea Artillery Ramblers, PAFC won 6–0. [107]
January 30	Played as a full back for PAFC away against Horndean, PAFC won 4–0, ACD scored 1 goal. [107]
February 13	Played in goal for PAFC at Garrison Recreation Ground against Stubbington Lodge School, PAFC won 3–1. [107]
February 20	Played as a full back for PAFC at Forton against RMLI, PAFC won 6–0. [107]
February 27	Played as a full back for PAFC at North End against Hayling Island, PAFC won 7–1. [107]
March 6	Played for PAFC (position unknown) at North End against Petersfield, PAFC won 13–1. [107]

1886

March 13	Played in goal for PAFC away against Portsmouth Grammar School, drew 1–1. [107]
March 20	Played in goal for PAFC at Officers' Recreation Ground against HMS Marlborough, PAFC lost 1–0. [107]
March 27	Played as a full back for PAFC away against Petersfield, drew 1–1. [107]
October 2	Played in goal for PAFC at Portsmouth against Woolston Works, result unknown. [107]
October 9	Played as a back for PAFC at Garrison Recreation Ground against the 2nd Worcestershire, PAFC lost 3–1. [107]
October 16	Played in goal for PAFC at Garrison Recreation Ground against Fareham, PAFC won 5–0. [107]
October 30	Played in goal for PAFC away against Petersfield, Portsmouth Senior Cup round one, PAFC won 6-1. [107]
November 3	Played as a full back for PAFC at Garrison Recreation Ground against United Services Men's Garrison, PAFC lost 3–2. [107]
November 6	Played as a full back for PAFC at Garrison Recreation Ground against the Worcestershire Regiment, PAFC lost 1–0. [107]
November 13	Played as a back for PAFC away against Portsmouth Grammar School, PAFC won 5–2, ACD scored an own goal. [107]
November 17	Played as a back for PAFC at Garrison Recreation Ground against the Royal Irish Rifles, drew 1–1. [107]
November 27	Played in goal for PAFC at Hilsea against 2/1 Welsh Division RA, PAFC won 3–0. [107]
December 15	Played as a full back for PAFC at Garrison Recreation Ground against Blandford, PAFC won 3–2, Hampshire Senior Cup round one. [107]
December 18	Played as a back for PAFC at Garrison Recreation Ground against Portsmouth Grammar School, PAFC won 3–0, Portsmouth Senior Cup round two. [107]

1887

January 15	Played as a back for PAFC at Garrison Recreation Ground against the Royal Irish Rifles, PAFC won 1–0 [107]
February 5	Played as a back for PAFC at United Services Officers' Ground against Freemantle, PAFC won 2–0. [107]
February 12	Played as a back for PAFC at United Men's Ground against the Royal Irish Rifles, PAFC won 4–2. [107]
March 5	Played as a back for PAFC away against Portsmouth Grammar School, PAFC won 5–1. [107]
March 19	Played in goal for PAFC away against Petersfield, drew 1–1. [107]
March 23	ACD played in goal for PAFC at United Services Men's Ground against Mr Richard's Garrison Team, PAFC won 2–0. [107]
March 26	Played in goal for PAFC at United Services Recreation Ground against Woolston Works; PAFC won 1–0, Portsmouth & District Challenge Cup. [107]
April 8	Played in goal for PAFC at United Services Recreation Ground against HMS Marlborough, PAFC won 2-0. [107]
October 29	Played as a full back for PAFC at Men's Recreation Ground against Hilsea Ramblers, PAFC lost 3–1. [107]
November 2	Played as a full back for PAFC at Recreation Ground, Portsmouth against Chichester G & AC, PAFC lost 3–0. [107]
November 12	Played in goal for PAFC at Recreation Ground, Portsmouth against the Royal Scots Greys, PAFC won 3–0. [107]
December 24	Played in goal for PAFC at United Service Men's Ground against Sunflowers, PAFC won 2–0. [107]

1888

January 7	Played in goal for PAFC at Officers' Recreation Ground against Hilsea Ramblers, PAFC lost 1–0, Portsmouth Senior Cup Semi-Final. [107]

1888

January 25	Played as a full back for PAFC at Officers' Recreation Ground against Hilsea Ramblers, PAFC lost 4–0, Portsmouth Senior Cup Semi-Final. [107]
February 4	Played in goal for PAFC at Bar End Cricket Ground against Woolston Works, PAFC lost 1–0, Hampshire Senior Cup. [107]
March 17	Played in goal for PAFC at Hilsea Recreation Ground against Portsmouth Grammar School, drew 0–0 in the Portsmouth Senior Cup Final First Round. [107]
October 13	Played as a full back for PAFC at United Services Men's Ground against the Royal Engineers (Chatham), PAFC lost 6–0. [107]
October 27	Played as a full back for PAFC at United Services Men's Ground against the United Services, drew 1–1. [107]
November 1	Played as a full back for PAFC at United Services Men's Ground against the South Yorkshire Regiment, PAFC won 2–0. [107]
November 3	Played as a full back for PAFC at Men's Recreation Ground against United Services Men's Team, PAFC lost 3–0, Portsmouth Senior Cup first round. [107]
December 13	Played as a full back for PAFC at United Services Men's Ground against Winchester, PAFC won 2–0. [107]
December 19	Played as a full back for PAFC at United Services Men's Ground against Fareham, PAFC won 6–0. [107]
December 22	Played as a full back for PAFC at United Services Men's Ground against United Services Men's Team, drew 0–0. [107]

1889

January 8	Played as a full back for PAFC at Aldershot against the King's Royal Rifles, PAFC won 4–0, Hampshire Senior Cup second round. [107]
January 19	Played as a full back for PAFC away against Fareham, PAFC won 3–1. [107]
January 26	Played as a full back for PAFC at Men's Recreation Ground against the Yorkshire Regiment, PAFC lost 1–0. [107]
February 2	Played as a full back for PAFC at North End against the YMCA, PAFC won 3–1. [107]
February 23	Played as a full back for PAFC at Men's Recreation Ground against Portsmouth Grammar School, PAFC won 2–0, Hampshire Senior Cup semi-final. [107]
March 2	Played as a full back for PAFC at County Ground, Southampton against the Royal Engineers (Aldershot), PAFC lost 5–1, Hampshire Senior Cup Final [107] played at Southampton. [8]
November 2	Played as a full back for PAFC away against Petersfield, PAFC won 3–0. [107]
November 20	Played as a full back for PAFC at United Services Men's Ground against Stubbington House School, PAFC won 1–0. [107]
November 23	Played as a full back for PAFC away against Fareham, PAFC won 5–0. [107]
November 30	Played as a full back for PAFC at Hilsea against Portsmouth Grammar School, PAFC won 6–0. [107]
December 28	Played as a full back for PAFC away against the Royal Engineers (Aldershot), PAFC lost 3–2, Hampshire Senior Cup second round. This was ACD's last appearance for Portsmouth Association Football Club. [107]

1890

September 24	ACD presided over the AGM of the Portsmouth Association Football Club at the Albany Hotel, Landport, Mr A.H. Wood was elected as captain. [415]

1900

May 19	ACD was captain of a Langman Hospital football team that played against the Imperial Yeomanry Field Hospital at Bloemfontein, South Africa, the result was a 1-1 draw. [494]

John Francis Innes Hay Doyle (Innes Doyle) and Cricket

Innes played second class cricket for Idlers 1892, Townley Park 1895, Royal Artillery Officers 1895, Royal Artillery Devonport 1896-1898, Hampshire Rovers 1896, 73rd Battery Royal Artillery 1897, Esher 1904, Authors 1904 & 1906, E.W. Hornungs XI 1907 and Marylebone Cricket Club (MCC) 1908-1909.

The team that Innes played for are named first in all entries.

1892
September 6	Idlers against Norwood Club at Norwood Green, he scored 25, match drawn, ACD, A.H. Wood and E.W. Hornung were also in Idlers team. [235]

1895
May 6	Royal Artillery Officers against Sweet Seventeen at Redlands Sports Ground, Weymouth, he scored 2, Sweet Seventeen won. [235]
August 5	Townley Park against Merton at John Innes Recreation Ground, Merton Park. He scored 8, Merton Park won [235]

1896
May 9	Royal Artillery Devonport against Ottery St. Mary at Salston Field, Ottery St. Mary, he scored 7, Ottery St. Mary won. [235]
May 27	Royal Artillery Devonport against Devonshire Regiment at Devonport, he scored 3, Devonshire Regiment won. [235]
August 10	Played on 10 and 11 for Hampshire Rovers against Littlehampton at the Sportsfield, Littlehampton, he scored 7 and then 16 not out and took 1 wicket and 1 catch, Littlehampton won. ACD and A.H. Wood were also in the Rovers team. [235]
August 22	Royal Artillery Devonport against Shobrooke at Shobrooke Park, Shobrooke, he scored 12 and zero and took 2 wickets, Shobrooke won. [235]

1897
May 12	Royal Artillery Devonport against Exeter at The County Cricket Ground, Exeter, he scored 2 and took 1 catch, Exeter won. [235]
May 19	Royal Artillery Devonport against Blundell's School at Blundell's School, Tiverton, he scored 11, Blundell's School won. [235]
May 26	Royal Artillery Devonport against Devonshire Regiment at Topsham Barracks, Exeter, he scored 15 and took 1 catch, he did nor bat in the second innings, match drawn. [235]
June 5	Royal Artillery Devonport against Wonford House at Wonford House, Exeter, he scored 25, Royal Artillery Devonport won. [235]
June 9	Royal Artillery Devonport against Devonshire Regiment at Topsham Barracks, Exeter, he scored 4 and took 1 catch, Devonshire Regiment won. [235]
July 1	Royal Artillery Devonport against Honiton at Topsham Barracks, Exeter, he scored 51 not out, match drawn. [235]
July 3	Royal Artillery Devonport against 4th Battalion Devonshire Regiment at Topsham Barracks, Exeter, he scored 5, 4th Battalion Devonshire Regiment won. [235]
July 10	Royal Artillery Devonport against St. Matthew's at Topsham, Exeter, he scored 2 and took 1 wicket, St. Matthew's won. [235]
August 4	73rd Battery Royal Artillery against 19th Battery Royal Artillery at Topsham Barracks, Exeter, he scored 27 and took 1 catch, 73rd Battery Royal Artillery won. [235]

1898
June 28	Royal Artillery Devonport against 4th Battalion Devonshire Regiment at Topsham Barracks, Exeter, he scored 3, match drawn. [235]

1904

May 14	Esher against Marlborough Blues at New Road, Esher, he scored 8, match drawn. ACD was also in the Esher team. [235]
May 20	Authors against the Artists at New Road, Esher, he scored 15, the Authors won. ACD and E.W. Hornung were also in the Authors team. [235]

1906

May 19	Authors against the Artists at New Road, Esher, he scored 51, the Artists won. ACD and E.W. Hornung were also in the Authors team. [235]

1907

May 31	E.W. Hornung's XI against the Artists at New Road, Esher, he scored 1 and took 1 catch, E.W. Hornung's XI won. ACD was also in E.W. Hornung's XI. [235]

1908

May 20	MCC against Christ's Hospital at Christ's Hospital Ground, Horsham, he scored 11, MCC won. [235]
June 20	MCC against Royal Military College Sandhurst at Royal Military Academy Ground, Camberley, he scored 2, Royal Military College Sandhurst won, E.W. Hornung also played for MCC scoring 1. [235]
August 12	MCC against East Grinstead at East Grinstead Sports Club Ground, he scored 3 and took 1 catch, match drawn. ACD played for MCC and scored 4 and took 1 catch. [235]

1909

May 29	MCC against Royal Military College Sandhurst at Royal Military Academy Ground, Camberley, he scored 6 and took 1 catch, match drawn. [235]

The grave of Sir Arthur & Lady Conan Doyle at All Saints Church, Minstead, Hampshire

BIOGRAPHIES & SEMI-BIOGRAPHICAL WORKS

Chronological Listing
Compiled By Brian W Pugh & Phil Bergem

Doyle, Arthur Conan. *Memories and Adventures.* (London: Hodder & Stoughton, 1924; Boston: Little, Brown, 1924; Revised edition – London: John Murray, 1930).

Olsson, Viktor. *Sir Arthur Conan Doyle*, Liv och minnen (Malmo: Varidslitteraturens Folag 1930). [Swedish]

Lamond, John. *Arthur Conan Doyle: A Memoir.* (London: John Murray, 1931; Port Washington, NY: Kennikat Press, 1972).

Pearson, Hesketh. *Conan Doyle: His Life and Art.* (London: Methuen & Co., 1943); as *Conan Doyle.* (New York: Walker & Company, 1961).

Doyle, Adrian Conan. *The True Conan Doyle.* (London: John Murray, 1945; New York: Coward-McCann, Inc., 1946).

Carr, John Dickson. *The Life of Sir Arthur Conan Doyle.* (London: John Murray, 1949; New York: Harper & Brothers, 1949).

Hardwick, Michael and Mollie Hardwick. *The Man Who Was Sherlock Holmes.* London: John Murray, 1964; (Garden City, NY: Doubleday, 1964).

Nordon, Pierre. *Sir Arthur Conan Doyle: l'homme et l'œuvre.* Paris: Librairie Marcel Didier, 1964; [French], as *Conan Doyle: A Biography*, translated by Frances Partridge, (London: John Murray, 1966; New York: Holt, Rinehart and Winston, 1967).

Hoehling, Mary. *The Real Sherlock Holmes: Arthur Conan Doyle.* (New York: Julian Messner, 1965). [For children]

Wood, James Playsted. *The Man Who Hated Sherlock Holmes: A Life of Sir Arthur Conan Doyle.* (New York: Pantheon Books, 1965). [For children]

Nordon, P. Weil. (Doyle, Adrian Conan, ed.). *Sir Arthur Conan Doyle Centenary, 1859-1959.* (London: John Murray, 1959; Garden City, NY: Doubleday & Co., 1959).

Brown, Ivor. *Conan Doyle: A Biography of the Creator of Sherlock Holmes.* (London: Hamish Hamilton, 1972).

Higham, Charles. *The Adventures of Conan Doyle: The Life of the Creator of Sherlock Holmes.* (London: Hamish Hamilton, 1976; New York: W. W. Norton, 1976; Toronto: George J. McLeod, Ltd., 1976).

Pearsall, Ronald. *Conan Doyle: A Biographical Solution.* (London: Weidenfeld and Nicolson, 1977; New York: St. Martin's Press, 1977).

Symons, Julian. *A Portrait of an Artist: Conan Doyle.* (London: Whizzard Press/André Deutsch, 1979); as *Conan Doyle: Portrait of an Artist.* (New York: The Mysterious Press, 1979; Sydney: Reed Books, 1980).

Edwards, Owen Dudley. *The Quest for Sherlock Holmes.* (Edinburgh: Mainstream Publishing, 1983; Totowa, NJ: Barnes & Noble, 1983).

Doyle, Arthur Conan. *The Uncollected Sherlock Holmes.* Edited by Richard Lancelyn Green. (Harmondsworth, Middlesex: Penguin Books, Ltd., 1983).

Rodin, Alvin E. and Jack D. Key. *Medical Casebook of Doctor Arthur Conan Doyle: From Practitioner to Sherlock Holmes and Beyond.* (Malabar, FL: Robert E. Krieger Publishing Company, Inc., 1984).

Cox, Don Richard. *Arthur Conan Doyle.* (New York: Frederick Ungar Publishing Co., 1985).

Lachtman, Howard. *Sherlock Slept Here.* (Santa Barbara, CA: Capra Press, 1985).

Jaffe, Jacqueline A. *Arthur Conan Doyle.* (Boston, MA: Twayne Publishers, 1987).

Stavert, Geoffrey. *A Study in Southsea: The Unrevealed Life of Doctor Arthur Conan Doyle.* (Portsmouth, Hampshire: Milestone Publications, 1987; Cincinnati, OH: Seven Hills Book Distributors, 1987).

Redmond, Christopher. *Welcome to America, Mr. Sherlock Holmes.* (Toronto: Simon & Pierre, 1987).

McCearney, James. *Arthur Conan Doyle.* (Paris: La Table Ronde, 1988). [French]

Jones, Kelvin I. *Conan Doyle and the Spirits.* (Wellingborough, Northamptonshire: The Aquarian Press, 1989; New York: Harper Collins, 1990).

Kawamura, Mikio. コナン・ドイル－ホームズ・SF・心霊主義 [*Conan Doyle: Holmes – SF – Spiritualism*]. (Tokyo: Koudansha, 1991). [Japanese]

Costello, Peter. *The Real World of Sherlock Holmes: True Crimes Investigated by Arthur Conan Doyle.* (London: Robinson Publishing, 1991; New York: Carroll & Graf Publishers, Inc., 1991). (Reissued in 2006, New York: Avalon Publishing Group, Inc. as *Conan Doyle, Detective*.)

Stone, Harry. *The Casebook of Sherlock Doyle: True Mysteries Investigated by Conan Doyle.* (Romford, Essex: Ian Henry Publications, 1991; Studio City, CA: Empire Publishing Service, 1992).

Payne, Malcolm and Philip Weller, eds. *Recollections of Sir Arthur Conan Doyle.* (Lee-on-Solent, Hampshire: Sherlock Publications, 1993).

Redmond, Christopher. *A Sherlock Holmes Handbook.* (Toronto: Simon & Pierre, 1993; Second edition, as *Sherlock Holmes Handbook.* (Toronto: Dundurn Press, 2009).

Coren, Michael. *Conan Doyle.* (London: Bloomsbury Publishing, 1995; Toronto: Stoddart, 1995).

Nollen, Scott Allen. *Sir Arthur Conan Doyle at the Cinema.* (Jefferson, NC: McFarland & Company, Inc., Publishers, 1996).

Lellenberg, Jon L., editor. *The Quest for Sir Arthur Conan Doyle.* (Carbondale, IL: Southern Illinois University Press, 1987). Second edition published on Compact Disk – Part of *The Works of Sir Arthur Conan Doyle.* (Franconia, VA: Insight Engineering, 1997).

Adams, Cynthia. *The Mysterious Case of Sir Arthur Conan Doyle.* (Greensboro, NC: Morgan Reynolds Incorporated, 1999). [For children]

Peacock, Judith. *Arthur Conan Doyle*, (Makato, MN: The Creative Company, 1999).

Moore, Pat. *Arthur Conan Doyle. A Brief Portrait*, (London: Lilburne Press, 1999).

Booth, Martin. *The Doctor, the Detective and Arthur Conan Doyle: A Biography of Arthur Conan Doyle.* (London: Hodder & Stoughton, 1997); as *The Doctor and the Detective: A Biography of Sir Arthur Conan Doyle.* (New York: Thomas Dunne Books, 2000).

Stashower, Daniel. *Teller of Tales: The Life of Arthur Conan Doyle.* (New York: Henry Holt and Company, 1999; London: Allen Lane, 2000).

Pascal, Janet B. *Arthur Conan Doyle: Beyond Baker Street.* (Oxford: Oxford University Press Children's Books, 2000). [For children]

Pugh, Brian W. *A Chronology of the Life of Sir Arthur Conan Doyle May 22nd 1859 to July 7th 1930.* (Lewes, Sussex: Privately printed, 2000); *Addenda and Corrigenda*, 2002; Second edition, 2003; *Addenda and Corrigenda*, 2005 (Lewes, Sussex: Privately printed); (First edition, London: MX Publishing Ltd., 2009; Second edition, London: MX Publishing Ltd., 2012, Third edition, London: MX Publishing Ltd., 2014 paperback & Ebook, *Addenda & Corrigenda*: London: MX Publishing Ltd., 2015, Fourth edition, London: MX Publishing Ltd., 2018).

Bergem, Phillip G. *The Family and Residences of Arthur Conan Doyle.* (St. Paul, Minnesota: Privately printed, 2001; Second edition, St. Paul, MN: Picardy Place Press, 2003, Second edition (revised) St. Paul, Minnesota: Privately printed 2007).

Hines, Stephen. *The True Crime Files of Sir Arthur Conan Doyle.* (New York: Berkley Publishing Group, 2001).

Doyle, Georgina. *Out Of The Shadows: The Untold Story of Arthur Conan Doyle's First Family.* (British Columbia, Ashcroft: Calabash Press 2004).

Bergem, Philip G., *A Bibliographic Listing of Stories, Poems, and Other Writings of A. Conan Doyle.* (St. Paul, Minnesota: 75 copies privately printed 2007, CD-ROM edition (with minor corrections and additions) 2010, with further additions 2012, 2013.

Lellenberg, Jon, Stashower, Daniel and Foley, Charles. *Arthur Conan Doyle: A Life in Letters.* (London: HarperPress, 2007; New York: The Penguin Press, 2007, Penguin Books, 2008).

Lycett, Andrew. *Conan Doyle: The Man Who Created Sherlock Holmes.* (London: Weidenfeld & Nicolson, 2007); as *The Man Who Created Sherlock Holmes: The Life and Times of Sir Arthur Conan Doyle.* (New York: Free Press, 2007).

Norman, Andrew. *Arthur Conan Doyle: Beyond Sherlock Holmes.* (Stroud, Gloucestershire: Tempus Publishing, Ltd, 2007).

Miller, Russell. *The Adventures of Arthur Conan Doyle.* (London: Harvill Secker, 2008); as *The Adventures of Arthur Conan Doyle: A Biography.* (New York: Thomas Dunne Books, 2008).

Stjepanovic-Pauly, Marianne. *Arthur Conan Doyle: Sherlock Holmes et au-delà.* (Paris: Éditions Du Jasmin, 2008). [French]

Pugh, Brian W. and Paul R. Spiring. *On the Trail of Arthur Conan Doyle.* (Brighton, Sussex: Book Guild Publishing, 2008).

Turner, Margaret Newman. *Arthur, Louise and the True Hound of the Baskervilles.* (Herefordshire: Logaston Press, 2010).

Pugh, Brian W., Spiring, Paul R. & Bhanji, Sadru. *Arthur Conan Doyle, Sherlock Holmes and Devon.* (London: MX Publishing Ltd., 2010).

Duncan, Alistair. *The Norwood Author: Arthur Conan Doyle & The Norwood Years (1891-1894)*. (London: MX Publishing Ltd., 2010).

Duncan, Alistair. *An Entirely New Country: Arthur Conan Doyle, Undershaw and the Resurrection of Sherlock Holmes*. (London: MX Publishing Ltd., 2011).

Doyle, Arthur Conan. *Dangerous Work: Diary of an Arctic Adventure*, edited by Lellenberg, Jon and Stashower, Daniel, (London: The British Library Publishing Division, 2012).

Salvatori, Gianluca, Solito, Enrico, & Vianello, Robert, (editors). *Sir Arthur Conan Doyle: Viaggio in Italia – Italian Journey*, (Italy: Bob Bazlen Servizi Editorali, Rome, 2012).

Bret, Emmanuel Le. *Conan Doyle Contre Sherlock Holmes*, (Paris: Editions du Moment, 2012). [French]

Duncan, Alistair, *No Better Place: Arthur Conan Doyle, Windlesham and Communications with the Other Side*, (London: MX Publishing Ltd., 2015).

Glücklich, Nicole (project editor) *The Adventures of Two British Gentlemen in Switzerland: In the Footsteps of Sir Arthur Conan Doyle and Sherlock Holmes* (Germany: DSHG Verlag, Ludwigshafen am Rhein, Germany, 2016).

Sims, Michael, *Arthur and Sherlock: Conan Doyle and The Creation of Holmes*, (London: Bloomsbury, 2017).

Montague, Charlotte, *Creating Sherlock Holmes: The Remarkable Story of Sir Arthur Conan Doyle*, (New York, USA: Chartwell Books, 2017).

Boström, Mattias, *From Holmes to Sherlock: The Story of the Men and Woman Who Created an Icon*, (New York: The Mysterious Press, 2017).

Facsimile Manuscripts That Have Been Published

The Adventure of the Priory School (Santa Barbara: Santa Teresa Press, 1985).
The Adventure of the Dying Detective (London: Westminster Libraries and The Arthur Conan Doyle Society, 1991).
The Adventure of the Lion's Mane (London: Westminster Libraries and The Sherlock Holmes Society of London, 1992).
A Regimental Scandal (Penyffordd, Chester: The Arthur Conan Doyle Society, 1995).
The Hound of the Baskervilles Chapter XI (New York: The Baker Street Irregulars in co-operation with the New York Public Library-Berg Collection, 2001).
Angels of Darkness: A Drama in Three Acts (New York: The Baker Street Irregulars in co-operation with the Toronto Public Library, 2001).
The Adventure of Shoscombe Old Place in *The Adventure of Shoscombe Abbey* (Lausanne: Bibliothèque cantonale et universitaire Lausanne, 2002).
The Horror of the Heights (Ashcroft: Calabash Press in co-operation with The Sherlock Holmes Collections, Department of Special Collections and Rare Books, University of Minnesota Libraries, The Arthur Conan Doyle Society and The Norwegian Explorers, 2004).
The Adventure of the Six Napoleons in *The Napoleon Bust Business Again* (New York: The Baker Street Irregulars in co-operation with the Henry E. Huntington Library and Art Gallery, 2004).
Reproduction of notes for *The Valley of Fear* in *Murderland* (New York: The Baker Street Irregulars, 2004).
The Red Circle in *Mandate for Murder* (New York: The Baker Street Irregulars in co-operation with the Lilly Library of Indiana University, 2006).
The Three Students in *So Painful a Scandal* (New York: The Baker Street Irregulars in co-operation with Houghton Library of the Harvard College Library, 2009).
A Scandal in Bohemia in *Bohemian Souls* (New York The Baker Street Irregulars in co-operation with The Harry Ransom Center at The University of Texas at Austin, 2011).
The Golden Pince-Nez in *The Wrong Passage* (New York: The Baker Street Irregulars in co-operation with The Harry Ransom Center at The University of Texas at Austin, 2012).
Log of the S.S. Hope 1880 in *Dangerous Work* (London: The British Library, 2012).
The Second Stain in *Irregular Stain* (New York: The Baker Street Irregulars in association with Magill Library at Haverford College, 2013).
How Watson Learned the Trick, (London: Walker Books Ltd. 2014).
The Empty House in *Out of the Abyss* (New York: The Baker Street Irregulars in association with The Rosenbach of the Free Library of Philadelphia, 2014).
The Dancing Men in *Dancing to Death* (New York: The Baker Street Irregulars with grateful acknowledgment to Brian Perkins, Sr. and Laura Perkins Mercer for permission to reproduce the manuscript, 2016).
The Adventure of the Abbey Grange (London: Sherlock Holmes Society of London and Fondation Martin Bodmer, 2016).
The Adventure of the Creeping Man (Winchester, UK: Winchester University Press, Winchester, UK, 2017).
His Last Bow (partial) in *Trenches: The War Service of Sherlock Holmes* (New York: The Baker Street Irregulars, 2017).

BIBLIOGRAPHY

A Chronological Listing of First and Early Appearances

Title	Published	Journal/Book
1879		
The Mystery of Sasassa Valley.	6 September	Chambers's Journal.
Gelseminum as a Poison.	20 September	British Medical Journal.
1880		
The American's Tale.	Christmas	London Society.
1881		
A Night among the Nihilists.	April	London Society.
After Cormorants with a Camera.	14 & 21 October	British Journal of Photography.
The Gully of Bluemansdyke.	Christmas	London Society.
That Little Square Box.	Christmas	London Society.
1882		
Notes on a Case of Leucoythaemia.	25 March	Lancet.
On the Slave Coast with a Camera.	31 March & 7 April	British Journal of Photography.
Bones, The April Fool of Harvey's Sluice.	April	London Society.
Our Derby Sweepstakes.	May	London Society.
Up an African River with the Camera.	28 July	British Journal of Photography.
That Veteran.	2 September	All the Year Round.
Dry Plates on a Wet Moor.	3 November	British Journal of Photography.
A Few Technical Hints.	December	British Journal of Photography Almanac.
My Friend the Murderer.	Christmas	London Society.
1883		
The Captain of the "Polestar".	January	Temple Bar.
Trial of Burton's Emulsion Process.	12 January	British Journal of Photography.
Life and Death in the Blood.	March	Good Words.
Gentlemanly Joe.	31 March	All the Year Round.
The Week. Topics of the Day.	16 June	The Medical Times.
Where to Go with the Camera. Southsea: Three Days in Search of Effects.	22 June	British Journal of Photography.
The Winning Shot.	11 July	Bow Bells.
The "New" Scientific Subject.	20 July	British Journal of Photography.
Where to Go with the Camera. To the Waterford Coast and Along It.	17 & 24 August	British Journal of Photography.
Selecting a Ghost. The Ghosts of Goresthorpe Grange.	December	London Society.
An Exciting Christmas Eve; or My Lecture on Dynamite.	December	Boy's Own Paper.
The Silver Hatchet.	Christmas	London Society.

1884

J. Habakuk Jephson's Statement.	January	The Cornhill Magazine.
The Heiress of Glenmahowley.	January	Temple Bar.
The Blood-Stone Tragedy.	16 February	Cassell's Saturday Journal.
John Barrington Cowles.	12 & 19 April	Cassell's Saturday Journal.
A Day on "The Island".	25 April	British Journal of Photography.
The Cabman's Story.	17 May	Cassell's Saturday Journal.
Easter Monday with the Camera.	23 May	British Journal of Photography.
The Tragedians.	20 August	Bow Bells.
The Remote Effects of Gout.	29 November	Lancet.
Crabbe's Practice.	Christmas	Boy's Own Paper.

1885

The Man from Archangel.	January	London Society.
Strange Tale of the Sea.	3 April	The Boston Herald.
The Lonely Hampshire Cottage.	2 May	Cassell's Saturday Journal.
The Great Keinplatz Experiment.	July	Belgravia Magazine.
Where to Go with the Camera. Arran in Autumn.	17 July	British Journal of Photography.
With a Camera on an African River.	30 October	British Journal of Photography.
The Wanderers' Irish Tour.	November	Stonyhurst Magazine.
The Fate of the Evangeline.	December	Boy's Own Paper.
Elias B. Hopkins. The Parson of Jackman's Gulch.	Christmas	London Society.

1886

Touch and Go: A Midshipman's Story.	April	Cassell's Family Magazine.
Testing Gas Pipes for Leakage.	19 November	Gas and Water Review.
Cyprian Overbeck Wells. A Literary Mosaic.	Christmas	Boy's Own Paper.

1887

Uncle Jeremy's Household.	8-19 January	Boy's Own Paper.
A Test Message.	2 July	Light.
A Study in Scarlet.	November	Beeton's Christmas Annual.
Corporal Dick's Promotion.	Christmas	Boy's Own Paper.
The Stone of Boxman's Drift.	Christmas	Boy's Own Paper.

1888

John Huxford's Hiatus.	June	The Cornhill Magazine.
A Study in Scarlet.	2 July	Ward, Lock & Co.
On the Geographical Distribution of British Intellect.	August	The Nineteenth Century.
The Mystery of Cloomber.	30 August-8 November	The Pall Mall Budget.
The Mystery of Cloomber.	17 December	Ward & Downey.

1889

Micah Clarke.	25 February	Longmans, Green & Co.
Micah Clarke.	8 June-28 September	Manchester Weekly Times.
The Bravoes of Market-Drayton.	24 August	Chambers's Journal.
The Firm of Girdlestone.	27 October 1889-13 April 1890	The People.

1890

The Ring of Thoth.	January	The Cornhill Magazine.
Mr. Stevenson's Methods in Fiction.	January	The National Review.
The Sign of the Four.	February	Lippincott's Monthly Magazine.
Mysteries and Adventures (collection)	1 March	Walter Scott.

The Gully of Bluemansdyke.
The Parson of Jackman's Gulch. ['Elis B. Hopkins']
My Friend the Murderer.
The Silver Hatchet.
The Man from Archangel.
That Little Square Box.
A Night among the Nihilists.

The Captain of the "Polestar" and Other Tales (collection)

                                                                  6 March   Longmans, Green & Co.

The Captain of the "Polestar."
J. Habakuk Jephson's Statement.
The Great Keinplatz Experiment.
The Man from Archangel.
That Little Square Box.
John Huxford's Hiatus.
A Literary Mosaic. [Cyprian Overbeck Wells. A Literary Mosaic]
John Barrington Cowles.
The Parson of Jackman's Gulch. [Elias B. Hopkins]
The Ring of Thoth.

The Firm of Girdlestone.	15 April	Chatto & Windus.
A Physiologist's Wife.	September	Blackwood's Edinburgh Magazine.
The Sign of Four.	1 October	Spencer Blackett.
The Duello in France.	December	The Cornhill Magazine.
Dr. Koch and his Cure.	December	Review of Reviews.
The Surgeon of Gaster Fell.	6-27 December	Chambers's Journal.
A Pastoral Horror.	21 December	The People.

1891

The White Company.	January-December	The Cornhill Magazine.
The Song of the Bow.	February	The Cornhill Magazine.
Our Midnight Visitor.	February	Temple Bar.
The Voice of Science.	March	The Strand Magazine.
A Straggler of '15.	21 March	Black & White.
The Song of the Bow.	10 May	The Sun.
The Franklin's Maid.	28 June	The Sun.
A Scandal in Bohemia.	July	The Strand Magazine.
The Doings of Raffles Haw.	12 July	Pittsburgh Commercial Gazette.
The Colonel's Choice.	26 July	Lloyd's Weekly Newspaper.
The Red-Headed League.	August	The Strand Magazine.
Woman's Wit.	8 August	Baltimore Weekly Sun.
A Case of Identity.	September	The Strand Magazine.
The Boscombe Valley Mystery.	October	The Strand Magazine.
The White Company.	26 October	Smith, Elder & Co.
The Five Orange Pips.	November	The Strand Magazine.
A Sordid Affair.	29 November	The People.
The Man with the Twisted Lip.	December	The Strand Magazine.
Portraits of Celebrities – A. Conan Doyle.	December	The Strand Magazine.

1891

The Doings of Raffles Haw.	12 December 1891 – 27 February 1892	Answers.
Between Two Fires.	19 December	The Gentlewoman.
Beyond the City.	Christmas	Good Cheer.
A False Start.	Christmas	The Gentlewomen.

1892

The Adventure of the Blue Carbuncle.	January	The Strand Magazine.
Out of the Running.	2 January	Black and White.
The Gamut of Humour.	30 January	The Speaker.
The Adventure of the Speckled Band.	February	The Strand Magazine.
The Storming Party.	6 February	The Speaker.
De Profundis.	18 February	The Independent.
De Profundis.	March	The Idler Magazine.
The Adventure of the Engineer's Thumb.	March	The Strand Magazine.
The Great Brown-Pericord Motor.	5 March	Ludgate Weekly Magazine.
The Doings of Raffles Haw.	5 March	Cassell & Co. Ltd.
The Frontier Line.	12 March	The Speaker.
The Adventure of the Noble Bachelor.	12 March	The Courier-Journal.
The Adventure of the Noble Bachelor.	April	The Strand Magazine.
The Adventure of the Beryl Coronet.	16 April	The Indianapolis News.
Strange Adventure. (The Engineer's Thumb)	30 April	Baltimore Weekly Sun.
A Talk with Dr. Conan Doyle.	May	The Bookman (London).
The Adventure of the Beryl Coronet.	May	The Strand Magazine.
A Regimental Scandal.	14 May	The Indianapolis News.
The Adventures of the Copper Beeches.	June	The Strand Magazine.
The Glamour of the Arctic.	July	The Idler Magazine.
A Question of Diplomacy.	Summer	The Illustrated London News.
A Day With Conan Doyle by Harry How.	August	The Strand Magazine.
Out of the Running.	5 August	Bow Bells.
Lot No 249.	September	Harper's Monthly.
"For Nelson's Sake" H.M.S. Foudroyant.	12 September	Daily Chronicle.
The Great Shadow.	1 October	The Saturday Globe.
The Adventures of Sherlock Holmes (collection)	14 October	George Newnes.
A Scandal in Bohemia.		
The Red-Headed League.		
A Case of Identity.		
The Boscombe Valley Mystery.		
The Five Orange Pips.		
The Man with the Twisted Lip.		
The Adventure of the Blue Carbuncle.		
The Adventure of the Speckled Band.		
The Adventure of the Engineer's Thumb.		
The Adventure of the Noble Bachelor.		
The Adventure of the Beryl Coronet.		
The Adventure of the Copper Beeches.		
The Great Shadow.	31 October	Arrowsmith's Christmas Annual.
Jelland's Voyage.	November	Phil May's Winter Annual.
The Los Amigos Fiasco.	December	The Idler Magazine.
The Adventure of Silver Blaze.	December	The Strand Magazine.
Critics and Criticism: Two Types of Reviews.	12 December	Morning Leader.

1893

The Refugees.	January-June	Harper's New Monthly Magazine.
My First Book VI. – Juvenilia.	January	The Idler Magazine.
The Adventure of the Cardboard Box.	January	The Strand Magazine.
The Adventure of the Yellow Face.	February	The Strand Magazine.
A Chat with Dr. Conan Doyle.	15 February	Cassell's Magazine.
An Arizona Tragedy. [The American's Tale]	25 February	The Minneapolis Journal.
The Adventure of the Stockbroker's Clerk.	March	The Strand Magazine.
The Adventure of the "Gloria Scott."	April	The Strand Magazine.
The Adventure of the Musgrave Ritual.	May	The Strand Magazine.
The Refugees.	17 May	Longmans, Green & Co.
The Green Flag.	June	The Pall Mall Magazine.
The Adventure of the Reigate Squire.	June	The Strand Magazine.
The Adventure of the Crooked Man.	July	The Strand Magazine.
The Great Shadow and Beyond the City.	August	J.W. Arrowsmith.
The "Slapping Sal."	August	The Vagabond's Annual.
Pennarby Mine.	August	The Pall Mall Magazine.
The Adventure of the Resident Patient.	August	The Strand Magazine.
The Adventure of the Greek Interpreter.	September	The Strand Magazine.
The Adventure of the Naval Treaty.	October & November	The Strand Magazine.
The Case of Lady Sannox.	29 October	The Courier-Journal.
The Case of Lady Sannox.	November	The Idler Magazine.
A Lay of the Links.	11 November	Today.
The Final Problem.	26 November	The Courier-Journal.
The Adventure of the Final Problem.	December	The Strand Magazine.
The Memories of Sherlock Holmes (collection)	13 December	George Newnes.
The Adventure of Silver Blaze.		
The Adventure of the Yellow Face.		
The Adventure of the Stockbroker's Clerk.		
The Adventure of the "Gloria Scott."		
The Adventure of the Musgrave Ritual.		
The Adventure of the Reigate Squires.		
The Adventure of the Crooked Man.		
The Adventure of the Resident Patient.		
The Adventure of the Greek Interpreter.		
The Adventure of the Naval Treaty.		
The Adventure of the Final Problem.		
Alpine Walk.	14 December	The Independent.

1894

The Ballad of the "Eurydice".	24 March	The Speaker.
The Doctors of Hoyland.	April	The Idler Magazine.
Paris in 1894: A Superficial Impression.	21 April	The Speaker.
Before My Bookcase.	5 May-20 June	Great Thoughts.
A Sordid Affair.	June	Illustrated Home Guest.
Sweethearts.	June	The Idler Magazine.
The Lord of Chateau Noir.	July	The Strand Magazine.
An Actor's Duel & The Winning Shot.	7 July	John Dicks.
My First Book.	August	McClure's Magazine.
Juvenilia published in My First Book.	September	Chatto & Windus.
A Chat with Conan Doyle.	October	The Idler Magazine.
The Stark Munro Letters.	October 1894 – November 1895	The Idler Magazine.
The Favourite Quotation.	4 October	New Age.

1894

Round the Red Lamp (collection)	23 October	Methuen & Co.
Behind the Times.		
His First Operation.		
A Straggler of '15.		
The Third Generation.		
A False Start.		
The Curse of Eve.		
Sweethearts.		
A Physiologist's Wife.		
The Case of Lady Sannox.		
A Question of Diplomacy.		
A Medical Document.		
Lot No 249.		
The Los Amigos Fiasco.		
The Doctors of Hoyland.		
The Surgeon Talks.		
Real Conversation…	November	McClure's Magazine.
The Parasite.	10 November	Harper's Weekly.
A Foreign Office Romance.	11 November	Indianapolis News.
Los Amigos Fiasco.	17 November	The Minneapolis Journal.
The Medal of Brigadier Gerard.	December	The Strand Magazine.
An Alpine Pass on "Ski."	December	The Strand Magazine.
The Parasite.	3 December	A. Constable.
The Stark Munro Letters.	13 December	Leslie's Illustrated Weekly.
A Foreign Office Romance.	Christmas	The Young Man & The Young Woman.

1895

How to Make a Really Happy New Year. Oh! The Happiness of a Smile!	January	Demorest's Family Magazine.
The Green Flag.	January	McClure's Magazine.
A Forgotten Tale.	January	Scribner's Magazine.
The Recollections of Captain Wilkie.	19 & 26 January	Chambers's Journal.
The Poor.	2 February	Great Thoughts.
Impartial Opinions from England.	10 February	The New York Times.
Literary Aspects of America.	March	The Ladies Home Journal.
How the Brigadier Held the King.	April	The Strand Magazine.
What are the Benefits of Bicycling?	May	Demorest's Family Magazine.
How the King Held the Brigadier.	May	The Strand Magazine.
How the Brigadier Slew the Brothers of Ajaccio.	June	The Strand Magazine.
How the Brigadier Came to the Castle Of Gloom.	July	The Strand Magazine.
How the Brigadier Took the Field against the Marshal Millefleurs.	August	The Strand Magazine.
How the Brigadier was Tempted by the Devil.	September	The Strand Magazine.
The Stark Munro Letters.	5 September	Longmans, Green & Co.
The Surgeon of Gaster Fell.	October	The People's Home Journal.
A Night Among the Nihilists.	November	Good Literature.
Novelists on their Works.	November	The Ludgate.
How the Brigadier Played for a Kingdom.	December	The Strand Magazine.

1896

Rodney Stone.	January-December	The Strand Magazine.

1896

Cycle Notes: Dr. Conan Doyle on Cycling.	18 January	Scientific American.
On the Egyptian Frontier.	8 February	The Speaker.
Christmas 1895.	15 February	Today.
The Exploits of Brigadier Gerard (collection)	15 February	George Newnes.
How the Brigadier Came to the Castle of Gloom.		
How the Brigadier Slew the Brothers of Ajaccio.		
How the Brigadier Held the King.		
How the King Held the Brigadier.		
How the Brigadier Took the Field against the Millefleurs.		
How the Brigadier Played for a Kingdom.		
How the Brigadier Won His Medal. [The Medal of Brigadier Gerard]		
How the Brigadier was Tempted by the Devil.		
Before the Campaign. I. A Letter from Cairo.	1 April	The Westminster Gazette.
Before the Campaign. II. Can the Fella Fight?	7 April	The Westminster Gazette.
From Cairo to Akasheh. Letters from Egypt. – III.	9 April	The Westminster Gazette.
The Scene at Assouan. Letters from Egypt. – IV.	13 April	The Westminster Gazette.
Correspondents and Camels. Letters from Egypt. – V.	20 April	The Westminster Gazette.
From Assouan to Korosko. Letters from Egypt. – VI.	27 April	The Westminster Gazette.
A Rover Chanty.	27 June	The Speaker.
The Conan Doyle Banquet at the Authors' Club.	4 July	Queen.
Dr. Conan Doyle on Cycling.	22 August	Hub.
The Three Correspondents.	October	The Windsor Magazine.
Rodney Stone.	13 November	Smith, Elder & Co.
The Field Bazaar.	20 November	The Student.

1897

Uncle Bernac – A Memory of the Empire.	January-March	The Cosmopolitan.
Life on a Greenland Whaler.	January	The Strand Magazine.
Tales of the High Seas: No. 1 – The Governor of St. Kitt's.	January	Pearson's Magazine.
Uncle Bernac.	8 January-5 March	Manchester Weekly Times.
A Ballad of the Ranks.	6 February	The Speaker.
Tales of the High Seas: No. 2 – The Two Barques.	March	Pearson's Magazine.
The Blind Archer.	20 March	The Speaker.
The Output of Authors.	April	Pearson's Magazine.
Tales of the High Seas: No. 3 – The Voyage of Copley Banks.	May	Pearson's Magazine.
The Tragedy of the Korosko.	May-Dec.	The Strand Magazine.
Uncle Bernac.	14 May	Smith, Elder & Co.
Tales of the High Seas: No. 4 – The Striped Chest.	July	Pearson's Magazine.
The Fiend of the Cooperage.	1 October	Manchester Weekly Times.

1898

The New Catacomb. [The Burger's Secret]		The Sunlight Year Book.
Cremona.	January	The Cornhill Magazine.
My Favorite Novelist and His Best Book.	January	Munsey's Magazine.
With the Chiddingfolds.	1 January	The Speaker.
The Confession.	17 January	The Star.
The Tragedy of the Korosko.	1 February	Smith, Elder & Co.
The Old Huntsman.	5 March	The Speaker.

1898

The Groom's Story.	27 March	The Sun.
The Groom's Story.	April	The Cornhill Magazine.
The Late Mr. James Payn. A Tribute from Dr. Conan Doyle.	2 April	The Illustrated London News.
The Beetle Hunter.	June	The Strand Magazine.
Songs of Action (collection)	8 June	Smith, Elder & Co.
The Song of the Bow.		
Cremona.		
The Storming Party.		
The Frontier Line.		
Corporal Dick's Promotion. A Ballad of '82.		
A Forgotten Tale.		
Pennarby Mine.		
A Rover Chanty.		
A Ballad of the Ranks.		
A Lay of the Links.		
The Dying Whip.		
Master.		
H.M.S. "Foudroyant."		
The Farnshire Cup.		
Songs of Action.		
The Groom's Story.		
With the Chiddingfolds.		
A Hunting Morning.		
The Old Grey Fox.		
Ware Holes.		
The Home-Coming of the Eurydice.		
The Inner Room.		
The Irish Colonel.		
The Blind Archer.		
A Parable.		
A Tragedy.		
The Passing.		
The Franklin's Maid. [From The White Company]		
The Old Huntsman.		
The King of the Foxes.	July	The Windsor Magazine.
The Man with the Watches.	July	The Strand Magazine.
The Lost Special.	August	The Strand Magazine.
The Sealed Room.	September	The Strand Magazine.
An Impression of the Army.	17 September	The Speaker.
The Black Doctor.	October	The Strand Magazine.
The Club-Footed Grocer.	November	The Strand Magazine.
Master.	19 November	The Living Age.
The Retirement of Signor Lambert.	December	Pearson's Magazine.
The Brazilian Cat.	December	The Strand Magazine.
A Shadow Before.	December	The Windsor Magazine.

1899

The Japanned Box.	January	The Strand Magazine.
The Jew's Breastplate.	February	The Strand Magazine.
B. 24.	March	The Strand Magazine.
A True Story of the Tragedy of Flowery Land.	19 March	The Courier-Journal.
A Duet with Occasional Chorus.	23 March	Grant Richards.
The Story of the Latin Tutor.	April	The Strand Magazine.
The Brown Hand.	May	The Strand Magazine.
The Arab Steed.	1 July	Daily News Weekly.

1899

The Croxley Master.	October-December	The Strand Magazine.
Who's That Calling? (poem)	18 October	Daily News.
The Crime of the Brigadier.	December	The Cosmopolitan.
My First Guinea.	December	Pearson's Magazine.

1900

The Crime of the Brigadier.	January	The Strand Magazine.
The Début of Bimbashi Joyce.	3 January	Punch.
Hilda Wade. XII. The Episode of the Dead Man Who Spoke.	February	The Strand Magazine.
Playing with Fire.	March	The Strand Magazine.
The Green Flag and Other Stories of War and Sport (collection)	27 March	Smith, Elder & Co.

The Green Flag.
Captain Sharkey I. How the Governor of St. Kitt's came Home.
Captain Sharkey II. The Dealings of Captain Sharkey with Stephen Craddock.
Captain Sharkey III. How Copley Banks slew Captain Sharkey.
The Crime of the Brigadier.
The Croxley Master.
The "Slapping Sal".
The Lord of Chateau Noir.
The Striped Chest.
A Shadow Before.
The King of the Foxes.
The Three Correspondents.
The New Catacomb.
The Début of Bimbashi Joyce.
A Foreign Office Romance.

My Friend the Villain.	April	The Hearthstone.
A First Impression.	6 April	The Friend.
Conan Doyle "In Luck".	16 April	Daily News.
Mr. Burdett-Coutt's Charges.	6 July	The Times.
The War in South Africa. The Epidemic of Enteric Fever in Bloemfontein.	7 July	British Medical Journal.
An Impression of the Regency.	August	Frank Leslie's Popular Monthly.
A Glimpse of the Army.	September	The Strand Magazine.
Some Military Lessons of the War.	October	The Cornhill Magazine.
The Great Boer War.	23 October	Smith, Elder & Co.
A Gaudy Death.	15 December	Tit-Bits.

1901

The Military Lessons of the War: A Rejoinder.	January	The Cornhill Magazine.
Strange Studies from Life. I. – The Holocaust of Manor Place.	March	The Strand Magazine.
The Edinburgh Burns Club Dinner. Address by Dr. Conan Doyle.	25 March	The Scotsman.
Strange Studies from Life. II. – The Affair of George Vincent Parker.	April	The Strand Magazine.
The Immortal Memory.	April	R. Mitchell & Sons.
The Great Boer War.	May 1901-June 1902	The Wide World Magazine.
Strange Studies from Life. III. – The Debatable Case of Mrs. Emsley.	May	The Strand Magazine.

1901
A British Commando. An Interview with Conan Doyle.
               June   The Strand Magazine.
The Hound of the Baskervilles.   August 1901-April 1902
                        The Strand Magazine.
Boer Critics on "The Great Boer War". September   The Cornhill Magazine.
A Hunting Morning.   October   Current Literature.

1902
The War in South Africa-Its Cause and Conduct. 16 January Smith, Elder, & Co.
The Hound of the Baskervilles.   25 March   George Newnes.
How the Brigadier Lost His Ear.   August   The Strand Magazine.
How the Brigadier Saved the Army.   November   The Strand Magazine.
How the Brigadier Rode to Minsk.   December   The Strand Magazine.

1903
A Duet. (A Duologue)   Samuel French.
Brigadier Gerard at Waterloo. Part I. The Adventure of the Forest Inn.
               January   The Strand Magazine.
Brigadier Gerard at Waterloo. Part II. The Adventure of the Nine Prussian Horsemen.
               February   The Strand Magazine.
The Brigadier in England.   March   The Strand Magazine.
Arthur Conan Doyle (interview/ article). April   The Bookman.
How the Brigadier Joined the Hussars of Conflans.
               April   The Strand Magazine.
How Etienne Gerard said goodbye to his Master.
               May   The Strand Magazine.
The Leather Funnel.   June   The Strand Magazine.
The Adventures of Gerard (collection)   22 September George Newnes.
How the Brigadier Lost His Ear.
How the Brigadier Captured Saragossa. [How the Brigadier Joined the Hussars of Conflans]
How the Brigadier Slew the Fox. [The Crime of the Brigadier]
How the Brigadier Saved an Army.
How the Brigadier Triumphed in England. [The Brigadier in England]
How the Brigadier Rode to Minsk.
How the Brigadier Bore Himself at Waterloo. I. The Story of the Forest Inn.
                       II. – The Story of the Nine Prussian Horsemen.
The Last Adventure of the Brigadier. [How the Etienne Gerard said Good-Bye to His Master]
The Adventure of the Empty House.   26 September Collier's Weekly.
The Adventure of the Empty House.   October   The Strand Magazine.
The Adventure of the Norwood Builder. 31 October   Collier's Weekly.
The Adventure of the Norwood Builder. November   The Strand Magazine.
The Adventure of the Dancing Men.   December   The Strand Magazine.
The Adventure of the Solitary Cyclist.   26 December Collier's Weekly.

1904
The Adventure of the Solitary Cyclist.   January   The Strand Magazine.
The Adventure of the Priory School.   30 January   Collier's Weekly.
The Adventure of the Priory School.   February   The Strand Magazine.
The Adventure of Black Peter.   27 February   Collier's Weekly.
The Adventure of Black Peter.   March   The Strand Magazine.
The Adventure of Charles Augustus Milverton. 26March   Collier's Weekly.
The Adventure of Charles Augustus Milverton. April   The Strand Magazine.
The Adventure of the Six Napoleons.   30 April   Collier's Weekly.
The Adventure of the Six Napoleons.   May   The Strand Magazine.
The Adventure of the Three Students.   June   The Strand Magazine.
The Adventure of the Golden Pince-nez. July   The Strand Magazine.

1904

The Adventure of the Missing Three-Quarter.	August	The Strand Magazine.
The Adventure of the Abbey Grange.	September	The Strand Magazine.
The Adventure of the Second Stain.	December	The Strand Magazine.

1905

The Adventure of the Second Stain. — 28 January — Collier's The National Weekly.

The Return of Sherlock Holmes (collection) — 7 March — George Newnes.
- The Adventure of the Empty House.
- The Adventure of the Norwood Builder.
- The Adventure of the Dancing Men.
- The Adventure of the Solitary Cyclist.
- The Adventure of the Priory School.
- The Adventure of Black Peter.
- The Adventure of Charles Augustus Milverton.
- The Adventure of the Six Napoleons.
- The Adventure of the Three Students.
- The Adventure of the Golden Pince-nez.
- The Adventure of the Missing Three-Quarter.
- The Adventure of the Abbey Grange.
- The Adventure of the Second Stain.

The Fiscal Question. — April — W. Henderson.
Sir Nigel. — December 1905 – December 1906 — The Strand Magazine.
Sir Nigel's Song. — 10 December — Associated Sunday Magazines.

1906

An Incursion into Diplomacy.	June	The Cornhill Magazine.
An Incursion into Diplomacy.	July	Smith, Elder & Co.
Sir Nigel.	15 November	Smith, Elder & Co.
Through the Magic Door.	December 1906-November 1907	Cassell's Magazine.

1907

Waterloo. (A one-act play based on A Straggler of '15) — Samuel French.
The Strange Case of George Edalji. — 2 & 3 January — The Daily Telegraph.
The Case of Mr. George Edalji. — 11 & 12 January — The Daily Telegraph.
The Case of George Edalji: A Question for Opthalmologists. — 19 January — British Medical Journal & Lancet.
The Story of Mr. George Edalji. — 20 January — T. Harrison Roberts.
The Croxley Master. — March 1907 — McClure, Phillips & Co.
Through the Magic Door. — 20 November — Smith, Elder & Co.

1908

A Pot of Caviare. — March — The Strand Magazine.
The Grey Dress. — May — The Flag.
A Heroic Roman. How Dorando failed to seize the Laurel. — 25 July — Daily Mail.
The Silver Mirror. — August — The Strand Magazine.
The Undoing of Archibald: A Composite Novelette. — August — The Strand Magazine.
The Singular Experience of Mr. J. Scott Eccles. — 15 August — Collier's The National Weekly.

1908
The Singular Experience of Mr. John Scott Eccles.
| | September | The Strand Magazine. |

Round the Fire Stories (collection) — 24 September — Smith, Elder & Co.
The Leather Funnel.
The Beetle Hunter.
The Man with the Watches.
The Pot of Caviare.
The Japanned Box.
The Black Doctor.
Playing with Fire.
The Jew's Breastplate.
The Lost Special.
The Club-Footed Grocer.
The Sealed Room.
The Brazilian Cat.
The Usher of Lea House School. [The Latin Tutor]
The Brown Hand.
The Fiend of the Cooperage.
Jelland's Voyage.
B. 24.
The Tiger of San Pedro. — October — The Strand Magazine.
The Adventure of the Bruce-Partington Plans. — December — The Strand Magazine.

1909
Shakespeare's Expostulation. — March — The Cornhill Magazine.
By the North Sea. — April — The Press Album.
Bendy's Sermon. — April — The Strand Magazine.
A Discord. Being a Break in a Duet. — June — Nash's Magazine.
The Lord of Falconbridge. — August — The Strand Magazine.
Some Recollections of Sport. — September — The Strand Magazine.
The Crime of the Congo. — October — Hutchinson & Co.
The Homecoming. — December — The Strand Magazine.

1910
1902-1909. — August — The Rifleman.
The Terror of Blue John Gap. — August — The Strand Magazine.
The Marriage of the Brigadier. — September — The Strand Magazine.
The Romance of Medicine. — 8 October — Lancet.
The Last Galley. — November — The London Magazine.
The Coming of the Huns. — November — Scribner's Magazine.
The Passing of the Legions. — December — The London Magazine.
The First Cargo. — December — Scribner's Magazine.
The Adventure of the Devil's Foot. — December — The Strand Magazine.

1911
The Red Star. — January — Scribner's Magazine.
The Contest. — March — Pearson's Magazines.
The Adventure of the Red Circle. — March & April — The Strand Magazine.
An Iconoclast. — 5 March — Associated Sunday Magazines.
Songs of the Road (collection) — 16 March — Smith, Elder & Co.
I. Narrative Verse and Songs.
Foreword.
A Hymn of Empire.
Sir Nigel's Song.
The Arab Steed.
A Post Impressionist.

1911

Songs of the Road (collection continued)
Empire Builders.
The Groom's Encore.
The Bayhorse.
The Outcasts.
The End.
1902-1909.
The Wanderer.
Bendy's Sermon.
II. Philosophic Verses.
Compensation.
The Banner of Progress.
Hope.
Religio Medici.
Man's Limitation.
Mind and Matter.
Darkness.
III. Miscellaneous Verses.
A Woman's Love.
By the North Sea.
December's Snow.
Shakespeare's Expostulation.
The Empire-1902.
A Voyage-1909.
The Orphanage.
Sexagenarius Loquitor.
Night Voices.
The Message. (From Heine)
The Echo. (After Heine)
Advice to a Young Author.
A Lilt of the Road.

The Blighting of Sharkey.	April	Pearson's Magazine.
A Career as a Medical Man.	April	Great Thoughts.
The Last Galley (collection)	26 April	Smith, Elder & Co.

The Last Galley.
The Contest.
Through the Veil.
An Iconoclast.
Giant Maximin.
The Coming of the Huns.
The Last of the Legions. [The Passing of the Legions]
The First Cargo.
The Homecoming.
The Red Star.
The Silver Mirror.
The Blighting of Sharkey.
The Marriage of the Brigadier.
The Lord of Falconbridge.
Out of the Running.
De Profundis.
The Great Brown-Pericord Motor.
The Terror of Blue John Gap.

Giant Maximin.	July	The Literary Pageant.
One Crowded Hour.	August	The Strand Magazine.
What Reform is Most Needed?	September	The Strand Magazine.

1911

Why He Is Now In Favour Of Home Rule.	26 September	Liberal Federation Department.
The Disappearance of Lady Frances Carfax.	December	The Strand Magazine.

1912

The Lost World.	24 March-21 July	Associated Sunday Magazines.
The Lost World.	April-November	The Strand Magazine.
Religio Medici.	April	Current Literature.
Ragtime!	30 April	The Daily Telegraph.
The Speckled Band. (A Play)	August	Samuel French Ltd.
The Case of Oscar Slater.	19 August	Hodder & Stoughton.
The Terror of Blue John Gap.	30 August	Privately Printed.
The Lost World.	15 October	Hodder & Stoughton.
The Fall of Lord Barrymore.	December	The Strand Magazine.

1913

Great Britain and the Next War.	February	The Fortnightly Review.
The Poison Belt.	March-July	The Strand Magazine.
The Golden Dog	29 March	Crowborough Weekly.
The Greatest Mystery of the Sea: The "Marie Celeste".	July	The Strand Magazine.
The Poison Belt.	13 August	Hodder & Stoughton.
Borrowed Scenes.	September	Harper's Bazaar.
How it Happened.	September	The Strand Magazine.
The Horror of the Heights.	November	The Strand Magazine.
The Adventure of the Dying Detective.	22 November	Collier's The National Weekly.
The Adventure of the Dying Detective.	December	The Strand Magazine.
Divorce. Reform of the Law Needed.	2 December	The Morning Post.
Divorce Law Reform. Sir Arthur Conan Doyle in Reply.	9 December	The Morning Post.

1914

Pulled Up. [The King of the Foxes]	14 June	Top Notch Magazine (USA).
Danger! Being the Log of Captain John Sirius.	July	The Strand Magazine.
What Naval Experts Think.	July	The Strand Magazine.
The Athabasca Trail.	2 July	Montreal Gazette.
The World-War Conspiracy.	27 August	Daily Chronicle.
The Valley of Fear.	September 1914 – May 1915	The Strand Magazine.
Great Britain and the Next War.	September	Small, Maynard & Co.
The Devil's Doctrine.	18 September	Daily Chronicle.
The Great German Plot.	26 September	Daily Chronicle.
"The War" As Seen By Sir Arthur Conan Doyle.	27 September	New York Tribune.
To Arms!	30 September	Hodder & Stoughton.
The "Contemptible Little Army."	10 October	Daily Chronicle.
A Policy of Murder.	26 October	Daily Chronicle.
Madness.	23 November	Daily Chronicle.
The German War.	December	Hodder & Stoughton.
The War. A Statement of the British Case.	December	The Strand Magazine (NY).

1915

Western Wanderings.	January	George H. Doran Company.
Western Wanderings.	January-April	The Cornhill Magazine.

1915

How I "Broke Into Print". II Arthur Conan Doyle.
| | February | The Strand Magazine. |

The Athabasca Trail.	April	The Cornhill Magazine.
The Valley of Fear.	3 June	Smith, Elder & Co.
An Outing in War-Time.	October	The Strand Magazine.
The Outlook on the War.	25 October	Daily Chronicle.
Stranger Than Fiction.	27 November	
		Collier's The National Weekly.
Stranger than Fiction.	December	The Strand Magazine.
Ypres.	December	The Queen's Gift Book.
Sir John French. An Appreciation.	20 December	Daily Chronicle.

1916

The Prisoner's Defence.	January	
		Collier's The National Weekly.
The Prisoner's Defence.	February	The Strand Magazine.
The British Campaign in France.	April 1916-June 1917	
		The Strand Magazine.
A Glimpse of the British Army.	13 – 15 June	Daily Chronicle.
A Glimpse of the French Line.	20 & 22 June	Daily Chronicle.
In the Argonne.	22 June	Daily Chronicle.
Under Fire on the Izonzo Front.	27 June	Daily Chronicle.
Warfare in the Carnic Alps.	29 June	Daily Chronicle.
A Visit to Three Fronts.	August	Hodder & Stoughton.
A New Revelation. Spiritualism and Religion.	4 November	Light.
The British Campaign in France and Flanders. Volume 1.		
	23 November	Hodder & Stoughton.
Spiritualism and Religion.	2 December	Light.

1917

Supremacy of the British Soldier.	19 April	Daily Chronicle.
The Guards Came Through.	23 June	The Times.
Is Sir Oliver Lodge Right? Yes.	July	The Strand Magazine.
The British Campaign in France and Flanders. Volume 2.		
	5 July	Hodder & Stoughton.
The Guns in Sussex.	27 July	The Times.
What will England be like in 1930?	August	The Strand Magazine.
His Last Bow.	September	The Strand Magazine.
His Last Bow (collection)	22 October	John Murray.
The Adventure of Wisteria Lodge.		
The Adventure of the Cardboard Box.		
The Adventure of the Red Circle.		
The Adventure of the Bruce-Partington Plans.		
The Adventure of the Dying Detective.		
The Disappearance of Lady Frances Carfax.		
The Adventure of the Devil's Foot.		
His Last Bow.		
Phenomena and Religion of Spiritualism. A New Revelation.		
	28 October	The Sunday Times.
The New Revelation.	10, 17 & 24 November	
		Light.
Some Personalia about Mr. Sherlock Holmes.	December	The Strand Magazine.

1918

| The New Revelation. | January | Metropolitan Magazine. |

1918

Three of Them I. A Chat about Children, Snakes and Zebus.	April	The Strand Magazine.
Three of Them II. About Cricket.	April	The Strand Magazine.
The British Campaign in France and Flanders. Volume 3.	9 April	Hodder & Stoughton.
The New Revelation.	29 April	Hodder & Stoughton.
The Battle of the Somme.	May-June	The Strand Magazine.
Three of Them III. Speculations.	July	The Strand Magazine.
Three of Them IV. The Leather Skin Tribe.	August	The Strand Magazine.
The Battle of Arras.	October	The Strand Magazine.
The Rent in the Line. (Breaking the Hindenburg Line).	3 October	The Times.
The Battle of Messines.	November	The Strand Magazine.
Life After Death. [A Form Letter]	5 November	Daily Chronicle.
Three of Them V. About Naughtiness and Frogs and Historical Pictures.	December	The Strand Magazine.
Danger! And Other Stories (collection)	4 December	John Murray.

Danger!
One Crowded Hour.
A Point of View.
The Fall of Lord Barrymore.
The Horror of the Heights.
Borrowed Scenes.
The Surgeon of Gaster Fell.
The Prisoner's Defence.
How it Happened.
Three of Them. I. A Chat about Children, Snakes and Zebus.
    II. About Cricket.
    III. Speculations.
    IV. The Leatherskin Tribe.

1919

Cambrai. The First Phase – Nov 20th-29th 1917.	January	The Strand Magazine.
The Volunteer.	22 January	Daily Express.
Cambrai. The Second Phase.	February	The Strand Magazine.
Life After Death.	March	The Strand Magazine.
The British Campaign in France and Flanders. Volume 4.	31 March	Hodder & Stoughton.
The Vital Message.	May, August & October	Nash's–Pall Mall Magazine.
A Full Report of a Lecture on Spiritualism. (Worthing 11/07/1919)	August	The Worthing Gazette.
The British Campaign in France and Flanders. Volume 5.	5 September	Hodder & Stoughton.
The Vital Message.	4 November	Hodder & Stoughton.
Uncharted Coast. I. The Law of the Ghost.	December	The Strand Magazine.
The Guards Came Through and Other Poems (collection)	16 December	John Murray.

The Guards Came Through.
Victrix.
Those Others.
Haig is Moving.
The Guns in Sussex.
Ypres.
Grousing.
The Volunteer.

1919
The Guards Came Through and Other Poems (collection continued)
The Night Patrol.
The Wreck on Loch McGarry.
The Bigot.
The Athabasca Trail.
Ragtime!
Christmas in Wartime. [Christmas in Trouble]
Lindisfaire.
A Parable.
Fate.

1920
Uncharted Coast. II. A New Light on Old Crimes.
                                                    January   The Strand Magazine.
Our Reply to The Cleric.   January
                                                                        The Spiritualists' National Union.
The British Campaign in France and Flanders. Volume 6.
                                                    23 January   Hodder & Stoughton.
Uncharted Coast. III. The Shadows on the Screen.
                                                    May   The Strand Magazine.
The Night Patrol.   May   The Student.
The Sideric Pendulum.   August   The Strand Magazine.
Spiritualism and Rationalism.   27 August   Hodder & Stoughton.
Uncharted Coast. IV. An Old Story Retold.   September   The Strand Magazine.
Uncharted Coast. V. The Absolute Proof.   November   The Strand Magazine.
Fairies Photographed-An Epoch Making Event. December   The Strand Magazine.

1921
The Evidence for Fairies.   March   The Strand Magazine.
Uncharted Coast. VI. A Worker of Wonders. May   The Strand Magazine.
The Wanderings of a Spiritualist.   29 May-10 July The Weekly Dispatch.
The Wanderings of a Spiritualist.   2 September   Hodder & Stoughton.
The Adventure of the Mazarin Stone.   October   The Strand Magazine.
The Bully of Brocas Court A Legend of the Ring.
                                                    November   The Strand Magazine.
The Nightmare Room.   December   The Strand Magazine.

1922
The Problem of Thor Bridge.   February & March
                                                                        The Strand Magazine.
The Book I Most Enjoyed Writing.   March   The Strand Magazine.
The Lift.   June   The Strand Magazine.
"Now Then Smith!"   July   The Strand Magazine.
A Point of Contact.   September   Hearst's International.
The Coming of the Fairies.   1 September   Hodder & Stoughton.
The Adventures of a Spiritualist in America. 3 September-17 December
                                                                             Lloyd's Sunday News.
The Poems of Arthur Conan Doyle-Collected Edition.
                                                    21 September   John Murray.

Contents:
Songs of Action. All are the same poems as in the volume of the same name.
Songs of the Road.
Four poems have been added to this section, and A Lilt of the Road has been omitted.
The Farewell.
"Now Then, Smith!"
To My Lady.

1922
The Poems of Arthur Conan Doyle-Collected Edition (continued)
A Reminiscence of Cricket.
The Guards Came Through and Other Poems Collection.
Seven Poems have been added to this section, and a verse play. One poem is revised.
The Bugles of Canada.
To Carlo.
Little Billy.
Take Heart.
Retrospect.
Comrades.
The Journey. (a one-act play)
Christmas in Trouble. (originally called Christmas in Wartime)
To Ronald Ross.
The Mystery of the Fox Sisters.   October
                The Quarterly Transactions of the British College of Psychic Science.
Spiritualism-Some Straight Questions and Some Direct Answers.
                                    14 October   Light.
The Centurion.   December   The Story-teller.
Billy Bones.   December   The Strand Magazine.
The Case for Spirit Photography.   14 December   Hutchinson & Co.

1923
The Cottingley Fairies. An Epilogue.   February   The Strand Magazine.
The Adventure of the Creeping Man.   March   The Strand Magazine.
Our American Adventure.   16 March   Hodder & Stoughton.
Haunting Dreams.   April   The Strand Magazine.
Psychic Phenomena are Real.   June   The London Magazine.
The Forbidden Subject.   August   The Strand Magazine.
Memories and Adventures.   October 1923-July 1924
                                                        The Strand Magazine.

Three of Them (collection)   November   John Murray.
A Chat about Children, Snakes and Zebras.
About Cricket.
Speculation.
The Leatherskin Tribe.
About Naughtiness and Frogs and Historical Pictures.
Billy Bones.
The Forbidden Subject.

1924
The Adventure of the Sussex Vampire.   January   The Strand Magazine.
Our Second American Adventure.   15 February   Hodder & Stoughton.
Early Psychic Experiences.   March   Pearson's Magazine.
What Comes After Death?   April   Pearson's Magazine.
Talk with the "Ghost" of Lenin.   30 May   Daily Express.
How Watson Learned the Trick.   June   Methuen.
Memories and Adventures.   18 September   Hodder & Stoughton.
Edward Irving and the Voices.   October
                The Quarterly Transactions of the British College of Psychic Science.
The Adventure of the Three Garridebs.   25 October
                                                        Collier's The National Weekly.
The Adventure of the Illustrious Client. 8 November
                                                        Collier's The National Weekly.
How Our Novelists Write Their Books.   December   The Strand Magazine.

1925

The Adventure of the Three Garridebs.	January	The Strand Magazine.
The Adventure of the Illustrious Client.	February & March	The Strand Magazine.
The Story of Swedenborg.	14 February	Light.
First Developments in America.	21 February	Light.
The Prophet of the New Revelation.	28 February, 7 & 14 March	Light.
The Land of Mist.	19 March	Hutchinson & Co.
The Eddy Brothers and the Holmeses.	21 March-18 April	Light.
The Land of Mist.	July 1925-March 1926	The Strand Magazine.
Psychic Experiences.	November	G.P. Putman's Sons.

1926

The History of Spiritualism (2 Volumes)	June	Cassell & Co.
The Adventure of the Three Gables.	18 September	Liberty.
The Adventure of the Three Gables.	October	The Strand Magazine.
The Adventure of the Blanched Soldier.	16 October	Liberty.
The Adventure of the Blanched Soldier.	November	The Strand Magazine.
The Adventure of the Lion's Mane.	27 November	Liberty.
The Adventure of the Lion's Mane.	December	The Strand Magazine.
The Adventure of the Retired Colourman.	18 December	Liberty.

1927

The Adventure of the Retired Colourman.	January	The Strand Magazine.
The Adventure of the Veiled Lodger.	22 January	Liberty.
The Adventure of the Veiled Lodger.	February	The Strand Magazine.
The British Army in Italy.	1 February	The Fortnightly Review.
A Sherlock Holmes Prize Competition.	March	The Strand Magazine.
The Adventure of Shoscombe Old Place.	5 March	Liberty.
Pheneas Speaks.	21 March	Psychic Press & Bookshop.
The Adventure of Shoscombe Old Place.	April	The Strand Magazine.
Ghosts I Have Seen – 1. The Spectral Friars.	1 May	The Weekly Dispatch.
The Sherlock Holmes Prize Competition Result-How I made my List.	June	The Strand Magazine.
The Case-Book of Sherlock Holmes (collection)	16 June	John Murray.
The Adventure of the Illustrious Client.		
The Adventure of the Blanched Soldier.		
The Adventure of the Mazarin Stone.		
The Adventure of the Three Gables.		
The Adventure of the Sussex Vampire.		
The Adventure of the Three Garridebs.		
The Problem of Thor Bridge.		
The Adventure of the Creeping Man.		
The Adventure of the Lion's Mane.		
The Adventure of the Veiled Lodger.		
The Adventure of Shoscombe Old Place.		
The Adventure of the Retired Colourman.		
W.G. Grace – A Memory.	July	The Strand Magazine.
Houdini the Enigma.	August-September	The Strand Magazine.
Ghost of the Moat.	4 August	Daily Express.
The Maracot Deep.	October 1927-February 1928	The Strand Magazine.

1927

The Alleged Posthumous Writings of Great Authors.	December	The Fortnightly Review.
The Great Characters of Fiction-"Which should I Most Like to have Created?"	December	The Strand Magazine.

1928

What Does Spiritualism Actually Teach and Stand For?	February	The Psychic Bookshop.
A Word of Warning.	February	The Psychic Press.
When the World Screamed.	25 February & 3 March	Liberty.
Thomas Lake Harris: A Strange Prophet.	April	The Quarterly Transactions of the British College of Psychic Science.
When the World Screamed.	April & May	The Strand Magazine.
Blood Sports-Should They Be Abolished?	May	The Strand Magazine.
Notes from a Strange Mail-bag-The Dreamers.	June	The Strand Magazine.
Can We Speak with the Dead?	October	The London Magazine.
The Story of Spedegue's Dropper.	October	The Strand Magazine.
The British Campaigns in Europe 1914-1918.	November	Geoffrey Bles.

1929

The Disintegration Machine.	January	The Strand Magazine.
The Lord of the Dark Face I. The Dangers of the Deep.	April & May	The Strand Magazine.
The Lord of the Dark Face II. The Crisis.	May	The Strand Magazine.
An Open Letter to Those of My Generation.	22 May	The Psychic Press.
The Maracot Deep (collection)	29 July	John Murray.
The Maracot Deep.		
The Disintegration Machine.		
The Story of Spedegue's Dropper.		
When the World Screamed.		
Our African Winter.	9 September	John Murray.
The Roman Catholic Church-A Rejoinder.	October	The Psychic Press.
The Death Voyage.	October	The Strand Magazine.

1930

The Edge of the Unknown (collection)	24 June	John Murray.
The Riddle of Houdini. [Houdini the Enigma]		
Shadows on the Screen.		
Notes from a Strange Mailbag.		
The Ghost of the Moat.		
The Law of the Ghost.		
The Alleged Posthumous Writings of Unknown Authors.		
Some Curious Personal Experiences.		
Dwellers on the Border.		
A Strange Prophet. [Thomas Lake Harris: A Strange Prophet]		
A London Ghost.		
The Half Way House of Matter.		
A Remarkable Man.		
The Rift in the Veil.		
A New Light on Old Crimes.		
Singular Records of a Circle.		
The Parish Magazine.	August	The Strand Magazine.
The Last Resource.	16 August	Liberty.
The End of Devil Hawker.	23 August	Saturday Evening Post.
The Passing of Conan Doyle.	September	The Strand Magazine.

1930

A Scandal in Bohemia.	September	The Strand Magazine.
Some Letters of Conan Doyle. With Notes and Comments by H. Greennough Smith.		
	October	The Strand Magazine.
The End of Devil Hawker.	November	The Strand Magazine.
The Last Resource.	December	The Strand Magazine.

1963

Strange Studies from Life. (collection)	January	The Candlelight Press.

The Holocaust of Manor Place.
The Love Affair of George Vincent Parker.
The Debatable Case of Mrs. Emsley.
A British Commando. An Interview with Conan Doyle.

Old Bill, Private Arthur Conan Doyle 1914

Miscellaneous Works
Selective List Of Miscellaneous Writings

Minor Contributions

A Selective List of Prefaces, Forwards, Collaborations, Translations and Introductions by ACD

TITLE	AUTHOR	ACD's CONTRIBUTION	
The Fate of Fenella.	Helen Mathers.	Between Two Fires.	1892
Jane Annie; Or, The Good Conduct Prize.	J.M. Barrie.	Second Act Lyrics.	1893
A Brief History of The Lotos Club.	John Elderkin.	Speech.	1894
Hilda Wade.	Grant Allen.	Chapter XII.	1900
Ballads of the War.	H.D. Rawnsley.	Prefatory Note.	1901
The Construction and Reconstruction of the Human Body.	Eugen Sandow.	Foreword.	1907
Great Britain and the Congo.	E.D. Morel.	Introduction.	1909
The Fair Land of Central America.	Maurice de Waleffe.	Preface.	1911
Divorce and Morality.	C.S. Bremner.	Preface.	1912
What the Worker Wants.	H.G. Wells.	A Rejoinder.	1912
Adam Lindsay Gordon.	Edith Humphris.	Dedication.	1912
What Irish Protestants Think.		Verbatim Report.	1912
Marriage and Divorce.	A. Hamilton.	Preface.	1913
Divorce and the Church.	Lord Hugh Cecil.	Reply.	1913
In Quest of Truth.	Captain H. Stansbury.	Correspondence.	1914
"G.H. Darby" Captain of the Wyrley Gang.	G.A. Atkinson.	Preface.	1914
The Evolution of the Olympic Games 1829 B.C.-1914 A.D.	F.A.M. Webster.	Preface.	1914
Songs of Sea Labour. (Chanties)	Frank T. Bullen.	Appreciation.	1914
The Portuguese Amnesty.	Earl of Lytton.	Verbatim Report.	1914
The Story of British Prisoners.	The Foreign Office.	Annotated/Preface.	1915
Glorious Battles of English History.	Major C.H. Wylly.	Foreword.	1915
Address Delivered Before the Canadian Club of Montreal.			1915
5,000.000 Men.	Lord Kitchener.	Appreciation.	1916
A Petition to the Prime Minister on behalf of Sir Roger Casement.			1916
"Is Spiritualism of the Devil?"	Revd. F. Fielding-Ould.	Introduction.	1917
The Song of Songs.	Hermann Sudermann.	Letter.	1917
The Undiscovered Country.	H. Bayley.	Introduction.	1918
Spiritualism, Its History, Phenomena and Doctrine.	J. Arthur Hill.	Introduction.	1918
An Amazing Séance and an Exposure.	Sydney A. Moseley.	Introduction.	1919
The Eternal Question.	Allen Clarke.	Foreword.	1919
Life is Movement.	Eugen Sandow.	Foreword.	1919
The Life Beyond the Veil.	Revd. G. Vale Owen.	Introduction.	1920
Rachel Comforted.	Mrs Fred Maturin.	A note.	1920
Verbatim Report of a Public Debate on "The Truth of Spiritualism."		Address.	1920
Life After Death.		Reply.	1920
Spiritualism Its Present-Day Meaning.			1920
A Message to Humanity.	Various.	Appreciation.	1920
The Unrepentant Northcliffe.	Ferdinand Hansen.	Letters.	1921
D.D. Home. His Life and Mission.	Mme. Dunglas Home.	Edited/Introduction.	1921
The Blue Island.	W.T. Stead.	ACD Letter.	1922
Old Offenders.	E.W. Hornung.	Preface.	1923

Under the Southern Cross.	Horace Leaf.	Introduction.	1923
Man! and His Future.	Harvey Metcalfe.	Preface.	1923
The Spiritualist's Reader.	Compiled by ACD.	Preface.	1924
The Case of Lester Coltman.	Lilian Walbrook.	Introduction.	1924
The Mystery of Joan of Arc.	Leon Denis.	Translated & Preface.	1924
The Great Stories of Real Life.	Various.	Edalji & Slater.	1924
The Book of the Queen's Dolls' House.	Various	Contribution.	1924
Survival.	Various.	Contribution.	1924
Phantoms of the Dawn.	Violet Tweedale.	Foreword.	1924
The Evolution of Spiritualism.	Harvey Metcalfe.	Preface.	1925
Brave Deeds of Brave Men.	C. Sheridan Jones.	Foreword.	1925
My Religion.	Various.	Address.	1925
From the Other Side.	J.H.D. Miller.	Foreword Letter.	1925
Other World People.	J.W. Herries.	Foreword.	1926
The Soul of Jack London.	Edward Biron Payne.	Prefatory Letter.	1926
Researches in the Phenomena of Spiritualism.	William Crookes.	Appendix.	1926
Leslie's Letters to his Mother.	Various.	Two Letters.	1926
The Case For and Against Psychical Belief.	Various.	Contribution.	1927
What I Think.	Various.		1927
The Truth about Oscar Slater.	William Park.	Statement/Introduction.	1927
I Escape.	Captain J.L. Hardy.	Introduction.	1927
The House of Wonder.	E.M.S.	Letter.	1927
The Great Problem and the Evidence for its Solution.	G.L. Johnson.	An Appreciation.	1928
A Commonsense View of Religion.	A Business Man.	Introduction.	1928
Psychical Experiences of a Musician.	Florizel von Reuter.	Foreword.	1928
Where Are the Dead?		Symposium.	1928
Alloquia.	D. Marinus.	Preface/Letter.	1928
Health, Its Recovery and Maintenance.	Abdul Latif.	Preface.	1928
Léon Denis Intime.	Claire Baumard.	Preface.	1929
The Spiritual Adventures of a Business Man.	T.A.R. Purchas.	Foreword.	1929
The New Nuctemeron.	Marjorie Livingston.	Preface.	1930
The Consoling Angel.	Florizel von Reuter.	Foreword.	1930

1st Edition Cover of *Three of Them* published 1923

The main room at Windlesham. 1907-1930

Works Consulted/Sources

On-line resources for the newspapers quoted can be found at the following:
The Times: http://infotrac.galegroup.com library membership number required.
New Zealand: www.paperspast.natlib.gov.nz free access.
Australia: http://trove.nla.gov.au/newspapers free access.
British: www.britishnewspaperarchive.co.uk subscription required.
Cricket Archive http://www.cricketarchive.com subscription required

1. Lamond, John, *Arthur Conan Doyle, A Memoir*, (London: John Murray 1931).
2. Pearson, Hesketh, *Conan Doyle, His Life & Art*, (London: Methuen & Co. Ltd. 1943).
3. Carr, John Dickson, *The Life of Sir Arthur Conan Doyle*, (London: John Murray 1949).
4. Nordon, Pierre, *Conan Doyle*, (London: John Murray 1966).
5. Edwards, Owen Dudley, *The Quest for Sherlock Holmes*, (Edinburgh: Mainstream 1983).
6. Green, Richard Lancelyn, and Gibson, John Michael, *A Bibliography of A. Conan Doyle*, (Oxford: Clarendon Press 1983).
7. Rodin, Alvin E & Key, J.D., *Medical Casebook of Doctor Arthur Conan Doyle* (Malabar, Flarador: Robert E. Krieger Publishing 1984).
8. Stavert, Geoffrey, *A Study in Southsea: The Unrevealed Life of Doctor Arthur Conan Doyle*, (Portsmouth: Milestone Publications 1987).
9. Redmond, Christopher, *Welcome To America, Mr. Sherlock Holmes*, (Toronto: Simon & Pierre 1987).
10. Doyle, Arthur Conan, *Memories & Adventures*, (London: Greenhill Books 1988).
11. A Chronology of Arthur Conan Doyle as in the *Oxford Sherlock Holmes Series*. General editor Owen Dudley Edwards, (Oxford: Oxford University Press 1994).
12. Green, Richard Lancelyn, *Conan Doyle of Wimpole Street*, (Penyffordd, Chester: The Arthur Conan Doyle Society 1994).
13. Doyle, Arthur Conan, *Western Wanderings*, (Penyffordd, Chester: The Arthur Conan Doyle Society 1994).
14. Booth, Martin, *The Doctor, The Detective and Arthur Conan Doyle*, (London: Hodder & Stoughton 1997).
15. Stashower, Daniel, *Teller of Tales The Life of Arthur Conan Doyle*, (New York: H. Holt & Company 1999).
16. Mrs Georgina Doyle, private correspondence and conversations with the author.
17. Redmond, Christopher, *The Sherlock Holmes Handbook*, (Toronto: Simon & Pierre 1993).
18. Green, Richard Lancelyn & Gibson, John Michael, *Letters to the Press*, (Iowa City: University of Iowa Press 1986).
19. Doyle, Arthur Conan, *The Future of Canadian Literature*, (Penyffordd, Chester: The Arthur Conan Doyle Society 1994).
20. Jones, Kelvin I., *Conan Doyle and the Spirits*, (Wellingborough: The Aquarian Press 1989).
21. Doyle, Arthur Conan, *Essays on Photography*, edited and introduced by John Michael Gibson & Richard Lancelyn Green, (London: Secker & Warburg 1982).
22. Doyle, Arthur Conan, *Wanderings of a Spiritualist*, (London: Hodder & Stoughton 1921).
23. Green, Richard Lancelyn, 'Conan Doyle's Sisters in their Governess Day' in Bruxner, Pamela (ed.) *A Gaggle of Governesses*, (London: The Sherlock Holmes Society of London 1997).
24. Rowlands, Peter, *Raffles and his Creator*, (London: Nexta 1999).
25. Costello, Peter, *The Real World of Sherlock Holmes*, (London: Robinson Publishing 1991).
26. Brandon, Ruth, *The Life and Many Deaths of Harry Houdini*, (London: Secker & Warburg 1993).
27. Monahan, Eric, 'Conan Doyle in Torbay' in *The Torr The Journal of The Poor Folk Upon the Moors Issue No. 13 Autumn 1998*.

28. Doyle, Arthur Conan, *A Full Report of a Lecture on Spiritualism*, (Cambridge: Rupert Books Monograph No.1).
29. Doyle, Arthur Conan, *The New Revelation*, (Cambridge: Rupert Books Monograph No.3).
30. House, Jack, *Square Mile of Murder*, (Glasgow: The Molendinar Press 1975).
31. Green, Richard Lancelyn, *The Uncollected Sherlock Holmes*, (London: Penguin 1983).
32. Green, Richard Lancelyn, *Back to Baker Street. Conan Doyle in London*, (London: The Sherlock Holmes Society of London 1994).
33. Green, Richard Lancelyn, 'Louisa Hawkins and her Family' in Smyth, Anna (ed.) *The Boscombe Valley Mystery Tour*, (London: The Sherlock Holmes Society of London 1999).
34. Trotter, W.R., *Conan Doyle at Hindhead, 1895-1907*, (ACD Journal Vol. 7 1996/7).
35. Crouch, John D., *Letter from John D. Crouch*, (ACD Journal Vol. 1 No. 2 1990).
36. Green, Richard Lancelyn, 'Sir Arthur Conan Doyle in Cornwall', in Bruxner, Pamela (ed.) *The Cornish Horror*, (London: The Sherlock Holmes Society of London 1998).
37. *The Life and Times of Crowborough Beacon Golf Club*, (Privately Printed).
38. Spencer, Frank, *The Piltdown Papers*, (Oxford: Oxford University Press 1990).
39. Cooke, Catherine, *Conan Doyle and Homes*, (ACD Journal Vol. 1 No. 1 1989).
40. Wilson, Philip K., *'Dear Price. Yours Sincerely, A. Conan Doyle'*, (ACD Journal Vol. 3 1992).
41. Pilot, R. and Rodin, A., *The Annotated Lost World*, (Indianapolis: Wessex Press, 1996).
42. Green, Richard Lancelyn, 'Conan Doyle and Hampshire' in Horrocks, Peter (ed.) *The Tri-Metallic Question*, (London: The Sherlock Holmes Society of London 1991).
43. Cooke, Catherine, *Notes from a Lumber-Room*, (ACD Society The Parish Magazine No. 12 April 1995).
44. Homer, M.W. & Roden, C., *The Movietone Interview: Arthur Conan Doyle*, (ACD Journal Vol. 6 1995).
45. Ernst, B.M. & Carrington, H. *Houdini and Conan Doyle*, (London: Hutchinson & Co. 1933).
46. Green, Richard Lancelyn & Gibson, John Michael, *A Bibliography of A. Conan Doyle*, (London: Hudson House 2000).
47. Doyle, Arthur Conan, *The Sign of Four*, (see Introduction by Christopher Roden), (Oxford University Press 1994).
48. Doyle, Arthur Conan, *The Adventures of Sherlock Holmes*, (see Introduction by Richard Lancelyn Green), (Oxford: Oxford University Press 1994).
49. Doyle, Arthur Conan, *The Hound of the Baskervilles*, (see Introduction by W. W. Robson), (Oxford University Press 1994).
50. Doyle, Arthur Conan, *The Return of Sherlock Holmes*, (see Introduction by Richard Lancelyn Green), (Oxford: Oxford University Press 1994).
51. Doyle, Arthur Conan, *The Valley of Fear*, (see Introduction by Owen Dudley Edwards), (Oxford: Oxford University Press 1994).
52. Doyle, Arthur Conan, *His Last Bow*, (see Introduction by Owen Dudley Edwards), (Oxford: Oxford University Press 1994).
53. Doyle, Arthur Conan, *The Memories of Sherlock Holmes*, (see Introduction by Christopher Roden), (Oxford: Oxford University Press 1994).
54. Spartacus Schoolnet 18/07/00.
55. Payne, Malcolm, (collected) Philip Weller (edited with some notes) *Recollections of Sir Arthur Conan Doyle by Residents of Crowborough*, (Fareham, Hampshire: Sherlock Publications 1993).
56. Marylebone Cricket Club Records supplied by Richard Greep.
57. Green, Richard Lancelyn, 'Conan Doyle's Norfolk Connection' in *Sail and Steam*, (London: The Sherlock Holmes Society of London 2000).
58. Census April 1881 supplied by Eric Monahan.
59. Weller, Philip, 'Would You Care To Register, Sir Arthur?' *The Devil's Foot Contract Reviewed* in The FMHC Interim Report June 2001, (Sherlock Publications 2001).
60. Engen, Rodney, *Richard Doyle*, (Stroud, Gloucestershire: Catalpa Press 1983).

61. Doyle, Arthur Conan, *The Hound of the Baskervilles*, (see introduction by Christopher Frayling), (London: Penguin Classics 2001).
62. Bates, R. & Scolding, B., *Five Walks around Mullion*, (Mullion, Devon: Mullion Parish Council & Cornwall County Council 1998).
63. Green, Richard Lancelyn, 'Conan Doyle and His Cricket', in Black, M.C. (ed.) *The Victorian Cricket Match between The Sherlock Holmes Society of London versus the P.G. Wodehouse Society*, (London: The Sherlock Holmes Society of London 2001).
64. Haggard, H. Rider, (Higgins, D.S. ed.) *The Private Diaries of Sir Henry Rider Haggard 1914 – 1925*, [Details supplied by Philip Weller], (London: Cassell & Co. Ltd. 1980).
65. Polidoro, Massimo, *Final Séance*, (New York: Prometheus Books 2001).
66. Roden, Christopher, *Conan Doyle the Cricketer: The Wanderers Tour of 1885*, (ACD Journal Vol. 5 1994).
67. Oddie, S. Ingleby, *Sir Arthur Conan Doyle and Jack The Ripper*, (Ripperologist No. 34 April 2001).
68. Bergem. Philip G. *The Family Residences of Arthur Conan Doyle*, (Privately Printed, St. Paul, Minnesota 2001).
69. Private correspondence between Horace Coates and the Author 2000.
70. Stevenson, Frances, (Taylor, A.J.P. ed.) *Lloyd George – A Diary*, (London: Hutchinson & Co. 1971).
71. Hedgcock, Murray (ed.) *Wodehouse at the Wicket*, (London: Hutchinson & Co. 1997, Arrow Books 2011).
72. *The Sherlock Holmes Journal* Vol. 18, No. 3, Winter 1987.
73. Gagan, Mark & Doyle, Steven T., *Arthur Conan Doyle Memorial Dedication Ceremony, Commemorative Booklet*, (The Illustrious Clients of Indianapolis 1994).
74. Doyle, Arthur Conan, *Our African Winter*, (London: Duckworth & Co. Ltd. 2001).
75. *Conan Doyle's Calgary Visit – June 1923*, (Web Site of geocities.com).
76. Sellens, Frank, *Sussex Notebook*, Crowborough Courier 14/12/01.
77. Private correspondence between Our Society and the Author.
78. *Under Doctor's Orders and Under the Italian Sun,* A Letter from Arthur Conan Doyle to William Gillette analysed by Philip Weller, (Uno Studio in Holmes, The Italian Sherlock Holmes Society 2002).
79. Green, Richard Lancelyn, *The Hound of the Baskervilles, Part One*, (London: The Sherlock Holmes Society of London Journal, Vol. 25 No. 3 Winter 2001).
80. Green, Richard Lancelyn, *The Hound of the Baskervilles, Part Two*, (London: The Sherlock Holmes Society of London Journal Vol. 25 No. 4 Summer 2002).
81. Personal correspondence with Eric Monahan 2002.
82. Copy of poster supplied by Michael Doyle. 2002.
83. Information supplied by Philip Bergem taken from the 1901 UK Census, RG 13, Piece 905, 2058, 616 & 4872, Folio 10, 88, 68 & 56, Pages 11, 12, 17, 26 & 30.
84. *The Parish Magazine* Number Eleven August 1994 (The News Magazine of The Arthur Conan Doyle Society, 1994).
85. *Conan Doyle in the Daily Mail*, (ACD Journal Vol. 9 June 1999).
86. Bogomoletz, Wladimir W., *Sir Arthur Conan Doyle's Seven Visits to Paris*, (ACD Journal Vol. 10 May 2000).
87. Private correspondence between Richard Lancelyn Green & Malcolm Payne, 14 August 1996.
88. *The Sherlock Holmes Society of London Journal* Vol. 18 No. 3 Winter 1987.
89. Conan Doyle (Crowborough) Establishment Archives.
90. Hunt, Peter, *Oscar Slater The Great Suspect*, (London: Carroll & Nicholson 1951).
91. Hodge, Harry, (ed.), *Famous Trials Number One* (London: Penguin Books 1954).
92. Green, Richard Lancelyn, (ed.), *Lend Me Your Ears'*, The Sherlock Holmes Society of London Excursion Handbook. 5–7 September 2003, (London: The Sherlock Holmes Society of London 2003).
93. Lownie, Andrew, *John Buchan-The Presbyterian Cavalier*, (London: Pimlico, 2002), p.123, [details supplied by P. Weller].

94. Lownie, Andrew, *John Buchan-The Presbyterian Cavalier*, (London: Pimlico, 2002), p. 326, note 9, [details supplied by P. Weller].
95. Devils Porridge, http://www.secretscotland.org.uk
96. American Family Immigration History Center, The Statue of Liberty–Ellis Island Foundation, Inc.
97. Grand Lodge of British Columbia and Yukon Famous Freemasons Website.
98. Doyle, Arthur Conan, *The Horror of the Heights*, A Facsimile of the author's holograph manuscript with commentary, with an introduction by Philip Bergem, (Ashcroft, Canada: Calabash Press 2004).
99. The Conan Doyle Collection, Christie's Of London Sale Catalogue, 19 May 2004.
100. Kalush, William & Sloman, Larry, *The Secret Life of Houdini The Making of America's First Superhero*, (New York: Atria Books 2006).
101. McClure, Michael & Susan, *When Doyle Visited Baker Street* in *Commanding Views From The Empty House*, Cochran, W.R. &. Speck, G.R. (eds.) (Indianapolis: Gasogene Books 1996).
102. http://www.ttsupportersclub
103. http://www.homepages.mcb.net/ttmuseum/1905.html
104. http://www.the-hindhead-golf-club.co.uk/history.asp
105. http://www.oldclassiccar.co.uk
106. Sellens. Frank, *Sussex Notebook*, Crowborough Courier 16 April 2004.
107. Smith, Kevin, *Sherlock Holmes Was A Pompey Keeper*, (Tiverton, Devon: Halsgrove Publications 2004).
108. Personal correspondence with Vinnie Brosnan January 2005.
109. cricinfoengland website 2005.
110. Lachtman, Howard, *Sherlock Slept Here*, (Santa Barbara, Calif.: Capra Press 1985).
111. Rodin, Alvin E. & Key, Jack D., *Our British Cousin: Highlights and Attitudes of Arthur Conan Doyle in America*, (ACD The Journal of The Arthur Conan Doyle Society Volume 3: 1992).
112. White, Ronald S., *Sir Arthur Conan Doyle in the Pacific Northwest*, (ACD The Journal of the Arthur Conan Doyle Society Volume 3: 1992).
113. Wills-Wood, Chris, *Dr. Conan Doyle, A Victorian Physician and Practitioner*, (ACD The Journal of the Arthur Conan Doyle Society Volume 3: 1992).
114. Doyle, Arthur Conan, *Arthur Conan Doyle on Sherlock Holmes: Speeches at the Stoll Convention Dinner*, (London: The Favil Press 1981).
115. 1861 Scotland Census.
116. 1871 Scotland Census.
117. 1891 England Census.
118. 1891 England Census.
119. 1891 English Census.
120. 1891 Scotland Census.
121. *Farnham, Haslemere & Hindhead Herald* Saturday 4 February 1899.
122. *Farnham, Haslemere & Hindhead Herald* Saturday 15 April 1899.
123. Guest Book of Undershaw and Windlesham supplied by Richard Sveum.
124. Doyle, Georgina, *Out of the Shadows*, (Canada: Calabash Press 2004).
125. Irwin-Brown, Ralph, *Hindhead's Turn Will Come*, (Bury St. Edmunds, Suffolk: St. Edmundsbury Press 1991).
126. From The Archives of Crowborough Courier 24 June 2005.
127. Sellens, Frank, *Sussex Notebook*, Crowborough Courier 19 August 2005.
128. Bob Persaud of the Royal College of Physicians of London.
129. Copy of Innes Doyle's diary entry courtesy of Mrs G. Doyle.
130. Surrey Police charge sheet.
131. *The Folkestone Herald* 2 September 1905.
132. *The Granta* January 1893.
133. The Society of Psychical Research Records.
134. Wood, Jeremy, *Speed on the Downs: Lewes Speed Trials 1924 – 1939*, (Billingshurst, West Sussex: JWFA Books 2005).

135. Private correspondence with Mr George Dibben, Joint Churchwarden, All Saints Church, Minstead.
136. Private correspondence with Bill Barnes in Australia, 6 January 2006.
137. Find my Past: Britain: outbound passenger list.
138. *The New York Times* 12 January 1909.
139. Hamilton, Victor, *Sir Arthur In Belfast Revisited*, The Chronicler 15, March 2006 The Quarterly Sherlockian Supplement of The Crew of the SS May Day, Belfast, and private correspondence with Oscar Ross.
140. Doyle, Arthur Conan, *The 'Baby Book' of Denis Stewart Percy Conan Doyle*, published with *The Land of Mist*, (London: Impala Press 2006).
141. Private correspondence with Jon Lellenberg, April 2006.
142. Correction by Christopher Roden by email, 21 April 2006.
143. Bird, Margaret, *An East Wind*, The East Coast Expedition of The Sherlock Holmes Society of London 1997, (London: The Sherlock Holmes Society of London 1997).
144. Green, Richard Lancelyn, *Conan Doyle: Ship's Surgeon,* in *Helping Out Hopeless Hopkins*, Bruxner, Pamela & Ellis, Bob (eds.), (London: The Sherlock Holmes Society of London 2001).
145. Marriott, Guy & Ellis, Bob, *Sherlock Holmes in Switzerland*, (The Sherlock Holmes Society of London 2005).
146. Mark Doyle, Australia, his source: dated letter from ACD on hotel stationary, addressed to the owner of the Adelaide Advertiser newspaper, also, its envelope postmarked that day.
147. Mark Doyle, Australia, his source: Australian Associated Press quoting Daily Express (London), indicating exhumation took place at dawn on Friday 1 July 1955.
148. Catalogue of sale in the collection of the author.
149. *The Baker Street Journal* volume 22, number 3, September 1972.
150. Doyle, Steven T., (ed.), *The Illustrious Clients Fifth Casebook: Sherlock Holmes in the Heartlands*, [See chapter 1 by Don Curtis & chapter 2 by Steven T. Doyle], (Indianapolis: Gasogene Books 2006).
151. Certified Copy of the Certificate of an entry in register of the Birth and Death of George Turnavine Budd.
152. Beveridge, A., *What became of Arthur Conan Doyle's father? The last years of Charles Altamont Doyle*, (published on line September 2006).
153. Certified Copy of an Entry given at The General Register Office of Birth and Death of Bertram Fletcher Robinson.
154. Crouch, John D., *Dr. Conan Doyle in Bloemfontein*, (ACD The Journal of the Arthur Conan Doyle Society, Volume 1, Number 3 September 1990, & Volume 2, Number 1 Spring 1991, & Volume 2, Number 3 Autumn 1991).
155. Dated report by ACD in *The Westminster Gazette* 20 April 1896, Correspondents and Camels.
156. Dated report by ACD in *The Westminster Gazette* 27 April 1896, From Assouan to Korosko.
157. *Western Morning News* Thursday 18 November 1909.
158. *Western Morning News* Thursday 24 November 1909.
159. *Western Morning News* Saturday 27 March 1915.
160. *Western Morning News* Wednesday 21 February 1923.
161. *Western Morning News* Thursday 22 February 1923.
162. *Western Morning News and Mercury* Saturday 24 February 1923.
163. Costello, Peter, *Conan Doyle Detective: True Crimes Investigated By The Creator Of Sherlock Holmes*, (London: Robinson 2006).
164. *Eastern Daily Press* Wednesday 8 November 1922.
165. *Eastern Daily Press* Thursday 9 November 1922.
166. Childress, David Hatcher, *Lost Cities & Ancient Mysteries of South America*, (London: Adventures Unlimited Press 1986).
167. *Western Morning News* Thursday 5 August 1920.
168. *Western Morning News* Friday 6 August 1920.

169. Stockman, Rocky, *The Hangman's Diary: A Calendar of Judicial Hangings*, (London: Headline Books 1993).
170. *The Belfast Newsletter* Wednesday 13 May 1925.
171. *The Northern Whig and Belfast Post* Wednesday 13 May 1925.
172. *The Irish News and Belfast Morning News* Wednesday 13 May 1925.
173. *The Belfast Newsletter* Friday 15 May 1925.
174. *The Northern Whig and Belfast Post* Thursday 14 May 1925.
175. *The Northern Whig and Belfast Post* Friday 15 May 1925.
176. *The Belfast Telegraph* Thursday 14 May 1925.
177. *The Belfast Telegraph* Saturday 16 May 1925.
178. *The Belfast Evening Telegraph* Friday 22 September 1911.
179. *The Irish Times* 1 November 1916.
180. Norman, Andrew, *Arthur Conan Doyle Beyond Sherlock Holmes*, (Stroud, Gloucestershire: Tempus Publishing 2007).
181. Private correspondence (2007) with Simon Blundell, the Reform Club Librarian.
182. Mrs Irene Ferguson, Assistant to University Archivist Special Collections, University of Edinburgh. Information supplied by email on 4 May 2007.
183. Photocopy of the thesis by Arthur Conan Doyle.
184. Terry, J.E., & Rose, Arthur, *The Return of Sherlock Holmes*, a play in four acts, (Romford, Essex: Ian Henry Publications 1993).
185. Personal opinion.
186. *The Shirburnian* June 1901, pp 96-98.
187. *The Cheltonian* June 1901, pp 139-142.
188. Green, Richard Lancelyn, 'A Note on the Handwriting in "A Scandal in Bohemia"' in *Reflections On A Scandal In Bohemia*, (New York: Magico Magazine 1986).
189. Wikipedia 2007.
190. Private correspondence with Richard Lancelyn Green.
191. *The Times* 20 July 1875.
192. Pybus, Sylvia, *Sherlock Holmes in Sheffield*, (Sheffield History Reporter, August/September 2006 Issue 107, pp 4-5).
193. *Who's Who* 2016.
194. Beare, Geraldine, (com. by) *Index To The Strand Magazine 1891–1950*, (Westpoint, Connecticut 1982).
195. Whitt, J.F. *The Strand Magazine: A Selective Checklist*, (1979).
196. *A. Conan Doyle 1859-1930*, (Tiger Books, Kent 1991).
197. Doyle, Arthur Conan, *The Blood-Stone Tragedy A Druidical Story*, edited and with an introduction by Christopher Roden & Barbara Roden, and an afterword by Owen Dudley Edwards, (The Arthur Conan Doyle Society, Penyfford, Chester 1995).
198. Bergem, Philip G., *A Bibliographic Listing of Stories, Poems, and Other Writings of A. Conan Doyle*, (Minneapolis, Minnesota, Privately Printed 2007).
199. Bergem, Philip G., *A Doylean and Sherlockian Checklist of The Strand Magazine*, (Andover, Minnesota, Privately Printed 2007).
200. Bergem, Philip G., *The Family and Residences of Arthur Conan Doyle*, (St. Paul, Minnesota, Privately Printed 2007 second edition).
201. Private correspondence with the National Automobile Museum, Reno, America.
202. Lycett, Andrew, *Conan Doyle: The Man Who Created Sherlock Holmes*, (London: Weidenfeld & Nicolson 2007).
203. Lellenberg, Jon, Stashower, Daniel & Foley, Charles (eds.) *Arthur Conan Doyle: A Life in Letters*, (London: Harper Press 2007).
204. 1891 England Census.
205. 1871 Scotland Census.
206. 1881 Scotland Census.
207. 1881 Scotland Census.
208. Photocopy of page from the Black Museum visitors book supplied by John Ross the curator.
209. *The Evening World* USA 19 April 1922.

210. Travis, John, *An Illustrated History of Lynton and Lynmouth 1770-1914*, (Derby: Breedon Publishing Company 1995).
211. *The Lady Conan Doyle Diary Canada Tour 1914* and *Arthur Conan Doyle's Note Book 1914* held at The Toronto Public Library, 2008.
212. The Library Chronicle of the University of Texas at Austin, New Series Number 8, Fall, 1974.
213. The Commonwealth War Graves Commission.
214. 1936 Grand Prix Season Part 5, http://www.kolumbus
215. Miller, Russell, *The Adventures Of Arthur Conan Doyle*, (London: Harvill Secker 2008).
216. 1851 Scotland Census.
217. 1871 England Census.
218. 1901 England Census.
219. 1881 England Census.
220. Edwards, Owen Dudley, *Conan Doyle and Stonyhurst*, ACD Journal Vol. 6 1995.
221. Alistair Duncan from *Norwood News* 27 May 1893.
222. Alistair Duncan from *Norwood News* 10 June 1893.
223. Alistair Duncan from *Norwood News* 24 June 1893.
224. Alistair Duncan from *Norwood News* 1 July 1893.
225. Alistair Duncan from *Norwood News* 8 July 1893.
226. Alistair Duncan from *Norwood News* 15 July 1893.
227. Alistair Duncan from *Norwood News* 15 July 1893.
228. Alistair Duncan from *Norwood News* 22 July 1893.
229. Alistair Duncan from *Norwood News* 29 July 1893.
230. http://www.rochestersqtemple.co.uk 2009.
231. Redmond, Chris, Massachusetts Welcomes Arthur Conan Doyle, *Baker Street Miscellanea* No.41, Spring 1985 (Chicago: The Sciolist Press 1985).
232. Rodin, Alvin E & Key, Jack D., The New Forest, Bignell Wood and Sir Arthur Conan Doyle, *Baker Street Miscellanea* No. 46, Summer 1986 (Chicago: The Sciolist Press 1986).
233. Cooke, Catherine & Rodin, Alvin E., Arthur Conan Doyle In London Part I: In Baker Street and Beyond, *Baker Street Miscellanea* No. 73, Summer 1993 (Chicago: The Sciolist Press 1993).
234. Rodin, Alvin E., Cooke, Catherine & Brown, Kevin, Arthur Conan Doyle In London Part II: St. Mary's Hospital: Medicine, Spiritualism and Scion, *Baker Street Miscellanea* No. 74, Winter 1994 (Chicago: The Sciolist Press 1994).
235. Cricket Archive (http://www.cricketarchive.com).
236. Duncan, Alistair, *Close To Holmes*, (London: MX Publishing 2009).
237. Alistair Duncan from *Norwood News* 14 July 1894.
238. *Psypioneer* Vol. 2, No. 3 March 2006, online electronic journal edited by Paul J. Gaunt.
239. *Psypioneer* Vol. 2, No. 7 July 2006, online electronic journal edited by Paul J. Gaunt.
240. *Psypioneer* Vol. 3, No. 9 September 2007, online electronic journal edited by Paul J. Gaunt.
241. *Psypioneer* Vol. 5, No. 5 May 2009, online electronic journal edited by Paul J. Gaunt.
242. The National Archives, London, via Find My Past.
243. Letter held at the Harry Ransom Research Center, Austin, USA, via Andrew Lycett.
244. The original top 10 holiday destinations, http://www.guardian.co.uk 30/10/09.
245. *Penny Illustrated Paper and Illustrated Times* 26 August 1905.
246. Doug Elliott, *The Prophet: Conan Doyle in Sydney* parts 1 & 2, The Log, The Journal of the Sydney Sherlock Holmes Society, Summer & Autumn Vol. 12 No. 3&4 2009, Vol. 13 No. 1&2 2009/2010.
247. Doyle, Arthur Conan, *Our American Adventure*, (London: Hodder & Stoughton 1923).
248. Doyle, Arthur Conan, *Our Second American Adventure*, (London: Hodder & Stoughton 1924).
249. Soames, Mary (editor), *Speaking for Themselves: The Personal Letters of Winston and Clementine Churchill*, (London: Doubleday 1998).
250. www.frazernash.co.uk

251. *The Standard* (London) 7 August 1894.
252. Find My Past – 1911 Census.
253. Carson, L., (editor) *The Stage Year Book*, (London: Carson & Comerford Ltd. 1909), [information supplied by Clifford Goldfarb].
254. *The Star* (Canterbury, New Zealand) 1 July 1903.
255. *Grey River Argus* (West Coast, New Zealand) 9 July 1912.
256. *Hawera & Normanby Star* (Taranaki, New Zealand) 10 May 1913.
257. *Grey River Argus* (West Coast, New Zealand) 27 November 1920.
258. *Evening Post* (Wellington, New Zealand) 3 December 1920.
259. *Evening Post* (Wellington, New Zealand) 6 December 1920.
260. *Evening Post* (Wellington, New Zealand) 8 December 1920.
261. *Thames Star* (Waikato, New Zealand) 13 December 1920.
262. *Evening Post* (Wellington, New Zealand) 10 December 1920.
263. *Evening Post* (Wellington, New Zealand) 8 & 9 December 1920.
264. *Evening Post* (Wellington, New Zealand) 11 December 1920.
265. *Evening Post* (Wellington, New Zealand) 14 December 1920.
266. *Evening Post* (Wellington, New Zealand) 13 December 1920.
267. *Evening Post* (Wellington, New Zealand) 1 December 1920.
268. *Evening Post* (Wellington, New Zealand) 11 December 1920.
269. *Ashburton Guardian* (Canterbury, New Zealand) 16 December 1920.
270. *NZ Truth* (National, New Zealand) 13 November 1920.
271. *NZ Truth* (National, New Zealand) 13 November 1920.
272. *NZ Truth* (National, New Zealand) 13 November 1920.
273. *NZ Truth* (National, New Zealand) 13 November 1920.
274. *Evening Post* (Wellington, New Zealand) 24 December 1920.
275. *Ashburton Guardian* (Canterbury, New Zealand) 13 January 1921.
276. *Evening Post* (Wellington, New Zealand) 1 February 1921.
277. *Evening Post* (Wellington, New Zealand) 2 August 1937.
278. *The Register* (Adelaide) 20 September 1920.
279. *The Register* (Adelaide) 30 September 1920.
280. *Brisbane Courier* (Brisbane) 6 January 1921.
281. *Brisbane Courier* (Brisbane) 11 January 1921.
282. *Brisbane Courier* (Brisbane) 12 January 1921.
283. *Brisbane Courier* (Brisbane) 12 February 1921.
284. *Brisbane Courier* (Brisbane) 17 February 1921.
285. *Sydney Morning* Herald (Sydney) 18 January 1921.
286. *Western Australian* (Perth) 19 February 1921.
287. *Daily Mail* (Brisbane) 15 January 1921.
288. *The Advertiser* (Adelaide) 18 September 1920.
289. *The Register* (Adelaide) 22 September 1920.
290. *The Register* (Adelaide) 25 September 1920.
291. *The Register* (Adelaide) 24, 28 & 30 September 1920.
292. *The Register* (Adelaide) 30 September 1920.
293. *The Register* (Adelaide) 2 October 1920.
294. *The Argus* (Melbourne) 2 October 1920.
295. *The Argus* (Melbourne) 7 October 1920.
296. *The Argus* (Melbourne) 8 October 1920.
297. *The Argus* (Melbourne 11 October 1920.
298. *The Argus* (Melbourne) 9 October 1920.
299. *The Argus* (Melbourne) 1 November 1920.
300. *The Argus* (Melbourne) 4 November 1920.
301. *The Argus* (Melbourne) 9 November 1920.
302. *The Argus* (Melbourne) 8 November 1920.
303. *The Argus* (Melbourne) 12 November 1920.
304. *The Argus* (Melbourne) 1 November 1920.
305. *Sydney Morning Herald* (Sydney) 13 November 1920.
306. *Sydney Morning Herald* (Sydney) 15 November 1920.

307. *Sydney Morning Herald* (Sydney) 16 November 1920.
308. *Sydney Morning Herald* (Sydney) 17 November 1920.
309. *Sydney Morning Herald* (Sydney) 20 November 1920.
310. *Sydney Morning Herald* (Sydney) 23 November 1920.
311. *Sydney Morning Herald* (Sydney) 26 November 1920.
312. *Sydney Morning Herald* (Sydney) 26 & 29 November 1920.
313. *Sydney Morning Herald* (Sydney) 29 November 1920.
314. *Sydney Morning Herald* (Sydney) 26 November & 2 December 1920.
315. *Sydney Morning Herald* (Sydney) 31 December 1920.
316. *Sydney Morning Herald* (Sydney) 10 January 1921.
317. *Sydney Morning Herald* (Sydney) 18 January 1921.
318. *Sydney Morning Herald* (Sydney) 31 January 1921.
319. *Sydney Morning Herald* (Sydney) 19 January 1921.
320. Duncan, Alistair, *The Norwood Author: Arthur Conan Doyle & The Norwood Years (1891-1894)*, (London: MX Publishing 2010).
321. Letter held at the National Archives of Scotland; reference AD21/5/43.
322. Duncan, Alistair, *An Entirely New Country: Arthur Conan Doyle, Undershaw and the Resurrection of Sherlock Holmes*, (London: MX Publishing 2011).
323. Malec, Andrew, *Molding The Image: William Gillette as Sherlock Holmes*, (Special Collections Gallery O. Meridith Wilson Library University of Minnesota, Minneapolis 1983).
324. 1861 England Census.
325. 1851 England Census.
326. *British Medical Journal* 9 April 1898.
327. Baptism Records supplied by Reverend Andrew Cornes, All Saints Church, Crowborough.
328. www.devilsporridge.co.uk
329. Sellens, Frank, *Sussex Notebook*, Kent & Sussex Courier 23 March 2012.
330. *Kent & Sussex Courier* 30 October 1925, supplied by John Hackworth.
331. *Kent & Sussex Courier* 6 November 1925, supplied by John Hackworth.
332. *Kent & Sussex Courier* 20 March 1925, supplied by John Hackworth.
333. Ardolino, Frank, *Sir Arthur Conan Doyle and Baseball*, The Baseball Research Journal, Vol. 41, No. 1, Spring 2012.
334. Homer, Michael W., *Arthur Conan Doyle's Adventure in Winnipeg*, Manitoba History, No. 25, Spring 1993.
335. Photocopy of programme of Grand Evening Concert at the Town Hall, Bloemfontein, 24 May 1900 supplied by Doug Wrigglesworth.
336. Doyle, Arthur Conan, *Dangerous Work: Diary of an Arctic Adventure*, (editors: Lellenberg, Jon & Stashower, Daniel), (London: The British Library Publishing Division, 2012).
337. Doug Wrigglesworth, private correspondence with the author.
338. Normanton, Helena, *The Trial of Norman Thorne*, (London: Geoffrey Bles, undated).
339. *Portsmouth Evening News* 2 November 1882.
340. *Portsmouth Evening News* 10 February 1883.
341. *Portsmouth Evening News* 12 March 1883.
342. *Portsmouth Evening News* 29 October 1883.
343. *Hampshire Telegraph* 24 November 1883.
344. *Portsmouth Evening News* 7 December 1883.
345. *London Standard* 18 December 1883.
345a. *London Daily News* 20 December 1883.
346. *Hampshire Telegraph* 19 January 1884.
347. *Hampshire Telegraph* 16 February 1884.
348. *Hampshire Telegraph* 1 March 1884.
349. *Hampshire Telegraph* 3 May 1884.
350. *Hampshire Telegraph* 27 September 1884.
351. *Hampshire Telegraph* 15 November 1884.
352. *Hampshire Telegraph* 23 May 1885.

353. *Glasgow Herald* 3 August 1885.
354. *Hampshire Telegraph* 19 September 1885.
355. *Portsmouth Evening News* 30 October 1885.
356. *Portsmouth Evening News* 11 January 1886.
357. *Portsmouth Evening News* 21 January 1886.
358. *Portsmouth Evening News* 4 March 1886.
359. *Hampshire Telegraph* 20 March 1886.
360. *Portsmouth Evening News* 2 April 1886.
361. *Portsmouth Evening News* 16 April 1886.
362. *Portsmouth Evening News* 4 May 1886.
363. *Portsmouth Evening News* 26 June 1886.
364. *Portsmouth Evening News* 3 July 1886.
365. *Hampshire Advertiser* 31 July 1886.
366. *Portsmouth Evening Post* 9 November 1886.
367. *Hampshire Telegraph* 27 November 1886.
368. *Portsmouth Evening News* 26 November 1886.
369. *Hampshire Telegraph* 11 December 1886.
370. *Hampshire Telegraph* 11 December 1886.
371. *Hampshire Telegraph* 25 December 1886.
372. *Hampshire Telegraph* 25 December 1886.
373. *Hampshire Telegraph* 22 January 1887.
374. *Hampshire Telegraph* 22 January 1887.
375. *Hampshire Telegraph* 19 March 1887.
376. *Hampshire Telegraph* 23 April 1887.
377. *Hampshire Telegraph* 30 April 1887.
378. *Hampshire Telegraph* 26 November 1887.
379. *Hampshire Telegraph* 3 December 1887.
380. *Hampshire Telegraph* 10 December 1887.
381. *Hampshire Telegraph* 10 December 1887.
382. *Hampshire Telegraph* 21 January 1888.
383. *Hampshire Telegraph* 28 January 1888.
384. *Hampshire Telegraph* 4 February 1888.
385. *Hampshire Telegraph* 18 February 1888.
386. *Hampshire Telegraph* 3 March 1888.
387. *Hampshire Telegraph* 17 March 1888.
388. *Hampshire Telegraph* 28 April 1888.
389. *Hampshire Telegraph* 3 November 1888.
390. *Hampshire Telegraph* 3 November 1888.
391. *Hampshire Telegraph* 22 December 1888.
392. *Hampshire Telegraph* 19 January 1889.
393. *Portsmouth Evening News* 24 January 1889.
394. *Hampshire Telegraph* 30 March 1889.
395. *Hampshire Telegraph* 30 March 1889.
396. *Hampshire Telegraph* 18 May 1889.
397. *Hampshire Advertiser* 8 June 1889.
398. *Portsmouth Evening News* 13 June 1889.
399. *Pall Mall Gazette* 3 August 1889.
400. *Hampshire Telegraph* 12 October 1889.
401. *Portsmouth Evening News* 15 October 1889.
402. *Hampshire Telegraph* 7 December 1889.
403. *Portsmouth Evening News* 27 January 1890.
404. *Portsmouth Evening News* 29 January 1890.
405. *Portsmouth Evening News* 7 February 1890.
406. *Hampshire Telegraph* 1 March 1890.
407. *Portsmouth Evening News* 17 March 1890.
408. *Portsmouth Evening News* 30 April 1890.
409. *Portsmouth Evening News* 14 May 1890.

410. *Portsmouth Evening News* 4 July 1890.
411. *Portsmouth Evening News* 18 July 1890.
412. *Portsmouth Evening News* 22 August 1890.
413. *Portsmouth Evening News* 10 September 1890.
414. *Hampshire Telegraph* 27 September 1890.
415. *Hampshire Telegraph* 27 September 1890.
416. *Portsmouth Evening News* 10 November 1890.
417. *Portsmouth Evening News* 28 November 1890.
418. *Portsmouth Evening News* 13 December 1890.
419. *Leeds Mercury* 25 February 1892.
420. *Pall Mall Gazette* 21 October 1892.
421. *The Era* 21 January 1893.
422. *Morning Post* 7 April 1893.
423. *Morning Post* 15 May 1893.
424. *Sunderland Daily Echo & Shipping Gazette* 13 May 1893.
425. *Glasgow Herald* 1 July 1893.
426. *Glasgow Herald* 28 September 1893.
427. *Leeds Mercury* 7 October 1893.
428. *Manchester Courier & Lancashire General Advertiser* 7 October 1893.
429. *Isle of Man Times* 24 October 1893.
430. *Lancaster Gazette* 28 October 1893.
431. *Glasgow Herald* 1 November 1893.
432. *Manchester Evening News* 8 November 1893.
433. *Manchester Evening News* 15 November & *Huddersfield Chronicle* 18 November 1893.
434. *Leeds Times* 18 November 1893.
435. *York Herald* 18 November 1893.
436. *Sheffield Independent* 17 November 1893.
437. *Manchester Evening News* 21 November 1893.
438. *Dundee Courier* 25 November 1893.
439. *Newcastle Courant* 2 December 1893.
440. *Glasgow Herald* 27 November 1893.
441. *Glasgow Herald* 2 December 1893.
442. *Nottinghamshire Guardian* 9 December 1893.
443. *Bristol Mercury* 7 December 1893.
444. *Yorkshire Evening Post* 9 December 1893.
445. *Yorkshire Evening Post* 9 December 1893.
446. *York Herald* 12 May 1894.
447. *Morning Post* 25 May 1894.
448. *Manchester Courier & Lancashire General Advertiser* 7 July 1894.
449. *Glasgow Herald* 26 November 1894.
450. *London Daily News* 18 December 1894.
451. *Huddersfield Chronicle* 19 December 1894.
452. *Pall Mall Gazette* 20 February 1895.
453. *Morning Post* 29 April 1895.
454. *Morning Post* 17 April 1896.
455. *Hampshire Telegraph* 16 May 1896.
456. *Northern Echo* 30 May 1896.
457. *Hampshire Telegraph* 6 & 13 June 1896.
458. *London Standard* 20 July 1896.
459. *Falkirk Herald* 29 July 1896.
460. *London Standard* 3 December 1896.
461. *London Standard* 6 February 1897.
462. *Portsmouth Evening News* 10 February 1897.
463. *Freeman's Journal* 10 March 1897.
464. *Freeman's Journal* 29 March 1897.
465. *Morning Post* 31 March 1897.
466. *Lloyd's Weekly Newspaper* 9 May 1897.

467. *Hampshire Telegraph* 22 May 1897.
468. *The Era* 5 June 1897.
469. *Morning Post* 26 June 1897.
470. *Pall Mall Gazette* 24 July 1897.
471. *Morning Post* 26 January 1898.
472. *London Daily News* 10 March 1898.
473. *The Era* 28 May 1898.
474. *Whitstable Times & Herne Bay Herald* 4 February 1899.
475. *The Era* 22 April 1899.
476. *Cheltenham Looker-On* 10 June 1899.
477. *Western Daily Press* 12 June 1899.
478. *Morning Post* 23 June 1899.
479. *Morning Post* 29 June 1899.
480. *London Standard* 19 July 1899.
481. *The Era* 1 July 1899.
482. *Portsmouth Evening News* 1 August 1899.
483. *The Era* 29 July 1899.
484. *Worcestershire Chronicle* 7 October 1899.
485. *Liverpool Mercury* 6 October 1899.
486. *Portsmouth Evening News* 13 October 1899.
487. *Reading Mercury* 7 October 1899.
487a. *Reading Mercury* 14 October 1899.
488. *Bath Chronicle & Weekly Gazette* 26 October 1899.
489. *Western Daily Press* 20 October 1899.
490. *Morning Post* 27 October 1899.
491. *Morning Post* 15 December 1899.
492. *Western Times* 6 January 1900.
493. *Morning Post* 26 February 1900.
494. Cooper, Ken, *Aide-De-Camp To Conan Doyle: The Boer War Diary of Charles Blasson*, (Great Briton: Amazon.co.uk.Ltd., Marston Gate 2013).
495. The Burts of the Langman Hospital, www.pelternet.co.za
496. *Morning Post* 16 May 1900.
497. *London Standard* 17 August 1900.
498. *Manchester Guardian & Lancashire General Advertiser* 18 August 1900.
499. *Morning Post* 21 August 1900.
500. *Sunderland Daily Echo & Shipping Gazette* 8 September 1900.
501. *Essex Newsman* 15 September 1900.
502. *Manchester Courier & Lancashire Advertiser* 25 September 1900.
503. *Glasgow Herald* 27 September 1900.
504. *Glasgow Herald* 29 September 1900.
505. *Pall Mall Gazette* 8 October 1900.
506. *London Standard* 23 October 1900.
507. *Morning Post* 6 November 1900.
508. *Manchester Courier & Lancashire General Advertiser* 13 October 1900.
509. *London Standard* 16 November 1900.
510. *Leeds Mercury* 17 December 1900.
511. *Huddersfield Chronicle* 17 December 1900.
512. *Shields Daily Gazette* 29 December 1900.
513. *Manchester Evening News* 12 February 1901.
514. *Tamworth Herald* 9 March 1901.
515. *Lichfield Mercury* 8 March 1901.
516. *Falkirk Herald* 27 March 1901.
517. *Dundee Courier* 25 March 1901.
518. *Aberdeen Press & Journal* 8 April 1901.
519. *Portsmouth Evening News* 27 April 1901.
520. *Portsmouth Evening News* 31 May 1901.
521. *The Cheltenham Looker-On* 15 June 1901.

522. *Sheffield Daily Telegraph* 11 July 1901.
523. *Portsmouth Evening News* 18 July 1901.
524. *Portsmouth Evening News* 20 July 1901.
525. *Manchester Courier & Lancashire Advertiser* 24 August 1901.
526. *Dundee Courier* 2 December 1901.
527. *Dundee Courier* 3 December 1901.
528. *Portsmouth Evening News* 27 December 1901.
529. *Sunderland Daily Echo & Shipping Gazette* 13 February 1902.
530. *Nottingham Evening Post* 12 July 1902.
531. *Dundee Evening Telegraph*, 13 September 1902.
532. *Western Daily Press* 15 October 1902.
533. *Yorkshire Evening Post* 6 November 1902.
534. *Derbyshire Times & Chesterfield Herald* 8 November 1902.
535. *Aberdeen Press & Journal* 1 December 1902.
536. *Dundee Evening Telegraph*, 29 November 1902.
537. *Dundee Courier* 29 November 1902.
538. *Sunderland Daily Echo & Shipping Gazette* 2 December 1902.
539. *Nottingham Evening Post* 27 January 1903.
540. *Portsmouth Evening News* 13 February 1903.
541. *Portsmouth Evening News* 26 March 1903.
542. *Portsmouth Evening News* 26 March 1903.
543. *Exeter & Plymouth Gazette* 11 April 1903.
544. *Portsmouth Evening News* 9 May 1903.
545. *Worcestershire Chronicle* 30 May 1903.
546. *Western Times* 26 August 1903.
547. *Edinburgh Evening News* 5 November 1903.
548. *Edinburgh Evening News* 5 November 1903.
549. *Edinburgh Evening News* 5 November 1903.
550. *Dundee Courier* 8 December 1903.
551. *Southern Reporter*, Selkirk 10 December 1903.
552. *Edinburgh Evening News* 12 December 1903.
553. *Portsmouth Evening News* 22 December 1903.
554. *Edinburgh Evening News* 9 January 1904.
555. *Shields Daily Gazette* 20 February 1904.
556. *Edinburgh Evening News* 5 March 1904.
557. *Southern Reporter* 17 March 1904.
558. *Surrey Mirror* 8 April 1904.
559. *Southern Reporter* 14 April 1904.
560. *Dover Express* 20 May 1904.
561. *Portsmouth Evening* News 25 May 1904.
562. *Dundee Evening Post*, Angus 21 June 1904.
563. *Dundee Courier* 23 June 1904.
564. *Southern Reporter* 30 June 1904.
565. *Southern Reporter* 30 June 1904.
566. *Exeter & Plymouth Gazette* 15 August 1904.
567. *Exeter & Plymouth Gazette* 17 August 1904.
568. *Southern Reporter* 15 September 1904.
569. *Southern Reporter* 20 October 1904.
570. *Sunderland Daily Echo & Shipping Gazette* 22 October 1904.
571. *Southern Reporter* 1 December 1904.
572. *Southern Reporter* 2 February 1905.
573. *Southern Reporter* 2 February 1905.
574. *Aberdeen Press & Journal* 22 March 1905.
575. *Southern Reporter* 6 April 1905.
576. *Southern Reporter* 6 April 1905
577. *Southern Reporter* 6 April 1905.
578. *Southern Reporter* 6 April 1905.

579. *Aberdeen Press & Journal* 20 April 1905.
580. *Manchester Courier & Lancashire General Advertiser* 11 May 1905.
581. *Dundee Courier* 1 June 1905.
582. *Surrey Mirror* 9 June 1905.
583. *Dover Express* 11 August 1905.
584. *Western Times* 28 August 1905.
585. *Manchester Courier & Lancashire General Advertiser* 28 August 1905.
586. *Southern Reporter* 14 September 1905.
587. *Southern Reporter* 14 September 1905.
588. *Manchester Courier & Lancashire General Advertiser* 19 October 1905.
589. *Western Times* 7 November 1905.
590. *Western Times* 22 November 1905.
591. *Southern Reporter* 7 December 1905.
592. *Manchester Courier & Lancashire General Advertiser* 11 December 1905.
593. *Cheltenham Chronicle* 30 December 1905.
594. *Hull Daily Mail* 29 December 1905.
595. *Southern Reporter* 11 January 1906.
596. *Southern Reporter* 11 January 1906.
597. *Dundee Courier* 11 January 1906.
598. *Southern Reporter* 18 January 1906.
599. *Southern Reporter* 18 January 1906.
600. *Surrey Mirror* 15 June 1906.
601. *Kent & Sussex Courier* 24 August 1906.
602. *Manchester Courier & Lancashire General Advertiser* 11 February 1907.
603. *Gloucester Citizen* 1 June 1907.
604. *Leamington Spa Courier* 19 July 1907.
605. *Leamington Spa Courier* 19 July 1907.
606. Salvatori, Gianluca, Solito, Enrico, & Vianello, Robert, *Sir Arthur Conan Doyle: Viaggo in Italia – Italian Journeys* (editors), (Italy: Bob Bazlen Servizi Editorali, Rome 2012).
607. *Kent & Sussex Courier* 6 December 1907.
608. *Manchester Courier & Lancashire General Advertiser* 2 May 1908.
609. *Dundee Evening Telegraph* 23 June 1908.
610. *Aberdeen Press & Journal* 20 October 1908.
611. *Cheltenham Looker-On* 24 October 1908.
612. *Dundee Evening Telegraph* 15 January 1909.
613. *Manchester Courier & Lancashire General Advertiser* 2 March 1909.
614. *Dundee Courier* 21 April 1909.
615. *Cheltenham Looker-On* 1 May 1909.
616. *Kent & Sussex Courier* 20 August 1909.
617. *Kent & Sussex Courier* 24 September 1909.
618. *Grantham Journal* 6 November 1909.
619. *North Devon Journal* 16 June 1910.
620. *Leamington Spa Courier* 24 June 1910.
621. *Aberdeen Press & Journal* 19 September 1910.
622. *Crowborough Weekly* 22 October 1910.
623. Ue, Tom, *Sherlock Holmes and Shakespeare*, Cameron Hollyer Memorial Lecture Series April 30, 2011, (The Friends of the Arthur Conan Doyle Collection, Toronto Public Library and Tom Ue 2011).
624. *Cheltenham Looker-On* 27 May 1911.
625. *Cheltenham Looker-On* 22 July 1911.
626. *Kent & Sussex Courier* 14 June 1912.
627. *Kent & Sussex Courier* 12 July 1912.
628. *Kent & Sussex Courier* 2 August 1912.
629. *Kent & Sussex Courier* 2 August 1912.
630. *Kent & Sussex Courier* 16 August 1912.
631. *Kent & Sussex Courier* 8 November 1912.

632. *Dundee Courier* 26 November 1912.
633. *Derby Daily Telegraph* 31 December 1912.
634. *Western Times* 27 January 1913.
635. *Kent & Sussex Courier* 31 January 1913.
636. *Kent & Sussex Courier* 7 February 1913.
637. *New York Times* 1 May 1913.
638. *Dundee Courier* 9 May 1913.
639. *Manchester Courier & Lancashire General Advertiser* 24 May 1913.
640. *Kent & Sussex Courier* 26 September 1913.
641. *Kent & Sussex Courier* 24 October 1913.
642. *Manchester Courier & Lancashire General Advertiser* 11 December 1913.
643. *Manchester Evening News* 13 January 1914.
644. *Kent & Sussex Courier* 30 January 1914.
645. *Kent & Sussex Courier* 6 February 1914
646. *Kent & Sussex Courier* 20 March 1914.
647. *Kent & Sussex Courier* 3 April 1914.
648. *Manchester Courier & Lancashire General Advertiser* 16 April1914.
649. *Kent & Sussex Courier* 17 April 1914.
650. *Kent & Sussex Courier* 17 July 1914.
651. *Liverpool Echo* 13 June 1914.
652. *Grantham Journal* 18 July.
653. *Kent & Sussex Courier* 4 September 1914.
654. *Kent & Sussex Courier* 2 October 1914.
655. *Kent & Sussex Courier* 2 October 1914.
656. *Kent & Sussex Courier* 9 October 1914.
657. *Kent & Sussex Courier* 11 December 1914.
658. *Dover Express* 5 February 1915.
659. *Kent & Sussex Courier* 5 March 1915.
660. *Dundee Courier* 12 March 1915.
661. *Newcastle Journal* 17 March 1915.
662. *Cheltenham Looker-On* 27 March 1915.
663. *Exeter and Plymouth Gazette* 26 March 1915.
664. *Liverpool Echo* 13 April 1915.
665. *Kent & Sussex Courier* 30 April 1915.
666. *Gloucester Citizen* 4 August 1915.
667. *Kent & Sussex Courier* 6 August 1915.
668. *Kent & Sussex Courier* 24 September 1915.
669. *Kent & Sussex Courier* 8 October 1915.
670. *Exeter & Plymouth Gazette* 16 October 1915.
671. *Kent & Sussex Courier* 3 December 1915.
672. *Western Daily Press* 4 February 1916.
673. *Kent & Sussex Courier* 17 March 1916.
674. *Kent & Sussex Courier* 23 June 1916.
675. *Kent & Sussex Courier* 7 July 1916.
676. *Gloucester Citizen* 5 August 1916.
677. *Kent & Sussex Courier* 22 September 1916.
678. *Kent & Sussex Courier* 13 October 1916.
679. *Kent & Sussex Courier* 17 November 1916.
680. *Western Times* 16 November 1916.
681. *Kent & Sussex Courier* 24 November 1916.
682. *Chelmsford Chronicle* 27 April 1917.
683. *Dundee Evening Telegraph* 9 August 1917.
684. *Gloucester Citizen* 8 September 1917.
685. *Taunton Courier* 17 October 1917.
686. *Kent & Sussex Courier* 1 March 1918.
687. *Kent & Sussex Courier* 15 March 1918.
688. *Chelmsford Chronicle* 3 May 1918.

689. *Hull Daily Mail* 13 February 1918.
690. *Nottingham Evening Post* 8 July 1918.
691. *Kent & Sussex Courier* 12 July 1918.
692. *Gloucester Citizen* 25 September 1918.
693. *Nottingham Evening Post* 26 November 1918.
694. *Liverpool Daily Post* 16 April 1915.
695. *Kent & Sussex Courier* 17 January 1919.
696. *Hull Daily Mail* 13 February 1919.
697. *Cheltenham Looker-On* 15 February 1919.
698. *Cheltenham Looker-On* 15 February 1919.
699. *Dundee Courier* 18 February 1919.
700. *Kent & Sussex Courier* 21 February 1919.
701. *Kent & Sussex Courier* 7 March 1919.
702. *Kent & Sussex Courier* 18 April 1919.
703. *Kent & Surrey Courier* 25 April 1919.
704. *Kent & Sussex Courier* 16 May 1919.
705. *Aberdeen Press & Journal* 12 November 1919.
706. *Aberdeen Press & Journal* 13 November 1919.
707. *Dundee Courier* 14 November 1919.
708. *Kent & Sussex Courier* 5 December 1919.
709. *Aberdeen Press & Journal* 22 January 1920.
710. *Hull Daily Mail* 9 February 1920.
711. *Dundee Evening Telegraph* 19 February 1920.
712. *Kent & Sussex Courier* 9 April 1920.
713. *Kent & Sussex Courier* 9 April 1920.
714. *Western Daily Press* 21 April 1920.
715. *Dundee Evening Telegraph* 2 June 1920.
716. *Kent & Sussex Courier* 25 June 1920.
717. *Hull Daily Mail* 14 March 1921.
718. *Aberdeen Press & Journal* 24 March 1921.
719. *Dundee Courier* 26 October 1921.
720. *Nottingham Evening Post* 5 November 1921.
721. *Nottingham Evening Post* 8 November 1921.
722. *Nottingham Evening Post* 25 October 1921.
723. *Western Times* 19 December 1921.
724. *Kent & Sussex Courier* 18 August 1922.
725. *Kent & Sussex Courier* 17 November 1922.
726. *Kent & Sussex Courier* 24 November 1922.
727. *Nottingham Evening Post* 26 January 1923.
728. *Kent & Sussex Courier* 16 February 1923.
729. *Kent & Sussex Courier* 2 March 1923.
730. *Nottingham Evening Post* 2 March 1923.
731. *Kent & Sussex* Courier 23 March 1923.
732. *Kent & Sussex Courier* 9 November 1923.
733. *Nottingham Evening Post* 3 March 1924.
734. *Nottingham Evening Post* 15 December 1924.
735. *Nottingham Evening Post* 23 December 1924.
736. *Nottingham Evening Post* 29 January 1925.
737. *Western Daily News* 6 July 1925.
738. *Aberdeen Press & Journal* 26 February 1926.
739. *Dundee Courier* 12 March 1926.
740. *Aberdeen Press & Journal* 9 February 1927.
741. *Western Times* 14 April 1927.
742. *Gloucester Citizen* 2 June 1927.
743. *Western Daily* Press 8 May 1928.
744. *Dundee Courier* 9 June 1928.
745. *Aberdeen Press & Journal* 10 July 1928.

746. *Dundee Courier* 12 July 1928.
747. *Nottingham Evening Post* 26 July 1928.
748. *Western Daily Press* 11 September 1928.
749. *Hull Daily Mail* 14 September 1928.
750. *Aberdeen Press & Journal* 27 October 1928.
751. *Derby Daily Telegraph* 6 April 1929.
752. *Nottingham Evening Post* 11 April 1929.
753. *Dundee Evening Telegraph* 22 April 1929.
754. *Dundee Evening Telegraph* 17 July 1929.
755. *Nottingham Evening Post* 12 October 1929.
756. *Western Morning News* 11 February 1930.
757. *Dundee Evening Telegraph* 25 March 1930.
758. *Nottingham Evening Post* 19 January 1931.
759. *Dundee Evening Telegraph* 8 June 1931.
760. *Dundee Evening Telegraph* 12 August 1931.
761. *Dundee Courier* 12 April 1932.
762. *Gloucester Citizen* 3 May 1932.
763. *Gloucester Citizen* 12 July 1932.
764. *Dundee Courier* 20 July 1932.
765. *Bath Chronicle & Weekly Gazette* 25 February 1933.
766. *Western Gazette* 25 January 1935.
767. *Gloucester Echo* 1 February 1935.
768. *Gloucester Citizen* 17 April 1935.
769. *Essex Newsman* 14 December 1935.
770. *Dundee Evening Telegraph* 2 July 1936.
771. *Western Daily Press* 19 August 1936.
772. *Hull Daily Mail 18 August* 1936.
773. *Gloucester Echo* 12 August 1938.
774. *Kent & Sussex Courier* 13 October 1939.
775. *Dundee Courier* 18 December 1942.
776. *Dundee Evening Telegraph* 4 July 1947.
777. *Western Gazette* 15 August 1947.
778. *Dundee Evening Telegraph* 5 March 1948.
779. *Aberdeen Press & Journal* 23 April 1949.
780. *Dundee Courier* 23 October 1950.
781. theweald.org
782. The Sherlock Holmes Society of South Australia press release.
783. Jenni Thurmer and Francesca Zilio, South Australian Museum, Adelaide.
784. *Referee* (Sydney) 6 October 1920.
785. *The Argus* (Melbourne) 19 October 1920.
786. *Evening News* (Sydney) 27 November 1929.
787. British India Office Ecclesiastical Returns – Marriages.
788. *Russkiye Vedomosti (Russian Bulletin)* 22 March 1916: Visiting British: Walk with Conan Doyle by Alexey N. Tolstoy [supplied by Alexander Orlov].
789. British Library website.
790. *The Fort William Daily Times* 14 June 1914 from an article in *The Chronicle-Journal*, Canada 23 March 2014
791. *The Sussex Agricultural Express* 6 June 1908.
792. *The Sussex Agricultural Express* 17 June 1910.
793. *The Sussex Agricultural Express* 8 July 1910.
794. *The Sussex Agricultural Express* 31 May 1912.
795. *Kent & Sussex Courier* 8 October 1909.
796. Goetz, Thomas, *The Remedy: Robert Koch, Arthur Conan Doyle, and The Quest To Cure Tuberculosis*, (New York: Gotham Books 2014).
797. *The Times* 9 June 1909.
798. Mullocks Specialist Auctioneers & Valuers website.
799. Letter from ACD to *New York Times* 22 June 1922.

800. *The Times* 20 June 1903.
801. David Knight (archivist) Stonyhurst College, Clitheroe, Lancashire.
802. *Kent & Sussex Courier* 27 April 1917.
803. *Daily Telegraph* 27 December 1921.
804. *Surrey Comet* 7 October 1899.
805. *La Patrie* 9 July 1923.
806. *The Montreal Gazette* 11 1923.
807. *Surrey Comet* 14 October 1899.
808. Email correspondence with Alexis Barquin and Phil Bergem.
809. The Arthur Conan Doyle Encyclopedia: https://www.arthur-conan-doyle.com
810. *Barrington Town-Warming* (Volume IV January 25-February 1942).
811. *Kent & Sussex Courier* 20 October 1889.
812. *Kent & Sussex Courier* 13 June 1930.
813. *Western Daily Press* 11 June 1930.
814. British Library, London from M.C. Black.
815. *Times Union*, (Albany) 2 June 2014 in a feature "On This Date In 1914…"
816. *Denton Publications Inc.* 12 June 2014 in a feature "One Hundred Years Ago June.
817. *Northern Whig*, (Belfast) 12 May 1925. (From Terry Eakin via Oscar Ross)
818. *Irish Times* 12 May 1925. (From Terry Eakin via Oscar Ross)
819. *Irish Independent* 15 May 1925. (From Oscar Ross)
820. *Kent & Sussex Courier* 12 June 1908.
821. *Kent & Sussex Courier* 19 June 1908.
822. *Sussex Agricultural Express* 16 May 1908.
823. *Sussex Agricultural Express* 4 July 1908.
824. *Sussex Agricultural Express* 26 March 1909.
825. *Sussex Agricultural Express* 21 May 1909.
826. *Sussex Agricultural Express* 5 November 1909.
827. *Sussex Agricultural Express* 21 January 1910.
828. *Sussex Agricultural Express* 1 April 1910.
829. *Sussex Agricultural Express* 24 June 1910.
830. *Sussex Agricultural Express* 2 June 1911
831. *Sussex Agricultural Express* 14 July 1911.
832. *Sussex Agricultural Express* 9 February 1912.
833. *Sussex Agricultural Express* 28 March 1913.
834. *Sussex Agricultural Express* 9 July 1914.
835. *Sussex Agricultural Express* 2 October 1914.
836. *Sussex Agricultural Express* 11 December 1914.
837. Photocopy of letter supplied by Evan Holzwasser.
838. *Sussex Agricultural Express* 21 August 1915.
839. *Sussex Agricultural Express* 24 September 195.
840. *Sussex Agricultural Express* 2 June 1916.
841. *Sussex Agricultural Express* 14 May 1920.
842. *Sussex Agricultural Express* 23 July 1920.
843. *Sussex Agricultural Express* 30 December 1921.
844. *Sussex Agricultural Express* 25 April 1924.
845. *Sussex Agricultural Express* 12 July 1929.
846. *Sussex Agricultural Express* 12 July 1929.
847. *Sussex Agricultural Express* 9 August 1929.
848. *Sussex Agricultural Express* 8 May 1931.
849. *Sussex Agricultural Express* 29 May 1931.
850. *Sussex Agricultural Express* 29 May 1931.
851. *Sussex Agricultural Express* 3 July 1931.
852. *Sussex Agricultural Express* 20 November 1931.
853. *Sussex Agricultural Express* 15 January 1932.
854. *Sussex Agricultural Express* 24 June 1932.
855. *Sussex Agricultural Express* 5 August 1932.
856. *Sussex Agricultural Express* 19 May 1933.

857. *Sussex Agricultural Express* 15 September 1933.
858. *Sussex Agricultural Express* 16 August 1935.
859. *Sussex Agricultural Express* 9 July 1937.
860. *Sussex Agricultural Express* 3 October 1947.
861. *Sussex Agricultural Express* 13 July 1951.
862. *Kent & Sussex Courier* 8 November 1907.
863. *Kent & Sussex Courier* 17 April 1908.
864. *Kent & Sussex Courier* 3 July 1908.
865. *Kent & Sussex Courier* 10 July 1908.
866. *Kent & Sussex Courier* 24 July 1908.
867. *Kent & Sussex Courier* 31 July 1908.
868. *Kent & Sussex Courier* 14 August 1908.
869. *Kent & Sussex Courier* 21 August 1908.
870. *Kent & Sussex Courier* 21 August 1908.
871. *Kent & Sussex Courier* 18 September 1908.
872. *Kent & Sussex Courier* 3 January 1913.
873. *Kent & Sussex Courier* 10 October 1913.
874. *Kent & Sussex Courier* 29 May 1914.
875. *Kent & Sussex Courier* 14 January 1916.
876. *The Times* 1 January 1916.
877. *Kent & Sussex Courier* 16 February 1917.
878. *Kent & Sussex Courier* 2 March 1917.
879. *Kent & Sussex Courier* 22 June 1917.
880. *Kent & Sussex Courier* 16 November 1917.
881. *Kent & Sussex Courier* 12 September 1919.
882. *Kent & Sussex Courier* 17 June 1921.
883. *Kent & Sussex Courier* 15 December 1922.
884. The Conan Doyle Encyclopedia https://arthur-conan-doyle.com
885. *Kent & Sussex Courier* 9 November 1923.
886. *Kent & Sussex Courier* 29 February 1924.
887. *Kent & Sussex Courier* 14 March 1924.
888. *Kent & Sussex Courier* 14 March 1924.
889. *Kent & Sussex Courier* 25 April 1924.
890. *Kent & Sussex Courier* 9 May 1924.
891. *Kent & Sussex Courier* 30 May 1924.
892. *Kent & Sussex Courier* 30 May 1924.
893. *Kent & Sussex Courier* 7 November 1924.
894. *Kent & Sussex Courier* 7 November 1924.
895. *Kent & Sussex Courier* 14 November 1924.
896. *Kent & Sussex Courier* 6 February 1925.
897. *Kent & Sussex Courier* 28 August 1925.
898. *Kent & Sussex Courier* 18 September 1925.
899. *Kent & Sussex Courier* 29 January 1926.
900. *Kent & Sussex Courier* 29 January 1926.
901. *Kent & Sussex Courier* 5 February 1926.
902. *Kent & Sussex Courier* 26 February 1926.
903. *Kent & Sussex Courier* 19 March 1926.
904. *Kent & Sussex Courier* 26 March 1926.
905. *Kent & Sussex Courier* 26 March 1926.
906. *Kent & Sussex Courier* 23 April 1926.
907. *Kent & Sussex Courier* 2 April 1926.
908. *Kent & Sussex Courier* 30 April 1926.
909. *Kent & Sussex Courier* 2 July 1926.
910. *Kent & Sussex Courier* 2 July 1926.
911. *The Times* 5 July 1926.
912. *The Times* 7 July 1926.
913. *Kent & Sussex Courier* 1 October 1926.

914. *Kent & Sussex Courier* 19 November 1926.
915. *Kent & Sussex Courier* 7 January 1927.
916. *Kent & Sussex Courier* 7 January 1927.
917. *Kent & Sussex Courier* 11 February 1927.
918. *Kent & Sussex Courier* 25 February 1927.
919. *Kent & Sussex Courier* 4 March 1927.
920. *Kent & Sussex Courier* 18 March 1927.
921. *Kent & Sussex Courier* 11 November 1927.
922. *Kent & Sussex Courier* 18 November 1927.
923. *Kent & Sussex Courier* 17 February 1928.
924. *Kent & Sussex Courier* 24 February 1928.
925. *Kent & Sussex Courier* 31 May 1929.
926. *Kent & Sussex Courier* 13 June 1930.
927. *Kent & Sussex Courier* 20 June 1930.
928. *Kent & Sussex Courier* 4 July 1930.
929. *Kent & Sussex Courier* 18 July 1930.
930. *Kent & Sussex Courier* 19 September 1930.
931. *Kent & Sussex Courier* 26 September 1930.
932. *Kent & Sussex Courier* 24 October 1930.
933. *Kent & Sussex Courier* 19 December 1930.
934. *Kent & Sussex Courier* 16 January 1931.
935. *Kent & Sussex Courier* 13 February 1931.
936. *Kent & Sussex Courier* 6 March 1931.
937. *Kent & Sussex Courier* 9 October 1931.
938. *Kent & Sussex Courier* 25 March 1932.
939. *Kent & Sussex Courier* 2 December 1932.
940. *Kent & Sussex Courier* 9 December 1932.
941. *Kent & Sussex Courier* 23 December 1932.
942. *Kent & Sussex Courier* 12 April 1935.
943. *Kent & Sussex Courier* 26 June 1936.
944. *Kent & Sussex Courier* 24 July 1936.
945. *Kent & Sussex Courier* 21 August 1936.
946. *Kent & Sussex Courier* 28 May 1937.
947. *Kent & Sussex Courier* 27 May 1938.
948. *Kent & Sussex Courier* 5 July 1940.
949. *Kent & Sussex Courier* 30 October 1931.
950. *Kent & Sussex Courier* 27 November 1931.
951. *Kent & Sussex Courier* 11 December 1931.
952. *Kent & Sussex Courier* 15 January 1932.
953. *Kent & Sussex Courier* 12 February 1932.
954. *Kent & Sussex Courier* 26 February 1932.
955. *Kent & Sussex Courier* 18 March 1932.
956. *Kent & Sussex Courier* 4 November 1932.
957. *Kent & Sussex Courier* 11 November 1932.
958. *Kent & Sussex Courier* 18 November 1932.
959. *Kent & Sussex Courier* 10 February 1933.
960. *Kent & Sussex Courier* 24 February 1933.
961. *Kent & Sussex Courier* 10 November 1933.
962. *Kent & Sussex Courier* 26 November 1934.
963. National Motor Museum Beaulieu, Hampshire.
964. *The Times* 24 February 1987.
965. *Liverpool Daily Post* 20 October 1914.
966. *Yorkshire Post & Leeds Intelligence* 5 December 1921.
967. *Kent & Sussex Courier* 2 December 1932.
968. *The Times* 23 November 1951.
969. *The Times* 7 February 1987.
970. *The Times* 3 August 1988.

971. *The Times* 2 August 1989.
972. *The Times* 1 August 1991.
973. *The Times* 28 September 1991.
974. *The Times* 11 January 1992.
975. *Hastings & St. Leonards Observer* 21 December 1907.
976. Wikipedia UK General Election 1900.
977. *Edinburgh Evening News* 5 October 1900.
978. Wikipedia UK General Election 1906.
979. *Edinburgh Evening News* 18 January 1906.
980. *Portsmouth Evening News* 9 February 1889.
981. King, W.D., *Henry Irving's Waterloo*, (America: University of California Press 1993).
982. Boström, Mattias & Laffey, Matt, *Sherlock Holmes and Conan Doyle in the Newspapers, Volume 1: 1881-1892*, (Indianapolis, America: Gasogene Books 2015).
983. *The Times* 19 October 1905.
984. *Yorkshire Post & Leeds Intelligencer* 12 March 1914.
985. *London Evening Standard* 29 June 1897.
986. *The Times* 11 November 1927.
987. *Motherwell Times* (Scotland) 18 November 1927.
988. *Surrey Mirror* 4 December 1903.
989. *Edinburgh Evening News* 12 December 1903.
990. *Southern Reporter* 10 December 1903.
991. *Southern Reporter* 3 December 1903.
992. *Yorkshire Post & Leeds Intelligencer* 27 April 1926.
993. 1936-37 Grand Prix Season http://www.kolumbus
994. *Racing Sports Cars* http://racingsportscars.com
995. *Motor Sport* August 1931.
996. *Motor Sport* September 1933.
997. *Motor Sport* September 1936.
998. *Motor Sport* April 1932.
999. *Motor Sport* August 1933.
1000. *Motor Sport* September 1934.
1001. *Motor Sport* July 1936.
1002. *Motor Sport* August 1936.
1003. *Motor sport* October 1936.
1004. Bill Barnes, Australia by email.
1005. Bonhams Catalogue of Auction on 18 March 2015.
1006. *Hawick News & Border Chronicle* 4 March 1904.
1007. *Hawick News & Border Chronicle* 11 March 1904.
1008. *Hawick News & Border Chronicle* 20May 1904.
1009. *Hawick News & Border Chronicle* 17 June 1904.
1010. *Hawick News & Border Chronicle* 24 June 1904.
1011. *Hawick News & Border Chronicle* 21 October 1904.
1012. *Hawick News & Border Chronicle* 11 November 1904.
1013. *Brisbane Courier* 25 July 1903.
1014. Costello, Peter, *What Became of Sir Arthur's Mysterious Aunt Kate* in *The Passengers' Log, The Journal of The Sydney Sherlock Holmes Society, The Sydney Passengers'*, 6 January 2015, Volume 18 No. 2.
1015. *Brisbane Courier* 11 January 1921.
1016. sleebooth.co.uk
1017. Correspondence with Oscar Ross.
1018. Higham, Charles. *The Adventures of Conan Doyle: The Life of the Creator of Sherlock Holmes*, (New York: W.W. Norton, 1976).
1019. Coren, Michael. *Conan Doyle*. (London: Bloomsbury Publishing, 1995).
1020. *The Times* 17 February 1906.
1021. Utechin, Nicholas, Cooke, Catherine, *Sherlock Holmes: The Man Who Never Lived and Will Never Die, Museum of London, A Catalogue*, (London & New York: The Quartering Press, 2015).

1022. Stock, Randall, *Unlocking "The Empty House": Its History and Manuscript* in *Out of the Abyss*, (USA: The Baker Street Irregular Press 2014).
1023. *Kent & Sussex Courier* 23 January 1925.
1024. *Kent & Sussex Courier* 6 February 1925.
1025. Facsimile of *The Adventure of the Lion's Mane*, Westminster Libraries & The Sherlock Holmes Society of London, (Bristol: The Longdunn Press Ltd. 1992).
1026. Facsimile of *A Regimental Scandal*, (Penyffordd, Chester, UK: The Arthur Conan Doyle Society 1995).
1027. Hyder, William, *Notes on the Manuscript* and Pilot, Roy *The Business Was a Bust* in the facsimile of *The Adventure of the Six Napoleons, That Napoleon Bust Business Again*, (USA: The Baker Street Irregulars in cooperation with the Henry E. Huntington Library and Art Gallery, 2004).
1028. Weller, Philip, *The Adventures of the Six Neapolitans* in the facsimile of *The Adventures of the Red Circle, Mandate for Murder*, (USA: The Baker Street Irregulars in cooperation with the Lilly Library of Indiana University, 2006).
1029. Blau, Peter E. & Austin, J. Bliss, *Some Notes on the Provenance of the Manuscript* in the facsimile of *The Adventures of the Red Circle, Mandate for Murder*, (USA: The Baker Street Irregulars in cooperation with the Lilly Library of Indiana University, 2006).
1030. Duncan, Alistair, *No Better Place: Arthur Conan Doyle, Windlesham and Communications with the Other Side*, (London: MX Publishing Ltd. 2015).
1031. *Gloucester Echo* 1 March 1920.
1032. *Gloucester Echo* 2 March 1923.77
1033. *Gloucester Echo* 18 February 1926.
1034. *Portsmouth Evening News* 26 March 1926.
1035. *Kent & Sussex Courier* 26 March 1926.
1036. *Portsmouth Evening News* 21 October 1926.
1037. *Portsmouth Evening News* 14 November 1889.
1038. *Portsmouth Evening News* 17 December 1897.
1039. *Portsmouth Evening News* 30 January 1898.
1040. *Portsmouth Evening News* 1 February 1905.
1041. *The Sportsman* 29 May 1905.
1042. *Portsmouth Evening News* 21 July 1905.
1043. *Portsmouth Evening News* 7 December 1905.
1044. *Portsmouth Evening News* 21 March 1911.
1045. *Portsmouth Evening News* 13 April 1915.
1046. *Portsmouth Evening News* 7 May 1921.
1047. *Portsmouth Evening News* 6 June 1921.
1048. *Portsmouth Evening News* 7 June 1921.
1049. *Portsmouth Evening News* 28 September 1921.
1050. *Portsmouth Evening News* 4 July 1922.
1051. *Portsmouth Evening News* 6 July 1922.
1052. *Portsmouth Evening News* 8 August 1922.
1053. *Portsmouth Evening News* 9 August 1922.
1054. *Portsmouth Evening News* 22 April 1924.
1055. *Portsmouth Evening News* 30 May 1924.
1056. *Portsmouth Evening News* 7 September 1925.
1057. *Portsmouth Evening News* 23 October 1925.
1058. *Portsmouth Evening News* 24 October 1925.
1059. *Portsmouth Evening News* 9 November 1925.
1060. *Portsmouth Evening News* 30 January 1926.
1061. *Portsmouth Evening News* 27 February 1926.
1062. *Portsmouth Evening News* 26 April 1926.
1063. *Portsmouth Evening News* 25 June 1926.
1064. *Portsmouth Evening News* 5 July 1926.
1065. *Portsmouth Evening News* 23 October 1926.
1066. *Portsmouth Evening News* 25 October 1926.

1067. *Portsmouth Evening News* 5 November 1926.
1068. *Portsmouth Evening News* 1 December 1926.
1069. *Portsmouth Evening News* 29 January 1930.
1070. *Portsmouth Evening News* 13 February 1931.
1071. *Portsmouth Evening News* 20 February 1931.
1072. *Portsmouth Evening News* 11 April 1932.
1073. *Portsmouth Evening News* 27 October 1932.
1074. *Portsmouth Evening News* 26 May 1934.
1075. *Portsmouth Evening News* 22 April 1941.
1076. *Sevenoaks Chronicle & Kentish Advertiser* 18 July 1902.
1077. *Sevenoaks Chronicle & Kentish Advertiser* 9 January 1903.
1078. *Sevenoaks Chronicle & Kentish Advertiser* 29 May 1903.
1079. *Sevenoaks Chronicle & Kentish Advertiser* 30 March 1906.
1080. *Sevenoaks Chronicle & Kentish Advertiser* 21 February 1919.
1081. *Sevenoaks Chronicle & Kentish Advertiser* 11 July 1919.
1082. *Sevenoaks Chronicle & Kentish Advertiser* 5 December 1919.
1083. *Sevenoaks Chronicle & Kentish Advertiser* 9 April 1920.
1084. *Sevenoaks Chronicle & Kentish Advertiser* 11 February 1921.
1085. *Sevenoaks Chronicle & Kentish Advertiser* 24 June 1921.
1086. *Sevenoaks Chronicle & Kentish Advertiser* 17 March 1922.
1087. *Sevenoaks Chronicle & Kentish Advertiser* 17 March 1922.
1088. *Sevenoaks Chronicle & Kentish Advertiser* 19 January 1923.
1089. *Sevenoaks Chronicle & Kentish Advertiser* 7 September 1923.
1090. *Sevenoaks Chronicle & Kentish Advertiser* 12 October 1923.
1091. *Sevenoaks Chronicle & Kentish Advertiser* 26 December 1924.
1092. *Sevenoaks Chronicle & Kentish Advertiser* 11 September 1925.
1093. *Sevenoaks Chronicle & Kentish Advertiser* 13 November 1925.
1094. *Derby Daily Telegraph* 6 December 1927.
1095. *Sevenoaks Chronicle & Kentish Advertiser* 29 June 1928.
1096. *Sevenoaks Chronicle & Kentish Advertiser* 22 November 1929.
1097. *Sevenoaks Chronicle & Kentish Advertiser* 4 July 1930.
1098. *Sevenoaks Chronicle & Kentish Advertiser* 23 December 1932.
1099. *Sevenoaks Chronicle & Kentish Advertiser* 6 November 1936.
1100. *Sevenoaks Chronicle & Kentish Advertiser* 9 September 1938.
1101. *Sevenoaks Chronicle & Kentish Advertiser* 21 July 1939.
1102. *Portsmouth Evening News* 2 November 1883.
1103. *Portsmouth Evening News* 7 December 1883.
1104. *Kent & Sussex Courier* 7 October 1949.
1105. *The Times* 13 June 1925.
1106. *The Times* 23 June 1925.
1107. *The Times* 20 February 1952.
1108. *The Times* 11 November 1925.
1109. http://silentmoviemonsters.tripod.com/TheLostWorld
1110. *Bath Chronicle & Weekly Gazette* 13 June 1925.
1111. *Wells Journal* 26 June 1925.
1112. *Wells Journal* 4 July 1907.
1113. *Cheltenham Chronicle* 7 November 1925.
1114. *Buckingham Advertiser and Free Press* 22 February 1919.
1115. *Gloucester Citizen* 1 February 1922.
1116. *Cheltenham Looker-On* 3 June 1899.
1117. *Cheltenham Chronicle* 10 June 1899.
1118. *Cheltenham Chronicle* 17 June 1899.
1119. *The Times* 18 March 1926.
1120. *The Times* 26 March 1926.
1121. *Western Morning News* 5 October 1926.
1122. *Hartlepool Mail* 17 November 1927

1123. Roden, Christopher, *The Holborn Restaurant Luncheon, Thursday, 29 July 1920*, (ACD The Journal of The Arthur Conan Doyle Society Volume 4: 1993).
1124. Jiggens, Clifford, *Cricketing Days: Conan Doyle of the MCC*, (ACD The Journal of The Arthur Conan Doyle Society Volume 5: 1995)
1125. Roden, Christopher & Demakos, Matthew, *ACD's Correspondence with The Belgravia*, (ACD The Journal of The Arthur Conan Doyle Society Volume 9 June 1999)
1126. *Kent & Sussex Courier* 24 May 1929.
1127. Vause, Mikel, *Sir Arthur Conan Doyle: The Righters of Wrongs* in *A Tangled Skein*, edited by Leslie S. Klinger, (New York: The Baker Street Irregulars 2008).
1128. Information received by email from Mark Alberstat 3 January 2016.
1129. Information received by email from Doug Wrigglesworth 4 January 2016.
1130. CAM Magazine Issue 75, Easter 2015, information supplied by Roger Straughan.
1131. Leonie Paterson at the Royal Botanic Garden Edinburgh Archives.
1132. *Yorkshire Evening Post* 26 July 1902.
1133. Tait, Derek, *Houdini: The British Tours*, (Driftwood Coast Publishing 2011).
1134. Boström, Mattias & Laffey, Matt, *Sherlock Holmes and Conan Doyle in the Newspapers, Volume 2: January-June 1893*, (Indianapolis, America: Gasogene Books 2016).
1135. Wingett, Matt, *Conan Doyle and The Mysterious World of Light 1887-1920*, (England: Life is Amazing 2016).
1136. *Northampton Mercury* 17 October 1919.
1137. *Leamington Spa Courier* 17 October 1919.
1138. *Lancashire Evening Post* 20 January 1920.
1139. *Lancashire Evening Post* 23 January 1920.
1140. *Yorkshire Post and Leeds Intelligencer* 18 February 1920.
1141. *Dublin Express* 24 August 1885.
1142. *Hampshire Telegraph* 14 November 1885.
1143. *Hampshire Telegraph* 12 December 1885.
1144. *Bexhill-on-Sea Observer* 6 November 1909.
1145. *Bexhill-on-Sea Observer* 7 May 1910.
1146. Telfer, Kevin, *Peter Pan's First XI*, (London: Sceptre 2010).
1147. Lear, Linda, *Beatrix Potter: A Life in Nature*, (London: Penguin Books 2007)
1148. *Western Daily Press* 12 June 1899.
1149. Obermuller-Bennett, Sarah, *Sir Arthur Conan Doyle and Sidmouth: An Exhibition Remembered*, in The Torr: The Journal of The Poor Folk Upon The Moors, Silver Jubilee Edition Issue No. 48 – Spring 2016.
1150. *The Era* 16 June 1906.
1151. *Derry Journal* 25 March 1912.
1152. *The Times* 21 March 1912.
1153. *The Times* 4 July 1911.
1154. *The Times* 20/21 July 1911.
1155. *Pittsburgh Post-Gazette* 24 April 2016.
1156. *The Era* 19 October 1895.
1157. Jaher, David, *The Witch of Lime Street*, (New York: Crown Publishers 2015)
1158. *Dundee Evening Telegraph* 2 September 1895.
1159. *Edinburgh Evening News* 29 March 1919.
1160. *The Scotsman* 5 April 1919.
1161. *Lancashire Evening Post* 10 April 1919.
1162. *Kent & Sussex Courier* 1 November 1889.
1163. www.teamdan.com/archive/book/beyond_1918
1164. *Hampshire Telegraph* 7 February 1885.
1165. *Hampshire Telegraph* 28 March 1885.
1166. *Hampshire Telegraph* 4 April 1885.
1167. *Hampshire Telegraph* 2 May 1885.
1168. *Hampshire Telegraph* 18 July 1885.
1169. *Hampshire Telegraph* 17 October 1885.
1170. *Hampshire Telegraph* 29 September 1888.

1171. *Hampshire Telegraph* 3 November 1888.
1172. *Dundee Advertiser* 23 November 1893.
1173. *Yorkshire Evening Post* 4 December 1893.
1174. History of Hankley Golf club website.
1175. *Warrensburgh News*, USA 4 June 1914.
1176. *Mid Sussex Times* 28 July 1908.
1177. *Mid Sussex Times* 11 June 1912.
1178. *Harrogate Herald* 24 March 1915.
1179. *Harrogate Herald* 30 May 1917.
1180. *The Montreal Gazette* 9 July 1923.
1181. https://arthur-conan-doyle.com
1182. *The London Gazette* 27 March 1942.
1183. Supplement to *The London Gazette* 21 July 1944.
1184. Supplement to *The London Gazette* 5 August 1947.
1185. Supplement to *The London Gazette* 19 August 1947.
1186. Supplement to *The London Gazette* 1 January 1948.
1187. Supplement to *The London Gazette* 5 April 1949.
1188. Supplement to *The London Gazette* 1 January 1952.
1189. Supplement to *The London Gazette* 2 April 1963.
1190. Supplement to *The London Gazette* 26 April 1963.
1191. Supplement to *The London Gazette* 8 June 1963.
1192. Supplement to *The London Gazette* 17 May 1966.
1193. *Oxford Dictionary of National Biography*, Doyle, Dame Jean Lena Annette Conan by Jane Potter.
1194. *The Times* 11 August 1885.
1195. *The Times* 25 November 1887.
1196. *The Times* 1 June 1892.
1197. *The Times* 3 June 1892.
1198. *The Times* 13 October 1892.
1199. *The Times* 5 April 1893.
1200. *The Times* 17 April 1893.
1201. *The Times* 1 July 1893.
1202. *The Times* 3 July 1893.
1203. *The Times* 7 May 1894.
1204. *The Times* 25 May 1894.
1205. *The Times* 1 June 1894.
1206. *The Times* 28 June 1894.
1207. *The Times* 7 August 1894.
1208. *The Times* 22 September 1894.
1209. *The Times* 18 December 1894.
1210. *The Times* 6 May 1895.
1211. *The Times* 6 May 1895.
1212. *The Times* 25 January 1896.
1213. *The Times* 15 June 1896.
1214. *The Times* 18 September 1896.
1215. *The Times* 10 December 1896.
1216. *The Times* 11 February 1897.
1217. *The Times* 2 March 1897.
1218. *The Times* 6 March 1897.
1219. *The Times* 1 April 1897.
1220. *The Times* 27 May 1897.
1221. *The Times* 8 October 1897.
1222. *The Times* 26 March 1898.
1223. *The Times* 31 March 1898.
1224. *The Times* 14 June 1898.
1225. *The Times* 17 June 1898.
1226. *The Times* 22 June 1898.

1227. *The Times* 12 December 1898.
1228. *The Times* 28 January 1899.
1229. *The Times* 30 January 1899.
1230. *The Times* 11 February 1899.
1231. *The Times* 7 March 1899.
1232. *The Times* 22 May 1899.
1233. *The Times* 7 June 1899.
1234. *The Times* 12 June 1899.
1235. *The Times* 31 August 1899.
1236. *The Times* 3 October 1899.
1237. *The Times* 1 November 1899.
1238. *Belfast News Letter* 7 November 1899.
1239. *The Times* 1 December 1899.
1240. *The Times* 7 February 1900.
1241. *The Times* 22 February 1900.
1242. *The Times* 22 February 1900.
1243. *The Times* 3 March 1900.
1244. *The Times* 6 July 1900.
1245. *The Times* 28 July 1900.
1246. *The Times* 31 July 1900.
1247. *The Times* 31 July 1900.
1248. *The Times* 9 August 1900.
1249. *The Times* 20 August 1900.
1250. *The Times* 25 September 1900.
1251. *The Times* 10 October 1900.
1252. *The Times* 15 November 1900.
1253. *The Times* 17 December 1900.
1254. *The Times* 18 December 1900.
1255. *The Times* 11 March 1901.
1256. *The Times* 18 April 1901.
1257. *The Times* 23 April 1901.
1258. *The Times* 3 May 1901.
1259. *The Times* 9 May 1901.
1260. *The Times* 17 May 1901.
1261. *The Times* 21 May 1901.
1262. *The Times* 24 May 1901.
1263. *The Times* 14 June 1901.
1264. *The Times* 26 June 1901.
1265. *The Times* 11 July 1901.
1266. *The Times* 18 July 1901.
1267. *The Times* 25 July 1901.
1268. *The Times* 17 August 1901.
1269. *The Times* 26 August 1901.
1270. *The Times* 2 September 1901.
1271. *The Times* 16 September 1901.
1272. *The Times* 28 October 1901.
1273. *The Times* 5 November 1901.
1274. *The Times* 22 January 1902.
1275. *The Times* 13 February 1902.
1276. *The Times* 2 June 1902.
1277. *The Times* 17 June 1902.
1278. *The Times* 25 June 1902.
1279. *The Times* 26 June 1902.
1280. *The Times* 4 July 1902.
1281. *The Times* 12 July 1902.
1282. *The Times* 17 July 1902.
1283. *The Times* 18 July 1902.

1284. *The Times* 26 July 1902.
1285. *The Times* 29 July 1902.
1286. *The Times* 9 September 1902.
1287. *The Times* 20 September 1902.
1288. *The Times* 25 October 1902.
1289. *The Times* 27 October 1902.
1290. *The Times* 26 November 1902.
1291. *The Times* 29 November 1902.
1292. *The Times* 16 December 1902.
1293. *The Times* 18 December 1902.
1294. *The Times* 5 January 1903.
1295. *The Times* 6 January 1903.
1296. *The Times* 31 January 1903.
1297. *The Times* 17 February 1903.
1298. *The Times* 26 February 1903.
1299. *The Times* 25 March 1903.
1300. *The Times* 4 May 1903.
1301. *The Times* 29 May 1903.
1302. *The Times* 1 July 1903.
1303. *The Times* 14 July 1903.
1304. *The Times* 25 July 1903.
1305. *The Times* 1 August 1903.
1306. *The Times* 28 September 1903.
1307. *The Times* 7 October 1903.
1308. *The Times* 16 October 1903.
1309. *The Times* 23 October 1903.
1310. *The Times* 14 November 1903.
1311. *The Times* 10 December 1903.
1312. *The Times* 1 January 1904.
1313. *The Times* 19 January 1904.
1314. *The Times* 27 January 1904.
1315. *The Times* 28 January 1904.
1316. *The Times* 10 February 1904.
1317. *The Times* 20 February 1904.
1318. *The Times* 5 March 1904.
1319. *The Times* 22 April 1904.
1320. *The Times* 23 April 1904.
1321. *The Times* 23 April 1904.
1322. *The Times* 5 May 1904.
1323. *The Times* 17 & 18 May 1904.
1324. *The Times* 31 May 1904.
1325. *The Times* 20 June 1904.
1326. *The Times* 30 June 1904.
1327. *The Times* 15 July 1904.
1328. *The Times* 19 July 1904.
1329. *The Times* 21 July 1904.
1330. *The Times* 10 September 1904.
1331. *The Times* 12 September 1904.
1332. *The Times* 18 October 1904.
1333. *The Times* 6 December 1904.
1334. *The Times* 17 December 1904.
1335. *The Times* 9 January 1905.
1336. *The Times* 17 January 1905.
1337. *The Times* 8 February 1905.
1338. *The Times* 18 May 1905.
1339. *The Times* 23 May 1905.
1340. *The Times* 5 June 1905.

1341. *The Times* 24 June 1905.
1342. *The Times* 1 July 1905.
1343. *The Times* 8 July 1905.
1344. *The Times* 21 July 1905.
1345. *The Times* 14 August 1905.
1346. *The Times* 1 September 1905.
1347. *The Times* 14 October 1905.
1348. *The Times* 18 October 1905.
1349. *The Times* 21 October 1905.
1350. *The Times* 7 November 1905.
1351. *The Times* 21 November 1905.
1352. *The Times* 1 January 1906.
1353. *The Times* 18 January 1906.
1354. *The Times* 1 March 1906.
1355. *The Times* 7 April 1906.
1356. *The Times* 24 April 1906.
1357. *The Times* 25 May 1906.
1358. *The Times* 11 June 1906.
1359. *The Times* 18 June 1906.
1360. *The Times* 5 July 1906.
1361. *The Times* 7 July 1906.
1362. *The Times* 24 July 1906.
1363. *The Times* 15 November 1906.
1364. *The Times* 19 January 1907.
1365. *The Times* 22 January 1907.
1366. *The Times* 24 January 1907.
1367. *The Times* 8 March 1907
1368. *The Times* 8 March 1907.
1369. *The Times* 19 March 1907.
1370. *The Times* 9 April 1907.
1371. *The Times* 16 April 1907.
1372. *The Times* 23 April 1907.
1373. *The Times* 24 April 1907.
1374. *The Times* 9 May 1907.
1375. *The Times* 16 May 1907.
1376. *The Times* 28 May 1907.
1377. *The Times* 22 June 1907.
1378. *The Times* 11 July 1907.
1379. *The Times* 12 July 1907.
1380. *The Times* 23 July 1907.
1381. *The Times* 16 August 1907.
1382. *The Times* 22 August 1907.
1383. *The Times* 29 August 1907.
1384. *The Times* 4 November 1907.
1385. *The Times* 18 December 1907.
1386. *The Times* 25 December 1907.
1387. *The Times* 24 April 1908.
1388. *The Times* 1 February 1908.
1389. *The Times* 23 May 1908.
1390. *The Times* 29 May 1908.
1391. *The Times* 3 June 1908.
1392. *The Times* 17 June 1908.
1393. *The Times* 25 June 1908.
1394. *The Times* 3 July 1908.
1395. *The Times* 11 July 1908.
1396. *The Times* 15 July 1908.
1397. *The Times* 22 July 1908.

1398. *The Times* 1 August 1908.
1399. *The Times* 16 November 1908.
1400. *The Times* 11 November 1908.
1401. *The Times* 21 November 1908
1402. *The Times* 20 November 1908.
1403. *The Times* 9 January 1909.
1404. *The Times* 12 January 1909.
1405. *The Times* 13 January 1909.
1406. *The Times* 14 January 1909.
1407. *The Times* 15 January 1909.
1408. *The Times* 16 January 1909.
1409. *The Times* 18 January 1909.
1410. *The Times* 22 January 1909.
1411. *The Times* 22 February 1909.
1412. *The Times* 2 March 1909.
1413. *The Times* 24 May 1909.
1414. *The Times* 1 June 1909.
1415. *The Times* 16 June 1909.
1416. *The Times* 23 June 1909.
1417. *The Times* 9 July 1909.
1418. *The Times* 21 July 1909.
1419. *The Times* 10 August 1909.
1420. *The Times* 20 August 1909.
1421. *The Times* 3 September 1909.
1422. *The Times* 11 September 1909.
1423. *The Times* 9 October 1909.
1424. *The Times* 12 October 1909.
1425. *The Times* 5 November 1909.
1426. *The Times* 10 November 1909.
1427. *The Times* 9 November 1909.
1428. *The Times* 20 November 1909.
1429. *The Times* 25 November 1909.
1430. *The Times* 24 December 1909.
1431. *The Times* 27 December 1909.
1432. *The Times* 29 January 1910.
1433. *The Times* 12 February 1910.
1434. *The Times* 21 February 1910.
1435. *The Times* 7 April 1910.
1436. *The Times* 29 April 1910.
1437. *The Times* 2 May 1910.
1438. *The Times* 4 May 1910.
1439. *The Times* 31 May 1910.
1440. *The Times* 1 June 1910.
1441. *The Times* 13 June 1910.
1442. *The Times* 6 June 1910.
1443. *The Times* 20 June 1910.
1444. *The Times* 1 July 1910.
1445. *The Times* 1 August 1910.
1446. *The Times* 14 July 1910.
1447. *The Times* 23 July 1910.
1448. *The Times* 28 July 1910.
1449. *The Times* 3 October 1910.
1450. *The Times* 4 October 1910.
1451. *The Times* 5 October 1910.
1452. *The Times* 7 October 1910.
1453. *The Times* 19 October 1910.
1454. *The Times* 29 October 1910.

1455. *The Times* 12 December 1910.
1456. *The Times* 19 December 1910.
1457. *The Times* 13 February 1911.
1458. *The Times* 25 February 1911.
1459. *The Times* 28 February 1911.
1460. *The Times* 6 March 1911.
1461. *The Times* 29 April 1911.
1462. *The Times* 2 May 1911.
1463. *The Times* 13 May 1911.
1464. *The Times* 24 May 1911.
1465. *The Times* 25 May 1911.
1466. *The Times* 30 May 1911.
1467. *The Times* 6 July 1911.
1468. *The Times* 8 July 1911.
1469. *The Times* 10 July 1911.
1470. *The Times* 10 July 1911.
1471. *The Times* 11 July 1911.
1472. *The Times* 12 July 1911.
1473. *The Times* 13 July 1911.
1474. *The Times* 14 July 1911.
1475. *The Times* 17 July 1911.
1476. *The Times* 17 July 1911.
1477. *The Times* 18 July 1911.
1478. *The Times* 19 July 1911.
1479. *The Times* 19 July 1911.
1480. *The Times* 21 July 1911.
1481. *The Times* 8 August 1911.
1482. *The Times* 23 August 1911.
1483. *The Times* 22 September 1911.
1484. *The Times* 5 October 1911.
1485. *The Times* 15 October 1911.
1486. *The Times* 9 December 1911.
1487. *The Times* 23 April 1912.
1488. *The Times* 25 June 1912.
1489. *The Times* 16 July 1912.
1490. *The Times* 24 July 1912.
1491. *The Times* 21 August 1912.
1492. *The Times* 7 November 1912.
1493. *The Times* 8 November 1912.
1494. *The Times* 8 February 1913.
1495. *The Times* 17 February 1913.
1496. *The Times* 12 April 1913.
1497. *The Times* 29 April 1913.
1498. *The Times* 8 May 1913.
1499. *The Times* 26 May 1913.
1500. *The Times* 9 July 1913.
1501. *The Times* 21 August 1913.
1502. *The Times* 13 September 1913.
1503. *The Times* 17 September 1913.
1504. *The Times* 14 October 1913.
1505. *The Times* 3 November 1913.
1506. *The Times* 4 November 1913.
1507. *The Times* 7 November 1913.
1508. *The Times* 18 November 1913.
1509. *The Times* 20 November 1913.
1510. *The Times* 28 November 1913.
1511. *The Times* 8 December 1913.

1512. *The Times* 10 December 1913.
1513. *The Times* 3 February 1914.
1514. *The Times* 9 February 1914.
1515. *The Times* 26 March 1914.
1516. *The Times* 28 May 1914.
1517. *The Times* 1 June 1914.
1518. *The Times* 6 July 1914.
1519. *The Times* 14 July 1914.
1520. *The Times* 29 July 1914.
1521. *The Times* 19 August 1914.
1522. *The Times* 9 September 1914.
1523. *The Times* 22 March 1914.
1524. *The Times* 13 April 1914.
1525. *The Times* 10 July 1914.
1526. *The Times* 29 July 1914.
1527. *The Times* 3 August 1914.
1528. *The Times* 14 January 1916.
1529. *The Times* 8 February 1916.
1530. *The Times* 21 February 1916.
1531. *The Times* 22 February 1916.
1532. *The Times* 29 May 1916.
1533. *The Times* 16 June 1916.
1534. *The Times* 6 July 1916.
1535. *The Times* 22 August 1916.
1536. *The Times* 19 December 1916.
1537. *The Times* 24 March 1917.
1538. *The Times* 13 April 1917.
1539. *The Times* 25 May 1917.
1540. *The Times* 14 June 1917.
1541. *The Times* 23 June 1917.
1542. *The Times* 27 July 1917.
1543. *The Times* 3 September 1917.
1544. *The Times* 12 September 1917.
1545. *The Times* 26 October 1917.
1546. *The Times* 1 January 1918.
1547. *The Times* 8 February 1918.
1548. *The Times* 13 March 1918.
1549. *The Times* 11 April 1918.
1550. *The Times* 4 May 1918.
1551. *The Times* 2 October 1918.
1552. *The Times* 11 October 1918.
1553. *The Times* 30 October 1918.
1554. *The Times* 29 October 1918.
1555. *The Times* 29 November 1918.
1556. *The Times* 28 January 1919.
1557. *The Times* 24 February 1919.
1558. *The Times* 28 April 1919.
1559. *The Times* 16 June 1919.
1560. *The Times* 23 June 1919.
1561. *The Times* 28 June 1919.
1562. *The Times* 12 July 1919.
1563. *The Times* 24 September 1919.
1564. *The Times* 3 January 1920.
1565. *The Times* 12 March 1920.
1566. *The Times* 10 May 1920.
1567. *The Times* 10 June 1920.
1568. *The Times* 30 July 1920.

1569. *The Times* 12 August 1920.
1570. *The Times* 28 September 1920.
1571. *The Times* 2 October 1920.
1572. *The Times* 6 November 1920.
1573. *The Times* 1 January 1921.
1574. *The Times* 3 January 1921.
1575. *The Times* 1 February 1921.
1576. *The Times* 24 March 1921.
1577. *The Times* 11 April 1921.
1578. *The Times* 12 April 1921.
1579. *The Times* 15 April 1921.
1580. *The Times* 18 April 1921.
1581. *The Times* 7 May 1921.
1582. *The Times* 10 May 1921.
1583. *The Times* 16 May 1921.
1584. *The Times* 27 May 1921.
1585. *The Times* 6 June 1921.
1586. *The Times* 25 August 1921.
1587. *The Times* 29 November 1921.
1588. *The Times* 30 November 1921.
1589. *The Times* 15 February 1922.
1590. *The Times* 3 April 1922.
1591. *The Times* 26 June 1922.
1592. *The Times* 19 July 1922.
1593. *The Times* 20 September 1922.
1594. *The Times* 20 November 1922.
1595. *The Times* 2 February 1923.
1596. *The Times* 29 March 1923.
1597. *The Times* 14 August 1923.
1598. *The Times* 10 October 1923.
1599. *The Times* 18 October 1923.
1600. *The Times* 5 December 1923.
1601. *The Times* 1 February 1924.
1602. *The Times* 25 April 1924.
1603. *The Times* 10 June 1924.
1604. *The Times* 29 October 1924.
1605. *The Times* 27 December 1924.
1606. *The Times* 27 December 1924.
1607. *The Times* 24 January 1925.
1608. *The Times* 28 February 1925.
1609. *The Times* 3 March 1925.
1610. *The Times* 7 & 8 April 1925.
1611. *The Times* 28 April 1925.
1612. *The Times* 25 July 1925.
1613. *The Times* 24 October 1925.
1614. *The Times* 28 October 1925.
1615. *The Times* 7 December 1925.
1616. *The Times* 12 February 1926.
1617. *The Times* 10 March 1926.
1618. *The Times* 20 May 1926.
1619. *The Times* 28 October 1926.
1620. *The Times* 30 November 1926.
1621. *The Times* 28 December 1926.
1622. *The Times* 21 March 1927.
1623. *The Times* 1 July 1927.
1624. *The Times* 16 July 1927.
1625. *The Times* 8 August 1927.

1626. *The Times* 29 August 1927.
1627. *The Times* 4 October 1927.
1628. *The Times* 27 October 1927.
1629. *The Times* 18 June 1928.
1630. *The Times* 25 July 1928.
1631. *The Times* 26 July 1928.
1632. *The Times* 26 September 1928.
1633. *The Times* 19 October 1928.
1634. *The Times* 11 June 1929.
1635. *The Times* 27 June 1929.
1636. *The Times* 16 August 1929.
1637. *The Times* 9 October 1929.
1638. *The Times* 14 November 1929.
1639. *The Times* 20 November 1929.
1640. *The Times* 5 February 1930.
1641. *The Times* 4 February 1930.
1642. *The Times* 3 June 1930.
1643. *The Times* 10 June 1930.
1644. *The Times* 19 June 1930.
1645. *The Times* 8 July 1930.
1646. *The Times* 12 July 1930.
1647. *The Times* 14 July 1930.
1648. *The Times* 20 October 1930.
1649. *The Times* 18 May 1931.
1650. *The Times* 9 October 1931.
1651. *The Times* 17 September 1932.
1652. *The Times* 3 May 1933.
1653. *The Times* 10 May 1933.
1654. *The Times* 22 November 1933.
1655. *The Times* 2 March 1934.
1656. *The Times* 12 April 1934.
1657. *The Times* 16 January 1935.
1658. *The Times* 1 February 1935.
1659. *The Times* 16 January 1936.
1660. *The Times* 19 February 1936.
1661. *The Times* 29 February 1936.
1662. *The Times* 9 March 1936.
1663. *The Times* 27 April 1936.
1664. *The Times* 4 June 1936.
1665. *The Times* 19 June 1936.
1666. *The Times* 19 August 1936.
1667. *The Times* 21 August 1936.
1668. *The Times* 12 December 1936.
1669. *The Times* 31 May 1937.
1670. *The Times* 9 June 1937.
1671. *The Times* 3 July 1937.
1672. *The Times* 1 November 1938.
1673. *The Times* 3 April 1940.
1674. *The Times* 28 June 1940.
1675. *The Times* 1 July 1940.
1676. *The Times* 23 August 1940.
1677. *The Times* 29 April 1941.
1678. *Dundee Evening Telegraph* 4 July 1947.
1679. *The Times* 12 July 1947.
1680. *The Times* 1 January 1948.
1681. *The Times* 2 February 1948.
1682. *The Times* 20 December 1948.

1683. *The Times* 23 April 1949.
1684. *The Times* 6 February 1950.
1685. *The Times* 7 November 1950.
1686. *The Times* 13 February 1951.
1687. *The Times* 22 May 1951.
1688. *The Times* 29 October 1951.
1689. *The Times* 21 January 1953.
1690. *The Times* 29 January 1953.
1691. *The Times* 22 April 1954.
1692. *The Times* 10 March 1955.
1693. *The Times* 16 March 1955.
1694. *The Times* 25 June 1955.
1695. *The Times* 8 July 1955.
1696. *The Times* 29 February 1956.
1697. *The Times* 26 March 1956.
1698. *The Times* 20 July 1956.
1699. *The Times* 12 February 1957.
1700. *The Times* 27 March 1957.
1701. *The Times* 9 October 1958.
1702. *The Times* 17 February 1959.
1703. *The Times* 21 May 1959.
1704. *The Times* 22 May 1959.
1705. *The Times* 23 March 1960.
1706. *The Times* 29 April 1960.
1707. *The Times* 10 November 1960.
1708. *The Times* 4 April 1962.
1709. *The Times* 14 November 1962.
1710. *The Times* 2 April 1963.
1711. *The Times* 27 April 1963.
1712. *The Times* 2 May 1963.
1713. *The Times* 1 July 1963.
1714. *The Times* 28 October 1963.
1715. *The Times* 7 November 1963.
1716. *The Times* 6 November 1963.
1717. *The Times* 13 December 1963.
1718. *The Times* 1 January 1964.
1719. *The Times* 8 February 1964.
1720. *The Times* 29 February 1964.
1721. *The Times* 5 March 1964.
1722. *The Times* 21 March 1964.
1723. *The Times* 23 July 1964.
1724. *The Times* 31 October 1964.
1725. *The Times* 5 December 1964.
1726. *The Times* 19 December 1964.
1727. *The Times* 11 February 1965.
1728. *The Times* 20 February 1965.
1729. *The Times* 13 May 1965.
1730. *The Times* 12 June 1965.
1731. *The Times* 5 October 1965.
1732. *The Times* 25 October 1965.
1733. *The Times* 12 November 1965.
1734. *The Times* 22 July 1967.
1735. *The Times* 4 June 1970.
1736. *The Times* 22 April 1972.
1737. *The Times* 25 April 1974.
1738. *The Times* 22 February 1975.
1739. *The Times* 10 May 1975.

1740. *The Times* 29 May 1975.
1741. *The Times* 14 June 1976.
1742. *The Times* 1 November 1976.
1743. *The Times* 11 October 1980.
1744. *The Times* 30 April 1981.
1745. *The Times* 3 August 1983.
1746. *The Times* 21 November 1983.
1747. *The Times* 1 August 1984.
1748. *The Times* 26 October 1984.
1749. *The Times* 31 July 1985.
1750. *The Times* 23 July 1986.
1751. *The Times* 29 July 1987.
1752. *The Times* 21 April 1989.
1753. *The Times* 7 March 1992.
1754. *The Times* 4 March 1993.
1755. *The Times* 4 June 1993.
1756. *The Times* 23 May 1994.
1757. *The Times* 11 November 1994.
1758. *The Times* 30 November 1995.
1759. *The Times* 19 November 1997.
1760. *The Times* 17 January 1998.
1761. *The Times* 30 January 1998.
1762. *The London Gazette* 4 April 1893.
1763. *The London Gazette* 29 May 1896.
1764. Supplement to *The London Gazette* 7 April 195.
1765. Supplement to *The London Gazette* 14 January 1916.
1766. Supplement to *The London Gazette* 1 January 1918.
1767. Supplement to *The London Gazette* 11 March 1919.
1768. *Daily Mirror* 4 April 1914.
1769. *East & South Devon Advertiser* 26 January 1907.
1770. *Western Morning News* 28 October 1903.
1771. *Western Morning News* 22 February 1909.
1772. *Barnsley Chronicle* 21 September 1901.
1773. *Warwick & Warwickshire Advertiser* 20 July 1907.
1774. *Warwick & Warwickshire Advertiser* 23 June 1910.
1775. *Warwick & Warwickshire Advertiser* 8 January 1916.
1776. *Independent* 21 September 1992.
1777. *Independent* 19 September 1994.
1778. *Hendon & Finchley Times* 1 July 1921.
1779. *Leeds Mercury* 7 December 1914.
1780. *Leeds Mercury* 3 December 1921.
1781. *Leeds Mercury* 5 December 1921.
1782. *Leeds Mercury* 12 August 1924.
1783. *The Brooklyn Daily Eagle* 1 February 1925. (Supplied by Alexis Barquin).
1784. *The Brooklyn Daily Eagle* 8 February 1925. (Supplied by Alexis Barquin).
1785. Lavas, J.R. (editor), *The Lost World: Sir Arthur Conan Doyle Collector's Edition*, (Auckland, New Zealand 2012).
1786. http://en.espn.co.uk/scrum/rugby/series/index.html
1787. *London Daily News* 14 October 1907.
1788. *The Times* 9 October 1920.
1789. *The Times* 31 May 1922.
1790. *The Times* 6 March 1925.
1791. *The Times* 10 March 1934.
1792. *The Times* 2 May 1934.
1793. *Athletic News* 27 February 1911.
1794. *New York Times* 8 December 1894.
1795. *New York Times* 8 December 1894.

1796. *New York Times* 19 September 1907.
1797. *New York Times* 21 May 1914.
1798. *New York Times* 28 May 1914.
1799. *New York Times* 29 May 1914.
1800. *New York Times* 31 May 1914.
1801. *New York Times* 1 June 1914.
1802. *New York Times* 27 July 1915.
1803. *New York Times* 9 April 1922.
1804. *New York Times* 13 April 1922.
1805. *New York Times* 14 April 1922.
1806. *New York Times* 22 April 1922.
1807. *New York Times* 5 May 1922.
1808. *New York Times* 8 May 1922.
1809. *New York Times* 22 May 1922.
1810. *New York Times* 25 May 1922.
1811. *New York Times* 7 April 1923.
1812. *New York Times* 9 April 1923.
1813. *New York Times* 16 April 1923.
1814. *New York Times* 27 April 1923.
1815. *New York Times* 29 April 1923.
1816. *New York Times* 14 January 1937.
1817. *New York Times* 4 June 1970.
1818. *Boston Sunday Globe* 23 April 1922.
1819. Glücklich, Nicole, (project editor), *The Adventures of Two British Gentlemen in Switzerland: In the Footsteps of Sir Arthur Conan Doyle and Sherlock Holmes*, (Germany: DSHG Verlag, Ludwigshafen am Rhein, Germany 2016).
1820. *Sporting Times* 16 September 1905.
1821. *Illustrated Sporting and Dramatic News* 29 March 1930.
1822. *The Sketch* 25 November 1896.
1823. www.irvineburnsclub.org
1824. *The Sphere* 19 January 1901.
1825. *The Sphere* 6 July 1901.
1826. *Whitefriars Journal* volume 3, number 7, January 1908.
1827. *Western Daily Press* 10 March 1926.
1828. *The Graphic* 8 October 1927.
1829. *The Sketch* 10 December 1930.
1830. *Irish Times* 30 May 1898.
1831. *Irish Times* 16 June 1904.
1832. *Irish Times* 17 January 1908.
1833. www.vintageedmonton.com
1834. Photocopies of letters in the collection of the author.
1835. www.firstworldwar.com
1836. Copy of advertising poster in the collection of the author.
1837. Find My Past: Passenger list leaving the UK 1890-1960.
1838. Boström, Mattias & Laffey, Matt, *Sherlock Holmes and Conan Doyle in the Newspapers, Volume 3: July-December 1893*, (Indianapolis, America: Gasogene Books 2017).
1839. *Light* 30 September 1916.
1840. *Light* 6 January 1917.
1841. *Light* 13 January 1917.
1842. *Light* 31 March 1917.
1843. *Light* 1 September 1917.
1844. *Light* 8 September 1917.
1845. *Light* 3 November 3 1917.
1846. *Light* 15 December 1917.
1847. *Light* 26 January 1918

1848. *Light* 4 May 1918.
1849. *Light* 2 November 1918.
1850. *Light* 9 November 1918.
1851. *Light* 16 November 1918.
1852. *Light* 18 January 1919.
1853. *Light* 25 January 1919.
1854. *Light* 8 February 1919.
1855. *Light* 1 March 1919.
1856. *Light* 22 March 1919.
1857. *Light* 5 April 1919.
1858. *Light* 19 April 1919.
1859. *Light* 7 June 1919.
1860. *Light* 6 September 1919.
1861. *Light* 20 September 1919.
1862. *Light* 27 September 1919.
1863. *Light* 11 October 1919.
1864. *Light* 25 October 1919.
1865. *Light* 24 January 1920.
1866. *Light* 31 January 1920.
1867. *Light* 14 February 1920.
1868. *Light* 6 March 1920.
1869. *Light* 28 March 1920.
1870. *Light* 6 March 1920.
1871. *Light* 13 March 1920.
1872. *Light* 27 March 1920.
1873. *Light* 10 April 1920.
1874. *Light* 3 April 1920.
1875. *Light* 17 April 1920.
1876. *Light* 1 May 1920.
1877. *Light* 8 May 1920.
1878. *Light* 22 May 1920.
1879. *Light* 26 June 1920.
1880. *Light* 17 July 1920.
1881. *Light* 7 August 1920.
1882. *Light* 11 September 1920.
1883. *Light* 25 September 1920.
1884. *Light* 1 January 1921.
1885. *Light* 16 April 1921.
1886. *Light* 23 April 1921.
1887. *Light* 28 May 1921.
1888. *Light* 18 June 1921.
1889. *Light* 16 July 1921.
1890. *Light* 1 October 1921.
1891. *Light* 15 October 1921.
1892. *Light* 19 November 1921.
1893. *Light* 24 December 1921.
1894. *Light* 7 January 1922.
1895. *Light* 21 January 1922.
1896. *Light* 30 December 1922.
1897. *Light* 11 February 1922.
1898. *Light* 18 February 1922.
1899. *Light* 25 March 1922.
1900. *Light* 6 May 1922.

1901. *Light* 3 June 1922.
1902. *Light* 8 July 1922.
1903. *Light* 29 July 1922.
1904. *Light* 5 August 1922.
1905. *Light* 23 September 1922.
1906. *Light* 9 October 1922.
1907. *Light* 14 October 1922.
1908. *Light* 21 October 1922.
1909. *Light* 18 November 1922.
1910. *Light* 2 December 1922.
1911. *Light* 6 January 1923.
1912. *Light* 20 January 1923.
1913. *Light* 10 February 1923.
1914. *Light* 3 March 1923.
1915. *Light* 21 April 1923.
1916. *Light* 5 May 1923.
1917. *Light* 12 May 1923.
1918. *Light* 18 August 1923.
1919. *Light* 8 September 1923.
1920. *Light* 27 October 1923.
1921. *Light* 3 November 1923.
1922. *Light* 17 November 1923.
1923. *Light* 24 November 1923.
1924. *Light* 19 January 1924.
1925. *Light* 9 February 1924.
1926. *Light* 16 February 1924.
1927. *Light* 23 February 1924.
1928. *Light* 1 March 1924.
1929. *Light* 3 May 1924.
1930. *Light* 10 May 1924.
1931. *Light* 24 May 1924.
1932. *Light* 25 October 1924.
1933. *Light* 8 November 1924.
1934. *Light* 6 December 1924.
1935. *Light* 13 December 1924.
1936. *Athletic News* 10 November 1913.
1937. *Sheffield Independent* 1 December 1921.
1938. *The Scotsman* 2 February 1922.
1939. *Sunderland Daily Echo* 29 November 1922.
1940. *Sporting Life* 4 July 1894.
1941. *Sporting Life* 7 July 1894.
1942. *Sporting Life* 3 August 1894.
1943. *Sporting Life* 25 June 1897.
1944. *Sporting Life* 21 July 1897.
1945. *Sporting Life* 4 August 1897.
1946. *Sporting Life* 6 August 1897.
1947. *Sporting Life* 9 August 1897.
1948. *Sporting Life* 13 August 1897.
1949. *Sporting Life* 18 August 1897.
1950. *Sporting Life* 27 August 1897.
1951. *Sporting Life* 1 September 1897.
1952. *Sporting Life* 3 August 1898.
1953. *Sporting Life* 6 August 1898.

1954. *Sporting Life* 8 August 1898.
1955. *Sporting Life* 10 May 1899.
1956. *Sporting Life* 6 June 1903.
1957. *Sporting Life* 15 July 1905.
1958. *Sporting Life* 25 October 1905.
1959. *Sporting Life* 29 May 1906.
1960. *Sporting Life* 28 May 1907.
1961. *Sporting Life* 7 June 1907.
1962. *Sporting Life* 31 July 1907.
1963. *Sporting Life* 15 August 1907.
1964. *Sporting Life* 12 February 1908.
1965. *Sporting Life* 31 May 1909.
1966. *Sporting Life* 30 August 1909.
1967. *Athletic News* 26 May 1913.
1968. *Light* 4 December 1920.
1969. *Hampshire Chronicle* 23 August 1890.
1970. *Cricket and Football Field* 30 May 1908.
1971. *Army and Navy Gazette* 24 July 1915.
1972. Schüler, C.J., *Writers, Lovers, Soldiers, Spies: A History of the Authors' Club of London, 1891-2016*, (London: Authors' Club, London 2016).
1973. Correspondence by email with C.J. Schüler, chairman of the Authors' Club 2008 to 2015.
1974. *Ballymena Weekly Telegraph* 23 March 1929.
1975. *Ballymena Weekly Telegraph* 26 June 1937.
1976. *Nottingham Journal* 23 November 1920.
1977. *Nottingham Journal* 6 December 1922.
1978. *Nottingham Journal* 9 May 1928.
1979. *Nottingham Journal* 14 June 1928.
1980. *Pall Mall Gazette* 19 September 1913.
1981. *The Times* 9 March 1948.
1982. Houdini, *A Magician Among the Spirits*, (USA: Harper & Brothers Ltd., New York 1924).
1983. *Northern Whig* 11 May 1927.
1984. *Northern Whig* 14 June 1928.
1985. *Northern Whig* 11 July 1928.
1986. *Northern Whig* 22 June 1936.
1987. *Northern Whig* 19 July 1937.
1988. *Northern Whig* 24 May 1944.
1989. *Northern Whig* 7 May 1945.
1990. *London Evening Standard* 29 November 1901.
1991. *London Evening Standard* 11 March 1902.
1992. *London Evening Standard* 2 July 1903.
1993. *London Evening Standard* 20 November 1903.
1994. *London Evening Standard* 25 January 1904.
1995. *London Evening Standard* 26 January 1904.
1996. *London Evening Standard* 8 February 1905.
1997. *London Evening Standard* 25 February 1905.
1998. *London Evening Standard* 10 July 1905.
1999. *London Evening Standard* 25 October 1905.
2000. *London Evening Standard* 22 February 1908.
2001. *London Evening Standard* 11 December 1908.
2002. *London Evening Standard* 4 May 1909.
2003. *London Evening Standard* 11 November 1909.
2004. *Shields Daily News* 8 December 1919.
2005. *Northern Daily Telegraph* 16 November 1898.
2006. *Northern Daily Telegraph* 20 April 1904.

2007. *Northern Daily Telegraph* 6 October 1904.
2008. *Wiltshire Times* 19 June 1897.
2009. *Wiltshire Times* 17 March 1951.
2010. Mackaill, Alan & Kemp, Dawn, *Conan Doyle & Joseph Bell: The Real Sherlock Holmes*, (Great Britain: Royal College of Surgeons of Edinburgh 2007).
2011. Kalbfleisch, John, *Tragedy's cause stumped even Conan Doyle*, (*Montreal Gazette* 3 June 2017, first published 5 June 2005).
2012. *Eastern Evening News* 7 May 1894.
2013. *Eastern Evening News* 30 August 1894.
2014. *Eastern Evening News* 1 September 1894.
2015. *Eastern Evening News* 7 June 1898.
2016. *Eastern Evening News* 16 November 1898.
2017. *Eastern Evening News* 24 February 1908.
2018. *Kentish Mercury* 7 September 1894.
2019. *Surrey Comet* 21 October 1893.
2020. *Surrey Comet* 4 June 1904.
2021. *Norwich Mercury* 8 October 1904.
2022. http://standrewsnorfolf.play-cricket.com
2023. *Hampshire Telegraph* 31 July 1897.
2024. Montague, Charlotte, *Creating Sherlock Holmes: The Remarkable Story of Sir Arthur Conan Doyle*, (New York, USA 2017).
2025. *The Adventure of the Abbey Grange Manuscript Facsimile*, (London: Sherlock Holmes Society of London and Fondation Martin Bodmer 2016).
2026. *The Second Stain* facsimile manuscript *The Irregular Stain*, see Uncovering "The Second Stain by Randall Stock, (New York: The Baker Street Irregulars in association with Magill Library at Harvard College 2013).
2027. *The Dancing Men* facsimile manuscript *Dancing to Death*, see Tracking "The Dancing Men" by Randall Stock, (New York: The Baker Street Irregulars 2016).
2028. The C. Frederick Kittle Collection of Doyleana held at The Newberry Library, Chicago.
2029. The Richard Lancelyn Green Collection Portsmouth.
2030. *The Morning Post* 22 June 1908.
2031. *The Morning Post* 25 June 1908.
2032. *Brighton Gazette* 6 November 1909.
2033. *Brighton Gazette* 1 December 1909.
2034. *Brighton Gazette* 15 December 1909.
2035. *Brighton Gazette* 18 December 1909.
2036. *Brighton Gazette* 22 June 1910.
2037. *Brighton Gazette* 13 August 1910.
2038. *Brighton Gazette* 21 September 1910.
2039. *Brighton Gazette* 28 September 1910.
2040. Brice, Stratford, *Arthur Conan Doyle and Glasshayes House: The 1912 Extension of the Lyndhurst Grand Hotel* by email.
2041. Information supplied by Mattias Boström.
2042. *Bognor Regis Observer* 24 August 1910.
2043. *West Sussex County Times* 6 December 1930.
2044. *Daily Herald* 11 June 1930.
2045. *Daily Telegraph & Courier* (London) 31 October 1899.
2046. *Daily Telegraph & Courier* (London) 1 May 1903.
2047. *Daily Telegraph & Courier* (London) 27 November 1903.
2048. *Daily Telegraph & Courier* (London) 9 April 1907.
2049. *Daily Telegraph & Courier* (London) 1 May 1907.
2050. *Daily Telegraph & Courier* (London) 20 December 1907.
2051. *Daily Telegraph & Courier* (London) 27 March 1909.
2052. *Daily Telegraph & Courier* (London) 12 March 1910.
2053. *The Sherlock Holmes Collections of Daniel Posnansy Auction 19 December 2017*.
2054. *Western Daily Mercury* 24 January 1912.
2055. Research received from Michael Morton.

2056. *Daily Herald* 3 July 1922.
2057. *Daily Herald* 8 October 1929.
2058. *Daily Herald* 11 November 1930.
2059. *Daily Herald* 11 June 1930.
2060. *Daily Herald* 2 July 1930.
2061. *Daily Herald* 8 July 1930.
2062. *Daily Herald* 6 June 1931.
2063. *Coventry Evening Telegraph* 7 September 1931.
2064. *Birmingham Daily Gazette* 7 September 1907.
2065. *Birmingham Daily Gazette* 24 March 1921.
2066. *Birmingham Daily Gazette* 10 November 1921.
2067. *Birmingham Daily Gazette* 21 January 1922.
2068. *Birmingham Daily Gazette* 16 June 1922.
2069. *Birmingham Daily Gazette* 1 March 1923.
2070. *Birmingham Daily Gazette* 15 December 1924.
2071. *Birmingham Daily Gazette* 7 September 1925.
2072. *Birmingham Daily Gazette* 7 September 1925.
2073. *Birmingham Daily Gazette* 11 September 1925.
2074. *Birmingham Daily Gazette* 22 March 1927.
2075. *Birmingham Daily Gazette* 16 April 1956.
2076. *Western Daily Press* 1 June 1910.
2077. *Sports Argus* 17 December 1910.
2078. *Reading Observer* 12 April 1913.
2079. *Northampton Chronicle & Echo* 4 October 1919.
2080. *Northampton Chronicle & Echo* 14 October 1919.
2081. *Reading Observer* 7 February 1920.
2082. *Reading Observer* 13 March 1920.
2083. *London Daily News* 5 May 1898.
2084. *The Stage* 6 May 1915.
2085. *The Sportsman* 26 August 1886.
2086. *The Sportsman* 19 March 1902.
2087. *The Sportsman* 5 August 1902.
2088. *The Sportsman* 9 August 1902.
2089. *The Sportsman* 13 August 1902.
2090. *The Sportsman* 19 August 1902.
2091. *The Sportsman* 8 August 1903.
2092. *The Sportsman* 28 May 1904.
2093. *The Sportsman* 9 August 1905.
2094. *The Sportsman* 19 August 1905.
2095. *The Sportsman* 22 August 1910.
2096. *The Sportsman* 2 September 1910.
2097. *The Sportsman* 10 June 1912.
2098. *The Sportsman* 18 June 1912.
2099. *The Sportsman* 5 August 1912.
2100. *The Sportsman* 11 April 1913.
2101. *The Sportsman* 15 January 1924.
2102. *His Last Bow* facsimile of the partial manuscript *Trenches: The War Service of Sherlock Holmes*, see Making "His Last Bow": Its History and Manuscript by Randall Stock, (New York: The Baker Street Irregulars 2017).
2103. *The Sportsman* 17 April 1905.
2104. *Belfast Newsletter* 15 July 1916.
2105. *London Evening Standard* 26 June 1909.
2106. *Inverness Courier* 1 December 1893.
2107. Northampton Chronicle & Echo 27 June 1929.
2108. www.doubledeclutch.com/?=delage-type-x
2109. Information supplied by Bibliothèque cantonale et universitaire Lausanne.
2110. *Light* 30 January 1926.

ABOUT THE CHRONOLOGIST

Brian W. Pugh lives in Lewes, East Sussex not far from the town of Crowborough (the home of Sir Arthur Conan Doyle 1907-1930), he was born in 1944 and has lived in Lewes all of his life. He first became interested in Sherlock Holmes in 1958 when he received his first Holmes book *The Complete Sherlock Holmes Short Stories*; this was followed in 1960 with *The Sherlock Holmes Long Stories*, both are still in his collection. His interest in Holmes was reawakened with the Jeremy Brett series on television and he joined The Franco-Midland Hardware Company and The Sherlock Holmes Society of London. On becoming increasingly interested in Conan Doyle he joined The Conan Doyle (Crowborough) Establishment and The Arthur Conan Doyle Society. He is a member of many of other Holmesian groups including The Poor Folk on the Moors, The Sydney Passengers' in Australia, plus many more. Brian is The Curator of The Conan Doyle (Crowborough) Establishment, which is a society dedicated to Arthur Conan Doyle; he is also responsible for maintaining the modest ACD collection that The Establishment holds of Conan Doyle photographs and ephemera. He also assists in research about ACD, his life, his family and his writings etc., and assists the media and general enquiries for research about Conan Doyle. The Establishment was instrumental in fund raising and arranging the erection of the Conan Doyle statue in Crowborough.

PUBLISHED WORKS:

He is the author of *A Chronology of the Life of Sir Arthur Conan Doyle* [privately printed, 2000, London: MX Publishing Ltd. 2009, London: MX Publishing Ltd., Revised & Expanded Edition 2012 & 2014, Addenda & Corrigenda 2014, revised and expanded edition 2018], *The Sir Arthur Conan Doyle Statue At Crowborough* [privately printed, 2001], *Buzzin In Sussex: An Investigation Into The Connections Of Sir Arthur Conan Doyle, His Family And Sherlock Holmes* [privately printed, 2005], *Bonfire Night in Lewes* [London: MX Publishing Ltd. 2011] and *The Budds of the West Country* [privately printed, 2012], *Cliffe Bonfire Society Through the Years 1853-2014* [London: MX Publishing Ltd. 2015]. And as joint author with John Hackworth, *The Conan Doyle Crowborough Walk* [privately printed, 2005]. He is also joint author with Paul R. Spiring of *On The Trail of Arthur Conan Doyle: An Illustrated Devon Tour* [Brighton: Book Guild Publishing Ltd, 2008], *Auf der Spur von Arthur Conan Doyle* [Mannheim: Dryas Verlag, 2008], *Bertram Fletcher Robinson: A Footnote to The Hound of the Baskervilles* [London: MX Publishing, 2008], *Tras las huellas de Arthur Conan Doyle* [London: MX Publishing Ltd. 2008] and joint author with Paul R. Spiring & Sadru Bhanji of *Arthur Conan Doyle, Sherlock Holmes and Devon: A Complete Tour Guide & Companion* [London: MX Publishing Ltd. 2010].

He has had a number of articles printed in various Sherlock Holmes societies journals and edits The Conan Doyle (Crowborough) Establishment Irregular Newsletter and The Annual Birthday File. He has been frequently interviewed on live radio programmes and has featured on various television programmes connected with ACD.

The Author and Curator of The Conan Doyle (Crowborough) Establishment

1st Crowborough Scouts Troup 138, 163
2nd Essex Regiment 149
3rd Essex Regiment 149
3rd Reserve Battalion 153
4th Army Corps 148
5th West Middlesex R.V. Regiment 92
6th Royal Sussex Volunteer Regiment 146
79th Battery Harrismith 93
'1902-1909' (poem, 1910) 128
Abbey Holme (ship) 4
Abbey, H.R.B. 127
Aberdeen 161
   His Majesty's Theatre 78
   Music Hall 162
Accra 20
ACD characters, Professor Challenger 11
Acme Library 62
Active (whaler) 15
An Actor's Duel (1894) 58
Adcock, A. St John 138
Addah 20
Addison, Albert 32, 35
'An Address to The Edinburgh University Tariff Reform League' (talk, 1904) 106
Addy, William 159, 162
Adelaide 170
   Art Gallery 166
   Auditorium 167
   Grand Central Hotel 166
   Humbug Scrub nature reserve 166
   Penfolds Winery (Magill) 166
   South Australian Museum 166
   Town Hall 166
Aden 200
Adirondacks (USA) 59
The Adventure of the Abbey Grange (1904) 103, 105, 154
The Adventure of the Beryl Coronet (1892) 47
The Adventure of Black Peter (1904) 100, 102, 222
The Adventure of the Blanched Soldier (1926) 192
The Adventure of the Blue Carbuncle (1892) 45, 46
The Adventure of the Cardboard Box (1893) 48, 51
The Adventure of Charles Augustus Milverton (1904) 100, 103, 178
The Adventure of the Copper Beeches (1892) 46, 48
The Adventure of the Creeping Man (1923) 179
The Adventure of the Crooked Man (1893) 53
The Adventure of the Dancing Men (1903) 99, 101, 157, 186
The Adventure of the Devil's Foot (1910) 130, 173, 174
The Adventure of the Dying Detective (1913) 139, 140
The Adventure of the Empty House (1903) 98, 100, 101, 151, 173
The Adventure of the Engineer's Thumb (1892) 46
The Adventure of the Final Problem (1893) 51, 55, 56
The Adventure of the "Gloria Scott" (1893) 51
The Adventure of the Golden Pince-Nez (1904) 105, 212
The Adventure of the Greek Interpreter (1893) 54, 221
The Adventure of the Illustrious Client (1924) 185, 186
The Adventure of the Lion's Mane (1926) 193, 222
The Adventure of the Man with the Twisted Lip (1891) 45
The Adventure of the Mazarin Stone (1921) 172

The Adventure of the Missing Three-Quarter (1904) 102, 105, 178
The Adventure of the Musgrave Ritual (1893) 50, 52
The Adventure of the Naval Treaty (1893) 54
The Adventure of the Noble Bachelor (1892) 47
The Adventure of the Norwood Builder (1903) 98, 101, 157
The Adventure of the Priory School (1904) 102, 173, 174, 186
The Adventure of the Red Circle (1911) 130, 173, 174
The Adventure of the Reigate Squire (1893) 52
The Adventure of the Resident Patient (1893) 53
The Adventure of the Retired Colourman (1926) 193
The Adventure of the Second Stain (1904) 106, 173, 174
The Adventure of Shoscombe Old Place (1927) 194
The Adventure of the Silver Blaze (1892) 50
The Adventure of Silver Blaze (1892) 48
The Adventure of the Six Napoleons (1904) 100, 103, 154
The Adventure of the Solitary Cyclist (1903) 98, 102, 173, 186
The Adventure of the Speckled Band (1892) 45, 47, 203, 212
The Adventure of the Stockbroker's Clerk (1893) 51
The Adventure of the Sussex Vampire (1924) 183
The Adventure of the Three Gables (1926) 192
The Adventure of the Three Garridebs (1924) 185, 186
The Adventure of the Three Students (1904) 101, 104, 154
The Adventure of the Veiled Lodger (1927) 193
The Adventure of Wisteria Lodge (1908) 118, 120
The Adventure of the Yellow Face (1893) 48, 51
The Adventures of Sherlock Holmes (1892) 49, 50, 154
The Adventures of Sherlock Holmes (silent film) 169
The Adventures of a Spiritualist in America (1922) 177
Aerial League of the British Empire 126
After Cormorants with a Camera (1881) 19
After Dinner Club 174
'The After Life' (lecture given by Denis Conan Doyle) 213
Air Forces Board 222
Aladdin Jr (play) 59
Alake of Abeokuta 104
Albany 142
  Union Station (Broadway) 143
Aldershot (Surrey) 113, 116
Alexander, Jack and Norah 116
Alexandra, Queen 93, 119, 133
Algiers 42
All the Year Round 21, 22
The Alleged Posthumous Writings of Known Authors (1927) 195
Allen, Grant 65, 77, 81
An Alpine Pass on "Ski" (1894) 58, 62
Alpine Walk (1893) 56
Amateur Billiards Championships 137, 163, 191
The Amateur Cracksman (Hornung) 75
Amateur Field Event Association 130
Amateur Swimming Association 124
Amateur Tennis Championships 184
American Copyright Act 44
American Psychical Institute & Laboratory 175
The American's Tale (1880) 18
Amherst
  Amherst House 60
  College Hall 60

Amodio, Marquis Julio de 214, 215
Amport House (Andover) 221
Amsterdam Colonial Museum 202
Andersen, Anna Charlotte *see* Doyle, Anne Charlotte
Anderson, Dr William Monro 166
Anerley Congregational Church 172, 173
Angel, Revd H. 215
Angell, Bryan Branford 84, 88, 114, 156, 167, 189, 199, 204, 210, 212
Angell, Bryan Mary Julia Josephine 'Dodo' (ACD's sister) 10, 11, 19, 23, 43, 66, 73, 76, 78, 88, 89, 97, 98, 99, 110, 113, 114, 115, 131, 139, 155, 193, 204, 212
Angell, Revd Charles Cyril 8, 73, 75, 78, 88, 89, 98, 112, 114, 115, 117, 131, 193, 204, 205, 212, 215
Angell, Julia 75, 78, 88
Angels of Darkness (drama 1888/1890) 35, 41
Anglo-African Writers' Club 79
Anglo-American Committee 75
Anglo-German Friendship Society 131
Answers 46
Anti-Slavery and Aborigines' Protection Society 129, 135
A.P. Watt (literary agent) 42, 43, 44
D. Appleton and Co. (New York) (publishers) 65, 97
'The Arab Steed' (poem, 1899) 79
'The Arctic Seas' (talk, 1883) 22, 23
Argonne Forest 151
An Arizona Tragedy (The American Tale) (1893) 51
Arlington Manor (Berkshire) 80
Armadale Castle (ship) 198
Arrowsmith's Christmas Annual 50
'The Art of Fiction' (talk, 1901) 87
Arthur Conan Doyle: A Memoir (by J. Lamond) 211
Arthur Conan Doyle. A Study of a Man and His Books (by A. St John Adcock, 1913) 138
Arthur Conan Doyle (interview, 1903) 98
Artists' General Benevolent Institution 139
Arundel Castle (Sussex) 128
Ashdown Forest Hotel (Forest Row, Sussex) 87, 88, 112
Ashley, Evelyn 40
Aspern (Austria) 220
Asquith, H.H. 146
Associated Newspapers Ltd 211
Associated Sunday Magazine 110, 130, 135
Association of American Correspondents 195
Association for the Oral Instruction of the Deaf and Dumb 136
Astor, William Waldorf 71
'At the Front' (lecture, 1920) 168
At the Waters of Strife: Some Little Verses (by Bryan Mary Angell, 1918) 155
The Athabasca Trail (1914) 145, 148
The Athenaeum Press (publishers) 212
Athens 117, 139
Atlantic City 174, 176
  Ambassador Hotel 176
Atlantic Union 82, 89, 100
Austin Ten (motor car) 217
Australia 165, 174
  Adelaide 167, 170
  Brisbane 169
  Fremantle 166, 170
  Geelong 167

Jenolan Caves (Blue Mountains) 170
  Medlow Bath Hotel (Blue Mountains) 169, 170
  Melbourne 166–7, 169, 170, 210
  Nerrin-Nerrin (Western Victoria) 167
  Sydney 166, 167–8, 169, 170, 212
  Toowoomba 169
  Unity Mine (Bendigo) 167
Australian High Command 158
Australian and New Zealand Luncheon Club 159
Austro-Daimler racing car 210, 211
Authors' Club 50, 51, 68, 72, 77, 78, 79, 81, 82, 87, 89, 92, 93, 95, 97, 99, 101, 102, 106, 108, 110, 111, 114, 115, 116, 118, 121, 130, 135, 141, 142, 153, 173, 178, 183, 184, 201, 211, 220
  Ladies Banquet (1927) 193
Authors' Club Billiards Handicap 138
Author's Edition (1903) 97, 100
The Avenue, Eltham (Kent) 19

Bailey, Charles 167, 170
Baldwin, Stanley 142
Balestier, Beatty 61
Balfour, Arthur J. 37, 108
Ball, Henry 28, 31
Ball, Jane Isabella *see* Doyle, Jane Isabella Ball
Ball, J.H. 65
'The Ballad of the "Eurydice"' (or 'The Home-Coming of the Eurydice') (poem, 1894) 57
'A Ballad of the Ranks' (poem, 1897) 70
Ballyclare (Co. Antrim) 214
Balmer, J.R. 219
Baltimore, Edgar Allan Poe monument 60
Baltimore Weekly Sun 45, 47
Bangor (Co. Down) 213
Bangs, John Kendrick 61, 74
Baring-Gould, Revd Sabine 49
Barnes, John 205
Barr, Robert 46, 49
Barrett, William Fletcher 38, 51
Barrie, J.M. 46, 47, 49, 50, 52, 65, 74, 88, 95, 103, 117, 126, 127, 136, 141, 146, 201
Barrington Town-Warming Lectures (Illinois, USA) 216
Barry-Doyle, Father Richard (ACD's 2nd cousin) 8, 157, 158, 212
Barrymore, Ethel 142
Baskerville, Henry 'Harry' 90, 114
Bath
  Assembly Rooms 163
  Dunkerton Rectory 189
  Empire Hotel 212
  Grand Pump Room Hotel 188
  Guildhall 112
  Royal Institution Assembly Rooms 81
  Widcombe Lodge 112
The Battle of Arras (1918) 158
Battle of Britain Service of Thanksgiving and Rededication (1992) 225
The Battle of Cambrai (1919) 159
The Battle of Messines (1918) 158
The Battle of the Somme (1918) 157
BBC 184, 189
Beach Hotel (Littlehampton) 128
The Beacon Brass Band 118

Beauchamp, Earl and Countess 115
Beaulieu Abbey 197
Beaulieu (France) 139
Beckenham Golf Club 51
The Beetle Hunter (1898) 75
Beeton's Christmas Annual 32
Before the Campaign: I. A Letter from Cairo (1896) 67
Before the Campaign: II. Can the Fella Fight? (1896) 67
Before My Bookcase (1894) 57
Belfast 159, 187
  City Hall 217
  Clarence Place (Manor Hall) 216
  Midland Hotel (York Street) 187
  Midland Station Hotel 187
  St George's Hall (High Street) 187
  Ulster Hall 187, 188
  Ye Olde Castle Restaurant (Castle Place) 187
Belfast Association of Spiritualists 188
Belfast Evening Telegraph 134
Belfast Rotary Club 187
Belgian Congo 121
Belgravia Magazine 26
Bell, Dr Joseph 3, 11, 12, 13, 87, 134
Bell, Colonel J.H. 178
Bellchambers, Eliza Mary 166
Bellchambers, Thomas Paine 166
Belleisle (Co. Fermanagh) 210
'Bendy's Sermon' (poem, 1909) 122
Beneficial Society's Hall (Portsea) 29
The Benefit of the Doubt (Pinero) 65
Benham, Dr 50
Bennett, Arnold 146
Bennett, Herbert John 87, 88
Bennett, John A. 159
Bentley Priory 222
Bergman, Dr Ernst von 41
Berlin 40, 41, 117, 190, 214
  Central Hotel 41
Berlin Olympic Games (1916) 136, 138
Bernhardt, Sarah 129
Berrington, Henry 187
The Beryl Coronet 45
Besant, Annie 195
Besant, Walter 32, 44, 70
Besinnet, Ada 175, 180
Between Two Fires (1891) 46
Beyond the City (1893) 53
Beyond the City. The Idyll of a Suburb (1891) 44, 46
'Beyond the Grave' (lecture, 1920) 169
Bignell Wood *see under* Minstead
Billiards Amateur Flying Handicap 164
Billiards Association 183, 215
  Amateur Championship 137, 138
Billiards Control Club (BCC) 141, 183, 192
Billington, James 88
Billington, Thomas 88
Billy Bones (1922) 178

Birmingham 14, 18, 19, 20, 23, 42, 98, 155
  Aston 20
    Clifton House (Ashton Road) 13, 219
    Harborne and Edgbaston Institute 55
    The Elms (Gravelly Hill) 20
    Town Hall 159, 173
The Birmingham Daily Post 52
Birmingham Gazette & Express 116
Birmingham Spiritualist Church 159, 173
Bisley (Surrey) 116
Black and White 43, 46
Blackburn 173
Blackpool, Hotel Metropole 162
Blackwood's Edinburgh Magazine 41
Blair, Captain Gordon Campbell 137
Blairerno House, Drumlithie (Aberdeenshire) 10, 13, 15, 19
Blake, F.T. 165
Blasson, Charles 83, 84
The Blighting of Sharkey (1911) 131
'The Blind Archer' (poem, 1897) 70
Bloemfontein
  Langman Hospital (Ramblers Ground) 198
  Polley's Hotel 198
'Blood Brotherhood' (speech, 1912) 135
Blood Sports - Should They Be Abolished? (1928) 196
The Blood-Stone Tragedy (1884) 23, 24
Blundell's School (Tiverton, Devon) 71
Boer Critics on 'The Great Boer War' (1901) 92
Boer War 80, 82–4, 96
Boex, Joseph Henri Honoré (aka J.H. Rosny aîné) 142
Bognor, Pier Hotel 177
Bolton 173
Bombay 78, 170, 199
  Taj Mahal Hotel 165
Bones, The April Fool of Harvey's Sluice (1882) 20
Bonfort, Madame 42
Bonnot, Jules 170
Bonny River (Nigeria) 20
The Book I Most Enjoyed Writing (1922) 174
The Book of the Queen's Doll's House (by A.C. Benson, 1924) 184
The Bookman 47, 98
Booksellers' Trade Dinner (1893) 51, 52
Booth, General 115
Border Burghs 101, 110
"Borrow"-ed Scenes (1913) 140
The Boscombe Valley Mystery (1891) 44, 45
Boston 60, 142, 174
  Association Hall 60, 61
  Symphony Hall 175
The Boston Herald 26
Botha, Marie Mandina 118
Boucicault, Dion, *Louis* (play) 12
Boulnois, Clara 125, 156, 168
Boulnois, Henry Percy 31, 36, 39, 40, 46, 76, 131
Boulnois, Stratten 36, 77, 112, 125
Bourhill, J.G. 128
Bournemouth 148

   Portman Lodge 151
   Royal Bath Hotel 131
   Winter Gardens 161
Bow Bells 22, 24, 49
Bowen, Revd T.R. 219
bowling clubs/teams
   Mewport Bowling Club 29
   Southsea Bowling Club 29
Bowshot Cottage (West Grinstead Park) 153, 154, 169
Box Hill (Dorking) 47
Boy Scouts 138, 189, 191
Boy Scouts London Appeal 194
Boyes, George 159
Boys' Empire League 96, 97, 99, 101, 102
Boy's Own Paper 23, 25, 28, 31, 32
Boz Club 106
Bradford 109, 148
   Eastbrook Wesleyan Mission 155
   Great Northern Victoria Hotel 103
   Mechanics' Institute 55
Bradford Textile Society 103
Bradley, H. Denis 185
Brampton (Huntingdonshire) 218
Branches park (Newmarket) 210
Brandon, Jocelyn 123
Messrs Brandon and Nicholson (solicitors) 123
Branger, Johannes 57, 63
Branger, Tobias 57
The Bravoes of Market Drayton (1888) 35, 38
Brazil 31
'A Breach of Liberty. Sir A. Conan Doyle Defends Spiritualists' (lecture, 1924) 185
Brett, Jeremy 225
Bridgend Register Office (Glamorgan) 214
C. Bridger and Sons (estate agents) 171
Bridges, Margaret 210
Bridgewater (Somerset) 85
The Brigadier and the Fox (reading, 1900) 84
Brigadier Gerard (play, 1906) 111, 112, 113
Brigadier Gerard (silent film, 1927) 195
Brigadier (horse) 69, 73
Bright, Addison 126
Brighton 148, 151, 158, 160, 174
   Dome Mission 125, 185, 210
   Hippodrome 164
   Hotel Metropole 125, 138
   Oddfellows Hall 158
   Old Ship Hotel 127
   Princes Hotel 136
   Royal Pavilion 125, 174
   Southwick cemetery 147
   Spiritualist Church 210
   Theatre Royal 128
Brighton Motor Rally and Gala Week (1930) 205
Brighton Spiritualist Brotherhood 161, 164
Brillat-Savarin, Jean Anthelme 190
Brindisi 66, 139
Brisbane 4, 135

Bellevue Hotel 169
　　Government House 170
　　His Majesty's Theatre 100, 169, 170
　　Redbank Plains apiary 170
　　Spiritual Church 170
Bristol 19, 110
　　Colston Hall 163, 164
　　Empire Theatre 188
　　Hippodrome 171
　　Literary and Philosophic Club 56
　　Prince's Theatre 59
　　Victoria Rooms 56
　　Victoria Rooms (Clifton) 81
British Air Forces of Occupation (Germany) 217
British Antarctic Expedition 124
The British Army in Italy (1927) 193
The British Campaign in France and Flanders Vol.1 (1916) 151, 153
The British Campaign in France and Flanders Vol.2 (1917) 155
The British Campaign in France and Flanders Vol.3 (1918) 157
The British Campaign in France and Flanders Vol.4 (1919) 160
The British Campaign in France and Flanders Vol.5 (1919) 161
The British Campaign in France and Flanders Vol.6 (1920) 162
British College of Psychic Science 176, 193, 211
British Empire League 167
British Expeditionary Force (BEF) 151, 153, 155
British Farmers' Red Cross Fund 154, 157
British Homeopathic Association 212
British III Corps 153
British Industries Fair (1926 & 1927) 191, 193
British Journal of Photography 19, 20, 21, 22, 24, 26, 27
British Journal of Photography Almanac 21
British Medical Association (BMA) Council 135
British Medical Journal (BMJ) 13, 84, 114
British Museum Fund for the Exploration of South Africa 188
British National Protest 141
British Olympic Council 140
British Red Cross Society 151, 154, 157
British-American Peace Centenary appeal (1913) 140
Brittain, Mrs Annie 164
Brittain, Harry 110
Brodrick, W. St. 97
Bromet, Air Vice-Marshall Sir Geoffrey Rhodes 45, 222, 223
Bromley New Council Hall 184
Bromley United Services Club Ltd 184
Brooklands Automobile Racing Club (BARC) 201
Brooklands (Surrey) 133, 210, 211
Brooklyn Robins (baseball) 175
Brown, Justice 187
The Bruce-Partington Plans (1908) 121
Buchan, John (author) 145, 186
Buchan, John (crew member on the *Hope*) 17, 191
Buchanan, Henry 73
Buckeburg 217
Buckingham Palace 96, 119, 151, 156, 223, 224
Buckle, George 45
Budd, Dr George Turnavine 2, 19, 20, 36
Buffalo 142, 174

Bugatti racing car 213, 214, 215
Bulawayo 198
　Grand Hotel 199
　Palace Theatre 199
The Bully of Brocas Court. A Legend of the Ring (1921) 173
Bungalow Bay (Saranac Lake, USA) 59
Burleigh, Bennett 83
Burn, Colonel C.R. 148
Burnham, Lord 104
Burns' Detective Agency 125, 138
Burns, William John 138, 143
Burton, Mary 6
Burton, Mr 24
Burton, Willie 22
Butler, Dr 73
Butt, Emily *see* Hawkins, Emily Butt
Butt, Louisa 43
Buxton 96
By the North Sea (1909) 122
Bylandt, Mr van 202

The Cabman's Story. The Mysteries of a London "Growler" (1884) 24
Caillard, Lady 213
Cairo
　Mena Hotel 200
　Pyramids and Sphinx 200
Calcutta 167, 189
Calgary 179
　Al Azhar Temple 182
Cambridge
　Guildhall 121
　Masonic Hall 209
　St Catherine's John Ray Society 192
Cambridge, Duke of 82
Cambridge Union 194
Cambridge University 211
Cambridge University Automobile Club 210
Cambridge University Quinquaginta Dance Club Ball (1930) 209
Cameron, Lieutenant-Governor Sir Douglas 145
Cameroons 215
Can We Speak with the Dead? (1928) 197
Canada 115
　Algoma Indian School (Sault Ste. Marie) 143
　Algonquin Provincial Park (Ontario) 144, 145
　Calgary 179, 182
　Edmonton 142, 143, 179, 182
　Fort William 142, 143, 144, 145
　Fort William Henry Hotel (Lake George) 143
　Grand Trunk Railroad 143
　Great Lakes 142, 143
　Jasper National Park (Canadian Rockies) 142, 143, 144, 182
　Lake Champlain 143
　Lake Ontario 145
　Lake Patricia 144
　Lake Superior 145
　London 143
　Loon Lake House (Saskatchewan) 182

   Medicine Lake 144
   Montreal 142, 143, 145, 179, 182
   Moose River 144
   Niagara Falls 61, 145
   Ottawa 143, 145
   Pyramid Lake 1144
   Sarnia 143
   Tête Jaune Cache 144
   Toronto 61, 142
   Vancouver 181–2
   Winnipeg 142, 143, 144, 179, 182
   Yellow Head Lake 144
Canadian Engineers 154
Canadian Pacific Railway 145
Canadian Pacific Steamship Company 181
Canary Islands 20
Candlelight Press, New York (publishers) 220
Candy (Ceylon) 170
Cannes 139
Cantello, Mrs 22
Cape Coast Castle (Gold Coast) 20
Cape Palmas, Monrovia (Liberia) 20
Cape Town
   City Hall 198
   Houses of Parliament 198
   Mount Nelson Hotel 82, 84, 198
The Captain of the Pole-star (1883) 22
The Captain of the Pole-star and Other Stories (1890) 39
'Captain Scott's Expedition' (lecture, 1913) 140
Captain Webb Fund 124
Cardiff 159
   Hillcrest (Penylan) 159
   Playhouse theatre 183
A Career as a Medical Man (1911) 131
Carlo (ACD's dog) 172
Carlyle, Thomas 28
Carmer, Count 133
Carpentier, George 140
The Case of George Edalji: A Question for Opthalmologists (1907) 113, 114
A Case of Identity (1891) 44, 45
The Case of Lady Sannox (1893) 55
'The Case of Lester Coltman' (lecture, 1925) 187
The Case of Oscar Slater (1912) 135, 136
The Case for Spirit Photography (1922) 178
The Case-Book of Sherlock Holmes (1927) 194, 218
Casement, Sir Roger 127, 130, 134, 151, 152
Cassell & Company (publishers) 45, 47, 191
Cassell's Family Magazine 29
Cassell's Magazine 113
Cassell's Saturday Journal 23, 24, 26, 51
Catalina Island, St Catherine Hotel 180
Caux 66
Central Association of Volunteer Training Corps 147
The Centurion (1922) 178
Chalk, Mrs 125
Chamberlain, Joseph 93
Chamber's Journal 13, 35, 38, 42, 63

Champion de Crespigny, Major Sir Claude 154, 157
Channel Fleet Shooting Trophy 106
Channel Tunnel 138, 141
Channell, Mr Justice 123
Chaplin, Charles 92
Messrs. Charles J. Parris (estate agents) 219
Charlton, Mr 143
Charmouth, Coach and Horses Hotel 57
A Chat with Conan Doyle (interview) (1894) 59
A Chat with Dr Conan Doyle (interview, 1893) 51
Chatto & Windus (publishers) 39, 58
Chelmsford Regent Theatre 213
Chelmsford Spiritualists' Society 213
Cheltenham 132, 133, 148, 159, 201
   Queen's Hotel 79, 131, 133, 159
   Town Hall 148, 159
Chester 153
   Greenfield house 134, 139
   Music Hall 149
Chesterton, G.K. 146
Chevrons Club 154
Chicago 56, 59, 60, 125, 141, 142, 174, 175, 179, 180
   2 Bank Street 60
   Central Music Hall 60
   Farmers' Fellowship Club 59
   Grand Pacific Hotel 59
   Opera House 59
   Orchestra Hall 180
   Twentieth Century Club (Michigan Avenue) 59
   Union League Club 59
Chicago Pageant of Progress 187
Chicago (US Navy ship) 57
Chiddingfold Hound 77
Chiddingfold Hunt 77, 109
Chiddingfold (Surrey) 73
Children's County Holiday Fund 115
Chimay (Belgium) 214, 220
Chiverton, Thomas 23
Choate, Joseph Hodges 84, 107
Christian, Princess 93
Christian Spiritualist Church (Philadelphia, Co. Durham) 209
'Christianity and Spiritualism' (lecture, 1923) 179
Christie's auction house (London) 151, 154, 157, 173, 221, 222, 223
'Christmas 1895' (poem, 1896) 66
Chukovsky, Korney 151
Church of England Waifs' and Strays Society 127
Church of Ireland Moral Welfare Association 216
Churchill, Clementine 124
Churchill, Winston 87, 88, 89
Churton Collins Memorial Fund 121
Cincinnati 56, 59, 142, 179
   Burnet House 59
   Emery Hall 180
   Odd Fellows Hall 59
City of York (hot air balloon) 91
Civilian National Reserve (later Home Guard) 146
'Civilian National Reserve' (pamphlet, 1914) 146

Clancy, Warden 143
Claremont, Dr C.C. 32
Claretie, Jules 52
Clarice (play by Gillette) 109
Clarkson, H.L. 143
Claxton, Isabella Ann Leckie 190, 191
Cleeve, Elizabeth 79
Cleeve, Thomas Rodney 79, 82
Cleveland 142, 179, 180
Cleveland Literary and Philosophical Society (Middlesborough) 55
Cliffe House, Ruyton-XI-Towns (Shropshire) 13
Cliftonville (Kent) 214
Cliveden (Maidenhead) 71
Clytonville Hotal (Margate) 96
College of Psychic Science 164
Collier's Weekly 101, 102, 103, 106, 120, 140, 150, 185
Collins, Churton 107, 113
Colombo (Ceylon) 165, 170, 204
The Colonel's Choice (1891) 45
Colonial and Indian troops 71
Colonial Premiers 95
Colonna, Cynthia 162
Colorado Springs 180
   Antlers Hotel 180
Columbia (ship) 162
Columbus (Ohio) 180
The Coming of the Fairies (1922) 177
'The Coming of the Fairies' (lecture by E.L. Gardner, 1921) 172
The Coming of the Huns (1910) 129, 178
Committee of Twenty-Five 202
Como 94
Compatriots' Club 103, 106
The Complete Sherlock Holmes Long Stories (1929) 201
The Complete Sherlock Holmes Short Stories (1928) 197
Compton (Surrey), Prior's Field 109
Comstock, F. Ray 143
'Conan Doyle & Gibbon' (lecture, 1908) 121
Conan Doyle, Arthur *see* Doyle, Arthur Ignatius Conan
The Conan Doyle Banquet at the Authors' Club. Dr Doyle tells the Story of his Career (1896) 68
Conan Doyle Cup (rifle shooting) 110, 116, 120
Conan Doyle family members *see* under 'Doyle'
Conan Doyle in "Luck" (1900) 83
'Conan Doyle on the Others. Fellow Authors Criticised. What He Thinks of Their Articles' (speech, 1925) 189
Conan Doyle Prize (Edinburgh University) 128
The Conan Doyle Stories (1929) 201
Conan Doyle (trawler) 147, 157, 159, 162
'Conan Doyle's Views on the War' (talk, 1900) 82
Conan, Elizabeth 3
Conan, Marianne/a (or Mary Ann) *see* Doyle, Marianne/a (or Mary Ann) Conan
Conan, Michael (ACD's great uncle) 3, 4, 10, 13, 14
Conan, Susan Frances Field 4, 10, 22
The Confessions (1898) 74
Congleton (Cheshire) 172
'Congo Atrocities (or Iniquities)' (speech, 1909) 124
Congo Reform Association 118, 124

'The Congo Reform Bill' (speech by E.D. Morel) 124, 125
Connyngham, Sir William 133
Conservative Party 33, 40, 75
Constable & Co (Publishers) 62
Constantinople 117
  Pera Palace 117
The "Contemptible Little Army" (1914) 147
The Contest (1911) 130
Coogan, Jackie 179, 181
Cooper, D. 92
Cooper, Rita 214
Copenhagen 133, 202, 203
  Holmens Kirke 134
  Hotel d'Angleterre 202
  Hvidøre palace 133
  Idrætshuset 202
  Odd Fellowpalæet 202
The Cornhill Magazine 22, 24, 25, 33, 39, 41, 42, 74, 87, 92, 111, 122, 135, 147, 148
'Corporal Dick's Promotion (An Epic of the Egyptian Campaign)' (poem, 1887) 32
Correspondents and Camels. Letters from Egypt (1896) 67
Cosham
  Spiritualist Church 213
  Trades' Hall (Southampton Road) 213
The Cosmopolitan 69, 81
The Cottage (Telfont Evias, Salisbury) 74
Cottingley Fairies 164, 168, 200
The Cottingley Fairies. An Epilogue (1923) 178
County Guild of Spiritualism for Sussex 175
County Volunteer Regiments 150
The Courier-Journal 47, 48, 55, 78
Court Treatt, Major Chaplin 191
Court Treatt, Stella 191
The Covered Wagon (silent film, 1923) 180
Cowan, Sir Henry 211
Cowan, Jean Lindsey 205
Cowan, Lady Winifrede 213
Crabbe's Practice (1884) 25
Cranston, Sir Robert 104
Cranston's Hotel Company Ltd 119, 132
Crawford, Francis R. 117
Crawford, Dr J.W. 159, 166
Crawfurd, Oswald 50
Craze, George 209
'Cremona. A Ballad of the Irish Brigade' (poem, 1898) 74
Crewe 160
Crewe Circle 172
cricket clubs/teams
  1st Army Corps 99
  1st King's Dragoon Guards 58
  Actors 116
  Addiscombe 44, 45, 48, 49, 53
  Aldershot Division 78
  Allahakbarries 42, 51, 71, 75, 79, 90, 99
  Ardingly College 41, 119, 127, 135
  Army Service Corps 67
  Artists 71, 75, 79, 90, 91, 95, 99, 104, 107, 108, 111, 115, 120
  Authors 69, 79, 91, 94, 95, 99, 104, 107, 108, 111, 115, 120, 134, 136

Beaumont College 48
Bedford County School 99
Bedford Grammar School 99
Bedford Modern School 99
Bellevue 128
Blackheath 79
Blackmoor 99
Blue Mantles 119, 120, 127, 128, 135, 136
Blundell's School 71
Border Regiment 34
Bournemouth 80
Brighton College 119, 127
Brixton Wanderers 29, 53
Broadwater 100, 108
Brook House 120
Buckinghamshire 85
Burlington Wanderers 58
Cambridgeshire 80, 85, 102
Captain Clark's Eleven 76
Cheltenham College 79, 91
Chislehurst 52
Christ's Hospital 119
Church of England Young Men's Society 72
Churt 75, 76
Clifton College 79
A. Conan Doyle & Crowborough & District 120
Dr Conan Doyle's XI 76, 104, 119
Corinthians 37, 38
Cornwall 96
Coventry 100
Coventry & North Warwickshire 116
Cricket Golfers 109
Crowborough Crocks 136
Croydon 47, 53, 58
Crystal Palace 40, 58
Derbyshire 90, 95, 115
Devon 96, 100
Devon Dumplings 105
Devonshire Regiment 68, 71, 75
Dorking 79
Dorset Regiment 34, 37
Dorsetshire 92
Dublin University 27
Dulwich 1st team 52
Dulwich College 48, 49
Eashing 95
East Dulwich 45
East Gloucester 79
East Grinstead 119, 120
East Lyss 68
Eastbourne 70, 71, 72, 135
Eastbourne College 131
Eastbourne Town CC 72
Egypt 115, 120
S. Ellis' XI 48
Emeriti 48
Epsom 49, 52

Erratics 44, 48
Esher 103
Eton College 120, 128
Exeter 70
Exmouth 105
Fareham 29, 30, 31, 33, 37, 40
Farnham 79
Forest Hill 53
Free Foresters 40
Frensham Hill 108
Fulham 119
Fun of the Bristol 26
Gala 96
The Gentlemen of Holland (Netherlands) 58
Gentlemen of Marylebone Cricket Club 91, 95, 108
Gentlemen of Warwickshire 99
Godalming 69
Grange Club 91
Granville (Lee) 45, 49, 58
Grayshott 75, 79, 80, 99, 100, 109
Grecians 48, 53
Green Jackets 40
F.H. Gresson's XI 119, 127, 131, 136
Hampshire Colts 41
Hampshire Hogs 37, 80
Hampshire Regiment 24
Hampshire Rovers 34, 40, 48, 67, 68, 69, 71, 72, 75, 78, 80, 91, 92, 107, 108, 115
Hampshire XI 41
Hampstead 48, 115, 136
Harrow 120
Harrow Blues 136
Haslemere 68, 69, 75, 76, 80, 85, 108
Havant 37, 38
Haverford College 105
Hawick 104
Hawick and Wilton Cricket Club 103
Heron's Ghyll 120
Hertfordshire 85
Hindhead School 75
Honiton 71
J.R. Hope's XI 120
Hornsey 44
E.W. Hornung's XI 115
Hythe Hill 108, 109
I Zingari 135
The Idlers 49
In the Ranks Dramatic Company 34
Incogniti 40, 72, 78, 79, 80, 90, 91, 105, 108, 119
Instow 100
Kenley 54
Kensington 68
Kent 104
Lansdowne 90
Dr Law's XI 53
Leamington Spa 116
Leamington Town 100
Leicestershire 89

Leighton 71
Leinster Club 27
Lewes Priory 119, 128, 131, 135
Liphook 75
Liss 109
Littlehampton 68, 72, 128
London & Westminster Bank 52, 57
London County 85, 91, 95, 103
London Playing Fields 92, 116
F. Loud's XII 58
Lowestoft Visitors 58
Lynchmere 75, 95, 99
Lythe Hill 105, 109
Mcc & Ground 116
Madcaps 128
Majilton Gay City Company 29
Manx Cats 136
Marlborough Blues 103, 105
G.M. Maryon-Wilson's XI 134
Mayfield 136
MCC 40, 48, 58, 72, 79, 80, 85, 89, 90, 91, 92, 95, 96, 99, 100, 102, 103, 104, 105, 109, 115, 119, 120, 123, 127, 128, 136, 200
MCC & Ground 111, 119
Middlesex Hospital 119
Minor Counties 91
Mitcham 58, 78
The Mote 120
Mr Turle's Eleven 76
Norbury Park 44, 49
Norfolk County Asylum 58, 72, 92
North Devon 95, 100
North Warwickshire 100
Northbrook 58
Northchapel 76, 85
Norwood Club 44, 45, 47, 48, 49, 52, 53, 54, 57, 58
Oaklands Park 80
Oakleigh Wanderers 44
Oatlands Park 99
Ockley 32
Old Cholmelians 72
Old Eastbournians 120
Old Malvernians 69, 72
Old Yelvertonians 72
Ordnance Survey 24, 34
Ottery St Mary 67
Oxfordshire 92
Peripatetics 72
Petersfield 85
Petworth 75
Phoenix 27
Plaistow 48, 72
Portsmouth Borough 24, 26, 29, 30, 31, 33, 34, 36, 37, 38, 41
Portsmouth Cricket Club 25, 26, 27, 29, 31, 32, 36, 37, 39, 40
Portsmouth Grammar School 38
Portsmouth XI cricket 9
Press 69
Publishers 134, 136

Reigate Priory 72
Richmond 79
Roving Friars 49
Royal Academy of Arts 116, 119, 136
Royal Artillery 36, 72
Royal Artillery Devonport 67, 68, 70, 71, 75
Royal Artillery Gosport 33
Royal Artillery Hilsea 33
Royal Artillery Northern Division 29
Royal Artillery Southern Division 37
Royal Engineers 24, 34, 94
Royal Engineers (Chatham) 99
Royal Marine Artillery (RMA) 37, 91
Royal Military College (Sandhurst) 91, 119, 123
Royal Navy 37, 71, 91, 108, 116
Royal Sussex Regiment 30
Rugby Town 100
Ryde 34, 38
St John's College 119, 127
St Matthew's 71
Sarisbury 27, 30
R.W. Sealy's XI 95, 100
Selkirk 96
Sherborne School 79, 90
Shere 42, 51
Shobrooke 68
Shottermill 80
Sidmouth 96, 100
South Croydon 49
South Hampshire Rovers 24, 29, 34, 37, 38, 41
South Lancashire Regiment 34, 36, 40
South Lynn 71
South Norwood 45
South of Scotland 104
Southampton Cricket Club 37
Southsea Rivals 24, 26
Southsea Rovers 36, 37
Spencer 57
Standard Athletic Club (Paris) 128
Stonyhurst College 27
Stonyhurst Wanderers 27
The Sudan 115, 120
Surbiton 80
Surrey Club & Ground 44, 71
Surrey Colts 78
Sussex Martlets 120, 127, 128, 131, 134, 135
Sutton 49
Teignbridge 96, 100
Theatre Royal 26
Thirteen Local Clubs 70
Dr Thomson's XI 53
Thorpe Asylum 58
Tonbridge School 119
C.M. Tuke's XI 79
Tunbridge Wells 119
Undershaw 76, 95, 100, 108, 109
United Services 92, 100, 107, 108, 115

United Services Portsmouth 29, 30, 33, 37, 38, 40, 41, 48, 68, 75, 78, 80
Upper Tooting 120
Uppingham Rovers 72, 78
Victoria College (Jersey) 40
Warwickshire Gentlemen 116, 127
West Kent 136
Westminster School 41
W.G. Grace's team 91
Willesden 44, 45, 48
Wilts Regiment 108
Wiltshire 80, 85, 92, 108
Winchester 34, 41
Windsor Home Park 45
Wonford House 71
Ye Olde Carawan 34

cricket grounds
Addiscombe Ground 53
Adhurst St Mary (Hants) 34
Agar's Plough (Eton College) 128
Ardingly College Ground (Hayward's Heath) 119, 127, 131, 135
Bar End Cricket Ground 33
Beacon Hill 76
Beaumont College Ground (Old Windsor) 48
Bedford County School Ground 99
Belmont Grounds (Sidmouth) 100
Blundell's School (Tiverton) 71
Boscawen Park (Truro) 96
Brighton College Ground 119, 127
Bristol 79
Broadwater 108
Broadway (Worcestershire) 71, 75, 79
Buccleuch Park (Hawick) 104
Butts Gound (Coventry) 100
Catisfield (Fareham) 30, 31, 32, 34
The Cedars (Lee) 45
Charlton Park (Gloucester) 79
Cheam Road (Sutton) 49
Cheltenham College Ground 91
Chiswick Park (London) 79
Christ's Hospital Ground (Horsham) 119
Clifton College Close Ground 79
College Ground (Cheltenham) 79
College Park (Dublin) 27
Cotmandene (Dorking) 79
Crystal Palace Park 85
Dean Park (Bournemouth) 80
Denmark Hill 79
Devonport 68, 100
Dripping Pan (Lewes) 119, 128, 131
East Gloucester Cricket Club Ground 79
East Grinstead Sports Club Ground 119, 120
Eastbourne College Ground 131
Epsom Down 49
Exeter County Ground 70, 105
Fairfield Ground (Croydon) 48
Fareham 29
Frensham Hill (Farnham) 99, 108

Godalming 100
Golf Links Road (Westward Ho!) 95, 100
The Grange (Church Road, Crowborough) 127, 136
Grayshott 100
Grayshott Hall 75
Haslemere 108
Havant Park 37
Heron's Ghyll House 120
Hilsea Recreation Ground 24, 29, 33, 34, 37, 38, 40, 68, 69, 80
Hove County Ground 136
Hurstpierpoint College Ground 119, 127
J.W. Hobbs Ground (Norbury) 48
Kelly College Ground (Tavistock) 96, 100
Laleham County Ground 92
Lansdowne Cricket Club (Coombe Park, Bath) 90
Leamington Cricket Club Grounds 100, 116
Leighton (Wiltshire) 71
Littlehampton Sportsfield 68, 72, 128
Lord's 69, 75, 80, 85, 89, 91, 92, 94, 95, 99, 105, 108, 109, 115, 116, 119, 120, 134, 136
Lymington Road (Hampstead) 48
Lynchmere Cricket Ground 99, 105, 108
Lythe Hill Park 68, 75, 85, 108, 109
Maer Ground (Exmouth) 105
Melbourne Cricket Ground (Australia) 166
Merchant Taylors' Ground (Northwood) 48, 58
Mossilee (Galashiels) 104
Mote Park (Maidstone) 120
Nevill Ground (Tunbridge Wells) 119, 120, 136, 138, 139
New Road (Esher) 91, 95, 99, 103, 104, 107, 115
Norfolk County Asylum 72
North End (Portsmouth) 24
Northbrook 45
Norwood Pavilion Ground (Norwood Green) 44, 45, 47, 48, 49, 52, 53, 54, 57, 58
Oatlands Park Cricket Club Ground (Weybridge) 80, 99
Observatory Lane, Rathmines (Dublin) 27
Officers Club Services Ground (Aldershot) 78
Officers' Recreation Ground (Portsmouth) 91, 108
Oval 78
Philiphaugh (Selkirk) 104
Phoenix Cricket Club Ground, Phoenix Park (Dublin) 27
Quarr Hill, Ryde (IoW) 34, 38
Recreation Ground (Portsmouth) 67
Rectory Field (Blackheath) 79
Richmond 67
Royal Marines Ground (Eastney, Southsea) 91
Royal Military Academy Ground (Camberley) 91, 111, 123
Royal Military College Ground (Camberley) 119
Rugby Town Club Ground 100
Saffrons (Eastbourne) 71, 72
The Saffrons (Eastbourne) 135
St Cross (Winchester) 40
St George's (Portsmouth) 24
St Quintin's Park (Kensington) 90
Salston Field (Ottery St Mary) 67
Sandhills (Instow) 100
Sandilands (Croydon) 45, 48
Searles (Fletching) 134

Sherborne School (Dorset) 79
Shobrooke Park 68
Southampton County Cricket Ground 24, 34, 37, 41, 80
Stoke 116
Stonyhurst College Ground, Clitheroe (Lancashire) 27
Surbiton 80
Sydney Cricket Ground (Australia) 168
Teignbridge 96, 100
Thorpe Asylum Ground, St Andrew's (Norfolk) 53, 58
Toleys Cricket Ground (Willesden) 45
Tonbridge School Ground 119
Topsham Barracks (Exeter) 71, 72, 75
Trowbridge Cricket Club Ground 80
Tunbridge Wells 127, 128, 135
Turney Road (Dulwich) 49
United Services Recreation (Men's) Ground (Portsmouth) 29, 30, 33, 34, 36, 37, 38, 40, 48, 68, 71, 75, 78, 92, 107, 115
Uppingham School 78
Victoria College Ground, St Helier (Jersey) 40
Vincent Square (Westminster) 41
Warwick Cricket Club Ground 99, 116
Wellbrook Ground (Mayfield) 136
West Hoathly 120
Winchester College Ground 41
Windsor Park 45
Wolfe Recreation Ground (Crowborough) 41
Wonford House (Exeter) 71
cricket tours abroad
  Holland 45, 46
  Jersey C.I. 40
Cricketers' National War Fund 97
Crighton Royal Institution (Dumfries) 46, 48, 54
The Crime of the Brigadier (1899) 81, 82
The Crime of the Congo (1909) 121, 124
Crimes Club *see* Our Society (Crimes Club)
Crippen, Dr Hawley Harvey 129
Critics and Criticism. Two Types of Reviews (1892) 50
Cromarsh, H. Ripley (pen name of ACD's sister 'Dodo') 99, 110, 113, 114
Cromer, Lady 66
Cromer, Lord 66, 125
Crosse, Dr 107
Crossman, Sir William 29
Crowborough 153
  All Saints Church 122, 130, 138
  Badminton Hall (Croft Road) 154
  Beacon Court 137
  Beacon Gardens 155
  Blackness 187
  Blue Anchor (Beacon Road) 212
  Bricklayers Arms 120
  Cemetery 150
  Christ Church Schoolroom 124
  Christ Church Schools 154
  Church Hall Room 138
  Constitutional Club 192
  Crest Hotel 124
  Croft Road Lecture Hall 126, 150

    Ex-Service Men's Club (Eridge Road) 177, 179, 184, 186, 190, 191, 196
    Forest Fold Baptist Chapel 212
    The Grange (Church Road) 193
    Gymnasium Club 129
    The Lodge 113
    Mark Cross Court 193, 201
    Mockett's Café 189
    Monkstown house 112, 113, 114, 116, 142, 213
    Moorside Dormy House 193
    Oddfellows Hall 126, 135, 137, 146, 157, 160
    Parish Church (Jarvis Brook) 214
    Parish Hall 177
    Picture Palace (Croft Road) 189
    Quarry Hill Farm (Lock's Farm, Fey House) (Hurtis Hill) 135, 141
    Railway Hotel (Jarvis Brook) 209
    Rookwood (Southview) 131
    Salvation Hall (Whitehill) 119
    Treblers Farm (Jarvis Brook) 137
    Walsh Manor (VAD Hospital) 156
    Waterloo Hall/Hut 192, 196
    Wesleyan Chapel 117
    Westminster Bank 217
    Windlesham Cottage 121, 154
    Windlesham (Hurtis Hill) 117, 118, 119, 120, 121, 124, 126, 129, 130, 133, 134, 135, 136, 137, 138, 139, 140, 141, 145, 147–64, 171, 172, 177, 183, 185, 186, 187, 188, 190, 192, 194, 195, 196, 200, 201, 204, 209–13, 216, 217, 218, 219
    Yew Trees (Southview Road) 147
    YMCA Recreation Hut 149, 150, 153, 154
Crowborough & District Billiard League 191, 192
Crowborough Camp (Canadian Soldiers) 154
Crowborough Cottage Hospital 193
Crowborough and District Cricket League 209
Crowborough and District War Memorial Fund 160
The Crowborough Edition (1930) 204
Crowborough Literary Association 126
Crowborough Literary Society 121
Crowborough P.S.A. 129
Crowborough Rifle Club 118, 120
Crowborough Silver Prize Band 126
Crowborough Volunteer Training Corps 150
Crowborough Weekly 138
The Crown Diamond. An Evening with Sherlock Holmes (play, 1921) 171, 172, 183, 217
The Croxley Master (1899) 80, 114
Croydon
    Adul School (Park Lane) 164
    Aerodrome 187
Crystal Palace Bowling Club 27
Crystal Palace Tavern, Fratton (Hants) 27
Curnow, Leslie 191
Current Literature 92, 135
The Curse of Eve (read at mtg of Authors' Club) 50, 56
Curtin, Mr 154
Cushman, Dr 175
Cycle Notes: Dr Conan Doyle on Cycling (1896) 66
Cyprian Overbeck Wells. A Literary Mosaic (1886) 31
Czar's Proposition 77

Dagmar, Empress of Russia 133
Daily Chronicle 49, 146, 147, 150, 151, 152, 154, 158
Daily Express 116, 117, 120, 124, 138, 139, 159, 184, 188, 194, 197
Daily Mail 120, 141
Daily Mirror 155, 174, 178
Daily News 81, 83
Daily News Weekly 79
Daily Telegraph 83, 113, 135, 173
Dalton, Dr 56
Danger! And Other Stories (1918) 159
Danger! Being the Log of Captain John Sirius (1914) 142, 145
Danish Club 221
Dante (play by Sardou) 98
Darling of the Gods (play by David Belasco) 104
Darlington 160
Dartmoor 20, 21, 88, 90
Das Gupta, K.N. 195
Daughter, J.S. 174
Davidson, Jo 204
Davies (friend) 22
Davos
  Curhaus Hotel 55
  Grand Hôtel and Pensione Belvedere 54, 55, 56, 57, 62–3
  Hotel Boul 63
  Hotel Victoria 63
  Kurhaus Hotel 55, 56
  Literary Scientific Society 61
Dawson, Charles 134
A Day with Dr Conan Doyle (interview, 1892) 49
A Day on the Island (1884) 24
Daylight Savings Bill 119, 122
Days with the Army (1900) 85
De Profundis (1892) 47
'Death and the Hereafter' (lecture, 1918) 158, 159, 160, 161, 162, 163, 164, 165, 166, 167, 169, 171, 178
The Death Voyage: The Kaiser and His Fleet (1929) 201
The Début of Bimbashi Joyce (1900) 82
'Deeds of Gallantry. Sir Arthur Conan Doyle and the Press Censor' (speech, 1914) 147
Delmonte Hotel (Delmonte) 162
Demorest's Family Magazine 63
Denmark 142, 146, 202
Dennis Company (Guildford) 105
Denver 179
  Brown Palace Hotel 180
  Orpheum Theatre 180
Detroit 56, 59, 142, 174
  Detroit Church of Our Father 60
  Russell House Hotel 60
The Devil's Doctrine (1914) 146
Devonshire, Duke of 153
Dewsbury National Spiritualist Church 185
Dharmapala, Anagarika 195
Dickens, Charles 102, 130
Dicks, John (publisher) 58
Dieppe 151
Disabled Officers' Garden Homes 212
The Disappearance of Lady Frances Carfax (1911) 134, 173

A Discord. Being a Break In a Duet (1909) 123
The Disintegration Machine (1929) 198
Divonne 94
Divorce Law Reform: An Essay 121
Divorce Law Reform Movement 110, 141, 155, 158
Divorce Law Reform. Sir Arthur Conan Doyle in Reply (1913) 140
Divorce Law Reform Union 121, 128, 131, 135, 155
Divorce. Reform of the Law Needed (1913) 140
Doble, Mr 143
The Doctors of Hoyland (1894) 57
'Does Death End All?' (spiritualist lecture) 14, 18
The Doings of Raffles Haw (1891) 42, 44, 45, 46, 47
Donaghadee (Co. Down) 187
Doncaster 160
Donnington 214
Dorset 57, 123, 151
Doubleday, Doran & Company Inc 204
Douglas, James 172
Dover (Kent), Grand Hotel 109
Downes, Mrs M.T. 181
Doyle, Adelaide 3, 4
Doyle, Adrian Malcolm Conan (ACD's son) 126, 129, 130, 131, 151, 156, 165, 166, 174, 175, 179, 183, 191, 193, 197, 198, 199, 201, 204, 205, 209, 210, 213–18, 220, 222, 224
Doyle, Angela Firmstone-Williams 221, 222, 223
Doyle, Ann Martha (or Annette) (later Sister Ignatius Aloysius) (ACD's aunt) 2, 7, 9, 12, 19, 81
Doyle, Ann Mary Frances 'Annette' or 'Nan' or 'Tottie' (ACD's sister) 5, 6, 22, 24, 30, 32, 35, 39
Doyle, Ann Ruml 219, 220, 221
Doyle, Anna Charlotte Andersen 126, 214, 215, 216, 218, 224
Doyle, Anna Maria 1, 7
Doyle, (Arthur Alleyne) Kingsley Conan (ACD's son) 50, 53, 56, 62, 67, 73, 88, 97, 98, 103, 110, 111, 112, 116, 118, 122, 123, 125, 126, 128, 129, 134, 135, 137, 141, 142, 146, 148, 151, 152, 153, 155, 158
Doyle, Arthur Ignatius Conan
  birth 5
  accepts Honorary Presidency of the Executive of the Federation International des Spiritistes of Paris 184
  accused of plagiarism 142
  active on Olympic Games committee 138
  agrees to stand as Unionist candidate 3
  applies for Reader's ticket at British Museum Reading Room 43
  appointed Cavaliere of the Crown of Italy 74
  appointed Honorary President of County Guild of Spiritualism for Sussex 175
  appointed medical examiner for Gresham Life Assurance Society 21
  appointed Vice-President of PLPS 190
  arrested/released in Bloemfontein 84
  attends classes at Royal Botanic Garden, Edinburgh 11–12
  attends fancy dress ball 63
  attends Suffragette trial 139
  attends/gives talks at meetings of PLSS 21, 22, 23, 24, 25, 26, 28, 29, 30, 31, 32, 33, 36, 37, 39, 40
  auction of effects from Windlesham 217
  awarded MD from University of Edinburgh 26
  becomes doctor's assistant in Sheffield & Birmingham 12, 13, 18
  becomes surgeon's clerk to Dr Bell 13
  buys a motor car 98
  buys property in Fort William, Canada 144

cameo performance in the film *Our Mutual Girl* 144
campaigns for channel tunnel 138
campaigns for use of body armour for the troops 152
caught speeding 107, 108, 109
co-edits school journal 9
confirmed 8
contributes to funds for Eastbourne spiritualist society 152
conversion to Irish Home Rule 47
court order in respect of dogs worrying sheep 193
created Knight of Grace 98
death of Touie 112
decides to sell his coin collection 139
declares his belief in spiritualism 150, 153
draws up his will 122, 204
edits journal at Jesuit school in Austria 10
education 7–10
elected captain of Portsmouth Cricket Club 32, 33
elected joint secretary of the PLSS 30
elected joint vice-president of the Hampshire Psychical Society 34, 38
elected President of Ex-Service Men's Club, Crowborough 191, 196
elected President of PLSS 47
elected President of UNLSS 48
elected Vice-President of the Crowborough & District Billiards League 192
elected Vice-President of PLPS 204
engagement and marriage to Jean Leckie 116, 117
entertains Boy Scouts 138, 189, 191
exhumation and reinterrment of remains 219
experiments with gelseminum (yellow jasmine) 13
farewell dinner in Southsea 42
filmed at Windlesham (1927 & 1928) 193, 197
finds Iguanodon fossil 134
first Englishman to cross Maienfelder Furka Pass 57
foreman at inquest in Crowborough 137
forms Home Guard unit 146
gives up medicine to become full-time writer 44, 45
goes sledging 63
has accident autowheeling to Brighton 138
health of 23, 44, 45, 56, 63, 94, 106, 114, 115, 121–2, 137, 146, 148, 199, 202, 203, 204, 205
holidays 7, 12, 19, 24, 35, 36, 40, 42–3, 47, 48, 49, 51, 53, 54, 55, 56–7, 64–7, 78, 87, 88–9, 94, 98, 112, 117, 123, 124, 126, 139–40, 143–5, 154, 194
initiated as a Freemason 31, 88
interest in spiritualism, paranormal, telepathy and fairies 12, 14, 25, 28, 31, 32, 51, 55, 57, 153–205, 164
interviews with 194, 196, 197
investigates cure for tuberculosis claim 40, 41
joins Beckenham Golf Club 51
joins the Langman Field Hospital in South Africa 82–4
joins the Reform Club 45, 48
joins the SPR 51
joins the WPB 146
lecture tour of Australia & New Zealand 165–70
lecture tour of Scandinavia and Holland 201–3
lecture tour of South Africa 197–200
lecture tours of USA & Canada 59–62, 174–6, 179–82
makes out his will 81, 122
marries Touie 27
memorial plaques 211, 218, 219, 225

memorial service for 209
motor accident 106
moves to London 43
nicknamed 'the great northern diver' after falling into the sea 15
oak grave marker erected 210
offered Honorary Degree of D.D. from Edinburgh 106
opposes building of Isolation Hospital in Crowborough 164
Paget's portrait of 73
papers stored at Westminster Bank, Crowborough 217
plays bandy (form of ice hockey) 63
plays billiards 14, 63, 84, 130, 135, 137, 138, 142, 153, 178, 179, 183, 192, 196
plays bowls 26, 29
plays cricket 9, 13, 19, 24, 26, 27, 29–34, 36–8, 40–2, 44–5, 47, 48–9, 51, 52, 58, 67–9, 70–2, 75–6, 78–80, 85, 89–92, 94–5, 99–100, 104–5, 107–9, 111, 115–16, 119–20, 127–8, 131, 134, 135–6
plays golf 61, 62, 101, 112, 113, 122, 123, 127, 129, 130, 131, 142, 184
plays, watches, umpires football 14, 25, 27–32, 33, 35, 36, 38–9, 41, 84
plays/watches baseball 143, 144
political interests 24, 32, 33, 37, 40, 101, 110
presented with dinner service 27
presides over AGM of PAFC 41
probate granted on his will 210
proposed as Rector of St Andrews University 186
proposes the toast 'The Immortal Memory' 88
receives a knighthood 94, 95, 96
receives LL.D from Edinburgh University 107
rejected to fight in Boer War 81
renounces the Catholic faith 20
resigns as chairman of UNLSS 57
resigns as Deputy Lieutenant of Surrey 173
resigns from Freemason Phoenix Lodge 35
resigns from SPR 204
resigns as President of London Spiritualist Alliance 205
selected as member of the MCC 79
share investments 38, 44, 46, 61, 124, 148
ship's doctor on SS *Mayumba* 20
student at University of Edinburgh Medical School 11, 13
subscriptions/donations 58, 137, 139, 142, 150, 154, 156, 157, 158, 159, 160, 162, 166, 176, 191, 192, 194
suggests use of inflatable rubber boats for the navy 147
surgeon on board whaling ship 14–18
takes an excursion in a bi-plane 131
takes an excursion in a hot air balloon 91, 93
takes and passes his exams 19
takes up boxing 15, 16, 135, 140, 149, 150
takes up hunting 73
takes up shooting 153
takes up skiing 49, 57, 63
talks, lectures, speeches 22, 23, 28, 32, 33, 35, 36, 50–5, 57, 59, 61, 62, 70, 71, 73, 77, 80, 81, 102, 110, 112, 115, 124, 127–30, 134–8, 141, 143, 145–75, 177–92, 194–5
visits front lines in France 151, 153, 154, 158
visits relatives in London 9
voted on to Council of PLSS 24
as war correspondent 66
watches baseball 175, 182
watches cricket matches in Australia 167, 168
watches rugby match at Colombes 171

    watches Volunteer Review 24
    witnesses a séance 159
    writes first story 6
    death and burial 205
Doyle, Bryan Mary Julia Josephine 'Dodo' (ACD's sister) *see* Angell, Bryan
Doyle, Caroline Mary Burton 'Lottie' (ACD's sister) *see* Oldham, Caroline
Doyle, Catherine 1, 2
Doyle, Catherine Amelia Angela (ACD's sister) 5
Doyle, Catherine 'Kate' Agnes Mullin Foley (ACD's aunt) 3, 4, 8, 100, 135
Doyle, Catherine Ruml 198
Doyle, Catherine Tynan (ACD's great-grandmother) 1
Doyle, Charles Altamont (ACD's father) 3, 4, 5, 6, 7, 8, 9, 10, 13, 15, 20, 26, 28, 33, 42, 43, 46, 48, 54, 100, 183
Doyle, Ida Claudia Clara Schwensen (ACD's daughter-in-law) 18, 130, 134, 139, 142, 146, 147, 151, 154, 155, 156, 159, 209, 224
Doyle, Constance Amelia Monica 'Connie' (ACD's sister) *see* Hornung, Constance Amelia Monica 'Connie' Doyle
Doyle, Denis Percy Stewart (ACD's son) 87, 122, 131, 156, 165, 166, 167, 174, 175, 179, 183, 191, 197, 199, 201, 204, 205, 209–13, 215, 216, 219, 220
Doyle, Francis 'Frank' 2, 3
Doyle, Francis Kingsley (ACD's grandson) 155, 205, 215, 216
Doyle, Henry Edward (ACD's uncle) 2, 6, 12, 19, 47, 192, 193
Doyle, James 1
Doyle, James (ACD's great-grandfather) 1, 4
Doyle, James Edmund William (ACD's uncle) 2, 9, 12, 19, 50
Doyle, Jane Adelaide Rose 'Ida' (ACD's sister) *see* Foley, Jane
Doyle, Jane Henrietta Hawkins (ACD's aunt) 3, 9, 12, 19, 188
Doyle, Jane Isabella Ball (ACD's aunt) 2, 6, 12, 107
Doyle, Jean Leckie (ACD's 2nd wife) 9, 19, 43, 67, 70, 71, 72, 73, 77, 85, 88, 91, 92, 94, 96, 103, 108, 113, 114, 115, 116, 117, 125, 126, 127, 128, 129, 130, 131, 132, 137, 138, 139, 142-5, 147, 148, 152, 154, 156, 159, 162, 163, 165, 168, 169, 171, 174–5, 176, 177, 178, 179, 180, 183, 185, 186, 187, 190, 191, 195, 197, 199–203, 205, 209–13, 214, 215, 216, 219
Doyle, Jean Lena Annette Conan 'Billie' (ACD's daughter) 137, 138, 156, 166, 174, 175, 183, 185, 191, 197, 199, 205, 209–25
Doyle, John Francis Innes Hay (ACD's brother) 8, 18, 19, 21, 23, 27, 39, 41, 43, 49, 51, 59, 61, 62, 66–73, 75–8, 87, 93, 96, 103, 104, 106, 112, 113, 115 21, 123, 125, 127, 128, 130, 133, 134, 139, 141, 142, 146, 148–51, 153–5, 156, 159, 160, 224
Doyle, John (pen-name 'H.B.') (ACD's grandfather) 1, 4, 7, 192, 193
Doyle, John Reinhold Innes (ACD's grandson) 139, 146, 151, 154, 205, 214, 215, 219, 220, 221, 222, 223, 224
Doyle, Louise/a 'Touie' Hawkins (ACD's 1st wife) 2, 4, 5, 6, 24–7, 31, 32, 35, 37, 42, 43, 50, 51, 53–8, 62, 63, 65–7, 72, 73, 77, 79, 82, 88, 92, 95, 96, 104–7, 111, 112, 114
Doyle, Marianne/a (or Mary Ann) Conan (ACD's grandmother) 1, 2, 3
Doyle, Mary Helena Monica Henrietta (or Harriet) (ACD's sister) 6
Doyle, Mary Josephine Elizabeth Foley (ACD's mother) 3, 4, 5, 6, 7, 8, 9, 13, 15, 19, 21, 22, 23, 27, 28, 39, 43, 50, 66, 73, 75, 78, 81, 88, 96, 105, 115, 153, 154, 156, 169, 171
Doyle, Mary Louise Conan 'Toots' (ACD's daughter) 36, 37, 39, 40, 43, 53, 54, 56, 62, 67, 70, 73, 77, 88, 93, 104, 107, 111, 113, 115–18, 121–3, 125, 126, 128, 129, 158, 162, 164, 170, 176, 177, 183, 186, 189, 190, 194, 205, 209, 215, 219, 222, 223
Doyle, Michael 1, 4
Doyle, Princess Nina Mdivani *see* Harwood, Nina Mdivani
Doyle, Richard 'Dickie' 2, 9, 12, 23
Doyle, Richard John Francis 220, 222
Doyle, William 1
Dr Barnardo's Homes 121
Dr Conan Doyle on Cycling (1896) 69
'Dr Conan Doyle and the Freemasons' (talk, 1901) 88

Dr Koch and His Cure (1890) 39
Drayson, General Alfred 22, 25, 36, 39, 40
Dreamland and Ghostland (anon, 1887) 32
Dresden 117, 118, 122, 128
Drew, John 142
Driver, L. 77
Drummond, Jessie 24
Dry Plates on a Wet Moor (1882) 21
Du Maurier, George 25
Dublin 27, 214
   St Andrew's Church 2
Dublin Daily Express 150
The Duello in France (1890) 39
A Duet (1899) 78, 96, 97
Dunbar, Roxburgh Hotel 112
Dundee
   Gilfillan Memorial Hall 162
   Kinnaird Hall 55
   Mount Roas, Seafield Road (Broughty Ferry) 55
Durban Marine Hotel 198
Durham, The Deanery 163
Dutch Treat Club 179
Dysart, Earl of 145

Earlam, J. 191
'The Early Christian Church and Spiritualism' (lecture, 1925) 188
Early Psychic Experiences (1924) 184
East Knowe, Brodick (Isle of Arran) 12
East Sussex County Council 164
Eastbourne 26, 149, 152, 152–3
   Claremont Hotel (Grand Parade) 71, 72
   Devonshire Park 149
   Grand Parade 147
   Holywell (Cliff Road) 209
   Mostyn Terrace 172
   St John's Church 156
   Town Hall 161
Easter Island 36
Easter Monday with the Camera (1884) 24
Easter Rising (Dublin, 1916) 152
Eclipse (whaler) 15, 17, 18
'The Edalji Case' (talk, 1907) 115
Edalji, George 101, 113, 114, 115, 116, 117, 140, 219
The Eddy Brothers and the Holmeses (1925) 187
Edgar Allan Poe Centenary Dinner (1909) 122
Edgar Allan Poe monument (Baltimore) 60
The Edge of the Unknown (1930) 205
Edgley, Mr 199
Edinburgh 10, 18, 47, 81, 88, 105, 122, 132, 133
   Abercromby Place 4
   Argyle Park Terrace 9, 11
   Balmoral Hotel 88, 107
   Clyde Street 4
   Constitutional Club 106
   Edinburgh Philosophical Institute (Queen Street Hall) 55
   George Square 12, 19
   Liberton Bank House 6

    Lonsdale Terrace 15, 19
    Nelson Street 4, 5
    Newington Academy (Salisbury Place) 7
    Nicholson Street 4
    North British Station Hotel 102
    Old Waverly Temperance Hotel 112
    Palace Theatre 93
    Picardy Place 5, 6, 218, 222
    Royal Botanic Garden 11
    Royal Edinburgh Asylum/Hospital (Morningside) 42, 46, 48
    Royal Infirmary 13
    St Andrew Square 3
    St Andrew's Hall 174
    St John Street 101
    St Mary's Roman Catholic Cathedral 4, 5, 6, 11
    Sciennes Hill Place 4, 7
    Scotland Street 4
    Scottish Court of Criminal Appeal 196
    Scottish Psychical Society (Stafford Street) 196
    Synod Hall 102, 125
    Tower Bank (Portobello) 6
    Usher Hall 148, 160, 173, 174
    Waverley Market 97
    Wilson's Park (Portobello) 6
Edinburgh Burns Club 88
Edinburgh, Leith and Granton Lifeboat Fund 93
Edinburgh Unionists 85
Edinburgh University 10, 26, 96, 97, 101, 106, 107, 128
Edinburgh University Club 54
Edinburgh University Medical School 8, 11, 19
Edmonton 142, 143, 179
    Allen Theatre 182
    King Edward Hotel 143
Edward Irving and the Voices (1924) 185
Edward VII 93, 95, 96, 104, 115, 119, 151, 156
Egypt 62, 65
    Assiout 66
    Assouan Hotel 67
    Aswan 66, 67
    Dendour 66
    Korosko 66, 67
    Luxor 66
    Mena House Hotel (Cairo) 65, 66
    Natron Lake 66
    Wadi Halfa 66, 67
Eira (whaler) 17
Ekman, Gösta 203
Elbe (steamship) 59
Elektra (opera, Richard Strauss) 129
Eliot, Revd Maurice 216
Elizabeth II 221
Ellen Terry Jubilee 111
Elliot, Dr Henry Francis 13
Ellis, Dr Erasmus 199
Ellis, John 129, 152
Elsinore (Sjælland) 134
Elwell, J.B. 186

Elworthy, Lord 225
Emery Down, New Forest (Hants) 36, 40
The End of Devil Hawker (1930) 209
Ends of the Earth Club (New York) 103
The Engineer's Thumb 45, 47
English-Holland Society 202
The Episodes of Marge: Memoirs of a Humble Adventuress ('H. Ripley Cromarsh' ACD's sister) 99
Erben, Rear-Admiral Henry 57
Erik (whaler) 14
Ernst, Bernard 164
Esher, Lord 126
An Essay upon the Vasomotor Changes of Tabes Dorsalis (ACD's MD thesis) (1885) 26
'The Etheric Body' (lecture, 1927) 194
Eton College 110, 112, 125
Evans, Air Chief Marshall Sir Donald 223
Evans, Commander Edward 'Teddy' 140
Evanson, W.A.D. 129
Evens, H. 138
Evens, J.T. 192
The Evidence for Fairies (1921) 170
An Exciting Christmas Eve; or My Lecture on Dynamite (1883) 23
Exeter 70, 96
   Hippodrome 165
   Victoria Hall 148
Exmouth, Imperial Hotel 194
'Exploits of the Anzacs' (speech, 1919) 159
The Exploits of Brigadier Gerard (1895) 63, 66
'Exposition of Unionist Principles' (speech, 1906) 110

Fairbanks, Douglas 179, 181
Fairies Photographed - An Epoch-Making Event (1920) 168
Fake Spiritualism Exposed (film, 1926) 192
The Fall of Lord Barrymore (1912) 137, 178
A False Start (1891) 46
Family Magazine 62
Fareham 25, 27, 28, 29, 30, 31, 32, 33, 34, 35, 37, 38, 40
'Farmers and the Red Cross' (speech, 1917) 154
Farnham Herald 171
The Fate of the Evangeline (1885) 28
The Favourite Quotation (1894) 59
Fawcett, Colonel Percy 130
Federation International des Spiritistes of Paris 184
Feldkirchian Gazette 10
Fenger, Dean 134
Fenstanton 204
Ferguson, G.H. 210
Fernando Po 20
Ferrari 500 TRC (racing car) 220
Festival of Britain (1951) 218
Festival of Empire (Crystal Palace) (1911) 131
A Few Technical Hints (1882) 21
Fiat Convertible 215
'Fiction as Part of Literature' (talk, 1893) 53
Fidgeon, C.E. 116
The Field Bazaar (1896) 69, 212
Field, Susan Frances *see* Conan, Susan Frances Field

Fielding, Henry 111, 112
The Fiend of the Cooperage (1897) 72
Financial News 102
The Fires of Fate (play, 1909) 123, 124, 125, 178
The Firm of Girdlestone. A Romance for the Unromantic (1885) 23, 26, 28, 38, 39
Firmstone-Williams, Angela *see* Doyle, Angela Firmstone-Williams
First Developments in America (1925) 186
A First Impression (1900) 83
First National Pictures (film company) 186
First World War 146, 151, 158
   Battle of the Somme 152
   Mons 146
   Ypres 149
The Fiscal Question (Tariff Reform) (1905) 107
The Five Orange Pips (1891) 44, 45, 46
The Flag 118
Fleming, B.H. 145
Fleming, Major 141
Fletcher, Bertram 85
Florence 65, 94, 177
Foley, Barbara 198, 212
Foley, Catherine 'Kate' Agnes Mullin (ACD's aunt) *see* Doyle, Catherine 'Kate'
Foley, Catherine Pack 1, 3, 4, 6
Foley, Charles 219
Foley, Claire 87, 92, 112
Foley, Innes Cliffe 'Pabby' 97, 156, 215, 219, 223
Foley, Jane Adelaide Rose 'Ida' Doyle (ACD's sister) 9, 19, 23, 54, 57, 62, 66, 71, 73, 74, 76, 82, 92, 94, 97, 104, 109, 114, 121, 133, 156, 205, 215, 223
Foley, Mary Josephine *see* Doyle, Mary Josephine Elizabeth Foley
Foley, Nelson 4, 62, 66, 71, 73, 74, 76, 82, 94, 97, 104, 114, 121, 215, 223
Foley, Percy Fitzgerald (Michael) 76, 92, 153, 198, 205, 212, 223
Foley, Peter 212
Foley, Robert 198
Foley, Ruth 219
Foley, William 'Bill' 1, 3, 217
Folkestone 153
   Hotel Metropole 150
   Nursing Home 205
   Royal Pavilion Hotel 148, 205
Football Association 140
football clubs/teams
   2/1 Welsh Division RA 30
   Albion Athletic 38
   Argyll & Sutherland Highlanders 27
   Blandford 30
   Chichester 25, 28, 32
   Collingwood (Australia) 166
   Cowes 25, 28
   Fareham 25, 28, 30, 35, 38
   Freemantle 31, 39
   Geneva Cross 39, 41
   Havant 25, 27, 28
   Hayling Island 25, 29
   Hilsea Artillery Ramblers 27, 28, 32, 33
   Hindhead 98
   HMS *Marlborough* 29, 31
   Horndean 28

    Imperial Yeomanry Field Hospital 84
    King's Royal Rifles 35
    Langman Hospital 84
    Midhurst 28
    Petersfield 29, 30, 31
    Portsmouth 98
    Portsmouth Association Football Club (PAFC) 25, 26, 27–33, 35, 36, 38, 39, 41
    Portsmouth Grammar School 29, 30, 31, 36, 39
    Post Office Portsmouth 38
    Richmond (Australia) 166
    Royal Engineers (Aldershot) 36, 39
    Royal Engineers (Chatham) 34
    Royal Irish Rifles 30, 31
    Royal Marines Light Infantry (RMLI) 28
    Royal Scots Greys 32
    South Norwood 45
    South Yorkshire Regiment 35
    Southsea 25
    Stubbington House (Lodge) School 28, 38
    Sunflowers 25, 28, 32
    Undershaw Football Club 73
    United Services Men's Garrison 30, 31, 34, 35
    Wimbourne 28
    Winchester 35
    Woolston Works 30, 31, 33
    2nd Worcestershire Regiment 28, 30
    YMCA 36
football cups
    Hampshire Association Junior Cup 41
    Hampshire Senior Cup 30, 33, 35, 36, 39
    Minor Cup 38, 102
    Portsmouth & District Challenge Cup 31
    Portsmouth Association Challenge Cup 39
    Portsmouth Senior Cup 30, 32, 33, 35
football grounds
    Aldershot 35
    County Ground Southampton 36
    East Hants Ground 25
    Forton 28
    Garrison Barracks Ground 28, 30, 31
    Governor's Green (Portsmouth) 38
    Hilsea Recreation Ground 30, 33, 39, 41
    Melbourne Ground (Australia) 166
    North End (Portsmouth) 25, 27, 28, 29, 36
    United Services Recreation Ground (Officer's and Men's) (Portsmouth) 29, 31, 32, 33, 34, 35, 36, 38
Forbes, Alex 'Alec' 149, 152
Forbes Arms, Alford (Aberdeenshire) 47
Forbes, J.B. 205
Forbes, Patrick Leckie 191, 214
Forbes, P.F. 151
Forbes, Sarah Mildred 191, 209
The Forbidden Subject (1923) 182
Ford, Dr Vernon 36, 40, 68, 72, 74, 77
Ford, Mrs Vernon 74, 77
Fordoun House (Scotland) 13, 20
A Foreign Office Romance (1894) 60, 62

Foreign Policy (play, 1893) 52
'A Forgotten Tale' (poem, 1895) 62
A Form Letter (1918) 158, 204
Forrester, Harding 199
Forster, R. Collingwood 111
Fort Ticonderoga 143
Forthunay, Paul 201
The Fortnightly Review 137, 193, 195
Foster, Governor General 167
Foster, Lady 167
Fox sisters (Margaret, Kate, Leah) 194
France, Anatole 141
'France as a Holiday Ground' (speech, 1912) 137
France's-day organisation 149
Franco-British Society 221
Franco-British Travel Union 137
Frank Leslie's Popular Monthly 85
'The Franklin's Maid' (poem, 1891) 44
Frazer Nash racing car *see* 'The Slug'
Freemasons
  Lodge Canongate Kilwinning (No.2) Edinburgh 101, 106
  Phoenix Lodge No. 257 (Southsea) 31, 35, 93, 130
  Rising Star Lodge No.1022 (Bloemfontein) 83
  St Mary's Chapel (No.I) (Edinburgh) 88
Freetown (Sierra Leone) 20
French, Constance Emily 179
French Navy 109
French Red Cross 149
French, Sir John 150
The Friend 83
Frinton-on-Sea (Essex), Tudor Lodge (Bagland Road) 139–40
Frohman, Charles 74
From Assouan to Korosko. Letters from Egypt (1896) 67
From Cairo to Akasheh. Letters from Egypt (1896) 67
The Frontier Line (poem, 1892) 47
Fry, C.B. 101, 106
Fry, Sidney H. 163
A Full Report of a Lecture on Spiritualism (1919) 161
Fullerton, Miss 12
'The Future of Canadian Literature' (speech, 1914) 143
'The Future of Life' (lecture, 1926) 191

'G' Company (Cinque Ports) Royal Sussex 135, 137, 141
Gaiola (Gulf of Gaeta) 73, 74, 82, 94, 104
Galashiels 3, 102, 107
  Gala House 105
  Gala Park 109
  Masonic Hall 106
  Town Hall 106, 109
  Volunteer Hall 110
Galsworthy, John 146, 186
The Gamut of Humour (1892) 46
Gardner, E.L. 172
Gas and Water Review 30
Gateshead Town Hall 160
A Gaudy Death (1900) 87
Gay and Hancock Ltd (publishers) 155

Gazette 173
Gelseminium as Prism (article, 1878) 13
Geneva 219, 220, 224
'The Genius of George Meredith' (lectures: 1888, 1892, 1893) 35, 50, 52, 53
Genoa 73, 215
Gentlemanly Joe (1883) 22
The Gentlewoman 46
Gentlewoman's Industrial Guild 118
George H. Doran Company, New York (publishers) 147
'George Meredith, Novelist and Poet' (talk, 1893) 55
George Newnes Ltd (publisher) 49, 56, 66, 94
George V (previously Prince of Wales) 105, 107, 191, 193
German Air Service Company 190
The German War (1914) 147
Germany
   Bremerhaven 132
   Cologne 132
   Hamburg 132, 203
   Munster 132
The Ghost of the Moat (1927) 194
Ghosts I Have Seen I. The Spectral Friars (1927) 195
Giant Maximin (1911) 132
Giant's Causeway (Ireland) 187
Gibraltar 165
Gilbert, Dr Philip 50
Gilbert, W.S. 111
Gilchrist, Marion 122
Giles, Dr William Anstey 166
Gill, Thomas Patrick 38
Gillette, William 77, 78, 81, 92, 93, 109, 119, 196
Girls Training Corps 217
Gissing, George 74
Gjedser 203
Gladstone, Herbert 114
Gladwin, L. Fane 121
The Glamour of the Arctic (1892) 48
Glasgow 122, 148, 160, 174
   Caledonia Road Church 55
   Queen's Park U.P. Church 56
   St Andrew's Hall 160, 173
The Glasgow Herald 52
Glebe House, Glebe (Lee) 43, 88
Glen Falls 143
   Opera House 61
Glenconner, Lord and Lady 155
A Glimpse of the Army (1900) 85
A Glimpse of the British Army (1916) 151
A Glimpse of the French Line (1916) 152
Gloucester, Duchess of 221
Goacher, E.J. 216
Godalming (Surrey) 113
   Peper Harow Church 115
   Prior's Field boarding school 93
   Public Hall 98
   Wesleyan Chapel 98
Goddard, Air Marshall Sir Victor 224
'The Golden Dog' (poem, 1913) 138

Golden Lion (Rheims) 132
Goldfinch, H. 123
golf championships/cups
  American Amateur Golf Championship 131
  British Amateur Golf Championship 131
  Lord Brassey Prize 127
  Spring Meeting Vice-Presidents Cup 142
  Verral Cup 160
golf clubs
  Beacon Golf Club (Crowborough) 112, 122, 123, 127, 128, 129, 130, 141, 142, 160, 184, 200
  Crowborough Beacon (Ladies Section) 132
  De La Warr Golf Club (Crowborough) 122, 184
  Hindhead Golf Club 69, 77, 106, 107, 108, 109, 110, 111, 112, 118
  Lelant Golf Club, St Ives (Cornwall) 51
  Royal Eastbourne Club 130
  Royal Musselburgh Golf Club 101
golf courses
  Cissbury (Worthing) 131
  Hankley 103
  Sheringham (Norfolk) 103
Golf Cricketers 109
Goligher family 159
Gonville and Caius College, Cambridge 201
Good Cheer (Christmas ed. of *Good Words*) 46
Good Literature 65
Good Words 44
Goodwood Races (Sussex) 72
Gore-Booth, Lord 223
Gorell, Lord 211
Gould, F. Carruthers 102
Gower, Miss 210
Gower, Sir Robert 172
GP Delage (racing car) 214
Grace, W.G. 85, 95
Graham, Revd H. 215
Grant Richards (publisher) 78, 99
Grasse 139
Grauman, Sid 180
Gray, Captain John 14, 15
Grayshott
  Institute 77
  St Luke's Church 112, 158, 169
Grayswood Beeches (Haslemere) 67, 68, 69
'The Great Battles of the War' (lecture, 1915) 148–9
The Great Boer War (1900) 85, 89, 94
Great Britain and the Next War (1913) 137, 146
'Great British Battles' (speech, 1915) 150
The Great Brown-Pericord Motor (1892) 47
The Great Characters of Fiction: "Which Should I Most Like to Have Created?" (1927) 195
The Great Detective (ballet, 1953) 219
The Great German Plot (1914) 146
The Great Keinplatz Experiment 26
Great Lakes (East Africa) 198
The Great Shadow (1892) 47, 49, 50, 53
Great Thoughts 63, 131
'Great Writers Have Known' (talk, 1920) 168
Great Wyrley (Staffordshire) 113, 116

The Greatest Mystery of the Sea: The "Marie Celeste" (1913) 139
Greece 139
Green, A. 195
The Green Flag (1893) 52, 62, 178
The Green Flag and Other Stories of War and Sport (1900) 83
Greenhill-Gardyne, Colonel 189
Greenock
   Philosophical Society 56
   Watt Museum Hall 56
Greenville House (Barnstable) 153
Gresham Life Assurance Society 21
Gresson, Mr and Mrs F.H. 193
Gretna, HM Arms Factory 153, 155
The Grey Dress (1908) 118
Griffiths, Arthur 69, 75
Griffiths, Frances 165
Griffiths, John L. 143
Groombridge Place (Sussex) 201
'The Groom's Story' (poem, 1898) 74
Grosser Kurfuerst (ship) 132
The Guards Came Through and Other Poems (1919) 162
'The Guards Came Through' (poem, 1917) 155
Guest, Ivor 65
Guggisberg, Frederick Gordon 100, 109, 116, 117
Guildford County Session 108
Guildford (Surrey) 107
Guildhall Club 80
The Gully of Bluemansdyke (1881) 19, 20
Gun, Air Marshall Sir George 222
'The Guns in Sussex' (poem, 1917) 155
Gurney Champion, A. 123

Haggard, Henry Rider 44, 74, 95, 108, 121, 159
The Hague 202, 210
   Dierentuin (the Zoo) 202
   Hotel des Indes 202
   Musee Moritz 202
Haig, Sir Douglas 154
Halahan, Miss 73
Haldane, J.B.S. 194
Halifax, Victoria Hall 172
Hall Barn (Beaconsfield, Bucks) 94, 104
Hall Caine, Derwent 194
Halle (Belgium) 159, 160
Halpert, Felix de 140
Halves (drama, 1899) 78, 79, 80
Ham House (Richmond) 145
Hamburg 132
   Hotel Atlantic 203
   Karl Hagenbesk's Zoo 203
Hamilton, Dora 70
Hamilton, Thomas Glendenning 182
Hamlet (Shakespeare) 9
Hampshire Psychical Society 34, 38
Hampshire Regiment, 1st Battalion 148, 151, 154
Hampshire Telegraph 34
Messr. Hampton 117

Hanley 161
  Spiritualist Church 163
Harding of Petherton, Field Marshall Lord 224
Hardy, Mrs Thomas 104
Hardy, Thomas 44, 49, 146, 195
Harper's Bazaar 140
Harper's Monthly 49
Harper's New Monthly Magazine 51
Harris, Susanna 167
Harris, William 201
T. Harrison Roberts (publishers) 114
Harrison, Superintendent 159
Harrogate
  Council Chamber 154
  Hotel Majestic 154
  The Kursaal 148
  Lord Furness's Hospital 154
  Ripon Road 148
  Royal Hall 163
Harrogate Literary Society 148
Harte, Bret 44
Hartz, Dr Henry 41
Harvard Library 175
Harvey, A. 110
Harward, Annie 31
Harward, Nancy 31
Harward, General Thomas 30, 31
Harwich 133
Harwood, Anthony 224
Harwood, Nina Mdivani 87, 213, 214, 219, 220, 222, 224
Haslemere 113
  Rectory Gardens 80
Haslemere Microscope and Natural History Society 73
Hastings 150, 159
  Congregational Church 159
  North Lodge (St Leonard's) 159
Hastings, Cuyler 100
Hawick 106
  Buccleuch Hotel 103
  Tower Hotel 106, 110
  Town Hall 105, 107, 109, 110
Hawick Burghs 3, 110
Hawick Theatre 102
Hawkinge (Kent) 219, 220
Hawkins, Emily Butt 2, 6, 9, 24, 25, 26, 27, 37, 43, 53, 72, 73, 77, 88, 109, 110
Hawkins, Emily 'Nem' 2, 4, 5, 6, 34, 42, 43, 48, 49, 53, 55, 72, 73, 104, 112, 116, 153, 155
Hawkins, Jane Henrietta *see* Doyle, Jane Henrietta Hawkins
Hawkins, Jeremiah Jnr 6, 43, 53
Hawkins, Jeremiah Snr 2, 6, 9
Hawkins, John 'Jack' 2, 4, 5, 6, 24, 25, 26
Hawkins, Louise/a 'Touie' *see* Doyle, Louise/a 'Touie' Hawkins
Hawkins, Mary 6
Hawkins, Robert Crawford 118
Hawley 163
Heard, Mr 143
Hearst's International 177
The Hearthstone 83

Heathfield (Sussex) 210
Heaven Has Claws (by Adrian Conan Doyle) 218
Hedley, J. Hall 130
Heggie, O.P. 128
The Heiress of Glenmahowley (1884) 23
Helyer (or Heyler), J. 191
W. Henderson, Hawick (publisher) 107
Henderson, Lady 117
Hendon Aerodrome 131
Henley, William Ernest 116
Henry VIII (Shakespeare) 128
Henze, Martin 112
A Heroic Roman. How Dorando failed to seize the Laurel (1908) 120
Hewlett, Maurice 141
Hichens, Robert 75
Hilda Wade XII: The Episode of the Dead Man Who Spoke (1900) 82
Hill House Hotel (Happisburgh, Norfolk) 98
Hilton, H.H. 134
Hindhead 65, 68, 125
  Beacon Hotel 76, 77
  Brecon Hill Hotel 76
  The Cottage 77, 110
  Free Church 103
  Free Church Hall 77, 105
  Hindhead Hall 74, 87
  Moorlands Hotel 67, 69, 70
  Royal Huts Hotel 98
  The Royal Huts 77
  Undershaw 65, 67, 68, 69, 71, 72, 73, 74, 75, 76, 77, 78, 79, 80, 81, 85, 88, 89, 93, 99, 101, 102, 104, 105, 109, 110, 111, 113, 114, 115, 116, 118, 126, 166, 167, 171
  Undershaw Hotel 175, 187, 213
  Wesleyan Church 105
Hindhead School (Churt, Surrey) 88
His Last Bow (1917) 154, 155
The History of the British Campaign in France (1915) 147
The History of Spiritualism (1926) 191
Hitchcock, Raymond 176
HMS *Collingwood* 216
'H.M.S. *Foudroyant*' (poem, 1892) 49
HMS *President* 222
HMS *Zulu* 151
Hoare, Amy J. Ratcliff 101, 109
Hoare, Josephine 'Joey' 48, 49, 76
Hoare, Josephine Ratcliff 76, 87, 99, 105
Hoare, Dr Reginald Ratcliff 13, 18, 19, 20, 23, 42, 48, 49, 74
hockey grounds
  Mayfield 210
  Nevill Ground (Tunbridge Wells) 210, 211, 212
  Nevill Ground (Worthing) 211
  Uckfield 210
  Worthing 212
hockey teams
  Benenden 211
  Hamilton House 210
  Hildenborough 212
  Old Palace (Mayfield) 210, 212
  Oxted 212

   Pilgrims 212
   St Clair 211
   Sevenoaks 211
   Tonbridge 211
   Tunbridge Wells Ladies (Nevill) "A" team 210, 211, 212
   Uckfield 20, 211
   Worthing 211
Hocking, Silas 53
Hodder & Stoughton (publishers) 136, 139, 147, 152, 153, 155, 157, 160, 161, 162, 165, 172, 177, 179, 184, 185
Hodder House (prep school for Stonyhurst) (Lancashire) 7
Hogg, James 20
Holden, Frederick Thomas 215
Holland 45, 201
Holland, Constance 'Tiny' 205
Holland, E.D. 106
Hollerday House (Lynton, Devon) 96, 127
Holley, George 182
Hollywood
   Samuel Goldwyn Studios 181
   Sid Grauman's Egyptian Theatre 180
Holmes, Oliver Wendell 59, 60, 175
Holmes, Sherlock 11, 44, 51, 77, 90, 127, 134, 147, 167, 169, 172, 183
'Home Defence' (speech, 1914) 147
Home Green (Littlestone-on-Sea) 223
The Homecoming (1909) 125
Hope (Hawkins), Anthony 74, 88, 99, 110, 111, 121, 135
Hope (whaler) 14–18, 137, 191, 211, 216
Hope, William 172
Hopkins, Elias B. (pseud of ACD) 28
Horam Road Men's Christian Society (YMCA) 210
Horn, O.F. 133
Hornung, Arthur Oscar 63, 73, 77, 88
Hornung, Constance Amelia Monica 'Connie' Doyle (ACD's sister) 7, 8, 12, 19, 23, 27, 28, 43, 45, 46, 48, 49, 51, 52, 54, 62, 73, 74, 75, 76, 77, 78, 88, 97, 98, 100, 115, 118, 123, 128, 133, 142, 153, 156, 171, 184, 198
Hornung, E.W. 'Willie' 6, 7, 45, 49, 50, 51, 52, 54, 57, 63, 73, 74, 75, 78, 88, 92, 98, 100, 101, 106, 110, 111, 112, 115, 116, 117, 118, 119, 126, 128, 142, 149, 153, 171
Hornung, John Peter 'Pitt' 89, 150
Hornung, Laura 89
Hornung, Miss 54
Hornung, Oscar 149
The Horror of the Heights (1913) 140
Horsham Drill Hall 209
Horton, Revd H. 215
Hospital of St John of Jerusalem 98
Houdini, Bess 164, 176
Houdini the Enigma (1927) 194
Houdini, Harry 21, 160, 163, 164, 175, 176, 180, 192
The Hound of the Baskervilles (1901) 88, 89, 90–2, 94
The Hound of the Baskervilles (film) 203, 211
House of Commons 89
House of Commons Channel Tunnel Committee 141
The House of Temperley (film, 1913) 140
The House of Temperley (play, 1909) 125, 126, 127, 137
House-to-House Electric Light Company Ltd 38
Hove 146, 174

Garden House (Upper Drive) 164
Town Hall 148, 161, 164, 174
How the Brigadier Bore Himself at Waterloo (1903) 97
How the Brigadier Came to the Castle of Gloom (read on US lecture tour, 1894) 59
How the Brigadier Held the King (1895) 63
How the Brigadier joined the Hussars at Conflans (1903) 98
How the Brigadier Lost His Ear (1902) 95
How the Brigadier Played for a Kingdom (1895) 66
How the Brigadier Rode to Minsk (1902) 97
How the Brigadier said Goodbye to his Master (1903) 98
How the Brigadier Saved the Army (1902) 96
How the Brigadier Slew the Fox (1900) 82
How the Brigadier Triumphed in England (1903) 98
How the Brigadier was Tempted by the Devil (1895) 65
How, Harry 49
How I "Broke Into Print" (1915) 148
How It Happened (1913) 140, 143
How Our Novelists Write Their Books (1924) 185
How to Make a Real Happy New Year. Oh! The happiness of a Smile (1895) 62
How Watson Learned the Trick (1924) 184, 185
Howard Association 141
Howdy Chicago! (film, 1921) 187
Howells, William Dean 33
Hub 69
Huddersfield 160
Hughes, William Morris 'Billy' 166
Hull Artillery Hall 125
Hullo London (skit on *The House of Temperley* by George Grossmith, 1910) 127
'The Human Argument' (lecture, 1920) 166, 167, 168, 169, 171
Humphry, Frank 141
Hunter, Mrs 167
A Hunting Morning (1901) 92
Hurst Springs, Sussex Petty Sessions (1927) 193
Hutchinson & Co (publishers) 124, 178, 187
Hutchinson, George 46
Hydesville 179

Ibsen, Henrik 51
An Iconoclast (1911) 130, 178
The Idler Magazine 46, 47, 48, 50, 51, 55, 57, 59
Idler's soirées 46
Igglesden, Charles 138, 142
Ignatius Aloysius, Sister *see* Doyle, Ann Martha (or Annette)
Ilford Psychical Research Society 185
Illustrated Home Guest 57
The Illustrated London News 49, 74
Illustrated Weekly News 62
'The Immortal Memory' (toast and publication, 1901) 88
Impartial Opinions from England (1895) 63
Imperial Airways 187
Imperial Sunday Alliance 123
Imperial Union 106
An Impression of the Army (1898) 76
An Impression of the Regency (1900) 85
In the Argonne (1916) 152
An Incursion into Diplomacy (1906) 111, 112
The Independent 47, 56

India 78
  Bombay 78, 165, 170, 199
  Calcutta 167, 189
  Mysore 219
Indian National Council of the YMCA 187
Indianapolis 56, 59, 179, 180
  Claypool Hotel 180
  Denison Hotel 59
  Indiana State Soldiers and Sailors Monument 59
  Murat Theatre 180
  Plymouth Congregational Church 59
The Indianapolis News 47, 60
Institution of Municipal and County Engineers 131
Inter-collegiate Competition (putting the weight) (1930) 204
International Arbitration and Peace Association 27
International Congress for Psychical Research 182
International Congress of Spiritualists 176, 188, 189, 197
International Federation of Spiritualists 197
International Press Conference 74
International Psychic Gazette 201
Inverness Music Hall (Inverness) 56
Ipplepen (Devon)
  Park Hill House 90
  St Andrew's Church 114
Iredale, G.H. 179
Ireland
  Dublin 2, 27, 214
  King's County 7
  Kingston (nr Dublin) 27
  Lismore, County Waterford 7, 19
Irish Brigade 70
Irish Home Rule 130, 134, 135
Irish Literary Society 70, 71
Irish National Literary Society 76
Irish Protestant Committee 137
Irvine Burns Club 82
Irving, Henry 9, 12, 47, 49, 51, 59, 71, 74, 78, 95, 98, 101, 104, 107, 108, 109
Irwin, Joseph 188
Is Sir Oliver Lodge Right? – "Yes" (1917) 155
'Is Spiritualism of the Devil' (speech, 1917) 154
Isle of Arran 12, 24
Isle of Man International Cup race 106, 107
Isle of May 19
Isle of Mull, Glenfors (Aros) 189
Isle of Wight 24, 37
  Seaview 128

J. Habakuk Jephson's Statement (1883/4) 22, 23
Jack the Ripper 107
Jackson, Frederick G. 73
Jacques, B. 216
Jakeman, Mary 131, 142, 144, 165, 166
Jam of Nawanaga 121
James, Henry 33, 49, 74
James Russell Powell Fund 56
Jan Mayen (whaler) 14, 15
Jan Mayen's Island (Arctic Circle) 15

Jane Annie; or, The Good-Conduct Prize (comic operetta, 1893) 50, 52, 53
Japan Society 123
Jeakes, Revd J.M. 112
Jeffries, Jim 125
Jelland's Voyage (1892) 50
Jerome, Jerome K. 46, 48, 49, 50, 117
Jerrard, A.W. 33
Jersey C.I. 40
  Opera House (St Helier) 121
  Victoria College (St Helier) 40
Jeune, Lady 80, 93, 97
Jeune, Sir Francis 80, 97
Jewish Spiritualist Society 173
Jewish Territorial Organization 111
Jilla, A.D. 195
Johannesburg
  Carlton Hotel 198
  Country Club 198
  Orpheum Theatre 198, 199
  Premier Diamond Mine 199
  Robinson gold mine 199
  Rotary Club 198
  Standard Theatre 198
John, Ambrose 215
John Barrington Cowles (1884) 24
John Huxford's Hiatus (1888) 33
John Murray (publishers) 146, 147, 155, 159, 162, 176, 177, 183, 194, 197, 201, 205, 211
John W. Lovell Company (publishers) 45
Johnson, Jack 125
Jones, E.G. 122
Jones, Henry Arthur 93, 173
Jones, H.L. 170
Jones, William George 100, 105
Jonson, Ashton 202, 203
Joseph, Leo 159
'Journey's End' (play by R.C. Sherriff, 1929) 203
Juvenilia (1894) 58
J.W. Arrowsmith (publishers) 53

Kampala (Uganda) 198
Kansas City 142, 179, 180
Karoa (ship) 199
Keedick, Lee 175
Kellogg, F.B. 186
Kempton, Mrs 198
Kennel, Lieutenant Willam 143
Kenny, William S. 143
Kent & Sussex Light Car Club 209–12
Kent Coal Concessions Group of Companies 148
Kenya 197
Kidbrook (Kent) 9
The King of the Foxes (1898) 75, 145, 178
King George V National Memorial Fund 214
Kingston (near Dublin) 27
Kingston (Surrey)
  Literary Society 54
  St James's Hall 54, 80

Spiritualist Church 194
   Spiritualist Society 185
Kipling, Rudyard 61, 95, 108, 141, 192
Kirkwood, Dorothy 123, 128, 141
Kirriemuir 47, 50
Kisumu 199, 200
Kitchener, Lord 146
Knapp, Elizabeth Laing 143
Knapp, Joseph Palmer 143
Knole (Kent) 140
København (*Copenhagen*) (sailing ship) 198, 202, 203
Koch, Robert 40, 41
Kristianstad (Sweden) 220
Kyffin, Evan 166

La Roque, Rul 195
Lacey, Sir F.E. 79
The Ladies Home Journal 63
Lagos 20
Lake Victoria Nyanza 199, 200
Lamb, John (steward on the *Hope*) 211
Lamond, Revd Dr John 211
Lancashire Fusilier Brigade 149
The Lancet 20, 25, 114, 129
The Land of Mist (1925) 185, 186, 187, 188, 190
Lang, Andrew 35
Langman, Archie 73, 75, 77, 82, 83–4, 117
Langman Field Hospital 82–4
Langman, John 82, 87, 91, 99, 117
Langman, Mary 99
Largs (Scotland) 123
Larnach-Nevill, Major Gus 212
The Last Galley (1910) 129, 131, 178
The Last of the Legions (1910) 130
The Last Resource (1930) 209
The Late Mr James Payn. A Tribute from Dr Conan Doyle (1898) 74
'The Later Battles of War' (lecture, 1915) 150
Latter, William 212, 216
Lawes, Charles 92
'A Lay of the Links' (poem, 1893) 55
Le Touquet 136
Le Touret 149
Leaf, Horace 171, 174, 183, 184
Leamington Spa 132
   Regent Hotel 100
   Town Hall 101, 161
The Leather Funnel (1903) 92, 178
Leckhampton (Gloucester) 6
Leckie, James Blyth 8, 19, 43, 88, 190, 191, 205, 213, 214
Leckie, Jean *see* Doyle, Jean Leckie
Leckie, Malcolm 19, 43, 88, 110, 116, 142, 146
Leckie, P. Stewart 114
Leckie, Patrick Comrie 19, 43, 88, 190
Leckie, Patrick Stewart 191, 205, 209
Leckie, Richard 205
Leckie, Robert 118
Leckie, Sara/h 19, 43

Leckie, Selina 8, 19, 43, 88, 1159
Leckie, Stuart 127
Leconsfield, Lord 73
Lee, Arthur 127
Leeds 172
  Albert Hall 173
  Coliseum Theatre (Cookridge Street) 56
  Mechanics' Institute 55
  Town Hall 158
Leeds Sunday Society 56
Leicester 153, 160
  Palace Theatre 162
Leinster Motor Cycle and Car Club 213
Lerwick (Scotland) 14, 18
  Commercial Hotel 14
  Queen's Hotel 14
Lett, Mr 1144
Leuchers, Mrs and Miss 77
Lewes
  County Hall 164
  Race Hill 209–12, 210
  Race Stand 155
  Southover Church 145
  Wickham Nursing Home 216
Lewes Assizes 187
Lewes Police Court 210
Lewis, Colonel 66
Liberal Colonial Club 135
Liberal Federation Department 134
Liberal Union Club Council 104, 105
Liberal Unionist Council Conference 110
Liberal Unionist Party 24, 32, 33, 40, 76, 91, 108
Liberal-Christian League 129
Liberty magazine 192, 193, 196, 209
Liege 182
  Grevignée Cemetery 182
Life After Death (A Form Letter) (1918) 158
Life After Death (interview with ACD 1919) 160
'Life after Death' (speech, 1919) 159, 163, 174, 202, 203
'Life After Death in the Third Sphere' (lecture, 1928) 198
'The Life Beyond' (lecture, 1921) 172, 181
The Life on a Greenland Whaler (1897) 69
'Life as it is Beyond the Veil' (lecture, 1929) 199
'Life in Spirit World Told by Conan Doyle' (lecture, 1923) 181
'The Life and Times of Gibbon' (lecture, 1904) 102
The Lift (1922) 175
Light Advertisement Compensation Fund 154
Light newspaper 32, 69, 151, 153, 155, 177, 179, 180, 182, 186, 187
Light Sustentation Fund 157, 159, 162
The Limes (Wallingford, Oxfordshire) 98
Lindau, Germany 10
Lindfield (Surrey) 164
Lindsay-Hogg, E.V. 121
Lindsay-Hogg, Nora Cicely 203
Lippincott, Craige 60
J.B. Lippincott (publisher) 58
Lippincott's Monthly Magazine 38, 39

Lisbon 39, 41
Literary Aspects of America (1895) 63
The Literary Pageant 132
Literary and Philosophical Society 55, 81
Literary Society Lectures 80
'Literature' (speech, 1910) 127
A Little Bit of Fluff (play by Walter W. Ellis) 153
Little Popo 20
Liverpool 10, 20, 24, 62, 92, 94, 145, 153, 174, 182, 187
  Adelphi Hotel 123
  Philharmonic Hall 148, 160
  Picton Lecture Hall 55
  Shakespeare Theatre 123
  Sun Hall 125
  Wavertree 8
Livesey, Mr 52
The Living Age 76
Lloyd George, David 145, 153, 154
Lloyd's Sunday News 177
Lloyd's Weekly Newspaper 45
Locard, Edmond 170
Loder-Symonds, Lily 91, 116, 150
Lodge, Sir Oliver 155, 194, 197, 216
London
  Abbey House (Baker Street) 218
  Abbey House (Victoria Street) 190, 192
  Albany (Piccadilly) 200
  Anerley (Bromley) 172, 173
  Annington Road (Muswell Hill) 131
  Arlington Street 117
  Battersea Town Hall 163
  Bayswater 3
  Belgrave Square 115
  Berners Street 2
  Blackheath 77
  Bouverie Street 79
  Brixton 153, 184
  Buckingham Palace Mansions (Victoria Street) 177, 178, 179, 184–5, 186, 188, 189, 190, 191, 192, 194, 196, 197, 201, 203, 204
  Buckingham Street 98
  Burroughes Hall (Soho Square) 164, 173
  Cambridge Terrace 3, 4
  Caxton Hall (Westminster) 106, 108, 157, 158, 176, 184, 188
  Cenotaph 183
  Central Hall (Westminster) 147
  Clifton Gardens (Maida Vale) 7, 9, 12, 19
  Common House (Kensington) 81
  Copthall Gardens (Twickenham) 223
  County Hall (Spring Gardens) 150, 185
  Curzon Street 218
  Devonshire Place 43, 44, 216
  Dorchester House 115
  Downing Street 154
  East Ham 163
  Eaton Terrace 114
  Ely-place (Holborn) 115
  Finborough Road (Chelsea) 9, 12, 19, 23

Great Windmill Street 141
Grosvenor Place 130
Guildhall 122, 127, 147
Harley Street 97
Hayter House (Cheniston-gardens Studios) 131
Hendon 92
Holborn Town Hall 96
Horton Street (Kensington) 111
Kensington Town Hall 195
Lansdowne House 108
Lewisham 163, 164, 178
Long Acre 114
Mansion House 77, 98, 107, 124, 130, 131, 152
Memorial Hall (Farringdon Street) 102, 137
Merchant Taylors' Hall (Threadneedle Street) 70
Messrs. Orme and Son's Hall (Soho) 138
Montague Place (Bloomsbury) 43
Mortimer Hall 171
Mulberry House (Smith Square) 212
Norfolk Square 67
Oakley Street (Chelsea) 65
Park Crescent (Portland Place) 192
Piccadilly 184
Pitt Street (Kensington) 88
Portland Place 221
Portman Rooms (Baker Street) 133
Printing House Square 158
Pump Court (Temple) 113
Queen Anne's Gate 155
Queen Square 174
Queen Street 178
Queen's Gate Hall (Kensington) 197, 200
Queensberry Place (South Kensington) 190
Raphael House (Moorfields) 195, 197
Regent Street Polytechnic 190
St James's Hall 99
St James's Place 50
St Stephen's House (Westminster) 98
Salisbury House (Finsbury Circus) 92, 93, 95, 105, 108, 112, 116, 120, 128, 133, 136, 145, 149, 152, 155, 158, 161
Stafford House (St James's) 85
Stanhope Terrace (Hyde Park) 82
Stationers' Hall 185
Stratford Place 183
Tavistock Square 177, 178
Tennison Road (South Norwood) 44, 45, 46, 47, 49, 50, 55, 57, 58, 62, 69
Toynbee Hall 77
Upper Wimpole Street 43, 44, 225
Welcome Lecture Hall, Westow Street (Upper Norwood) 57
Wellington House (Buckingham Gate) 146
Westbourne Park Institute 80
Westbourne Terrace 105
Westminster Town Hall 32
White City 191, 193
Whitechapel 107
Whitehall Court 50, 77, 81, 87, 92, 95, 97, 102, 104, 106, 110, 114, 118, 211
Winchester House (Old Broad Street) 93, 172, 177, 183, 185, 189, 192

Woburn Square 218
   Woolwich Town Hall 177
   YMCA (Gower Street) 187
London Academy of Music 91
London Border Counties Association 79
London Churches/Cemeteries
   The Belfry (West Halkin Street) 213
   Brompton Oratory 110, 224
   Church House (Westminster) 187
   City Temple 129, 195
   Corpus Christi (Covent Garden) 225
   Dutch Church (Austin Friars) 118
   Ethical Church (Bayswater) 141
   Golders Green Crematorium (Hendon) 109, 213
   Holy Trinity (Brompton) 221
   Jewish Cemetery (Willesden) 192
   King's Weigh House Church 129
   London Spiritualist Church 185
   Munster Wesleyan Church (Fulham) 179
   Norwood Cemetery (Lambeth) 3, 4, 7
   Our Lady of the Rosary (Marylebone Road) 9
   Paddington Cemetery (Willesden) 74
   Rochester Square Spiritualist Temple 192
   St Bride's Church (Fleet Street) 99
   St Clement Danes (Strand) 114, 222, 223, 224, 225
   St George's (Hanover Square) 97, 106
   St James' Church (Spanish Place) 210
   St Luke's Spiritualist Church (Queen's Road, Forest Hill) 183
   St Margaret's (Westminster) 117, 197, 223
   St Martin-in-the-Fields 225
   St Mary's Roman Catholic Cemetery (Kensal Green) 23, 47, 107
   St Pancras Church 4
   St Paul's Cathedral 9, 97, 101, 116
   St Paul's Chapter House 127
   St Paul's (Covent Garden) 164
   St Peter's (Eaton Square) 121
   St Peter's and St Edward's Roman Catholic Church (Palace Street, Westminster) 54
   St Saviour's Church (Warrington Crescent) 74
   Spanish Chapel, Charles Street (Marylebone) 6
   Spiritualist Church (Southwark Bridge Road) 194
   Westbourne Chapel 80
   Westminster Abbey 9, 49, 109, 195, 221, 224, 225
   Whitefields Tabernacle 124
London Cinemas
   Capitol (Haymarket) 195
   Marble Arch Electric Palace 141
   Marble Arch Pavilion 192, 194
   New Gallery Cinema (Regent Street) 188
   West End Cinema (Coventry Street) 140
London Clubs, Societies, Institutions
   After-Dinner Club (Suffolk Street) 179
   Athenaeum 23, 87, 88, 89, 92, 93, 94, 95, 102, 138, 184, 191, 192
   City Liberal Club (Walbrook) 137
   Devonshire Club 91
   East India, Devonshire, Sports and Public Schools' Club (St James's Square) 154
   Institute of Lecturers 142
   Liberal Union Club (Great George Street) 77

Lyceum Club 107, 157, 177, 209
National Liberal Club 147
National Sporting Club (Covent Garden) 140, 157
Playgoers Club 51
Reform Club 45, 48, 50, 51, 52, 54, 55, 57, 62, 69, 70, 73, 78, 80, 82, 92, 151
Royal Aero and Lansdown Club (Fitzmaurice Place) 221, 222
Royal Air Force Club 223
Royal Automobile Club 99
Royal Geographical Society 130
Royal Medical and Chirurgical Society of London 107
Royal Societies Club (St James's) 69, 70, 73, 123, 127
Royal Society 81
Royal Society of Arts (John Adam Street) 70
Royal Society of British Artists (Suffolk Street) 153, 155
Royal Society of Medicine (Hanover Square) 123
Royal United Service Institution 92
St Mary's Hospital Medical Society 162
Savage Club 190
Savile Club 35
South Place Institute (Finsbury) 176, 184
Union Jack Club (Waterloo Road) 97, 98, 99, 100, 105, 115
London County Council (LCC) 108
London Courts
  Bow Street Magistrates Court 139
  Central Criminal Court (Old Bailey) 129
  Clerkenwell Court (London) 213
  Gray's Inn 89
  Old Bailey 151
  Southwark Police Court 105
  Westminster Police Court 197
London Daily News 109
London District Council 184
London Fund for the Relief of the Distressed in the West and South West of Ireland 75
London Gazette 159
A London Ghost (1924) 184
London Hospitals
  Charing Cross Hospital Charity 126
  London Clinic 216
  Middlesex Hospital 121
  St Mary's Hospital (Paddington) 81, 128, 134, 152, 156, 162
  St Pancras Hospital 214
  St Thomas's Hospital 157, 158, 173
London Hotels, Restaurants, Pubs 220
  Berkeley Hotel (Piccadilly) 122, 154, 178
  Café Monico (Regent Street) 70, 71, 115
  Café Royal 137, 213
  Canon Street Hotel 141, 148
  Carlton Hotel 96
  Carlton Rooms (Baker Street) 136
  Champion Hotel (Aldersgate Street) 81
  Charlton Hotel 102
  Claridge's Hotel 82, 101, 108
  Connaught Rooms (Great Queen Street) 134, 138, 148, 159, 177, 195
  Criterion Restaurant (Piccadilly) 51, 91, 95, 111, 115, 134
  De Keyser's Royal Hotel 137
  Dorchester Hotel 214, 221
  Egyptian Hall (Mansion House) 53

    Frascati's Restaurant (Oxford Street) 69
    Freemason's Tavern (Great Queen Street) 63
    Gaiety Restaurant 115, 117
    Golden Cross Hotel (Charing Cross) 95, 99, 103
    Grand Hotel (Trafalgar Square) 57, 79, 99, 104, 105, 110, 111, 113, 114, 115, 116, 119, 128
    Grosvenor House Hotel 70, 158, 163, 165, 173, 212
    Holborn Restaurant 48, 51, 52, 57, 68, 69, 70, 74, 75, 81, 87, 89, 123, 129, 140, 165, 197
    Hotel Albemarle (Piccadilly) 72
    Hotel Cecil 60, 75, 76, 87, 89, 92, 99, 100, 103, 107, 108, 111, 114, 126, 142, 196
    Hotel Dieudonné (Ryder Street) 140
    Hotel Great Central (Marylebone Road) 113
    Hotel Metropole (Whitehall Rooms) (Northumberland Avenue) 44, 54, 81, 104, 108, 115, 117, 122, 123, 126, 127, 128, 129, 130, 136, 137, 139, 140, 141, 146, 149, 150
    Hyde Park Hotel 191, 195
    Imperial Hotel 139
    Langham Hotel (Portland Place) 38, 46, 224
    Morley's Hotel (Cockspur Street/Trafalgar Square) 85
    Morley's Hotel (Trafalgar Square) 72, 75, 91
    Pagani's Restaurant (Great Portland Street) 46
    Palace Hotel (Bloomsbury Street) 191
    Park Lane Hotel 210
    Piccadilly Hotel 125, 140
    Prince's Restaurant (Piccadilly) 99, 123
    Queen's Hall (Langham Place) 70
    Ritz Hotel 127
    St James's Restaurant/Hall 57
    Savoy Hotel 104, 106, 111, 131, 135, 137, 141, 154, 190, 195, 222
    The Ship Tavern (Greenwich) 22, 25
    Strand Palace Hotel 210
    Trocadero Restaurant (Shaftesbury Avenue) 96, 97, 103, 118, 123, 131, 172
    Victoria Hotel (Northumberland Avenue) 124, 194
    Westminster Palace Hotel 52, 135, 141
    Ye Olde Cheshire Cheese (Fleet Street) 192
London Library (St James's Square) 69, 128
The London Magazine 129, 130, 181, 197
London Museums/Galleries
  Black Museum, New Scotland Yard 50
  British Museum 43
  Brooke Galleries 183
  Grafton Galleries 95
  Madame Tussaud's (Baker Street) 9, 93, 102
  National Portrait Gallery 192, 193, 220
  Royal Academy of Arts (Burlington House) 13, 57, 67, 69, 81, 85, 196, 201
  Suffolk Street Galleries 174
  Tower of London 9
  Westminster Aquarium 13
London Press Club 63, 96
London Prisons
  Holloway 50
  Newgate 50
  Pentonville 129, 152
  Wandsworth 187
London Society of East Anglians 111
London Society magazine 18, 20, 21, 23, 25, 28
London and South-Western Railway Rifle Club 98
London Spiritualist Alliance 153, 154, 155, 158, 163, 174, 178, 184, 185, 190, 195, 197, 205
London Spiritualist Alliance Ltd Council 169

London Spiritualist Association 186
London Spiritualist Church 183
London Territorial Force 126
London Theatres/Entertainment spaces
  Aeolian Hall (New Bond Street) 177, 187, 189, 191, 193, 196, 213
  Brixton Theatre 149
  Coliseum 171, 172, 183
  Comedy Theatre 65
  Crystal Palace 91, 93, 95, 131, 139
  Drury Lane 98, 111, 116
  Duke of York's 79, 93, 109
  Empire Theatre 127
  Everyman Theatre (Hampstead) 192
  Fortune Theatre 209, 211
  Garrick 62, 79, 80
  Globe Theatre 128, 129
  Grotrian Hall (Wigmore Street) 189, 190, 191, 194, 195, 196, 200
  Hampstead Conservatoire 81
  Haymarket 52, 101, 123, 124
  Her Majesty's 75
  Hippodrome 135
  His Majesty's 104, 108, 128
  Holloway Theatre 184
  Imperial Theatre 105, 111
  Independent Theatre 57
  Lyceum Theatre 9, 71, 74, 75, 78, 92, 93, 94, 95
  Lyric 111, 112, 123, 124
  Marlborough Theatre (Holloway) 126
  New People's Palace (Mile End Road) 173, 191
  Palace Theatre 187
  Prince of Wales 71
  Princes Theatre 183
  Princess's Theatre (Oxford Street) 123
  Queen's Hall (Langham Place) 118, 148, 160, 161, 163, 164, 170, 171, 183, 184, 185, 186, 190, 191, 203
  Royal Adelphi (Strand) 125, 126, 127
  Royal Albert Hall 70, 92, 105, 108, 115, 125, 141, 160, 192, 195, 209
  Royal Opera House (Covent Garden) 129
  Royalty Theatre 45, 173, 183
  Sadler's Wells Theatre 219
  St Jame's Theatre 172, 173
  Savoy 52, 53
  Scala Theatre 113
  Steinway Hall (Lower Seymour Street) 96, 111, 185
  Strand Theatre 130
  Terry's Theatre 52
  Theatre Royal (Drury Lane) 108
  Thurston's Grand Hall (Leicester Square) 163
London Zoo 215
Lone Dhow (by Adrian Conan Doyle, 1963) 221
The Lonely Hampshire Cottage (1885) 26
Longmans, Green, and Co. 36, 39, 52, 65, 185
Longman's School Magazine 46
Longstaff, Captain Will 196
The Lord of Chateau Noir (1894) 58
The Lord of the Dark Face I. The Dangers of the Deep (1929) 200
The Lord of the Dark Face II. The Crisis (1929) 200

The Lord of Falconbridge. A Legend of the Ring (1909) 123
The Los Amigos Fiasco (1892) 50
Los Amigos Fiasco (1894) 61
Los Angeles 164, 170, 179
   Ambassador Hotel 180, 181
   City Club 181
   Grand Theatre 180
   Sid Grauman's Million Dollar Theatre 188
   Trinity Auditorium 181
   Ventura oil fields 181
The Lost World (1912) 134, 135, 136
The Lost World (silent film, 1925) 178, 186, 187, 188, 190
Lot No.249 (1892) 49
Low, Sir James 55
Lowell Memorial 48
Lucens Castle 222, 224
The Ludgate 65
Ludgate Weekly Magazine 47
Lunn, Dr Henry 53
Lushing, Lieutenant 137
Luton 178
Lyndhurst 192
   Grand Hotel 135, 188
   The Okefield 185
Lynton (Devon) 96, 127
Lyons 170

Mabie, Hamilton W. 62
McBean's Orchids Ltd. 219
McCabe, Joseph 163, 170
McCall, M.P. 144
McClure, Philips & Co. 112, 114
McClure Publishing Company 61
McClure, Samuel Sidney 61, 101
McClure's Magazine 58, 62
Macedonia 100
McIlwaine, Judge 199
McKenzie, Peter (whaler on board the *Hope*) 216
McKim, Revd Joseph 98
McLean, Colin 137
MacLellan, Mrs Knight 167
Madeira 20, 197
Madness (1914) 147
Maeterlinck, Maurice 196
Mahan, Captain Alfred 57
Mahé (Seychelles) 218
Maheno (ship) 168
Maloja 57, 94
Malone, John 22, 23
Malta 146, 200
The Man Beyond (film starring Houdini, 1922) 175
The Man from Archangel (1884) 25
The Man with the Mattock (aka *A Pastoral Horror*) (1884) 24
'The Man in the Street' (lecture, 1920) 167
The Man with the Twisted Lip (1891) 46
The Man with the Watches (1898) 74, 75
Manchester 152, 160

   Ardwick Picture House 184
   Edinburgh University Club 54
   Free Trade Hall 76, 155, 172
   New Windsor Chapel (Salford) 55
   Sale Public Hall 54
   Town Hall 125
Manchester Weekly Times 69, 72
Manchester Weekly Times Supplement 37
Manning, William Herbert 123
Mansion House Indian Fund 70
Maoris 169
Mar, Rupert 154
The Maracot Deep (1927) 194, 195
The Maracot Deep and Other Stories (1929) 201
Maresfield (Sussex) 201
   Parish Church 205, 211, 213
   Village Hall 211
Margate 118
Marlborough Hotel (Southwold) 92
The Marriage of the Brigadier (1910) 128
'Marriage and Parenthood: Their Ideals and Dangers' conference (1918) 157
Marseilles 139, 165, 170, 200
   Hotel du Louvre 170
Marshall, W.B. 163
Marshall-Hall, Sir Edward 163
'The Marvels of Psychic Knowledge' (lecture, 1928) 198
Mary, Queen 191, 193
Marylebone Spiritualist Association 177, 185, 193, 209
Masefield, John 146
Masongill Cottage (North Yorkshire) 21, 22, 23, 42, 43, 50, 77, 81, 130, 153
Masongill Estate (North Yorkshire) 11
Masongill House (North Yorkshire) 21, 43, 88
Masongill (North Yorkshire) 27
Massachusetts
   Association Hall (Worcester) 60
   Greek Revival Mansion (Round Hill) (Northampton) 60
   Mount Auburn Cemetery (Cambridge) 60
   Northampton City Hall 60
'Master' (poem, 1898) 76
Masterman, Charles 145, 146
'The Material Side of the Psychic Movement' (speech, 1919) 162
'Materialisation' (lectures by Horace Leaf) 171
Matheson, Robert 4
Mathieson (crew member on the *Hope*) 17
Mdivani, Princess Elizabeth 213
Mdivani, Princess Nina *see* Harwood, Nina Mdivani
Mdivani, Prince Zachary 213
The Medal of Brigadier Gerard (1894) 60, 62
The Medical Times 22
Medicine Man (play by Trail & Hichens) 75
'Mediums and the Law' (lecture, 1925) 190
Meister, Dr J. von 133
Melbourne 166, 169, 170, 210
   Grand Hotel 166, 167
   Masonic Hall (Collins Street) 167
   Menzies Hotel 166, 167
   Parliament House 167

The Playhouse 167
Melksham (Wiltshire) 218
Melville Testimonial Committee 101, 102
Melville, William 102
The Memoirs of Sherlock Holmes (1893) 56
Memories and Adventures (1923) 182, 185
Mentone 139
Mercedes Benz SSK 211, 212, 213, 214
'A Mere Dream' (speech, 1914) 141
Meredith, George 47, 122, 136
Merlin airship 95
Merthyr Tydfil 162
  Theatre Royal 159
'Messages From Beyond the Grave' (lecture by E.T. Powell, 1921) 171
'Messages from Lord Northcliffe' (lecture, 1924) 186
Methuen & Co (publishers) 60, 184
Metropole Hotel (Monte Carlo) 121
Metropolis (film, 1927) 194
Metropolitan Association for Befriending Young Servants 70
Metropolitan Magazine 155
Meyer, Professor Milo de 36
Micah Clark (1889, 1892) 25, 31, 32, 33, 35, 36, 37, 46, 178
Middlesbrough 148
Midleton, Viscount 115
Milan 43, 65, 94
The Military Lessons of the War: A Rejoinder (1901) 87
Military Tournament 104
Milne, A.A. 116
Milne, Andrew Haggie 15
Milner, Lord 84
Milwaukee 56, 59
  Plymouth Congregational Church 60
Minden, Battle of 149
Minneapolis All-Stars (baseball) 182
The Minneapolis Journal 51, 61
Minstead
  All Saints Church 215, 219, 223
  Bignell Wood house 189, 192, 194, 195, 197, 200, 201, 204
Mitchel, John Purroy, Mayor of New York 143
Mitchell-Hedges, F.A. 218
'Modern Psychic Knowledge' (lecture, 1924) 183
'Modern Psychic Thought' (lecture, 1921) 173
Møhl, Steffen 156
Mombasa (Kenya) 199
  Manor Hotel 200
Monaco 139
Money, Catherine 131
Monmouth 26
Monsieur Beaucaire (play by Booth Tarkington, 1914) 147
Montreal 142, 143, 145, 179
  Bonaventure Station 143
  Canadian Club 143
  Mount Royal Hotel 182
  Ritz Carlton Hotel (Sherbrooke Street) 143
  Windsor Hotel 143
Montreal Gazette 145
Montreuil 151

Montrose Royal Lunatic Asylum (Sunnyside), Kincardineshire (now Angus) 26, 43, 46
Moore, Decima 109
Morayshire Club 97
Morel, Edmund Dene 56, 123, 124, 125, 127
Morel National Testimonial 128
Morning Leader 50
The Morning Post 51, 140
Morocco 124
Morris, Lady 176
Morris, Sir Malcolm 45, 176
Morris, Mrs Louisa Ann Meurig 209, 211
motor racing competitions/trophies
  Anglo-German motor race (1911) 132
  Cambridge Speed Trials 204
  Clayton Cup 204
  County Down Trophy Race 213
  Crawshay Challenge Trophy 201
  GP des Frontiéres 220
  GP Napoli 220
  GP Sverige 220
  Junior Car Club International 214
  Leinster Trophy 214, 215
  Lewes Speed Trials 201, 204, 205, 209, 210, 212
  Normanhurst Challenge Cup and Replica 210
  Prince Henry of Prussia Cup 132–3
  Racing Car Unlimited Group race 210
  St Etienne 220
  Skegness Sand Races 210
  Ulster Trophy 214
  Unlimited Super Sports Car Race 209–12
  Varsity Hill Club Climb 211
  VI Internationales Avus Rennen Grand Prix 214
  West Surrey Automobile Club Challenge Cup 109
  XII Grand Prix Des Frontiéres 214
  XIII Grand prix De Picardie 214
Motor Union of Great Britain and Ireland 113
Mount Auburn Cemetery (Cambridge, Massachusetts) 175
Mount Robson (British Columbia) 144
Mr Burdett-Coutts's Charges (1900) 84
'Mr Morel and the Congo' (speech, 1910) 129
Mr Stevenson's Methods in Fiction (1890) 39
Mrs Wiggs of the Cabbage Patch (play by Anne Crawford Flexner) 115
Müller, J.P. 122, 137
Munsey's Magazine 74
Murray, Captain 15
Murray, Sir Andrew 218
Murray, W.L. 92
The Musgrave Ritual (film, 1914) 141
'My Experiences' (talk, 1920) 163
My Favourite Novelist and His Best Book (1898) 74
My First Book (1894) 58
My First Book VI - Juvenilia (1893) 51
My First Guinea (1899) 81
My Friend the Murderer (1882) 21
My Friend the Villain (1900) 83
'My Psychic Experiences' (lecture, 1926) 191, 199
Myers, Frederic 54

Mysore 219
Mysteries and Adventures (1890) 39
The Mystery of Cloomber (1888) 33, 34, 35
The Mystery of the Fox Sisters (1922) 177
The Mystery of Sasassa Valley (1879) 13

Nairobi (Kenya) 198
  Athi Plains 199
  Grand Hotel 200
  Norfolk Hotel 199, 200
  Theatre Royal 199, 200
Nakuru 199
Nansen, Dr Fridtjof 70, 186
Naples 66, 73, 74, 82, 94, 112
  Hotel Du Vesuve 117
  Parkers Hotel 117
Nash, Dick 201
Nash, Percy 164
Nashimoto, Prince and Princess 123
Nash's Magazine 123
Nash's Pall Mall Magazine 160
Natal
  Imperial Hotel 198
  Town Hall 198
Nathan, Sir Matthew 170
National Defence Association 128
National Flag and London Schools Fund 115
National Institute for the Blind Fund 142
National League for Opposing Women's Suffrage 139
National Memorial Service for the Fallen of the War (1919) 160
National Police Fund 191
National Purity Crusade 117
The National Review 39
National Rifle Association 91, 110, 116, 123
National Society for the Prevention of Adulteration and Food Sophistication 129
National Sporting Club 94
National Union of Spiritualists 157, 160, 162, 172, 176, 184, 188
National Volunteer Home Defence Force, Holborn Battalion 148
Naulakha house (Brattleboro, Vermont) 61
Nederlansche Vereeniging van Spiritisten "Harmonia" 202
Needle Makers Company 70
Neilson-Terry, Dennis 183
Nelson's History of the War (John Buchan, editor 1914) 145
Netley Hospital (Hants) 41
New Age 59
'The New Army' (speech, 1916) 150
The New Catacomb (The Burger's Secret) (1898) 74
New Forest 38, 182, 188
  Minstead 215, 219, 223
New Jersey
  Alexander Hall (Princeton) 61
  Essex Lyceum (Newark) 60
  Firt Presbyterian Church (Jersey) 62
  Morristown 61
  Paterson's Association Hall (Paterson) 62
  St Batholomew's School for Boys (Morristown) 61
  State Fair Ground (Trenton) 60

New Kidbrooke (Kent) 8
The New Revelation (1917) 155, 156, 157, 187
'The New Revelation or Death and the Hereafter' (lecture, 1919) 162
'The New Revelation' (lecture, 1917) 155, 159, 173, 177, 179, 202
A New Revelation. Spiritualism and Religion (1916) 153
The "New" Scientific Subject (1883) 22
New South Wales Institute of Journalists 168
New Vagabond Club 51, 68, 69, 74, 75, 76, 81, 87, 95, 97, 111, 114, 118, 126, 130, 138
New York 59, 142, 174–5, 175, 214, 215, 218, 222
    Academy of Music 59
    Academy of Music (Brooklyn) 60, 175
    Aldine Club 59, 61, 62
    Ambassador Hotel 174, 175, 176
    American Art Association 173, 174
    American Art Galleries 178
    Astor Theatre 186
    Biltmore Hotel 179, 182, 218
    Bittenhouse (Pebble Beach) 162
    Brighton Casino 143
    Buffalo 81
    Calvary Baptist Church 59
    Carnegie Hall 175, 179
    The Carroll Theatre 176
    Central Park 179
    City Hall 142
    Coney Island Police Station 143
    Daly's Theatre 60, 61
    First Reformed Church (Schenectady) 61
    Flushing (Queen's County) 62
    Garrick Theatre 81, 84
    Gladstone Hotel 218
    Hamilton Club (Remsen Street, Brooklyn) 60
    Liberty Theatre 125
    Lotus Club 59, 61
    McAlpine Hotel 176
    Plaza Hotel 142
    Plaza Summer Garden and Air Terrace 143
    Plymouth Spiritualist Church (Rochester) 194
    Poe Cottage (Fordham) 176
    Polo Grounds 143
    Prince George Hotel 175
    Rathbun House Hotel (Elmira) 61
    St Andrew's Club (Yonkers) 61
    Savoy Theatre 113
    Shelburne Hotel 143
    Shore Acres (Bay Ridge) 143
    Sing Sing prison 142
    Star Theatre (Buffalo) 81
    Times Square Theatre 175
    Tombs Prison 122, 142
    Town Hall (Jamaica, Queen's County) 62
    Trinity Place Public School (New Rochelle) 61
    West Seventieth Street 186
    Whitehall Club 142
    Women's Union Hall (Buffalo) 61
    Yonkers Lawn Tennis Club 61
New York Giants (baseball) 175

New York Police Forgery Department 174
The New York Times 63, 185
New York Tribune 146
New York Yankees (baseball) 143
New Zealand 165, 168, 174
   Auckland 166, 168, 169
   Christchurch 166, 169
   Dunedin 166, 169
   Pa of Kaiopoi 169
   Wellington 166, 168, 169
Newbury 133
   Town Hall 80
Newcastle upon Tyne 53, 56, 109, 132, 133, 178
   Theatre Royal 53
   Town Hall 124
   Tyne Theatre 56
Newnes, Sir George 4, 42, 96, 117, 127
Newnes Ltd 44
Newport Bowling Club 26
Newport Market Refuge and Industrial Schools 61, 62
Newspaper Society 196
Newsvendors' Benevolent Institute 137
Newton Abbot (Devon) 90
Niagara Falls 61, 145, 175
   Prospect Hotel 61
Nice 139
A Night Among the Nihilists (1881) 18, 65
'The Night Patrol' (poem, 1920) 164
The Nightmare Room (1921) 173
The Nineteenth Century 34
Nitocris (Nile boat) 66
No. 46 (County of Sussex) ATS, RAF Company 215
'No Change in Death' (lecture, 1928) 198
The Noble Bachelor 45
Norddeutscher Lloyd 132
Normandy 54
Northampton 160
   Town Hall 161
Northampton Spiritualist Society 161
Northcliffe, Lord 141, 158
Northern Reform Tariff Federation 109
Norway 48, 49, 202
Norwich
   Maid's Head Hotel 105
   St Andrew's Hall 177
Norwich Medico-Chirurgical Society 105
Norwich Prison 88
Norwood, Dr F.W. 195
Norwood, Eille 167, 169, 172, 183
Not Forgotten Association 223, 224
Notes on a Case of Leucoythaemia (article, 1882) 20
Notes from a Strange Mailbag - The Dreamers (1928) 196
Nottingham 172
   Albert Hall 173
   Gladstone Hall 173
   Mechanics' Hall 56, 158
Nova Scotia Historical Society 93

Nova Zembla (whaler) 14
Novelists on their Works (1895) 65
Novices' Boxing Championship 154
'Now Then Smith!' (poem, 1922) 176

Oakland 181
Oaten, Ernest 183
O'Callaghan, Robert 83
Oddie, S. Ingleby 107
Officers' Pension Society 222
Old Calabar 20
'The Old Huntsman' (poem, 1898) 74
Oldham, Caroline Mary Burton 'Lottie' (sister of ACD) 6, 8, 12, 19, 22, 24, 34, 41, 43, 50, 51,
   55, 62, 66, 67, 73, 78, 80, 84, 85, 94, 104, 105, 112, 133, 149, 153, 156, 205, 216, 225
Oldham, Claire Annette 112, 133, 153, 205, 225
Oldham, Captain Leslie 80, 84, 85, 104, 105, 112, 133, 149, 225
O'Leary, Fr. J. 135
Olympic Games 120, 136, 138, 139
Olympic Sports Club 109
Omar Khayyam Club 69, 70
On the Egyptian Frontier (1896) 66
On the Geographical Distribution of British Intellect (1888) 34
'On the Outlook for 1926' (lecture, 1926) 190
On the Slave Coast with a Camera (1882) 20
One Crowded Hour (1911) 133
Onslow, Colonel 122
An Open Letter to Those of My Generation (1929) 200
Orange County, Music Hall 61
Order of the Hospital of St John of Jerusalem in England 151, 154, 157
Order of the Mejidic 117
Order of the Shefkat Nisham 117
The Origin and Outbreak of War (1916) 150
Orkney 14
Messrs. Orme and Son 138
'The Oscar Slater Case' (talk, 1911) 134
Oslo 202
   Aulaen (Christiana) 203
   Grand Hotel 203
Ottawa 143
   Canadian Club 139
   Chateau Laurier 139
   Grand Central Station 145
   Grosvenor House 145
Our African Winter (1929) 201, 202
Our American Adventure (1922) 177, 179
Our Derby Sweepstake (1882) 20
'Our Knowledge of the Brain' (talk by Dr C.C. Claremont, 1887) 32
'Our Life After Death' (speech, 1927) 194
Our Midnight Tragedy (1884) 24
Our Midnight Visitor (1891) 42
Our Mutual Girl (series of silent films, 1914) 144
'Our Reply to the Cleric' (lecture, 1919) 161, 162
Our Second American Adventure (1924) 184
Our Society (Crimes Club) 102, 105, 107, 113, 115, 126, 134, 140, 157, 162, 193, 195, 200
Out of the Running (1892) 46, 49
An Outing in War-Time (1915) 150
The Outlook from Sarras (1896) 67

The Outlook on the War (1915) 150
The Output of Authors (1897) 70
Outward Bound (play by Sutton Vane) 183
Owen, Revd George Vale 164, 172, 184, 185
Oxford 118, 132
Oxford University 211

Pack, Catherine *see* Foley, Catherine Pack
Packe, Colonel 157
Page, John 169
Pagent Literary Agency (New York) 173
Paget, Sidney 5, 73, 118
Paget, Walter 213
Pain, Barry 46
The Pall Mall Budget 34
Pall Mall Gazette 38
Pall Mall Magazine 52, 53, 57, 140
Paloona (ferry) 169
Paquebot Stambul (ship) 117
The Parasite (1894) 62
Pares, Mr 25
Paris 10, 43, 54, 62, 94, 107, 151, 170, 200, 219
'Paris in 1894: A Superficial Impression' (article, 1894) 57
Paris
  Avenue Wagram 10, 14, 22
  British Embassy church 220
  Eiffel Tower 35
  Hotel Byron 57
  Hotel du Louvre 170
  Hotel Regina 117, 188, 189
  Hotel Ritz 219
  Le Nouveau Cirque 35
  Les Invalides 35
  Louvre 35
  Luxembourg Gardens 35
  Musée de Cluny 35
  Musée Grévin 35
  Panorame de Bastille 35
  Panorame de Gravelotte 35
  Pantheon 35
  Saint Ouen cemetery 14
  Salle Wagram 189
  Stade de Colombes 171
  Theatre Albert 189
  Théâtre Sarah Bernhardt 137
The Parish Magazine (1930) 209
Parker, Sir Gilbert 54, 211
Parkman Land (Adirondack, USA) 59
The Parson of Jackman's Gulch (1885) 28
'The Passage of the Red Sea' (poem, 1873) 9
The Passing of Conan Doyle (by Greenhough Smith, 1930) 209
The Passing of the Legions (1910) 130
A Pastoral Horror (aka *The Man with the Mattock*) (1890) 24, 42
Patras 139
'Patriotism of Modern Writers. Sir A. Conan Doyle's Criticism' (speech, 1922) 173
Paulton (Somerset) 193
Payn, James 25, 45, 74, 78

Payne, William 111
Paynter, Joan 45
Peall, A. 173
Pearson's Magazine 69, 70, 76, 81, 130, 131, 184
Peary, Commander Robert 127
Pecorano (young Italian) 175
Peel, Mr 22
Peerless, Miss 147
Peking 87
Pemberton, Max 117
Pennarby Mine (poem, 1893) 53
Pentecost, George 212
Penzance Arcadians Amateur Dramatic Society 122
The People 38, 42, 46
The People's Home Journal 65
Peronne 214
'Personal Psychic Experiences' (lecture, 1923) 180
Peterhead Prison 122, 195
Peterhead (Scotland) 14, 18
Peters, Alfred Vout 153, 155, 174
Pettigrew, William 162
Pevensey Castle (Sussex) 126
Pheneas Speaks (1927) 193
Pheneas (spirit guide) 173, 178
Phenomena and Religion of Spiritualism. A New Revelation (1917) 155
Phil May's Illustrated Winter Annual 50
Philadelphia 60, 142, 174
    Musical Fund Hall 60
Philadelphia Athletics 143
Phillimore, Miss Mercy 197
Phillpots, Eden 46
Photographic Journal 24
'Photos of Fairies' (lecture, 1928) 198
A Physiologist's Wife (1890) 41
Pickering, Dr Latimer 61
Pickford, Mary 179, 181
'Pictures of Psychic Phenomena' (lecture, 1920) 166, 167, 168, 169
Pierrepont, Thomas 187
Piers, N. 63
Pietri, Dorando 120
Pilgrims Society/Club 96, 99, 101, 104, 106, 108, 111, 131, 135, 142, 152, 154, 186, 194
Pillo (Indian friend of Mary's) 177
Pinero, Arthur Wing 65
Pinwell Revue (New York) 176
Pittsburgh 142, 179
    Carnegie Music Hall (Oakland) 180
    William Penn Hotel (Grant Street) 180
Pittsburgh Commercial Gazette 44
The Pittsburgh Gazette Times 180
Plaat, Frau Lotte 203
Playfer, H. 120
Playford, P. 179
Playing with Fire (1900) 82
PLSS *see* Portsmouth Literary and Scientific Society
Plymouth 21, 36, 124, 163
    Durnford Street (Stonehouse) 20
    Elliot Terrace (The Hoe) 20, 179

   Grand Hotel 179
   Guildhall 179
Pocock, Julia 'Aunt Juey' 113, 123, 128, 176
Podmore, Frank 57
Poe, Edgar Allen 122, 176
   monument at Baltimore 60
   Poe Cottage (Fordham) 176
The Poems of Arthur Conan Doyle - Collected Edition (1922) 177
A Point of Contact (1922) 177
The Poison Belt (1913) 136, 137, 138, 139, 142
Poldhu Hotel (Mullion, Cornwall) 122, 126
Police and Observer Corps Ball (1930) 209
A Policy of Murder (1914) 147
Pontifex, Clare Verus 196
Pooley, Michael 222
The Poor (1895) 63
Port Elizabeth
   Humewood Hotel 198
   Opera House 198
Port Said 139, 165, 170
Port Soudan 200
Portland Borstal (Rochester, Kent) 173
Portland Public Auditorium 181
Portraits of Celebrities at Different Times in Their Lives (Strand Magazine, 1891) 46
Portsea Workingmen's Conservative Club, Arundel Street (Landport) 37
Portsmouth 21, 157, 160
   Albany Hotel, Commercial Road (Landport) 25, 32, 33, 39, 41
   Barrard's Amphitheatre (Gunwharf Road) 29, 33, 37
   Blue Anchor (Kingston's Cross) 25, 26
   Doyle Avenue 211
   Freemason's Hall (Landport) 31
   Garrison Recreation Ground 28, 30, 31
   George Hotel 37
   Golden Fleece (Commercial Road) 25
   Governor's Green 26
   Grand Jury Room (New Town Hall) 41
   Guildhall (High Street) 32, 33, 35, 36, 37, 192
   Hippodrome 164
   Kingston Lodge 31
   Old Portsmouth Theatre 32
   Penny Street Lecture Hall 22, 23, 24, 25, 28, 29, 30, 31
   Portland Hall 161
   Portland Hotel 72
   Portsdown Hill 24
   Portsmouth Grammar School 33
   Portsmouth Institute 30
   Protestant Buildings, Lower Hall 30
   St James Church (Milton) 39
   Soldiers' Institute, Sailor Boys' Room 28, 30, 32
   Town Hall 72, 73, 161, 171
   Victoria Hall (Commercial Road) 32
   Wesley Church (Arundel Street) 192
   see also Southsea
Portsmouth & Southsea Synagogue, Queen Street (Portsea) 35
Portsmouth Conservatives 75
The Portsmouth Evening News 22, 171, 176, 182, 189
Portsmouth Finance Committee 211

Portsmouth Grammar School 41
Portsmouth Hostel for Boys 209
Portsmouth House of Commons Debating Society 30
Portsmouth Jewish Literary and Debating Society 35
Portsmouth Literary and Philosophical Society (PLPS) 190
Portsmouth Literary and Scientific Society (PLSS) 21, 22, 23, 24, 25, 26, 28, 29, 30, 31, 32, 33, 36, 37, 39, 40, 41, 47, 73, 90
Portsmouth Road Works and Drainage Committee 211
Portsmouth and South Hampshire Electricity Supply Company 38
Portsmouth and South Hants Eye and Ear Infirmary 26, 36, 41, 71
Portsmouth Spritualist Brotherhood 192
Portsmouth Waltonian Angling Society 25
Portugal 7, 28, 39, 43, 51, 124
Portuguese Political Prisoners 141
Posillipo (Italy) 220
A Pot of Caviare (1908) 118
A Pot of Caviare (play, 1908) 121, 126
Potter, Beatrix 92
Powell, Sir Douglas 54
Powell, Ellis T. 171
Powell, Evan 161, 179
Powell, James Russell 56
Practical Psychology Club 187
The Press Album 122
Preston, Edmund 174
Preston Public Hall 162
Pretty, Air Marshall Sir Walter 223
Prichard, Hesketh 77
Prichard, Kate O'Brian 77
Prince of Wales Jubilee Fund 71, 75
The Princess's Nose (play by H.A. Jones) 93
Princess's Theatre Syndicate Ltd 123
The Prisoner's Defence (1916) 150
The Problem of Thor Bridge (1922) 174, 223
'The Proof of Survival' (lecture, 1921) 173
'Proofs of Immortality' (lecture, 1921) 173, 180, 182, 187, 188
The Prophet of the New Revelation (1925) 187
Psychic Bookshop, Library and Museum (Victoria Street, London) 186, 188, 193, 195, 196, 197, 211
'The Psychic in Crime' (lecture, 1919) 162
'Psychic Developments' (wireless lecture, 1924) 184
Psychic Experiences (1925) 190
'Psychic Experiences' (lecture, 1925) 187, 196
Psychic Lecture Week (1924) 185
'The Psychic Movement' (lecture, 1926) 191
Psychic Phenomena are Real (1923) 181
'Psychic Photography' (lecture, 1921) 172
The Psychic Press (publishers) 193, 195, 200, 201
Psychic Research Society *see* Society for Psychical Research (SPR)
Psychical Research Circle 209
Psychical Research Laboratory (National Laboratory of Psychical Research) (Kensington) 194
'The Psychical Research Society' (lecture by W.F. Barrett, 1893) 51
Pulborough 189
Pulled Up (1914) 145
Pullen, Mr 212
Punch magazine 79
Purchase, Frederick 23

G.P. Putnam's Sons (publishers) 190

The Quarterly Transactions of the British College of Psychic Science 177, 185, 196
Queen magazine 68
Queen's Club (Baron's Court, London) 184
Queen's Edinburgh Rifle Volunteer Brigade 97
The Queen's Gift Book 150
Queens Park Lecture Association (Glasgow) 56
Queenstown (Ireland) 82
A Question of Diplomacy (1892) 49, 52
A Question of Diplomacy (play, 1910) 126
Quiller-Couch, Arthur 'Q' 47
Quittah 20

R. Mitchell and Sons (publishers) 88
Rabbich, H.P. 165
Rabbich, J. 179
Raffles, A.J. (fictional character) 74
'Ragtime!' (poem, 1912) 135
Ranjitsinhji, Kumar Shri 'Ranji' 121
Raphael Tuck & Sons (Ltd) (publishers) 92, 93, 95, 105, 108, 112, 116, 120, 128, 133, 136, 145, 149, 152, 155, 158, 161, 165, 172, 177, 183, 185, 189, 192, 193, 195, 197, 201
Rathbone, Basil 222
The Ravens Dramatic Club 103
Re-union Concert for ex-Servicemen (1925) 190
Readers' Pension Fund 118
'Reading from my Books' (talk, 1899) 77
Reading Spiritualist Mission 163
Reading Town Hall 163
'Readings and Reminiscences' (talk, 1894) 61
Real Conversation (1894) 60
'Recent Evidences as to Man's Survival of Death' (talk by F. Myers, 1893) 54
'Recent Psychic Research' (lecture, 1921) 173, 174, 180
The Recollections of Captain Wilkie (1895) 63
The Red-Headed League (1891) 44, 45
Redhill Volunteers 158
Redway, George 32
Referees' Union 119, 139
The Refugees. A Tale of Two Continents (1893) 46, 47, 51, 52, 178
A Regimental Scandal (1892) 48, 223
The Register 166
Reid, George 127
Reid, Lady 127
Reid, Thomas Wemyss 74, 76
Reid, Whitelaw 108
Reigate 53
Reigate Borough Cemetery 110
'Religio Medici' (poem, 1912) 135
'The Religious Argument' (lecture, 1920) 166, 167, 171
'Religious and Scientific Aspects' (lecture, 1921) 173
A Remarkable Man (The Career of D.D. Home) (1921) 171
The Remote Effects of Gout (1884) 25
Rendel, Robert 211
The Rent in the Line (Breaking the Hindenburg Line) (1918) 158
Research Defence Society 118, 123
   Brighton and Sussex branch 124, 125, 126
'Responsible and Irresponsible Criminals' (talk, 1910) 126

'The Results of the Psychic Research' (lecture, 1929) 203
The Retirement of Signor Lambert (1898) 76
The Return of Sherlock Holmes (1903) 100, 106
The Return of Sherlock Holmes (play by Terry & Rose) 183
'The Revelation' (lecture, 1922) 177
The Review of Reviews 41
Reynolds, Mr 23
Rheims 171
Rhodes, Cecil 199
Rhodesia 197
  Bulawayo 198, 199
  Khami Ruins (Zimbabwe) 198, 199
  Matoppo Hills 198, 199
  Salisbury 198, 199
  Savoy Hotel (Beira) 199
  Victoria Falls 198, 199
Richard, Mr 31
Richardson, Dr Charles Sidney 12
Richmond Park 133
Richmond School, Richmond (Yorkshire) 27
The Riddle of Houdini (1927) 194
The Rifleman 128
The Ring of Thoth (1890) 39
RMS *Adriatic* 176, 182
RMS *Aquitania* 214
RMS *Austral* 94
RMS *Dunottar Castle* 124
RMS *Mongolia* 204
RMS *Olympic* 142, 179
RMS *Saturnia* 215
RMS *Windsor Castle* 197–8
Roberts, Ada 68
Roberts, Estelle 209
Roberts, Lady 84
Roberts, Lord 84, 95, 104
Roberts, Sydney 131
Robespierre (play by Victorien Sardou) 78
Robinson, Bertram Fletcher 8, 62, 87, 88, 89, 90, 102, 104, 113, 114
Robinson, Frederick William 46
Robinson, Harry S. 159
Robinson, Sir John 52, 74
Robinson, Mr 21
Robinson, Nugent 81
Rochdale 160
Rochester (USA) 81, 142, 179
  Powers Hotel 61
  YMCA Music Hall 61
Rockliffe family 10
Rodney Stone (1896) 65, 66, 69, 178
Rodney Stone (film, 1920) 164
Rogers, Colonel Maynard 143, 1144
Rogers, Mrs Maynard 143, 144
The Roman Catholic Church - A Rejoinder (1929) 201
'The Romance of Medicine' (speech & article 1910) 128, 129
Rome 65, 66, 73, 74, 117, 139
  Manzoni Theatre 117
  Trattoria Colonna 74

Roosevelt, Theodore 126, 127
Rose, Arthur 183
Rosebery, Lord 93
Rosebrook Cottage, Dixton (Monmouthshire) 5
Roskell, Arthur 9
Roskell, Richard, Bishop of Nottingham 8
Rotherfield Parish Church 203
Rotterdam Gebouw voor Kunsten en Wetenschappen 202
Rotterdamsche Vereeniging van Spiritisten "Harmonia" 202
Rotunda Lecture Hall 54
Round the Fire Stories (1908) 120
Round the Red Lamp (1894) 60
'A Rover Chanty' (poem, 1896) 68
Rowe, Arthur George 23
Rowe's Duchy Hotel (Princeton, Devon) 88, 90
Roy (ACD's collie dog) 138
Royal Academy Soirée (1926) 192
Royal Air Force (RAF) 215
Royal Albert Yacht Club 72
Royal Army Medical Corps (RAMC) 134, 136
Royal Automobile Club (RAC) 133
Royal Botanic Gardens (Regents Park) 108, 123
Royal Commission on the War in South Africa 98
The Royal Cornwall Gazette 51
Royal Field Artillery 51, 106
Royal Horse Artillery 78
Royal Horticultura Society (RHS) 219
Royal Links Hotel (Cromer, Norfolk) 72, 87, 89
Royal Literary Fund 127
Royal Military Academy (Sandhurst) 111
Royal Military Academy (Woolwich) 39, 43
Royal Navy 106
Royal Normal College and Academy for the Blind 50
Royal Scots Fusilliers 82
Royal Society for the Protection of Birds (RSPB) 141
Royal Star and Garter Home (Richmond) 222
Royal Surgical Aid Society 153
Royal Sussex Regiment, 'D' Crowborough Company 5th Battalion 149, 151, 152, 161
Ruml, Annn *see* Doyle, Ann Ruml
Ruml, Mr and Mrs Beardsley 219
Rumsey, Colonel 127
Rutherford, Professor William 11
Ruyton-XI-Towns (Shropshire) 13
Ryan, Elizabeth C. 75
Ryan, James 75
Ryan, Jimmie 12

Sackville, Lord 140, 192
St Andrews University 186
St Donat's Castle 214
St Dunstan's 164
St George's Rifles 82
St Ives Police Court (Huntingdonshire) 204
St Jean de Luz 171
St John's Church (Withyham, Sussex) 122
St Leonard's (Sussex) 147
  North Lodge 159

St Louis (ship) 74
St Louis (USA) 142, 179, 180
   American Theatre 180
   Hotel Chase 180
St Marylebone Borough Council (London) 218
Saint Mary's Hospital Gazette 129
St Paul's Cathedral Fund 186
St Vincent (Cape Verde Islands) 82
Saintsbury, H.A. 127
Salisbury, Lord 95
Salisbury (Rhodesia) 198, 199
   Meifle's Hotel 199
   Psychic Society 199
Salt Lake City 179
   Hotel Utah 180
   Mormon Tabernacle 180
Salvation Army 115
Samson, Mr and Miss 73
Samuel French Ltd (publishers) 97, 113, 136
San Diego Trinity Auditorium 180
San Francisco 179, 216
   Clift Hotel 181
   Dreamland Auditorium 181
   Muir Woods 181
   Redwood Grove 181
   Sausalito 181
   Tamalpais Mountain 181
San Remo 62, 106
Sandow, Eugen 92
Sandroyd School (Oxshott Heath, Surrey) 97, 112
Saturday Evening Post 209
The Saturday Globe 49
Sawyer, Julia 164
A Scandal in Bohemia (1891) 43, 44, 209
Scandinavia 201
The Scene at Assouan. Letters from Egypt (1896) 67
Scheveningen 202
Schwanenflügel, Peter Vilhelm von 202, 203
Schwensen, Clara *see* Doyle, Ida Claudia Clara Schensen
Schwensen, Reinhold 130
'Science, Spiritualism and Religion' (lecture, 1917) 153
Scientific American 66
Scolia Folk Song Quartette 186, 189, 194
Scott, Admiral Percy 97, 108
'Scott, Baden-Powell and Scouting' (speech, 1913) 138
Scott, O. 122
Scott, Robert Falcon 124
Scott, Dr Sydney 57
Scottish Border Amateur Athletic Association 103
Scottish Office of Works 4, 10
Scranton 81
A Scrap of Paper (play by Victorien Sardou) 142
Scribner's Magazine 62, 129, 130
Scull, W.D. 150
Sculptograph 100, 105
Seaforth 106
Seaforth Highlanders 149, 152

Seaman, Owen 127
Seattle 179, 181
  Public Arena 181
Seaver, Revd Canon R.W. 187
A Second Form Letter (1930) 204
Second World War 216
The Secret of the Moor Cottage ('H. Ripley Cromarsh' ACD's sister 'Dodo') 110, 113
Selbit, P.T. 160, 182
Selby 147
Selecting a Ghost (1883) 22, 23
Selkirk 102
  New Bridge 101
  Victoria Hall 101, 106, 110
  Volunteer Hall 110
Selkirk Unionist Party 101
Selwyn, Canon Edward Carus 118
Semmering 43
Sevenoaks Chronicle & Kentish Advertiser 190
Sevenoaks (Kent) 91, 93
Shackleton, Ernest H. 123
A Shadow Before (1898) 76, 178
Shakespeare, William 9
'Shakespeare's Exposition' (poem, 1909) 122
Shalford (Surrey) 107
Sharp, Frederick E. 159
Shasta Springs 181
Shaw, George Bernard 77, 141, 186
Shaw, Thomas 101, 110
Sheffield 12, 157, 172
  Music Hall (Surrey Street) 55
  Nelson Terrace (Spital Hill) 12
  Victoria Hall 173
Sheldon, Elizabeth Somerville 99
Shelton, Anne 225
Shenandoah (play) 59
Sheringham (Norfolk) 103
The Sherlock Holmes Competition - Mr Sherlock Holmes to his Readers (1927) 193
Sherlock Holmes (drama, Gillette & ACD) (1899) 79, 81, 84, 92, 93, 94, 100, 109, 117
The Sherlock Holmes Exhibition (1951) 218
The Sherlock Holmes Prize Competition - How I Made My List (1927) 194
Sherlock Holmes Society of London 220, 224
Shetland Islands 14, 18
Short, Edward 173
Shrewsbury 133, 148
'Sidelights on History' (lecture, 1899) 80, 81
The Sideric Pendulum (1920) 165
Sidmouth
  Belmont Grounds 96
  Royal York Hotel 96, 100
The Sidmouth Herald 96
Siedeberg, H.G. 183
Sierra Leone 20
The Sign of Four (1890) 38, 39, 41
The Sign of the Six or The Problem of the Sholtos see The Sign of Four
Silbert, Frau 176
Silk, J.N. 195
The Silver Hatchet (1883) 23

The Silver Mirror (1908) 120
Silver, Tom 107
Simmonds, William 77
'Simplicity in Religion. Sir A. Conan Doyle on the Brotherhood of Man' (lecture, 1924) 185
Singapore 221
The Singular Experience of Mr J. Scott Eccles (1908) 120
The Sins of Society (play by Cecil Ralegh & Henry Hamilton) 116
'Sir A. Conan Doyle and Divorce Law' (speech, 1917) 155
'Sir A. Conan Doyle and His Spiritual Guide' (lecture, 1924) 185
'Sir Arthur Conan Doyle on the Outrages' (speech, 1913) 139
Sir John French. An Appreciation (1915) 150
Sir Nigel (1905) 108, 109, 110, 112, 113, 178, 186
Sir Nigel's Song (1899) 79, 110
Skegness 214
Sladen, Miss 73
The "Slapping Sal" (1893) 53
Slater, David 159
Slater Memorial Hall (Norwich, Connecticut) 60
Slater, Oscar 122, 126, 135, 136, 140, 141, 195, 196, 217
Slatterie, Lizzie 30
'The Slug' (Anzani Frazer Nash racing car) 201, 204, 205, 209, 210, 211
Small, Maynard & Company (publishers) 110, 146
Smith, A.C. 92
Smith, Elder & Co. London (publishers) 22, 45, 69, 71, 75, 83, 93, 97, 100, 112, 113, 118, 120, 130, 131, 147, 149
Smith, Herbert Greenhough 88, 89, 117, 213
Smith, Reg 108
Smith, Theodore 195
Smith, William G (or S) 166
Smithers, Charles 8
Smyrna 117
Société des Savantes 189
Society of Advanced Psychic Research (Altadena, California) 181
Society of American Magicians 175, 176
Society of Authors 44, 48, 70, 89, 103, 107, 115, 134, 140, 195
Society of Authors Pension Fund 89
Society of Authors, Playwrights and Composers 177, 191
Society for Psychical Research (SPR) 51, 55, 57, 177, 178, 187, 204, 211
Society of Somerset Men 115
Society for the Study of Supernormal 164
A Soldier's Prayer (1899) 79
Some Curious Personal Experiences (1927) 195
'Some Facts About Fiction' (talk, 1893) 54, 55, 56
Some Letters of Conan Doyle (1930) 209
'Some New Photographs' (lecture, 1923) 178
Some Personalia about Mr Sherlock Holmes (1917) 155
Some Recollections of Sport (1909) 124
'The Song of the Bow' (poem, 1891) 42, 44
Songs of Action (1898) 75
Songs of the Road (1911) 130
Sopley RAF Station 221
A Sordid Affair (1891, 1894) 46, 57
Sotheby & Co. (London) 139, 205, 212, 217, 218
South Africa 96, 103, 197
  Bethulie 83
  Bloemfontein 82, 84, 98, 102, 198
  Brandfort 84

    Burgersdrop 83
    Cape Town 82, 84, 198
    Cathcart 82
    Durban 198
    East London 83
    Johannesburg 84, 198
    Mafeking 199
    Orange River Colony 93
    Port Elizabeth 198
    Pretoria 84, 198
    Queenstown 82
    Ramblers Cricket Ground (Bloemfontein) 83
    Rhodesia 198, 199–200
    Springfontein 83
    Stellenbosch 198
    Sterkstroom 83
    Table Bay 82
South African Hospital Commission 85
Southampton 59, 84, 103, 132, 195, 209, 223
    Holy Trinity Schoolrooms (Northam Road) 34
Southern Counties Union of Spiritualists 165
Southport 162
    Ainsdale Sands 204
    Birkdale Sands 211, 212, 214
    Cambridge Hall 80
Southport Motor Racing Club 204, 210, 213, 214
Southsea 23, 92, 161
    Ashburton Hall 190
    Barley Mow pub (Castle Road) 33
    Bush Hotel 21, 27, 29
    Bush Villas (Elm Grove) 21, 22, 23, 24, 27, 28, 29, 31, 32, 33, 35, 38, 39, 40, 41
    Clarence Parade 157
    Co-operative Hall (Albert Road) 209
    Emanuel Road 43
    Esplanade Hotel 40
    Green Road 30
    Grosvenor Hotel 39, 42, 67
    Grosvenor Street 22
    Grove Road 22
    Highland Road Cemetery 25, 216
    Hope House Day School (Green Road) 21
    Kingsley Hall (Fawcett Road) 192
    Portland Hall 36, 71, 171
    Portsmouth Temple of Spiritualism (Victoria Road) 184, 192
    Queens Gate (Osborne Road) 24, 25
    Royal Pier Hotel 107, 216
    St James's Church 216
    St Jude's Church 216
    St Paul's 31
    St Simon's School Room (Clarendon Road) 29
    St Vincent Lodge (Kent Road) 29
    South View Lodge (Kent Road) 68
    Southsea Terrace 67
    see also Portsmouth
Southsea Bowling Club 22, 26, 27, 29
Souvenir of the Charing Cross Hospital Bazaar 79
Spain 124

The Speaker 46, 47, 57, 66, 68, 70, 74, 76
The Speckled Band (play, 1910) 127, 128, 129, 130, 136, 141, 149, 172, 173
'Speech with the Dead' (talk, 1920) 165
Spencer Blackett (publisher) 41
Spencer, Mrs Stanley 95
Spencer, Percival 91
'Spirit Forms in Photography' (lecture by E.L. Gardner, 1921) 172
'Spirit' photographs exhibition (1924) 184, 185, 189
'Spirit Photographs' (lecture, 1920) 168, 177
'The Spirit World. Psychic Photographs' (lecture, 1920) 169
'Spiritual Communion in the Home Circle' (lecture, 1925) 188
'Spiritualism: A Reply to Critics' (lecture, 1920) 168
'Spiritualism: Its Religious Side' (lecture, 1920) 168
Spiritualism - Some Straight Questions and Direct Answers (leaflet, 1922) 177
Spiritualism (1927) 193
'Spiritualism and Christianity' (lecture, 1922) 177
'Spiritualism' (lecture given by Denis Conan Doyle) 209
Spiritualism and Rationalism (1920) 165
Spiritualism and Religion (1916) 153
Spiritualist Armistice Sunday Service (1925) 190
Spiritualist Church of New South Wales (Australia) 168
Spiritualist Community Services 187, 188, 190, 194, 195, 196, 200
Spiritualist Fellowship Centre (Hendon) 172
Spiritualist Services of Remembrance 192, 195, 203
Spiritualistic Churches & Lyceums (Melbourne) 167
'Spiritualists and Fallen' (lecture, 1925) 190
Spiritualists of Sussex 174
Spiritualists of the United Kingdom 165, 197
SS *America* 218
SS *Baltic* 174–5
SS *Briton* 84–5
SS *Egypt* 80
SS *Etruria* (ship) 62
SS *Graphic* 187, 188
SS *Harmonic* 143
SS *Königin Luise* 73
SS *Mayumba* 20
SS *Megantic* 145
SS *Modasa* 200
SS *Nagoya* 167
SS *Naldera* 165–6, 170, 199
SS *Oriental* 82, 83
SS *Orsova* 170
SS *Paloma* 169
SS *Port Caroline* 210
SS *Princess Victoria* 181
SS *Rawalpindi* 189
Stable, Laura 174
Stable, Revd S.R. 27
Stanger-Leathes, L.G. 213
Stanley, Madeleine Cecilia Carlyle 97
The Star 74
The Stark Munro Letters (1894) 53, 56, 59, 62, 65
'The State of Spiritualism in 1925' (lecture, 1926) 190
Stead, W.T. 77, 179
Steedman, Sir Alasdair 224
Stella Mautina, Feldkirch (Austria) 10

Stern, Major Albert 153
Stockholm 202, 203
  British Embassy 203
  Grand Hotel 203
  Konserthuset 203
  Oscarsteatern (Oscar Theatre) 203
Stockholm Spiritualist Society 203
Stoddart, Joseph Marshall 38
Stoker, Bram 115, 117
Stoll Convention Dinner (1921) 172
Stoll Film Company 167, 169, 172
The Stone of Boxman's Drift (1887) 32
Stonyhurst College (Lancashire) 7–10
Stonyhurst Figaro (journal) 9
Stonyhurst Magazine 27
Storey Institute Lecture Society (Lancaster) 55
'The Storming Party' (poem, 1892) 47
Storr, Mary 116, 125
The Story of B.24 (1899) 78
The Story of the Black Doctor (1898) 76
The Story of the Brazilian Cat (1898) 76
The Story of the Brown Hand (1899) 78
The Story of the Club-Footed Grocer (1898) 76
'The Story of the Irish Brigade' (talk, 1897) 73
The Story of the Japanned Box (1899) 77
The Story of the Jew's Breastplate (1899) 77
The Story of the Latin Tutor (1899) 78
The Story of the Lost Special (1898) 76
The Story of Mr George Edalji (1907) 113, 114
The Story of the Sealed Room (1898) 74, 76
The Story of Spedegue's Dropper (1928) 197
The Story of Swedenborg (1925) 186
A Story of Waterloo (play) (1894) 59, 61, 62, 71, 74, 75, 101, 108, 113, 149
The Storyteller magazine 178
A Straggler of '15 (1891) 43, 47, 59, 113
The Strand Magazine 39, 42, 43, 44, 45, 46, 47, 48, 49, 50, 51, 52, 53, 54, 56, 58, 60, 62, 63, 65,
    66, 69, 70, 75, 76, 77, 78, 80, 82, 85, 87, 88, 89, 90, 92, 97, 98, 101, 102, 103, 105, 106, 110,
    118, 120, 121, 122, 123, 124, 125, 128, 130, 133, 134, 135, 137, 138, 139, 140, 145, 146, 147,
    148, 150, 151, 153, 155, 157, 158, 159, 160, 162, 164, 165, 167, 168, 170, 172, 173, 174, 175,
    176, 178, 179, 182, 183, 185, 186, 188, 192, 193, 194, 195, 196, 197, 198, 200, 201, 209
Strange Adventure (aka *The Engineer's Thumb*) 47
A Strange Prophet (1928) 196
Strange Studies from Life (1963) 220
Strange Studies from Life II: The Love Affair of George Vincent Parker (1901) 88
Strange Studies from Life III: The Debatable Case of Mrs Emsley (1901) 89
Strange Tale of the Sea (1885) 26
Stranger than Fiction (1915) 150
Stranges Studies from Life I: The Holocaust of Manor Place (1901) 87
Strathview House (Kirriemuir) 47, 50
Streatham Volunteer Corps 149
The Student magazine 69, 164
A Study in Scarlet (formerly *A Tangled Skein*) (1887/88) 29, 30, 32, 33, 34
Suakim 200
Suez 170, 200
suffragists, suffragettes 138, 139
Sullivan, Arthur 111
'Summary and General Conclusion' (lecture, 1921) 171

The Sun 44, 74
Sunday Express 160, 172, 195
The Sunday Times 155
Sunderland 178
  Victoria Hall 148
The Sunlight Year Book 74
Super Sports Car Unlimited Group 210, 211, 212
Supremacy of the British Soldier (1917) 154
Surbiton Assembly Rooms 185
Surbiton New Spiritualist Church 194
The Surgeon of Gaster Fell (1890) 42, 65
Surrey County Dinner (1906) 111
Surrey County Football Association Council 102
Surrey Liberal Unionists Association 114
Surrey (Princess of Wales) Imperial Yeomanry Fund 79
'Survival and Communication' (speech, 1927) 194
Sussex Agricultural Express 132
Sussex Archaeological Society 126
Sussex Duty and Discipline Committee 151
Sussex Volunteer Regiment 155
Sutherland, Duke of 85
Swanage, Dorset 123
Sweden 202
Sweethearts (1894) 57
Swindon Swimming Baths 163
Switzerland 49
  Arosa 57
  Basle 10
  Berghotel Schwarenberg 54
  Clavedel 63
  Davos 51, 54, 55, 56, 57, 58, 61, 62–3, 94
  Engadine (Maloja) 65
  Findelen Glacier 53, 54
  Gemmi Pass 54
  Geneva 219, 220, 224
  Grand Hotel (Caux) 65
  Grand Hotel Victoria (Glion-sur-Montreux) 65
  Hotel de l'Europe (Lucerne) 53
  Interlaken 139
  Klosters 62
  Lausanne 129
  Lucerne 65
  Maienfelder Furka Pass 57
  Maloja 65
  Meiringen 53
  Mürren 139
  Old Catholic Church (Lucerne) 53
  Posthotel Löwen (Mühlen) 63
  Reichenbach Falls 51, 53
  Rorschach 10
  St Moritz 63, 94
  Villa Berna (Grindelwald) 186
  Zermatt 53, 54
  Zurich 94
Sydney 166, 167–8, 170
  Dispensary Hall (Enmore Road) 170
  Farmers 168

   Harbour Bridge 212
   Manly Congregational Church 168
   Pacific Hotel (Manly) 168
   Petty's Hotel (York Street) 168
   Sargent's Restaurant 168
   Stanmore Road Spiritualist Church 168, 170
   Taronga Zoo (Mosman) 168
   Town Hall 168
Sydney Herald 168
Sydney Millions Club (Australia) 168
Sydney Spiritualists (Australia) 168
Symonds, Katherine 63
Syracuse 81

Tacoma 181
   Scottish Cathedral 181
   Tacoma Hotel 181
The Tailor of Wallingham ('H. Ripley Cromarsh' ACD's sister 'Dodo') 114
Tait, George Reid 14
The Tale of Peter Rabbit (Potter) 92
Tales of Adventure and Medical Life/The Man from Archangel and Other Tales of Adventure (1922) 176
Tales of the High Seas. No.I The Governor of St Kitt's (1897) 69
Tales of the High Seas. No.II The Two Barques (1897) 70
Tales of the High Seas. No.III The Voyages of Copley Banks (1897) 70
Tales of the High Seas. No.IV The Striped Chest (1897) 71
Tales of Long Ago/The Last of the Legions and Other Tales of Long Ago (1922) 146
Tales of Love and Hate (by Adrian Conan Doyle, 1960) 220
Tales of Pirates and Blue Water/The Dealings of Captain Sharkey and Other Tales of Pirates (1922) 176
Tales of the Ring and Camp/The Croxley Master and Other Tales of the Ring and Camp (1922) 176
Tales of Terror and Mystery/The Black Doctor and Other Tales of Terror and Mystery (1922) 176
Tales of Twilight and the Unseen/The Great Keinplatz Experiment and Other Tales of Twilight and the Unseen (1922) 176
'Talk on Books' (talk, 1910) 129
A Talk with Dr. Conan Doyle (interview, 1892) 47
A Talk with the "Ghost" of Lenin (1924) 184
'A Talk on Survival' (lecture given by Denis Conan Doyle) 213
Tangier 217
A Tangled Skein see A Study in Scarlet
Tanner, General 199
Tariff Reform 89, 101, 105
Tariff Reform League 106, 107, 108, 109
Tarlton, Henry 199
Tatler 104, 105
Tauchnitz, Baron Christian Bernhard von 45
Tauchnitz, Baroness Henriette Morgenstern 45
Tavistock (Devon) 20, 21
Teck, Duke of 133
Teignmouth (Devon) 95
Temple Bar 22, 23, 24, 42
Teneriffe 20
Tenniel, Sir John 89
Tennyson, Alfred, Lord 49
Tennyson, Hallam 108

Territorial Volunteers Association Conference 155
The Terror of the Blue John Gap (1910) 128, 136
Terry, Ellen 49, 111
Terry, J.E. 183
Tessier, T. 107
A Test Message (1887) 32
Testing Gas Pipes for Leakage (1886) 30
That Little Square Box (1881) 20
That Veteran (1882) 21
'The Art of Killing' (talk by Alfred Drayson, 1889) 39
'The man who carries the gun' (song, 1916) 151
Thérèse Raquin (play by Émile Zola) 45
'Thomas Carlyle and his Works' (talk, 1886 & 1888) 28, 35
Thomas Lake Harris: A Strange Prophet (1928) 196
Thomas, Massie 166
Thomas, Revd Drayton 205
Thomas, Sybil Margaret, Viscountess Rhonda 188
Thomas, Tom 159
Thompson, Mrs E. 130
Thompson, Sir Henry 81, 93
Thomson, David 46
Thorne, Norman 187
Thornton in Lonsdale (Yorkshire) 27, 66
    St Oswald's Church 27, 78
The Three Correspondents (1896) 69
Three Men in a Boat (Jerome K. Jerome) 151
Three of Them: I. A Chat about Children, Snakes and Zebus (1918) 157
Three of Them: II. About Cricket (1918) 157
Three of Them: III. Speculations (1918) 157
Three of Them: IV. The Leather Skin Tribe (1918) 157
Three of Them: V. About Naughtiness and Frogs and Historical Pictures (1918) 158
Three of Them (1923) 183
'Three years residence in the Congo' (talk, 1887) 32
Through the Magic Door (1906) 113, 117, 118
Through the Mists I. The Coming of the Huns (1910) 129
Through the Mists II. First Cargo "Ex ovo omnia" (1910) 130
Through the Mists III. The Red Star (1911) 130
Ticknor, John 175
Tiflis (Tbilisi) 224
Tiko (a python) 215
The Times 82, 84, 89, 91, 94, 114, 118, 126, 134, 139, 155, 158, 161, 166, 167, 217
Tit-Bits 46, 87, 90
To Arms! (1914) 147
To the Rocky Mountains (1915) 147
Today 55
Toledo (USA) 56, 59, 60, 142, 174, 175, 180
    National Union League 59
Tolstoy, Alexey 151
Tolstoy, Leo 51
Top Notch Magazine (USA) 145
Topley, William James 144
Topsham (Devon) 68
Torbay (Devon), Grand Hotel 148
Toronto 61, 142, 174
    Massey Music Hall 61, 175
Torquay (Devon) 45, 87, 123, 178
    Boltons Boarding House 88

   The Pavilion 148, 179
   Town Hall 165
   Victoria and Albert Hotel 179
Touch and Go: A Midshipman's Story (1996) 29
The Tragedians (1884) 24
The Tragedy of the Korosko (1897) 70, 74, 123
Traill, H.D. 75
Transvaal War Fund 81
'Travels in Bolivia' (talk, 1888) 33
Tree, Herbert Beerbohm 104, 128
Trenchard, Lord 221
Trevor, Mrs 77
Trevor, Philip 76, 77, 117, 127
Trial of Burton's Emulsion Process (1883) 22
A Trial by Jury (G&S) 111
A True Story of the Tragedy of Flowery Land (1899) 78
Tuck, Sir Adolph 192, 193
Tuck, Gustave 195
Tunbridge Wells 117, 118, 147, 148
   Borough Cemetery 214
   Castle Hotel 218
   Great Hall 81, 121, 140, 147
   Great Hall Cinema 211
   Municipal Cemetery 205
   Pump Room 118
   School of Arms 135
   School of Music 124
   Sunnyhaven (Rusthall Park) 190
   Technical Institute and School of Arts 195
   Town Hall 153, 172, 185, 195
Tunbridge Wells Cripples' Branch (Dr Barnardo's Homes) 121
Tunbridge Wells Hospital Pay Day Fund 182
Turnavine, Dr George 20
Turner, Major-General 141
Twickenham and Richmond Music Festival 215
Twidle, Arthur 213
'Two Great Battles - 2nd Ypres and Loos' (speech, 1916) 150
Tynan, Catherine *see* Doyle, Catherine Tynan
Tyneside Sunday Lecture Society (Newcastle upon Tyne) 56
'Typhoid and the Army' (speech, 1901) 92

Uckfield (Sussex) 210
Ugandan Railway 199
The Unchartered Coast I. Law of the Ghost (1919) 162
The Unchartered Coast II. A New Light on Old Crimes (1920) 162
The Unchartered Coast III. Shadows on the Screen (1920) 164
The Unchartered Coast IV. An Old Story Retold (1920) 165
The Unchartered Coast V. The Absolute Proof (1920) 167
The Unchartered Coast VI. A Worker of Wonders (1921) 171
Uncle Bernac - A Memory of the Empire (1897) 66, 68, 69, 71
Uncle Jeremy's Household (1887) 31
Under Fire on Izonzo Front (1916) 152
Undershaw *see under* Hindhead
Undershaw Rifle Club 87, 91
The Undoing of Archibald. A Composite Novelette by Fifty Popular Novelist (1908) 120
Union Church Young Peoples' Society (Heathfield) 210
United Irish League of Great Britain 147

UNLSS *see* Upper Norwood Literary and Scientific Society
'The Unseen World' (lecture, 1926) 192
Up an African River with the Camera (1882) 21
Upper Norwood Literary and Scientific Society (UNLSS) 48, 50, 51, 52, 54, 57
Uppingham School 118
'The Use of Spiritualism' (lecture, 1928) 196
The Usher of Lea House School (1899) 78
Usoga (steamer) 200
Uxbridge 220, 221

Vagabond's Annual (*Arrowsmith's Summer Annual*) 53
The Valley of Fear (1914) 141, 142, 146, 149, 178
Vancouver 179, 181
Venice 43, 94
  Hotel Royal Danieli 117, 219
Verdun 202
Verrall, Ivy 145
Versailles 35
  Trianon Palace Hotel 219
Veteran Relief Fund 118
Veterans' Club Association 149, 152
Victoria 20
Victoria (Canada)
  Capitol Theatre 181
  Empress Hotel (Inner Harbour) 181
Victoria Cricket Association 81
Victoria League 153
Victoria, Queen 84
Victoria Station (London) 42
Victorian Spiritualists (Melbourne) 170
Vienna 41, 42–3
  Hotel Kummer 42
  Pension Bomfort (Universitat Strasse) 42
A Visit to Three Fronts (1916) 152
The Vital Message (1919) 160, 161, 162
The Voice of Science (1891) 43
Volkhovski, Felix 51
'The Volunteer' (poem, 1919) 159
Volunteer Review, Portsmouth (1884) 24

Waggoner's Wells (Hindhead) 73
Wagner, Inez 181
Waifs and Strays Society 130
Waite, Edgar Ravenswood 166
Wall & Co. 124
Wall, Walter H. 159
Wallace, Alfred Russell 196
Waller, Ada 88
Waller, Bryan Charles 8, 9, 11, 12, 15, 19, 21, 27, 43, 66, 68, 88
Waller, Julia 27
Waller, Lewis 111, 112, 113, 147, 150
Waller, Victor 113
Walsall 159
Walter Scott Club 93
Walter Scott Publishing Co. 39
Walters, P. 184
'The Wanderers' Irish Tour' (poem, 1885) 27

The Wanderings of a Spiritualist (1921) 171, 172
The War. A Statement of the British Case (1914) 147
"The War" As Seen By Sir Arthur Conan Doyle (1914) 146
War Office 149
War Propaganda Bureau (WPB) 145, 146
The War in South Africa - Its Cause and Conduct (1901) 93
The War in South Africa. The Epidemic of Enteric Fever at Bloemfontein (1900) 84
Warburton, Mr 22
Ward and Downey (publishers) 35
Ward, Lock & Company (publishers) 30, 33, 34
Warfare in the Carnic Alps (1916) 152
Warnemunde 203
Warrington 172
  Orford Church 172
  Parr Hall 172
Warrington, Mr Justice 126
Warsaw 140
Washington 174, 175
  The Arlington 60
  Metserott Music Hall 60
  National Capital Press Club 60
Washington, Brooker 129
Waterloo see A Story of Waterloo (play)
Waterloo Station (London) 96
Watson, Dr Archibald 166
Watson, Phyllis Lindsay 106
Webb, Matthew 124
The Week. Topics of the Day (1883) 22
The Weekly Dispatch 171, 195
Weigall, Sir Archibald 166
Weldon, Miss Elmore 19
Welldon, Bishop 163
Wells, Bombardier 140
Wells, H.G. 74, 78, 146, 194
Wells (Somerset) 139, 188
West Grinstead 184
West Grinstead Park 118
West Surrey Automobile Club 107
Western Morning News 178, 179
Western Wanderings (1915) 147
Westham (Sussex)
  The Horns (Hankham) 215
  St Mary's Church 215
Westminster, Duke of 102
The Westminster Gazette 66, 67
Westport Catastrophe 58
W.G. Grace - A Memory (1927) 194
Whaling in the Arctic Ocean (1897) 69
What are the Benefits of Bicycling? (1895) 63
What Comes After Death? (1924) 184
What Does Spiritualism Actually Teach and Stand For? (1928) 195
What Naval Experts Think (1914) 145
What Reform is Most Needed? (1911) 134
'What Spiritualism gives the World' (lecture, 1926) 191
What Will England Be Like in 1930? (1917) 155
When the World Screamed (1928) 196
'Where Are the Dead?' (lecture, 1928) 196

Where to Go with the Camera: Arran in Autumn (1885) 26
Where to Go with the Camera (1883) 22
'The White Ant' (lecture on Maeterlinck's book, 1928) 196
The White Company (1891) 36, 38, 39, 40, 42, 45, 108, 157
White, E. 127
White, Field-Marshall Sir George 137
White Star Line 109, 145, 174, 179, 182
White, Dr William 60
Whitefriars Club 87, 118
Whitesmith Buildings (Hawksdale, Carlisle) 88
Whitfield, G.S. 127
Whitfield, T.S. 127
Whitington, Ernest 166
Whitley Ridge (Brockenhurst) 222
Whitsuntide Golf Competition 123
'Who's That Calling?' (poem, 1899) 81
Why He Is Now In Favour of Home Rule (1911) 134
Whydah (Dahomey) 20
Wickland, Dr 180, 201
Wickland, Mrs 201
The Wide World Magazine 89
Wigan 211
Wilde, Oscar 38, 44
  A Woman of No Importance 52
  The Picture of Dorian Gray 38
Wilde, Percival 143
Wilkes-Barre 81
'Will This War End Christianity' (lecture given by Denis Conan Doyle) 216
William Black Memorial Fund 78
William (engineer) 74
Messrs William Watson & Sons (Hawick) 110
Williams, A.C.R. 117
Williams, A.R. 73
Williams, David 159
Williams, E. 109
Williamson, Jack 17
Wilson, Colonel F.A. 211
Wimbledon 158
  King's Palace Picture Theatre 161
Windermere 132, 133
Windlesham Billiards Competition 178
Windlesham Cottage and house *see under* Crowborough
'Windlesham variety. Memoria Denis Conan Doyle' (orchid) 219
Windsor Castle 119
The Windsor Magazine 69, 75, 76
Windsor Park 133
Windward (whaler) 14
The Winning (1894) 58
The Winning Shot (1883) 22
Winnipeg 142, 143, 179
  Canadian Club 143
  Fort Garry Hotel 144, 182
  Union Hotel 143
  Union Station 182
  Walker Theatre 182
  Wesley Park 182
Winnipeg Arenas (baseball) 182

With a Camera on an African River (1885) 27
'With the Chiddingfolds' (poem, 1898) 74
Wodehouse, P.G. 116
Wolseley, Lord 76, 78, 81
Wolseley-Siddeley Car Company 121
Wolverhampton 161
Woman of the Year Luncheon (1965) 222
Woman's Auxiliary Air Force 215
Woman's Services Rifle match (1957) 220
Woman's Wit (1891) 45
Women's Royal Air Force Officers' Association 221, 222
Women's Royal Air Force (WRAF) 215, 217, 218, 220
'The Wonders of Psychic Knowledge' (lecture, 1928) 198, 199
Wontner, Sir Hugh 225
Wood, Alfred Herbert 6, 30, 33, 34, 37, 38, 40, 41, 48, 49, 72, 76, 87, 90, 91, 92, 95, 99, 104, 106, 107, 108, 110, 112, 115, 116, 117, 120, 122, 131, 135, 137, 146, 149, 165, 166, 168, 177, 179, 187, 209, 216
Wood, Emily 131
Wood, Sholto 109, 113
Woolwich and Plumstead Spiritualist Society 177
Worcester 160, 161, 162
Worcester Cathedral 161
A Word of Warning (1928) 195
World Congress of Spiritualism 210
The World-War Conspiracy (1914) 146
Wormesly, Mr 179
Worthing 120, 160
   Connaught Hall 161
   Spiritualist Mission Church (Grafton Road) 191
The Worthing Gazette 161
Wright, Arthur 164
Wright Cup Handicap (billiards) 192
Wright, Elsie 164, 165
Wright, Francis J. 159
Wynne, Agar 167
Wynter, Major J.R. 197
Wynyard, Captain E.G. 79

Yale 142, 174
Yarmouth Town Hall (Norfolk) 177
Yates, Miss V. 197
Yelverton, R.D. 113
Yeo, John 125
The Young Man and The Young Woman magazine 62
Youth and Survival League 211
Ypres (1915) 150

Zangwill, Dina 133
Zangwill, Israel 46, 133, 146
Zerdin, Noah 213
Zermatt Riffelalp Hotel 53, 54
Zola, Émile 45

www.ingramcontent.com/pod-product-compliance
Lightning Source LLC
Chambersburg PA
CBHW080850010526
44116CB00012B/2089